1976

This book may be kept

FOURTEEN DAYS

HAWTHORNE: THE CRITICAL HERITAGE

THE CRITICAL HERITAGE SERIES

GENERAL EDITOR: B. C. SOUTHAM, M.A., B.LITT. (OXON)

Formerly Department of English, Westfield College, University of London

Volumes in the series include

JANE AUSTEN	B. C. Southam
BROWNING	Boyd Litzinger and Donald Smalley
BYRON	Andrew Rutherford
COLERIDGE	J. R. de J. Jackson
DICKENS	Philip Collins
DRYDEN	James and Helen Kinsley
HENRY FIELDING	Ronald Paulson and Thomas Lockwood
THOMAS HARDY	R. G. Cox
HAWTHORNE	J. Donald Crowley
HENRY JAMES	Roger Gard
JAMES JOYCE (2 vols)	Robert H. Deming
KIPLING	Roger Lancelyn Green
D. H. LAWRENCE	R. P. Draper
MILTON	John T. Shawcross
SCOTT	John O. Hayden
SPENSER	R. N. Cummings
SWIFT	Kathleen Williams
SWINBURNE	Clyde K. Hyder
TENNYSON	J. D. Jump
THACKERAY	Geoffrey Tillotson and Donald Hawes
TROLLOPE	Donald Smalley
OSCAR WILDE	Karl Beckson

HAWTHORNE

THE CRITICAL HERITAGE

Edited by

J. DONALD CROWLEY

Associate Professor of English
University of Missouri

NEW YORK

BARNES & NOBLE, INC.

First published in Great Britain 1970
Published in the United States of America 1970
by Barnes & Noble, Inc., New York, N.Y.
© J. Donald Crowley 1970
SBN 389 04055 x

Printed in Great Britain

General Editor's Preface

The reception given to a writer by his contemporaries and near-contemporaries is evidence of considerable value to the student of literature. On one side we learn a great deal about the state of criticism at large and in particular about the development of critical attitudes towards a single writer; at the same time, through private comments in letters, journals or marginalia, we gain an insight upon the tastes and literary thought of individual readers of the period. Evidence of this kind helps us to understand the writer's historical situation, the nature of his immediate reading-public, and his response to these pressures.

The separate volumes in the *Critical Heritage Series* present a record of this early criticism. Clearly, for many of the highly productive and lengthily reviewed nineteenth- and twentieth-century writers, there exists an enormous body of material; and in these cases the volume editors have made a selection of the most important views, significant for their intrinsic critical worth or for their representative quality—perhaps even registering incomprehension!

For earlier writers, notably pre-eighteenth century, the materials are much scarcer and the historical period has been extended, sometimes far beyond the writer's lifetime, in order to show the inception and growth of critical views which were initially slow to appear.

In each volume the documents are headed by an Introduction, discussing the material assembled and relating the early stages of the author's reception to what we have come to identify as the critical tradition. The volumes will make available much material which would otherwise be difficult to access and it is hoped that the modern reader will be thereby helped towards an informed understanding of the ways in which literature has been read and judged.

B.C.S.

TO
SUE, CHRIS, AND ANNE

Contents

CONTENTS

CONTENTS

Tanglewood Tales (1853)

Mosses from an Old Manse (1854)

The Marble Faun [Transformation] (1859–61)

Our Old Home (1863–4)

xi

CONTENTS

(C) *Passages from the French and Italian Note-Books* (1872)

Preface and Acknowledgments

This book gathers together those materials that make up the primary record of Hawthorne's literary reputation from 1828 to 1883. The documents collected here thus trace the reception of Hawthorne's fiction, both in America and in England, from the publication of *Fanshawe* to that of the Riverside Edition of his *Complete Works*, which established the basic Hawthorne canon and has been, until the appearance of the Centenary Edition now being published, the standard scholarly text. The 142 selections give a representative account of the reaction to all of Hawthorne's works and are, with a few exceptions, arranged chronologically.

Most of the items printed here are reviews and notices, not only because they are generally the most valuable critical statements, but also because they have been much less accessible than comments in memoirs, biographies, and other book-length publications. Besides the classical statements of Poe, Melville, and Henry James and the prominent appraisals of such writers as E. P. Whipple, George W. Curtis, Richard Holt Hutton, Leslie Stephen, and Anthony Trollope, the entries include many other reviews and letters which reflect the intensity as well as the range of the contemporary opinion of Hawthorne's works. Hawthorne himself was, throughout his career, especially concerned about the place of the artist in American society, and those portions of his Prefaces in which he addresses himself to the question of his relation with his audience are therefore included here as an enlightening comment both on his own works and on the popular taste. Still other opinions from letters and private journals are mentioned in the headnotes and in the Introduction. Nevertheless, so full and numerous are the contemporary statements—these documents amount to less than half the mass of criticism examined—that it has been necessary to extract from many of the essays included here.

The attempt has been to present as fully and faithfully as possible for the years 1828 to 1883 the popular and critical reaction to Hawthorne as a literary artist, and to reconstruct the milieu in which Hawthorne shaped his art.

I am grateful to the University of Missouri Research Council for granting me a summer research fellowship for this project. The texts of Hawthorne's prefaces to *The Scarlet Letter*, *The House of the Seven Gables*, *The Blithedale Romance*, and *The Marble Faun*; the text of the Postscript to *The Marble Faun*; and the passages from 'The Custom-House' are reprinted from the Centenary Edition of the Works of Nathaniel Hawthorne, edited by William Charvat, Roy Harvey Pearce, Claude M. Simpson, Matthew J. Bruccoli, and Fredson Bowers, a publication of the Ohio State University Centre for Textual Studies and the Ohio State University Press. Copyright © 1963, 1965, 1968 by the Ohio State University Press. All rights reserved. Grateful acknowledgment is also due to the Houghton Mifflin Company for permission to quote from Hawthorne's Prefaces in the 1883 Riverside Edition of his works and from George Parsons Lathrop's *A Study of Hawthorne* (1876); the New York Public Library for permission to quote letters from the Duyckinck Collection and from the Henry W. and Albert A. Berg Collection; the Harvard College Library for permission to quote from the Hawthorne-Fields and the Hawthorne-Longfellow correspondence; Yale University Press for permission to quote from *The Letters of Herman Melville*, edited by Merrell R. Davis and William H. Gilman; Columbia University Press for permission to quote from Ralph L. Rusk's edition of *The Letters of Ralph Waldo Emerson*; Harvard University Press for permission to quote from *The Letters of Emily Dickinson*, edited by Thomas H. Johnson and Theodora Ward, and *Selected Mark Twain-Howells Letters*, edited by Frederick Anderson, William M. Gibson, and Henry Nash Smith; Professor Norman Holmes Pearson for permission to quote from a Hawthorne letter in his private collection. The librarians of the University of Missouri, the University of Illinois, and Yale University were most kind in making available materials for this collection. I owe a special debt to Bertha Faust, whose *Hawthorne's Contemporaneous Reputation* (1939) has been a basic reference for research on this subject.

I would also like to thank the proprietors and editors of the following magazines and newspapers for permission to reprint reviews and notices from their files: *Atlantic Monthly*, *Blackwood's Magazine*, the *Cornhill Magazine* (John Murray, Ltd.), *Harper's Magazine*, the *Nation* (New York), the *New Statesman* (for notices from the *Athenaeum*), the *Spectator*, and *The Times*.

J. DONALD CROWLEY

Introduction

I

THE EARLY WRITINGS: LACK OF RECOGNITION

Nathaniel Hawthorne, wrote Poe in 1847, 'is *the* example, *par excellence*, in this country, of the privately-admired and publicly-unappreciated man of genius' (No. 41). Poe's assessment is a basically accurate one and points to perhaps the central paradox in Hawthorne's contemporary reputation: although his fiction was from the very beginning reviewed favourably, even enthusiastically, neither the fiction nor the reviews captured the attention of the common reading public. If the lack of a wide popular audience was a general condition faced by almost every serious writer in nineteenth-century America, it is fitting nevertheless that Poe should have seen the problem as defining Hawthorne's special plight. In 1851, shortly after the publication of *The Scarlet Letter*, Hawthorne, looking back on the reception of his first collection of tales, wrote in his Preface to *Twice-Told Tales* (No. 67) that the 'circulation of the two volumes was chiefly confined to New England; nor was it until long after this period, if it even yet be the case, that the Author could regard himself as addressing the American public, or, indeed, any public at all. He was merely writing to his known or unknown friends.' Although Melville, Whitman, and Poe himself suffered something of the same kind of fate, it was Hawthorne who seemed to confront most fully the problem of an inadequate reading public and whose works were most shaped by that problem. The need to create an acceptably wide audience for himself was a matter of constant urgency throughout most of his career. Emily Dickinson could characterize her own poetry as '. . . my letter to the World/ That never wrote to me—' and be at ease with the thought. Hawthorne, however, had to speak of his *Twice-Told Tales* somewhat desperately as 'his attempts, and very imperfectly successful ones, to open an intercourse with the world'.

The American literary scene in the early nineteenth century was by no means inviting, especially to the serious, professional writer. Sydney Smith, one of the founders of the *Edinburgh Review*, could with

justification ask, 'Who reads an American book?' In 1828, the year
Hawthorne published *Fanshawe*, his first book, James Fenimore Cooper
complained in *Notions of the Americans* of the lack of an international
copyright law and the economic consequences for American literature:

> The fact that an American publisher can get an English work without money
> must for a few years longer . . . have a tendency to repress a national literature.
> No man will pay a writer for an epic, a tragedy, a sonnet, a history, or a romance,
> when he can get a work of equal merit for nothing. . . .
>
> A capital American publisher has assured me that there are not a dozen
> writers in this country whose works he should feel confidence in publishing at
> all, while he reprints hundreds of English books without the least hesitation.
> This preference is by no means so much owing to any difference in merit, as to
> the fact that, when the price of the original author is to be added to the uniform
> hazard which accompanies all literary speculations, the risk becomes too great.

It was a complaint that Hawthorne would later repeat. Although
Washington Irving and then Cooper himself gained a certain popularity,
especially in England, it was still possible for Alexis de Tocqueville to
write in 1835 that the 'inhabitants of the United States have, then, at
present, properly speaking, no literature. The only authors whom I
acknowledge as American are the journalists.' Even as a young man,
Hawthorne, writing to his mother about his future, saw clearly the
difficulties of authorship: 'What do you think of my becoming an
author, and relying for support upon my pen? . . . How proud you
would feel to see my works praised by the reviewers, as equal to the
proudest productions of the scribbling sons of John Bull. But authors
are always poor devils, and therefore Satan may take them.'[1]

More than any other writer of his time, Hawthorne was to make the
difficulties of authorship in America one of the central *données* of his
fiction. Oberon, his *persona* in 'The Devil in Manuscript' (1835), for
example, is a frustrated young writer who objects that 'no American
publisher will meddle with an American work,—seldom if by a known
writer, and never if by a new one,—unless at the writer's risk'. Hawthorne was undoubtedly looking back on his experience with *Fanshawe*, which, according to his sister, he had had to publish at his own
expense. But he also had in mind his failure to find a publisher for his
first projected collection of short fiction, a volume he intended to call
Seven Tales of My Native Land. Full of despair, he is thought to have
burned the manuscript much as he later has Oberon burn his unpublished tales. Before he succeeded in putting himself before the
public in the one-volume edition of *Twice-Told Tales* in 1837, he

suffered further disappointments. Arrangements for publishing two other completed collections, *Provincial Tales* (1829) and *The Story-Teller* (1834), fell through, and Hawthorne was reduced to regarding himself as 'the obscurest man of letters in America'. As the titles, *The Story-Teller* and *Twice-Told Tales*, suggest, Hawthorne's failure to present his work in book form led him in his fiction to focus still more sharply on the plight of the artist and his relation to an audience. Indeed, the unity of the 1834 collection was supposed to have been based on the character of 'a travelling story-teller, whose shiftings of fortune were to form the interludes and links between the separate stories'.[2]

Such circumstances as these were instrumental in compelling Hawthorne, first, to turn away from the full-length romance, and then to rely altogether on magazines and gift-book annuals for the publication of his tales and sketches. Unable to find publishers for his collections, he met instantly with enthusiastic approval and success in that the editors of the most prestigious American periodicals of the day gladly accepted his short fiction. It was not long before editors in New York and Washington joined those in Boston who were inviting Hawthorne to contribute to their magazines and annuals. And for good reason: many of his finest stories he wrote during the early 1830s. S. G. Goodrich, editor of the Boston *Token*, which became the most widely read of the gift-book annuals, accepted four of Hawthorne's tales—'The Wives of the Dead', 'Roger Malvin's Burial', 'My Kinsman, Major Molineux', and 'The Gentle Boy'—for the 1832 volume, saying that 'they are as good, if not better, than anything else I get. My estimate of the pieces is sufficiently evinced by the use I have made of them, and I cannot doubt that the public will coincide with me.'[3] Between 1831 and 1838 Hawthorne published twenty-seven tales and sketches in the *Token*— eight of them in 1837 alone, when his contributions comprised a large part of the volume. The majority of his other tales he published separately in two monthly magazines: in the mid-1830s eighteen appeared in the *New-England Magazine* and in the late 1830s and early 1840s twenty-two were printed in the *United States Magazine and Democratic Review*. There was a brisk demand for his fiction and, always striving to discover and widen his audience, he published approximately thirty other tales and sketches in a variety of newspapers, monthlies and annuals.

Hawthorne's last tale, 'Feathertop', was published in 1852 in the *International Magazine*—almost a quarter of a century after his first attempts had seen print. His was a sad initiation, and it exacted heavy penalties, the first of which was economic. Although he received $100 for that last story, the largest amount he had ever been paid for short fiction, he said that he 'would not write another for the same price', and thus declined Rufus W. Griswold's proposal that he write twelve tales to be published in monthly instalments. Writing for the magazines had long been for him what he called 'the most unprofitable business in the world'. In a letter to his friend Horatio Bridge in 1843, Hawthorne stated the paradox of his situation: 'nobody's scribblings seem to be more acceptable to the public than mine; and yet I shall find it a tough scratch to gain a respectable support by my pen.'[4] For the eight tales Hawthorne contributed to the 1837 *Token* he was paid only $108, or a mere dollar per page, and the best estimates are that the twenty-seven pieces he published there could not have brought him more than $343.[5] If Goodrich was unquestionably exploiting Hawthorne, editors of other periodicals made equally paltry payments. Park Benjamin, editor of the *New-England Magazine*, confessed that the rate of 'one dollar by the page for prose . . . is all that the magazine can afford'. John O'Sullivan of the *Democratic Review*, soliciting Hawthorne's work in 1837 in an effort to lend prestige to his new journal, promised $5 a page, but he was apparently always irregular in his payments and by 1844 could offer no more than $20 for any story, whatever its length. Benjamin paid Hawthorne nothing for four stories he originally accepted for the *New-England Magazine*, but printed instead in the *American Monthly Magazine* when he suddenly changed editorial posts. 'Ethan Brand' likewise brought Hawthorne nothing. Altogether his experiences with the magazines compelled him to complain to Bridge that the 'pamphlet and piratical system has so broken up all regular literature, that I am forced to write hard for small gains'.[6]

As acute as they were, Hawthorne's economic difficulties were almost the least of his problems. He learned quickly not to rely on a steady income from his serious literary efforts alone and sought to maintain himself and his family by a variety of other labours. For six months in 1836 he edited the *American Magazine of Useful and Entertaining Knowledge* in Boston, and later that year he wrote *Peter Parley's Universal History*, a compendium which became popular children's reading immediately and made a large profit for Goodrich, its publisher. In 1839 and 1840 Hawthorne, trying to make himself financially stable enough to marry, took a political appointment as measurer of salt and coal in the Boston Custom House at an annual salary of $1,500. A year later he joined the Brook Farm experiment and invested his savings there in the misguided hope that the community would enable him to support a family. After his first years of marriage at the Old Manse in Concord, during which he edited his friend Bridge's *Journal of an African Cruiser*, Hawthorne received, in 1846, another political appointment—this one the surveyorship in the Custom House at Salem, a position he held until the summer of 1849 and an account of which he gives in his essay introductory to *The Scarlet Letter*. From 1853 to 1857 he was the U.S. Consul in Liverpool, a position he was rewarded with as the campaign biographer and friend of President Franklin Pierce. Such efforts, however, were as much demanded by Hawthorne's personality and life-style as by his financial situation. As the recurrence of the theme in his fiction suggests, he was deeply suspicious of his tendencies as an artist to remove himself from society and its common concerns, and he therefore from time to time felt compelled to take an active role in the daily, practical affairs of his world. During such periods his literary productivity was, unfortunately, sharply curtailed.

A more subtle and lasting effect of periodical publication on Hawthorne was that its conditions seriously delayed the recognition he obviously deserved. The conventions of the trade encouraged—in a way, forced—Hawthorne to write anonymously or pseudonymously. Even after the publication of the 1837 *Twice-Told Tales*, the first work to carry his name on the title-page, Hawthorne continued to use a variety of signatures for his separately published tales. During the 1830s many of those tales were anonymous; others he signed as 'By the Author of "The Gentle Boy"', and later ones, trying to publicize himself as the author of a book, he ascribed to 'The Author of *Twice-Told Tales*'. Not until after the expanded 1842 *Twice-Told Tales*, however, did he regularly sign his own name to periodical publications. Bridge, urging Hawthorne to bring out the 1837 volume under his own name, analysed the writer's situation:

I've been thinking of how singularly you stand among the writers of the day; known by name to very few, and yet your writings more admired than any others with which they are ushered forth. One reason of this is that you scatter your strength by fighting under various banners. In the same book you appear as the author of 'The Gentle Boy,' the author of 'The Wedding Knell,' 'Sights from a Steeple,' and, besides, throw out two or three articles with no allusion to the author, as in the case of 'David Snow,' [*sic*] and 'The Prophetic Pictures,' which I take to be yours. Your articles in the last 'Token' alone are enough to give you a respectable name, if you were known as their author.[7]

It is not surprising that editors such as Goodrich and Benjamin, both of whom relied on Hawthorne for embarrassingly large numbers of contributions to individual volumes, deliberately exploited his reticence about acknowledging his stories. The extent to which Hawthorne was indeed unknown is dramatically illustrated by the fact that in 1837 one Massachusetts newspaper, in reprinting 'The Shaker Bridal', attributed the story to Catherine Sedgwick, one of the many female contributors to gift-book annuals.

Hawthorne did not record his motives for such anonymity, but one of his reasons, certainly, was that he had no desire to have his name linked with those of other contributors. The annuals and magazines of the day were generally offerings to the feminine sensibility, many edited by women and all encouraging new amateur authoresses to submit specimens of elegantly moral amusement. *The Gem, The Amulet, The Casket, Pearls of the West,* and *Friendship's Offering*—names typical of those annuals that flourished in the 1830s—reflect the kind of overweening taste and sentiment found in gift-book literature. The influence of such writers as Miss Sedgwick, Miss Lydia Sigourney, and Mrs. Sarah Hale led Hawthorne to complain that 'America is now wholly given over to a damned mob of scribbling women, and I should have no chance of success while the public is occupied with their trash— and should be ashamed of myself if I did succeed'.[8] Having to look to such periodicals as outlets for his fiction, Hawthorne was forced to compete directly with a facile and sentimental form of literature whose qualities he correctly felt almost precluded the possibility of the audience's understanding his darker and more ambiguous art. Goodrich put his finger on the public's preference for the simple and happy when he compared Hawthorne with Nathaniel P. Willis, a gift-book favourite whom Goodrich valued as his most admired contributor:

Willis was all sunshine and summer, the other, chill, dark, and wintry; the one was full of love and hope, the other of doubt and distrust . . . it is, perhaps, neither a subject of surprise or regret, that the larger portion of the world is so happily constituted as to have been more ready to flirt with the gay muse of the one, than to descend into the spiritual charnel house, and assist at the psychological dissections of the other.[9]

II

HAWTHORNE AS SELF-CRITIC: HIS BASIC UNCERTAINTY

These general conditions of periodical publication—the lack of economic success, the convention of unsigned authorship, and the necessity of competing directly with an inferior and unserious literature—had an unquestionably large and continuing effect on Hawthorne's thought and fiction. 'The best things come, as a general thing, from the talents that are members of a group', wrote Henry James; 'every man works better when he has companions working in the same line, and yielding the stimulus of suggestion, comparison, emulation.'[10] Denied that 'comfort and inspiration of belonging to a class' one feels Hawthorne especially might have profited from, he was a solitary worker many of whose strengths and weaknesses stemmed from his never being quite comfortable in that role. If those conditions saved Hawthorne from the temptation to imitate the techniques and clichés of the popular literature of his day and turned his art inward to discover its own resources, they also, in denying him a viable tradition and milieu by which he could measure his individual talent, made him uncertain about his role and his powers as an artist. In a letter to Longfellow he wrote:

As to my literary efforts, I do not think much of them—neither is it worthwhile to be ashamed of them. They would have been better, I trust, if written under more favorable circumstances. I have no external excitement—no consciousness that the public would like what I wrote, nor much hope, nor a very passionate desire that they should do so. Nevertheless, having nothing else to be ambitious of, I have felt considerably interested in literature; and if my writings had made any decided impression, I should probably have been stimulated to greater exertions; but there has been no warmth of approbation, so that I have always written with benumbed fingers.[11]

Part of Hawthorne's characteristic self-depreciation in his remarks about his fiction must be understood as cultivated public style, but a fundamental lack of confidence persists nevertheless in those remarks. While many writers have had large doubts about their work, few have been plagued as unremittingly as Hawthorne.

This legacy of mistrust about the relative merits of his work Hawthorne expresses nowhere more pointedly than in a letter to James T. Fields questioning the advisability of publishing *The Scarlet Letter* by itself rather than as part of yet another collection of tales, this one to go by the name of 'Old-Time Legends; Together with Sketches, Experimental and Ideal':

Keeping so close to its point as the tale does, and diversified not otherwise than by turning the same dark idea to the reader's eye, it will weary very many people and disgust some. Is it safe, then, to stake the fate of the book entirely on this one chance? A hunter loads his gun with a bullet and several buckshot, and following his sagacious example, it was my purpose to conjoin the one long story with half a dozen shorter ones; so that failing to kill the public outright with my biggest and heaviest lump of lead, I might have other chances with the smaller bits, individually, and in the aggregate.[12]

Variety Hawthorne saw as a primary and positive value in fiction, and the need he felt for a variety of moods and effects in his stories sprang in part from his uncertainty about the merits of each work individually considered. Thus his 'buckshot' theory.

That theory is evident as a kind of organizational motif in almost all of Hawthorne's volumes of short fiction. It looms large, certainly, in Hawthorne's oftentimes puzzling selection of tales and sketches for his collections, which are always characterized by as many different kinds as he could offer. Choosing eighteen of thirty-six separately published tales and sketches for his 1837 *Twice-Told Tales*, he spoke of them as his '"twice-told" tediousness' and said unenthusiastically that they were 'such articles as seemed best worth offering to the public a second time'.[13] Although it is inconceivable that Hawthorne did not use extreme care in selecting stories for his collections, he had little faith in his ability to distinguish between tales of greater and lesser merit. After making the selections for the 1842 *Twice-Told Tales*, for example, Hawthorne evaluated the rejected tales for E. A. Duyckinck, then editor of *Arcturus*:

Several (which for aught I know, are as good as the rest) will be left out of the collection. In the Token for 1832 are some of the first stories which I wrote— 'The Wives of the Dead'—'Major Molineux'—'Roger Malvin's Burial'—in that for 1833, 'The Canterbury Pilgrims'—for 1837, 'The Man of Adamant,' and 'Monsieur du Miroir'—for 1838, 'Sylph Etherege.' In the New England Magazine is 'Young Goodman Brown.'[14]

It has been a source of amazement for modern readers, who see 'My Kinsman, Major Molineux' as one of his finest and most complex symbolic tales, that Hawthorne failed to collect that story until 1852 in *The Snow-Image*, his last collection, in which he gathered together almost all of his hitherto uncollected fiction. At the same time he included in earlier volumes a number of pieces, such as 'Mrs. Bullfrog', which he himself thought to be obviously inferior. That sort of choice is to be accounted for finally by Hawthorne's lack of confidence and by his consequent desire to provide sufficient variety of style and subject to attract what he called 'the broadest class of sympathies' of the reading public. Hawthorne could not have said with as much apparent ease as

Fielding had in *Tom Jones* that 'An author ought to consider himself, not as a gentleman who keeps private or eleemosynary treat, but rather as one who keeps a public ordinary, at which all persons are welcome for their money'. Nevertheless, his desire to have as much variety as possible in his collections is a sign of his commitment to art as a pre-eminently public and popular form of expression.

So large were Hawthorne's doubts about the merit and appeal of his writings that they remained with him even after the success of *The Scarlet Letter* transformed his career. On 15 July 1851 he wrote Fields to comment on a recent review of his works, and his remarks show the old attitudes persisting:

There is praise enough to satisfy a greedier author than myself. I set it aside, as not being able to estimate how far it is deserved. I can better judge of the censure, much of which is undoubtedly just; and I shall profit by it if I can. But, after all, there would be no great use in attempting it. There are weeds enough in my mind, to be sure, and I might pluck them up by the handfull; but, in so doing, I should root up the few flowers along with them. It is also to be considered, that what one man calls weeds, another classifies among the choicest flowers in the garden.[15]

The self-effacing and apologetic tone resolves itself here in an assess-ment of his work that is decidedly fatalistic. Whatever he might try, Hawthorne seems to be saying, is doomed, if not to failure, then to a very mixed reception. Such statements—and Hawthorne makes many of them, both public and private—reflect his deep ambivalence toward his own work. He himself, one is led to believe, is both the readers he describes here: he sees his fiction both as weed and as choicest flower. His uncertainty was such that, compelled on the one hand to write the kind of fiction he did, he was no less compelled, later, to almost systematically criticize and reject it. He had no sooner published *Fan-shawe* anonymously in 1828 than, so the story has it, he tried to recall all the copies. So complete was his disavowal of the book that he kept the secret even from Mrs. Hawthorne. Likewise he apparently burned a large number of early manuscripts of tales and sketches. Preferring *The House of the Seven Gables* to *The Scarlet Letter*, he nevertheless wrote of the former that 'Sometimes, when tired of it, it strikes me that the whole is an absurdity from beginning to end . . . my prevailing idea is, that the book ought to succeed better than 'The Scarlet Letter,' though I have no idea that it will.'[16] The same kind of acceptance-rejection complex is evident in his comment about *The Marble Faun*, which on one occasion he called his 'best romance': 'To confess the truth', he told Fields, 'I admire it exceedingly at intervals, but am liable to cold fits, during which I think it the most infernal nonsense.'[17] The pattern of such a response haunted Hawthorne to the end of his career, and if it is by no means the primary cause of his inability to finish his last attempted romances, it must be seen as a significant factor among those contributing to the disintegration of his creative talent. In 1860, writing again to Fields, Hawthorne made a final, weary evaluation of his art:

My own opinion is, that I am not really a popular writer, and that what popularity I have gained is chiefly accidental, and owing to other causes than my own kind or degree of merit. Possibly I may (or may not) deserve something better than popularity; but looking at all my productions, and especially this latter one [*The Marble Faun*], with a cold or critical eye, I can see that they do not make their appeal to the common mind. It is odd enough, moreover, that my own individual taste is for quite another class of works than those which I myself am able to write. If I were to meet with such books as mine, by another writer, I don't believe I should be able to get through them.[18]

The publication of *The Scarlet Letter* had transformed Hawthorne's career only to the extent that it freed him from periodical publication and gave him widespread critical acclaim. It did not succeed in making him a favourite of the common reader.

III

THE SALES OF HAWTHORNE'S BOOKS

The story of the sales of Hawthorne's various literary productions is, to a surprising degree, given their stature as American classics and, after 1850, the astute promotional techniques of his new publisher, James T. Fields, merely a later instalment of the sad terms of his periodical publication. His first acknowledged volume, the 1837 *Twice-Told Tales*, although issued in an edition of only 1,000 copies, sold slowly in spite of Longfellow's laudatory review (No. 14). The 1842 *Twice-Told Tales*, expanded to two volumes and issued again in a small edition of 1,000 copies, fared so poorly that three years later Hawthorne had to reissue from 600 to 700 of those copies in a false edition.[19] Dissatisfied with what he called 'the New-England system of publication', Hawthorne tried his luck with still another publisher, Wiley & Putnam in New York, when in 1846 he collected twenty-three more pieces in *Mosses from an Old Manse*. That book went through more than one issue—it was the first of Hawthorne's major works to be printed from stereotype plates—but his total income for most of 1851 and 1852 from the sales of that collection was less than $150.[20] What is more astonishing is that *The Scarlet Letter*—widely praised in reviews and with 6,000 copies, in three American editions, exhausted within six months of its publication —was by no means an overwhelming commercial success in Hawthorne's lifetime. The total copies sold in America between 1850 and 1864 amounted to no more than 13,500, and Hawthorne's earnings from them were a mere $1,500.[21] It is instructive to recall here that Dickens initially viewed *Martin Chuzzlewit* as a failure because the serialized printing was only 23,000, and that Trollope estimated that, before copyright expired, sales of *Pickwick Papers* reached 800,000.[22]

But Hawthorne's situation had changed markedly, none the less. The wide critical acclaim *The Scarlet Letter* received spurred him to increased literary labours, as did the promptings of Fields. The next three years were to be his most productive, two romances and three more juvenile collections following hard on one another. 'As long as people will buy', Hawthorne wrote to Bridge, 'I shall keep at work, and I find that my facility for labor increases with the demand for it.'[23] Hawthorne plainly relished the brisk sales of his books during this period and Fields continually urged him to 'keep the pot a-boiling':

Will it not be a good plan [he wrote Hawthorne], for you to get ready a volume of Tales for the fall, to include those uncollected stories . . .? And then a book of stories for children for next season would do wonderfully well. . . . It is a good thing to follow up success in the Book way and your works are becoming every day more popular and commanding extensive sales. When the House of Seven Gables is out . . . I judge that the demand will be very great. . . . The republication of the Twice Told Tales seems to delight every-one.[24]

Thus Fields breathed new life into Hawthorne's old works as well as encouraging new ones. In 1851 new editions of both *Biographical Stories* and of *Twice-Told Tales*, the latter now accompanied by Hawthorne's famous Preface, preceded the publication of *Seven Gables*. *The Snow-Image, and Other Twice-Told Tales*, with its Preface, and a new juvenile collection, *A Wonder-Book for Girls and Boys*, Fields pressed Hawthorne to publish immediately after the romance in 1852. In his efforts to push Hawthorne's works '*à la* Steam Engine', as he put it, he even tried— albeit unsuccessfully—to persuade Hawthorne to acknowledge and reprint *Fanshawe*. Although Hawthorne was adamant in his refusal, he did manage in the same year to complete *The Blithedale Romance*, the third romance he published in as many years. From this he turned immediately to the task of writing the campaign biography of his old college friend, *Life of Franklin Pierce* (1852). The following year saw him complete *Tanglewood Tales, for Girls and Boys*, and in 1854 Fields, having purchased the copyright of *Mosses from an Old Manse*, persuaded him to add a couple of vagrant pieces from the magazines, and then ballyhooed the 'new' edition as 'Carefully revised by the Author'.

Fields's strategy, obviously, was to flood the market with as many of Hawthorne's volumes as possible so as to compensate for the steady but undramatic sales of each of the works. *The House of the Seven Gables*, which Hawthorne was convinced would stand its ground still better than *The Scarlet Letter*, was in fact slightly less popular, a total of 6,710 American copies being sold in its first six months and 11,500 during Hawthorne's lifetime.[25] Likewise, although the 2,000 copies of the new edition of *Twice-Told Tales* sold quickly, only about 3,000 more were needed from later impressions before 1864. Sales of the other individual volumes were no less unimpressive, but Fields was aiming for a cumulative effect. His plan succeeded in keeping Hawthorne's name before the public, and it increased the writer's income from these American editions to something more than $1,000 annually. More important, perhaps, Fields had been able to make arrangements for publication of the volumes in England. Delf publishers and then Chapman distributed *The Scarlet Letter*, and by 1851 five other houses, including Routledge and Bohn, were publishing editions in the British Isles. Chapman imported both *Twice-Told Tales* and *Seven Gables*, and Bohn and Routledge printed other English editions of those books. The Bohn editions of *The Snow-Image* and *A Wonder Book* appeared almost simultaneously with the American editions. Routledge printed an edition of the 1846 *Mosses* in 1851, and by 1852 Hawthorne's works were popular enough in England that Fields convinced Chapman and Hall, Dickens's publishers, to pay Hawthorne £200 for *The Blithedale Romance* copyright. Even the campaign biography of Pierce was imported, and Routledge advertised an edition in late 1852.[26] In 1853, Hawthorne, in Liverpool as the American Consul, was advertised as allowing Chapman and Hall, who paid £50 for the copyright, to publish *Tanglewood Tales* before the American edition appeared.

Thus ended Hawthorne's busiest literary years. From 1853 to 1857 his consular duties permitted him no writing other than his English note-books. He did not publish anything again until 1860, when he completed *The Marble Faun*. It is a sad irony that financial independence came to him not from his fiction, but, indirectly, from a political biography. His reward came finally in his appointment as Consul at Liverpool, a position in which he managed to save $30,000 during his tenure. If it is no wonder that at times Hawthorne felt that his success was 'chiefly accidental, and owing to other causes than my own kind or degree of merit', it is also true that he had widened his audience appreciably and could say that he 'stands foremost . . . [in England], as an American fiction-monger'.[27] His last romance, *The Marble Faun*, was first published there under the title *Transformation* by Smith, Elder & Co., who paid him £600 for the British copyright.[28] The American edition sold in greater numbers than the total sales of any of his previous romances, 14,500 copies of the two-volume work being exhausted within the year, and on the Continent Tauchnitz, which had previously published *The Scarlet Letter*, issued another edition of *Transformation*.[29] Three years later, Smith and Elder paid Hawthorne £180 for the English copyright to *Our Old Home*, a collection of essays from Hawthorne's consular days which, having been printed earlier in the *Atlantic Monthly* in instalments, was again published simultaneously in England and America in book form.

Our Old Home was the last volume published before his death in 1864, but his works were more marketable than they had ever been and, during the next twenty years, Fields and members of Hawthorne's family published parts of Hawthorne's various note-books and *Fanshawe* (1876), as well as his last fragmentary romances—*Pansie* (1864), *Septimius* (1872), *The Dolliver Romance* (1876), and *Dr. Grimshawe's Secret* (1883). New editions of individual volumes were numerous both in America and in England, and editions of his complete works included the Illustrated Library (1871), Little Classics (1875), Fireside (1879), Globe (1880), and Riverside (1883). If he had not quite become what we call a best-seller, he had come to be more than 'publicly appreciated': he was widely recognized as the writer of America's most serious and significant fiction.

IV

THE CONTEMPORARY RESPONSE
The Anonymous Years

Fanshawe was published anonymously in October 1828 by Marsh and Capen in Boston, Hawthorne, then twenty-four, having underwritten part if not all of the cost of publication. There is no evidence that the volume made its way to England. With one notably pithy exception (No. 1), reviews of the book were favourable, even encouraging. They were also vague and conventional in their praise and written by the very gift-book ladies whose influence and taste Hawthorne had come to detest. Several saw the book as helping to develop an authentic national literature, and one gave it the supreme praise of suggesting that Willis, the darling of the sentimental school of writers, was its creator. Although they are generally unperceptive, the reviews often rely on critical assumptions which had a wide currency. Thus one reviewer (No. 5) praises *Fanshawe*, rather curiously, for its realism—it is 'true to nature' and contains no 'violation of probability'—while another, William Leggett (No. 6), criticizes the plot as lacking probability and the characters as caricatures. Conversely, the former reviewer points to 'a falling off in the book . . . in the throwing in of light and shade to give effect to the picture', while the latter extols Hawthorne's ability to describe 'the heavens in all their different aspects of storm and sunshine'. Like the reviewers, Hawthorne himself was always concerned about getting enough variety—that is, 'sunshine and shadow'—into his fiction, and these terms were an important part of the critical vocabulary of the day.

Despite its friendly critical reception and its having been widely advertised, the volume did not sell well, and Hawthorne's disenchantment with it was such that he tried to dissociate himself from it altogether, enjoining family and friends to secrecy and encouraging them to believe that he was calling in all copies to destroy them. That version of events still persists, but critics have yet to discover whether Hawthorne's unhappiness over the book was caused by his dissatisfaction with its artistry or his disappointment with its negligible sales. The work provoked lively exchanges after Hawthorne's death when, for example, George W. Curtis called it a work characteristic of Hawthorne's mind and was later answered by George Parsons Lathrop, who argued that the story was 'not quite consonant with his native bent'. 'What separates this story', he says, 'from the rest of Hawthorne's work is an intricate plot, with passages of open humor, and a rather melodramatic tone in the conclusion.'[30]

Hawthorne's next publications, among them some of his finest tales, appeared in the *Token*. The reviewing of books at this period in America was very irregular, and gift-book annuals normally attracted only casual and brief notices in scattered newspapers and periodicals.

Consequently, Hawthorne's stories commanded no public comment until 1835 in Benjamin's review of the 1836 *Token* (No. 8). Eleven of his tales thus escaped notice altogether. The only recorded responses to 'My Kinsman, Major Molineux' and others were Goodrich's private remarks in letters to Hawthorne. 'The Gentle Boy', the first of his tales to receive public praise, was often singled out in later reviews of *Twice-Told Tales*, and in 1839 Hawthorne published a small separate edition with a dedication to Sophia Peabody (No. 18). Benjamin's reviews (Nos. 8 and 10), like so many American notices of the day, had the character of 'puffs' rather than of serious critiques. Taken up with facile and flattering comparisons of Hawthorne to better-known writers—Irving and Willis—Benjamin's statements reflect the casual, extra-literary nature of many contemporary reviews. In the second of his reviews, for example, the first to refer to Hawthorne by name, it is clear that Benjamin is eager to embarrass Goodrich, his competitor, by mentioning the large number of unsigned tales by Hawthorne in the 1837 *Token*. Interestingly, however, he expresses what must have been Hawthorne's own view that in America popularity and literary merit tended to be mutually exclusive, and that Hawthorne's best chance for success lay in England. The implicit reference to the superiority of British taste suggests that Benjamin may have seen Henry Chorley's review in the *Athenaeum* (No. 9), which had given Hawthorne much pleasure and encouragement because the critic was English and had mentioned all three of Hawthorne's pseudonymous tales as superior to the rest and striking in their use of native materials. Those sombre tales—'The Wedding Knell', 'The Minister's Black Veil', 'The Maypole of Merry Mount'—were among those Hawthorne included along with 'The Gentle Boy' in his first collection. Such, then, was the extent of Hawthorne's reputation after nearly a decade of writing for the periodicals.

The Tales: 1837–50

The *Twice-Told Tales*, made up of eighteen previously published pieces, was issued by the American Stationers Company (Boston) in March 1837, and ended Hawthorne's anonymity. Although the book sold slowly, it was received most favourably by those reviewers who mentioned it at all. References to Hawthorne's 'delicate taste', his 'elegance of style' and 'bold imagination', his 'quiet humor' and his 'fine tone of sadness'—all terms that were to become commonplace in nineteenth-century reviews of Hawthorne—were never far from these critics' thoughts. Hawthorne had in the collection tried to represent the full range of his art, but the reviews are predisposed to favour the descriptive sketches, such as 'Sights from a Steeple', and the simpler, more explicit allegories, such as 'Fancy's Show-Box', rather than Hawthorne's brooding and ambiguous historical tales. Charles Fenno Hoffman (No. 16), calling for another collection of Hawthorne's tales, praises him via a romantic rhetoric which sees him as 'a stricken deer in the forest of life' and then, as if trapped by the conflicting claims of his own language, suggests that this gentleness of intellect makes Hawthorne one of America's 'minor authors' who lack the masculine vigour and robustness necessary to express the national mind and imagination. Hoffman's views, themselves derivative from Longfellow's (No. 14), are especially noteworthy because they are so close to those attitudes towards himself and his work that Hawthorne was to express in his 1851 Preface to the tales (No. 67).

It is Longfellow's friendly review that enunciates most fully the critical dicta that shape the conventional response to Hawthorne's early work. The statement is pre-eminently an appreciation—personal, romantic, and impressionistic—rather than a systematic analysis of the works themselves. Aware that his is an anti-poetic culture, Longfellow exhorts his readers to receive Hawthorne as an artist whose tales and sketches represent a 'Poetry and Romance' of the 'Present' and are thus a truly national—that is, New England—literature. Quoting long passages in the manner of many reviews of the day, Longfellow chooses 'The Vision of the Fountain' and 'Sunday at Home' to illustrate Hawthorne's 'bright, poetic style', and reprints the whole of 'A Rill from the Town-Pump'. Most important, he celebrates the character of the writer himself and assumes that his personality is a clue to the spiritual qualities in the work: 'In order to judge the truth and beauty of his sketches', he says, 'we must at least know the point of view, from which he drew them.' Thus Longfellow can be said to have begun the cult of personality that would come to play so large a role, not only in Hawthorne criticism, but in his works themselves.[31] Longfellow's critical assumptions undoubtedly encouraged Hawthorne to start writing Prefaces (see, for example, Nos. 18 and 21) in which he presents himself as a person and establishes a relationship with his readers. Longfellow himself was much like Hawthorne in feeling that he had to ensure the value of literature and imaginative experience by describing the moral reliability of the author. The insistent moralistic attitudes of such critics as Andrew Preston Peabody (No. 17) regarding fictions that 'usurp the realm of fact' suggest the deep fear of and antagonism towards literary experience current in Hawthorne's America, and thus the need for Longfellow to emphasize Hawthorne's humanity as an author.

In the next review of major significance (No. 24), E. A. Duyckinck addresses himself to the general question of Hawthorne's lack of recognition, and then praises Hawthorne as an artist who is nobly above the issue of popularity and success. He is not only poetic; he is original. If, in his originality, he is, like Hamlet, a maimed genius, his imagination 'leads him into all possible conditions of being'—he is full of pathos, gloom, and terror, but also delight, cheerfulness, and sympathy. Again, the reviewer finds that Hawthorne's fiction reflects the man. Although Duyckinck's terms are outmoded, his review is a serious and not unsuccessful effort to come to grips with Hawthorne's sensibility.

After trying his hand at a collection of juvenile stories in 1841 (see Nos. 21, 22, and 23), Hawthorne issued the expanded, two-volume *Twice-Told Tales* in January 1842. The reviews were all favourable and celebrative of Hawthorne's genius, but there is an occasional hint—for example, in Longfellow's second review (No. 26)—of a lack of confidence that Hawthorne's works will ever be widely popular. Chorley (No. 31) again approves warmly, but exhorts Hawthorne to guard against monotony. Orestes Brownson (No. 28), while placing Hawthorne 'at the head of American literature' and comparing him with Dickens in his potential national importance, states that the tales 'are not precisely what he owes his country'. Like Hawthorne's other friendly critics, Brownson here seems the captive of the conflicting claims of his own rhetoric. Such reviewers first extol Hawthorne's 'poetic' virtues— his 'feminine' sensibility, his introspective depth, his treatment of the supernatural—and their vocabulary itself has a feminine or genteel aura about it. Having defined Hawthorne's superior genius in these terms, however, they then, seemingly unconscious of any contradiction, lament the lack of an intense and robust masculinity in Hawthorne's manner and subject. What the writer owes his country, what a fully democratic and popular literature demands, so their assumption goes, is an imagination vigorously turned outward and dramatizing present actuality rather than one that retires inward and meditates on the meanings of an imagined past. That Hawthorne himself shared the ambivalence and the confusion of this conflict is clear from his remark that he had 'nothing but thin air to concoct [his] stories of' and that the two or three in which he had portrayed 'a glimpse of the real world . . . please [him] better than the others'. The direction of the reviews led

Duyckinck in his next appraisal (No. 32) to counteract it by picturing Hawthorne as 'a man of a rugged frame of body' in whose stories there is a 'vein which no woman could ever reach, an intimacy with the sterner powers of life which we wish no woman to attain'.

Poe is the one critic whose assumptions differ markedly from those of the other reviewers. He wishes to discuss not Hawthorne and his sensibility, but his method and his style, and he is the first of the reviewers to prefer Hawthorne's tales to his sketches. While he too initially sees Hawthorne as an artist 'original at all points', he defines the proper goal of art to be the creation of sustained illusion and powerful effects on the reader rather than the earnest expression of truth by a sensitive and morally upright author. So absorbed is he in aesthetic concerns that his first full review (No. 29) becomes a defence of the tale *per se* and its high place among literary forms. Five years later, however, when reviewing *Mosses from an Old Manse*, which Wiley and Putnam had published in June 1846, Poe (No. 41) completely reverses these judgments about Hawthorne's merits. Then, because he thought—erroneously—that Hawthorne was a member of the Transcendentalist school of writers for the *North American Review*, he accuses him of addressing a coterie of friends and of being merely 'idiosyncratic' and 'peculiar' rather than original. Hawthorne's lack of popular success, Poe had come to believe, was in fact caused by his being '*not* original in any sense', and his peculiarity was the 'strain of allegory' Poe found dominating his stories and interfering with the demands of verisimilitude. Thus, Poe initiates the discussion of an issue that has been one of the primary concerns of Hawthorne criticism into the twentieth century.

Hawthorne's choices for *Mosses*—including a preponderance of allegorical tales and essay tales—reflect the desire he had expressed to Longfellow to put his fiction into closer touch with 'present actualities'. It was but one of many of his attempts to bridge the gap between his imagination and his readers by making the terms of his art clearer and more explicit. Although a great admirer of 'The Celestial Railroad', Emerson, apparently on the basis of a reading of *Mosses*, faulted Hawthorne for his strategy. 'Hawthorne', he says, 'invites his readers too much into his study, opens the process before them. As if the confectioner should say to his customers, "Now, let us make the cake." '[32]

Other reviews of the book, both in America and in England, had more than enough praise to compensate for Poe's displeasure and Emerson's doubts. Chorley (No. 36), in fact, commends most of Hawthorne's allegorical pieces, especially 'Earth's Holocaust', which is 'in the grandest style of allegory'. While the anonymous reviewer in *Blackwood's* (No. 37) begins in a highly negative way, calling Hawthorne's characters not only improbable but impossible, he ends by citing the virtues of most of the tales and sketches, whether allegorical or not. The praise is the more impressive in view of the critic's stern judgments in the same essay about other American writers, among them Poe. Charles Wilkins Webber's essay (No. 39) is a significant attempt to define Hawthorne's art, not only as bearing on the terms of contemporary political life, but as representing the most fitting expression of the national life—a middle way between the sentimental school and that of the exaggeration in frontier humour. His is the first serious and sustained effort to analyse Hawthorne's fiction in terms of the 'Real' and the 'Ideal', two pivotal criteria in nineteenth-century critical attitudes. At the opposite end of the critical spectrum from Poe, Webber cites 'Young Goodman Brown', a tale Poe thought represented the worst allegorical tendency in Hawthorne, as a prime example of how Hawthorne 'Humanizes the Unreal'. Like Samuel Dutton (No. 40), who admired especially the essay tales in the collection, Webber thinks *Mosses* superior to *Twice-Told Tales*.

Webber's view looks forward to many of the better-known ideas Melville developed in his long essay (No. 38) published in 1850 when he was struggling to finish *Moby Dick*. It is a notoriously extravagant piece of romantic criticism which, in its 'shock of recognition' of Hawthorne's genius, is the first to rank him with Shakespeare instead of Irving, Cooper, Lamb, Addison, Steele, and Tieck, as other reviewers had. Centrally concerned with Hawthorne's lack of popularity, he ends exuberantly and chauvinistically by urging the American public to buy 'by the hundred thousand'. And yet the essay is not uncontrolled. Melville's remarks make it clear that he was familiar with Hawthorne criticism—the view of Hawthorne as 'flowery' and as 'a man who means no meanings', of *Mosses* as 'a rare, quiet book, perhaps too deserving of popularity to be popular'. Beginning with an appreciation of those descriptive and meditative sketches that exemplify Hawthorne's quality of 'noonday repose', and thus were his best chance of appealing to the sentimentality of the reading public, Melville moves on to his now-famous consideration of the 'other' Hawthorne, who is 'shrouded in a blackness, ten times black'. Like other reviewers, then, Melville sees a feminine-masculine duality in Hawthorne's genius. Unlike them, he seems to have praised the 'daylight' Hawthorne, whom the public had made 'sequestered, harmless' only as a way of illustrating what an

'absurd misconception' of the man this view finally was. To see Hawthorne thus, he argues, is to miss the 'dark' Hawthorne, who is capable
of comparison with the Shakespeare of *Lear*. It is to miss, he implies, the
real Hawthorne. Although Longfellow surprisingly endorsed all Melville says about Hawthorne and although Melville himself attempts to
put the sunlight and shadow back together again, his essay introduces
the uneasy notion of an irreconcilable split in the character of Hawthorne's writings that twentieth-century criticism is still concerned to
evaluate. Neither Melville nor later critics have been able to resolve this
conflict as facilely as James Russell Lowell does in his description of
Hawthorne in 'A Fable for Critics':

> When Nature was shaping him, clay was not granted
> For making so full-sized a man as she wanted,
> So to fill out her model, a little she spared
> From some finer-grained stuff for a woman prepared.
> And she could not have hit a more excellent plan
> For making him fully and perfectly man.

The Scarlet Letter

Poe's attack on Hawthorne's allegorical bent clearly had little effect on
Hawthorne, if we can judge by the nature of his great romance, published on 16 March 1850 by Ticknor, Reed and Fields. Nevertheless,
even though after *The Scarlet Letter* many of the old critical issues disappeared and new ones arose, the dispute about the nature and merit of
Hawthorne's allegory persisted. That Hawthorne could no longer be
called altogether unknown is itself the main source of change in these
issues. His earlier Prefaces, especially 'The Old Manse', suggested themselves as ways of exploiting the reviewers' and the public's interest in
autobiographical statements and of simultaneously satisfying their
insistence—and his own—on a rendering of 'the Present, the Immediate,
the Actual'. 'The Custom-House', meeting their demands for sunshine
and actuality, was, among other things, his way of compensating for the
unrelieved darkness and ambiguity of his allegorical and symbolic
vision in the romance itself.

The book created a great stir among the reviewers, who invariably
saw it as a major literary event. Its subject was controversial and happily
established Hawthorne in the public consciousness. Such reviewers as
Duyckinck (No. 44) and Whipple (No. 46) describe the work as a rich
fulfilment of Hawthorne's modes of romance and sketch, the intense

gloom of the spiritual laws of the one being relieved sufficiently by 'the pleasant, personal descriptions' of the other. They accept the book not as a novel, but as a psychological romance, and thus understand its lack of incident as appropriate to 'a drama in which thoughts are acts'. Only later would critics complain of what in 1879 Henry James, following them, calls 'a want of reality and an abuse of the fanciful element' in the book. For the first reviewers, however, the story's power was worrisome. Even Chorley (No. 47), in his approbation, doubts that its 'passions and tragedies . . . are the legitimate subjects for fiction'. Three other critics—Anne W. Abbott (No. 48), Orestes Brownson (No. 50), and Arthur Cleveland Coxe (No. 51)—were moved to make direct attacks on both the characters as improbable and Hawthorne's moral vision as inadequately Christian and orthodox. 'Is the French era actually begun in our literature?' asks Coxe. One of the more perceptive of the reviewers, George Bailey Loring (No. 49), answers Abbott's objections by describing the book as 'extraordinary, as a work of art, and as a vehicle of religion and ethics'. Hawthorne would undoubtedly have been pleased had such a charge as Coxe's reached the proportions of a scandal and thereby boosted sales, but all evidence points to the fact that, as Hawthorne himself believed, 'The Custom-House' essay was chiefly responsible for the book's popularity. There was at the time, though, in private statements as well as the reviews, a sense about the book, as James was later to say, that 'Something might at last be sent to Europe as exquisite in quality as anything that had been received, and the best of it was that the thing was absolutely American; it belonged to the soil, to the air; it came out of the very heart of New England.'[33]

The House of the Seven Gables

As great as the power and effect of *The Scarlet Letter* were, Hawthorne, when he sat down to write his next romance, was determined to tell a different kind of story. Whipple had concluded his review hoping for 'a romance equal to The Scarlet Letter in pathos and power, but more relieved by touches of that beautiful and peculiar humor, so serene and so searching, in which he excels almost all living writers'. It is more accurate to say that Hawthorne agreed instinctively with Whipple and other critics here than that he was influenced by them to change the direction of his art. No one lamented more than Hawthorne himself what he called his lack of a faculty to write a sunshiny book, and he was convinced, as were his family and friends, that the *Seven Gables* was 'a more natural and healthy product of [his] mind'.[34] Combining the materials of both sketch and romance, it was a more difficult book for him to write, requiring, he said, 'more care and thought', because 'The Scarlet Letter being all in one tone, I had only to get my pitch, and could then go on interminably'.[35] Even so, he wrote to Fields that the book 'darkens damnably towards the close' and he tried to 'pour some setting sunshine over it'.[36] Again Hawthorne relied on a personal Preface explaining the special latitude of the romance to help dispel the romance's gloom. About five months in the writing of it, Hawthorne published the volume on 9 April 1851.

The reviews were enthusiastic and unanimous in their praise of the romance's range and variety. That it was quite different from *The Scarlet Letter* was taken to be a strong confirmation of Hawthorne's genius. Chorley claimed for him a place among the finest modern 'novelists', and Browning is said to have thought Hawthorne 'the finest genius that has appeared in English literature in many years'.[37] Hawthorne's descriptive powers are, as usual, frequently celebrated in the reviews, various sequences and episodes, such as those of Hepzibah in her shop, the Pyncheon garden, and the death of Judge Pyncheon, often being singled out as authentic and powerful. Although Chorley found Hawthorne's meditative speculations on the Judge's death getting in the way of the plot, most reviewers considered the scene 'a masterpiece of fantastic description'. The plot was hailed for its greater 'elaborateness' and its combination of the legendary past and the commonplace incidents of modern life. Equally important to Hawthorne, the characters themselves, in contrast to those of *The Scarlet Letter*, were often singled out as 'living realities'. Hepzibah and Phoebe, Judge Pyncheon, Clifford, and Uncle Venner some reviewers described almost in the manner of Trollope's characters—that is, as real people who have 'such a genuine expression of flesh and blood, that we cannot doubt we have known them all our days'. Hawthorne undoubtedly was secretly pleased when a reader complained that one of his ancestors, a Judge Pyncheon, had been maligned in Hawthorne's characterization. While Amory Dwight Mayo argues that Hawthorne is not 'a truthful delineator of character', he says that the reason for this is that Hawthorne's interest is in 'the relation of spiritual laws to character'. Henry James echoes the consensus of these contemporary reviews when he praises the book's 'greater richness of tone and density of detail' and its 'literal actuality' while defending its art as 'vague, undefinable, ineffable'. Although Hawthorne had a 'high sense of reality', he was no realist, James summarizes, and 'his local and national quality' is to be found 'between the lines of his writing and in the *indirect* testimony of his tone, his accent, his temper, of his very omissions and suppressions'.[38] He finds Hawthorne's characters conceived descriptively rather than rendered dramatically, but 'if their reality is light and vague, it is sufficient, and it is in harmony with the low relief and dimness of outline of the objects that surround them'.[39] While James calls the work 'a magnificent fragment', in the end he repeats the contemporary praise: 'It is a large and generous production, pervaded with that vague hum, that indefinable echo, of the whole multitudinous life of man, which is the real sign of a great work of fiction.'[40]

The Blithedale Romance

Hawthorne's commitment to variety and versatility is again reflected in his following *Seven Gables* with *A Wonder-Book*, *The Blithedale Romance*, a political autobiography, and another juvenile collection, *Tanglewood Tales*. Just before beginning *Blithedale*, he wrote to Bridge: 'I don't know what I shall write next. Should it be a romance, I mean to put an extra touch of the devil into it, for I doubt whether the public will stand two quiet books in succession without my losing ground.'[41] He felt uneasy about the book and gave the manuscript to Whipple to read when Fields, in Europe, could not oversee its publication in July 1852. It is not unexpected, then, in view of his pre-publication involvement with the book, that Whipple, in his review (No. 82), calls it 'the most perfect in execution of any of Hawthorne's works, and as a work of art, hardly equaled by any thing else which the country has produced'. Although the reviewers were again basically complimentary and British critics often lavished praise on the book, few American critics were as impressed as Whipple. Fields himself was plainly disappointed, and his terse comment probably reflects his sense of the publishing world's response to the book: 'I hope Hawthorne will give us no more Blithedales.'[42] More than one critic worried over that 'touch of the devil'. The anonymous reviewer for the *Westminster Review*—George Eliot has been suggested as the author[43]—condemns Hawthorne's analysis of his characters' states of mind as a 'poetry of the hospital . . . and the dissecting room'. Another anonymous critic (No. 86) expresses a common complaint when he accuses Hawthorne of a 'lack of tenderness' that makes him animate 'shadowy people with worse passions and more imperfect souls than we meet with in the world'. Emerson quite understandably found Hawthorne's sceptical treatment of social reform unsatisfactory, as did Charles Hale (No. 79). The reviews in general fall in between Whipple's and Fields' assessments, but their criticism is almost invariably enveloped in an attitude of appreciation for Hawthorne's genius and reputation. The *Westminster Review* critic, for example, calls the book 'unmistakably the finest production of genius in either hemisphere, in this quarter at least'. The *Spectator* review (No. 77) faults Hawthorne's plot, but then goes on to say that his art lies in descriptive details rather than in a multitude of incidents, and it ends by praising the book's conservative political philosophy and its moral lessons. In another of several statements coloured by political preferences, Orestes Brownson (No. 85), while taking Hawthorne to task for his treatment of Zenobia's suicide, praises the book as 'calculated to bring modern philanthropists into disrepute, and to cure the young and enthusiastic of their socialistic tendencies and dreams of world reform'.

Despite Hawthorne's disclaimer in his Preface (No. 76) that he was not writing about Brook Farm, most of the reviewers did not accept his assertion that the characters 'are entirely fictitious' and speculated about who the life-models for Zenobia, Hollingsworth, Priscilla, Westervelt, and Coverdale were. Their interest and concern here point up the increased strain Hawthorne had put on the limits of romance by bringing his scene so close to contemporary events and people. The work has had few champions. Browning told Hawthorne that it was his favourite, and, in 1895, William Dean Howells said he always liked it best because it 'is more nearly a novel, and more realistic than the others'.[44] James found himself engrossed in Miles Coverdale and Hawthorne's management of point of view, and he saw Zenobia as 'the nearest approach Hawthorne has made to the complete creation of a *person*'.[45] But his praise was at best partial. There are almost no comments about the book from Hawthorne himself. He had no sooner finished it than he planned another romance, 'which, if possible', he says, 'I mean to make more genial than the last'.[46]

The Marble Faun [*Transformation*]

Published in England as *Transformation* in late February 1860 and in America as *The Marble Faun* on 1 March, Hawthorne's last completed romance was his most heavily reviewed, and provoked a wide range of response. While controversy was spirited about most aspects of the story and its characters, there was a persistent complaint that, as the critic in the *Saturday Review* put it, Hawthorne's plot 'comes absolutely to nothing'.[47] Two British friends, Chorley (No. 102) and Henry Bright,[48] also objected to the haziness of the conclusion, its 'want of finish'. Hawthorne himself, even before seeing these reviews, had come to have similar doubts, for just a few days after the book's publication he wrote the Postscript (No. 103), which was added to later printings by 16 March.[49] In typical fashion, however, Hawthorne uses the occasion more to object to his readers' insistence on definite information about the characters than to satisfy their demands. The addition becomes what most of his Prefaces are: an attempt to distinguish the romance from the novel and to justify the romance's tenuous combination of 'the Real and the Fantastic'. It can hardly be said to represent a capitulation to public taste. That he was not totally successful in his efforts is best suggested by the fact that the Postscript itself inspired a parody in the *Knickerbocker*, '*The Marble Faun*: Completed' (No. 108), and that a later reviewer tried to explain away the story's indefiniteness by inventing an elaborate allegorical structure for it.[50] Relatively few of the critics agreed with John Lothrop Motley, who liked the 'misty way in which the story is indicated rather than revealed'. The reviewer for the *Dublin University Magazine*[51] took up the task of answering the objections of *The Times* review (No. 107), and in America Curtis joined Lowell (No. 104) in asserting that an effect of mysteriousness is a legitimate aspect of the romance. Although Whipple (No. 110) accuses Hawthorne of leaving his readers 'in the end bewildered in a labyrinth of guesses', he does so while insisting, as had another reviewer, Charles Card Smith, that the book 'must, on the whole, be considered the greatest of his works'.[52]

Most reviewers granted the romance an impressive and powerful theme, but disagreement about Hawthorne's characters and setting was animated and extensive. Opinion about Donatello ranged from his being 'one of the subtlest conceptions of human genius' to his being 'a monster'. Miriam, Hilda, and Kenyon were more often than not criticized as unoriginal and reminiscent of characters in both *The Blithedale Romance* and *The House of the Seven Gables*. One reviewer, Eliza W. Robbins, found their story 'nothing but a reproduction of "The Scarlet Letter"'.[53] She also felt that 'Were the art-criticisms with which it abounds the only thing in the volume, it would still be intrinsically valuable'. Hawthorne having incorporated into the romance many descriptive passages from his note-books, the book was indeed known widely for its guide-book-like passages of Rome. Reviews both praised and criticized it as an 'art-novel'. American critics were in general more favourably disposed than the British to such passages, but among British reviewers Chorley, Bright, and *The Times* critic approved of all Hawthorne's circumstantial detail, the last calling the book 'worth all the guide-books we ever met with'. Others, however, found Hawthorne too much in awe of the landscape and the galleries, and attributed to his interest in them the central weakness of the book. The *Universal Review* critic (No. 111) summed up a common view when he described the effect of the description as 'a feebleness of purpose, which makes the book a compromise between an art-novel and a psychological study'. Later critics have tended to agree that the accumulation of such detail is at cross-purposes with Hawthorne's intention of establishing what in his Preface (No. 101) he calls a 'poetic or fairy precinct, where actualities would not be so terribly insisted upon'. In 1879 James judged the book to be the most popular of Hawthorne's works, but he repeats much of the contemporary criticism, finding the genre 'an inferior one', Donatello 'rather vague and improbable', and 'the element of the unreal . . . pushed too far'.[54]

The General Estimates and Retrospective Views

All of Hawthorne's other works—the juvenile collections, *The Snow-Image*, *Life of Pierce*, *Our Old Home*, the note-books and the fragments—received critical notice at the time of their publication. Some of these minor pieces attracted little comment, while others captured the public's interest and commanded serious attention on the part of reviewers. That *A Wonder-Book* and *The Snow-Image* occasioned only a few reviews in major literary periodicals suggests not that they were singularly unpopular—Emerson, for example, wrote that the juvenile stories were 'the study of all children in America'[55]—but that after 1850 Hawthorne's audience had very quickly come to view the full-length romance as his special province. Whereas *Tanglewood Tales* and an enlarged edition of *Mosses* likewise attracted little attention, those works reflecting a concern for contemporary political and social realities—*Life of Pierce* and *Our Old Home*—were controversial enough to cause a rash of heated opinion. 'The masses', said Duyckinck, 'want facts and deeds, clear narration, and everyday probability of motive' (see No. 88), and these works aroused widespread interest. The diversity of Hawthorne's efforts here was celebrated by some readers as bringing him into 'a healthy encounter with living interests' and frowned upon by others as taking him out of his proper element. The appearance of the note-books and fragments was likewise marked by lively disagreement. Some reviewers found the 'marks of Hawthorne's inimitable genius' to be on those unfinished works (see, for example, No. 124); other critics were happy to see these posthumous publications, slight as they felt them to be, for the light they would throw on Hawthorne's personality. Perhaps a majority, agreeing with the critic of the *British Quarterly Review* (No. 130), found that his family, in publishing such pieces, had made Hawthorne 'the worst used of men'. That reviewer's complaint was a common one—namely, that while Hawthorne himself had hoped that no biography would be written of him and had always been noted for a 'fastidiousness' of style, he was now exploited by the publication of personal and unpolished statements 'to the detriment (were it possible) rather than to the increase of his reputation'.

Of greater weight than these reviews are the general estimates of Hawthorne's works that begin to appear shortly after the publication of *The Scarlet Letter* and, together with the reviews of the major works, best represent the gradual formulation of the basic nineteenth-century British and American attitudes towards Hawthorne. The statements included in this collection are representative of the most interesting of the general estimates published in other periodicals and in book form in the three decades following the appearance of Hawthorne's master-piece. They are retrospective glances over Hawthorne's career, and, though many are taken up with a chronological survey of the works, all develop at least partially a noteworthy thesis about the nature of Hawthorne's art. Several of the essays attempt to place Hawthorne by contrasting him with other writers, such as Poe (see Nos. 99 and 128), George Eliot (see No. 109), and Trollope (see No. 141). The questions these general assessments ask most persistently have to do with the reliability of Hawthorne's moral vision, the nature of allegory and the relationship between the actual and the ideal, the terms of Hawthorne's nationalistic genius, and, finally, Hawthorne's very personality or character. Indeed, nineteenth-century criticism, lacking the analytical methods to treat the first three issues satisfactorily and having, at the same time, a biographical bent, often came to see those issues in relation to Hawthorne's life and the question of what kind of man Hawthorne, the creator of the tales, was. His Prefaces are, indeed, one of Hawthorne's chief ways of coping with the first two issues: in them he sought to present a reliable author and explain the requirements of the romance as opposed to those of the novel. In so far as his Prefaces encouraged the critics in the direction of biographical concerns, he can be said to have shaped contemporary opinion at least as much as he was influenced by it. That the reviewers often cited passages from the Prefaces to explain various aspects of his works is evidence that Hawthorne, as a critic, deserves to be called one of the true 'architects of American literary culture'.[56]

Both Hawthorne and his reviewers were, in fact, acting upon the same large critical assumptions stemming from an essentially mid-nineteenth-century organic theory of literature and of the relationship between the artist and his work and the artist and his audience. Whitman's radical version of the theory he stated about himself and his *Leaves of Grass*: 'Whoso touches this book touches a man.' There is an implied organicism of this kind in Emerson's seemingly innocent remark that he thought Hawthorne 'a greater man than any of his works betray'. Richard Henry Stoddard (No. 93) was one of the first Hawthorne critics to state the theory baldly: 'If ever an author was revealed in his books, Hawthorne is the man.' He is also, along with Curtis, one of the first to express the view of Hawthorne as solitary and secluded: 'Quiet, unobtrusive, and retired, has been the life of Hawthorne, and such are his books. Had his life been different, his books could not well have been what they are.' As Hawthorne makes clear in 'The Old Manse', he was typically ambivalent about these implications of the organic theory: 'So far as I am a man of really individual attributes I veil my face; nor am I, nor have I ever been, one of those supremely hospitable people who serve up their own hearts, delicately fried, with brain sauce, as a tidbit for their beloved public.' But although in one sense he resisted self-exposure, in another he simply could not avoid it: 'veiling his face' meant for Hawthorne not only the writing of self-revelatory, if decorous, Prefaces, but even the furnishing of Stoddard with an autobiographical paragraph which positively encouraged the construction of what has come to be called the Hawthorne myth (see No. 94).

Caught as he was between equally strong impulses towards self-concealment and self-revelation, Hawthorne knew perhaps better than his critics the extent to which that myth had been their mutual creation. In his Preface to the 1851 *Twice-Told Tales* (No. 67) he speaks of how he had come 'to be regarded as a mild, shy, gentle, melancholic, exceedingly sensitive, and not very forcible man, hiding his blushes under an assumed name', and how he was uncertain 'that some of his subsequent

productions have not been influenced and modified by a natural desire
to fill up so amiable an outline, and to act in consonance with the
character assigned him'. Hawthorne's art, as Hawthorne himself knew
and as nearly all the reviewers pointed out, led him into an exploration
of various conditions of solitude, isolation, and alienation. But Hawthorne and most of his reviewers shared organicism's uneasiness about
the artist's pursuit of such themes. Hawthorne gave expression to that
suspicion many times, but nowhere more pointedly than in his analysis
of the artist in 'The Prophetic Pictures': 'It is not good for man to
cherish a solitary ambition. Unless there be those around him by whose
example he may regulate himself, his thoughts, his desires, and hopes
will become extravagant, and he the semblance, perhaps the reality, of a
madman.' The organic theory stressed that there should exist between
the artist and his reader a bond of sympathy which would allow the
reader to participate in the creative process of the artist. For both
Hawthorne and his critics that idea was axiomatic. The reviewer for
Blackwood's (No. 100), for example, condemns Hawthorne's works as
'singular' and his audience as 'peculiar', arguing that his stories are
'manufactured' and 'do not grow with a sweet progresion of nature':
'they are not stories', he says, 'into which you enter and sympathise,
but dramas of extraordinary dumb show'. Stoddard and other reviewers, however, insist that 'we feel in reading his books what he
must have felt in writing them'. It is, then, particularly in the light of
this organic theory that Hawthorne's remarks in his Prefaces and letters
take on their full significance as invitations for his readers to enter into
and reproduce the processes of his imagination.

The theory itself, unfortunately, had built-in contradictions in that
on the one hand it called for a very intense and individualized relationship between author and reader, while on the other it demanded that
the writer address a large audience, for, as the *Blackwood's* reviewer put
it, 'the novelist's true audience is the common people—the people of
ordinary comprehension and everyday sympathies'. Hawthorne
attempted to meet both demands, at times characterizing his tales as
attempts to 'open an intercourse with the world' and at others speaking
of 'that Gentle Reader for whom all my books were written' (see No.
106). Likewise, by encouraging the reviewers to promulgate the story
of his secluded years in Salem, he invited them and the larger public to
validate the dark themes of solitude in his work at the same time that he
hoped his Prefaces would allow him to illustrate his geniality, his
humour, and his involvement with the world of actuality. In writing

the Prefaces, Hawthorne was, whether consciously or not, attempting, again according to the dictates of organicism, to bring his works into a closer and fuller correspondence with his life. The strategy was one by which he hoped to mediate between his art and his audience while being true to both.

The interest in the 'unwordly' Hawthorne led inevitably to a view of Hawthorne as the victim of his art. Hawthorne thought E. P. Whipple the most perceptive critic of his works, and it is Whipple who has been called 'the purest example extant of the Victorian development of Romantic organicism'.[57] In his fullest treatment of Hawthorne's works and the organic theory (No. 110) Whipple gives explicit expression to the notion of Hawthorne as victimized by his art: 'His great books appear not so much created by him as through him. They have the character of revelations,—he, the instrument, being often troubled with the burden they impose on his mind.' But Whipple is not alone in seeing Hawthorne as controlled by his special genius. Stoddard had already explained Hawthorne's lack of a popular audience by saying that his "excellences have been his worst enemies'. In the 1870s the anonymous critic for the *Southern Review* (No. 135) joined other critics, such as William Brighty Rands (No. 137) and Trollope (No. 140), in the belief that with Hawthorne 'we are made to think that he could not have been anything else if he would'. Likewise, in another essay instrumental in popularizing the solitary Hawthorne (No. 120), Curtis, trying to explain what for him were Hawthorne's unsatisfactory attitudes regarding slavery and the Civil War, describes him as 'a disembodied intelligence' whose 'genius obeyed its law'.

There were various attempts by Hawthorne's family to discredit the views of Curtis. In 1868 Mrs. Hawthorne, in her Introduction to *Passages from the American Note-Books*, tried to dispel the notion that Hawthorne had a 'morbid shyness'. So too did George Parsons Lathrop in his 1876 critical biography of Hawthorne (see No. 139) and Julian Hawthorne in *Hawthorne and His Wife*. Previous critics, Lathrop argues, had made 'the grossest errors' in using passages from Hawthorne's works as a direct explanation of his personality. The Hawthorne he characterizes is a much simpler, more conventional man: 'a large, healthy nature' who 'shared the average human history', liked animals and wild nature, and was 'one of the great believers of his generation'. In the end, however, Lathrop feels compelled to admit that 'it is impossible to define Hawthorne's personality precisely', since 'his real and inmost character was a mystery even to himself'.

The primary heir of this contemporary opinion—British and American—about Hawthorne was, of course, Henry James. His *Hawthorne*, the only volume written about an American author for the English Men of Letters Series, is, far from being the new critical appraisal it has often been taken to be, an astute synthesis and richly personal restatement of a long tradition of accumulated opinion in two countries.[58] His book reflects the nineteenth century's continuing attempt to define Hawthorne's individual sensibility and his essentially American consciousness through his fiction. A representative of the new realism, the young James had to come to grips with the psychological romance. The expatriate, he was called upon to explain for a British audience his old countryman, whom he had earlier called 'the last pure American' (No. 133). Even James's sometimes patronizing tone regarding Hawthorne's 'provinciality' and his use of allegory cannot obscure the fact that Hawthorne was the large presence he had to confront as he strived to establish his own identity as an American artist. The Hawthorne he confronted was a man whose career he, like earlier critics, saw as formed by the influence of the 'solitary years'. He cites an entry of 4 October 1840 from the *American Note-Books*—a 'singularly beautiful and touching passage' in which Hawthorne speaks of his sense of the world's having called him forth. Part of that passage describes the lonely years from 1825 to 1837:

Here I sit in my old accustomed chamber, where I used to sit in days gone by. . . . Here I have written many tales—many that have been burned to ashes, many that have doubtless deserved the same fate. This claims to be called a haunted chamber, for thousands upon thousands of visions have appeared to me in it; and some few of them have become visible to the world. If ever I should have a biographer, he ought to make mention of this chamber in my memoirs, because so much of my lonely youth was wasted here, and here my mind and character were formed . . .

If the terms of the description are romanticized and exaggerated, they nevertheless represent a personal and, given Hawthorne's cultural situation, necessary myth-making. As such, they have had for Hawthorne, for James, and for much of the history of Hawthorne criticism the force of truth.

V

THE CRITICAL TRADITION AFTER 1883

Unlike Poe, Melville, Whitman, and Emily Dickinson, who were to be discovered or rediscovered in the twentieth century, Hawthorne,

having finally achieved within his lifetime a substantial recognition, became, in the twenty years after his death, a fixture in the national
consciousness. The feeling was widespread that the country had at last
in Hawthorne an authentic and authentically national literary genius.
To judge by the unparalleled encomiums in both prose and poetry, his
death had all the dimensions of a cultural episode for a people struggling
to claim an identity for American art. A St. Louis Public Library survey
in 1886 ranked *The Scarlet Letter* along with *Don Quixote*, *Les Miserables*,
Ivanhoe, and works of Thackeray, Dickens, and Eliot as among the
world's ten best novels, and listed *The Marble Faun* among the top
twenty. Again, of the topics from which members of the 1884 English
literature class at Yale could choose their Junior Essays, only one—
'Hawthorne's Imagination'—had to do with an American writer. His
inclusion in such a list (some other titles were 'Development of the
Novel', 'Wordsworth's Place among the English Poets', and 'Shakespeare's Female Characters') bespeaks the fact that in the last quarter of
the century Hawthorne came to be regarded as a singular American
classic.

   Nor has his fame ever suffered a dramatic reversal. Hawthorne, unlike
Longfellow, Lowell, and Holmes, has survived radical shifts in literary
taste, and his work continues, in spite of revolutionary changes in the
techniques of fiction, to command a deep respect, attention, and belief.
The canons of realism and naturalism have long since been sounded and
modernism has come and gone, but Hawthorne still remains. Robert
Lowell, in a poem commemorating the 1964 Hawthorne centenary,
put it most eloquently when he spoke of Hawthorne as a hardened
veteran of battle.[59] Hawthorne clearly represents for Lowell a still
viable and compelling imaginative possibility whose truths have not
been compromised either by the demands of realism or by the events
of more recent history. But if his reputation has been steady, it has not
been a safe or static one. Hawthorne's fiction has been controversial as
well as impressive to every generation of readers and writers since 1883,
and it has been attacked from several quarters since Coxe's condemnation of *The Scarlet Letter* in 1840. Mark Twain, for example, though he
ranked Hawthorne supreme among American stylists, wrote to William
Dean Howells: 'I can't stand George Eliot, and Hawthorne and those
people; I see what they are at a hundred years before they get to it, and
they just tire me to death.'[60] In 1909 W. C. Brownell found Hawthorne
not only 'allegory-mad', but lacking in seriousness.[61] Whereas many
nineteenth-century critics romanticized Hawthorne's detachment,

several biographers and critics of the 1920s—notably Herbert Gorman, Floyd Morris, and the historian V. L. Parrington—intensified Curtis's complaint that Hawthorne was much too ignorant of the political and social life around him. The best-known and perhaps the most important negative statement about Hawthorne's art is Yvor Winter's 'Maule's Curse, or Hawthorne and the Problem of Allegory' (1937), which faulted Hawthorne for having turned away from the allegorical perfection in *The Scarlet Letter* to the novel, a literary form totally inconsistent with his genius. A more recent attack is Martin Green's 'The Hawthorne Myth: A Protest',[62] which insists that Hawthorne, far from being a great writer, is not even a good one, and that it was his aim in his fiction to write Gothic romances in the manner of Mrs. Radcliffe and so please the Victorian tastes of his audience and himself. Hawthorne's present reputation, Green argues, is inflated, the creation of academic critics who confuse what Green calls Hawthorne's 'habit of equivocation' with conscious techniques of irony and ambiguity.

While such charges stand in sharp contrast to the overwhelming weight of Hawthorne criticism, that criticism at its best has not characteristically been of the nature of mere appreciation. Almost from the very beginning there has been, as a recent casebook phrased it, 'the Hawthorne Question'. Hawthorne's imagination—and the nature of reality as he projects it in his works—has continued to trouble and perplex the American literary consciousness and to engage the interest of some of our best critical minds. Especially after James's *Hawthorne*, the terms of Hawthorne's art provided the issues around which nineteenth-century American literary criticism grew up. Howells made Hawthorne a critical touchstone in the 'realism war' of the 1890s and used his fiction to illustrate the differences not only between the romance and the realistic novel, but also between the serious or Hawthorian romance and the popular, sentimental romance. Edwin H. Cady has pointed to the extraordinary power of Hawthorne's influence: James and Howells, he writes, 'as features of their very rebellion against "the Mage", repeatedly created—and in psychological, moral, and even mystical, as well as aesthetic, development—significant variations upon themes by Hawthorne'.[63] Something of the same kind of paradox is evident in twentieth-century criticism. For example, Philip Rahv can say that 'a good deal of [Hawthorne's] writing, despite his gift for precise observation, consists of fantasy unsupported by the convention of reality'.[64] Lionel Trilling, on the other hand, has suggested that Hawthorne 'always consented to the power of his imagination being controlled by the power of the world'.[65] That both statements have a validity is a sign of Hawthorne's power and is at least a partial explanation for the massive amount of recent writing about him and his work.

Much indeed has been written about Hawthorne, especially since 1932, when Randall Stewart's edition of Hawthorne's *American Notebooks* was published.[66] Just since 1960 there have been over forty doctoral dissertations written on Hawthorne alone. Countless shorter studies about almost every conceivable aspect of his life—his family history, his early years, his years at Bowdoin, his editorships, his removal from the Custom House, his consulship—have followed. The definitive scholarly edition of his works is now being published. Critical volumes of every persuasion abound—psychological and psychoanalytic criticism, myth criticism and Marxist, and historical criticism. All of the twentieth-century techniques of formalist, scientific analysis have been brought to bear on the Hawthorne question. There have been studies of Hawthorne's aesthetic theories and of his political views, of his attitudes toward Puritanism, Transcendentalism, and Brook Farm, studies of his reading and literary borrowings, of his methods of composition and revision, studies of his influence on James, Melville, and other writers, studies of each of his works and his projected works. Few other American authors have in these years been scrutinized so thoroughly, and, although in the last several years Melville, James, and Faulkner have generated a slightly higher critical interest than Hawthorne, it is still unquestionably true for us as it was for Emily Dickinson that 'Hawthorne appals, entices—'.[67]

For the twentieth century as for the nineteenth the man and his fiction have had something of the inscrutable about them. Even so, the changes in attitude in Hawthorne criticism, especially in the area of biographical studies, have been phenomenal. The view of Hawthorne's contemporaries and of the nineteenth century in general, a view that saw Hawthorne as a retiring genius who shrank from most social relationships as well as from political issues and the currents of national life, has in the past several decades been almost completely reversed. Since 1940 no fewer than seven biographies have appeared: Edward Mather [Jackson], *Nathaniel Hawthorne, A Modest Man* (1940), Lawrence Sargeant Hall, *Hawthorne: Critic of Society* (1944), Robert Cantwell, *Nathaniel Hawthorne: The American Years* (1948), Randall Stewart, *Nathaniel Hawthorne: A Biography* (1948), Mark Van Doren, *Hawthorne* (1949), Edward Wagenknecht, *Nathaniel Hawthorne: Man and Writer* (1961), and Hubert Hoeltje, *Inward Sky: The Mind and Heart of Nathaniel*

Hawthorne (1962). Only the first of these does not insist that Hawthorne was a more worldly man who was a keen student of his environment and an active spokesman, both as man and writer, for democratic society. The years from 1825 to 1837 Stewart tries to demythologize altogether as 'active, busy, productive ones' in which 'Hawthorne was doing just what a young author ambitious of enduring fame should and must do. He was reading much and writing much.'[68]

One of the central curiosities of the modern view is that while the biographers have tended to paint an outward life of sunshiny conventionality for Hawthorne, our criticism has paid more and more exclusive attention to those tales which the nineteenth century had much less use for—tales eliciting that 'blackness of darkness' Melville was the first to speak of. Whereas Hawthorne's audience preferred its fiction to be sentimental and simple and expected its writers to be mysterious and even, perhaps, eccentric, many twentieth-century critics have come to view Hawthorne's life as normal, commonplace, even dull while focusing on that part of his fiction which echoes with darkness, mystery, complexity, and ambiguity. Many of our most influential studies—most notably F. O. Matthiessen's *American Renaissance* (1941), Marius Bewley's *The Complex Fate* (1952), R. W. B. Lewis's *The American Adam* (1955), Richard Chase's *The American Novel and Its Tradition* (1957), Charles Feidelson, Jr.'s, *Symbolism and American Literature* (1953), and Harry Levin's *The Power of Blackness* (1958)—have considered Hawthorne in relation to his milieu and then emphasized the darkness of his wisdom. It is startling to realize that 'My Kinsman, Major Molineux' went unmentioned in Hawthorne criticism before the 1950s. Now, along with 'Young Goodman Brown', 'The Minister's Black Veil', 'Ethan Brand', 'Rappaccini's Daughter', 'The Birthmark', and 'The Artist of the Beautiful', it is what we measure the greatness of his short fiction by. Several of the most basic critical studies announce our leading preoccupation in their titles: Richard Harter Fogle's *Hawthorne's Fiction: The Light and the Dark* (1952), William Bysshe Stein's *Hawthorne's Faust: A Study in Myth-making* (1953), and Roy R. Male's *Hawthorne's Tragic Vision* (1957). Hawthorne's son Julian, when he read his father's brooding works, said that he could not understand how 'a man such as I knew my father to be could have written such books. He did not talk in that way and his moods had not seemed to be of that color.'[69] Seeing in our biographies and critical studies the same discrepancies between man and writer, we are no longer amazed by them. A book, as Proust has said, is the work of a self different from the self we manifest in our social and private life. The works of such writers as Kafka, Faulkner, Camus, and Nathaniel West—to say nothing of the events of our time—have prepared us to accept the terrifying and absurd as existing side by side with the commonplace and conventional, and thus they too help explain our continuing interest in Hawthorne and his art.

Several years ago Irving Howe questioned: 'How much of Hawthorne, apart from one superb novel and seven or eight first-rate stories, remains worth reading? How much of the rest is truly alive and not merely propped up by academic piety?'[70] Clearly, we do read some of Hawthorne's works initially only because they are by the author of *The Scarlet Letter* and, clearly, there is much that cannot be claimed as a masterpiece. But precisely the same must be said of so many of our great writers. The phenomenon of failure is not unknown in American literature, and, as Tocqueville long ago reminded us, failure has in a genuinely democratic literature a special significance and value. We do not go to Hawthorne only for well-wrought urns. He is not the kind of writer we go to merely for answers. We go to him instead for our questions, for our sense of the difficult and intransigent, and in reading him we rediscover, among other things, the burden and tragedy of the creative process. Perhaps the true measure of his greatness is that he was able to make his failures our problems.

NOTES

1 Letter, 13 March 1821, *Hawthorne and His Wife* (1884), Julian Hawthorne, i.108.
2 George Parsons Lathrop, *A Study of Hawthorne* (1876), pp. 173–4.
3 Letter, 31 May 1831, *Hawthorne and His Wife*, i.132.
4 Letter, 3 May 1843, *Personal Recollections of Nathaniel Hawthorne* (1893), Horatio Bridge, p. 94.
5 See Seymour L. Gross, 'Hawthorne's Income from *The Token*', *Studies in Bibliography* (1956), vii.236–9.
6 Letter, 1 April 1844, *Personal Recollections of Nathaniel Hawthorne*, p. 98.
7 Letter, 25 September 1836, *Hawthorne and His Wife*, i.138–9.
8 Letter, 12 October 1854, to W. D. Ticknor, 'A Group of Hawthorne Letters', *Harper's Monthly Magazine*, Julian Hawthorne (March 1904), cviii.606–7.

9 S. G. Goodrich, *Recollections of a Lifetime* (1857), ii.262.

10 *Hawthorne*, ed. Tony Tanner (1967), p. 45.

11 Letter, 11 June 1837, MS., Houghton Library, Harvard University.

12 Letter [20 January 1851], Hawthorne-Fields Letter Book, Houghton Library, Harvard University. William Charvat first identified the date of this letter.

13 Letter, 7 March 1837, to Longfellow, MS., Houghton Library, Harvard University.

14 Letter, 22 December 1841, Duyckinck Collection, MS. Division, New York Public Library.

15 Hawthorne-Fields Letter Book, Houghton Library, Harvard University.

16 Letter [undated] to James T. Fields, *Yesterdays with Authors* (1871), James T. Fields, pp. 55–6.

17 Letter, 10 October 1859, *Yesterdays with Authors*, p. 85.

18 Letter, 11 February 1860, *Yesterdays with Authors*, pp. 87–8.

19 See my essay, 'A False Edition of Hawthorne's *Twice-Told Tales*', *Papers of the Bibliographical Society of America* (Second Quarter, 1965), lix.182–8.

20 Randall Stewart, *Nathaniel Hawthorne: A Biography* (1948), p. 141.

21 See William Charvat's 'Introduction' to the Centenary Edition of *The Scarlet Letter*, ed. William Charvat, Roy Harvey Pearce, and Claude M. Simpson (1962), I.xvi.

22 See George H. Ford, *Dickens and His Readers* (1965), p. 43.

23 Letter, 22 July 1851, *Personal Recollections of Nathaniel Hawthorne*, p. 127.

24 Letter, 12 March 1851, to Hawthorne, MS., Berg Collection, New York Public Library.

25 See Charvat's 'Introduction' to the Centenary Edition of *The House of the Seven Gables* (1965), II.xx. For further details, see W. S. Tryon and William Charvat, *The Cost Books of Ticknor and Fields, 1832–1858* (1949).

26 Data for various editions mentioned in this paragraph are given in Jacob Blanck, *Bibliography of American Literature* (1963), iv.3–13.

27 Letter, 18 October 1852, to Bridge, *Personal Recollections of Nathaniel Hawthorne*, p. 131.

28 See Claude M. Simpson's 'Introduction' to the Centenary Edition of *The Marble Faun*, ed. William Charvat *et al.* (1968), IV.xxiv.

29 *Ibid.*, pp. xxix–xxx.

30 *A Study of Hawthorne*, p. 131. For Curtis's views see No. 120 in this book. For a fuller discussion of the publication of *Fanshawe*, see also Roy Harvey Pearce's 'Introduction' to the Centenary Edition (1964), iii.302–10.

31 See the headnote to No. 14 for Hawthorne's letter to Longfellow on the occasion of this review.

32 Edward Waldo Emerson and Waldo Emerson Forbes (eds.), *The Journals of Ralph Waldo Emerson* (1912), vii.188.

33 *Hawthorne*, p. 109.

34 Letter, 27 April 1851, to Duyckinck, Duyckinck Collection, MS. Division, New York Public Library.

35 Letter, 3 November 1850, to Fields, MS., Houghton Library, Harvard University.

36 Letter, 29 November 1850, to Fields, MS., Collection of Norman Holmes Pearson. Cited in Charvat's 'Introduction' to *The House of the Seven Gables*, II.xxii.

37 See Rose Hawthorne Lathrop, *Memories of Hawthorne* (1897), p. 174.

38 *Hawthorne*, pp. 118–19.

39 *Ibid.*, pp. 119–20.

40 *Ibid.*, p. 124.

41 Letter, 22 July 1851, *Personal Recollections of Nathaniel Hawthorne*, p. 127.

42 Letter [undated] to Miss Mary Russell Mitford, *Nathaniel Hawthorne: A Biography*, p. 123.

43 See Gordon S. Haight (ed.), *The George Eliot Letters* (1954), ii.55n.

44 *My Literary Passions* (1895), p. 186.

45 *Hawthorne*, p. 127.

46 Letter, 18 October 1852, to Bridge, *Personal Recollections of Nathaniel Hawthorne*, p. 131.

47 17 March 1860, ix.341–2. Reprinted in *Littell's Living Age*, 12 May 1860, lxv.323–5.

48 Bright's review appeared in the *Examiner*, 31 March 1860, p. 197.

49 For a fuller discussion of the reception of *The Marble Faun* see Simpson, IV.xxviii–xxxviii.

50 Martha Tyler Gale, '*The Marble Faun*, with a Key to its Interpretation', *New Englander*, October 1861, xix.860–70. Reprinted in the same magazine, January 1892, lvi.26–36, with a note suggesting that Hawthorne had approved of Mrs. Gale's analysis.

51 June 1860, lv.679–88.

52 *North American Review*, April 1860, xc.557–8.

53 *New Englander*, May 1860, xviii.441–52.

54 *Hawthorne*, pp. 152ff.

55 Letter, 15 December 1852, to Lidian Emerson, *The Letters of Ralph Waldo Emerson*, ed. Ralph L. Rusk (1939), v.331.

56 *The Development of American Literary Criticism*, ed. Floyd Stovall (1955), p. 8.

57 Richard H. Fogle, 'Organic Form in American Criticism, 1840–1870', in *The Development of American Literary Criticism*, p. 106.

58 James was in all probability aware of the four French reviews published in the 1850s and 1860s: E. D. Forgues's 'Poètes et Romanciers Americain', *Revue des deux mondes* (15 April 1852), lxxxvi.337–65, a general comment on Hawthorne's works which views the Prefaces as autobiography; Emile Montegut's review of *The Blithedale Romance*, 'Un Roman Socialiste en Amerique', *Revue des deux mondes* (1 December 1852), lxxxviii.809–41;

L. Etienne's 'Les Conteurs Americains', *Revue Contemporaine* (May 1857), xxxi.633–63, an attempt to describe, especially in relation to *The House of the Seven Gables*, what the reviewer sees as Hawthorne's American and Puritan sense of evil; and Montegut's 'Un Romancier Pessimiste en Amerique', (1 August 1860), n.s. xxviii.668–703. Montegut's second essay James refers to in his study, objecting to the French critic's description of Hawthorne as a post-Puritan pessimist as 'very much beside the mark', because Hawthorne, far from having the old Puritan convictions, looked at them 'from the poetic and aesthetic point of view, the point of view of entertainment and irony' (*Hawthorne*, pp. 68, 69). Although these reviews are lengthy, serious statements printed in the leading literary journals, they make few original insights, and at times indulge in long plot summaries or repeat attitudes voiced by British and American critics. As attempts to attract a French audience for Hawthorne's fiction, the reviews, all basically favourable, have to be called failures: Hawthorne's works, according to Roger Asselineau, have never stimulated the lively French interest that those of Poe and Emerson have ('Hawthorne Abroad', *Hawthorne Centenary Essays*, pp. 381–5). The story of Hawthorne's reputation in both the nineteenth and twentieth centuries has been a decidedly Anglo-American one.

59 'Hawthorne', *Hawthorne Centenary Essays*, pp. 3–4.
60 Letter, 21 July 1885, *Selected Mark Twain-Howells Letters*, ed. Frederick Anderson, William M. Gibson, and Henry Nash Smith (1968), p. 250.
61 *American Prose Masters* (1909), pp. 63–130.
62 *Essays and Studies* (1963), xvi.16–36. Collected in Martin Green, *Re-appraisals: Some Commonsense Readings in American Literature* (1965), pp. 61–85.
63 '"The Wizard Hand": Hawthorne, 1864–1900,' *Hawthorne Centenary Essays*, p. 333. See also his discussion of the 'literary personality cult' which he says typifies so much of the writing done about Hawthorne in the later nineteenth century (pp. 320–4).
64 'The Cult of Experience in American Writing', *Literature in America*, ed. Philip Rahv (1957), pp. 365–6.
65 'Our Hawthorne', *Hawthorne Centenary Essays*, p. 454.
66 For a fuller treatment of recent Hawthorne scholarship see Seymour L. Gross and Randall Stewart, 'The Hawthorne Revival', *Hawthorne Centenary Essays*, pp. 335–66.
67 Letter, [?] December 1879, to Thomas Wentworth Higginson, *The Letters of Emily Dickinson*, ed. Thomas H. Johnson and Theodora Ward (1958), ii.649.
68 *Nathaniel Hawthorne: A Biography*, p. 44.
69 'The Salem of Hawthorne', *Century Magazine* (May 1884), xxviii.6.
70 [Review of Hawthorne Centenary Essays], *American Literature* (March 1965), xxxvii.81.

Note on the Text

The reviews and other commentaries in this volume follow the original texts in all important respects. It has been necessary at times to delete digressive or repetitive passages, lengthy plot summaries, and extracts from Hawthorne's works when these are quoted merely to illustrate the general style of the novel or tale in question. All these omissions are clearly indicated in the text. Typographical errors in the originals have been silently corrected, but a few variant spellings have been allowed to stand. The editor's footnotes are numbered; footnotes that are part of the text are asterisked, daggered etc. The texts of the Prefaces to the five romances follow the Centenary Edition of the *Works of Nathaniel Hawthorne* now being published by the Ohio State University Press; the texts of all other Prefaces are taken from the Riverside Edition of the *Complete Works*, edited by George Parsons Lathrop in twelve volumes, Cambridge, Mass., 1883.

FANSHAWE

1828, 1851

I. Notice in the *New England Galaxy*

31 October 1828, xi, 3

Hawthorne's first romance, published anonymously and never acknowledged by him, was advertised frequently in New England newspapers. This earliest notice, probably the work of Joseph T. Buckingham, editor of the *Galaxy*, is the only one to fault the book seriously.

Fanshawe. . . . A love story with this title has just been published by Marsh and Capen. It has, like ten thousand others, a mystery, an elopement; a villain, a father, a tavern, almost a duel, a horrible death, and— heaven save the mark! . . . an end.

2. [Sarah Josepha Hale] from a review in the *Ladies' Magazine*

November 1828, i, 526–7

The editor, Mrs. Hale, who edited *Godey's Lady's Book* from 1837 to 1877, is best remembered as the author of 'Mary had a Little Lamb'. One of those literary ladies whose sentimental tastes conditioned the American book trade, she was said to write reviews which were altogether uncritical and sentimental.

We must . . . recommend the book to all those who wish to encourage the talents of our own writers. But do not depend on obtaining it for perusal from a circulating library, or from a friend. Purchase it, reader. There is but one volume, and trust me that is worth placing in your library.

The time has arrived when our American authors should have something besides empty praise from their countrymen. Not that we wish to see a race of mere book-worm authors fostered among us. Our institutions and character, demand activity in business; the useful should be preferred before the ornamental; practical industry before speculative philosophy; reality before romance. But still the emanations of genius may be appreciated, and a refined taste cultivated among us, if our people would be as liberal in encouraging the merits of our own writers, if they would purchase the really excellent productions which depict our own country, scenes and character, as they do the vapid and worn-out descriptions of European manners, fashions and vices.

3. Unsigned notice in the *Yankee and Boston Literary Gazette*

6 November 1828, i, 358

This book, although it bears marks of haste or inexperience in composition, has nevertheless considerable merit. Many parts of it are powerful and pathetic, and there are not a few specimens scattered about the work of excellent descriptive pencilling. The story possesses considerable interest, and although the author has not as yet added greatly to his country's literature, he should be encouraged to persevering efforts by a fair prospect of future success. We have no more room to devote to Fanshawe than this slight notice will occupy.

4. Unsigned notice in the [Boston] *Bower of Taste*

8 November 1828, i, 718

This little volume, as a novel, contains about its due proportion of love and romance; the author appears to be less used to sketching eccentric characters than many others are. Nevertheless, much good reasoning and fine sentiment may be found in its pages, as also many classical allusions, which prove the writer of Fanshawe to be a scholar of no ordinary attainments. We were much interested in its perusal.

5. From an unsigned review in the *Boston Weekly Messenger*

13 November 1828, xviii, 1

The story of Fanshawe is, apparently, the first effort of a Collegian, and, naturally enough, he has resorted to the neighborhood and history of his own Alma Mater for the scenery and incidents of the tale. . . . [The plot] has great merit. It is true to nature, and in no part does it shock us by a violation of probability. Indeed, wherever there is a falling off in the book, it is not in the design, but in the filling up—in the throwing in of light and shade to give effect to the picture. We attribute this, in some degree, to the author's want of confidence in his own power. He is fearful of going too far, and does not proceed far enough. His reserve and diffidence have hindered him from throwing that spirit into his dialogues, which we believe is at his command. Hence we find that they are never sufficiently detailed. A practised writer would have made two or three large duodecimos from no more material than is contained in these 140 pages, and they would have been far more interesting than if he had left one half that amount to be supplied by the reader's fancy.

The characters in Fanshawe are not wholly original. The prototype of the nominal hero, is the Wilfred of Scott's Rokeby. Dr. Melmoth reminds us too forcibly of Dominie Sampson, and there are a few touches in the nameless stranger,—who, by the way, is excellently drawn,—that are in the Dirk Hatteraick style. Ellen does not stand out quite so boldly as we could wish, but then there is something quite admirable in the management of Hugh Crombie, the red-nosed tavern-keeper. Edward Walcott is the master-spirit of the piece, and with a very few exceptions we like him, exceedingly. He drinks wine and breaks looking-glasses with all the grace of a modern Sophomore, and considering the distance of his residence from the city, he is really, quite *au fait* in all that pertains to the gentleman in high life.

To the elegance of language which frequently occurs in this volume, we are pleased to bear testimony. There are some beauties of more than an ordinary kind, and they give promise of better things hereafter.

6. [William Leggett], from a review in the *Critic*

22 November 1828, i, 53–5

Leggett, a minor author and a leading abolitionist in New York, was part owner of the *Evening Post* and assistant editor under William Cullen Bryant.

Who wrote this book? Yet what need is there to know the name of the author, in order to pronounce a decision? Be he whom he may, this is not his first attempt, and we hope it will not be his last. The mind that produced this little, interesting volume, is capable of making great and rich additions to our native literature; and it will, or we shall be sadly mistaken. The author is a scholar, though he makes no ostentatious display of scholarship; he is a poet, though there are not two dozen metrical lines in the volume with which to substantiate the assertion; he is a gentleman, though the nearest approach to gentlemen in his pages, are two country college boys; and he possesses a heart alive to the beauties of nature, and the beauties of sentiment, and replete with all those kindly feelings which adorn and dignify human nature. His story is told in language, simple, chaste and appropriate; describing, so that the eye of the reader sees them, all the beautiful and varied traits of the landscape in which he has chosen to locate his narrative; describing the heavens in all their different aspects of storm and sunshine, in the gray twilight of morning, the sleepy splendour of noonday, and the gorgeous effulgence of sunset; and describing (a more difficult thing than all) the human heart, both as it lightly flutters in a young, pure, happy maiden's bosom, and as it heavily beats beneath the yellow and shrivelled skin of an octogenarian virago; both as it animates the dark recesses of a ruffian's breast, and the young, ardent, impetuous bosom of an honourable and thoughtless lad of eighteen. It takes a poet to do this. The delicacy of Fanshawe's attachment; the nice propriety of conduct which both he and his rival observe towards the object of their affection, and towards each other; the frankness with which one asked, and the refined and courteous manner in which the other granted, his forgiveness, after some harsh words had escaped between them—and a thousand other circumstances—are convincing proofs that the author is a gentleman; for none but a gentleman understands these things. There is no parade of manners, no mock sentiment, no stuff, about him; but there is sincerity, and ease, and urbanity, and an ever wakeful regard for others' feelings, all of which he imparts to his characters, giving them an irresistible attraction. . . .

But the book has faults. The plot lacks probability; there is too much villany in some of the characters; or rather, there are too many bad characters introduced; their number is disproportioned to that of the good ones. The fight of the heroine is without sufficient motive, especially as her nature was but little spiced with romance; her rescue is effected by improbable means; and finally, the gullibility and unsophisticatedness of the amiable principal of Harley College, is rather a caricature than a portrait.

We will not impair the interest of such of our readers as may intend perusing this delightful little volume, by giving a synopsis of its fable. . . . But we will extract one passage, that our remarks may be accompanied by proof that we have not eulogized without cause. It is a death-bed scene, at which the villain of the piece had been led to be present . . .

[Quotes ch. 8, 'Ellen had no heart' to 'out of the cottage'.]

We have quoted the most sombre scene in the volume. There is a great deal of gayety and buoyancy of spirit evinced by the writer, in other parts; but when poor Fanshawe occupies the page, he will sometimes excite the reader's tears in despite of himself. We love to read and love to review a work like this, where one can conscientiously shake hands with the author, and bid him, All hail, and be sure on leaving him, that no unkindly feelings have been created, to rankle in his breast, making both the critic and the criticised unhappy. Beside those already mentioned, we have no fault to find with the author of Fanshawe; but we shall have, if he does not erelong give us another opportunity of reading one of his productions. Is it not quite possible that Willis wrote this book? We merely *guess*.

7. Hawthorne, from a letter to James T. Fields

12 January 1851

MS., Hawthorne-Fields Letter Book, Houghton Library, Harvard University.

You make an inquiry about some supposed former publication of mine. I cannot be sworn to make correct answers as to all the literary or other follies of my nonage; and I earnestly recommend you not to brush away the dust that may have gathered over them. Whatever might do me credit, you may be pretty sure that I should be ready enough to bring forward. Anything else, it is our mutual interest to conceal; and so far from assisting your researches in that direction, I especially enjoin it on you not to read any unacknowledged page which you may suppose to be mine.

THE TOKEN

1835–7

---

8. [Park Benjamin], from a review of *The Token* for 1836, *New-England Magazine*

October 1835, ix, 294–8

Benjamin (1809–64), editor and publisher, achieved a large notoriety for his abusive reviews and his willingness, when editor of the *New World*, to reprint British works without paying the authors. In 1835 Hawthorne had accused him of running off with several pieces of his fiction. As editor of the *New-England Magazine*, Benjamin had agreed to publish serially Hawthorne's second projected collection of tales, *The Story-Teller*, but when the journal was absorbed by the *American Monthly Magazine* Benjamin apparently took four unpaid for manuscripts from that collection and subsequently printed them without Hawthorne's permission. The pieces Benjamin refers to in this review Hawthorne had published earlier in *The Token*; 'The Wedding Knell', 'The Minister's Black Veil', and 'The May-Pole of Merry Mount' are those that appeared in the 1836 volume.

. . . The stories are by Miss Sedgwick, by W. L. Stone, by the authors of 'The Affianced One,' 'Sights from a Steeple,' and 'The Gentle Boy,' —by Miss Leslie, Grenville Mellen, and John Neal; besides those who have the grace to be anonymous. The author of 'The Gentle Boy,' whom we regard as the most pleasing writer of fanciful prose, except Irving, in the country, and 'John Neal,' have displayed their usual freshness and originality.

9. [Henry F. Chorley], from a review of *The Token* for 1836, *Athenaeum*

7 November 1835, 830–1

Chorley (1808–72), whose career as a reviewer for the *Athenaeum* spanned almost forty years, commented on nearly all of Hawthorne's works. His criticism had the reputation of being impartial and discriminating, if hardly original in its perceptions. Hawthorne, seeing this review, wrote his family: 'My worshipful self is a very famous man in London, the "Athenaeum" having noticed all my articles in the last Token, with long extracts' (George Parsons Lathrop, *A Study of Hawthorne* [1876], p. 173).

The Token.—The proprietors of this Annual fairly and justly pride themselves on producing a volume, without having had recourse to the aid of British artists . . . we have two stories of darker colour, 'The Wedding Knell,' and 'The Minister's Black Veil,' each of which has singularity enough to recommend it to the reader. The sketch from which we shall make our extract, gives us a picturesque group of our old friends the Cavaliers and the Pilgrims, with (for once) a change in their characters; the latter being the aggressors, and waging war against that gay centre of English sports, 'The May-pole of Merry Mount.'

[Quotes most of the tale in four long extracts.]

10. [Park Benjamin], from a review of *The Token* for 1837, *American Monthly Magazine*

October 1836, n.s., ii, 405–7

The review is noteworthy because it marks the end of Hawthorne's anonymity. Benjamin, in being the first critic to publicly identify Hawthorne's authorship, lists all of his contributions to the 1837 *Token* except 'Mrs. Bullfrog', a piece so unlike Hawthorne that Benjamin may not have known it to be his.

We shall not observe the order of the volume in commenting upon the literary pretensions of the work. The stories are, for the most part, written in a chaste and agreeable style; and are superior, as a whole, to those of any previous American Souvenir. They are as interesting as many others are stupid, which is very exalted praise. . . . The author of 'Sights from a Steeple,' of 'The Gentle Boy,' and of 'The Wedding Knell,' we believe to be one and the same individual. The assertion may seem very bold, yet we hesitate not to call this author second to no man in the country, except Washington Irving. We refer simply to romance writing; and trust that no wise man of Gotham will talk of Dewey, and Channing, and Everett, and Verplanck. Yes, to us the style of NATHANIEL HAWTHORNE is more pleasing, more fascinating, than any one's, except their dear Geoffrey Crayon! This mention of the real name of our author may be reprobated by him. His modesty is the best proof of his true excellence. How different does such a man appear to us from one who anxiously writes his name on every public post! We have read a sufficient number of his pieces to make the reputation of a dozen of our Yankee scribblers; and yet, how few have heard the name above written! He does not even cover himself with the same anonymous shield at all times; but liberally gives the praise which, concentrated on one, would be great, to several unknowns. If Mr. Hawthorne would but collect his various tales and essays, into one volume, we can assure him that their success would be brilliant—certainly in

England, perhaps in this country. His works would, probably, make twice as many volumes as Mr. Willis's! How extended a notoriety has the latter acquired on productions, whose quantity and quality are both far inferior to those of this voluntarily undistinguished man of genius!

'The Token' would be richly worth its price for 'Monsieur du Miroir,' 'Sunday at Home,' 'The Man of Adamant,' and 'The Great Carbuncle,' if every other piece were as flat as the editor's verses. 'David Swan' is, if we mistake not, from the same graphic hand; and so is 'Fancy's Show-Box'; we are sure of 'The Prophetic Pictures.' A little volume, containing these stories alone, would be a treasure. 'The Great Carbuncle' is eminently good; and, like all the rest of our author's tales, both here and elsewhere, conveys an important moral. . . . We commend the Editor for his good taste in the selection of his prose papers, and we can think of only one method by which he can do better than he has done;—this is, next year to employ Hawthorne to write the whole volume, and not to look at it himself till it be for sale by all booksellers in town and country.

11. [Lewis Gaylord Clark], from a review of *The Token* for 1838, *Knickerbocker Magazine*

November 1837, x, 447–9

Clark (1808–73), editor of the *Knickerbocker*, one of the foremost American literary magazines of the time, did much to promote a national literature by encouraging contributions from American writers, among them Hawthorne, who in 1837 had published several tales and sketches there. Clark mentions all of the pieces Hawthorne contributed to the 1838 *Token*, but he seems not to recognize 'Sylph Etherege' and 'Night Sketches' as Hawthorne's.

'Peter Goldthwaite's Treasure' is from the pen, and in the peculiar vein, of the author of 'Twice-Told Tales,' whose writings are *well* known, in every sense, to our readers. We think we are not in error in attributing the spirited sketch, 'Endicott and the Red Cross,' to the same source. 'The Shaker Bridal,' may be traced to a kindred paternity not less unerringly by the table of contents, than by a certain style, which, although *sui generis*, partakes nevertheless of many of the simple graces of the fine old English prose writers. . . . There are pleasant love stories for the ladies, and young lovers of both sexes, as 'The Love Marriage,' by Mrs. Hale, [and] 'Sylph Etherege.' . . . 'Night Sketches beneath an Umbrella,' and 'Martha Washington,' the latter by Mrs. Sigourney, are the only prose articles which we have not named, and they are in all respects worthy the excellent company they keep.

TWICE-TOLD TALES

1837

---

12. Unsigned review in the *Salem Gazette*

14 March 1837, li, 2

We noticed very hastily, last week, the volume of 'Twice Told Tales,' . . . by Nath'l Hawthorne, which might be repeated many times without wearying the reader. There is real genius shewn in every page of his writing—a delicate taste and quick perception which create the finest touches of feeling and fancy; a brilliant and bold imagination which leads him far out of the beaten track of common story tellers; and a beautiful simplicity and elegance of style, which place him among the very first of American writers. Every story in this little volume is marked by some distinctive beauty and excellence. Mr. Hawthorne's quiet and cheerful humor brightens every view of human nature, while a tone of pensive feeling breathes out even from the lightest sports of his fancy. It is this combination which makes him so fascinating a writer, and which has been said to be an unfailing characteristic of true genius. A fine moral tone pervades all the creations of his fancy, which gives them a still stronger hold upon our regard. We cannot but hope to hear again from one so eminently qualified to take a conspicuous rank among those who have already gained a wide and enduring fame.

We are glad to perceive that the book is printed in the neat and beautiful style which marks every work that is published by the American Stationers' Co.

We have placed on our first page a tale ['Fancy's Show-Box'] taken at random from the volume, on account of its convenient length; but which will serve to illustrate favorably the talents of the writer.

13. From an unsigned review in the *Knickerbocker Magazine*

April 1837, ix, 422–5

This modest volume, which comes before us without preface, or any sort of appeal to the public regard, is well calculated to stand on its own merits, and to acquire enduring popularity. The author possesses the power of winning immediate attention, and of sustaining it, by a certain ingenuous sincerity, and by the force of a style at once simple and graceful. In all his descriptions, whether of scenes or emotions, nature is his only guide. He reminds us, continually, of the author of 'Outre-Mer,' who, it is but just praise to say, stands nearer to Washington Irving, in his peculiar walk of literature, than any American writer of our day. Let the reader peruse the following, from an essay entitled 'A Rill from the Town Pump,' and tell us if any thing could be more *Lamb*-like in its natural humor and beauty. The scene is at the corner of two principal streets in Salem, where the Town Pump is 'talking through its nose'.

[Quotes 'NOON, by the north' to 'have the gout?' and 'Your pardon' to 'your true toper'.]

The annexed contains a delicate hint, which should not be lost upon the *ultra* advocates of temperance, who have done no small injury to the good cause by their own intemperance:

[Quotes 'Ahem! Dry work' to 'the TOWN-PUMP!']

In the 'Sights from a Steeple' are conspicuously displayed the happy skill in grouping, and the felicity of expression, so characteristic of our author. A passage or two are subjoined:

[Quotes several long passages with deletions.]

Next to the discourse of the pump, we should rank 'Sunday at Home,' of which we have before spoken in these pages, 'Mr. Higginbotham's Catastrophe,' 'The Gentle Boy,' and 'Little Annie's Ramble.' 'The Minister's Black Veil,' and 'The Prophetic Pictures,' are less to our

fancy; but they are marked by good taste, and managed with adroitness. In short, in quiet humor, in genuine pathos, and deep feeling, and
in a style equally unstudied and pure, the author of 'Twice-Told Tales'
has few equals, and with perhaps one or two eminent exceptions, no
superior in our country. We confidently and cordially, therefore, commend the beautiful volume before us to the attention of our readers.

14. [Henry Wadsworth Longfellow], from a review in the *North American Review*

July 1837, xxxxv, 59-73

Hawthorne felt a special kinship with Longfellow (1807–82), a
fellow classmate at Bowdoin, whose literary reputation in 1837
gave Hawthorne hope of success. Hawthorne sent Longfellow a
copy of *Twice-Told Tales* and later wrote several times to the
poet suggesting that they collaborate on a volume of juvenile
stories. It was to Longfellow, too, that Hawthorne first spoke of
his 'solitary years'. In a letter dated 11 June 1837 he wrote: 'I
seldom venture abroad till after dark. By some witch craft or
other—for I really cannot assign any reasonable why and wherefore—I have been carried apart from the main current of life, and
find it impossible to get back again. Since we last met . . . I have
secluded myself from society; and yet I never meant any such
thing, nor dreamed what sort of life I was going to lead. I have
made a captive of myself and put me into a dungeon . . .' (MS.,
Houghton Library, Harvard University).

When a new star rises in the heavens, people gaze after it for a season
with the naked eye, and with such telescopes as they may find. In the
stream of thought, which flows so peacefully deep and clear, through
the pages of this book, we see the bright reflection of a spiritual star,
after which men will be fain to gaze 'with the naked eye, and with the
spy-glasses of criticism.' This star is but newly risen; and ere long the

observations of numerous star-gazers, perched up on arm-chairs and editors' tables, will inform the world of its magnitude and its place in the heaven of poetry, whether it be in the paw of the Great Bear, or on the forehead of Pegasus, or on the strings of the Lyre, or in the wing of the Eagle. Our own observations are as follows.

To this little work we would say, 'Live ever, sweet, sweet book.' It comes from the hand of a man of genius. Every thing about it has the freshness of morning and of May. These flowers and green leaves of poetry have not the dust of the highway upon them. They have been gathered fresh from the secret places of a peaceful and gentle heart. There flow deep waters, silent, calm, and cool; and the green trees look into them, and 'God's blue heaven.' The book, though in prose, is written nevertheless by a poet. He looks upon all things in the spirit of love, and with lively sympathies; for to him external form is but the representation of internal being, all things having a life, an end and aim. The true poet is a friendly man. He takes to his arms even cold and in-animate things, and rejoices in his heart, as did St. Bernard of old, when he kissed his Bride of Snow. To his eye all things are beautiful and holy; all are objects of feeling and of song, from the great hierarchy of the silent, saint-like stars, that rule the night, down to the little flowers which are 'stars in the firmament of the earth.' . . .

There are some honest people into whose hearts 'Nature cannot find the way.' They have no imagination by which to invest the ruder forms of earthly things with poetry. . . . But it is one of the high attributes of the poetic mind, to feel a universal sympathy with Nature, both in the material world and in the soul of man. It identifies itself likewise with every object of its sympathy, giving it new sensation and poetic life, whatever that object may be, whether man, bird, beast, flower, or star. As to the pure mind all things are pure, so to the poetic mind all things are poetical. To such souls no age and no country can be utterly dull and prosaic. They make unto themselves their age and country; dwelling in the universal mind of man, and in the universal forms of things. Of such is the author of this book.

There are many who think that the ages of Poetry and Romance are gone by. They look upon the Present as a dull, unrhymed, and prosaic translation of a brilliant and poetic Past. Their dreams are of the days of Eld; of the Dark Ages, of the days of Chivalry, and Bards, and Trouba-dours and Minnesingers. . . . We also love ancient ballads. Pleasantly to our ears sounds the voice of the people in song, swelling fitfully through the desolate chambers of the past, like the wind of evening among ruins. And yet this voice does not persuade us that the days of balladry were more poetic than our own. The spirit of the past pleads for itself, and the spirit of the present likewise. If poetry be an element of the human mind, and consequently in accordance with nature and truth, it would be strange indeed, if, as the human mind advances, poetry should recede. The truth is, that when we look back upon the Past, we see only its bright and poetic features. All that is dull, prosaic, and common-place is lost in the shadowy distance. . . . With the Present it is not so. We stand too near to see objects in a picturesque light. What to others at a distance is a bright and folded summer cloud, is to us, who are in it, a dismal, drizzling rain. Thus to many this world, all beautiful as it is, seems a poor, working-day world. . . . Thus has it been since the world began. Ours is not the only Present, which has seemed dull, common-place, and prosaic.

The truth is, the heaven of poetry and romance still lies around us and within us. If people would but lay aside their 'abominable spectacles,' the light of The Great Carbuncle* would flash upon their sight with astonishing brightness. So long as truth is stranger than fiction, the elements of poetry and romance will not be wanting in common life. If, invisible ourselves, we could follow a single human being through a single day of its life, and know all its secret thoughts, and hopes, and anxieties, its prayers, and tears, and good resolves, its passionate delights and struggles against temptation,—all that excites, and all that soothes the heart of man,—we should have poetry enough to fill a volume. Nay, set the imagination free, like another Bottle-imp, and bid it lift for you the roofs of the city, street by street, and after a single night's observation you shall sit you down and write poetry and romance for the rest of your life.

We deem these few introductory remarks important to a true understanding of Mr. Hawthorne's character as a writer. It is from this point that he goes forth; and if we would go with him, and look upon life and nature as he does, we also must start from the same spot. In order to judge of the truth and beauty of his sketches, we must at least know the point of view, from which he drew them. Let us now examine the sketches themselves.

---

* See Mr. Hawthorne's story with this title. If some persons, like the cynic here mentioned, cannot see the gems of poetry which shine before them, because of their colored spectacles, others resemble the alchymist in the same tale, who 'returned to his laboratory with a prodigious fragment of granite which he ground to powder, dissolved in acids, melted in the crucible, and burnt with the blowpipe, and published the result of his experiments in one of the heaviest folios of the day.'

The Twice-told Tales are so called, we presume, from having been first published in various annuals and magazines, and now collected together, and told a second time in a volume by themselves. And a very delightful volume do they make; one of those, which excite in you a feeling of personal interest for the author. A calm, thoughtful face seems to be looking at you from every page; with now a pleasant smile, and now a shade of sadness stealing over its features. Sometimes, though not often, it glares wildly at you, with a strange and painful expression. . . .

One of the most prominent characteristics of these tales is, that they are national in their character. The author has wisely chosen his themes among the traditions of New England; the dusty legends of 'the good Old Colony times, when we lived under a king.' This is the right material for story. It seems as natural to make tales out of old tumble-down traditions, as canes and snuff-boxes out of old steeples, or trees planted by great men. The puritanical times begin to look romantic in the distance. . . . Truly, many quaint and quiet customs, many comic scenes and strange adventures, many wild and wondrous things, fit for humorous tale, and soft, pathetic story, lie all about us here in New England. There is no tradition of the Rhine nor of the Black Forest, which can compare in beauty with that of the Phantom Ship. The Fly-ing Dutchman of the Cape, and the Klabotermann of the Baltic, are nowise superior. The story of Peter Rugg, the man who could not find Boston, is as good as that told by Gervase of Tilbury, of a man who gave himself to the devils by an unfortunate imprecation, and was used by them as a wheelbarrow; and the Great Carbuncle of the White Mountains shines with no less splendor, than that which illuminated the subterranean palace in Rome, as related by William of Malmesbury. . . .

Another characteristic of this writer is the exceeding beauty of his style. It is as clear as running waters are. Indeed he uses words as mere stepping-stones, upon which, with a free and youthful bound, his spirit crosses and recrosses the bright and rushing stream of thought. Some writers of the present day have introduced a kind of Gothic architecture into their style. All is fantastic, vast, and wondrous in the outward form, and within is mysterious twilight, and the swelling sound of an organ, and a voice chanting hymns in Latin, which need a translation for many of the crowd. To this we do not object. Let the priest chant in what language he will, so long as he understands his own mass-book. But if he wishes the world to listen and be edified, he will do well to choose a language that is generally understood.

And now let us give some specimens of the bright, poetic style we praise so highly. Here is the commencement of a sketch entitled 'The Vision of the Fountain.' What a soft and musical flow of language! And yet all as simple as a draught of water from the fountain itself.

[Quotes 'At fifteen, I' to 'it had ever been'.]

Here are a few passages from a sketch called 'Sunday at Home.'

[Quotes several long passages with deletions.]

We are obliged to forego the pleasure of quoting from the Tales. A tale must be given entire, or it is ruined. We wish we had room for 'The Great Carbuncle,' which is our especial favorite among them all. It is, however, too long for this use. Instead thereof, we will give one of those beautiful sketches, which are interspersed among the stories, like green leaves among flowers. But which shall we give? Shall it be 'David Swan'; or 'Little Annie's Ramble'; or 'The Vision of the Fountain'; or 'Fancy's Show-Box'; or 'A Rill from the Town Pump'? We decide in favor of the last.

[Quotes the entire sketch.]

These extracts are sufficient to show the beautiful and simple style of the book before us, its vein of pleasant philosophy, and the quiet humor, which is to the face of a book what a smile is to the face of man. In speaking in terms of such high praise as we have done, we have given utterance not alone to our own feelings, but we trust to those of all gentle readers of the Twice-told Tales. Like children we say, 'Tell us more.'

15. Notice in the *Family Magazine*

November 1837, v, 280

Eighteen as pretty little tales as ever were told; so good indeed, that the titlepage tells us they are here 'twice told.' Several of these are fully equal to any in the 'Sketch Book'. 'Sunday at Home,' 'Sights from a Steeple,' and 'A Rill from the Town Pump,' are sketches that will be remembered as long as the 'Broken Heart,' or the 'Legend of Sleepy Hollow.' In our judgement, there has been no book published these twelve months, worthy a higher place in one's affections, than this same 'Twice Told Tales.'

16. [Charles Fenno Hoffman], a review in the *American Monthly Magazine*

March 1838, n.s., v, 281–3

Hoffman (1806–84), an author well known for travel literature and popular poetry, had editorial positions on several New York periodicals. Hawthorne contributed only a few pieces to the *American Monthly.*

A rose bathed and baptized in dew—a star in its first gentle emergence above the horizon—are types of the soul of Nathaniel Hawthorne; every vein of which (if we may so speak) is filled and instinct with beauty. It has expanded like a blossom, in the gay sunshine and sad shower, slowly and mutely to a rich and natural maturity. The 'Twice-told Tales' are well worth twice telling. They are the offspring of a calm, meditative fancy, enlivened at times with a flickering ray of humor.

Minds, like Hawthorne's, seem to be the only ones suited to an American climate. Quiet and gentle intellect gives itself, in our country, oftener to literature, than intellect of a hardier and more robust kind. Men endowed with vigorous and sturdy faculties are, sooner or later, enticed to try their strength in the boisterous current of politics or the Pactolian stream of merchandize. Would that some few of them had the will and the energy to cast off the heavy fetters of politics (or wear them lightly, if they needs must be worn,) and nurse their capacities for nobler tasks! Thus far American authors, who have been most triumphant in winning a name, have been of the gentler order. We can point to many Apollos, but Jove has not as yet assumed his thunder, nor hung his blazing shield in the sky.

Never can a nation be impregnated with the literary spirit by minor authors alone. They may ripple and play round the heart, and ensnare the affections, in their placid flow; but the national mind and imagination are to be borne along only on the ocean-stream of a great genius. Yet men like Hawthorne are not without their use; nay, they are the writers to smooth and prepare the path for nobler (but not better) visitants, by softening and ameliorating the public spirit. Of this latter class we know no better and no pleasanter companion than the author of 'Twice-told Tales.' To be read fitly, he should be read in the right mood and at the proper hour. To be taken up in haste and opened at random, would do him great wrong.

He should be perused in the holy calm of a summer's eve, or in the contemplative cheerfulness of a shiny autumn morning. Reading thus, we will be charmed with the book and the author. Quiet beauties (unseen of vulgar eyes) will steal out, and win their entrance into the soul unawares. Pleasant thoughts will glide out of the silent page, and gain access to the affections; and as we muse over the closed volume, we will say to ourselves, 'Surely life is a shadow, fringed with sunshine: sorrow is the main burthen of the history; happiness and gladness are merely episodes—and thus it passes away!' The copy of Hawthorne's Tales, which we chanced to peruse, had unfortunately fallen, before we received it, into the hands of one of those volunteer annotators, whose business it is to scribble on margins and at the foot of the page, erudite comments for the benefit of their successors. At the end of sundry stories in this duodecimo, *our* learned Theban has written 'Poor!' 'Slim and stupid!' &c. and at the close of the tale entitled 'The Minister's

Black Veil,' he has affixed 'Slim and Poor.' Unknown and pitiable creature! whithersoever thy fate has, by this time, borne thee—a malison be upon thee—mayest thou fall into the hands of Philistines and attornies—and may thy next two notes (for thy hand-writing betrays thee mercantile) lie over at the bank! Poor drudge! thou hast wronged, foully wronged one of the finest spirits in the land; and in thy critical note on that last tale (pregnant as it is with pathetic thought and profound meditation,) hast thou enlisted under Dogberry in the great Company of Dunces, and written thyself down as ass! Vanish, meanest of mankind, vanish—and give us leave once more to be with the author.

A writer like Hawthorne, who restricts himself to subjects in which individual feelings are expressed, is, of course, confined to a narrower range than the writer who undertakes to become the speaker for many kinds and classes of men. The essayist moves in a small and charmed circle; the novelist and the dramatic author have the circumference of the globe itself, in which to disport. The former, it is true, furnishes us with a more perfect mirror of the author's thoughts and actions, and lets us into the secret of his life; and hence arises the charm and the glory of the essay and the personal story. When a noble spirit, like Hawthorne, condescends to throw open to us the leaves of his private life, and to make us familiar with him in his little household of joys and sorrows, we should deal kindly with his errors, if any there be; and admire his gentle beauties with generous and heart-deep enthusiasm. The perusal of the 'Twice-told Tales' has excited in us many feelings 'too deep for tears.'

We have been led by it to contemplate the author in the twilight of a dim regret, and to picture him to ourselves as a stricken deer in the forest of life.

Some rending and ever-remembered sorrow seems to hover about his thoughts, and color them with the shadow of their presence. Almost every story in the volume is filled with a pervading sadness. In these pages sunshine is a transient visitor; cloud and darkness and a softer gloom, perpetual guests.

We think that the main peculiarity of Hawthorne, as a writer, and that which distinguishes him from any other with whom we are acquainted, is this same fine tone of sadness that pervades his best tales and sketches. One class of writings in this volume reminds us of Lamb, although without the antique, humorous, and high-sounding phrases which render the style of Elia so singular and profound of its kind. 'The Rill from the Town-Pump' is very much in this vein.

A second class of Hawthorne's sketches rivals Irving himself in occasional graphic thoughts and phrases, and partakes not a little of his picturesque mode of viewing a topic. We would instance 'Dr. Heidegger's Experiment,' where four venerable personages, in the withered extreme of age, are transformed into as many gay, frisking creatures in 'the happy prime of youth,' by a draught from the famous Fountain of Youth. It struck us as a very apt companion-piece to Irving's 'Mutability of Literature.' 'Fancy's Show-Box' has a sentence, here and there, flavored strongly with the Sketch Book humor. In the third species of writing in this volume, Hawthorne follows no model, imitates no predecessor, that we can recollect. He is himself. And these, to our mode of thinking, appear to be the gems and jewels of the work. The style is flowing, smooth, serious. The tone of the pieces, mellowed, calm, meditative. The manner of diffusing his subject, peculiar to himself, and original. The sketches and stories in which these characteristics predominate, outnumber, as might be expected, those of a different kind. 'Sunday at Home,' 'The Wedding Knell,' 'The Minister's Black Veil,' 'The Prophetic Pictures,' 'Sights from a Steeple,' are as fine essays of their kind as may be found in the English language. In fact, we scarcely know where to look for productions with which to compare them.

Many have written more pathetic and mournful stories, many have indulged in a tender, moralizing sorrow, as they looked upon the world and humanity: this many have accomplished admirably—Addison, Mackenzie, Lamb, and others. But nowhere do you find the new strain in which Hawthorne so eloquently pours forth his individual feelings.

His pathos, we would call New England pathos, if we were not afraid it would excite a smile; it is the pathos of an American, a New Englander. It is redolent of the images, objects, thoughts, and feelings that spring up in that soil, and nowhere else. The author of 'Twice-told Tales' is an honor to New England and to the country. These tales have passed through their first edition. When shall we have a second, enlarged by the delightful papers Mr. Hawthorne has lately produced?

17. A[ndrew] P[reston] P[eabody], from a review in the *Christian Examiner*

November 1838, xxv, 182–90

Peabody (1811–93), a leading Unitarian clergyman and later a Harvard Professor of Christian Morals, became editor and owner of the *North American Review* in 1853.

The mental and moral influence of the most faultless novels and tales of the fashion now current is at least questionable. There is reason to apprehend, that no mind could feed much upon them, without finding its notions of life unsettled, and the balance of its moral judgment disturbed. And the fault lies, not in any depravity of taste or perversion of feeling in the writers, but in the peculiar *kind* of composition. Fictions of this class create, where there is a creation already. They usurp the realm of fact, and change its order into anarchy. They disturb and displace the fabric of things as they are, and build up their ideal world in the very same space, which the actual world occupies. But true poetry, (from which higher fiction differs only in form,) takes for the theatre of its creations space unoccupied by grosser shapes and material agencies. Its province lies beyond, beneath, and within the world of matter and of fact. It leaves things as they are; but breathes into them a vital glow, writes upon them the image of the unseen and spiritual, and robes them in a softer light, a richer charm, a purer beauty. This is the character of the Tales before us. For this we prize and admire them. They are poetry from the deepest fountains of inspiration. Their interest consists in the development, not of events, but of sentiment. Many of them have neither plot nor catastrophe, indeed, are not tales in the common sense of the word; but are simply flower-garlands of poetic feeling wreathed around some everyday scene or object.

We thank and love the man, who draws aside for us the veil between sense and spirit, who reveals to us the inward significance, the hidden harmonies of common things, who bathes in poetic teints the prosiac elements of daily life. We welcome such a work, and deem it truly great, however humble or unostentatious the form in which it is wrought. We feel that Mr. Hawthorne has done this for us, and we thank him. We thank him also for having given us creations so full of moral purity and beauty.

We are charmed by the naiveté of these tales. Their style is perfectly transparent. The author shows himself in all of them; and we feel, after the perusal of this little volume, as if we had always been familiarly acquainted with him. The best pieces in the volume are those, which give us merely a transcript of the author's own musings, with barely a thread of incident to bind them together. The 'Sunday at Home' could have been written only by one, who revelled in the hushed calm and holy light of the Sabbath, whose soul was attuned to its harmonies, but of so fastidious a taste and delicate a sensibility, as to be repelled and chilled by the dissonances of the multitude's worship. 'Sights from a Steeple' is a graphic and beautiful sketch (à la 'Diable Boiteux,') of the scenes and adventures, discernible in a half hour's gaze from a church steeple,—a picture which, as every one knows, must needs borrow its shapes and colors much more from the author's own mind, than from the city of his residence. 'A Rill from the Town-pump' is an outgush (in the form of a soliloquy by the pump) of those manifold and party-colored associations and feelings, which always cluster around an object, however humble, which has been familiar to the eye from infancy; and the object is in itself so bare, barren, unsuggestive, as to give us the clearer insight into the mind, which could weave its ungraceful trunk, and arm, and trough, into a charming little idyll, as clear and refreshing as its own cool stream. There is hardly anything in the volume, which pleases us more than 'Little Annie's Ramble,' which is a mere sketch, simple, natural, full of child-like feeling, of a child's stroll with her friend through the gay streets of the town, by the print-shops and the toy-shops, through all the little worlds of gorgeous sights, which arrest infancy's lingering steps on its earliest walks.

The chief fault, which we can find with these delicious phantasies, is, that some of them are too vague and dreamy, drawn with dim and shadowy outlines only. If we may be allowed to prophesy, we pronounce this volume, beautiful as we deem it, as but a gathering of early windfalls,—the earnest of future rich, ripe, mellow harvests, we hope, for half a century to come. A mind so rich, a heart so pure and so enamored with purity, a love of nature so confiding and child-like, an imagination so teeming with gorgeous fancies, cannot blossom and shed its first-fruits, without awakening the fondest hopes and betraying the brightest promise.

There is hardly one of these Tales, grave or gay, which we would not gladly give our readers; and we hardly know where to make our choice. We should like to transfer 'The Gentle Boy' to our pages; but it is too long, and would not bear the scissors. We will content ourselves with 'David Swan,'—a leaf out of the every-day book of life, illustrating the safe and narrow path by which a kind Providence guides us between hidden precipices and chasms, by unseen pitfalls both of sorrow and of deceptive joy.

[Summarizes the story and quotes four long passages with deletions.]

Our author's peculiar talent seems to be that disclosed in the Tale just quoted,—that, not of weaving a material plot, but of gathering a group of spirit phantoms around some scene or moment in itself utterly uneventful.

These Tales abound with beautiful imagery, sparkling metaphors, novel and brilliant comparisons. They are everywhere full of those bright gems of thought, which no reader can ever forget. They contain many of those bold master-strokes of rhetoric, which dispatch whole pages of description in a single word. Thus, for instance, an adopted child is spoken of as 'a domesticated sunbeam' in the family, which had adopted him. How full of meaning is that simple phrase! How much does it imply, and conjure up of beauty, sweetness, gentleness, and love! How comprehensive, yet how definite! Who, after reading it, can help recurring to it, whenever he sees the sunny, happy little face of a father's pride or a mother's joy? This is but one of many of our author's similes, which we find branded into our own memory, as instinct with life and beauty.

We have spoken of the high moral tone of these pages. It is for this, for their reverence for things sacred, for their many touching lessons concerning faith, Providence, conscience, and duty, for the beautiful morals so often spontaneously conveyed, not with purpose prepense, but from the fulness of the author's own heart, that we are led to notice them in this journal. We close our notice by extracting two or three passages, which will convey some idea of the holy breathings that pervade the book. Our first extract is from the 'Sunday at Home.'

[Quotes 'On the Sabbath, I' to 'it will return again.']

We must not forget the beautiful close of 'Little Annie's Ramble.' Annie's mother, alarmed by her absence, has commissioned the town-crier to look her up.

[Quotes 'Stop, stop' to 'dear little Annie!']

Who does not recognise in this extract, and in the whole playful little piece which it closes, a beautiful, though unintended commentary on the divine act of Him, who, to allay the heated passions and jealousies of wrathful and selfish men, 'called a little child unto him, and set him in the midst of them'?

THE GENTLE BOY;
A THRICE-TOLD TALE

1839

---

18. Hawthorne, from the Preface

1839

The Tale, of which a new edition is now offered to the Public, was among the earliest efforts of its Author's pen; and, little noticed on its first appearance, in one of the Annuals [*The Token* for 1832], appears ultimately to have awakened the interest of a larger number of readers, than any of his subsequent productions. For his own part, he would willingly have supposed that a more practised hand, and cultivated fancy, had enabled him to excel his first artificial attempts; and there are several among his TWICE-TOLD TALES, which, on re-perusal, affect him less painfully with a sense of imperfect and ill-wrought conception, than THE GENTLE BOY. But the opinion of many (whose judgment, even in cases where they and he might be equally unprejudiced, would be far preferable to his own,) compels him to the conclusion, that Nature here led him deeper into the Universal heart, than Art has been able to follow. It was no gift within himself—no effort that could be renewed at pleasure—but a Happiness that alighted on his pen, and lent it somewhat of power over human sympathies, which he may vainly strive to snatch again.

19. Notice in the *New York Review*

April 1839, iv, 493

Of this exquisite story, so generally and deservedly admired, we need say nothing more than that this edition is put out to accompany an etching after the manner of Retzsch, by Miss Sophia A. Peabody, which for beauty and grace well merits the approbation it has received from our greatest painter, and which might well excite the gratification Mr. Hawthorne has expressed in his charming preface.

20. Notice in the *Literary Gazette*

22 June 1839, 392

We confess we cannot tell what to make of this sentimental rhapsody. There is a pretty outline illustration.

21. Hawthorne, Preface

1841

In writing this ponderous tome, the author's desire has been to describe the eminent characters and remarkable events of our annals in such a form and style that the YOUNG may make acquaintance with them of their own accord. For this purpose, while ostensibly relating the adventures of a chair, he has endeavored to keep a distinct and unbroken thread of authentic history. The chair is made to pass from one to another of those personages of whom he thought it most desirable for the young reader to have vivid and familiar ideas, and whose lives and actions would best enable him to give picturesque sketches of the times. On its sturdy oaken legs it trudges diligently from one scene to another, and seems always to thrust itself in the way, with most benign complacency, whenever an historical personage happens to be looking round for a seat.

There is certainly no method by which the shadowy outlines of departed men and women can be made to assume the hues of life more effectually than by connecting their images with the substantial and homely reality of a fireside chair. It causes us to feel at once that these characters of history had a private and familiar existence, and were not wholly contained within that cold array of outward action which we are compelled to receive as the adequate representation of their lives. If this impression can be given, much is accomplished.

Setting aside Grandfather and his auditors, and excepting the adventures of the chair, which form the machinery of the work, nothing in the ensuing pages can be termed fictitious. The author, it is true, has sometimes assumed the license of filling up the outline of history with details for which he has none but imaginative authority, but which, he hopes, do not violate nor give a false coloring to the truth. He believes that, in this respect, his narrative will not be found to convey ideas and impressions of which the reader may hereafter find it necessary to purge his mind.

The author's great doubt is, whether he has succeeded in writing a book which will be readable by the class for whom he intends it. To make a lively and entertaining narrative for children, with such unmalleable material as is presented by the sombre, stern, and rigid characteristics of the Puritans and their descendants, is quite as difficult an attempt as to manufacture delicate playthings out of the granite rocks on which New England is founded.

22. Notice, in the *Athenaeum*

4 June 1842, pp. 501–2

Liberty Tree, with the *Last Words of Grandfather's Chair* . . . We hold the 'Twice Told Tales' aforesaid in such pleasant remembrance, as to have opened 'Liberty Tree' with higher expectations than it is fair to bring to a child's book; yet, on the whole, we have not been disappointed: and as a collection of stories of American history, it will be welcome on this as well as the other side of the Atlantic.

23. [James Russell Lowell], from a review of *Historical Tales for Youth, Pioneer*

January 1843, i, 41–2

Lowell (1819–91), was editor of the *Pioneer*, in which Hawthorne's 'The Hall of Fantasy' and 'The Birthmark' first appeared. The periodical lasted for just three issues, being too discriminating to appeal sufficiently to the sentimental-moral popular taste.

When a man of acknowledged genius gives himself to the task of writing books for children, we know not whether to feel more surprise or grateful delight. That one whose pen always commands the loving admiration of his countrymen, should quietly turn aside from the alluring road which was leading him right onward to the height of ambition, to do a work of humble charity, whose silent consciousness must be its only reward, is a rare thing, and as purely beautiful as it is rare. But we are used to look for beautiful things from the author of 'Twice Told Tales.'

It has too long been a vulgar error, more deadly than any which the wise Sir Thomas Browne rooted out, that no elderly male or female (of good character) could be too stupid to write a book for children. While the quantity of a child's imagination was as yet hypothetical, it was ingeniously supposed that it had none at all, and, while romance was sternly outlawed from the nursery, pedantic commonplace and mathematical morality, inculcated till dulness and virtue grew in the childish mind to be convertible terms, reigned paramount there. . . . Now Mr. Hawthorne is making our New England history as delightful to the children as he has already to the parents. We hope he will not let his labors for the youthful deprive us of his instructions for the more mature, for we all need him, old as well as young. Like a true genius, he has made his own heart the centre from which all his artistic power has emanated, and found his materials around his very door. He has woven the softening halo of romance around the iron visages of the puritans, and intertwined the gentle flowers of love and poesy with the self-inflicted crown of thorns which encircled their gloomy and sallow brows. He has painted the old New England character in true, but soft and harmonious, colors, and illustrated the gentle and more graceful elements of it by the retired simplicity of his life. May the tears which his own tender and exquisite pathos draw from us, be all that we shall ever be called on to shed for him!

24. E. A. Duyckinck: Hawthorne's early work, from an unsigned essay, 'Nathaniel Hawthorne', in *Arcturus*

May 1841, i, 330–7

Duyckinck (1816–78), who was to become a close friend of Haw-thorne's and arrange for the publication of *Mosses from an Old Manse* (1846), was one of the most eminent literary men of the country. Editor of *Arcturus* and, later, of the *Literary World*, Duyckinck co-edited with his brother George the *Cyclopaedia of American Literature* (1855; revised 1866). Late in 1841 Duyckinck requested contributions from Hawthorne for *Arcturus*, and Hawthorne, in answering, spoke of this review:

Perhaps it would be decorous in me to decline some considerable part of the approbation there bestowed, as being quite beyond my deserts; but I cannot find it in my heart to do it. It is true, the public will never ratify it; but at least, the writer felt what he expressed; and therefore I have a right to receive it as genuine testimony to the impressions which I have produced. And, certainly, I would far rather receive earnest praise from a single individual, than to be claimed a tolerably pleasant writer by a thousand or a million. (22 December 1841, Duyckinck Collection, MS. Division, New York Public Library.)

In his own peculiar walk of fiction and sentiment, there is perhaps no author in English literature who could supply to us the few natural beautiful sketches of Nathaniel Hawthorne. Of the American writers destined to live, he is the most original, the one least indebted to foreign models or literary precedents of any kind, and as the reward of his genius he is the least known to the public. It might be thought that in the small band of true native authors there would be none neglected; that here among a people tenacious of national character, the reputation of the author would be secure; that out of a nation of readers, originality and genius would call forth numerous friends and devotees; that if the authors of the country were few, 'the fewer men, the greater share of honor.' But it is not so, reputation is dependent upon other qualities than worth alone, or we would not have at this day material for an article upon the genius of Hawthorne.

Doubtless Hawthorne has many admirers: his native New England must contain many who love his awe-stricken tales of the old colony times, of the era of the Province House, of the terror of Salem Witchcraft, of the picturesque gathering at the siege of Louisbourg; there are others who may unwittingly owe him thanks for pure descriptions of nature, passages of refined sentiment and graceful thought, that have found their way into the newspapers without any mention of the author. The loss of notoriety in this way we are sure would be no cause of regret to Hawthorne, for in the noiseless utterance of his reflections through the omnipresent press he might in all humility recognise an element of beneficence, free as the air of summer, carrying everywhere the blessing of the Unseen Benefactor. Notoriety, contemporary reputation,—they are but weak voices of that sound of Fame which breathes from the lips of the author, to live through his country and beyond his age, though it be heard only in the still small voice of conscious thought, or have its most enduring record imprinted on the flushed countenance of the lonely reader.

It need be no cause of regret to the friends of Hawthorne that he is not popular in the common acceptation of the word, for popularity is not essential to his success. He has written, not because others admire, but because he himself feels. His motive was from within. He could not have written better if a publisher had stood by his side feeding the flame of authorship with checks on the banker, or a body of editors been ready with paste and scissors to manufacture his wares in the best possible shape for the public. His merit does not need the verdict of multitudes to be allowed. It is not with him as with a novelist or dramatist who catches at the favor of the moment, and is everything or nothing according to the issue of his experiment. The writings of Hawthorne can bear the delay of favor, they cannot perish, for they spring from the depths of a true heart. They are part of the genuine recorded experience of humanity, and must live.★

★ We would be pleased to find that our author is more popular than we have represented him, but we have mentioned his name to many, who then heard it for the first time, and some of them book makers as well as book readers. We do not remember any mention of his name in English journals, save on one occasion in the small print of the London Literary Gazette, where his fine tale of The Gentle Boy, beautifully illustrated by a design drawn by Miss Peabody, was pronounced incomprehensible and absurd! It occurred to us

It will be seen that we attribute a deeper philosophy, a higher influence to these writings, than the description tales and essays, might seem to warrant. In truth, though written in prose, they are poems of a high order. The poetical temperament is beneath every page, moulding, modifying every thought, coloring every topic of commonplace with the hues of fancy and sensibility. The genius of Hawthorne is peculiar as that of Charles Lamb, with fewer external aids from books and conventional literary expressions. He does not, like the popular author, express the reluctant thoughts and images of other people's minds, but calls the rest to look upon, wonder at, admire, and then love, his own. His writings, like those of all strictly original writers, are the solution of a new problem, the exhibition of the human heart and intellect, under a new array of circumstances. From the depths of New England, the culture of her old history, her domestic faithfulness to simple-hearted living, amid the repulsive anti-poetical tendencies of the present day, the soul of a young man speaks to us in fanciful reveries, a passionate sense of life, in words of gloom and sorrow. Sadness deepened into awe and fear, is the constant attendant of his pen, but it is the sadness of youth—it is the young man's melancholy, with nought of the despair of age, or the cold hardness of practical life. His grave images are the visions of a dreamer who dreams of realities; he is weighed down by an ever present consciousness of real life, but wanting courage to grasp the real action, he catches only the shadow. Not irreverently, with the rashness often attributable to critics, would we say he has in his character much of Hamlet. His imagination leads him into all possible conditions of being; he is purely romantic, conscious all the while of the present world about him, which he lingers around without the energy of will to seize upon and possess. He has, with a higher impulse, something of the waywardness of his own character, Mr. Wakefield the London citizen, who one day absented himself from his wife, and lived twenty years in the next street, in the daily habit of seeing her, without even speaking to her or visiting his own door. So Hawthorne lives rather near the present time than actually belonging to it. His literary life is a fascinated dream, an abstraction. The confessions of an imaginary

that the country had for once produced something too refined to be measured by a hack reviewer. 'The Rill from the Town Pump,' the best known of Hawthorne's sketches, was stolen by a cunning London bookseller, the author's name omitted, and circulated as a temperance tract. In the 96th number of the North American Review, Longfellow has written an admirable eulogy of the 'Twice Told Tales,' and in the late American Monthly Magazine for March, 1838, there is an article worthy of the subject. We are not aware of any others.

character, one Oberon, in a paper entitled The Journal of a Solitary Man, betray the secret of the sombre half-disappointed spirit that breathes through his pages. It is the maiden Sympathy, sitting on her cold monument, smiling at grief, having never wedded manly Action.

[Quotes 'If there be any thing bitter' to 'the soul of woman', but with several deletions.]

The distinctive mark of Hawthorne's writings, is a fanciful pathos delighting in sepulchral images. Like the ancient Egyptians, he exhibits the skull and insignia of mortality to temper the gaiety of the feast. His style, pure, serene, cheerful, is dashed with fearful shadows of gloom, as on the brightest midsummer day a passing cloud veils the earth in momentary darkness. This quaint love of the tomb, which he employs as an antagonist force to an exceeding sense of the beauty and grace of life, not from an unhealthy morbid temperament, he has in common with several of the master minds of English literature. The dramatist Webster, who was originally a sexton, casts a strange fascinating gloom over his tragedies by his similes from the charnel house; Jeremy Taylor, in his Holy Dying, indulges in this luxury of wo—we read on, impressed by the profusion of the author's fancy covering the cold walls of the tomb with the drapery of grief and sorrow, till the mind, reposing perhaps on the humanity of the scene, is filled and diverted with a comforting sense of pleasure. The Hydriotaphia of Sir Thomas Browne is a joyous comment on the tomb, the intellect speculating on vanity and decay, and triumphant over death: "Tis all one to lie in St. Innocent's church-yard, as in the sands of Egypt. Ready to be anything, in the ecstasy of being ever, and as content with six foot as the moles of Adrianus!'

The Wedding Knell and the Minister's Black Veil, two of our author's 'Twice-Told Tales,' exhibit an ingenious refinement of terror wrought up with none of the ordinary machinery of gloom, no death's heads, or goblins or mysterious portraits, gleaming from the wall, no Radcliffean horror, but a metaphysical exposition of the dark places of the human soul, a preacher's exhibition and warning of guilt and death. Fancy's Show Box, the title of another sketch, is a skilful analysis of the deceitful human heart, tented to the quick. The following are picture-esque passages, not exactly in the vein we have described, but such as may more readily be detached from the narrative than the others, and they are taken from papers not collected in the volume of Tales. Here is a picture of that handmaiden of Death, Nurse Ingersoll.

[Quotes 'An awful woman!' to 'the judgment seat!' but with several revisions.]

One of the most fantastic visions of Hawthorne, is the Old Maid in the Winding Sheet, but like all his reveries, it has a groundwork of reality in the moral of the tale. The passage that follows, however, is purely fanciful:

[Quotes 'A lonely woman' to 'upon the tombstone!']

Though sketches of this kind abound in his pages, Hawthorne is not a gloomy writer—his melancholy is fanciful, capricious—his spirit of love for all things, his delight in childhood, his reverence for woman, his sympathy with nature, are constant. We are made better by all that he writes. If he shows the skilful touches of the physician in probing the depths of human sorrow, and noting the earliest stains of guilt upon the soul, he has too a fund of cheerfulness and sympathy that can minister to the mind diseased. What winning accents he might use from the pulpit—what lay sermons, full of hope and tranquillity and beauty, he may yet give the world in his writings!

25. [Nathan Hale, Jr.], from a review in the *Boston Miscellany*

February 1842, i, 92

Hale (1818–71), the brother of Edward Everett Hale, was a journalist, and edited the *Boston Miscellany*, in which Hawthorne was to publish 'A Virtuoso's Collection'.

Mr. Hawthorne's stories rarely contain much external action. He contents himself with unveiling the movements of the inner man, and the growth of motive and reflection, while the outward world is quiet or forgotten. Not that he does not often give to his pieces a high dramatic interest, but his favorite study is that of the affections and inward impulses of man. There is often an air of mystery about the person and actions of his characters, while they are still real characters, accurately defined and delicately shaded and colored. Ghost stories are evidently his delight; and without actually startling his readers by directly *asserting* the improbable, he often brings before them agents whom they almost believe to be shadows from another world, and exhibits his scenes and his actors under a light which must be miraculous and unearthly. The intense interest which he gives to his simple stories, is the result and the proof of the skill, with which he bears himself through these dangerous imaginative paths.

His writings, half tale and half essay, are unique in their form and language. The most engaging simplicity,—in which art wholly conceals the art,—the truest purity of thought and feeling, a warm and kind moral sense, and a polished ease of sentiment and expression, are their constant characteristics. They are mostly of a subdued and pensive cast; they remind us of the hours of twilight, and the fantastic shadows then thrown on our walls and ceiling by the flickering fire. Mirth and passion both come to us as if mellowed in the story of a sober and thoughtful man. He seems to have an acute perception of the ridiculous, and his humor is ready and delicate; but there is no inclination to the boisterous, and the shafts of the former seem to be tempered by a pity for its objects, and the latter seeks rather to wreathe the calm face with a smile than to distort it into laughter.

We may conclude by again expressing our pleasure at seeing these tales collected, and particularly at the evidence that the volumes give, that their author has not deserted the beautiful path, which was so much his own.

26. [Henry Wadsworth Longfellow], review in the *North American Review*

April 1842, lvi, 496–9

The lovers of delicate humor, natural feeling, observation 'like a blind man's touch,' unerring taste, and magic grace of style, will greet with pleasure this new, improved, and enlarged edition of Hawthorne's 'Twice-told Tales.' The first volume appeared several years since, and received notice and fit commendation in a former Number of our Journal. The second volume is made up of tales and sketches, similar in character to those of the first volume, and not inferior in merit. We are disposed, on the strength of these volumes, to accord to Mr. Hawthorne a high rank among the writers of this country, and to predict, that his contributions to its imaginative literature will enjoy a permanent and increasing reputation. Though he has not produced any elaborate and long-sustained work of fiction, yet his writings are most strikingly characterized by that creative originality, which is the essential life-blood of genius. He does not see by the help of other men's minds, and has evidently been more of an observer and thinker, than of a student. He gives us no poor copies of poor originals in English magazines and souvenirs. He has caught nothing of the intensity of the French, or the extravagance of the German, school of writers of fiction. Whether he writes a story or a sketch, or describes a character or a scene, he employs his own materials, and gives us transcripts of images painted on his own mind. Another characteristic merit of his writings is, that he seeks and finds his subjects at home, among his own people, in the characters, the events, and the traditions of his own country. His writings retain the racy flavor of the soil. They have the healthy vigor and free grace of indigenous plants.

Perhaps there is no one thing for which he is more remarkable than his power of finding the elements of the picturesque, the romantic, and even the supernatural, in the every-day, common-place life, that is constantly going on around us. He detects the essentially poetical in that which is superficially prosaic. In the alembic of his genius, the subtle essence of poetry is extracted from prose. The history, the traditions, the people, and the scenes of New England, have not generally been supposed favorable to the romance-writer or the poet; but, in his hands, they are fruitful and suggestive, and dispose themselves into graceful attitudes and dramatic combinations. In his little sketch called 'David Swan,' the subject is nothing more or less than an hour's sleep, by the way-side, of a youth, while waiting for the coach that is to carry him to Boston; yet how much of thoughtful and reflective beauty is thrown round it, what strange and airy destinies brush by the youth's un- conscious face, how much matter for deep meditation of life and death, the past and future, time and eternity, is called forth by the few incidents in this simple drama. As illustrations of the same power, we would refer to 'The Minister's Black Veil,' 'The Seven Vagabonds,' and 'Edward Fane's Rosebud,' not to speak of many others, in which this peculiarity is more or less perceptible.

One of Mr. Hawthorne's most characteristic traits is the successful manner in which he deals with the supernatural. He blends together, with a skilful hand, the two worlds of the seen and the unseen. He never fairly goes out of the limits of probability, never calls up an actual ghost, or dispenses with the laws of nature; but he passes as near as possible to the dividing line, and his skill and ingenuity are sometimes tasked to explain, by natural laws, that which produced upon the reader all the effect of the supernatural. In this, too, his originality is conspicuously displayed. We know of no writings which resemble his in this respect.

His genius, too, is characterized by a large proportion of feminine elements, depth and tenderness of feeling, exceeding purity of mind, and a certain airy grace and arch vivacity in narrating incidents and delineating characters. The strength and beauty of a mother's love are er that exquisite story, which we are tempted to pronounce, whole, the finest thing he ever wrote,—'The Gentle Boy.' ute delicacy of touch, and womanly knowledge of a child's character, are perceptible in 'Little Annie's Ramble.' How iiet pathos is contained in 'The Shaker Bridal,' and of tranquil The Three-fold Destiny.' His female characters are sketched with a pencil equally fine and delicate; steeped in the finest hues of the imagination, yet not

> too bright and good
> For human nature's daily food.

Every woman owes him a debt of gratitude for those lovely visions of womanly faith, tenderness, and truth, which glide so gracefully through his pages.

All that Mr. Hawthorne has written is impressed with a strong family likeness. His range is not very extensive, nor has he any great versatility of mind. He is not extravagant or excessive in any thing. His tragedy is tempered with a certain smoothness; it solemnizes and impresses us, but it does not freeze the blood, still less offend the most fastidious taste. He stoops to no vulgar horrors or physical clap-traps. The mind, in its highest and deepest moods of feeling, is the only subject with which he deals. There is, however, a great deal of calm power, as well as artist-like skill, in his writings of this kind, such as 'Howe's Masquerade,' 'The White Old Maid,' 'Lady Eleanor's Mantle.' In his humor, too, there is the same quiet tone. It is never riotous, or exuberant; it never begets a laugh, and seldom a smile, but it is most unquestioned humor, as any one may see, by reading 'A Rill from the Town Pump,' or 'Chippings with a Chisel.' It is a thoughtful humor, of kindred with sighs as well as tears. Indeed, over all that he has written, there hangs, like an atmosphere, a certain soft and calm melancholy, which has nothing diseased or mawkish in it, but is of that kind which seems to flow naturally from delicacy of organization and a meditative spirit. There is no touch of despair in his pathos, and his humor subsides into that minor key, into which his thoughts seem naturally cast.

As a writer of the language merely, Mr. Hawthorne is entitled to great praise, in our judgment. His style strikes us as one of marked and uncommon excellence. It is fresh and vigorous, not formed by studying any particular model, and has none of the stiffness which comes from imitation; but it is eminently correct and careful. His language is very pure, his words are uniformly well chosen, and his periods are moulded with great grace and skill. It is also a very perspicuous style, through which his thoughts shine like natural objects seen through the purest plate-glass. He has no affectations or prettinesses of phrases, and none of those abrupt transitions, or of that studied inversion and uncouth abruptness, by which attention is often attempted to be secured to what is feeble or commonplace. It is characterized by that same unerring good taste, which presides over all the movements of his mind.

We feel that we have hardly done justice to Mr. Hawthorne's claims in this brief notice, and that they deserve an extended analysis and criticism; but we have not done this, partly on account of our former attempt to do justice to his merits, and partly because his writings have now become so well known, and are so justly appreciated, by all discerning minds, that they do not need our commendation. He is not an author to create a sensation, or have a tumultuous popularity. His works are not stimulating or impassioned, and they minister nothing to a feverish love of excitement. Their tranquil beauty and softened tints, which do not win the notice of the restless many, only endear them the more to the thoughtful few. We commend them for their truth and healthiness of feeling, and their moral dignity, no less than for their literary merit. The pulse of genius beats vigorously through them, and the glow of life is in them. It is the voice of a man who has seen and thought for himself, which addresses us; and the treasures which he offers to us are the harvests of much observation and deep reflection on man, and life, and the human heart.

27. [Edgar Allan Poe], from a review in *Graham's Magazine*

April 1842, xx, 254

Among the pieces Poe (1809–49) published in *Graham's* during his literary editorship in 1841 and 1842 are 'The Masque of the Red Death', 'The Murders in the Rue Morgue', and 'The Philosophy of Composition'. The following review and its companion piece (see No. 29) are the first and the most approving of five statements Poe made on Hawthorne's works.

We have always regarded the *Tale* (using this word in its popular acceptation) as affording the best prose opportunity for display of the highest talent. It has peculiar advantages which the novel does not admit. It is, of course, a far finer field than the essay. It has even points of superiority over the poem. An accident has deprived us, this month, of our customary space for review; and thus nipped in the bud a design long cherished of treating this subject in detail; taking Mr. Hawthorne's volumes as a text. In May we shall endeavor to carry out our intention. At present we are forced to be brief.

With rare exception—in the case of Mr. Irving's 'Tales of a Traveller,' and a few other works of a like cast—we have had no American tales of high merit. We have had no skilful compositions—nothing which could bear examination as works of art. Of twattle called tale-writing we have had, perhaps, more than enough. We have had a superabundance of the Rosa-Matilda effusions—gilt-edged paper all *couleur de rose*: a full allowance of cut-and-thrust blue-blazing melodramaticisms; a nauseating surfeit of low miniature copying of low life, much in the manner, and with about half the merit, of the Dutch herrings and decayed cheeses of Van Tuyssel—of all this, *eheu jam satis!*

Mr. Hawthorne's volumes appear to us misnamed in two respects. In the first place they should not have been called 'Twice-Told Tales'—for this is a title which will not bear *repetition*. If in the first collected edition they were twice-told, of course now they are thrice-told.—May we live to hear them told a hundred times! In the second place, these compositions are by no means *all* 'Tales.' The most of them are essays properly so called. It would have been wise in their author to have modified his title, so as to have reference to all included. This point could have been easily arranged.

But under whatever titular blunders we receive this book, it is most cordially welcome. We have seen no prose composition by any American which can compare with *some* of these articles in the higher merits, or indeed in the lower; while there is not a single piece which would do dishonor to the best of the British essayists.

'The Rill from the Town Pump' which, through the *ad captandum* nature of its title, has attracted more of public notice than any one other of Mr. Hawthorne's compositions, is perhaps, the *least* meritorious. Among his best, we may briefly mention 'The Hollow of the Three Hills;' 'The Minister's Black Veil;' 'Wakefield;' 'Mr. Higginbotham's Catastrophe;' 'Fancy's Show-Box;' 'Dr. Heidegger's Experiment;' 'David Swan;' 'The Wedding Knell;' and 'The White Old Maid.' It is remarkable that all these, with one exception, are from the first volume.

The style of Mr. Hawthorne is purity itself. His *tone* is singularly effective—wild, plaintive, thoughtful, and in full accordance with his themes. We have only to object that there is insufficient diversity in these themes themselves, or rather in their character. His *originality* both of incident and of reflection is very remarkable; and this trait alone would ensure him at least *our* warmest regard and commendation. We speak here chiefly of the tales; the essays are not so markedly novel. Upon the whole we look upon him as one of the few men of indisputable genius to whom our country has as yet given birth. As such, it will be our delight to do him honor; and lest, in these undigested and cursory remarks, without proof and without explanation, we should appear to do him *more* honor than is his due, we postpone all further comment until a more favorable opporunity.

28. [Orestes Brownson], from a review in the *Boston Quarterly Review*

April 1842, v, 251–2

Brownson (1803–76), a Universalist minister who became a Unitarian and later, in 1844, a Roman Catholic, was an ardent liberal thinker and advocate of the rights of the working man. A prolific writer, he contributed heavily to the magazines he edited.

. . . These volumes are not introduced for the purpose of being criticised, for their author, in his own department, is one of those very few men, born to give law to criticism, not to receive the law from it; nor are they introduced for the sake of being commended to the public, for they are already well known; and no lover of American literature can be presumed to be ignorant of them. We notice them simply, to tell the author that these Tales, excellent as they are, are not precisely what he owes to his country. In them he has done much, and shown us that he can do more. He is a genuine artist. His mind is creative; more so than that of any other American writer that has yet appeared, with the exception, perhaps, of Washington Irving. He has wit, humor, pathos, in abundance; an eye for all that is wild, beautiful, or picturesque in nature; a generous sympathy with all forms of life, thought, and feeling, and warm, deep, unfailing love of his race. He has withal a vigorous intellect, and a serene and healthy spirit. He is gentle, but robust and manly; full of tenderness, but never maudlin. Through all his writings there runs a pure and living stream of manly thought and feeling, which characterizes always the true man, the Christian, the republican, and the patriot. He may be, if he tries, with several improvements, to the literature of his country, all that Boz is to that of England. He possesses a higher order of intellect and genius than Boz, stronger, and purer. He has more earnestness. The creator of 'The Gentle Boy' compares advantageously with the creator of 'Little Nell'. The Gentle Boy is indeed but a sketch; yet a sketch that betrays in every stroke the hand of the master; and we think, it required a much higher order of genius to conceive it, so gentle, so sweet, so calm, so full of life, of love, than it did to conceive the character of Little Nell, confessedly the most beautiful of Dickens's creations.

But we have no room for remarks. We have wished merely to enrol ourselves among those, who regard Mr. Hawthorne as fitted to stand at the head of American Literature. We see the pledge of this in his modesty, in his simplicity, and in his sympathy with all that is young, fresh, childlike; and above all in his originality, and pure, deep feeling of nationality. We pray him to remember that, while we approve his love of children, and admire much the books he has sent out for them, we do not forget that he is capable of writing for men, for all ages; and we ask him to attempt a higher and a bolder strain than he has thus far done. To those, if such there are, who have not read these Twice-Told Tales, we recommend them as being two as pleasant volumes to read, as pure and as healthy in their influence, as any two that can be found in the compass of our literature.

29. [Edgar Allan Poe], a review in *Graham's Magazine*

May 1842, xx, 298–300

We said a few hurried words about Mr. Hawthorne in our last number, with the design of speaking more fully in the present. We are still, however, pressed for room, and must necessarily discuss his volumes more briefly and more at random than their high merits deserve.

The book professes to be a collection of *tales*, yet is, in two respects, misnamed. These pieces are now in their third republication, and, of course, are thrice-told. Moreover, they are by no means *all* tales, either in the ordinary or in the legitimate understanding of the term. Many of them are pure essays; for example, 'Sights from a Steeple,' 'Sunday at Home,' 'Little Annie's Ramble,' 'A Rill from the Town-Pump,' 'The Toll-Gatherer's Day,' 'The Haunted Mind,' 'The Sister Years,' 'Snow-Flakes,' 'Night Sketches,' and 'Foot-Prints on the Sea-Shore.' We mention these matters chiefly on account of their discrepancy with that

marked precision and finish by which the body of the work is distinguished.

Of the Essays just named, we must be content to speak in brief. They
are each and all beautiful, without being characterised by the polish and
adaptation so visible in the tales proper. A painter would at once note
their leading or predominant feature, and style it *repose*. There is no
attempt at effect. All is quiet, thoughtful, subdued. Yet this repose may
exist simultaneously with high originality of thought; and Mr. Hawthorne has demonstrated the fact. At every turn we meet with novel
combinations; yet these combinations never surpass the limits of the
quiet. We are soothed as we read; and withal is a calm astonishment
that ideas so apparently obvious have never occurred or been presented
to us before. Herein our author differs materially from Lamb or Hunt
or Hazlitt—who, with vivid originality of manner and expression, have
less of the true novelty of thought than is generally supposed, and whose
originality, at best, has an uneasy and meretricious quaintness, replete
with startling effects unfounded in nature, and inducing trains of
reflection which lead to no satisfactory result. The Essays of Hawthorne
have much of the character of Irving, with more of originality, and less
of finish; while, compared with the Spectator, they have a vast superiority at all points. The Spectator, Mr. Irving, and Mr. Hawthorne have
in common that tranquil and subdued manner which we have chosen
to denominate *repose*; but, in the case of the two former, this repose is
attained rather by the absence of novel combination, or of originality,
than otherwise, and consists chiefly in the calm, quiet, unostentatious
expression of commonplace thoughts, in an unambitious unadulterated
Saxon. In them, by strong effort, we are made to conceive the absence
of all. In the essays before us the absence of effort is too obvious to be
mistaken, and a strong under-current of *suggestion* runs continuously
beneath the upper stream of the tranquil thesis. In short, these effusions
of Mr. Hawthorne are the product of a truly imaginative intellect,
restrained, and in some measure repressed, by fastidiousness of taste, by
constitutional melancholy and by indolence.

But it is of his tales that we desire principally to speak. The tale
proper, in our opinion, affords unquestionably the fairest field for the
exercise of the loftiest talent, which can be afforded by the wide
domains of mere prose. Were we bidden to say how the highest genius
could be most advantageously employed for the best display of its own
powers, we should answer, without hesitation—in the composition of
a rhymed poem, not to exceed in length what might be perused in an

hour. Within this limit alone can the highest order of true poetry exist. We need only here say, upon this topic, that, in almost all classes of composition, the unity of effect or impression is a point of the greatest importance. It is clear, moreover, that this unity cannot be thoroughly preserved in productions whose perusal cannot be completed at one sitting. We may continue the reading of a prose composition, from the very nature of prose itself, much longer than we can persevere, to any good purpose, in the perusal of a poem. This latter, if truly fulfilling the demands of the poetic sentiment, induces an exaltation of the soul which cannot be long sustained. All high excitements are necessarily transient. Thus a long poem is a paradox. And, without unity of impression, the deepest effects cannot be brought about. Epics were the offspring of an imperfect sense of Art, and their reign is no more. A poem *too* brief may produce a vivid, but never an intense or enduring impression. Without a certain continuity of effort—without a certain duration or repetition of purpose—the soul is never deeply moved. There must be the dropping of the water upon the rock. De Béranger has wrought brilliant things—pungent and spirit-stirring—but, like all immassive bodies, they lack *momentum*, and thus fail to satisfy the Poetic Sentiment. They sparkle and excite, but, from want of continuity, fail deeply to impress. Extreme brevity will degenerate into epigrammatism; but the sin of extreme length is even more unpardonable. *In medio tutissimus ibis.*[1]

Were we called upon, however, to designate that class of composition which, next to such a poem as we have suggested, should best fulfil the demands of high genius—should offer it the most advantageous field of exertion—we should unhesitatingly speak of the prose tale, as Mr. Hawthorne has here exemplified it. We allude to the short prose narrative, requiring from a half-hour to one or two hours in its perusal. The ordinary novel is objectionable, from its length, for reasons already stated in substance. As it cannot be read at one sitting, it deprives itself, of course, of the immense force derivable from *totality*. Worldly interests intervening during the pauses of perusal, modify, annul, or counteract, in a greater or less degree, the impressions of the book. But simple cessation in reading would, of itself, be sufficient to destroy the true unity. In the brief tale, however, the author is enabled to carry out the fulness of his intention, be it what it may. During the hour of perusal the soul of the reader is at the writer's control. There are no external or extrinsic influences—resulting from weariness or interruption.

[1] *In medio tutissimus ibis*: In the middle way you will go most safely.

A skilful literary artist has constructed a tale. If wise, he has not fashioned his thoughts to accommodate his incidents; but having conceived, with deliberate care, a certain unique or single *effect* to be wrought out, he then invents such incidents—he then combines such events as may best aid him in establishing this preconceived effect. If his very initial sentence tend not to the outbringing of this effect, then he has failed in his first step. In the whole composition there should be no word written, of which the tendency, direct or indirect, is not to the one pre-established design. And by such means, with such care and skill, a picture is at length painted which leaves in the mind of him who contemplates it with a kindred art, a sense of the fullest satisfaction. The idea of the tale has been presented unblemished, because undisturbed; and this is an end unattainable by the novel. Undue brevity is just as exceptionable here as in the poem; but undue length is yet more to be avoided.

We have said that the tale has a point of superiority even over the poem. In fact, while the *rhythm* of this latter is an essential aid in the development of the poem's highest idea—the idea of the Beautiful—the artificialities of this rhythm are an inseparable bar to the development of all points of thought or expression which have their basis in *Truth*. But Truth is often, and in very great degree, the aim of the tale. Some of the finest tales are tales of ratiocination. Thus the field of this species of composition, if not in so elevated a region on the mountain of Mind, is a table-land of far vaster extent than the domain of the mere poem. Its products are never so rich, but infinitely more numerous, and more appreciable by the mass of mankind. The writer of the prose tale, in short, may bring to his theme a vast variety of modes or inflections of thought and expression—(the ratiocinative, for example, the sarcastic or the humorous) which are not only antagonistical to the nature of the poem, but absolutely forbidden by one of its most peculiar and in-dispensable adjuncts; we allude of course, to rhythm. It may be added, here, *par parenthese*, that the author who aims at the purely beautiful in a prose tale is laboring at great disadvantage. For Beauty can be better treated in the poem. Not so with terror, or passion, or horror, or a multitude of such other points. And here it will be seen how full of prejudice are the usual animadversions against those *tales of effect* many fine examples of which were found in the earlier numbers of Black-wood. The impressions produced were wrought in a legitimate sphere of action, and constituted a legitimate although sometimes an exag-gerated interest. They were relished by every man of genius: although there were found many men of genius who condemned them without just ground. The true critic will but demand that the design intended be accomplished, to the fullest extent, by the means most advantageously applicable.

We have very few American tales of real merit—we may say, indeed, none, with the exception of 'The Tales of a Traveller' of Washington Irving, and these 'Twice-Told Tales' of Mr. Hawthorne. Some of the pieces of Mr. John Neal abound in vigor and originality; but in general, his compositions of this class are excessively diffuse, extravagant, and indicative of an imperfect sentiment of Art. Articles at random are, now and then, met with in our periodicals which might be advantageously compared with the best effusions of the British Magazines; but, upon the whole, we are far behind our progenitors in this department of literature.

Of Mr. Hawthorne's Tales we would say, emphatically, that they belong to the highest region of Art—an Art subservient to genius of a very lofty order. We had supposed, with good reason for so supposing, that he had been thrust into his present position by one of the impudent *cliques* which beset our literature, and whose pretensions it is our full purpose to expose at the earliest opportunity; but we have been most agreeably mistaken. We know of few compositions which the critic can more honestly commend than these 'Twice-Told Tales.' As Americans, we feel proud of the book.

Mr. Hawthorne's distinctive trait is invention, creation, imagination, originality—a trait which, in the literature of fiction, is positively worth all the rest. But the nature of originality, so far as regards its manifestation in letters, is but imperfectly understood. The inventive or original mind as frequently displays itself in novelty of *tone* as in novelty of matter. Mr. Hawthorne is original at *all* points.

It would be a matter of some difficulty to designate the best of these tales; we repeat that, without exception, they are beautiful. 'Wakefield' is remarkable for the skill with which an old idea—a well-known incident—is worked up or discussed. A man of whims conceives the purpose of quitting his wife and residing *incognito*, for twenty years, in her immediate neighborhood. Something of this kind actually happened in London. The force of Mr. Hawthorne's tale lies in the analysis of the motives which must or might have impelled the husband to such folly, in the first instance, with the possible causes of his perseverance. Upon this thesis a sketch of singular power has been constructed.

'The Wedding Knell' is full of the boldest imagination—an imagination fully controlled by taste. The most captious critic could find no flaw in this production.

'The Minister's Black Veil' is a masterly composition of which the sole defect is that to the rabble its exquisite skill will be *caviare*. The *obvious* meaning of this article will be found to smother its insinuated one. The *moral* put into the mouth of the dying minister will be supposed to convey the *true* import of the narrative; and that a crime of dark dye, (having reference to the 'young lady') has been committed, is a point which only minds congenial with that of the author will perceive.

'Mr. Higginbotham's Catastrophe' is vividly original and managed most dexterously.

'Dr. Heidegger's Experiment' is exceedingly well imagined, and executed with surpassing ability. The artist breathes in every line of it.

'The White Old Maid' is objectionable, even more than the 'Minister's Black Veil,' on the score of its mysticism. Even with the thoughtful and analytic, there will be much trouble in penetrating its entire import.

'The Hollow of the Three Hills' we would quote in full, had we space;—not as evincing higher talent than any of the other pieces, but as affording an excellent example of the author's peculiar ability. The subject is commonplace. A witch subjects the Distant and the Past to the view of a mourner. It has been the fashion to describe, in such cases, a mirror in which the images of the absent appear; or a cloud of smoke is made to arise, and thence the figures are gradually unfolded. Mr. Hawthorne has wonderfully heightened his effect by making the ear, in place of the eye, the medium by which the fantasy is conveyed. The head of the mourner is enveloped in the cloak of the witch, and within its magic folds there arise sounds which have an all-sufficient intelligence. Throughout this article also, the artist is conspicuous—not more in positive than in negative merits. Not only is all done that should be done, but (what perhaps is an end with more difficulty attained) there is nothing done which should not be. Every word *tells*, and there is not a word which does *not* tell.

In 'Howe's Masquerade' we observe something which resembles a plagiarism—but which *may be* a very flattering coincidence of thought. We quote the passage in question.

With a dark flush of wrath upon his brow they saw the general *draw his sword* and *advance to meet* the figure *in the cloak* before the latter had stepped one pace upon the floor.

'*Villain, unmuffle yourself,*' cried he, 'you pass no farther!'

The figure, without blenching a hair's breadth from the sword which was pointed at his breast, made a solemn pause, and *lowered the cape of the cloak* from his face, yet not sufficiently for the spectators to catch a glimpse of it. But Sir William Howe had evidently seen enough. The sternness of his countenance gave place to a look of wild amazement, if not horror, while he recoiled several steps from the figure, *and let fall his sword* upon the floor.'—See vol. 2, page 20.

The idea here is, that the figure in the cloak is the phantom or re-duplication of Sir William Howe; but in an article called 'William Wilson,' one of the 'Tales of the Grotesque and Arabesque,' we have not only the same idea, but the same idea similarly presented in several respects. We quote two paragraphs, which our readers may compare with what has been already given. We have italicized, above, the immediate particulars of resemblance.

The brief moment in which I averted my eyes had been sufficient to produce, apparently, a material change in the arrangement at the upper or farther end of the room. A large mirror, it appeared to me, now stood where none had been perceptible before: and as I stepped up to it in extremity of terror, mine own image, but with features all pale and dabbled in blood, *advanced* with a feeble and tottering gait to meet me.

Thus it appeared I say, but was not. It was Wilson, who then stood before me in the agonies of dissolution. Not a line in all the marked and singular lineaments of that face which was not even identically mine own. *His mask and cloak lay where he had thrown them, upon the floor.'*—Vol. 2, p. 57.

Here it will be observed that, not only are the two general conceptions identical, but there are various *points* of similarity. In each case the figure seen is the wraith or duplication of the beholder. In each case the scene is a masquerade. In each case the figure is cloaked. In each, there is a quarrel—that is to say, angry words pass between the parties. In each the beholder is enraged. In each the cloak and sword fall upon the floor. The 'villain, unmuffle yourself,' of Mr. H. is precisely paralleled by a passage at page 56 of 'William Wilson.'

In the way of objection we have scarcely a word to say of these tales. There is, perhaps, a somewhat too general or prevalent *tone*—a tone of melancholy and mysticism. The subjects are insufficiently varied. There is not so much of *versatility* evinced as we might well be warranted in expecting from the high powers of Mr. Hawthorne. But beyond these trivial exceptions we have really none to make. The style is purity itself. Force abounds. High imagination gleams from every page. Mr. Hawthorne is a man of the truest genius. We only regret that the limits of our Magazine will not permit us to pay him that full tribute of commendation, which, under other circumstances, we should be so eager to pay.

30. [G. P. R. James], from 'American Works of Fiction', in the *Foreign and Colonial Quarterly Review*

October 1843, ii, 458–88

James (1799–1860) is best remembered as a writer of historical novels, such as *Richelieu* and other popular historical works, parodied by Thackeray in *Novels by Eminent Hands*.

. . . a whole volume of collected Miscellanies of great excellence is here before us. We mean Mr. Hawthorne's 'Twice-Told Tales,' which will one day or other be naturalized into our library of Romance, if truth, fancy, pathos, and originality have any longer power to diffuse a reputation. He has caught the true fantastic spirit which somewhere or other exists in every society, be it ever so utilitarian and practical, linking the seen to the unseen, the matter-of-fact to the imaginative. To such a mind the commonest things become suggestive; the oldest truths appear clad in a garb of 'grace and pleasure.' The pump in the middle of the little town, recalls the days when the spring welled brightly out in the wilderness, and 'the Indian sagamores drank of it;' a walk with a child through the range of shop-window sights, enables the thoughtful man to draw aside the veils which hide our deepest associations and our saddest thoughts; the figure of a sleeping wayfarer under a tuft of maples by the wayside, invites him to consider the number of events which *all but* happen to every mortal; and this in aid of a vein of temperate and poetical elegance of imagery, the like of which is possessed by none of our writers of prose—Mrs. Southey, perhaps, excepted. As a recounter of mere legends, Mr. Hawthorne claims high praise. He reminds us of Tieck, in spite of the vast difference in the materials used by the two artists. Whether he revive the tradition of 'The Gray Champion,' —that supernatural hero who has existed in every country since the days of Ogier the Dane, to come forth and deliver, when the emergency presses hardest,—or tell how the 'May-pole of Merry Mount' was felled by the stern axe of Endicott, the Puritan governor,—or describe the meeting of the pilgrims in quest of that fabulous jewel, 'The Great Carbuncle,'—or relate the result of Dr. Heidegger's experiments with the Water of Youth,—he does his spiriting 'gently,' in the old romantic sense of the word, exercising his craft with a quiet power which is rare, the time and the subject and the place considered. We cannot too heartily commend this book, as the best addition to what may be called our Faëry Library, which has been made for many years; hoping, moreover, that the author is capable of producing more than the one slim volume which has made its way to England.

31. [Henry F. Chorley], from a review in the *Athenaeum*

23 August 1845, pp. 830–1

Although Chorley mentions no date here, it seems clear that the notice refers to the 1845 false edition of *Twice-Told Tales*. His remarks come after a long review of *Dashes at Life with a Free Pencil*, by N. P. Willis, the most popular and one of the few financially successful American writers of the day.

And now, a word of friendly welcome to Mr. Hawthorne. We have already so often expressed our pleasure in his gem-like tales (being the first, we believe, to recommend them to the notice of English tale-readers)—that none, we apprehend, will mistake for covert censure the recommendation we must now give him on the appearance of this second volume—to beware of monotony. We do not say this because he chiefly loves the by-gone times of New England,—nor, because of his manifest propensity towards the spiritual and supernatural (few since Sir Walter Scott telling 'a ghost-story' so gravely well as Mr. Hawthorne); and we love the dreamy vein of speculation in which he indulges, when it is natural; not entered dramatically and 'of good set purpose' by those who think that 'mobled queen is good,' and fantasy a taking device to entertain and engage an audience. But we conceive our author to be a retired and timid man, who only plays on his two strings because he lacks courage or energy to master a third. We have thus given him the support of friendly counsel, and have only to observe that his second volume of 'Twice-Told Tales' would be equal to his first, were it not too closely like it.

32. E. A. Duyckinck: Hawthorne as an established writer, from an unsigned essay, 'Nathaniel Hawthorne' in the *Democratic Review*

April 1845, xvi, 376–84

Nathaniel Hawthorne has passed that period of his literary life in which it is necessary to enter upon a systematic examination of his writings, in the old approved critical style. He is admitted to be a genuine author, simple, natural, and perfect in his peculiar department of writing, and stands upon that vantage ground, where his position being a thing established, one may write of him with freedom, and speak warmly of those points which may appeal most forcibly to his individual taste. This, we confess, is the species of criticism in which we take most delight—leaving to others the measuring and drilling of the raw recruit in literature, we prefer the ease and freedom—the *abandon* of conversation with the officers in the mess-room. Happy author he who has this privilege of being listened to with eagerness and enthusiasm, whose noble sayings are not dragged down to a little standard, whose trifles even are informed with the pregnant meaning of genius. Happy critic who can keep such glorious company. At such times be the *nil admirari* far from us—let the soul slake her thirst for excellence in one full untroubled draught. What care we if there *are* greater authors in the world? We can forget Shakspeare and Milton and Dante and Tasso, Cervantes and the other gods of the upper air, for the lesser deities. We are content with demigods, but they must be genuine.

Deprecating, then, all pretences to criticism, we take the liberty of setting in for a few moments' familiar colloquy with the writings of Hawthorne. We would write for the reader as we would talk to a friend who has a general acquaintance with the Essays (all readers of the Democratic have this) and who cared for the particular grounds of our admiration.

Imagine a man of a rugged frame of body and a delicate mind, of a physical hardihood to tempt all extremes of weather and suffer no annoyance as a ploughman in the heat of midsummer, or an amateur traveller breasting the storm for mere pleasurable excitement, with a fancy within airy, fragile and sensitive as a maiden's; the rough hairy rind of the cocoa-nut enclosing its sweet whiteness; fancy all this as a type of Nathaniel Hawthorne, and you have some idea of the peculiarities which impart their strength and their weakness to his writings. The perfectness of his style, the completeness of form, the unity of his subject and of all his subjects, are masculine: the light play of fancy, the sentiment, are feminine. There is a deeper vein which no woman could ever reach, an intimacy with the sterner powers of life which we should wish no woman to attain. At the first perusal of the writings of Hawthorne, the reader remarks the singular clearness, the fountain-like beauty of the style, 'more splendid than crystal;' a beauty not put on or occasional, but though doubtless supplied beneath by secret springs welling up here and there in the sedges irregularly, yet presenting the smoothness and placidity of the river at its surface. Such calm, be assured, indicates strength and a genuine nature. No apprentice at the use of language, no novice in thought, can write thus. Before the metal pours forth smooth and lustrous upon the floor of the smelting room there must have been the toiling fire in the furnace. Of what heterogeneous materials, of what storms and passions, of what petty and miserable weaknesses, is the quiet of the manly soul composed. Many costly ingredients, many rude ones, like rings and crucifixes tumbled in with masses of ore in the casting of some old church bell, have been melted down and purified together before there is music in the heart. There is nothing in human life that should sooner draw tears from a refined and reflecting nature than the contemplation of the utter peacefulness, the childlike nature, the deference to youth, eagerness, perhaps, mere waywardness of some well-disciplined man who has gone to school in life and come forth, wise, humble, chastened. Do not stop with Hawthorne's style as if it were a happy gift of nature; so it is, but it is more, it is the expression of Art. We begin then to look beneath, and presently find indications of something more than the agreeable essayist who amuses the world by laughing at its little follies or tickles his fancy with its picturesque exhibitions. There is a deep moral sentiment and an original exhibition of the elements of character which mark the author to some extent as a Creator. We feel that we are not reading every day after-dinner writing, but that we are continually coming upon something which is strange and individual. This something, whatever it turn out to be, is the measure of the man's originality; it is that by which he differs from other essayists. We can describe it as nothing else than a power of fascination which is exercised over the mind by the occasional gloom and pale glimpses as it were of fiends starting up on the page. The readers of the German Hoffmann will understand what is meant by this allusion, though his genius is more idiosyncratic, and his devils are more tangible and fearful than Hawthorne's. Hoffmann brings in peculiar grinning old men, very nasty and very marvellous, full of witchcraft, as living representations of the evil spirit; Hawthorne indicates nothing more than a cloud passing over the sky at midsummer, a frown on the face of a maiden, a flickering ripple on the stream. But put all these intimations together and they are frequent in Hawthorne's writings, and you have a certain novel and original element in his compositions. It is the shadow which Sin and Death in their twin flights are for ever casting upon the world; shadows which fall alike upon the so called evil and the so called good, which darken all that is pure, and defile all that is sacred, but not more than in actual life. Writers of a light character are so accustomed to look only upon what appears fair and good, or rather in their fair and good men and women are accustomed to find nothing else but what is good, that we are startled in the class of composition chosen by Hawthorne with these revelations. Many readers may run hastily over his compositions without suspecting the morality, though few can hesitate to observe such striking passages as 'Fancy's show box,' 'The Minister's Black Veil' and 'the Wedding Knell.' The tender melancholy which is inspired after reading these tales is, as we have remarked, allied to a kind of fascination. 'I fear thee, Ancient Mariner!' No conventionalist art thou, or respecter of show and outside, but as keensighted a moralist as tempest-stricken Lear whose sagacity flashes forth from his exceedingly vexed soul like the lightning from the storm-driven clouds. In great moments, under the influence of great passions, the soul sees clearly. No pretence or hypocrisy can avail before the sentiment of our moralist. It pierces the snowy folds of the preacher's vestment and the whiter covering of the maiden's heart. Alas! is all evil? No! but the very Heavens of this world are not pure. There is one tale of Hawthorne's which he has not collected in his published volumes, the incidents of which fully disclose the secret of many of his writings. It is called 'Young Goodman Brown,' and the scene is laid in Salem, witch-hunting Salem, where the author passed many years in 'the ordeal of retirement,' and the peculiar historical atmosphere of which contributed to many of the ghostly fancies which he has carried elsewhere. . . .

[Quotes 'With Heaven above' to 'with the coldest dew'.]

In all this there is simply an enforcement of the old, well-known, often illustrated truth, that there is a capacity for evil in the best of us, and that it rests very much within our own choice whether we shall be angels or devils, or in what proportion we shall mix the ingredients. But how dramatically is the truth conveyed, how naturally are these strange scenes managed! they show the possession of a power which it is 'excellent to have' but 'tyrannous to use.' The writer makes amends for this gloomy night-picture by the sunshine of his 'Little Annie.' It is so cheerful a sketch and so full of pleasant imagery that we give it entire to the reader without apology.

[Quotes the entire sketch.]

Such writings as these are sure to find their way to the heart; they steal upon it unawares and silently take possession of the fortress without encountering any of the critical guards and defences of passport, draw-bridge, and countersign. Bolder speculators have to battle for their opinions and fight their way to fame through the swords and pitfalls of reviews and reviewers; strictly original men who break ground for the first time in the uncultivated field of native literature, have to encounter the perils and hardships of the wilderness,—many long years and much patient cultivation must be undergone before the crop is an easy one here,—but writers of this stamp have the happy lot of being admitted and welcomed at once. Many, we may be sure, will neglect them, for all have not the simplicity and refinement of character to appreciate excellence in so chaste a form, but few will oppose, and when an admirer is gained he will be worth possessing.

It afforded us no little pleasure, not long since, to find the following notice of Hawthorne in an article in the English Foreign and Colonial Quarterly Review, said to be from the pen of Mr. James, the novelist. . . .

[Quotes Mr. James's review (see No. 30).]

Only the first volume of Hawthorne's collected 'Twice-Told Tales,' had been seen by this reviewer. He would have found additional material to support his high eulogy in the second volume in the Tales of the Province House, The Seven Vagabonds, The White Old Maid, Endicott and the Red Cross, Edward Fane's Rosebud (let the reader take this up after Mrs. Gamp, in Chuzzlewit), and The Sister Years, which has the merit, we believe, of being the only classic Newspaper Carrier's New-year Address ever printed! A third and fourth volume are yet behind, unpublished in book form, unknown to the shelves of the trade, and there are the 'Allegories of the Heart,' including the extra leaf to Bunyan, 'The Celestial Rail-road,' and various little volumes of Biography and American History, the best of their kind, and that kind one of the rarest—books for Children.

A truly pure, gentle and acceptable man of Genius is NATHANIEL HAWTHORNE!

33. Hawthorne among the humorists, from an unsigned essay, 'American Humor' in the *Democratic Review*

September 1845, xvii, 212–9

In this survey of writers of humorous prose, Hawthorne is placed with such essayists as Benjamin Franklin and John Wirt rather than with writers of fiction.

. . . Hawthorne whose strength lies in a combination of rich quaint sombre fancy, with a delicate melancholy coloring. The Tieck of this American literature of ours (though the gayer fancy of the German is clouded in his case by a slight tinge of the gloom of puritanical New England, in itself one of the sources of romantic interest and in his case of the mildest tinge and softest hues) has shown gleams and streaks of humor in most of his tales, his best writings by far. Whether in his essays or his meditative sketches, he sometimes discloses a vein of genuine humor, like himself however, rather of a gentle than of a forcible character. With more of Goldsmith than of Rabelais in it, though with little of the former and nothing of the latter. A graceful, pleasing humor, neither riant nor grotesque, nor very copious; sometimes only just enough to satisfy the reader of its existence at all, and often with nothing more whatever.

34. Hawthorne, from 'The Old Manse'

1846

When Hawthorne was gathering together the tales and sketches for the new collection, he wrote Duyckinck:

It is rather a sad idea—not that I am to write no more of this kind, but that I cannot better justify myself for having written at all. As the first essays and tentatives of a young author, they would be well enough—but it seems to me absurd to look upon them as conveying any claim to a settled literary reputation. I thank God, I have grace enough to be utterly dissatisfied with them, considered as the productions of a literary life—or in any point of view whatever; not but what I see the degrees of merit they possess. If they were merely spring blossoms, we might look for good fruit hereafter; but I have done nothing but blossom all through the Summer. I am ashamed—and there's an end. (Letter, 24 January 1846, Duyckinck Collection, MS. Division, New York Public Library.)

Receiving the specimen copy on 10 March 1846, Hawthorne wrote that the volume 'seemed rather stale to me; but my wife was pleased to like it'.

The treasure of intellectual good which I hoped to find in our secluded dwelling had never come to light. No profound treatise of ethics, no philosophic history, no novel even, that could stand unsupported on its edges. All that I had to show, as a man of letters, were these few tales and essays, which had blossomed out like flowers in the calm summer of my heart and mind. Save editing (an easy task) the journal of my friend of many years, the African Cruiser, I had done nothing else. With these idle weeds and withering blossoms I have intermixed some that were produced long ago,—old, faded things, reminding me of flowers pressed between the leaves of a book,—and now offer the bouquet, such as it is, to any whom it may please. These fitful sketches, with so little of external life about them, yet claiming no profundity of purpose,—so reserved, even while they sometimes seem so frank,—often but half in earnest, and never, even when most so, expressing satisfactorily the thoughts which they profess to image,—such trifles, I truly feel, afford no solid basis for a literary reputation. Nevertheless, the public—if my limited number of readers, whom I venture to regard rather as a circle of friends, may be termed a public—will receive them the more kindly, as the last offering, the last collection, of this nature which it is my purpose ever to put forth. Unless I could do better, I have done enough in this kind. For myself the book will always retain one charm—as reminding me of the river, with its delightful solitudes, and of the avenue, the garden, and the orchard, and especially the dear old Manse, with the little study on its western side, and the sunshine glimmering through the willow branches while I wrote.

Let the reader, if he will do me so much honor, imagine himself my guest, and that, having seen whatever may be worthy of notice within and about the Old Manse, he has finally been ushered into my study. There, after seating him in an antique elbow chair, an heirloom of the house, I take forth a roll of manuscript and entreat his attention to the following tales—an act of personal inhospitality, however, which I never was guilty of, nor ever will be, even to my worst enemy.

35. Notice in *Graham's Magazine*

August 1846, xxix, 107-8

Under this somewhat quaint title Mr. Hawthorne has given us an exquisite collection of essays, allegories, and stories, replete with fancy, humor and sentiment. Many of them have been published before in the magazines, but are well worthy of their present permanent form. The description of the Old Manse, Buds and Bird Voices, The Hall of Fantasy, The Celestial Railroad, The Procession of Life, P's Correspondence, and Earth's Holocaust, are among the most striking in the collection; and, in the finer qualities of mind and style, rank among the best productions of American literature. There is a felicity and evanescent grace to Mr. Hawthorne's humor, to which no other American can lay claim. We fear that it is almost too fine for popularity. It provokes no laughter, yet makes the 'sense of satisfaction ache' with its felicity of touch, and nicety of discrimination. He is even a finer and deeper humorist, we think, than Addison or Goldsmith, or Irving, though not so obvious and striking in his mirth. As he is a poet and man of genius in his humor, he is as felicitous in his representation of the serious as of the comic side of things; or rather, he so interlaces the serious with the comic that their division lines are scarcely observable. These 'Mosses,' and the 'Twice-Told Tales,' are certain of a life far beyond the present generation of readers.

36. [Henry F. Chorley], from a review in the *Athenaeum*

8 August 1846, pp. 807–8

We have had occasion, lately, to dwell with pleasure on the faëry tales of Andersen; and Mr. Hawthorne's stories for 'children of a larger growth' have been (as our readers know) equally welcome to us—and on similar grounds. Their unworldliness is charming. While nothing is so revolting as acted simplicity—unless it be acted philanthropy—there is no preacher to whom we love better to listen than one whose sympathies and convictions have been cherished and matured apart from the crowd; and who, not therefore ceasing to love his species, looks upon them—yet is not *of* them. Prejudice must, of course, under such circumstances, be allowed for;—the shadow of thought, if not austerity, from amid which the recluse looks out, causing him to see the sunshine by which others are surrounded through his own dark medium. We must be prepared, too, for a far-sightedness which is apt to grow morbid—inasmuch as it substitutes speculation for action. Nevertheless, it is to teachings from 'old manses,' where Poets 'dwell apart,' that we owe some of our best pleasures.

But, in addition to our love of Mr. Hawthorne's tone, there is much to content us in the manner in which his legends are presented. Few prose writers possess so rich a treasury in the chambers of their imagination; while our author's riches never make him extravagant. He gives us what suffices for our thorough enchantment and fullest credence— but nothing more. In such a tale, for instance, as that of 'Rappaccini's Daughter,'—the narrative of a Paduan magician, who, by way of endowing his innocent daughter with power and sovereignty, had nourished her on delicious poisons, till she communicated death to everything which she approached,—any less consummate master of the marvellous would have heaped horror on horror, till the monstrosity of the invention became intolerable. Mr. Hawthorne only leads us by imperceptible degrees into the fearful garden, full of its sumptuous blossoms—then insinuates the dark sympathy between the nature of the lady and her sisters, the death-flowers—then gradually fascinates us, even as she fascinated her lover, to feel a love and a sorrow for the Sorceress greater than our terror, and to attend at the catastrophe with those mingled feelings which no spell less powerful than Truth's can command. Thus it is with most of Mr. Hawthorne's stories. We have elsewhere said, that they resemble Tieck's faëry tales, in their power of translating the mysterious harmonies of Nature into articulate meaning. They may claim kindred, too, in their high finish and purity of style, with the Genevese novels of the late Töpffer; which have been kept out of sight by their unobtrusiveness,—only, we apprehend, that they may steadily advance to a permanent European popularity. There is another author, far dearer to all Englishmen than either Tieck or Töpffer, of whom Mr. Hawthorne reminds us;—who but the excellent John Bunyan? The orthodox will be thrown into fits by our saying that the writings of both have a touch of Puritanical quaintness which is anything but ungraceful. In short, we like this writer and his stories well; and are not afraid that any among the 'fit audience,' whom the more delicate and thoughtful order of creators prefer to assemble, will be disappointed if, attracted by our panegyric, they take up the book.

We shall extract a few passages descriptive of the 'Old Manse' and its 'surroundings.' One is the placid river Concord:—

[Quotes 'The river of peace' to 'of plunging in' and 'Here we are' to 'blow upon the head'.]

Here is another river-picture—worth, to our thinking, many *Turners*, brilliant with gamboge, and flushed with rose-pink:—

[Quotes 'Rowing our boat' to 'another to sleep' and 'Gentle and unobtrusive' to 'than we did'.]

Our last extract will show some of the author's philosophy—and, eke, his quiet humour:—

[Quotes 'Were I to adopt' to 'such philosophers'.]

We desire to recommend these 'Mosses'—only objectionable from the pedantry of their designation—to the reading of such as are select in their pleasures; and, to this end, have drawn upon the prologue rather than the play. Yet, better wonder-stories do not exist than 'The Birth-mark,' and 'Young Goodman Brown':—while 'The Celestial Railroad' deserves to be bound up with the Victorian edition of 'The Pilgrim's Progress'; and 'Earth's Holocaust' merits praise, as being in the grandest style of allegory—whether as regards the accumulation of imagery or the largeness of the truth propounded. Other of the tales, too, are excellent. The one other fault, in addition to the title, which we find with these volumes is, their author's intimation that he intends to write no more short tales. 'This'—as the *Edinburgh Review* said of Wordsworth, but in a totally different spirit—'will never do!'

37. From an unsigned review, 'The American Library', in *Blackwood's Magazine*

November 1847, lxii, 587–92

'*Mosses from an Old Manse,*' by Nathaniel Hawthorne, is the somewhat quaint title given to a series of tales, and sketches, and miscellaneous papers, because they were written in an old manse, some time tenanted by the author, a description of which forms the first paper in the series. We have already intimated our opinion of this writer. In many respects he is a strong contrast to the one we have just left. For whereas Mr. Poe is indebted to whatever good effect he produces to a close detail and agglomeration of facts, Mr. Hawthorne appears to have little skill and little taste for dealing with matter of fact or substantial incident, but relies for his favourable impression on the charm of style, and the play of thought and fancy.

The most serious defect in his stories is the frequent presence of some palpable improbability which mars the effect of the whole—not improbability, like that we already remarked on, which is intended and wilfully perpetrated by the author—not improbability of incident even, which we are not disposed very rigidly to inquire after in a novelist— but improbability in the main motive and state of mind which he has undertaken to describe, and which forms the turning-point of the whole narrative. As long as the human being appears to act as a human being would, under the circumstances depicted, it is surprising how easily the mind, carried on by its sympathies with the feelings of the actor, forgets to inquire into the probability of these circumstances. Unfortunately, in Mr Hawthorne's stories, it is the human being himself who is not probable, nor possible.

It will be worth while to illustrate our meaning by an instance or two, to show that, far from being hypercritical, our canon of criticism is extremely indulgent, and that we never take the bluff and surly objection—it cannot be!—until the improbability has reached the core of the matter. In the first story, 'The Birth Mark,' we raise no objection to the author, because he invents a chemistry of his own, and supposes his hero in possession of marvellous secrets which enable him to diffuse into the air an ether or perfume, the inhaling of which shall displace a red mark from the cheek which a beautiful lady was born with; it were hard times indeed, if a novelist might not do what he pleased in a chemist's laboratory, and produce what drugs, what perfumes, what potable gold or charmed elixir, he may have need of. But we do object to the preposterous motive which prompts the amateur of science to an operation of the most hazardous kind, on a being he is represented as dearly loving. We are to believe that a good *husband* is afflicted, and grievously and incessantly tormented by a slight red mark on the cheek of a beautiful woman, which, as a *lover*, never gave him a moment's uneasiness, and which neither to him nor to any one else abated one iota from her attractions. We are to suppose that he braves the risk of the experiment—it succeeds for a moment, then proves fatal, and destroys her—for what? Merely that she who was so very beautiful should attain to an ideal perfection. 'Had she been less beautiful,' we are told, 'it might have heightened his affection. But, seeing her otherwise so perfect, he found this one defect grow more and more intolerable, with every moment of their united lives.' And then, we have some further bewildering explanation about 'his honourable love, so pure and lofty that it would accept nothing less than perfection, nor miserably make itself contented with an earthlier nature than he had dreamed of.' Call you this 'pure and lofty love,' when a woman is admired much as a connoisseur admires a picture, who might indeed be supposed to fume and fret if there was one little blot or blemish in it. Yet, even a connoisseur, who had an exquisite picture by an old master, with only one trifling blemish on it, would hardly trust himself or another to repair and retouch, in order to render it perfect. Can any one recognise in this elaborate nonsense about ideal perfection, any approximation to the feeling which a man has for the wife he loves? If the novelist wished to describe this egregious connoisseurship in female charms, he should have put the folly into the head of some insane mortal, who, reversing the enthusiasm by which some men have loved a picture or a statue as if it were a real woman, had learned to love his beautiful wife as if she were nothing else than a picture or a statue.

Again, in the 'Story of the Artist of the Beautiful,' we breathe not a word about the impossibility of framing out of springs and wheels so marvellous a butterfly, that the seeming creature shall not only fly and move its antennæ, and fold and display its wings like the living insect, but shall even surpass the living insect by showing a fine sense of human character, and refusing to perch on the hand of those who had not a genuine sentiment of beauty. The novelist shall put what springs and wheels he pleases into his mechanism, but the springs and wheels he places in the mechanist himself, must be those of genuine humanity, or the whole fiction falls to the ground. Now the mechanist, the hero of the story, the 'Artist of the Beautiful,' is described throughout as animated with the feelings proper to the artist, not to the mechanician. He is a young watchmaker, who, instead of plodding at the usual and lucrative routine of his trade, devotes his time to the structure of a most delicate and ingenious toy. We all know that a case like this is very possible. Few men, we should imagine, are more open to the impulse of emulation, the desire to do that which had never been done before, than the ingenious mechanist; and few men more completely under the dominion of their leading passion or project, because every day brings some new contrivance, some new resource, and the hope that died at night is revived in the morning. But Mr Hawthorne is not contented with the natural and very strong impulse of the mechanician; he speaks throughout of his enthusiastic artisan as of some young Raphael intent upon 'creating the beautiful.' Springs, and wheels, and chains, however fine and complicate, are not 'the beautiful.' He might as well suppose the diligent anatomist, groping amongst nerves and tissues, to be stimulated to *his* task by an especial passion for the beautiful.

The passion of the ingenious mechanist we all understand; the passion of the artist, sculptor, or painter, is equally intelligible; but the confusion of the two in which Mr Hawthorne would vainly interest us, is beyond all power of comprehension. These are the improbabilities against which we contend. Moreover, when this wonderful butterfly is made—which he says truly was 'a gem of art that a monarch would have purchased with honours and abundant wealth, and have treasured among the jewels of his kingdom, as the most unique and wondrous of them all,'—the artist sees it crushed in the hands of a child and looks 'placidly' on. So never did any human mechanist who at length had succeeded in the dream and toil of his life. And at the conclusion of the story we are told, in not very intelligible language,—'When the artist rose high enough to achieve the Beautiful, the symbol by which he made it perceptible to mortal senses became of little value to his eyes, while his spirit possessed itself in the enjoyment of the reality.'

It is not, perhaps, to the *stories* we should be disposed to refer for the happier specimens of Mr Hawthorne's writing, but rather to those papers which we cannot better describe than as so many American *Spectators* of the year 1846—so much do they call to mind the style of essay in the days of Steele and Addison.

We may observe here, that American writers frequently remind us of models of composition somewhat antiquated with ourselves. While, on the one hand, there is a wild tendency to snatch at originality at any cost—to coin new phrases—new *probabilities*—to '*intensify*' our language with strange '*impulsive*' energy—to break loose, in short, from all those restraints which have been thought to render style both perspicuous and agreeable; there is, on the other hand—produced partly by a very intelligible reaction—an effort somewhat too apparent to be classical and correct. It is a very laudable effort, and we should be justly accused of fastidiousness did we mention it as in the least blameworthy. We would merely observe that an effect is sometimes produced upon an English ear as if the writer belonged to a previous era of our literature, to an epoch when to produce smooth and well modulated sentences was something rarer and more valued than it is now. . . .

In some of Mr Hawthorne's papers we are reminded, and by no means disagreeably, of the manner of Steele and Addison. 'The Intelligence Office' presents, in some parts, a very pleasing imitation of this style. . . .

There is a nice bit of painting, as an artist might say, under the title of 'The Old Apple-dealer.' We have seen the very man in England. We had marked it for quotation, but it is too long, and we do not wish to mar its effect by mutilation.

In the 'Celestial Railroad,' we have a new Pilgrim's Progress performed by *rail*. Instead of the slow, solitary, pensive pilgrimage which John Bunyan describes, we travel in fashionable company, and in the most agreeable manner.

The story of 'Roger Malvin's Burial' is well told, and is the best of his narrative pieces. 'The New Adam and Eve,' and several others, might be mentioned for an agreeable vein of thought and play of fancy. In one of his papers the author has attempted a more common species of humour, and with some success. For variety's sake, we shall close our notice of him, and for the present, of 'The American Library,' with an extract from 'Mrs Bullfrog.'

[Quotes 'To divert my mind' to ' "Bullfrog that I am!" ']

38. [Herman Melville], 'Hawthorne and His Mosses. By a Virginian Spending His Summer in Vermont', in the *Literary World*

17 and 24 August 1850, vii, 125–7, 145–7

Scholarship has not yet determined whether or not Melville had written this essay before meeting Hawthorne on 5 August 1850. The two men saw much of each other during the following year, and Melville celebrated their friendship by dedicating *Moby Dick* to Hawthorne. As enthusiastic as Melville's praise of *Mosses* is, he came to prefer the *Twice-Told Tales*. In 1851 he wrote to Duyckinck that the *Twice-Told*

far exceed the 'Mosses'—they are, I fancy, an earlier vintage from his vine. Some of those sketches are wonderfully subtle. Their deeper meanings are worthy of a Brahmin. Still there is something lacking—a good deal lacking—to the plump sphericity of the man. What is that?—He doesn't patronise the butcher—he needs roast-beef, done rare.—Nevertheless, for one, I regard Hawthorne (in his books) as evincing a quality of genius, immensely loftier, & more profound, too, than any other American has shown hitherto in the printed form. (*The Letters of Herman Melville*, ed. Merrell R. Davis and William H. Gilman [1960], p. 121.)

A papered chamber in a fine old farm-house, a mile from any other dwelling, and dipped to the eaves in foliage—surrounded by mountains, old woods, and Indian ponds,—this, surely, is the place to write of Hawthorne. Some charm is in this northern air, for love and duty seem both impelling to the task. A man of a deep and noble nature has seized me in this seclusion. His wild, witch-voice rings through me; or, in softer cadences, I seem to hear it in the songs of the hill-side birds that sing in the larch trees at my window.

Would that all excellent books were foundlings, without father or mother, that so it might be we could glorify them, without including their ostensible authors! Nor would any true man take exception to this; least of all, he who writes, 'When the Artist rises high enough to achieve the Beautiful, the symbol by which he makes it perceptible to mortal senses becomes of little value in his eyes, while his spirit possesses itself in the enjoyment of the reality.'

But more than this. I know not what would be the right name to put on the title-page of an excellent book; but this I feel, that the names of all fine authors are fictitious ones, far more so than that of Junius; simply standing, as they do, for the mystical, ever-eluding spirit of all beauty, which ubiquitously possesses men of genius. Purely imaginative as this fancy may appear, it nevertheless seems to receive some warranty from the fact, that on a personal interview no great author has ever come up to the idea of his reader. But that dust of which our bodies are composed, how can it fitly express the nobler intelligences among us? With reverence be it spoken, that not even in the case of one deemed more than man, not even in our Saviour, did his visible frame betoken anything of the augustness of the nature within. Else, how could those Jewish eyewitnesses fail to see heaven in his glance!

It is curious how a man may travel along a country road, and yet miss the grandest or sweetest of prospects by reason of an intervening hedge, so like all other hedges, as in no way to hint of the wide land-scape beyond. So has it been with me concerning the enchanting land-scape in the soul of this Hawthorne, this most excellent Man of Mosses. His 'Old Manse' has been written now four years, but I never read it till a day or two since. I had seen it in the book-stores—heard of it often—even had it recommended to me by a tasteful friend, as a rare, quiet book, perhaps too deserving of popularity to be popular. But there are so many books called 'excellent,' and so much unpopular merit, that amid the thick stir of other things, the hint of my tasteful friend was disregarded; and for four years the Mosses on the Old Manse never refreshed me with their perennial green. It may be, how-ever, that all this while the book, likewise, was only improving in flavor and body. At any rate, it so chanced that this long procrastination eventuated in a happy result. At breakfast the other day, a mountain girl, a cousin of mine, who for the last two weeks has every morning helped me to strawberries and raspberries, which, like the roses and pearls in the fairy tale, seemed to fall into the saucer from those straw-berry-beds, her cheeks—this delightful creature, this charming Cherry says to me—'I see you spend your mornings in the haymow; and yesterday I found there "Dwight's Travels in New England." Now I have something far better than that, something more congenial to our summer on these hills. Take these raspberries, and then I will give you some moss.' 'Moss!' said I. 'Yes, and you must take it to the barn with you, and good-by to "Dwight".'

With that she left me, and soon returned with a volume, verdantly bound, and garnished with a curious frontispiece in green; nothing less than a fragment of real moss, cunningly pressed to a fly-leaf. 'Why, this,' said I, spilling my raspberries, 'this is the "Mosses from an Old Manse".' 'Yes,' said cousin Cherry, 'yes, it is that flowery Hawthorne.' 'Hawthorne and Mosses,' said I, 'no more: it is morning: it is July in the country: and I am off for the barn.'

Stretched on that new mown clover, the hill-side breeze blowing over me through the wide barn-door, and soothed by the hum of the bees in the meadows around, how magically stole over me this Mossy Man! and how amply, how bountifully, did he redeem that delicious promise to his guests in the Old Manse, of whom it is written—'Others could give them pleasure, or amusement, or instruction—these could be picked up anywhere—but it was for me to give them rest. Rest, in a life of trouble! What better could be done for weary and world-worn spirits? What better could be done for anybody, who came within our magic circle, than to throw the spell of a magic spirit over him?' So all that day, half-buried in the new clover, I watched this Hawthorne's 'Assyrian dawn, and Paphian sunset and moonrise, from the summit of our Eastern Hill.'

The soft ravishments of the man spun me round about in a web of dreams, and when the book was closed, when the spell was over, this wizard 'dismissed me with but misty reminiscences, as if I had been dreaming of him.'

What a wild moonlight of contemplative humor bathes that Old Manse!—the rich and rare distilment of a spicy and slowly-oozing heart. No rollicking rudeness, no gross fun fed on fat dinners, and bred in the lees of wine,—but a humor so spiritually gentle, so high, so deep, and yet so richly relishable, that it were hardly inappropriate in an angel. It is the very religion of mirth; for nothing so human but it may be advanced to that. The orchard of the Old Manse seems the visible type of the fine mind that has described it—those twisted and contorted old trees, 'that stretch out their crooked branches, and take such hold of the imagination, that we remember them as humorists and odd-fellows.' And then, as surrounded by these grotesque forms, and hushed in the noon-day repose of this Hawthorne's spell, how aptly might the still fall of his ruddy thoughts into your soul be symbolized by 'the thump of a great apple, in the stillest afternoon, falling without a breath of wind, from the mere necessity of perfect ripeness!' For no less ripe than ruddy are the apples of the thoughts and fancies in this sweet Man of Mosses—

'Buds and Bird-voices—'

What a delicious thing is that! 'Will the world ever be so decayed, that Spring may not renew its greenness?' And the 'Fire-Worship.' Was ever the hearth so glorified into an altar before? The mere title of that piece is better than any common work in fifty folio volumes. How exquisite is this:—'Nor did it lessen the charm of his soft, familiar courtesy and helpfulness, that the mighty spirit, were opportunity offered him, would run riot through the peaceful house, wrap its inmates in his terrible embrace, and leave nothing of them save their whitened bones. This possibility of mad destruction only made his domestic kindness the more beautiful and touching. It was so sweet of him, being endowed with such power, to dwell, day after day, and one long, lonesome night after another, on the dusky hearth, only now and then betraying his wild nature, by thrusting his red tongue out of the chimney-top! True, he had done much mischief in the world, and was pretty certain to do more, but his warm heart atoned for all; He was kindly to the race of man.'

But he has still other apples, not quite so ruddy, though full as ripe; —apples, that have been left to wither on the tree, after the pleasant autumn gathering is past. The sketch of 'The Old Apple-Dealer' is conceived in the subtlest spirit of sadness; he whose 'subdued and nerveless boyhood prefigured his abortive prime, which, likewise, contained within itself the prophecy and image of his lean and torpid age.' Such touches as are in this piece cannot proceed from any common heart. They argue such a depth of tenderness, such a boundless sympathy with all forms of being, such an omnipresent love, that we must needs say that this Hawthorne is here almost alone in his generation,—at least, in the artistic manifestation of these things. Still more. Such touches as these,—and many, very many similar ones, all through his chapters— furnish clues whereby we enter a little way into the intricate, profound heart where they originated. And we see that suffering, some time or other and in some shape or other,—this only can enable any man to depict it in others. All over him, Hawthorne's melancholy rests like an

Indian-summer, which, though bathing a whole country in one softness, still reveals the distinctive hue of every towering hill and each far-winding vale.

But it is the least part of genius that attracts admiration. Where Hawthorne is known, he seems to be deemed a pleasant writer, with a pleasant style,—a sequestered, harmless man, from whom any deep and weighty thing would hardly be anticipated—a man who means no meanings. But there is no man, in whom humor and love, like mountain peaks, soar to such a rapt height as to receive the irradiations of the upper skies;—there is no man in whom humor and love are developed in that high form called genius; no such man can exist without also possessing, as the indispensable complement of these, a great, deep intellect, which drops down into the universe like a plummet. Or, love and humor are only the eyes through which such an intellect views this world. The great beauty in such a mind is but the product of its strength. What, to all readers, can be more charming than the piece entitled 'Monsieur du Miroir;' and to a reader at all capable of fully fathoming it, what, at the same time, can possess more mystical depth of meaning?—yes, there he sits and looks at me,—this 'shape of mystery,' this 'identical Monsieur du Miroir.' 'Methinks I should tremble now, were his wizard power of gliding through all impediments in search of me, to place him suddenly before my eyes.'

How profound, nay appalling, is the moral evolved by the Earth's Holocaust; where—beginning with the hollow follies and affectations of the world,—all vanities and empty theories and forms are, one after another, and by an admirably graduated, growing comprehensiveness, thrown into the allegorical fire, till, at length, nothing is left but the all-engendering heart of man; which remaining still unconsumed, the great conflagration is naught.

Of a piece with this, is the 'Intelligence Office,' a wondrous symbolizing of the secret workings in men's souls. There are other sketches still more charged with ponderous import.

'The Christmas Banquet,' and 'The Bosom Serpent,' would be fine subjects for a curious and elaborate analysis, touching the conjectural parts of the mind that produced them. For spite of all the Indian-summer sunlight on the hither side of Hawthorne's soul, the other side —like the dark half of the physical sphere—is shrouded in a blackness, ten times black. But this darkness but gives more effect to the ever-moving dawn, that for ever advances through it, and circumnavigates his world. Whether Hawthorne has simply availed himself of this mystical blackness as a means to the wondrous effects he makes it to produce in his lights and shades; or whether there really lurks in him, perhaps unknown to himself, a touch of Puritanic gloom,—this, I cannot altogether tell. Certain it is, however, that this great power of blackness in him derives its force from its appeals to that Calvinistic sense of Innate Depravity and Original Sin, from whose visitations, in some shape or other, no deeply thinking mind is always and wholly free. For, in certain moods, no man can weigh this world without throwing in something, somehow like Original Sin, to strike the uneven balance. At all events, perhaps no writer has ever wielded this terrific thought with greater terror than this same harmless Hawthorne. Still more: this black conceit pervades him through and through. You may be witched by his sunlight,—transported by the bright gildings in the skies he builds over you; but there is the blackness of darkness beyond; and even his bright gildings but fringe and play upon the edges of thunder-clouds. In one word, the world is mistaken in this Nathaniel Hawthorne. He himself must often have smiled at its absurd misconception of him. He is immeasurably deeper than the plummet of the mere critic. For it is not the brain that can test such a man; it is only the heart. Yet cannot come to know greatness by inspecting it; there is no glimpse to be caught of it, except by intuition; you need not ring it, you but touch it, and you find it is gold.

Now, it is that blackness in Hawthorne, of which I have spoken, that so fixes and fascinates me. It may be, nevertheless, that it is too largely developed in him. Perhaps he does not give us a ray of his light for every shade of his dark. But however this may be, this blackness it is that furnishes the infinite obscure of his back-ground,—that background, against which Shakspeare plays his grandest conceits, the things that have made for Shakspeare his loftiest but most circumscribed renown, as the profoundest of thinkers. For by philosophers Shakspeare is not adored as the great man of tragedy and comedy.—'Off with his head; so much for Buckingham!' This sort of rant, interlined by another hand, brings down the house,—those mistaken souls, who dream of Shakspeare as a mere man of Richard-the-Third humps and Macbeth daggers. But it is those deep far-away things in him; those occasional flashings-forth of the intuitive Truth in him; those short, quick probings at the very axis of reality;—these are the things that make Shakspeare, Shakspeare. Through the mouths of the dark characters of Hamlet, Timon, Lear, and Iago, he craftily says, or sometimes insinuates the things which we feel to be so terrifically true, that it were all but madness for any good man, in his own proper character, to utter, or even hint of them. Tormented into desperation, Lear, the frantic king, tears off the mask, and speaks the same madness of vital truth. But, as I before said, it is the least part of genius that attracts admiration. And so, much of the blind, unbridled admiration that has been heaped upon Shakspeare, has been lavished upon the least part of him. And few of his endless commentators and critics seem to have remembered, or even perceived, that the immediate products of a great mind are not so great as that undeveloped and sometimes undevelopable yet dimly-discernible greatness, to which those immediate products are but the infallible indices. In Shakspeare's tomb lies infinitely more than Shakspeare ever wrote. And if I magnify Shakspeare, it is not so much for what he did do as for what he did not do, or refrained from doing. For in this world of lies, Truth is forced to fly like a scared white doe in the woodlands; and only by cunning glimpses will she reveal herself, as in Shakspeare and other masters of the great Art of Telling the Truth,—even though it be covertly and by snatches.

But if this view of the all-popular Shakspeare be seldom taken by his readers, and if very few who extol him have ever read him deeply, or perhaps, only have seen him on the tricky stage (which alone made, and is still making him his mere mob renown)—if few men have time, or patience, or palate, for the spiritual truth as it is in that great genius;— it is then no matter of surprise, that in a contemporaneous age, Nathaniel Hawthorne is a man as yet almost utterly mistaken among men. Here and there, in some quiet armchair in the noisy town, or some deep nook among the noiseless mountains, he may be appreciated for something of what he is. But unlike Shakspeare, who was forced to the contrary course by circumstances, Hawthorne (either from simple disinclination, or else from inaptitude) refrains from all the popularizing noise and show of broad farce and blood-besmeared tragedy; content with the still, rich utterance of a great intellect in repose, and which sends few thoughts into circulation, except they be arterialized at his large warm lungs, and expanded in his honest heart.

Nor need you fix upon that blackness in him, if it suit you not. Nor, indeed, will all readers discern it; for it is, mostly, insinuated to those who may best understand it, and account for it; it is not obtruded upon every one alike.

Some may start to read of Shakspeare and Hawthorne on the same page. They may say, that if an illustration were needed, a lesser light might have sufficed to elucidate this Hawthorne, this small man of yesterday. But I am not willingly one of those who, as touching Shak-speare at least, exemplify the maxim of Rochefoucault, that 'we exalt the reputation of some, in order to depress that of others;'—who, to teach all noble-souled aspirants that there is no hope for them, pro-nounce Shakspeare absolutely unapproachable. But Shakspeare has been approached. There are minds that have gone as far as Shakspeare into the universe. And hardly a mortal man, who, at some time or other, has not felt as great thoughts in him as any you will find in Hamlet. We must not inferentially malign mankind for the sake of any one man, whoever he may be. This is too cheap a purchase of contentment for conscious mediocrity to make. Besides, this absolute and unconditional adoration of Shakspeare has grown to be a part of our Anglo-Saxon superstitions. The Thirty-Nine articles are now Forty. Intolerance has come to exist in this matter. You must believe in Shakspeare's un-approachability, or quit the country. But what sort of a belief is this for an American, a man who is bound to carry republican progressiveness into Literature as well as into Life? Believe me, my friends, that men, not very much inferior to Shakspeare, are this day being born on the banks of the Ohio. And the day will come when you shall say, Who reads a book by an Englishman that is a modern? The great mistake seems to be, that even with those Americans who look forward to the coming of a great literary genius among us, they somehow fancy he will come in the costume of Queen Elizabeth's day; be a writer of dramas founded upon old English history or the tales of Boccaccio. Whereas, great geniuses are parts of the times, they themselves are the times, and possess a correspondent coloring. It is of a piece with the Jews, who, while their Shiloh was meekly walking in their streets, were still praying for his magnificent coming; looking for him in a chariot, who was already among them on an ass. Nor must we forget that, in his own lifetime, Shakspeare was not Shakspeare, but only Master William Shakspeare of the shrewd, thriving, business firm of Condell, Shakspeare & Co., proprietors of the Globe Theatre in London; and by a courtly author, of the name of Chettle, was looked at as an 'upstart crow,' beautified 'with other birds' feathers.' For, mark it well, imitation is often the first charge brought against real originality. Why this is so, there is no space to set forth here. You must have plenty of sea-room to tell the Truth in; especially when it seems to have an aspect of newness, as America did in 1492, though it was then just as old, and perhaps older than Asia, only those sagacious philosophers, the common sailors, had never seen it before, swearing it was all water and moonshine there.

Now I do not say that Nathaniel of Salem is a greater than William of Avon, or as great. But the difference between the two men is by no means immeasurable. Not a very great deal more, and Nathaniel were verily William.

This, too, I mean, that if Shakspeare has not been equalled, give the world time, and he is sure to be surpassed, in one hemisphere or the other. Nor will it at all do to say, that the world is getting grey and grizzled now, and has lost that fresh charm which she wore of old, and by virtue of which the great poets of past times made themselves what we esteem them to be. Not so. The world is as young to-day as when it was created; and this Vermont morning dew is as wet to my feet, as Eden's dew to Adam's. Nor has nature been all over ransacked by our progenitors, so that no new charms and mysteries remain for this latter generation to find. Far from it. The trillionth part has not yet been said; and all that has been said, but multiplies the avenues to what remains to be said. It is not so much paucity as superabundance of material that seems to incapacitate modern authors.

Let America, then, prize and cherish her writers; yea, let her glorify them. They are not so many in number as to exhaust her good-will. And while she has good kith and kin of her own, to take to her bosom, let her not lavish her embraces upon the household of an alien. For believe it or not, England, after all, is in many things an alien to us. China has more bonds of real love for us than she. But even were there no strong literary individualities among us, as there are some dozens at least, nevertheless, let America first praise mediocrity even, in her own children, before she praises (for everywhere, merit demands acknowledgment from every one) the best excellence in the children of any other land. Let her own authors, I say, have the priority of appreciation. I was much pleased with a hot-headed Carolina cousin of mine, who once said,—'If there were no other American to stand by, in literature, why, then, I would stand by Pop Emmons and his "Fredoniad," and till a better epic came along, swear it was not very far behind the Iliad.' Take away the words, and in spirit he was sound.

Not that American genius needs patronage in order to expand. For that explosive sort of stuff will expand though screwed up in a vice, and burst it, though it were triple steel. It is for the nation's sake, and not for her authors' sake, that I would have America be heedful of the increasing greatness among her writers. For how great the shame, if other nations should be before her, in crowning her heroes of the pen! But this is almost the case now. American authors have received more just and discriminating praise (however loftily and ridiculously given, in certain cases) even from some Englishmen, than from their own countrymen. There are hardly five critics in America; and several of them are asleep. As for patronage, it is the American author who now patronizes his country, and not his country him. And if at times some among them appeal to the people for more recognition, it is not always with selfish motives, but patriotic ones.

It is true, that but few of them as yet have evinced that decided originality which merits great praise. But that graceful writer, who perhaps of all Americans has received the most plaudits from his own country for his productions,—that very popular and amiable writer, however good and self-reliant in many things, perhaps owes his chief reputation to the self-acknowledged imitation of a foreign model, and to the studied avoidance of all topics but smooth ones. But it is better to fail in originality, than to succeed in imitation. He who has never failed somewhere, that man cannot be great. Failure is the true test of greatness. And if it be said, that continual success is a proof that a man wisely knows his powers,—it is only to be added, that, in that case, he knows them to be small. Let us believe it, then, once for all, that there is no hope for us in these smooth, pleasing writers that know their powers. Without malice, but to speak the plain fact, they but furnish an appendix to Goldsmith, and other English authors. And we want no American Goldsmiths: nay, we want no American Miltons. It were the vilest thing you could say of a true American author, that he were an American Tompkins. Call him an American and have done, for you cannot say a nobler thing of him. But it is not meant that all American writers should studiously cleave to nationality in their writings; only this, no American writer should write like an Englishman or a Frenchman; let him write like a man, for then he will be sure to write like an American. Let us away with this leaven of literary flunkeyism towards England. If either must play the flunkey in this thing, let England do it, not us. While we are rapidly preparing for that political supremacy among the nations which prophetically awaits us at the close of the present century, in a literary point of view, we are deplorably unprepared for it; and we seem studious to remain so. Hitherto, reasons might have existed why this should be; but no good reason exists now. And all that is requisite to amendment in this matter, is simply this: that while fully acknowledging all excellence everywhere, we should refrain from unduly lauding foreign writers, and, at the same time, duly recognise the meritorious writers that are our own;—those writers who breathe that unshackled, democratic spirit of Christianity in all things, which now takes the practical lead in this world, though at the same time led by ourselves—us Americans. Let us boldly contemn all imitation, though it comes to us graceful and fragrant as the morning; and foster all originality, though at first it be crabbed and ugly as our own pine knots. And if any of our authors fail, or seem to fail, then, in the words of my Carolina cousin, let us clap him on the shoulder, and back him against all Europe for his second round. The truth is, that in one point of view, this matter of a national literature has come to such a pass with us, that in some sense we must turn bullies, else the day is lost, or superiority so far beyond us, that we can hardly say it will ever be ours.

And now, my countrymen, as an excellent author of your own flesh and blood,—an unimitating, and, perhaps, in his way, an inimitable man—whom better can I commend to you, in the first place, than Nathaniel Hawthorne. He is one of the new, and far better generation of your writers. The smell of your beeches and hemlocks is upon him; your own broad prairies are in his soul; and if you travel away inland into his deep and noble nature, you will hear the far roar of his Niagara. Give not over to future generations the glad duty of acknowledging him for what he is. Take that joy to yourself, in your own generation; and so shall he feel those grateful impulses on him, that may possibly prompt him to the full flower of some still greater achievement in your eyes. And by confessing him you thereby confess others; you brace the whole brotherhood. For genius, all over the world, stands hand in hand, and one shock of recognition runs the whole circle round.

In treating of Hawthorne, or rather of Hawthorne in his writings (for I never saw the man; and in the chances of a quiet plantation life, remote from his haunts, perhaps never shall); in treating of his works, I say, I have thus far omitted all mention of his 'Twice-told Tales' and 'Scarlet Letter.' Both are excellent, but full of such manifold, strange, and diffusive beauties, that time would all but fail me to point the half of them out. But there are things in those two books, which, had they been written in England a century ago, Nathaniel Hawthorne had utterly displaced many of the bright names we now revere on authority. But I am content to leave Hawthorne to himself, and to the infallible finding of posterity; and however great may be the praise I have bestowed upon him, I feel that in so doing I have more served and honored myself, than him. For, at bottom, great excellence is praise enough to itself; but the feeling of a sincere and appreciative love and admiration towards it, this is relieved by utterance; and warm, honest praise, ever leaves a pleasant flavor in the mouth; and it is an honorable thing to confess to what is honorable in others.

But I cannot leave my subject yet. No man can read a fine author, and relish him to his very bones while he reads, without subsequently fancying to himself some ideal image of the man and his mind. And if you rightly look for it, you will almost always find that the author himself has somewhere furnished you with his own picture. For poets (whether in prose or verse), being painters of nature, are like their brethren of the pencil, the true portrait-painters, who, in the multitude of likenesses to be sketched, do not invariably omit their own; and in all high instances, they paint them without any vanity, though at times with a lurking something that would take several pages to properly define.

I submit it, then, to those best acquainted with the man personally, whether the following is not Nathaniel Hawthorne;—and to himself, whether something involved in it does not express the temper of his mind,—that lasting temper of all true, candid men—a seeker, not a finder yet:—

A man now entered, in neglected attire, with the aspect of a thinker, but somewhat too roughhewn and brawny for a scholar. His face was full of sturdy vigor, with some finer and keener attribute beneath; though harsh at first, it was tempered with the glow of a large, warm heart, which had force enough to heat his powerful intellect through and through. He advanced to the Intelligencer, and looked at him with a glance of such stern sincerity, that perhaps few secrets were beyond its scope.

'I seek for Truth,' said he.

Twenty-four hours have elapsed since writing the foregoing. I have just returned from the hay-mow, charged more and more with love and admiration of Hawthorne. For I have just been gleaning through the Mosses, picking up many things here and there that had previously escaped me. And I found that but to glean after this man, is better than to be in at the harvest of others. To be frank (though, perhaps, rather foolish) notwithstanding what I wrote yesterday of these Mosses, I had not then culled them all; but had, nevertheless, been sufficiently sensible of the subtle essence in them, as to write as I did. To what infinite height of loving wonder and admiration I may yet be borne, when by repeatedly banqueting on these Mosses I shall have thoroughly incorporated their whole stuff into my being,—that, I cannot tell. But already I feel that this Hawthorne has dropped germinous seeds into my soul. He expands and deepens down, the more I contemplate him; and further and further, shoots his strong New England roots into the hot soil in my Southern soul.

By careful reference to the 'Table of Contents,' I now find that I have gone through all the sketches; but that when I yesterday wrote, I had not at all read two particular pieces, to which I now desire to call special attention,—'A Select Party,' and 'Young Goodman Brown.' Here, be it said to all those whom this poor fugitive scrawl of mine may tempt to the perusal of the 'Mosses,' that they must on no account suffer themselves to be trifled with, disappointed, or deceived by the triviality of many of the titles to these sketches. For in more than one instance, the title utterly belies the piece. It is as if rustic demijohns containing the very best and costliest of Falernian and Tokay, were labelled 'Cider,' 'Perry,' and 'Elder-berry wine.' The truth seems to be, that like many other geniuses, this Man of Mosses takes great delight in hood-winking the world,—at least, with respect to himself. Personally, I doubt not that he rather prefers to be generally esteemed but a so-so sort of author; being willing to reserve the thorough and acute appreciation of what he is, to that party most qualified to judge—that is, to himself. Besides, at the bottom of their natures, men like Hawthorne, in many things, deem the plaudits of the public such strong presumptive evidence of mediocrity in the object of them, that it would in some degree render them doubtful of their own powers, did they hear much and vociferous braying concerning them in the public pastures. True, I have been braying myself (if you please to be witty enough to have it so), but then I claim to be the first that has so brayed in this particular matter; and therefore, while pleading guilty to the charge, still claim all the merit due to originality.

But with whatever motive, playful or profound, Nathaniel Hawthorne has chosen to entitle his pieces in the manner he has, it is certain that some of them are directly calculated to deceive—egregiously deceive, the superficial skimmer of pages. To be downright and candid once more, let me cheerfully say, that two of these titles did dolefully dupe no less an eager-eyed reader than myself; and that, too, after I had been impressed with a sense of the great depth and breadth of this American man. 'Who in the name of thunder' (as the country-people say in this neighborhood), 'who in the name of thunder, would anticipate any marvel in a piece entitled "Young Goodman Brown?"' You would of course suppose that it was a simple little tale, intended as a supplement to 'Goody Two Shoes.' Whereas, it is deep as Dante; nor

can you finish it, without addressing the author in his own words—
'It is yours to penetrate, in every bosom, the deep mystery of sin.' And
with Young Goodman, too, in allegorical pursuit of his Puritan wife,
you cry out in your anguish:

'Faith!' shouted Goodman Brown, in a voice of agony and desperation; and
the echoes of the forest mocked him, crying—'Faith! Faith!' as if bewildered
wretches were seeking her all through the wilderness.

Now this same piece, entitled 'Young Goodman Brown,' is one of
the two that I had not all read yesterday; and I allude to it now, because
it is, in itself, such a strong positive illustration of that blackness in Hawthorne, which I had assumed from the mere occasional shadows of it, as
revealed in several of the other sketches. But had I previously perused
'Young Goodman Brown,' I should have been at no pains to draw the
conclusion, which I came to at a time when I was ignorant that the book
contained one such direct and unqualified manifestation of it.

The other piece of the two referred to, is entitled 'A Select Party,'
which, in my first simplicity upon originally taking hold of the book,
I fancied must treat of some pumpkin-pie party in old Salem, or some
chowder-party on Cape Cod. Whereas, by all the gods of Peedee, it is
the sweetest and sublimest thing that has been written since Spenser
wrote. Nay, there is nothing in Spenser that surpasses it, perhaps nothing that equals it. And the test is this: read any canto in 'The Faery
Queen,' and then read 'A Select Party,' and decide which pleases you
most,—that is, if you are qualified to judge. Do not be frightened at
this; for when Spenser was alive, he was thought of very much as Hawthorne is now,—was generally accounted just such a 'gentle' harmless
man. It may be, that to common eyes, the sublimity of Hawthorne
seems lost in his sweetness,—as perhaps in that same 'Select Party' of
his; for whom he has builded so august a dome of sunset clouds, and
served them on richer plate than Belshazzar when he banqueted his lords
in Babylon.

But my chief business now, is to point out a particular page in this
piece, having reference to an honored guest, who under the name of
'The Master Genius,' but in the guise 'of a young man of poor attire,
with no insignia of rank or acknowledged eminence,' is introduced to
the man of Fancy, who is the giver of the feast. Now, the page having
reference to this 'Master Genius,' so happily expresses much of what I
yesterday wrote, touching the coming of the literary Shiloh of America,
that I cannot but be charmed by the coincidence; especially, when it

shows such a parity of ideas, at least in this one point, between a man
like Hawthorne and a man like me.

And here, let me throw out another conceit of mine touching this
American Shiloh, or 'Master Genius,' as Hawthorne calls him. May it
not be, that this commanding mind has not been, is not, and never will
be, individually developed in any one man? And would it, indeed,
appear so unreasonable to suppose, that his great fullness and overflowing may be, or may be destined to be, shared by a plurality of men of
genius? Surely, to take the very greatest example on record, Shakspeare
cannot be regarded as in himself the concretion of all the genius of his
time; nor as so immeasurably beyond Marlow, Webster, Ford, Beau-
mont, Jonson, that these great men can be said to share none of his
power? For one, I conceive that there were dramatists in Elizabeth's
day, between whom and Shakspeare the distance was by no means
great. Let any one, hitherto little acquainted with those neglected old
authors, for the first time read them thoroughly, or even read Charles
Lamb's Specimens of them, and he will be amazed at the wondrous
ability of those Anaks of men, and shocked at this renewed example of
the fact, that Fortune has more to do with fame than merit,—though,
without merit, lasting fame there can be none.

Nevertheless, it would argue too ill of my country were this maxim
to hold good concerning Nathaniel Hawthorne, a man, who already,
in some few minds, has shed 'such a light, as never illuminates the earth
save when a great heart burns as the household fire of a grand intellect.'
The words are his,—'in the Select Party;' and they are a magnificent
setting to a coincident sentiment of my own, but ramblingly expressed
yesterday, in reference to himself. Gainsay it who will, as I now write, I
am Posterity speaking by proxy—and after times will make it more
than good, when I declare, that the American, who up to the present day
has evinced, in literature, the largest brain with the largest heart, that
man is Nathaniel Hawthorne. Moreover, that whatever Nathaniel
Hawthorne may hereafter write, 'The Mosses from an Old Manse' will
be ultimately accounted his master-piece. For there is a sure, though a
secret sign in some works which proves the culmination of the powers
(only the developable ones, however) that produced them. But I am by
no means desirous of the glory of a prophet. I pray Heaven that Hawthorne may *yet* prove me an impostor in this prediction. Especially, as I
somehow cling to the strange fancy, that, in all men, hiddenly reside
certain wondrous, occult properties—as in some plants and minerals—
which by some happy but very rare accident (as bronze was discovered

by the melting of the iron and brass at the burning of Corinth) may chance to be called forth here on earth; not entirely waiting for their better discovery in the more congenial, blessed atmosphere of heaven.

Once more—for it is hard to be finite upon an infinite subject, and all subjects are infinite. By some people this entire scrawl of mine may be esteemed altogether unnecessary, inasmuch 'as years ago' (they may say) 'we found out the rich and rare stuff in this Hawthorne, whom you now parade forth, as if only *yourself* were the discoverer of this Portuguese diamond in our literature.' But even granting all this—and adding to it, the assumption that the books of Hawthorne have sold by the five thousand,—what does that signify? They should be sold by the hundred thousand; and read by the million; and admired by every one who is capable of admiration.

39. Charles Wilkins Webber; Hawthorne and a national literature, from an unsigned essay, 'Hawthorne', in the *American Whig Review*

September 1846, iv, 296–316

Webber (1819–56), who used the pseudonym 'Charles Winterfield', is best known as a friend of Audubon and as a writer of Wild West tales and two volumes of natural history.

It happens that we have not only found Conservatism, but a good many other things we have asked for, in our national literature, expressed through the pages of Nathaniel Hawthorne. . . . We don't mean to say that Nathaniel Hawthorne is necessarily a '*nonpareil*,' and therefore above or beyond any body or thing else in all the land! We distinctly say that there are many of our 'Native' writers who, in their particular departments of thought and style, surpass him—or rather any particular effort of his—in their chosen and practiced line. It would be ridiculous to say or think otherwise; for the great fault we have to find with our Authors is, not that they lack earnestness or purpose, but that they have been too apt to dissipate both in a rash and heady intensification of their energies upon subjects not sufficiently universal in interest, and which, in view of results, might have been more wisely treated under many modifications. But we do say, quite as distinctly, that taking the plain level of results aimed at and ends accomplished, our author covers the broadest and the highest field yet occupied by the Imaginative Literature of the country, and deserves to be set forth, in very many particulars, as 'the glass of fashion and the mould of form' to those who are to come after, at least! To be sure, an officious wit, such as we have before endeavored to rebut, might be found, with the hardihood to say that he might do for some of his cotemporaries to glass themselves in! But we as decisively as heretofore repudiate any such heterodoxy! We are surely not accountable should he choose to say of our 'great Original Translator' that, could he only be induced to study Hawthorne earnestly and faithfully, there might be some hope that the manly self-reliance— the quiet, unobtrusive dignity—with which he asserts himself, and compels a loving recognition of his own peculiar modes, would cert- ainly touch and rouse the innate integrity even of an 'Appropriator's' life, until, with burning cheek, he would descend from the 'high-swung chariot' of his shame, and be content, like any other true man, to trust to his own ten toes—which, by the way, are good enough in themselves, and have carried him gracefully through the windings of many a 'soft Lydian measure!' Or if he should point 'our most distinguished Novelist' to the fine satires of Hawthorne, in which he has lashed the vices of his countrymen and times with unequaled keenness and effect, and yet has handled his cat-o'-nine-tails of scorpions with such exquisite dexterity and benevolent humor, that even those who winced and suffered most have been compelled to smile and look in his eyes, that they might drink out healing from the Love there. . . .

Hawthorne has a fine passage in the introductory chapter to the 'Mosses from an Old Manse,' relating to this morbid activity—this vehement and overstraining intellection—concerning which we have spoken so much, as the main and unpleasant characteristic of the age, but more particularly of our national literature and temper. We give it, for it suggests the same remedy which, not we alone, but many far- reaching minds of the day, have felt to be called for, and prayed might come. . . .

[Quotes 'Were I to adopt' to 'heighten the delerium'.]

. . . But we do say distinctly that we are very happy to perceive in him something of that breadth, depth, repose, and dignified reliance, which we have, perhaps unreasonably, asked as worthy characteristics of a truly National Literature—as they certainly are of a polished and elegant cultivation. It is very sure, if we ever aspire to any higher rank than that of mere imitators, we must fall back with an entire and un-hesitating confidence upon our own resources. All we think, write and say, must be tempered and modified by the *Real*—both moral and physical—around us. We cannot coquette here, alter there, and bodily appropriate elsewhere, from English or any other Foreign Literature, without subjecting ourselves to contempt in the end. Ours must be an honestly American—if it be not too much to say—an Aboriginal Literature! as distinct from all others as the plucked crown and scalp-lock of the red Indian—as vast, as rude, as wildly magnificent as our Mississippi, our mountains, or our Niagara—as still as our star-mirror-ing lakes at the North—as resistless in its roused strength as the tameless waves which tumble on 'the vexed Bermoothes' at the South! With-out these idiosyncrasies—unless we are high, free, calm, chivalric and stern—who will recognize us in the outward world? Hawthorne is national—national in subject, in treatment and in manner. We could hardly say anything higher of him, than that he is Hawthorne, and *'nothing else!'* He has never damned himself to the obese body of a Party. He belongs to *all of them*! . . .

It is greatly refreshing to meet with a straight-up-and-down flat-footed man, who stands on his own bottom, and asserts himself as Hawthorne does. A friend at my elbow suggests that there is a strong family likeness between the above sentence and one of Carlyle's in his essay upon Emerson. As we have no recollection of ever having seen the said sentence, we must simply congratulate Mr. Carlyle upon the happy coincidence. Hawthorne, too, speaks of Emerson, and in doing so, finely touches up this brawling tribe of Innovators—each one of whom imagines he has certainly found the Archimidean lever, and is heaving at it in the effort to turn the world topsy-turvy. We give it entire, since some of the finest characteristics of our author are here furnished:

[Quotes 'Severe and sober' to 'such philosophers'.]

But we have dwelt somewhat upon the universality of Hawthorne's mind, and his honestly philosophical readiness to recognize all truths, of whatever character, that may be presented by the different schools of avowed Reformers. It is somewhat curious to observe how quietly and unobtrusively this trait makes itself felt and recognized through his writings. Every now and then you stumble upon a passage which shows that he has extracted the honey from them all, and left what is merely the rough husk to the laws of decay. . . . We can, therefore, from this point of view, entirely appreciate the language he puts into the mouth of the 'new Adam and Eve,' when their fresh and unsophisticated minds have at once, through creation, been introduced to a great city of our civilization, from which, by a sudden 'judgment,' all the existing population has been swept, without the alteration of any physical expression of its condition at the time; with houses, ships, stores, streets, hotels, and private dwellings, left just as they were when the annihilating visitation overtook them! They have been long wandering amidst the labyrinth of doors and ways, filled with childlike and unspeakable amazement at all the inexplicable appliances they saw about them, when we find them curiously sauntering through the rooms of a modern mansion of luxury.

[Quotes 'by a most unlucky' to 'life within them'.]

But there is a still more interesting and even wiser exhibition of the Ethical Conservatism of his mind given in that fine allegory, 'Earth's Holocaust.' Here he represents a saturnalia of the Reformers who have carried the day, and induced the whole world to consent to make a great Holocaust of all things sacred in the past, concerning which there has been controversy. Of course as there has been controversy about everything, everything must be burnt, and a clean sweep be made—all things be wiped out, that the Race might begin anew! All things, true and false alike, were flung by the maddened multitude—even to the Book of Books—which refused to be burnt. When this has been accomplished and the reaction comes, the natural doubt begins to arise, whether the purified world would realize the expectation of benefit from such a sacrifice. This doubt is shared by the most dispassionately acute of the lookers-on in common with the murderers and criminals of every grade—but of course for very different reasons. A personage of very ominous character, who had been looking on with a quiet sneer, approaches these last with comforting words, as they are saying, 'This is no world for us any longer.'

[Quotes 'Poh, poh, my good' to 'my own brain!']

Would to God that we had more Teachers of such a creed as this in our Literature! Here we have embodied and illustrated, with a beautiful simplicity—not surpassed by that of the Greek fables or the Decameron —what is the fundamental thought of that Higher Conservatism upon the eternal base of which all wise and true Whigs have planted their feet. It is ridiculous to contend or hope that Political Creeds ever were or can be separated from the Ethical and Religious. One always has and always will grow out of the other. . . .

But it is to Hawthorne's Literary and Artistical character that we must now turn, and with equal pleasure. One of his finest traits is a sort of magical subtlety of vision, which, though it sees the true form of things through all the misty obscurations of humbug and cant, yet possesses the rare power of compelling others to see their naked shapes through a medium of its own. This is really the 'miraculous organ' of Genius, which projects out of its own life a '*couleur de Rose*,' with which everything it touches is imbued, and through which every one must look with it—or, if there is a purpose to be attained, throws forward a '*couleur de Diable*' with equal facility. A strong common sense in Hawthorne brushes away all cobwebs which obscure his subjects, except such as are dew-jewelled in the morning sun, and for these his rare fancy pleads sympathetically against that inexorable tribunal as exquisite illusions, mirthful fantasies of our old mother Nature, who thus presents her own creatures anew to our sated sense, through a glorifying kaleidoscope! . . . After all our Mother is the highest artist! It is a favorite expression with regard to Hawthorne, that he '*Idealizes*' everything. Now what does this Idealization mean? Is it that he *improves* upon Nature? Pshaw! this is a Literary cant which it is full time should be exploded! God is Nature! and if he be not the highest Artist, who is? Talk to me of *Idealizing* the violet, and you talk nonsense. Can you idealize the glories of an Autumn evening sunset, or *improve* the azure robe which 'lends enchantment' to the distant mountain's brow? Can you improve upon an Alpine Rose, with its contrasted accessories of desolation, in bare rugged cliffs, chill airs, inconstant storms of hail, and sleet, and snow, to vex the summer in its purple breast? When you can do this you may talk to us of idealizing God's own handy-work! Nature is never elevated, but it may be *approached*. It can never be '*improved*,' but it may be modified, as you may modify the rose into something like a red cabbage! But have you thereby made it into more than a rose? You have only distorted it! The beauty of the outward world is absolute—it depends upon our own eyes whether we see it so or not. . . . Now, Hawthorne does not endeavor to improve upon the Actual, but with a wise emulation attempts—first to reach it, and then to modify it suitably with the purpose he has to accomplish. Of course he is led by his fine taste to desire to see it himself, and make you see it in precisely that light in which it shows best—in which its highest beauty is revealed. It is the object of the Teacher to make us in love with Nature, and consequentially with Truth. He therefore presents Nature in her most effective and lovable attitudes. As he has, in painting the Day, a choice between all its periods he of course would not select the alert and laughing Morning, were his purpose to make us in love with shady langour; nor would he choose the sultry Noon to illustrate for, and fill us with images of buoyant life and action. He has all to select from, and the superiority of the Artist, is shown not only in the skill with which his objects are presented, but as well in the tact with which the conditions in which they are to be presented are selected; and this, after all, is what is truly meant by Idealizing them, though the greater portion of those who use the term suppose it to convey something mysteriously and inexpressibly significant.

We can't get away from the physical, and just as our material vision informs the inner life will that inner life know Wisdom. When some of our crude Theorists have learnt to realize this truth they will have learned too to toss their vagaries to the wind; for they will have come to the knowledge that one Fact of the external Life is worth a thousand Dreams, and that they need not waste their lives in seeing sights that have no substance, and dreaming Dreams that have no reality; for if they will only wake up, and look at the real World as it absolutely is, they will find they have a Paradise made to their hand—and that all that is wanted for their own, and the 'Perfectability' of the Race, is the requisite physical training and conditions which will furnish them with the capabilities for enjoying this Paradisaical state a benevolent Providence has offered them. . . . As an Artist, in this respect, Hawthorne possesses the most consummate skill. He sees a 'halo over common things,' and so brings up his readers, whether they will or not, to his point of view. . . . We know no modern writer more eminent than Hawthorne in this particular faculty. He is to the Present and the Future what Charles Lamb was to the Past. Lamb is a favorite of Conservative Literature—in that he held all the teachings of 'by-gones' as sacred—lived in memory, and furnishes us with that contrast of the Elder Experience with the Present Progress which we feel to be so indispensable as a guide to our Future. . . . Who will do it for us?

It is certain that neither Lamb, nor any other modern Prose Writer has ever walked more critically that difficult and narrow line between the Natural and Supernatural. This is a most perilous place to tread; and Hawthorne's clear eye and calm nerve does it with a steadiness and skill scarcely equaled. Take the first story in the Legends of the Province House, for example, in his earlier book, 'Twice-told Tales.' We defy anybody, after reading 'Howe's Masquerade,' to decide at once whether the 'mysterious pageant' with which the entertainment of the last Royal Governor of Massachusetts is interrupted, comes really from the Shadow-Land, or is merely a skillfully devised Masque of the rebellious Citizens! We are ourselves, to this very day, somewhat doubtful, though we have read it many times. When one comes to really analyze the Story in soberness, he finds himself a little puzzled in spite of his common sense; for though there can be no question as to the character of that strange figure, from a view of the face of which Sir William Howe recoils in horror and amazement—dropping his sword, which he had been about to use in his wrath—and though there can be as little room for mistake when, 'last of all, comes a figure shrouded in a military cloak, tossing his clenched hands into the Air, and stamping his iron-shod boots upon the broad freestone steps with a semblance of feverish despair, *but without the sound of a foot-tramp!*'—yet this sentence concludes the Story; and the Real and Unreal have been mingled throughout with so many consummate touches—such as when Colonel Joliff and his grand-daughter, who are both stout Rebels, leave, 'it was supposed that the Colonel and the young Lady possessed some secret intelligence in relation to the mysterious pageant of that night.' Now this passage is thrown in with a most admirable skill for the purpose of the Author; which is to continue a half-defined illusion in the reader's mind to the last, as to the true character of the scene he is perusing— whether these figures be of earth, or 'goblin damned!' This is the highest accomplishment of a peculiar skill which all imaginative writers have emulated. Its perfect type is found in the Old Ballads. Walter Scott and Fouque have been masters; while in Poetry Coleridge has triumphed supremely in Christabel. Hawthorne equals either of them in skill— but his subjects do not possess the breadth or Histrionic Grandeur of Scott's. His style and treatment have not equaled, though they have approached, the airy grace and tenderness of 'Undine;' or attained to the mysterious dread which creeps through music in unequaled Christabel. Yet we think his story of 'Young Goodman Brown' will bear to be contrasted with anything of this kind that has been done.

The subject of course wants many imposing elements—for it is merely an Allegory of simple New England Village Life—but as a Tale of the Supernatural it certainly is more exquisitely managed than anything we have seen in American Literature, at least! He wins our confidence at once, by his directness and perfect simplicity. We have no puerile announcement to begin with of 'A Tale of the Supernatural'—like the Painter's 'This is a Cow,' over his picture of that animal. We are left to find this out for ourselves in the due and proper time. In the meanwhile we are kept in a most titillating condition of uncertainty. . . .

[Quotes five long passages and summarizes the tale.]

. . . This story is only one of many, which equal it in all the attributes of Artistic effect, but few of which approach it in power. The singular skill with which our sympathy is kept 'halting between two opinions'— by which we are compelled throughout to recognize the flesh and blood reality of Goodman Brown; and necessarily, to enter into all the actual relations of the man, is only surpassed by the terrible elaboration with which this human embodiment of Doubt is compelled, through awe and madness, to struggle with the beings—almost equally human— of a self-created Hell. The effect, through all the sombre horror, is to keep our eyes 'upon the brim' with tenderness for the stout, deep-hearted Puritan and his sweet, gentle 'Faith'—with 'the pink ribbons in her cap!' But such effects are not, by any means, all that Hawthorne is capable of producing. We see through everything that he has done, the same faculty, not of *Idealizing* the Real—as it is called—but of Human-izing the Unreal—giving it thews, sinews and a life-blood! Nothing that is an image to us, or can be a subject of thought to us, is Unreal but through our own ignorance. They are all ours; and if we but possess the delicate intuition, may become familiars and the playmates of our moods! So Hawthorne, in his 'Virtuoso's Collection,' has given a real substance and entity to everything our childhood ever knew, from Aladdin's Lamp, and Cinderella's Slipper, [which he himself tried on,] to the skin of the 'Vulture' which preyed upon the liver of Prometheus, and even to 'Prospero's Magic Wand,' and, indeed, to the 'Magic Wand of Cornelius Agrippa,' with the veritable 'Iron Mask,' corroded with rust! All these we accept at his hands—just as our Childhood accepted 'Robinson Crusoe'—because we can't help it! So with all Hawthorne's stories—we never stop to ask whether they are 'sure 'nough' or not—it is sufficient that *he has made them Real*, and beguiled us for a time into the belief, that we are as wise as our Childhood was!

Ineffable wisdom of Simplicity! Why are there so many Infants among us, with foreheads in which 'the big imagination' is swelled out as we may conceit it to have been in the matured Shakspeare, which yet are wilted up, as they progress towards manhood, into the narrow quilting of a monkey's brow? Will 'Infantine' Wisdom answer us—or will Hawthorne? Hawthorne *might* do it!—for we see 'glimpses' in him that make him worthy.

The noblest Philosophers, of course, are those who have kept the Old Adam youngest in their veins! and necessarily such Philosophers must say the wisest and the gentlest things. . . .

The true Poet is the highest Philosopher; and it is as the true Poet that we most profoundly respect Hawthorne! There is a better Poetry than that which affiances itself to Rhythm—though it may be questioned whether it is a higher! Poetry has wedded itself to Music; though it may be doubted whether it can get away from the measured and according harmony of 'feet.' Yet we say, as Poetry is something above 'all rule or art,' it is necessarily above all 'metre,'—a pervading, uncontrollable Presence, which *will* stutter with a Human tongue the thoughts of Seraphim! and even in this imperfect speech work highest music out! Poetry is the music of Truth; and let it come through what medium it may, it is always musical while it is True! Thus it is that Hawthorne constantly writes Poems while he only pretends to be writing Tales! Who of our Poets can point to a deeper Poetry than is expressed in 'Rappaccini's Daughter.' Where, out of Hell or Byron, will you find anything to compass the cold, intellectual diabolicism of the famous Doctor 'Giacomo Rappaccini'? And where—certainly *not* in Byron!—will you find a sublimer retribution visited upon that presumptuous Thought, which dared the INEFFABLE and died!—than he there quietly gives? Not only in this, but in a dozen other Allegories—or Stories, as you choose to call them—can we point out 'Our Hawthorne' as 'Noticeable!' We had intended to have particularized in quotation many of those finer traits of spiritual beauty which have almost intruded themselves upon us, but we are compelled here, for want of space, to stop. We can only say, that in the 'Mosses of an Old Manse,' it seems to us that his Life has deepened since that which gave us 'The Twice-told Tales,' and that we hope and pray he may not spare us a future volume, though they may be even the Thrice-told Tales of Hawthorne!

40. S[amuel] W. S. D[utton]: Hawthorne and the natural style, from 'Nathaniel Hawthorne' in the *New Englander*

January 1847, v, 56–69

Dutton (1814–66), pastor of the North Church in New Haven, Connecticut, wrote various essays and critical pieces for the *New Englander*, most of them on current religious questions.

The works of Nathaniel Hawthorne place him, in our judgment, in the first rank of American authors, in the department of imaginative literature.

A curiosity to know something of the history of those who instruct or interest us, and honor our country, by their writings, is quite natural. Our readers, doubtless, would be gratified to know more of Mr. Hawthorne's history than we are able to give: for our knowledge of it is very limited. . . . His residence at Concord was, perhaps, either cause or effect of his sympathy with the amiable and highly cultivated, but misty and groping, philanthropists of the 'Concord sect' and the 'Roxbury Phalanx.' This sympathy, we regret to see and to say, appears, here and there, in his last volumes. It seems however, to be more a sympathy of heart and sentiment, than of intellect and conviction. For his native good sense evidently distrusts, and declines to adopt, their loose doctrines, and their unsubstantial plans and theories.

The volumes before us are four: two entitled Twice-Told Tales . . . and two entitled Mosses from an Old Manse. . . . They consist of various Tales, Essays, Allegories, and *Pieces*—we know of no term more specific which will answer our purpose.

Mr. Hawthorne's style of writing greatly pleases us. While it is lively, graphic, and picturesque, and occasionally forcible, it is very natural and quiet. There is nothing strained, and no painfully manifest aim and effort to be brilliant and effective. We have become so wearied with these faults in modern writers, that it is really refreshing to read one who writes unambitiously, and without this apparent labor—one who

135

tells us his thoughts and emotions, without a manifest consciousness of himself, and naturally, 'like the oubreaking of a fountain from the earth.' . . .

There is none of this diseased self-consciousness and this laborious self-display in Hawthorne's writing. His pleasant, truthful and earnest thoughts come forth noiselessly, and pass quietly on, as the clear water rises from the well-spring, and flows on in a gentle stream. His style is the simple clothing of his thought. There is nothing to draw our attention to it as style—to make us think of it, rather than of the thought which it communicates. . . . Mr. Hawthorne's style reminds us of Addison's, and of Charles Lamb's, and also of Scott's: though his simplicity is not so majestic and rich as Scott's, whose narration seems to us unequalled.

Mr. Hawthorne is a very minute observer. His eye seems to take in, at once, the whole, and each of the parts; and his narratives and pictures have often a particularity, which gives them a charming completeness and individuality—revealing minute traits, which we immediately and pleasantly recognize, but should not ourselves have thought of record-ing. He shows, in his descriptions of natural scenery, the quick and accurate and comprehensive eye of the true painter. And, then, mingled with his narrative or description, there is a kind of thinking aloud, or talking to himself, very truthful and pleasant—a sort of practical com-mentary on nature. We will give an illustration. Take this from his Buds and Bird-Voices.

[Quotes 'The trees, in our' to 'gather on them', 'Among the delights' to 'imagination for reality', and 'Thank Providence' to 'type of the Movement!']

We will take another illustration from his 'Snow-Flakes,' a picture of very different scenery.

[Quotes 'There is snow' to 'by our fireside', 'Now look we' to 'matter for the pen', and 'Such fantasies' to 'flock of snow-birds'.]

The same minuteness and accuracy of observation, and picturesque expression are seen in Mr. H.'s representations of the scenery of human life and character. He sees deeply into the interior of human character. He observes particularly and exactly its outward manifestations. And he sketches many varieties of it, in his usual easy and quiet style, but with great liveliness, and, indeed, dramatic skill and power. His person-ages are not all the same, with different names and in different circum-stances, but they preserve their individuality, and so stand out upon the canvass that we immediately recognize them. He is fond of seeing a great variety of characters. He frequently takes a position, whence he can see, at a glance, or in quick succession, a great many persons, as they actually appear. As, for instance, in his 'Sights from a Steeple,' whence he can see, not only the clouds, which he makes as full of varied life as the earth below, and, in the distance, on the one side, the culti-vated fields, villages, white country seats, the waving lines of rivulets, little placid lakes, and the knolls and hills, and, on the other side, the sea stretching away to a viewless distance, and the broad harbor on which is the town—but can also see the varied persons that appear to the eye and to the pocket spy-glass. . . . Or, as in his 'Toll-Gatherer's Day,' he takes his position at a toll-gate, on a frequently traveled road, and there observes all who pass from morning till night, reading their minds and hearts and condition, in their faces and general appearance and few passing words. Or, as in his 'Chippings with a Chisel,' he spends day after day in the workshop of a carver of tomb-stones, noting and reading the various persons who come to employ him. He is especially fond of bringing out the inward character. He loves to paint what he or some one else has called 'the moral picturesque,' and makes his accurate and lively description of the outward but the medium of vision into the inward.

Mr. Hawthorne has a very pleasant and good natured, yet successful and effective way of hitting off, or satirizing the faults and foibles and errors of individuals and cliques, of schools, and communities, and ages. And, while he looks with a kindly eye on human nature, and appreciates all its good qualities, he seems to be aware of its dark depths and its universal fountain of corruption. As illustrations of this trait, we would refer to The New Adam and Eve, The Intelligence Office, P. S. Correspondence, The Hall of Fantasy, The Procession of Life, Chip-pings with a Chisel, Peter Goldthwaite's Treasure, The Artist of the Beautiful—indeed we might go through the whole catalogue. But that which, in this respect, surpasses all his other writings, and we were about to say the writings of all but John Bunyan, is 'The Celestial Railroad:' which in respect to ease and rapidity, bears a relation to the road of John Bunyan's Pilgrim, like to that which a modern railroad bears to an old fashioned turnpike or county road—a pleasant but keen and truthful satire on modern easy modes of getting to heaven. We can not refrain from the endeavor to give our readers some idea of this work.

[Quotes nine long passages and summarizes the tale.]

We are greatly pleased with a gentle yet earnest humanity—a true interest in man and whatever pertains to him—which pervades all that Hawthorne writes. Its manifestations, however, are all of the indirect kind. There is no parade of it. There is no declamation about it. There is no manifest aim nor self-conscious effort, to be, and appear a phil-anthropist. His writings are instinct with a love of man as man, which appears, not because it desires to be seen, but because it is there and naturally comes forth toward its object. It speaks, not because it wishes to be heard, but because it has something pertinent and weighty to say. While Mr. H. has no hostility or envy towards the great and the opulent, and recognizes and appreciates their real manhood and worth, he is, evidently, most fond of the lowly and mediocral scenes and characters of life. He prefers to penetrate the humble externals of poverty, and to admire, or sympathize with, and picture, what is within, rather than to linger in marble halls and gorgeous dwellings, and amid the garniture and appliances and indulgences of luxury. And yet, there is in his writ-ings nothing of mawkish sympathy with the poor, no philanthropic cant, no hobby-riding upon humanity.

Of course Mr. H. has no favor to bestow upon that feeling of caste, to which the human heart is, in prosperity, so prone—the pride, which prompts its possessor to place himself above the sympathies of our common nature, above the sympathies of all except a select circle or class; which fills him with the thought that he is of better clay or mould than the mass of men, and can mingle with them only by condescension. A spirit of indirect, but decided, hostility to it, pervades all his writings. And some of his tales (for instance Lady Eleanore's Mantle) have a moral, which visits it with skillful and forcible rebuke. Mr. Hawthorne is said to belong to the democratic party. He certainly has that sympathy with every thing human which belongs to the true men of all parties. And he is very unlike many, who, with 'equal and exact justice to all men' and 'the largest liberty' on their lips, are the most inveterate haters of a particular class of men, the most obstinate withholders of 'equal and exact justice' from them, and the apologists, or advocates, or guardians of a system of their bitter oppression.

There is an unfavorable criticism which we feel bound to make on one of Hawthorne's tales. It is respecting a fault which offends our reverence and affection for the early New Englanders. This occurs in his story entitled 'The Gentle Boy,' founded on the persecutions of the Quakers—a tale, which, as a work of imagination, is excellent—varied, graphic, and surpassingly tender and beautiful. He exaggerates, in his story, the spirit of hostility, among the New England Puritans, to the Quakers. And he fails to make a very obvious and just distinction between persecution of the Quakers for heresy, and their punishment for civil offenses—for absolute breaches of the peace—for publicly vilifying the magistracy, for open and boisterous disturbance of worshiping congregations on the Sabbath, and for violent and abusive interruptions of clergymen in their discourses. It is true, indeed, that the utterance of heretical opinions was accounted, in the colonies of New England, (as it was in the parent country, in a greater degree, especially by those attached to the Episcopal hierarchy,) a civil crime. This was an error. It is to be acknowledged and regretted. But it was an error of the age; and one from which the Puritans were more free than most of their contemporaries. Oliver Cromwell, for example, was almost two hundred years in advance of his age, in respect to intellectual and religious tolerance. The early New Englanders ought to be admired for going so far toward entire freedom of opinion, in an age of ecclesiastical establishments, and of intellectual and religious servitude, rather than blamed for not going on to the perfection of toleration and spiritual freedom, which, by gradual steps, their posterity have attained. Many of the Quakers, in the wildness of their enthusiasm, felt called to be, and actually were, serious disturbers of the peace. And they were punished, with the severity of those rigid times towards offenders against good order and good manners, more for those breaches of the peace, than for the utterance of heresy. Though we do not deny that there were cases, where the utterance of heresy was made, partly at least, matter of accusation and of punishment. This was a stain upon the age, and upon our fathers, in that age. Let it not be denied. But, in the name of all that is worthy of reverence in any ancestry, let it not be magnified and blackened.

We regret this injustice by Mr. Hawthorne towards the New England Puritans. We are somewhat surprised at it. For he has shown, in other parts of his works, that he highly appreciates their character. True, the plan of the story of 'The Gentle Boy' was quite a temptation to exaggerate the persecution of the Quakers. But an author of Mr. H.'s genius has no need of the aid of exaggeration.

Hawthorne is generally quite successful, when he employs the supernatural. But, sometimes, he makes the lesson he would teach thereby so obscure, that it is not apprehended by many readers, who, to say the least, are not obtuse. For instance. His story of 'Young Goodman Brown' is designed to teach a moral lesson. But the design fails of accomplishment by the obscurity of execution. The lesson is not apprehended by nine out of ten of intelligent readers. The story is to them unintelligible. They do not know what the writer would be at. They can, perhaps, see the lesson, after some fortunate one has discovered and explained it. But such an explanation should be unnecessary. An allegory with crutches is a poor affair. An illustration, that needs to be illustrated, may well be spared.

But we have little except praise to offer respecting Hawthorne. We hope that he will write and publish often. For it is pleasant to observe, that the more he writes the better he writes. Mosses from an Old Manse —his last volumes—are decidedly superior to his Twice Told Tales.

Involuntarily, while we have been reading Hawthorne, Washington Irving comes up in our mind in comparison with him. Irving has labored successfully in a department of literature which Hawthorne has not entered. They can not, therefore, be compared, except in that kind of imaginative literature, which they have cultivated in common; and therein, we think Hawthorne quite equal to Irving. While he is not inferior to him in easy, graceful style of expression, and scarcely inferior in that exquisite gentleness and sensibility which is Irving's forte, he has a wider and deeper insight into human character, a greater fondness and capability for the moral picturesque, more dramatic power, and is a profounder thinker on the subjects of which he treats.

We hope Mr. Hawthorne will quit the custom house, and devote himself wholly to literature. His pen, now that it has won for him so high a reputation, will doubtless yield him an ample support, and in a way more congenial to his taste, and far more useful and honorable to his country. There are many hungry politicians who are competent to perform the duties of his office in the port of Salem, who have no great gift for benefiting the country in any other way. It is a waste of a kind of genius, which we can not well spare, to shut up Nathaniel Hawthorne in a custom house.

41. Edgar A. Poe: The attack on Hawthorne's allegory, from 'Tale Writing—Nathaniel Hawthorne', in *Godey's Lady's Book*

November 1847, xxxv, 252–6

In the May issue of *Godey's*, Poe had once again spoken favourably of Hawthorne in a brief mention which he quotes at the beginning of this review. Hawthorne, undoubtedly pleased by Poe's comments on *Twice-Told Tales* (see Nos. 27 and 29), had sent a complimentary copy of *Mosses* to Poe.

In the preface to my sketches of New York Literati, while speaking of the broad distinction between the seeming public and real private opinion respecting our authors, I thus alluded to Nathaniel Hawthorne:—

For example, Mr. Hawthorne, the author of 'Twice-Told Tales,' is scarcely recognized by the press or by the public, and when noticed at all, is noticed merely to be damned by faint praise. Now, my own opinion of him is, that although his walk is limited and he is fairly to be charged with mannerism, treating all subjects in a similar tone of dreamy *innuendo*, yet in this walk he evinces extraordinary genuis, having no rival either in America or elsewhere; and this opinion I have never heard gainsaid by any one literary person in the country. That this opinion, however, is a spoken and not a written one, is referable to the facts, first, that Mr. Hawthorne is a poor man, and secondly, that he *is not* an ubiquitous quack.

The reputation of the author of 'Twice-Told Tales' has been confined, indeed, until very lately, to literary society; and I have not been wrong, perhaps, in citing him as *the* example, *par excellence*, in this country, of the privately-admired and publicly-unappreciated man of genius. Within the last year or two, it is true, an occasional critic has been urged, by honest indignation, into very warm approval. Mr. Webber, for instance (than whom no one has a keener relish for that kind of writing which Mr. Hawthorne has best illustrated,) gave us, in a late number of 'The American Review,' a cordial and certainly a full tribute to his talents; and since the issue of the 'Mosses from an Old Manse,' criticisms of similar tone have been by no means infrequent in our more authoritative journals. I can call to mind few reviews of Hawthorne published *before* the 'Mosses.' One I remember in 'Arcturus' (edited by Matthews and Duyckinck) for May, 1841; another in the 'American Monthly' (edited by Hoffman and Herbert) for March, 1838; a third in the ninety-sixth number of the 'North American Review.' These criticisms, however, seemed to have little effect on the popular taste—at least, if we are to form any idea of the popular taste by reference to its expression in the newspapers, or by the sale of the author's book. It was never the fashion (until lately) to speak of him in any summary of our best authors. The daily critics would say, on such occasions, 'Is there not Irving and Cooper, and Bryant and Paulding, and—Smith?' or, 'Have we not Halleck and Dana, and Longfellow and —Thompson?' or, 'Can we not point triumphantly to our own Sprague, Willis, Channing, Bancroft, Prescott and—Jenkins?' but these unanswerable queries were never wound up by the name of Hawthorne.

Beyond doubt, this inappreciation of him on the part of the public arose chiefly from the two causes to which I have referred—from the facts that he is neither a man of wealth nor a quack;—but these are insufficient to account for the whole effect. No small portion of it is attributable to the very marked idiosyncrasy of Mr. Hawthorne himself. In one sense, and in great measure, to be peculiar is to be original, and than the true originality there is no higher literary virtue. This true or commendable originality, however, implies not the uniform, but the continuous peculiarity—a peculiarity springing from ever-active vigor of fancy—better still if from ever-present force of imagination, giving its own hue, its own character to everything it touches, and, especially, *self impelled to touch everything*.

It is often said, inconsiderately, that very original writers always fail in popularity—that such and such persons are too original to be comprehended by the mass. 'Too peculiar,' should be the phrase, 'too idiosyncratic.' It is, in fact, the excitable, undisciplined and child-like popular mind which most keenly feels the original. The criticism of the conservatives, of the hackneys, of the cultivated old clergymen of the 'North American Review,' is precisely the criticism which condemns and alone condemns it. 'It becometh not a divine,' saith Lord Coke, 'to be of a fiery and salamandrine spirit.' Their conscience allowing them to move nothing themselves, these dignitaries have a holy horror of being moved. 'Give us *quietude*,' they say. Opening their mouths with proper caution, they sigh forth the word '*Repose*.' And this is, indeed, the one thing they should be permitted to enjoy, if only upon the Christian principle of give and take.

The fact is, that if Mr. Hawthorne were really original, he could not fail of making himself felt by the public. But the fact is, he is *not* original in any sense. Those who speak of him as original, mean nothing more than that he differs in his manner or tone, and in his choice of subjects, from any author of their acquaintance—their acquaintance not extending to the German Tieck, whose manner, in *some* of his works, is absolutely identical with that *habitual* to Hawthorne. But it is clear that the element of the literary originality is novelty. The element of its appreciation by the reader is the reader's sense of the new. Whatever gives him a new and insomuch a pleasurable emotion, he considers original, and whoever frequently gives him such emotion, he considers an original writer. In a word, it is by the sum total of these emotions that he decides upon the writer's claim to originality. I may observe here, however, that there is clearly a point at which even novelty itself would cease to produce the legitimate originality, if we judge this originality, as we should, by the effect designed: this point is that at which *novelty becomes nothing novel*; and here the artist, *to preserve his originality*, will subside into the common-place. No one, I think, has noticed that, merely through inattention to this matter, Moore has comparatively failed in his 'Lalla Rookh.' Few readers, and indeed few critics, have commended this poem for originality—and, in fact, the effect, originality, is not produced by it—yet no work of equal size so abounds in the happiest originalities, individually considered. They are so excessive as, in the end, to deaden in the reader all capacity for their appreciation.

These points properly understood, it will be seen that the critic (unacquainted with Tieck) who reads a single tale or essay by Hawthorne, may be justified in thinking him original; but the tone, or manner, or choice of subject, which induces in this critic the sense of the new, will—if not in a second tale, at least in a third and all subsequent ones—not only fail of inducing it, but bring about an exactly antagonistic impression. In concluding a volume, and more especially in concluding all the volumes of the author, the critic will abandon his first design of calling him 'original,' and content himself with styling him 'peculiar.'

With the vague opinion that to be original is to be unpopular, I could, indeed, agree, were I to adopt an understanding of originality which, to my surprise, I have known adopted by many who have a right to be called critical. They have limited, in a love for mere words, the literary to the metaphysical originality. They regard as original in letters, only such combinations of thought, of incident, and so forth, as are, in fact, absolutely novel. It is clear, *however*, not only that it is the novelty of *effect* alone which is worth consideration, but that this effect is *best* wrought, for the end of all fictitious composition, pleasure, by shunning rather than by seeking the absolute novelty of combination. Originality, thus understood, tasks and startles the intellect, and so brings into undue action the faculties to which, in the lighter literature, we least appeal. And thus understood, it cannot fail to prove unpopular with the masses, who, seeking in this literature amusement, are positively offended by instruction. But the true originality—true in respect of its purposes—is that which, in bringing out the half-formed, the reluctant, or the unexpressed fancies of mankind, or in exciting the more delicate pulses of the heart's passion, or in giving birth to some universal sentiment or instinct in embryo, thus combines with the pleasurable effect of *apparent* novelty, a real egoistic delight. The reader, in the case first supposed, (that of the absolute novelty,) is excited, but embarrassed, disturbed, in some degree even pained at his own want of perception, at his own folly in not having himself hit upon the idea. In the second case, his pleasure is doubled. He is filled with an intrinsic and extrinsic delight. He feels and intensely enjoys the seeming novelty of the thought, enjoys it as really novel, as absolutely original with the writer —*and* himself. They two, he fancies, have, alone of all men, thought thus. They two have, together, created this thing. Henceforward there is a bond of sympathy between them, a sympathy which irradiates every subsequent page of the book.

There is a species of writing which, with some difficulty, may be admitted as a lower degree of what I have called the true original. In its perusal, we say to ourselves, not 'how original this is!' nor 'here is an idea which I and the author have alone entertained,' but 'here is a charmingly obvious fancy,' or sometimes even, 'here is a thought which I am not sure has ever occurred to myself, but which, of course, has occurred to all the rest of the world.' This kind of composition (which still appertains to a high order) is usually designated as 'the natural.' It has little external resemblance, but strong internal affinity to the true original, if, indeed, as I have suggested, it is not of this latter an inferior degree. It is best exemplified, among English writers, in Addison, Irving and *Hawthorne*. The 'ease' which is so often spoken of as its distinguishing feature, it has been the fashion to regard as ease in appearance alone, as a point of really difficult attainment. This idea, however, must be received with some reservation. The natural style is difficult only to those who should never intermeddle with it—to the unnatural. It is but the result of writing with the understanding, or with the instinct, that the *tone*, in composition, should be that which, at any given point or upon any given topic, would be the tone of the great mass of humanity. The author who, after the manner of the North Americans, is merely at *all* times *quiet*, is, of course, upon *most* occasions, merely silly or stupid, and has no more right to be thought 'easy' or 'natural' than has a cockney exquisite or the sleeping beauty in the wax-works.

The 'peculiarity' or sameness, or monotone of Hawthorne, would, in its mere character of 'peculiarity,' and without reference to what is the peculiarity, suffice to deprive him of all chance of popular appreciation. But at his failure to be appreciated, we can, *of course*, no longer wonder, when we find him monotonous at decidedly the worst of all possible points—at that point which, having the least concern with Nature, is the farthest removed from the popular intellect, from the popular sentiment and from the popular taste. I allude to the strain of allegory which completely overwhelms the greater number of his subjects, and which in some measure interferes with the direct conduct of absolutely all.

In defence of allegory, (however, or for whatever object, employed,) there is scarcely one respectable word to be said. Its best appeals are made to the fancy—that is to say, to our sense of adaptation, not of matters proper, but of matters improper for the purpose, of the real with the unreal; having never more of intelligible connection than has something with nothing, never half so much of effective affinity as has the substance for the shadow. The deepest emotion aroused within us by the happiest allegory, *as* allegory, is a very, very imperfectly satisfied sense of the writer's ingenuity in overcoming a difficulty we should have preferred his not having attempted to overcome. The fallacy of the idea that allegory, in any of its moods, can be made to enforce a truth—that metaphor, for example, may illustrate as well as embellish an argument—could be promptly demonstrated: the converse of the supposed fact might be shown, indeed, with very little trouble—but these are topics foreign to my present purpose. One thing is clear, that if allegory ever establishes a fact, it is by dint of overturning a fiction. Where the suggested meaning runs through the obvious one in a *very* profound under-current, so as never to interfere with the upper one without our own volition, so as never to show itself unless *called* to the surface, there only, for the proper uses of fictitious narrative, is it available at all. Under the best circumstances, it must always interfere with that unity of effect which, to the artist, is worth all the allegory in the world. Its vital injury, however, is rendered to the most vitally important point in fiction—that of earnestness or verisimilitude. That 'The Pilgrim's Progress' is a ludicrously over-rated book, owing its seeming popularity to one or two of those accidents in critical literature which by the critical are sufficiently well understood, is a matter upon which no two thinking people disagree; but the pleasure derivable from it, in any sense, will be found in the direct ratio of the reader's capacity to smother its true purpose, in the direct ratio of his ability to keep the allegory out of sight, or of his *in*ability to comprehend it. Of allegory properly handled, judiciously subdued, seen only as a shadow or by suggestive glimpses, and making its nearest approach to truth in a not obtrusive and therefore not unpleasant *appositeness*, the 'Undine' of De La Motte Fouqué is the best, and undoubtedly a very remarkable specimen.

The obvious causes, however, which have prevented Mr. Hawthorne's *popularity*, do not suffice to condemn him in the eyes of the few who belong properly to books, and to whom books, perhaps, do not quite so properly belong. These few estimate an author, not as do the public, altogether by what he does, but in great measure—indeed, even in the greater measure—by what he evinces a capability of doing. In this view, Hawthorne stands among literary people in America much in the same light as did Coleridge in England. The few, also, through a certain warping of the taste, which long pondering upon books as books merely never fails to induce, are not in condition to view the errors of a scholar as errors altogether. At any time these gentlemen are prone to think the public not right rather than an educated author wrong. But the simple truth is, that the writer who aims at impressing the people, is *always* wrong when he fails in forcing that people to receive the impression. How far Mr. Hawthorne has addressed the people at all, is, of course, not a question for me to decide. His books afford strong internal evidence of having been written to himself and his particular friends alone.

There has long existed in literature a fatal and unfounded prejudice, which it will be the office of this age to overthrow—the idea that the mere bulk of a work must enter largely into our estimate of its merit. I do not suppose even the weakest of the Quarterly reviewers weak enough to maintain that in a book's size or mass, abstractly considered, there is anything which especially calls for our admiration. A mountain, simply through the sensation of physical magnitude which it conveys, does, indeed, affect us with a sense of the sublime, but we cannot admit any such influence in the contemplation even of 'The Columbiad.' The Quarterlies themselves will not admit it. And yet, what else are we to understand by their continual prating about 'sustained effort?' Granted that this sustained effort has accomplished an epic—let us then admire the effort, (if this be a thing admirable,) but certainly not the epic on the effort's account. Common sense, in the time to come, may possibly insist upon measuring a work of art rather by the object it fulfils, by the impression it makes, than by the time it took to fulfil the object, or by the extent of 'sustained effort' which became necessary to produce the impression. The fact is, that perseverance is one thing and genius quite another; nor can all the transcendentalists in Heathendom confound them.

Full of its bulky ideas, the last number of the 'North American Review,' in what it imagines a criticism on Simms, 'honestly avows that it has little opinion of the mere tale;' and the honesty of the avowal is in no slight degree guaranteed by the fact that this Review has never yet been known to put forth an opinion which was *not* a very little one indeed.

The tale proper affords the fairest field which can be afforded by the wide domains of mere prose, for the exercise of the highest genius. Were I bidden to say how this genius could be most advantageously employed for the best display of its powers, I should answer, without hesitation, 'in the composition of a rhymed poem not to exceed in length what might be perused in an hour.' Within this limit alone can the noblest order of poetry exist. I have discussed this topic elsewhere, and need here repeat only that the phrase 'a long poem' embodies a paradox. A poem must intensely excite. Excitement is its province, its essentiality. Its value is in the ratio of its (elevating) excitement. But all excitement is, from a psychal necessity, transient. It cannot be sustained through a poem of great length. In the course of an hour's reading, at most, it flags, fails; and then the poem is, in effect, no longer such. Men admire, but are wearied with the 'Paradise Lost;' for platitude follows platitude, *inevitably*, at regular interspaces, (the depressions between the waves of excitement,) until the poem, (which, properly considered, is but a succession of brief poems,) having been brought to an end, we discover that the sums of our pleasure and of displeasure have been very nearly equal. The absolute, ultimate or aggregate effect of any epic under the sun is, for these reasons, a nullity. 'The Iliad,' in its form of epic, has but an imaginary existence; granting it real, however, I can only say of it that it is based on a primitive sense of Art. Of the modern epic nothing can be so well said as that it is a blindfold imitation of a 'come-by-chance.' By and by these propositions will be understood as self-evident, and in the meantime will not be essentially damaged as truths by being generally condemned as falsities.

A poem *too* brief, on the other hand, may produce a sharp or vivid, but never a profound or enduring impression. Without a certain continuity, without a certain duration or repetition of the cause, the soul is seldom moved to the effect. There must be the dropping of the water on the rock. There must be the pressing steadily down of the stamp upon the wax. De Beranger has wrought brilliant things, pungent and spirit-stirring, but most of them are too immassive to have *momentum*, and, as so many feathers of fancy, have been blown aloft only to be whistled down the wind. Brevity, indeed, may degenerate into epigrammatism, but this danger does not prevent extreme length from being the one unpardonable sin.

Were I called upon, however, to designate that class of composition, which, next to such a poem as I have suggested, should best fulfil the demands and serve the purposes of ambitious genius, should offer it the most advantageous field of exertion, and afford it the fairest opportunity of display, I should speak at once of the brief prose tale. History, philosophy, and other matters of that kind, we leave out of the question, of course. *Of course*, I say, and in spite of the graybeards. These graver topics, to the end of time, will be best illustrated by what a discriminating world, turning up its nose at the drab pamphlets, has agreed to understand as *talent*. The ordinary novel is objectionable, from its length, for reasons analogous to those which render length objectionable in the poem. As the novel cannot be read at one sitting, it cannot avail itself of the immense benefit of *totality*. Worldly interests, intervening during the pauses of perusal, modify, counteract and annul the impressions intended. But simple cessation in reading would, of itself, be sufficient to destroy the true unity. In the brief tale, however, the author is enabled to carry out his full design without interruption. During the hour of perusal, the soul of the reader is at the writer's control.

A skillful artist has constructed a tale. He has not fashioned his thoughts to accommodate his incidents, but having deliberately conceived a certain *single effect* to be wrought, he then invents such incidents, he then combines such events, and discusses them in such tone as may best serve him in establishing this preconceived effect. If his very first sentence tend not to the outbringing of this effect, then in his very first step has he committed a blunder. In the whole composition there should be no word written of which the tendency, direct or indirect, is not to the one pre-established design. And by such means, with such care and skill, a picture is at length painted which leaves in the mind of him who contemplates it with a kindred art, a sense of the fullest satisfaction. The idea of the tale, its thesis, has been presented unblemished, because undisturbed—an end absolutely demanded, yet, in the novel, altogether unattainable.

Of skillfully-constructed tales—I speak now without reference to other points, some of them more important than construction—there are very few American specimens. I am acquainted with no better one, upon the whole, than the 'Murder Will Out' of Mr. Simms, and this has some glaring defects. The 'Tales of a Traveler,' by Irving, are graceful and impressive narratives—'The Young Italian' is especially good—but there is not one of the series which can be commended as a whole. In many of them the interest is subdivided and frittered away, and their conclusions are insufficiently *climacic*. In the higher requisites of composition, John Neal's magazine stories excel—I mean in vigor of thought, picturesque combination of incident, and so forth—but they ramble too much, and invariably break down just before coming to an end, as if the writer had received a sudden and irresistible summons to dinner, and thought it incumbent upon him to make a finish of his story before going. One of the happiest and best-sustained tales I have seen, is 'Jack Long; or, The Shot in the Eye,' by Charles W. Webber, the assistant editor of Mr. Colton's 'American Review.' But in general skill of construction, the tales of Willis, I think, surpass those of any American writer—with the exception of Mr. Hawthorne.

I must defer to the better opportunity of a volume now in hand, a full discussion of his individual pieces, and hasten to conclude this paper with a summary of his merits and demerits.

He is peculiar and not original—unless in those detailed fancies and detached thoughts which his want of general originality will deprive of the appreciation due to them, in preventing them forever reaching the public eye. He is infinitely too fond of allegory, and can never hope for popularity so long as he persists in it. This he will not do, for allegory is at war with the whole tone of his nature, which disports itself never so well as when escaping from the mysticism of his Goodman Browns and White Old Maids into the hearty, genial, but still Indian-summer sunshine of his Wakefields and Little Annie's Rambles. Indeed, *his* spirit of 'metaphor run-mad' is clearly imbibed from the phalanx and phalanstery atmosphere in which he has been so long struggling for breath. He has not half the material for the exclusiveness of authorship that he possesses for its universality. He has the purest style, the finest taste, the most available scholarship, the most delicate humor, the most touching pathos, the most radiant imagination, the most consummate ingenuity; and with these varied good qualities he has done *well* as a mystic. But is there any one of these qualities which should prevent his doing doubly as well in a career of honest, upright, sensible, prehensible and comprehensible things? Let him mend his pen, get a bottle of visible ink, come out from the Old Manse, cut Mr. Alcott, hang (if possible) the editor of 'The Dial', and throw out of the window to the pigs all his odd numbers of 'The North American Review.'

THE SCARLET LETTER

1850–1

42. Hawthorne, from 'The Custom-House'

1850

On 4 February 1850, having finished the romance, Hawthorne wrote to Horatio Bridge that the publisher

speaks of [the book] in tremendous terms of approbation; so does Mrs. Hawthorne, to whom I read the conclusion, last night. It broke her heart and sent her to bed with a grievous headache—which I look upon as triumphant success! Judging from its effect on her and the publisher, I may calculate on what bowlers call a ten-strike! Yet I do not make any such calculation. Some portions of the book are powerfully written; but my writings do not, nor ever will, appeal to the broadest class of sympathies, and therefore will not attain a very wide popularity. Some like them very much; others care nothing for them, and see nothing in them. There is an introduction to this book—giving a sketch of the Custom-House, with an imaginative touch here and there—which perhaps may be more widely attractive than the main narrative. The latter lacks sunshine. To tell you the truth, it is . . . positively a h-ll-fired story, into which I found it almost impossible to throw any cheering light. (MS., Houghton Library, Harvard University.)

. . . as thoughts are frozen and utterance benumbed, unless the speaker stand in some true relation with his audience—it may be pardonable to imagine that a friend, a kind and apprehensive, though not the closest friend, is listening to our talk; and then, a native reserve being thawed by this genial consciousness, we may prate of the circumstances that lie around us, and even of ourself, but still keep the inmost Me behind its veil. To this extent and within these limits, an author, methinks, may be autobiographical, without violating either the reader's rights or his own.

It will be seen, likewise, that this Custom-House sketch has a certain propriety, of a kind always recognized in literature, as explaining how a large portion of the following pages came into my possession, and as offering proofs of the authenticity of a narrative therein contained. This, in fact,—a desire to put myself in my true position as editor, or very little more, of the most prolix among the tales that make up my volume,—this, and no other, is my true reason for assuming a personal relation with the public.

★

"What is he?" murmurs one gray shadow of my forefathers to the other. "A writer of story-books! What kind of a business in life,—what mode of glorifying God, or being serviceable to mankind in his day and generation,—may that be? Why, the degenerate fellow might as well have been a fiddler!" Such are the compliments bandied between my great-grandsires and myself, across the gulf of time! And yet, let them scorn me as they will, strong traits of their nature have intertwined themselves with mine.

★

Moonlight, in a familiar room, falling so white upon the carpet, and showing all its figures so distinctly,—making every object so minutely visible, yet so unlike a morning or noontide visibility,—is a medium the most suitable for a romance-writer to get acquainted with his illusive guests. There is the little domestic scenery of the well-known apartment; the chairs, with each its separate individuality; the centre-table, sustaining a work-basket, a volume or two, and an extinguished lamp; the sofa; the book-case; the picture on the wall;—all these details, so completely seen, are so spiritualized by the unusual light, that they seem to lose their actual substance, and become things of intellect. Nothing is too small or too trifling to undergo this change, and acquire dignity thereby. A child's shoe; the doll, seated in her little wicker carriage; the hobby-horse;—whatever, in a word, has been used or played with, during the day, is now invested with a quality of strangeness and remoteness, though still almost as vividly present as by daylight. Thus, therefore, the floor of our familiar room has become a neutral territory, somewhere between the real world and fairy-land, where the Actual and the Imaginary may meet, and each imbue itself with the nature of the other. Ghosts might enter here, without affrighting us. It would be too much in keeping with the scene to excite surprise, were we to look about us and discover a form, beloved, but gone hence, now sitting quietly in a streak of this magic moonshine, with an aspect that would make us doubt whether it had returned from afar, or had never once stirred from our fireside.

The somewhat dim coal-fire has an essential influence in producing the effect which I would describe. It throws its unobtrusive tinge throughout the room, with a faint ruddiness upon the walls and ceiling, and a reflected gleam from the polish of the furniture. This warmer light mingles itself with the cold spirituality of the moonbeams, and communicates, as it were, a heart and sensibilities of human tenderness to the forms which fancy summons up. It converts them from snow-images into men and women. Glancing at the looking-glass, we behold —deep within its haunted verge—the smouldering glow of the half-extinguished anthracite, the white moonbeams on the floor, and a repetition of all the gleam and shadow of the picture, with one remove farther from the actual, and nearer to the imaginative. Then, at such an hour, and with this scene before him, if a man, sitting all alone, cannot dream strange things, and make them look like truth, he need never try to write romances.

But, for myself, during the whole of my Custom-House experience, moonlight and sunshine, and the glow of fire-light, were just alike in my regard; and neither of them was of one whit more avail than the twinkle of a tallow-candle. An entire class of susceptibilities, and a gift connected with them,—of no great richness or value, but the best I had,—was gone from me.

It is my belief, however, that, had I attempted a different order of composition, my faculties would not have been found so pointless and inefficacious. I might, for instance, have contented myself with writing out the narratives of a veteran shipmaster, one of the Inspectors, whom I should be most ungrateful not to mention; since scarcely a day passed that he did not stir me to laughter and admiration by his marvellous gifts as a story-teller. Could I have preserved the picturesque force of his style, and the humorous coloring which nature taught him how to throw over his descriptions, the result, I honestly believe, would have been something new in literature. Or I might readily have found a more serious task. It was a folly, with the materiality of this daily life pressing so intrusively upon me, to attempt to fling myself back into another age; or to insist on creating the semblance of a world out of airy matter, when, at every moment, the impalpable beauty of my soap-bubble was broken by the rude contact of some actual circumstance. The wiser effort would have been, to diffuse thought and imagination through the opaque substance of to-day, and thus to make it a bright transparency; to spiritualize the burden that began to weigh so heavily; to seek, resolutely, the true and indestructible value that lay hidden in the petty and wearisome incidents, and ordinary characters, with which I was now conversant. The fault was mine. The page of life that was spread out before me seemed dull and commonplace, only because I had not fathomed its deeper import. A better book than I shall ever write was there; leaf after leaf presenting itself to me, just as it was written out by the reality of the flitting hour, and vanishing as fast as written, only because my brain wanted the insight and my hand the cunning to transcribe it. At some future day, it may be, I shall remember a few scattered fragments and broken paragraphs, and write them down, and find the letters turn to gold upon the page.

43. Hawthorne, Preface to the Second Edition

30 March 1850

Much to the author's surprise, and (if he may say so without additional offence) considerably to his amusement, he finds that his sketch of official life, introductory to THE SCARLET LETTER has created an unprecedented excitement in the respectable community immediately around him. It could hardly have been more violent, indeed, had he burned down the Custom-House, and quenched its last smoking ember in the blood of a certain venerable personage, against whom he is supposed to cherish a peculiar malevolence. As the public disapprobation would weigh very heavily on him, were he conscious of deserving it, the author begs leave to say, that he has carefully read over the introductory pages, with a purpose to alter or expunge whatever might be found amiss, and to make the best reparation in his power for the atrocities of which he has been adjudged guilty. But it appears to him, that the only remarkable features of the sketch are its frank and genuine good-humor, and the general accuracy with which he has conveyed his sincere impressions of the characters therein described. As to enmity, or ill-feeling of any kind, personal or political, he utterly disclaims such motives. The sketch might, perhaps, have been wholly omitted, without loss to the public, or detriment to the book; but, having undertaken to write it, he conceives that it could not have been done in a better or a kindlier spirit, nor, so far as his abilities availed, with a livelier effect of truth.

The author is constrained, therefore, to republish his introductory sketch without the change of a word.

44. [E. A. Duyckinck], from a review in the *Literary World*

30 March 1850, vi, 323–5

Mr. Hawthorne introduces his new story to the public, the longest of all that he has yet published, and most worthy in this way to be called a romance, with one of those pleasant personal descriptions which are the most charming of his compositions, and of which we had so happy an example in the preface to his last collection, the Mosses from an Old Manse. In these narratives everything seems to fall happily into its place. The style is simple and flowing, the observation accurate and acute; persons and things are represented in their minutest shades, and difficult traits of character presented with an instinct which art might be proud to imitate. They are, in fine, little cabinet pictures exquisitely painted. The readers of the Twice Told Tales will know the pictures to which we allude. They have not, we are sure, forgotten Little Annie's Ramble, or the Sights from a Steeple. This is the Hawthorne of the present day in the sunshine. There is another Hawthorne less companionable, of sterner Puritan aspect, with the shadow of the past over him, a reviver of witchcrafts and of those dark agencies of evil which lurk in the human soul, and which even now represent the old gloomy historic era in the microcosm and eternity of the individual; and this

Hawthorne is called to mind by such tales as the Minister's Black Veil or the Old Maid in the Winding Sheet, and reappears in the Scarlet Letter, a romance. Romantic in sooth! Such romance as you may read in the intensest sermons of old Puritan divines, or in the mouldy pages of that Marrow of Divinity, the ascetic Jeremy Taylor.

The Scarlet Letter is a psychological romance. The hardiest Mrs. Malaprop would never venture to call it a novel. It is a tale of remorse, a study of character in which the human heart is anatomized, carefully, elaborately, and with striking poetic and dramatic power. Its incidents are simply these. . . .

[Summarizes the story.]

. . . the scarlet letter . . . is the hero of the volume. The denouement is the death of the clergyman on a day of public festivity, after a public confession in the arms of the pilloried, branded woman. But few as are these main incidents thus briefly told, the action of the story, or its passion, is 'long, obscure, and infinite.' It is a drama in which thoughts are acts. The material has been thoroughly fused in the writer's mind, and springs forth an entire, perfect creation. We know of no American tales except some of the early ones of Mr. Dana, which approach it in conscientious completeness. Nothing is slurred over, superfluous, or defective. The story is grouped in scenes simply arranged, but with artistic power, yet without any of those painful impressions which the use of the words, as it is the fashion to use them, 'grouping' and 'artistic' excite, suggesting artifice and effort at the expense of nature and ease.

Mr. Hawthorne has, in fine, shown extraordinary power in this volume, great feeling and discrimination, a subtle knowledge of character in its secret springs and outer manifestations. He blends, too, a delicate fancy with this metaphysical insight. We would instance the chapter towards the close, entitled 'The Minister in a Maze,' where the effects of a diabolic temptation are curiously depicted, or 'The Minister's Vigil,' the night scene in the pillory. The atmosphere of the piece also is perfect. It has the mystic element, the weird forest influences of the old Puritan discipline and era. Yet there is no affrightment which belongs purely to history, which has not its echo even in the unlike and perversely commonplace custom-house of Salem. Then for the moral. Though severe, it is wholesome, and is a sounder bit of Puritan divinity than we have been of late accustomed to hear from the degenerate successors of Cotton Mather. We hardly know another writer who has lived so much among the new school who would have handled this delicate subject without an infusion of George Sand. The spirit of his old Puritan ancestors, to whom he refers in the preface, lives in Nathaniel Hawthorne.

We will not mar the integrity of The Scarlet Letter by quoting detached passages. Its simple and perfect unity forbids this. Hardly will the introductory sketch bear this treatment without exposing the writer to some false impressions; but as evidence of the possession of a style faithfully and humorously reflective of the scenes of the passing hour, which we earnestly wish he may pursue in future volumes, we may give one or two separable sketches.

There is a fine, natural portrait of General Miller, the collector; equal in its way to the Old Inspector, the self-sufficing gourmand lately presented in our journal; and there are other officials as well done. A page, however, of as general application, and of as sound profit as any in this office-seeking age, is that which details, in its mental bearing,

THE PARALYSIS OF OFFICE.

[Quotes 'An effect—which' to 'manly character'.]

The personal situation of Nathaniel Hawthorne—in whom the city by his removal lost an indifferent official, and the world regained a good author—is amusingly presented in this memoir of

A DECAPITATED SURVEYOR.

[Quotes 'A remarkable event' to 'a literary man'.]

And a literary man long may he remain, an honor and a support to the craft, of genuine worth and fidelity, to whom no word is idle, no sentiment insincere. Our literature has given to the world no truer product of the American soil, though of a peculiar culture, than Nathaniel Hawthorne.

45. [George Ripley], from a review in the *New York Tribune Supplement*

1 April 1850, ix, 2

Ripley (1802–80), a Unitarian minister and a liberal thinker and reformer, is best known for his Transcendentalist theories and his role in organizing Brook Farm. He founded *The Dial* and from 1849 to 1880 was the book reviewer for the *Tribune*. With Charles Dana he edited the *New American Cyclopaedia* (1858–63).

The weird and ghostly legends of the Puritanic history present a singularly congenial field for the exercise of Mr. Hawthorne's peculiar genius. From this fruitful source, he has derived the materials for his most remarkable creations. He never appears so much in his element as when threading out some dim, shadowy tradition of the twilight age of New England, peering into the faded records of our dark-visaged forefathers for the lingering traces of the preternatural, and weaving into his gorgeous web of enchantment the slender filaments which he has drawn from the distaff of some muttering witch on Gallows-Hill. He derives the same terrible excitement from these legendary horrors, as was drawn by Edgar Poe from the depths of his own dark and perilous imagination, and brings before us pictures of death-like, but strangely fascinating agony, which are described with the same minuteness of finish—the same slow and fatal accumulation of details—the same exquisite coolness of coloring, while everything creeps forward with irresistible certainty to a soul-harrowing climax—which made the last-named writer such a consummate master of the horrible and infernal in fictitious composition. Hawthorne's tragedies, however, are always *motived* with a wonderful insight and skill, to which the intellect of Poe was a stranger. In the most terrific scenes with which he delights to scare the imagination, Hawthorne does not wander into the region of the improbable; you scarcely know that you are in the presence of the supernatural, until your breathing becomes too thick for this world; it is the supernatural relieved, softened, made tolerable, and almost attractive, by a strong admixture of the human; you are tempted onward by the mild, unearthly light, which seems to shine upon you like a healthful star; you are blinded by no lurid glare; you acquiesce in the necessity of the wizard journey; instead of being provoked to anger by a superfluous introduction to the company of the devil and his angels.

The elements of terror, which Mr. Hawthorne employs with such masterly effect, both in the original conceptions of his characters and the scenes of mystery and dread in which they are made to act, are blended with such sweet gushes of natural feeling, such solemn and tender relations of the deepest secrets of the heart, that the painful impression is greatly mitigated, and the final influence of his most startling creation is a serene sense of refreshment, without the stupor and bewilderment occasioned by a drugged cup of intoxication.

The 'Scarlet Letter,' in our opinion, is the greatest production of the author, beautifully displaying the traits we have briefly hinted at, and sustained with a more vigorous reach of imagination, a more subtle instinct of humanity, and a more imposing splendor of portraiture, than any of his most successful previous works.

[Summarizes the story and quotes several long passages.]

We have not intended to forestall our readers with a description of the plot, which it will be perceived abounds in elements of tragic interest, but to present them with some specimens of a genuine native romance, which none will be content without reading for themselves. The moral of the story—for it has a moral for all wise enough to detect it—is shadowed forth rather than expressed in a few brief sentences near the close of the volume.

[Quotes ch. 24, 'But there was' to 'such an end!']

The introduction, presenting a record of savory reminiscences of the Salem Custom House, a frank display of autobiographical confessions, and a piquant daguerreotype of his ancient colleagues in office, while surveyor of that port, is written with Mr. Hawthorne's unrivalled force of graphic delineation, and will furnish an agreeable amusement to those who are so far from the scene of action as to feel no wound in their personal relations, but the occasional too sharp touches of the caustic acid, of which the 'gentle author' keeps some phials on his shelf for convenience and use. The querulous tone in which he alludes to his removal from the Custom House, may be forgiven to the sensitiveness of a poet, especially as this is so rare a quality in Uncle Sam's office-holders.

46. [E. P. Whipple], a review in *Graham's Magazine*

May 1850, xxxvi, 345–6

Whipple (1819–86) was ranked with Poe and Lowell among American critics of the day, and his opinions were especially valued by Hawthorne. Among his collected works are *Essays and Reviews* (1849) and *Recollections of Eminent Men* (1887).

In this beautiful and touching romance Hawthorne has produced something really worthy of the fine and deep genius which lies within him. The 'Twice Told Tales,' and 'Mosses from an Old Manse,' are composed simply of sketches and stories, and although such sketches and stories as few living men could write, they are rather indications of the possibilities of his mind than realizations of its native power, penetration, and creativeness. In 'The Scarlet Letter' we have a complete work, evincing a true artist's certainty of touch and expression in the exhibition of characters and events, and a keen-sighted and far-sighted vision into the essence and purpose of spiritual laws. There is a profound philosophy underlying the story which will escape many of the readers whose attention is engrossed by the narrative.

The book is prefaced by some fifty pages of autobiographical matter, relating to the author, his native city of Salem, and the Custom House, from which he was ousted by the Whigs. These pages, instinct with the vital spirit of humor, show how rich and exhaustless a fountain of mirth Hawthorne has at his command. The whole representation has the dreamy yet distinct remoteness of the purely comic ideal. The view of Salem streets; the picture of the old Custom House at the head of Derby's wharf, with its torpid officers on a summer's afternoon, their chairs all tipped against the wall, chatting about old stories, 'while the frozen witticisms of past generations were thawed out, and came bubbling with laughter from their lips'—the delineation of the old Inspector, whose 'reminiscences of good cheer, however ancient the date of the actual banquet, seemed to bring the savor of pig or turkey under one's very nostrils,' and on whose palate there were flavors 'which had lingered there not less than sixty or seventy years, and were still apparently as fresh as that of the mutton-chop which he had just devoured for his breakfast,' and the grand view of the stout Collector, in his aged heroism, with the honors of Chippewa and Fort Erie on his brow, are all encircled with that visionary atmosphere which proves the humorist to be a poet, and indicates that his pictures are drawn from the images which observation has left on his imagination. The whole introduction, indeed, is worthy of a place among the essays of Addison and Charles Lamb.

With regard to 'The Scarlet Letter,' the readers of Hawthorne might have expected an exquisitely written story, expansive in sentiment, and suggestive in characterization, but they will hardly be prepared for a novel of so much tragic interest and tragic power, so deep in thought and so condensed in style, as is here presented to them. It evinces equal genius in the region of great passions and elusive emotions, and bears on every page the evidence of a mind thoroughly alive, watching patiently the movements of morbid hearts when stirred by strange experiences, and piercing, by its imaginative power, directly through all the externals to the core of things. The fault of the book, if fault it have, is the almost morbid intensity with which the characters are realized, and the consequent lack of sufficient geniality in the delineation. A portion of the pain of the author's own heart is communicated to the reader, and although there is great pleasure received while reading the volume, the general impression left by it is not satisfying to the artistic sense. Beauty bends to power throughout the work, and therefore the power displayed is not always beautiful. There is a strange fascination to a man of contemplative genius in the psychological details of a strange crime like that which forms the plot of The Scarlet Letter, and he is therefore apt to become, like Hawthorne, too painfully anatomical in his exhibition of them.

If there be, however, a comparative lack of relief to the painful emotions which the novel excites, owing to the intensity with which the author concentrates attention on the working of dark passions, it must be confessed that the moral purpose of the book is made more definite by this very deficiency. The most abandoned libertine could not read the volume without being thrilled into something like virtuous resolution, and the roué would find that the deep-seeing eye of the novelist had mastered the whole philosophy of that guilt of which practical roués are but childish disciples. To another class of readers, those who have theories of seduction and adultery modeled after the

French school of novelists, and whom libertinism is of the brain, the volume may afford matter for very instructive and edifying contemplation; for, in truth, Hawthorne, in The Scarlet Letter, has utterly undermined the whole philosophy on which the French novels rest, by seeing farther and deeper into the essence both of conventional and moral laws; and he has given the results of his insight, not in disquisitions and criticisms, but in representations more powerful even than those of Sue, Dumas, or George Sand. He has made his guilty parties end, not as his own fancy of his own benevolent sympathies might dictate, but as the spiritual laws, lying back of all persons, dictated to him. In this respect there is hardly a novel in English literature more purely objective.

As everybody will read The Scarlet Letter, it would be impertinent to give a synopsis of the plot. The principal characters, Dimmesdale, Chillingworth, Hester, and little Pearl, all indicate a firm grasp of individualities, although from the peculiar method of the story, they are developed more in the way of logical analysis than by events. The descriptive portions of the novel are in a high degree picturesque and vivid, bringing the scenes directly home to the heart and imagination, and indicating a clear vision of the life as well as forms of nature. Little Pearl is perhaps Hawthorne's finest poetical creation, and is the very perfection of ideal impishness.

In common, we trust, with the rest of mankind, we regretted Hawthorne's dismissal from the Custom House, but if that event compels him to exert his genius in the production of such books as the present, we shall be inclined to class the Honorable Secretary of the Treasury among the great philanthropists. In his next work we hope to have a romance equal to The Scarlet Letter in pathos and power, but more relieved by touches of that beautiful and peculiar humor, so serene and so searching, in which he excels almost all living writers.

47. [Henry F. Chorley], a review in the *Athenaeum*

15 June 1850, p. 634

This is a most powerful but painful story. Mr. Hawthorne must be well known to our readers as a favourite with the *Athenæum*. We rate him as among the most original and peculiar writers of American fiction. There is in his works a mixture of Puritan reserve and wild imagination, of passion and description, of the allegorical and the real, which some will fail to understand, and which others will positively reject,—but which, to ourselves, is fascinating, and which entitles him to be placed on a level with Brockden Brown and the author of 'Rip Van Winkle.' 'The Scarlet Letter' will increase his reputation with all who do not shrink from the invention of the tale; but this, as we have said, is more than ordinarily painful. When we have announced that the three characters are a guilty wife, openly punished for her guilt,—her tempter, whom she refuses to unmask, and who during the entire story carries a fair front and an unblemished name among his congregation,—and her husband, who, returning from a long absence at the moment of her sentence, sits himself down betwixt the two in the midst of a small and severe community to work out his slow vengeance on both under the pretext of magnanimous forgiveness,—when we have explained that 'The Scarlet Letter' is the badge of Hester Prynne's shame, we ought to add that we recollect no tale dealing with crime so sad and revenge so subtly diabolical, that is at the same time so clear of fever and of prurient excitement. The misery of the woman is as present in every page as the heading which in the title of the romance symbolizes her punishment. Her terrors concerning her strange elvish child present retribution in a form which is new and natural:—her slow and painful purification through repentance is crowned by no perfect happiness, such as awaits the decline of those who have no dark and bitter past to remember. Then, the gradual corrosion of heart of Dimmesdale, the faithless priest, under the insidious care of the husband, (whose relationship to Hester is a secret known only to themselves,) is appalling; and his final confession and expiation are merely a relief, not a reconciliation.—We are by no means satisfied that passions and tragedies like these are the legitimate subjects

163

for fiction: we are satisfied that novels such as 'Adam Blair' and plays such as 'The Stranger' may be justly charged with attracting more persons than they warn by their excitement. But if Sin and Sorrow in their most fearful forms are to be presented in any work of art, they have rarely been treated with a loftier severity, purity, and sympathy than in Mr. Hawthorne's 'Scarlet Letter.' The touch of the fantastic befitting a period of society in which ignorant and excitable human creatures conceived each other and themselves to be under the direct 'rule and governance' of the Wicked One, is most skilfully administered. The supernatural here never becomes grossly palpable:—the thrill is all the deeper for its action being indefinite, and its source vague and distant.

48. [Anne W. Abbott], from a review in the *North American Review*

July 1850, lxxi, 135–48

Miss Abbott, one of that 'damned mob of scribbling women' as Hawthorne called them, wrote various reviews for the *North American* and edited the *Child's Friend*, a literary journal for young people.

. . . we confess that, to our individual taste, this naughty chapter [the 'Custom-House'] is more piquant than any thing in the book; the style is racy and pungent, not elaborately witty, but stimulating the reader's attention agreeably by original turns of expression, and unhackneyed combinations of words, falling naturally into their places, as if of their own accord, and not obtained by far seeking and impressment into the service. The sketch of General Miller is airily and lightly done. . . . The delineations of wharf scenery, and of the Custom House, with their appropriate figures and personages, are worthy of the pen of Dickens; and really, so far as mere style is concerned, Mr. Hawthorne has no reason to thank us for the compliment; he has the finer touch, if not more genial feeling, of the two. Indeed, if we except a few expressions which savor somewhat strongly of his late unpoetical associations, and the favorite metaphor of the guillotine, which, however apt, is not particularly agreeable to the imagination in such detail, we like the preface better than the tale.

No one who has taken up the Scarlet Letter will willingly lay it down till he has finished it; and he will do well not to pause, for he cannot resume the story where he left it. He should give himself up to the magic power of the style, without stopping to open wide the eyes of his good sense and judgment, and shake off the spell; or half the weird beauty will disappear like a 'dissolving view'. . . . That the author himself felt this sort of intoxication as well as the willing subjects of his enchantment, we think, is evident in many pages of the last half of the volume. His imagination has sometimes taken him fairly off his feet, insomuch that he seems almost to doubt if there be any firm ground at all,—if we may so judge from such mistborn ideas as the following:

But, to all these shadowy beings, so long our near acquaintances,—as well Roger Chillingworth as his companions,—we would fain be merciful. It is a curious subject of observation and inquiry, whether hatred and love be not the same thing at bottom. Each, in its utmost development, supposes a high degree of intimacy and heart-knowledge; each renders one individual dependent for the food of his affections and spiritual life upon another; each leaves the passionate lover, or the no less passionate hater, forlorn and desolate by the withdrawal of his object. Philosophically considered, therefore, the two passions seem essentially the same, except the one happens to be seen in a celestial radiance, and the other in a dusky and lurid glow. In the spiritual world, the old physician and the minister—mutual victims as they have been—may, unawares, have found their earthly stock of hatred and antipathy transmuted into golden love.

Thus devils and angels are alike beautiful, when seen through the magic glass; and they stand side by side in heaven, however the former may be supposed to have come here. As for Roger Chillingworth, he seems to have so little in common with man, he is such a gnome-like phantasm, such an unnatural personification of an abstract idea, that we should be puzzled to assign him a place among angels, men, or devils. . . . Hester at first strongly excites our pity, for she suffers like an immortal being; and our interest in her continues only while we have hope for her soul, that its baptism of tears will reclaim it from the foul stain which has been cast upon it. We see her humble, meek, self-denying, charitable, and heartwrung with anxiety for the moral welfare of her wayward child. But anon her humility catches a new tint, and we find it pride; and so a vague unreality steals by degrees over all her most humanizing traits—we lose our confidence in all—and finally, like Undine, she disappoints us, and shows the dream-land origin and nature, when we were looking to behold a Christian.

There is rather more power, and better keeping, in the character of Dimmesdale. But here again we are cheated into a false regard and interest, partly perhaps by the associations thrown around him without the intention of the author, and possibly contrary to it, by our habitual respect for the sacred order, and by our faith in religion, where it has once been rooted in the heart. We are told repeatedly, that the Christian element yet pervades his character and guides his efforts; but it seems strangely wanting. 'High aspirations for the welfare of his race, warm love of souls, pure sentiments, natural piety, strengthened by thought and study, and illuminated by revelation—all of which invaluable gold was little better than rubbish' to Roger Chillingworth, are little better than rubbish at all, for any use to be made of them in the story. Mere suffering, aimless and without effect for purification or blessing to the soul, we do not find in God's moral world. The sting that follows crime is most severe in the purest conscience and the tenderest heart, in mercy, not in vengeance, surely; and we can conceive of any cause constantly exerting itself without its appropriate effects, as soon as of a seven years' agony without penitence. But here every pang is wasted. A most obstinate and unhuman passion, or a most unwearying conscience it must be, neither being worn out, or made worse or better, but such a prolonged application of the scourge. Penitence may indeed be life-long; but as for this, we are to understand that there is no penitence about it. . . .

But Little Pearl—gem of the purest water—what shall we say of her? That if perfect truth to childish and human nature can make her a mortal, she is so; and immortal, if the highest creations of genius have any claim to immortality. Let the author throw what light he will upon her, from his magical prism, she retains her perfect and vivid human individuality. When he would have us call her elvish and imp-like, we persist in seeing only a capricious, roguish, untamed child, such as many a mother has looked upon with awe, and a feeling of helpless incapacity to rule. Every motion, every feature, every word and tiny shout, every naughty scream and wild laugh, come to us as if our very senses were conscious of them. The child is a true child, the only genuine and consistent mortal in the book; and wherever she crosses the dark and gloomy track of the story, she refreshes our spirit with pure truth and radiant beauty, and brings to grateful remembrance the like ministry of gladsome childhood, in some of the saddest scenes of actual life. We feel at once that the author must have a 'Little Pearl' of his own, whose portrait, consciously or unconsciously, his pen sketches out. Not that we would deny to Mr. Hawthorne the power to call up any shape, angel or goblin, and present it before his readers in a striking and vivid light. But there is something more than imagination in the picture of 'Little Pearl.' . . .

We know of no writer who better understands and combines the elements of the picturesque in writing than Mr. Hawthorne. His style may be compared to a sheet of transparent water, reflecting from its surface blue skies, nodding woods, and the smallest spray or flower that peeps over its grassy margin; while in its clear yet mysterious depths we espy rarer and stranger things, which we must dive for, if we would examine. . . . One cannot but wonder, by the way, that the master of such a wizard power over language as Mr. Hawthorne manifests should not choose a less revolting subject than this of the Scarlet Letter, to which fine writing seems as inappropriate as fine embroidery. The ugliness of pollution and vice is no more relieved by it than the gloom of the prison is by the rose tree at its door. There are some palliative expressions used, which cannot, even as a matter of taste, be approved. . . .

We hope to be forgiven, if in any instance our strictures have approached the limits of what may be considered personal. We would not willingly trench upon the right which an individual may claim, in common courtesy, not to have his private qualities or personal features discussed to his face, with everybody looking on. But Mr. Hawthorne's example in the preface, and the condescending familiarity of the attitude he assumes therein, are at once our occasion and our apology.

49. [George Bailey Loring], from a review in the *Massachusetts Quarterly Review*

September 1850, iii, 484–500

Loring (1817–1891) was a physician and political leader whose essays normally dealt with politics and agriculture. Something of a popular orator, his views reflected a religious conservatism tempered by a scientific pragmatism.

No author of our own country, and scarcely any author of our times, manages to keep himself clothed in such a cloak of mystery as Nathaniel Hawthorne. From the time when his 'Twice-Told Tales' went, in their first telling, floating through the periodicals of the day, up to the appearance of 'The Scarlet Letter,' he has stood on the confines of society, as we see some sombre figure, in the dim light of the stage scenery, peering through that narrow space, when a slouched hat and a muffling cloak do not meet, upon the tragic events which are made conspicuous by the glare of the footlights. From nowhere in particular, from an old manse, and from the drowsy dilapidation of an old custom-house, he has spoken such oracular words, such searching thoughts, as sounded of old from the mystic God whose face was never seen even by the most worthy. It seems useless now to speak of his humor, subtle and delicate as Charles Lamb's; of his pathos, deep as Richter's; of his penetration into the human heart, clearer than that of Goldsmith or Crabbe; of his apt and telling words, which Pope might have envied; of his description, graphic as Scott's or Dickens's; of the delicious lanes he opens, on either hand, and leaves you alone to explore, masking his work with the fine *'faciebat'* which removes all limit from all high art, and gives every man scope to advance and develop. He seems never to trouble himself, either in writing or living, with the surroundings of life. He is no philosopher for the poor or the rich, for the ignorant or the learned, for the righteous or the wicked, for any special rank or condition in life, but for human nature as given by God into the hands of man. He calls us to be indignant witnesses of no particular social, religious, or political enormity. He asks no admiration for this or that individual or associated virtue. The face of society, with its manifold features, never comes before you, as you study the extraordinary experience of his men and women, except as a necessary setting for the picture. They might shine at tournaments, or grovel in cellars, or love, or fight, or meet with high adventure, or live the deepest and quietest life in unknown corners of the earth,—their actual all vanishes before the strange and shifting picture he gives of the motive heart of man. In no work of his is this characteristic more strikingly visible than in 'The Scarlet Letter;' and in no work has he presented so clear and perfect an image of himself, as a speculative philosopher, an ethical thinker, a living man. Perhaps he verges strongly upon the supernatural, in the minds of those who would recognize nothing but the corporeal existence of human life. But man's nature is, by birth, *super*natural; and the deep mystery which lies beneath all his actions is far beyond the reach of any mystical vision that ever lent its airy shape to the creations of the most intense dreamer. . . . It is, as we had a right to expect, extraordinary, as a work of art, and as a vehicle of religion and ethics.

Surrounded by the stiff, formal dignitaries of our early New England Colony, and subjected to their severe laws, and severer social atmosphere, we have a picture of crime and passion. It would be hard to conceive of a greater outrage upon the freezing and self-denying doctrines of that day, than the sin for which Hester Prynne was damned by society, and for which Arthur Dimmesdale damned himself. For centuries, the devoted and superstitious Catholic had made it a part of his creed to cast disgrace upon the passions; and the cold and rigid Puritan, with less fervor, and consequently with less beauty, had driven them out of his paradise, as the parents of all sin. There was no recognition of the intention or meaning of that sensuous element of human nature which, gilding life like a burnishing sunset, lays the foundation of all that beauty which seeks its expression in poetry, and music, and art, and gives the highest apprehension of religious fervor. Zest of life was no part of the Puritan's belief. . . . The state of society which this grizzly form of humanity created, probably served as little to purify men as any court of voluptuousness; and, while we recognize with compressed lip that heroism which braved seas and unknown shores, for opinion's sake, we remember, with a warm glow, the elegances and intrepid courage and tropical luxuriance of the cavaliers whom they left behind them. Asceticism and voluptuarism on either hand, neither fruitful of the finer and truer virtues, were all that men had arrived at in the great work of sensuous life.

It was the former which fixed the scarlet letter to the breast of Hester Prynne, and which drove Arthur Dimmesdale into a life of cowardly and selfish meanness, that added tenfold disgrace and ignominy to his original crime. In any form of society hitherto known, the sanctity of the devoted relation between the sexes has constituted the most certain foundation of all purity and all social safety. Imperfect as this great law has been in most of its development, founded upon and founding the rights of property, instead of positively recognizing the delicacy of abstract vitue, and having become, of necessity, in the present organization, a bulwark of hereditary rights, and a bond for a deed of conveyance, it nevertheless appeals to the highest sense of virtue and honor which a man finds in his breast. In an age in which there is a tendency to liberalize these, as well as all obligations, in order to secure those which are more sacred and binding than any which have been born of the statute-book, we can hardly conceive of the consternation and disgust which overwhelmed our forefathers when the majesty of virtue, and the still mightier majesty of the law, were insulted. It was as heir of these virtues, and impressed with this education, that Arthur Dimmesdale, a clergyman, believing in and applying all the moral remedies of the times, found himself a criminal. . . . In this way, he presented the twofold nature which belongs to us as members of society; —a nature born from ourselves and our associations, and comprehending all the diversity and all the harmony of our individual and social duties. Violation of either destroys our fitness for both. And when we remember that, in this development, no truth comes except from harmony, no beauty except from a fit conjunction of the individual with society, and of society with the individual, can we wonder that the great elements of Arthur Dimmesdale's character should have been overbalanced by a detestable crowd of mean and grovelling qualities, warmed into life by the hot antagonism he felt radiating upon himself and all his fellow-men—from the society in which he moved, and from which he received his engrafted moral nature? He sinned in the arms of society, and fell almost beyond redemption; his companion in guilt became an outcast, and a flood of heroic qualities gathered around her. Was this the work of social influences?

In this matter of crime, as soon as he became involved, he appeared before himself no longer a clergyman, but a man—a human being. He answered society in the cowardly way we have seen. He answered himself in that way which every soul adopts, where crime does not penetrate. The physical facts of crime alone, with which society has to do, in reality constitute sin. Crimes are committed under protest of the soul, more or less decided, as the weary soul itself has been more or less besieged and broken. The war in the individual begins, and the result of the fierce struggle is the victory of the sensual over the spiritual, when the criminal act is committed. If there is no such war, there is no crime; let the deed be what it may, and be denominated what it may, by society. The soul never assents to sin, and weeps with the angels when the form in which it dwells violates the sacred obligations it imposes upon it. When this human form, with its passions and tendencies, commits the violation, and, at the same time, abuses society, it is answerable to this latter tribunal, where it receives its judgment; while the soul flees to her God, dismayed and crushed by the conflict, but not deprived of her divine inheritance. Between the individual and his God, there remains a spot, larger or smaller, as the soul has been kept unclouded, where no sin can enter, where no mediation can come, where all the discords of his life are resolved into the most delicious harmonies, and his whole existence becomes illuminated by a divine intelligence. Sorrow and sin reveal this spot to all men—as, through death, we are born to an immortal life. They reveal what beliefs and dogmas becloud and darken. They produce that intense consciousness, without which virtue can not rise above innocency. They are the toil and trial which give strength and wisdom, and which, like all other toil, produce weariness and fainting and death, if pursued beyond the limit where reaction and the invigorating process begin. We can not think with too much awe upon the temptations and trials which beset the powerful. The solemn gloom which shuts down over a mighty nature, during the struggle, which it recognizes with vivid sense, between its demon and its divinity, is like that fearful night in which no star appears to relieve the murky darkness. And yet, from such a night as this, and from no other, the grandeur of virtue has risen to beautify and warm and bless the broad universe of human hearts, and to make the whole spiritual creation blossom like the rose. The Temptation and Gethsemane,—these are the miracles which have redeemed mankind.

Thus it stands with the individual and his soul. With himself and society come up other obligations, other influences, other laws. The tribunal before which he stands as a social being cannot be disregarded with impunity. The effects of education and of inheritance cling around us with the tenacity of living fibres of our own bodies, and they govern, with closest intimacy, the estimate of deeds which constitute the catalogue of vice and virtue, and which in their commission elevate or depress our spiritual condition.

We doubt if there is a stronger element in our natures than that which forbids our resisting with impunity surrounding social institutions. However much we may gain in the attempt, it is always attended with some loss. The reverence which enhanced so beautifully the purity and innocence of childhood, often receives its death-blow from that very wisdom out of which comes our mature virtue. Those abstractions whose foundation is the universe, and without an apprehension of which we may go handcuffed and fettered through life, may draw us away from the devotion which deepened and gilded the narrow world in which we were strong by belief alone. The institutions in which we were born controlled in a great degree the mental condition of our parents, as surrounding nature did their physical, and we owe to these two classes of internal and external operations the characters we inherit. An attack, therefore, upon these institutions, affects us to a certain degree as if we were warring against ourselves. Reason and conscience, and our sublimest sense of duty, may call us to the work of reform,—instinct resists. . . . Arthur Dimmesdale, shrinking from intimate contact and intercourse with his child, shrunk from a visible and tangible representation of the actual life which his guilty love had created for himself and Hester Prynne;—love, guilty, because, secured as it may have been to them, it drove them violently from the moral centre around which they revolved.

We have seen that this was most especially the case with the man who was bound and labelled the puritan clergyman; that he had raised a storm in his own heavens which he could not quell, and had cast the whirlwind over the life of his own child. How was it with Hester Prynne?

On this beautiful and luxuriant woman, we see the effect of open conviction of sin, and the continued galling punishment. The heroic traits awakened in her character by her position were the great self-sustaining properties of woman, which, in tribulation and perplexity, elevate her so far above man. The sullen defiance in her, was imparted to her by society. Without, she met only ignominy, scorn, banishment, a shameful brand. Within, the deep and sacred love for which she was suffering martyrdom,—for her crime was thus sanctified in her own apprehension, —was turned into a store of perplexity, distrust, and madness, which darkened all her heavens. Little Pearl was a token more scarlet than the scarlet letter of her guilt; for the child, with a birth presided over by the most intense conflict of love and fear in the mother's heart, nourished at a breast swelling with anguish, and surrounded with burning marks of its mother's shame in its daily life, developed day by day into a void little demon perched upon the most sacred horn of the mother's altar. Even this child, whose young, plastic nature caught the impress which surrounding circumstances most naturally gave, bewildered and maddened her. The pledge of love which God had given her, seemed perverted into an emblem of hate. And yet how patiently and courageously she labored on, bearing her burthen the more firmly, because, in its infliction, she recognized no higher hand than that of civil authority! . . .

Her social ignominy forced her back upon the true basis of her life. She alone, of all the world, knew the length and breadth of her own secret. Her lawful husband no more pretended to hold a claim, which may always have been a pretence; the father of her child, her own relation to both, and the tragic life which was going on beneath that surface which all men saw, were known to her alone. How poor and miserable must have seemed the punishment which society had inflicted! The scarlet letter was a poor type of the awful truth which she carried within her heart. Without deceit before the world, she stand forth the most heroic person in all that drama. When, from the platform of shame she bade farewell to that world, she retired to a holier, and sought for such peace as a soul cast out by men may always find. This was her right. No lie hung over her head. Society had heard her story, and had done its worst. And while Arthur Dimmesdale, cherished in the arms of that society which he had outraged, glossing his life with a false coloring which made it beautiful to all beholders, was dying of an inward anguish, Hester stood upon her true ground, denied by this world, and learning that true wisdom which comes through honesty and self-justification. In casting her out, the world had torn from her all the support of its dogmatic teachings, with which it sustains its disciples in their inevitable sufferings, and had compelled her to rely upon that great religious truth which flows instinctively around a life of agony, with its daring freedom. How far behind her in moral and religious excellence was the accredited religious teacher, who was her companion in guilt! Each day which bound her closer and closer to that heaven which was now her only home, drove him farther and farther from the spiritual world, whose glories he so fervently taught others.

It is no pleasant matter to contemplate what is called the guilt of this woman; but it may be instructive, nevertheless. We naturally shrink from any apparent violation of virtue and chastity, and are very ready to forget, in our eager condemnation, how much that is beautiful and holy may be involved in it. We forget that what society calls chastity is often far the reverse, and that a violation of this perverted virtue may be a sad, sorrowful, and tearful beauty, which we would silently and reverently contemplate,—silently, lest a harsh word of the law wound our hearts,—reverently, as we would listen to the fervent prayer. While we dread that moral hardness which would allow a human being to be wrecked in a storm of passion, let us not be unmindful of the holy love which may *long and pray for its development.* Man's heart recognizes this, whether society will or not. The struggle and the sacrifice which the latter calls a crime, the former receives as an exhilarating air of virtue. . . .

Is there no violation of social law more radical and threatening than any wayward act of passion can be? It may be necessary, perhaps, that the safety of associated man demands all the compromises which the superficiality of social law creates, but the sorrow may be none the less acute because the evil is necessary. We see in the lives of Arthur Dimmesdale and Hester Prynne, that the severity of puritanic law and morals could not keep them from violation; and we see, too, that this very severity drove them both into a state of moral insanity. And does any benefit arise from such a sacrifice? Not a gentle word, or look, or thought, met those two erring mortals. Revenge embittered the heart of the old outraged usurper. Severity—blasting, and unforgiving, and sanctimonious—was the social atmosphere which surrounded them. We doubt not that, to many minds, this severity constitutes the saving virtue of the book. But it is always with a fearful sacrifice of all the gentler feelings of the breast, of all the most comprehensive humanity, of all the most delicate affections and appreciations, that we thus rudely shut out the wanderer from us; especially when the path of error leads through the land whence come our warmest and tenderest influences. We gain nothing by this hardness, except a capability to sin without remorse. . . .

The father, the mother, and the child, in this picture,—the holy trinity of love,—what had the world done for them? And so they waited for the divine developments of an hereafter. Can this be a true and earnest assurance that we may hope for the best development there? This imaginary tale of wrong, is but a shadow of the realities which daily occur around us. . . . But is it not most sad and most instructive that Love, the great parent of all power and virtue and wisdom and faith, the guardian of the tree of knowledge of good and evil, the effulgence of all that is rich and generous and luxuriant in nature, should rise up in society to be typified by the strange features of 'The Scarlet Letter?'

50. [Orestes Brownson], from a review in *Brownson's Quarterly Review*

October 1850, n.s., v, 528–32

Mr. Hawthorne is a writer endowed with a large share of genius, and in the species of literature he cultivates has no rival in this country, unless it be Washington Irving. His *Twice-told Tales,* his *Mosses from an Old Manse,* and other contributions to the periodical press, have made him familiarly known, and endeared him to a large circle of readers. The work before us is the largest and most elaborate of the romances he has as yet published, and no one can read half a dozen pages of it without feeling that none but a man of true genius and a highly cultivated mind could have written it. It is a work of rare, we may say of fearful power, and to the great body of our countrymen who have no well defined religious belief, and no fixed principles of virtue, it will be deeply interesting and highly pleasing.

We have neither the space nor the inclination to attempt an analysis of Mr. Hawthorne's genius, after the manner of the fashionable criticism of the day. Mere literature for its own sake we do not prize, and we are more disposed to analyze an author's work than the author himself. Men are not for us mere psychological phenomena, to be studied, classed, and labelled. They are moral and accountable beings, and we look only to the moral and religious effect of their works. Genius perverted, or employed in perverting others, has no charms for us, and we turn away from it with sorrow and disgust. We are not among those who join in the worship of passion, or even of intellect. God gave us our faculties to be employed in his service and in that of our fellow-creatures for his sake, and our only legitimate office as critics is to inquire, when a book is sent us for review, if its author in producing it has so employed them.

Mr. Hawthorne, according to the popular standard of morals in this age and this community, can hardly be said to pervert God's gifts, or to exert an immoral influence. Yet his work is far from being unobjectionable. The story is told with great naturalness, ease, grace, and delicacy, but it is a story that should not have been told. It is a story of crime, of an adulteress and her accomplice, a meek and gifted and highly popular Puritan minister in our early colonial days,—a purely imaginary story, though not altogether improbable. Crimes like the one imagined were not unknown even in the golden days of Puritanism, and are perhaps more common among the descendants of the Puritans than it is at all pleasant to believe; but they are not fit subjects for popular literature, and moral health is not promoted by leading the imagination to dwell on them. There is an unsound state of public morals when the novelist is permitted, without a scorching rebuke, to select such crimes, and invest them with all the fascinations of genius, and all the charms of a highly polished style. In a moral community such crimes are spoken of as rarely as possible, and when spoken of at all, it is always in terms which render them loathsome, and repel the imagination.

Nor is the conduct of the story better than the story itself. The author makes the guilty parties suffer, and suffer intensely, but he nowhere manages so as to make their sufferings excite the horror of his readers for their crime. The adulteress suffers not from remorse, but from regret, and, from the disgrace to which her crime has exposed her, in her being condemned to wear emblazoned on her dress the Scarlet Letter which proclaims to all the deed she has committed. The minister, her accomplice, suffers also, horribly, and feels all his life after the same terrible letter branded on his heart, but not from the fact of the crime itself, but from the consciousness of not being what he seems to the world, from his having permitted the partner in his guilt to the disgraced, to be punished, without his having the manliness to avow his share in the guilt, and to bear his share of the punishment. Neither ever really repents of the criminal deed; nay, neither ever regards it as really criminal, and both seem to hold it to have been laudable, because they *loved* one another,—as if the love itself were not illicit, and highly criminal. No man has the right to love another man's wife, and no married woman has the right to love any man but her husband. Mr. Hawthorne, in the present case seeks to excuse Hester Prynne, a married woman, for loving the Puritan minister, on the ground that she had no love for her husband, and it is hard that a woman should not have some one to love; but this only aggravated her guilt, because she was not only forbidden to love the minister, but commanded to love her husband, whom she had vowed to love, honor, cherish, and obey. The modern doctrine that represents the affections as fatal, and wholly withdrawn from voluntary control, and then allows us to plead tham in justification of neglect of duty and breach of the most positive precepts of both the natural and the revealed law, cannot be too severely reprobated.

Human nature is frail, and it is necessary for every one who standeth to take heed lest he fall. Compassion for the fallen is a duty which we all owe, in consideration of our own failings, and especially in consideration of the infinite mercy our God has manifested to her erring and sinful children. But however binding may be this duty, we are never to forget that sin is sin, and that it is pardonable only through the great mercy of God, on condition of the sincere repentance of the sinner. But in the present case neither of the guilty parties repents of the sin. . . . They hug their illicit love; they cherish their sin; and after the lapse of seven years are ready, and actually agree, to depart into a foreign country, where they may indulge it without disguise and without restraint. Even to the last, even when the minister, driven by his agony, goes so far as to throw off the mask of hypocrisy, and openly confess his crime, he shows no sign of repentance, or that he regarded his deed as criminal.

The Christian who reads *The Scarlet Letter* cannot fail to perceive that the author is wholly ignorant of Christian asceticism, and that the highest principle of action he recognizes is pride. In both the criminals, the long and intense agony they are represented as suffering springs not from remorse, from the consciousness of having offended God, but mainly from the feeling, especially on the part of the minister, that they have failed to maintain the integrity of their character. They have lowered themselves in their own estimation, and cannot longer hold up their heads in society as honest people. It is not their conscience that is wounded, but their pride. *He* cannot bear to think that he wears a disguise, that he cannot be the open, frank, stainless character he had from his youth aspired to be, and *she*, that she is driven from society, lives a solitary outcast, and has nothing to console her but her fidelity to her paramour. There is nothing Christian, nothing really moral, here. The very pride itself is a sin; and pride often a greater sin than that which it restrains us from committing. There are thousands of men and women too proud to commit carnal sins, and to the indomitable price of our Puritan ancestors we may attribute no small share of their external morality and decorum. It may almost be said, that, if they had less of that external morality and decorum, their case would be less desperate; and often the violation of them, or failure to maintain them, by which their pride receives a shock, and their self-complacency is shaken, becomes the occasion, under the grace of God, of their conversion to truth and holiness. As long as they maintain their self-complacency, are satisfied with themselves, and feel that they have outraged none of the decencies of life, no argument can reach them, no admonition can startle them, no exhortation can move them. Proud of their supposed virtue, free from all self-reproach, they are as placid as a summer morning, pass through life without a cloud to mar their serenity, and die as gently and as sweetly as the infant falling asleep in its mother's arms. We have met with these people, and after laboring in vain to waken them to a sense of their actual condition, till completely discouraged, we have been tempted to say, Would that you might commit some overt act, that should startle you from your sleep, and make you feel how far pride is from being either a virtue, or the safeguard of virtue, —or convince you of your own insufficiency for yourselves, and your absolute need of Divine grace. Mr. Hawthorne seems never to have learned that pride is not only sin, but the root of all sin, and that humility is not only a virtue, but the root of all virtue. No genuine contrition or repentance ever springs from pride, and the sorrow for sin because it mortifies our pride, or lessens us in our own eyes, is nothing but the effect of pride. All true remorse, all genuine repentance, springs from humility, and is sorrow for having offended God, not sorrow for having offended ourselves.

Mr. Hawthorne also mistakes entirely the effect of Christian pardon upon the interior state of the sinner. He seems entirely ignorant of the religion that can restore peace to the sinner,—true, inward peace, we mean. He would persuade us, that Hester had found pardon, and yet he shows us that she had found no inward peace. Something like this is common among popular Protestant writers, who, in speaking of great sinners among Catholics that have made themselves monks or hermits to expiate their sins by devoting themselves to prayer, and mortification, and the duties of religion, represent them as always devoured by remorse, and suffering in their interior agony almost the pains of the damned. . . .

Again, Mr. Hawthorne mistakes the character of confession. He does well to recognize and insist on its necessity; but he is wrong in supposing that its office is simply to disburden the mind by communicating its secrets to another, to restore the sinner to his self-complacency, and to relieve him from the charge of cowardice and hypocrisy. Confession is a duty we owe to God, and a means, not of restoring us to our self-complacency, but of restoring us to the favor of God, and reëstablishing us in his friendship. The work before us is full of mistakes of this sort, in those portions where the author really means to speak like a Christian, and therefore we are obliged to condemn it, where we acquit him of all unchristian intention.

As a picture of the old Puritans, taken from the position of a moderate transcendentalist and liberal of the modern school, the work has its merits; but as little as we sympathize with those stern old Popery-haters, we do not regard the picture as at all just. We should commend where the author condemns, and condemn where he commends. Their treatment of the adulteress was far more Christian than his ridicule of it. But enough of fault-finding, and as we have no praise, except what we have given, to offer, we here close this brief notice.

51. [Arthur Cleveland Coxe], from 'The Writings of Hawthorne', in the *Church Review*

January 1851, iii. 489–511

Coxe (1818–96) was an Episcopal bishop whose theological conservatism informed all that he wrote and stands in sharp contrast to that of Loring. His attack on *The Scarlet Letter* was partially reprinted in *Notorious Literary Attacks*, ed. Albert Mordell (1926).

Current Literature, in America, has generally been forced to depend, for criticism, upon personal partiality or personal spleen. We have had very little reviewing on principle; almost none with the pure motive of building up a sound and healthful literature for our country, by cultivating merit, correcting erratic genius, abasing assumption and imposture, and insisting on the fundamental importance of certain great elements, without which no literature can be either beneficial or enduring. Our reviews have, accordingly, exercised very little influence over public taste. They have been rather tolerated than approved; and, for the most part, have led a very precarious existence, rather as attempts than as achievements; creditable make-believes; tolerable domestic imitations of the imported article; well enough in their way, but untrustworthy for opinion, and worthless for taste. Their reviewals of cotemporary authors have too commonly been a mere daubing of untempered mortar, or else a deliberate assault, with intent to kill. In either case the reviewer has betrayed himself, as writing, not for the public, but for the satisfaction or the irritation of the author; and the game of mock reviewing has become as notorious as that of mock auctions. The intelligent public hears the hammering and the outcry, but has got used to it, and passes by. Nobody's opinion of a book is the more or less favorable for anything that can be said in this or that periodical. . . .

We make no apology, therefore, for becoming reviewers, when we acknowledge our earnest hope, not only that we may do something to assist the literary and theological studies of Anglo-American Churchmen, but that we may make the voice of the Church more audible to the American public in general, and thus may exercise, for the benefit of popular authors, some salutary influence upon public taste. Our mission —to borrow a little cant from the times—is, indeed, rather religious than literary; yet, in an age when literature makes very free with religion, we must be pardoned for supposing that religion owes some attention to literature. We grant that we have little taste for popular criticism, and if anybody chooses to assert that we are not qualified critics, we concede it entirely. . . . We know not the literary world, except from a distant view, and have nothing in common with its aims or its occupations; but we think it high time that the literary world should learn that Churchmen are, in a very large proportion, their readers and book-buyers, and that the tastes and principles of Churchmen have as good a right to be respected as those of Puritans and Socialists. It is in this relation to our subject that we have taken up the clever and popular writings of Hawthorne; and we propose to consider them, without any attempt to give them a formal review, just in the free and conversational manner which is permitted to table-talk or social intercourse. . . .

[Hawthorne] is a writer, who, under other influences, might have contributed to our literature a variety of sterling and valuable works, admitting of no dispute as to their merit, or who would have made even popular tales the vehicle of deep and earnest suggestion to the young, as well as of pure amusement to all classes. We would exhort him against becoming a trifler, as one who must give account for gifts that might be prolific of good to the world. If, even now, he would resolve to make his future career one of high moral principle, and to use his talents not so much for 'making himself a rank among the world's *dignitaries*,' as for doing good in his day and generation, we know of no one more likely to succeed in becoming one of the world's *benefactors*, and gaining quite enough of its empty admiration beside. Not that we would have him change his songs into sermons, or his tales and romances into moral essays. We are not of those who question the utility of fairy fiction as the costume of severe and homely truth. Parable and allegory have been the vehicle of wisdom, among all cultivated nations; yes, of inspired wisdom, too; of Nathan's rebuke, when he pointed the arrows of the Law at the sinner's conscience, and of the love of JESUS CHRIST, when he opened to the sick and needy the healing waters of the Gospel. The principle thus established leaves nothing for the casuist to prescribe, but that stories should be always of moral benefit to those whole faculties of soul, and mind, and heart, with which GOD claims to be loved and served. Here is the standard, therefore, by which we are to estimate the tale-writer. In the one case, he may be justly regarded as a preceptor who has mastered the difficult art of imparting instruction, with impressions of pastime, and who has managed to make even the recreations of the mind, subservient to its most laborious exercises: in the other he is, in short, a nuisance in society, which it becomes the duty of good citizens to abate. . . .

The success which seems to have attended this bold advance of Hawthorne, and the encouragement which has been dealt out by some professed critics,* to its worst symptoms of malice prepense, may very naturally lead, if unbalanced by a moderate dissent, to his further compromise of his literary character. We are glad, therefore, that 'The Scarlet Letter' is, after all, little more than an experiment, and need not be regarded as a step necessarily fatal. It is an attempt to rise from the composition of petty tales, to the historical novel; and we use the expression *an attempt*, with no disparaging significance, for it is confessedly a trial of strength only just beyond some former efforts, and was designed as part of a series. It may properly be called a novel, because it has all the ground-work, and might have been very easily elaborated

* See a late article in the Massachusetts Quarterly.

into the details, usually included in the term; and we call it *historical*, because its scene-painting is in a great degree true to a period of our Colonial history, which ought to be more fully delineated. We wish Mr. Hawthorne would devote the powers which he only partly discloses in this book, to a large and truthful portraiture of that period, with the patriotic purpose of making us better acquainted with the stern old worthies, and all the *dramatis personæ* of those times, with their yet surviving habits, recollections, and yearnings, derived from maternal England. Here is, in fact, a rich and even yet an unexplored field for historic imagination; and touches are given in 'The Scarlet Letter,' to secret springs of romantic thought, which opened unexpected and delightful episodes to our fancy, as we were borne along by the tale. . . .

There is a provoking concealment of the author's motive, from the beginning to the end of the story; we wonder what he would be at; whether he is making fun of all religion, or only giving a fair hint of the essential sensualism of enthusiasm. But, in short, we are astonished at the kind of incident which he has selected for romance. It may be such incidents were too common, to be wholly out of the question, in a history of the times, but it seems to us that good taste might be pardoned for not giving them prominence in fiction. . . .

And this brings inquiry to its point. Why has our author selected such a theme? Why, amid all the suggestive incidents of life in a wilderness; of a retreat from civilization to which, in every individual case, a thousand circumstances must have concurred to reconcile human nature with estrangement from home and country; or amid the historical connections of our history with Jesuit adventure, savage invasion, regicide outlawry, and French aggression, should the taste of Mr. Hawthorne have preferred as the proper material for romance, the nauseous amour of a Puritan pastor, with a frail creature of his charge, whose mind is represented as far more debauched than her body? Is it, in short, because a running undertide of filth has become as requisite to a romance, as death in the fifth act to a tragedy? Is the French era actually begun in our literature? And is the flesh, as well as the world and the devil, to be henceforth dished up in fashionable novels, and discussed at parties, by spinsters and their beaux, with as unconcealed a relish as they give to the vanilla in their ice cream? We would be slow to believe it, and we hope our author would not willingly have it so, yet we honestly believe that 'The Scarlet Letter' has already done not a little to degrade our literature, and to encourage social licentiousness:

it has started other pens on like enterprises, and has loosed the restraint of many tongues, that have made it an apology for 'the evil communications which corrupt good manners.' We are painfully tempted to believe that it is a book made for the market, and that the market has made it merchantable, as they do game, by letting everybody understand that the commodity is in high condition, and smells strongly of incipient putrefaction.

We shall entirely mislead our reader if we give him to suppose that 'The Scarlet Letter' is coarse in its details, or indecent in its phraseology. This very article of our own, is far less suited to ears polite, than any page of the romance before us; and the reason is, we call things by their right names, while the romance never hints the shocking words that belong to its things, but, like Mephistophiles, insinuates that the archfiend himself is a very tolerable sort of person, if nobody would call him Mr. Devil. . . . We are not sure we speak quite strong enough, when we say, that we would much rather listen to the coarsest scene of Goldsmith's 'Vicar,' read aloud by a sister or daughter, than to hear from such lips, the perfectly chaste language of a scene in 'The Scarlet Letter,' in which a married wife and her reverend paramour, with their unfortunate offspring, are introduced as the actors, and in which the whole tendency of the conversation is to suggest a sympathy for their sin, and an anxiety that they may be able to accomplish a successful escape beyond the seas, to some country where their shameful commerce may be perpetuated. Now, in Goldsmith's story there are very coarse words, but we do not remember anything that saps the foundations of the moral sense, or that goes to create unavoidable sympathy with unrepenting sorrow, and deliberate, premeditated sin. The 'Vicar of Wakefield' is sometimes coarsely virtuous, but 'The Scarlet Letter' is delicately immoral. . . .

In Hawthorne's tale, the lady's frailty is philosophized into a natural and necessary result of the Scriptural law of marriage, which, by holding her irrevocably to her vows, as plighted to a dried up old bookworm, in her silly girlhood, is viewed as making her heart an easy victim to the adulterer. The sin of her seducer too, seems to be considered as lying not so much in the deed itself, as in his long concealment of it, and, in fact, the whole moral of the tale is given in the words—'Be true—be true,' as if sincerity in sin were virtue, and as if 'Be clean—be clean,' were not the more fitting conclusion. 'The untrue man' is, in short, the hang-dog of the narrative, and the unclean one is made a very interesting sort of a person, and as the two qualities are united in the hero, their composition creates the interest of his character. . . .

We assure Mr. Hawthorne, in conclusion, that nothing less than an earnest wish that his future career may redeem this misstep, and prove a blessing to his country, has tempted us to enter upon a criticism so little suited to our tastes, as that of his late production.

TRUE STORIES FROM HISTORY AND BIOGRAPHY

1851

52. Notice in *Graham's Magazine*

February 1851, xxxviii, 134

This work consists of two parts—'Grandfather's Chair,' and 'Biographical Stories,' and the purpose of both is to enlighten and amuse young readers. 'Grandfather's Chair' is devoted to a delightful conversational narrative of the principal events in the history of New England, and the exquisite simplicity of the style is the beautiful medium of exciting incidents, characteristic portraiture, and just reflections. The 'Biographical Stories' are devoted to Benjamin West, Newton, Johnson, Cromwell, Franklin and Queen Christina; and in producing the highest effects of biography are much superior to many 'lives' of more pretension. The genius of Hawthorne is visible throughout the book, and its ductility is evinced in the ease with which it is accommodated to the comprehension of young readers. In a simple, cosy, conversational manner he conveys the result of much study, thought, and imaginative life in the past; historical characters are so represented that they have the reality of actual men and women; and the heroic and romantic in their natures are delineated so completely in the narrative of their actions, that the reader unconsciously builds up their characters in his own imagination, and finds at the end that he has living and distinct ideas of persons, who were before mere names and shadowy abstractions. Every boy and girl in the land should have a copy of this delightful book, and to children of a larger growth it will be found full of instruction and entertainment.

53. Notice in the *Southern Quarterly Review*

April 1851, n.s., iii, 571–2

A series for youth, by one of our most pleasant story-tellers and essayists. The historical sketches are mostly drawn from the chronicles of New-England; the biographical are drawn indiscriminately from Great Britain and America. The good taste, excellent sense and thoughtful morality of the writer are ample securities for the propriety of this volume in the hands of the young. It is adorned by several wood cuts, and 'got up' in pretty style.

THE HOUSE OF THE SEVEN GABLES

1851

---

54. Hawthorne, Preface

27 January 1851

When a writer calls his work a Romance, it need hardly be observed that he wishes to claim a certain latitude, both as to its fashion and material, which he would not have felt himself entitled to assume, had he professed to be writing a Novel. The latter form of composition is presumed to aim at a very minute fidelity, not merely to the possible, but to the probable and ordinary course of man's experience. The former—while, as a work of art, it must rigidly subject itself to laws, and while it sins unpardonably, so far as it may swerve aside from the truth of the human heart—has fairly a right to present that truth under circumstances, to a great extent, of the writer's own choosing or creation. If he think fit, also, he may so manage his atmospherical medium as to bring out or mellow the lights and deepen and enrich the shadows of the picture. He will be wise, no doubt, to make a very moderate use of the privileges here stated, and, especially, to mingle the Marvellous rather as a slight, delicate, and evanescent flavor, than as any portion of the actual substance of the dish offered to the Public. He can hardly be said, however, to commit a literary crime, even if he disregard this caution.

In the present work, the Author has proposed to himself (but with what success, fortunately, it is not for him to judge) to keep undeviatingly within his immunities. The point of view in which this Tale comes under the Romantic definition, lies in the attempt to connect a by-gone time with the very Present that is flitting away from us. It is a Legend, prolonging itself, from an epoch now gray in the distance, down into our own broad daylight, and bringing along with it some of its legendary mist, which the Reader, according to his pleasure, may either disregard, or allow it to float almost imperceptibly about the characters and events, for the sake of a picturesque effect. The narrative, it may be, is woven of so humble a texture as to require this advantage, and, at the same time, to render it the more difficult of attainment.

Many writers lay very great stress upon some definite moral purpose, at which they profess to aim their works. Not to be deficient, in this particular, the Author has provided himself with a moral;—the truth, namely, that the wrong-doing of one generation lives into the successive ones, and, divesting itself of every temporary advantage, becomes a pure and uncontrollable mischief;—and he would feel it a singular gratification, if this Romance might effectually convince mankind (or, indeed, any one man) of the folly of tumbling down an avalanche of ill-gotten gold, or real estate, on the heads of an unfortunate posterity, thereby to maim and crush them, until the accumulated mass shall be scattered abroad in its original atoms. In good faith, however, he is not sufficiently imaginative to flatter himself with the slightest hope of this kind. When romances do really teach anything, or produce any effective operation, it is usually through a far more subtile process than the ostensible one. The Author has considered it hardly worth his while, therefore, relentlessly to impale the story with its moral, as with an iron rod—or rather, as by sticking a pin through a butterfly—thus at once depriving it of life, and causing it to stiffen in an ungainly and unnatural attitude. A high truth, indeed, fairly, finely, and skilfully wrought out, brightening at every step, and crowning the final developement of a work of fiction, may add an artistic glory, but is never any truer, and seldom any more evident, at the last page than at the first.

The Reader may perhaps choose to assign an actual locality to the imaginary events of this narrative. If permitted by the historical connection, (which, though slight, was essential to his plan,) the Author would very willingly have avoided anything of this nature. Not to speak of other objections, it exposes the Romance to an inflexible and exceedingly dangerous species of criticism, by bringing his fancy-pictures almost into positive contact with the realities of the moment. It has been no part of his object, however, to describe local manners, nor in any way to meddle with the characteristics of a community for whom he cherishes a proper respect and a natural regard. He trusts not to be considered as unpardonably offending, by laying out a street that infringes upon nobody's private rights, and appropriating a lot of land which had no visible owner, and building a house, of materials long in use for constructing castles in the air. The personages of the Tale—

though they give themselves out to be of ancient stability and considerable prominence—are really of the Author's own making, or, at all events, of his own mixing; their virtues can shed no lustre, nor their defects redound, in the remotest degree, to the discredit of the venerable town of which they profess to be inhabitants. He would be glad, therefore, if—especially in the quarter to which he alludes—the book may be read strictly as a Romance, having a great deal more to do with the clouds overhead, than with any portion of the actual soil of the County of Essex.

55. Herman Melville, from a letter to Hawthorne, in *The Letters of Herman Melville* (ed. Merrell R. Davis and William H. Gilman [1960])

16(?) April(?) 1851, pp. 123-5

The contents of this book do not belie its rich, clustering, romantic title. With great enjoyment we spent almost an hour in each separate gable. This book is like a fine old chamber, abundantly, but still judiciously, furnished with precisely that sort of furniture best fitted to furnish it. There are rich hangings, wherein are braided scenes from tragedies! There is old china with rare devices, set out on the carved buffet; there are long and indolent lounges to throw yourself upon; there is an admirable sideboard, plentifully stored with good viands; there is a smell as of old wine in the pantry; and finally, in one corner, there is a dark little black-letter volume in golden clasps, entitled 'Hawthorne: A Problem.' It has delighted us; it has piqued a re-persual; it had robbed us of a day, and made us a present of a whole year of thoughtfulness; it has bred great exhilaration and exultation with the remembrance that the architect of the Gables resides only six miles off, and not three thousand miles away, in England, say. We think the book, for pleasantness of running interest, surpasses the other works of the author. The curtains are more drawn; the sun comes in more; genialities peep out more. Were we to particularize what most struck us in the deeper passages, we would point out the scene where Clifford, for a moment, would fain throw himself forth from the window to join the procession; or the scene where the judge is left seated in his ancestral chair. Clifford is full of an awful truth throughout. He is conceived in the finest, truest spirit. He is no caricature. He is Clifford. And here we would say that, did circumstances permit, we should like nothing better than to devote an elaborate and careful paper to the full consideration and analysis of the purport and significance of what so strongly characterizes all of this author's writings. There is a certain tragic phase of humanity which, in our opinion, was never more powerfully embodied than by Hawthorne. We mean the tragicalness of human thought in its own unbiassed, native, and profounder workings. We think that into no recorded mind has the intense feeling of the visable truth ever entered more deeply than into this man's. By visable truth, we mean the apprehension of the absolute condition of present things as they strike the eye of the man who fears them not, though they do their worst to him,—the man who, like Russia or the British Empire, declares himself a sovereign nature (in himself) amid the powers of heaven, hell, and earth. He may perish; but so long as he exists he insists upon treating with all Powers upon an equal basis. If any of those other Powers choose to withhold certain secrets, let them; that does not impair my sovereignty in myself; that does not make me tributary. And perhaps, after all, there is *no* secret. We incline to think that the Problem of the Universe is like the Freemason's mighty secret, so terrible to all children. It turns out, at last, to consist in a triangle, a mallet, and an apron,—nothing more! We incline to think that God cannot explain His own secrets, and that He would like a little information upon certain points Himself. We mortals astonish Him as much as He us. But it is this *Being* of the matter; there lies the knot with which we choke ourselves. As soon as you say *Me,* a *God,* a *Nature,* so soon you jump off from your stool and hang from the beam. Yes, that word is the hangman. Take God out of the dictionary, and you would have Him in the street.

There is the grand truth about Nathaniel Hawthorne. He says NO! in thunder; but the Devil himself cannot make him say *yes.* For all men who say *yes,* lie; and all men who say *no,*—why, they are in the happy condition of judicious, unincumbered travellers in Europe; they cross the frontiers into Eternity with nothing but a carpet-bag,—that is to say, the Ego. Whereas those *yes*-gentry, they travel with heaps of baggage, and, damn them! they will never get through the Custom House. What's the reason, Mr. Hawthorne, that in the last stages of metaphysics a fellow always falls to *swearing* so? I could rip an hour. You see, I began with a little criticism extracted for your benefit from the 'Pittsfield Secret Review,' and here I have landed in Africa. . . .

P.S. The marriage of Phoebe with the daguerreotypist is a fine stroke, because of his turning out to be a *Maule*. If you pass Hepzibah's cent-shop, buy me a Jim Crow (fresh) and send it to me by Ned Higgins.

56. James Russell Lowell, from a letter to Hawthorne, in *Hawthorne and His Wife*

24 April 1851 [1884], i, 390–2

I have been so delighted with 'The House of the Seven Gables' that I cannot help sitting down to tell you so. I thought I could not forgive you if you wrote anything better than 'The Scarlet Letter;' but I cannot help believing it a great triumph that you should have been able to deepen and widen the impression made by such a book as that. It seems to me that the 'House' is the most valuable contribution to New England history that has been made. It is with the highest art that you have typified (in the revived likeness of Judge Pyncheon to his ancestor the Colonel) that intimate relationship between the Present and the Past in the way of ancestry and descent, which historians so carefully overlook. Yesterday is commonly looked upon and written about as of no kin to To-day, though the one is legitimate child of the other, and has its veins filled with the same blood. And the chapter about Alice and the Carpenter,—Salem, which would not even allow you so much as Scotland gave Burns, will build you a monument yet for having shown that she did not hang her witches for nothing. I suppose the true office of the historian is to reconcile the present with the past.

I think you hardly do justice (in your preface to 'Twice-Told Tales') to your early reception. The augury of a man's popularity ought to be looked for in the intensity and not the vulgairty of his appreciation. . . .

57. [E. A. Duyckinck], from a review in the *Literary World*

26 April 1851, viii, 334–5

In the preface to this work, the anxiously looked-for successor to the Scarlet Letter, Mr. Hawthorne establishes a separation between the demands of the novel and the romance, and under the privilege of the latter, sets up his claim to a certain degree of license in the treatment of the characters and incidents of his coming story. This license, those acquainted with the writer's previous works will readily understand to be in the direction of the spiritualities of the piece, in favor of a process semi-allegorical, by which an acute analysis may be wrought out and the truth of feeling be minutely elaborated; an apology, in fact, for the preference of character to action, and of character for that which is allied to the darker elements of life—the dread blossoming of evil in the soul, and its fearful retributions. The House of the Seven Gables, one for each deadly sin, may be no unmeet adumbration of the corrupted soul of man. It is a ghostly, mouldy abode, built in some eclipse of the sun, and raftered with curses dark; founded on a grave, and sending its turrets heavenward, as the lightning rod transcends its summit, to invite the wrath supernal. Every darker shadow of human life lingers in and about its melancholy shelter. There all the passions allied to crime,— pride in its intensity, avarice with its steely gripe, and unrelenting con- science, are to be expiated in the house built on injustice. Wealth there withers, and the human heart grows cold: and thither are brought as accessories the chill glance of speculative philosophy, the descending hopes of the aged laborer, whose vision closes on the workhouse, the poor necessities of the humblest means of livelihood, the bodily and mental dilapidation of a wasted life. . . .

Yet the sunshine casts its rays into the old building, as it must, were it only to show us the darkness.

In truth there is sunshine brought in among the inmates, and these wrinkled, cobwebbed spiritualities with gentle Phœbe,—but it is a playful, typical light of youth and goodness,—hardly crystallizing the vapory atmosphere of the romance into the palpable concretions of actual life.

Yet, withal, these scenes and vivid descriptions are dramatic and truthful; dramatic in the picturesque and in situation rather than in continuous and well developed action; true to the sentiment and inner reality, if not to the outer fact. The two death scenes of the founder of the family and of his descendant, Judge Pyncheon, possess dramatic effect of a remarkable character; and various other groupings, at the fountain and elsewhere, separate themselves in our recollection. The chief, perhaps, of the dramatis personæ, is the house itself. From its turrets to its kitchen, in every nook and recess without and within, it is alive and vital, albeit of a dusty antiquity. We know it by sunlight and moonlight; but the elm which surmounts its roof, the mosses in its crevices, and its supernatural mist-swept blackness. Truly is it an actor in the scene. We move about trembling among its shadows,—the darkness of poverty and remorse dogging ruthlessly at our heels.

Verily this Hawthorne retains in him streaks of a Puritan ancestry. Some grave beater of pulpit cushions must lie among his ancestry; for of all laymen he will preach to you the closest sermons, probe deepest into the unescapable corruption, carry his lantern, like Belzoni among the mummies, into the most secret recesses of the heart; and he will do this with so vital a force in his propositions that they will transcend the individual example and find a precedent in every reader's heart. So true is it that when you once seize an actual thing you have in it a picture of universal life.

His Old Maid (Hepzibah) sacrificing pride to open her shop of small wares in one of the gables of the building, and her reluctant experiences of the first day, is not only a view of family pride in its shifts and reluctance, but covers all the doubts and irresolutions which beset a sensitive mind on the entrance upon any new sphere of duty in the great world.

These pictures are clear, distinct, full. The description is made out by repeated touches. There is no peculiar richness in the style: in some respects it is plain, but it flows on pellucid as a mountain rivulet, and you feel in its refreshing purity that it is fed by springs beneath.

You must be in the proper mood and time and place to read Hawthorne, if you would understand him. We think any one would be wrong to make the attempt on a rail-car, or on board a steamboat. It is not a shilling novel that you are purchasing when you buy the House of the Seven Gables, but a book—a book with lights and shades, parts and diversities, upon which you may feed and pasture, not exhausting the whole field at an effort, but returning now and then to uncropped fairy rings and bits of herbage. . . .

[Summarizes the story and quotes several long passages.]

Such is the material of Hawthorne's legend—with every 'coigne of vantage' for his procreant, melancholy fancy to work in, hanging his airy cobwebs about, not without a glitter on them of dew and sunshine. In tenderness and delicacy of sentiment, no writer of the present day can go beyond this book. This is Hawthorne's province of the world. In it his life is original, fanciful, creative.

58. Unsigned review in the *Christian Examiner*

May 1851, l, 508–9

The Twice-Told Tales were the first fruits of Mr. Hawthorne's genius; and their simple beauty and quiet pathos are doubtless familiar to many of our readers. They display the same mental characteristics that he has shown in his later works; and in the present elegant edition, which is enriched with an original Preface and a finely engraved head of the author, they can hardly fail for finding many new admirers.

In the Preface to The House of the Seven Gables, our author claims for the book 'a certain latitude, both as to its fashion and material, which he would not have felt himself entitled to assume, had he professed to be writing a Novel'; and he further tells us, that 'it has been no part of his object, however, to describe local manners, nor in any way to meddle with the characteristics of a community for whom he cherishes a proper respect and a natural regard.' He has, however, a moral constantly in view, which is, to show that 'the wrong-doing of one generation lives into the successive ones, and, divesting itself of every temporary advantage, becomes a pure and uncontrollable mischief'; and the same idea is presented once and again in the course of the romance itself. The work whose character and aim are thus described is a production of great power, though inferior in interest to The Scarlet Letter. The impression which it leaves on the reader's mind is, indeed, much pleasanter than that produced by its predecessor; but its plot is more complex, the characterization more exaggerated, and the artistic execution less perfect. Viewed as a whole, it will stand much higher than when considered in its separate parts; for the general outline is well conceived, but the filling up is not of equal excellence. There is too much of disquisition, and too little of narrative and dialogue. Consequently we have fewer descriptive passages of so great beauty and so tender pathos as we find in The Scarlet Letter and in some of the Twice-Told Tales, while there are scattered through the volume many sparkling gems of thought and incidental sketches of character which are alike striking and admirable. It will add to Mr. Hawthorne's reputation, and be greatly admired by a large class of readers.

We may say here, what we should have said at greater length had we noticed The Scarlet Letter, that it contains the grossest and foulest falsification of truth in history and personal character, that we have ever encountered, in romance or narrative.

59. From an unsigned review in *Harper's New Monthly Magazine*

May 1851, ii, 855–6

The House of the Seven Gables . . . is strongly marked with the bold and unique characteristics that have given its author such a brilliant position among American novelists. The scene, which is laid in the old Puritanic town of Salem, extends from the period of the witchcraft excitement to the present time, connecting the legends of the ancient superstition with the recent marvels of animal magnetism, and affording full scope for the indulgence of the most weird and sombre fancies. Destitute of the high-wrought manifestations of passion which distinguished the 'Scarlet Letter,' it is more terrific in its conception, and not less intense in its execution, but exquisitely relieved by charming portraitures of character, and quaint and comic descriptions of social eccentricities. A deep vein of reflection underlies the whole narrative, often rising naturally to the surface, and revealing the strength of the foundation on which the subtle, aerial inventions of the author are erected. His frequent dashes of humor gracefully blend with the monotone of the story, and soften the harsher colors in which he delights to clothe his portentous conceptions. In no former production of his pen, are his unrivalled powers of description displayed to better advantage. . . .

Nor are the characters of the story drawn with less sharp and vigorous perspective. They stand out from the canvas as living realities. In spite of the supernatural drapery in which they are enveloped, they have such a genuine expression of flesh and blood, that we can not doubt we have known them all our days. They have the air of old acquaintance—only we wonder how the artist got them to sit for their likenesses. The grouping of these persons is managed with admirable artistic skill. Old Maid Pyncheon, concealing under her verjuice scowl the unutterable tenderness of a sister—her woman-hearted brother, on whose sensitive nature had fallen such a strange blight—sweet and beautiful Phebe, the noble village-maiden, whose presence is always like that of some shining angel—the dreamy, romantic descendant of the legendary wizard—the bold, bad man of the world, reproduced at intervals in the bloody Colonel, and the unscrupulous Judge—wise old Uncle Venner—and inappeasable Ned Higgins—are all made to occupy the place on the canvas which shows the lights and shades of their character in the most impressive contrast, and contributes to the wonderful vividness and harmony of the grand historical picture. On the whole, we regard 'The House of the Seven Gables,' though it exhibits no single scenes that may not be matched in depth and pathos by some of Mr. Hawthorne's previous creations, as unsurpassed by any thing he has yet written, in exquisite beauty of finish, in the skillful blending of the tragic and comic, and in the singular life-like reality with which the wildest traditions of the Puritanic age are combined with the every-day incidents of modern society.

60. [E. P. Whipple], a review in *Graham's Magazine*

May 1851, xxxviii, 467–8

On 23 May 1851 Hawthorne commented on Whipple's reviews: 'Whipple's notices have done more than please; for they have helped me to see my book. Much of the censure I recognize as just. I wish I could feel the praise to be so fully deserved. I hope the book has sold respectably. Being better (which I insist it is) than the Scarlet Letter, I have never expected it to be so popular' (Letter, to James T. Fields, Hawthorne-Fields Letter Book, Houghton Library, Harvard University).

'The wrong-doing of one generation lives into the successive ones, and, divesting itself of every temporary advantage, becomes a pure and uncontrollable mischief;' this is the leading idea of Hawthorne's new romance, and it is developed with even more than his usual power. The error in 'The Scarlet Letter,' proceeded from the divorce of its humor from its pathos—the introduction being as genial as Goldsmith or Lamb, and the story which followed being tragic even to ghastliness. In 'The House of the Seven Gables,' the humor and the pathos are combined, and the whole work is stamped with the individuality of the author's genius, in all its variety of power. The first hundred pages of the volume are masterly in conception and execution, and can challenge comparison, in the singular depth and sweetness of their imaginative humor, with the best writing of the kind in literature. The other portions of the book have not the same force, precision, and certainty of handling, and the insight into character especially, seems at times to follow the processes of clairvoyance more than those of the waking imagination. The consequence is that the movement of the author's mind betrays a slight fitfulness toward the conclusion, and, splendid as is the supernaturally grotesque element which this ideal impatience introduces, it still somewhat departs from the integrity of the original conception, and interferes with the strict unity of the work. The mental nerve which characterizes the first part, slips occasionally into mental nervousness as the author proceeds.

We have been particular in indicating this fault, because the work is of so high a character that it demands, as a right, to be judged by the most exacting requirements of art. Taken as a whole, it is Hawthorne's greatest work, and is equally sure of immediate popularity and permanent fame. Considered as a romance, it does not so much interest as fasten and fascinate attention; and this attractiveness in the story is the result of the rare mental powers and moods out of which the story creatively proceeds. Every chapter proves the author to be, not only a master of narrative, a creater of character, an observer of life, and richly gifted with the powers of vital conception and combination, but it also exhibits him as a profound thinker and skillful metaphysician. We do not know but that his eye is more certain in detecting remote spiritual laws and their relations, than in the sure grasp of individual character; and if he ever loses his hold upon persons it is owing to that intensely meditative cast of his mind by which he views persons in their relations to the general laws whose action they illustrate. There is some discord in the present work in the development of character and sequence of events; the dramatic unity is therefore not perfectly preserved; but this cannot be affirmed of the unity of the law. That is always sustained, and if it had been thoroughly embodied, identified, and harmonized with the concrete events and characters, we have little hesitation in asserting that the present volume would be the deepest work of imagination ever produced on the American continent.

Before venturing upon any comments on the characters, we cannot resist the temptation to call the attention of our readers to the striking thoughts profusely scattered over the volume. These are generally quietly introduced, and spring so naturally out of the narrative of incidents, that their depth may not be at first appreciated. Expediency is the god whom most men really worship and obey, and few realize the pernicious consequences and poisonous vitality of bad deeds performed to meet an immediate difficulty. Hawthorne hits the law itself in this remark: 'The act of the present generation is the germ which may and must produce good or evil fruit, in a far distant time; for, together with the seed of the merely temporary crop, which mortals term expediency, they inevitably sow the acorns of a more enduring growth, which may darkly overshadow their posterity.' In speaking of the legal murder of old Matthew Maule for witchcraft, he says that Matthew 'was one of the martyrs to that terrible delusion, which should teach us, among its other morals, that the influential classes, and those who take upon themselves to be leaders of the people, are fully liable to all the passionate error that had ever characterized the maddest mob.' In reference to the hereditary transmission of individual qualities, it is said of Colonel Pyncheon's descendants, that 'his character might be traced all the way down, as distinctly *as if the colonel himself, a little diluted, had been gifted with a sort of intermittent immortality on earth.*' In a deeper vein is the account of the working of the popular imagination on the occasion of Col. Pyncheon's death. This afflicting event was ascribed by physicians to apoplexy; by the people to strangulation. The colonel had caused the death of a reputed wizard; and the fable ran that the lieutenant-governor, as he advanced into the room where the colonel sat dead in his chair, *saw a skeleton hand* at the colonel's throat, which vanished away as he came near him. Such touches as these are visible all over the volume, and few romances have more quotable felicities of thought and description.

The characters of the romance are among the best of Hawthorne's individualizations, and Miss Hepzibah and Phœbe are perhaps his masterpieces of characterization, in the felicity of their conception, their contrast, and their inter-action. Miss Hepzibah Pyncheon, the inhabitant of the gabled house, is compelled at the age of sixty to stoop from her aristocratic isolation from the world, and open a little cent shop, in order that she may provide for the subsistence of an unfortunate brother. The chapters entitled 'The Little Shop-Window,' 'The First Customer,' and a 'Day Behind the Counter,' in which her ludicrous humiliations are described, may be placed beside the best works of the most genial humorists, for their rapid alterations of smiles and tears, and the perfect April weather they make in the heart. The description of the little articles at the shop-window, the bars of soap, the leaden dragoons, the split peas, and the fantastic Jim Crow, 'executing his world-renowned dance in gingerbread;' the attempts of the elderly-maiden to arrange her articles aright, and the sad destruction she makes among them, crowned by upsetting that tumbler of marbles, 'all of which roll different ways, and each individual marble, devil-directed, into the most difficult obscurity it can find;' the nervous irritation of her deportment as she puts her shop in order, the twitches of pride which agonize her breast, as stealing on tiptoe to the window, 'as cautiously as if she conceived some bloody-minded villain to be watching behind the elmtree, with intent to take her life,' she stretches out her long, lank arm to put a paper of pearl-buttons, a Jew's harp, or what not, in its destined place, and then straitway vanishing back into the dusk, 'as if the world need never hope for another glimpse of her;' the 'ugly and spiteful little din' of the door-bell, announcing her first penny customer; all these, and many more minute details, are instinct with the life of humor, and cheerily illustrate that 'entanglement of something mean and trivial with whatever is noblest in joy and sorrow,' which it is the office of the humorist to represent and idealize.

The character of Phœbe makes the sunshine of the book, and by connecting her so intimately with Miss Hepzibah, a quaint sweetness is added to the native graces of her mind and disposition. The 'homely witchcraft' with which she brings out the hidden capabilities of every thing, is exquisitely exhibited, and poor Uncle Venner's praise of her touches the real secret of her fascination. 'I've seen,' says that cherry mendicant, 'a great deal of the world, not only in people's kitchens and back-yards, but at the street corners, and on the wharves, and in other places where my business calls me; but I'm free to say that I never knew a human creature do her work so much like one of God's angels as this child Phœbe does!' Holgrave, the young gentleman who carries off this pearl of womanhood, appears to us a failure. It is impossible for the reader to like him, and one finds it difficult to conceive how Phœbe herself can like him. The love scenes accordingly lack love, and a kind of magnetic influence is substituted for affection. The character of Clifford is elaborately drawn, and sustained with much subtle still, but he occupies perhaps too much space, and lures the author too much into metaphysical analysis and didactic disquisition. Judge Pyncheon is powerfully delineated, and the account of his death is a masterpiece of fantastic description. It is needless, perhaps, to say that the characters of the book have, like those in 'The Scarlet Letter,' a vital relation to each other, and are developed not successively and separately, but mutually, each implying the other by a kind of artistic necessity.

The imagination in the 'House of Seven Gables,' is perhaps most strikingly exhibited in the power with which the house itself is pervaded with thought, so that every room and gable has a sort of human interest communicated to it, and seems to symbolize the whole life of the Pyncheon family, from the grim colonel, who built it, to that delicate Alice, 'the fragrance of whose rich and delightful character lingered about the place where she lived, as a dried rose-bud scents the drawer where it has withered and perished.'

In conclusion, we hope to have the pleasure of reviewing a new romance by Hawthorne twice a year at least. We could also hope that if

Holgrave continues his contributions to the magazines, that he would send Graham some such a story as 'Alice Pyncheon,' which he tells so charmingly to Phœbe. 'The Scarlet Letter,' and 'The House of Seven Gables,' contain mental qualities which insensibly lead some readers to compare the author to other cherished literary names. Thus we have seen Hawthorne likened for this quality to Goldsmith, and for that to Irving, and for still another to Dickens; and some critics have given him the preference over all whom he seems to resemble. But the real cause for congratulation in the appearance of an original genius like Hawthorne, is not that he dethrones any established prince in literature, but that he founds a new principality of his own.

61. [Henry F. Chorley], from a review in the *Athenaeum*

24 May 1851, pp. 545–7

The invention of 'The Scarlet Letter' involved so much crime and remorse, that—though never was tragedy on a similar theme more clear of morbid incitements,—we felt that in a journal like ours the tale could be characterized only, not illustrated by extracts. So powerful, however, was the effect of that novel—even on those who, like ourselves, were prepared to receive good things from Mr. Hawthorne's hands—as to justify no ordinary solicitude concerning his next effort in fiction. This is before us—in 'The House of the Seven Gables': a story widely differing from its predecessor,—exceeding it, perhaps, in artistic ingenuity—if less powerful, less painful also—rich in humours and characters—and from first to last individual. It is thus made evident that Mr. Hawthorne possesses the fertility as well as the ambition of Genius: and in right of these two tales few will dispute his claim to rank amongst the most original and complete novelists that have appeared in modern times. . . . We know nothing better than the manner in which he presses superstition into his service as a romancer: leaving the reader to guess and explain such marvels as at first seen down the dim vista of Time, are reproduced more faintly in the world of the real Present. . . .

[Summarizes the story and quotes several long passages.]

Before, however, we leave this book, we have to note a fault in it not chargeable upon 'The Scarlet Letter,'—and one which, as having introduced Mr. Hawthorne to the English public, we mention in friendly jealousy, lest it grow into an affection with him. That affluence of fancy, that delight in playing with an idea and placing it in every chameleon light of the prism, and that love of reverie, which are so fascinating in a humorous essayist—become importunate if employed in scenes of emotion and junctures of breathless suspense. The speculations, for instance, upon him who sat in the deserted house on the day of the catastrophe fret the reader with their prosy and tantalizing ingenuity. They would have been in their place in the study of a single figure; but as interrupting the current which is sweeping the fortunes of many persons to the brink of the cataract—they are frivolous and vexatious. We beg our vigorous inventor and finely finishing artist (Mr. Hawthorne is both) to mistrust himself whenever he comes to his second simile and his third suggestion. They weaken the reader's faith,—they exhaust, not encourage, in him that desire to consider 'what might have happened' in such or such other cases which it is so essentially the privilege of first-class stories to generate.

62. Unsigned review in the *Southern Quarterly Review*

July 1851, n.s., iv, 265–6

Mr. Hawthorne is rapidly making himself a high reputation, as a writer of prose fiction. He is a tale writer, rather than a novelist, and exhibits some very peculiar endowments in this character. He has a rare and delicate fancy, with an imagination capable, in particular, of that curious distribution of light and shade—'that little glooming light, most like a shade,'—which constitutes the singular faculty of some of the most remarkable of the Italian painters. He is truthful, also, in his delineations of character, though his range is a limited one. He enters, with the art of Sterne, into the heart of his single captive, and, with exquisite adroitness, unfolds to you, and to the victim's self, the hurts of the secret nerve, its morbid condition, and how it operates upon, and affects by sympathy, the whole system. In these revelations, our author shows himself a minute philosopher. He goes farther than the simple delineation of the sore and secret places—he shows you why they became sore, and how they failed to keep their secrets from him. As a writer of prose fancies, fresh and delicate, of simple truths of the heart, which are obscure, in other hands, only from the absence of those exquisite antennæ which he employs, he exhibits a grace and felicity which show him to be a master. His province is peculiarly this fine one of the heart, with its subtler conditions, its eccentric moods, the result of secret weaknesses or secret consciousnesses, which it dare not confess and dare not overcome—its aberrations of soul or temper—its morbid passions, which fester without action, and are thus quite as vicious as if they had become developed by the actual commission of crime. Of the particular story before us, we have only to add that it exhibits happily the characteristic faculty of the author, in the delineation of morbid and peculiar conditions—in the curious distribution of light and shadow, and in the utterance of graceful and happy fancies, in close connection with moral philosophies and mental feelings, which are at once true to nature and agreeable to art. As a story, the 'House of the Seven Gables' will probably prove less attractive to the general reader than the 'Scarlet Letter,' as exhibiting a less concentrative power; but it is a more truthful book, and, if less ambitious in plan and manner, is not less earnest of purpose, nor less efficient in the varieties of character.

63. Hawthorne, from a letter to Horatio Bridge, in *Personal Recollections of Nathaniel Hawthorne*

22 July 1851 [1893] pp. 126–7

Why did you not write and tell me how you liked, or how you did not like, the 'House of the Seven Gables'? . . . I rather think I have reached that stage when I do not care, very essentially one way or the other, for anybody's opinion on any one production. On this last romance, for instance, I have heard and seen such diversity of judgment that I should be altogether bewildered if I attempted to strike a balance. So I take nobody's estimate unless it happens to agree with my own. I think it a work more characteristic of my mind, and more proper and natural for me to write, than 'The Scarlet Letter'; but for that very reason, less likely to interest the public. Nevertheless it appears to have sold better than the former, and, I think, is more sure of retaining the ground it acquires. Mrs. Kemble writes that both works are popular in England. . . .

64. Rufus W. Griswold on Hawthorne, from an unsigned essay, 'Nathaniel Hawthorne', in the *International Magazine*

1 May 1851, iii, 156–60

Griswold (1815–57), a journalist and anthologist, is best remembered as the author of a generally unreliable and malicious biography of Poe. His anthologies both formed and reflected current taste, and in his *Prose Writers of America* (1847) he included four Hawthorne pieces—'A Rill from the Town Pump', 'David Swan', 'The Celestial Railroad', and an excerpt from 'Buds and Bird Voices'. This review is noteworthy not only because it includes one of the first printed references to *Fanshawe*, but also because it is characteristic of the way Hawthorne criticism after 1850 began focusing on biographical details and using Hawthorne's Prefaces as autobiographical statements.

The author of *The House of Seven Gables* is now about forty-five years of age. He was born in Salem, Massachusetts, and is of a family which for several generations has 'followed the sea.' Among his ancestors, I believe, was the 'bold Hawthorne,' who is celebrated in a revolutionary ballad as commander of the 'Fair American.' He was educated at Bowdoin College in Maine, where he graduated in 1825.

Probably he appeared in print before that time, but his earliest volume was an anonymous and never avowed romance which was published in Boston in 1832. It attracted little attention, but among those who read it with a just appreciation of the author's genius was Mr. S. G. Goodrich, who immediately secured the shrouded star for *The Token*, of which he was editor, and through which many of Hawthorne's finest tales and essays were originally given to the public. He published in 1837 the first and in 1842 the second volume of his *Twice-Told Tales*, embracing whatever he wished to preserve from his contributions to the magazines; in 1845 he edited *The Journal of an African*

Cruiser; in 1846 published *Mosses from an Old Manse*, a second collection of his magazine papers; in 1850 *The Scarlet Letter,* and in the last month the longest and in some respects the most remarkable of his works, *The House of Seven Gables.*

In the introductions to the *Mosses from an Old Manse* and *The Scarlet Letter* we have some glimpses of his personal history. He had been several years in the Custom-House at Boston, while Mr. Bancroft was collector, and afterwards had joined that remarkable association, the 'Brook Farm Community,' at West Roxbury, where, with others, he appears to have been reconciled to the old ways, as quite equal to the inventions of Fourier, St. Simon, Owen, and the rest of that ingenious company of schemers who have been so intent upon a reconstruction of the foundations of society. In 1843, he went to reside in the pleasant village of Concord, in the 'Old Manse,' which had never been profaned by a lay occupant until he entered it as his home. In the introduction to *The Mosses* he says:

[Quotes 'A priest had' to 'to be disturbed'.]

In his home at Concord, thus happily described, in the midst of a few congenial friends, Hawthorne passed three years; and, 'in a spot so sheltered from the turmoil of life's ocean,' he says, 'three years hasten away with a noiseless flight, as the breezy sunshine chases the cloud-shadows across the depths of a still valley.' But at length his repose was invaded by that 'spirit of improvement,' which is so constantly marring the happiness of quiet-loving people, and he was compelled to look out for another residence.

[Quotes 'Now came hints' to 'heart and mind'.]

The *Mosses from an Old Manse* he declared the last offering of their kind he should ever put forth; 'unless I can do better,' he wrote in this Introduction, 'I have done enough in this kind.' He went to his place in the Custom House, in his native city, and if President Taylor's advisers had not been apprehensive that in his devotion to ledgers he would neglect the more important duties of literature, perhaps we should have heard no more of him; but those patriotic men, remembering how much they had enjoyed the reading of the *Twice-Told Tales* and the *Mosses*, induced the appointment in his place of a whig, who had no capacity for making books, and in the spring of last year we had *The Scarlet Letter.*

Like most of his shorter stories, The Scarlet Letter finds its scene and time with the earlier Puritans. Its argument involves the analysis and action of remorse in the heart of a person who, himself unsuspected, is compelled to assist in the punishment of the partner of his guilt. This peculiar and powerful fiction at once arrested attention, and claimed for its author the eminence as a novelist which his previous performances had secured for him as a writer of tales. Its whole atmosphere and the qualities of its characters demanded for a creditable success very unusual capacities. The frivolous costume and brisk action of the story of fashionable life are easily depicted by the practised sketcher, but a work like The Scarlet Letter comes slowly upon the canvas, where passions are commingled and overlaid with the deliberate and masterly elaboration with which the grandest effects are produced in pictorial composition and coloring. It is a distinction of such works that while they are acceptable to the many, they also surprise and delight the few who appreciate the nicest arrangement and the most high and careful finish. The Scarlet Letter will challenge consideration in the name of Art, in the best audience which in any age receives Cervantes, Le Sage, or Scott.

Following this romance came new editions of *True Stories from History and Biography*, a volume for youthful readers, and of the *Twice-Told Tales*. In the preface to the latter, underrating much the reputation he has acquired by them, he says:

[Quotes 'The author of *Twice-Told Tales*' to 'chimney on fire'; 'As he glances' to 'of blank pages'; and 'The author would regret' to 'far better than fame'.]

That there should be any truth in this statement that the public was so slow to recognize so fine a genius, is a mortifying evidence of the worthlessness of a literary popularity. But it may be said of Hawthorne's fame that it has grown steadily, and that while many who have received the turbulent applause of the multitude since he began his career are forgotten, it has widened and brightened, until his name is among the very highest in his domain of art, to shine there with a lustre equally serene and enduring.

Mr. Hawthorne's last work is *The House of Seven Gables*, a romance of the present day. It is not less original, not less striking, not less powerful, than The Scarlet Letter. We doubt indeed whether he has elsewhere surpassed either of the three strongly contrasted characters of the book. An innocent and joyous child-woman, Phœbe Pyncheon, comes from a farm-house into the grand and gloomy old

mansion where her distant relation, Hepzibah Pyncheon, an aristo-
cratical and fearfully ugly but kind-hearted unmarried woman of
sixty, is just coming down from her faded state to keep in one of her
drawing-rooms a small shop, that she may be able to maintain an elder
brother who is every moment expected home from a prison to which
in his youth he had been condemned unjustly, and in the silent solitude
of which he has kept some lineaments of gentleness while his hair has
grown white, and a sense of beauty while his brain has become dis-
ordered and his heart has been crushed and all present influences of
beauty have been quite shut out. The House of Seven Gables is the
purest piece of imagination in our prose literature.

The characteristics of Hawthorne which first arrest the attention are
imagination and reflection, and these are exhibited in remarkable
power and activity in tales and essays, of which the style is distinguished for great simplicity, purity and tranquillity. His beautiful
story of Rappacini's Daughter was originally published in the Democratic Review, as a translation from the French of one M. de l'Aubépine, a writer whose very name, he remarks in a brief introduction,
(in which he gives in French the titles of some of his tales, as *Contes
deux foix racontées, Le Culte du Feu,* etc.) 'is unknown to many of his
countrymen, as well as to the student of foreign literature.' He describes himself, under this *nomme de plume,* as one who—

Seems to occupy an unfortunate position between the transcendentalists (who
under one name or another have their share in all the current literature of the
world), and the great body of pen-and-ink men who address the intellect and
sympathies of the multitude. If not too refined, at all events too remote, too
shadowy and unsubstantial, in his mode of development, to suit the taste of the
latter class, and yet too popular to satisfy the spiritual or metaphysical requisi-
tions of the former, he must necessarily find himself without an audience, except
here and there an individual, or possibly an isolated clique.

His writings, to do them justice, he says—

Are not altogether destitute of fancy and originality; they might have won him
greater reputation but for an inveterate love of allegory, which is apt to invest
his plots and characters with the aspect of scenery and people in the clouds, and
to steal away the human warmth out of his conceptions. His fictions are sometimes historical, sometimes of the present day, and sometimes, so far as can be
discovered, have little or no reference either to time or space. In any case, he
generally contents himself with a very slight embroidery of outward manners,
—the faintest possible counterfeit of real life,—and endeavors to create an inter-

est by some less obvious peculiarity of the subject. Occasionally a breath of nature, a rain-drop of pathos and tenderness, or a gleam of humor, will find its way into the midst of his fantastic imagery, and make us feel as if, after all, we were yet within the limits of our native earth. We will only add to this cursory notice, that M. de l'Aubépine's productions, if the reader chance to take them in precisely the proper point of view, may amuse a leisure hour as well as those of a brighter man; if otherwise, they can hardly fail to look excessively like nonsense.

Hawthorne is as accurately as he is happily described in this curious piece of criticism, though no one who takes his works in the 'proper point of view,' will by any means agree to the modest estimate which, in the perfect sincerity of his nature, he has placed upon them. He is original, in invention, construction, and expression, always picturesque, and sometimes in a high degree dramatic. His favorite scenes and traditions are those of his own country, many of which he has made classical by the beautiful associations that he has thrown around them. Everything to him is suggestive, as his own pregnant pages are to the congenial reader. All his productions are life-mysteries, significant of profound truths. His speculations, often bold and striking, are presented with singular force, but with such a quiet grace and simplicity as not to startle until they enter in and occupy the mind. The gayety with which his pensiveness is occasionally broken, seems more than any thing else in his works to have cost some effort. The gentle sadness, the 'half-acknowledged melancholy,' of his manner and reflections, are more natural and characteristic.

His style is studded with the most poetical imagery, and marked in every part with the happiest graces of expression, while it is calm, chaste, and flowing, and transparent as water. There is a habit among nearly all the writers of imaginative literature, of adulterating the conversations of the poor with barbarisms and grammatical blunders which have no more fidelity than elegance. Hawthorne's integrity as well as his exquisite taste prevented him from falling into this error. There is not in the world a large rural population that speaks its native language with a purity approaching that with which the English is spoken by the common people of New England. The vulgar words and phrases which in other states are supposed to be peculiar to this part of the country are unknown east of the Hudson, except to the readers of foreign newspapers, or the listeners to low comedians who find it profitable to convey such novelties into Connecticut, Massachusetts, and Vermont. We are glad to see a book that is going down to the next ages as a representative of national manners and character in all respects correct.

Nathaniel Hawthorne is among the first of the first order of our writers, and in their peculiar province his works are not excelled in the literature of the present day or of the English language.

65. Henry T. Tuckerman: Hawthorne as a psychological novelist, from 'Nathaniel Hawthorne', in the *Southern Literary Messenger*

June 1851, xvii, 344–9

Tuckerman (1813–71), a poet and critic, represents, with Duyc-kinck and others, a romantic criticism influential in mid-century America. Among his works are romantic travel books, a volume of Irvingesque sketches, and several literary biographies. Haw-thorne appears to have thought highly of Tuckerman's essay and wrote the following letter, which appeared with a reprint of the review in *Littell's Living Age,* 11 June 1864, lxxxi, 518–24:

I have received the *Southern Literary Messenger,* and have read your beautiful article on my, I fear, unworthy self. It gave me, I must confess, the pleasantest sensation I have ever experienced, from any cause connected with literature; not so much for the sake of the praise as because I felt that you saw into my books and understood what I meant. I cannot thank you enough for it.

What the scientific use of lenses—the telescope and the microscope—does for us in relation to the external universe, the psychological writer achieves in regard to our own nature. He reveals its wonder and beauty, unfolds its complex laws and makes us suddenly aware of the mysteries within and around individual life. In the guise of attractive fiction and sometimes of the most airy sketches, Hawthorne thus deals with his reader. His appeal is to consciousness and he must, therefore, be met in a sympathetic relation; he shadows forth,—hints,—makes signs,—whispers,—muses aloud,—gives the keynote of melody—puts us on a track;—in a word, addresses us as nature does—that is unostentatiously, and with a significance not to be realized without reverent silence and gentle feeling—a sequestration from bustle and material care, and somewhat of the meditative insight and latent sensibility in which his themes are conceived and wrought out. Sometimes they are purely descriptive, bits of Flemish painting—so exact and arrayed in such mellow colors, that we unconsciously take them in as objects of sensitive rather than imaginative observation; the 'Old Manse' and the 'Custom House' —those quaint portals to his fairy-land, as peculiar and rich in contrast in their way, as Boccaccio's sombre introduction to his gay stories—are memorable instances of this fidelity in the details of local and personal portraiture; and that chaste yet deep tone of colouring which secure an harmonious whole. Even in allegory, Hawthorne imparts this sympathetic unity to his conception; 'Fire Worship,' 'The Celestial Railroad', 'Monsieur du Miroir,' 'Earth's Holocaust,' and others in the same vein, while they emphatically indicate great moral truth, have none of the abstract and cold grace of allegorical writing; besides the ingenuity they exhibit, and the charm they have for the fancy, a human interest warms and gives them meaning to the heart. On the other hand, the imaginative grace which they chiefly display, lends itself quite as aptly to redeem and glorify homely fact in the plastic hands of the author. 'Drowne's Wooden Image,' 'The Intelligence Office,' and other tales derived from common-place material, are thus moulded into artistic beauty and suggestiveness. Hawthorne, therefore, is a prose-poet. He brings together scattered beauties, evokes truth from apparent confusion, and embodies the tragic or humorous element of a tradition or an event in lyric music—not, indeed, to be sung by the lips, but to live, like melodious echoes, in the memory. We are constantly struck with the felicity of his invention. What happy ideas are embodied in 'A Virtuoso's Collection,' and 'The Artist of the Beautiful'—independent of the grace of their execution! There is a certain uniformity in Hawthorne's style and manner, but a remarkable versatility in his subjects; and each as distinctly carries with it the monotone of a special feeling or fancy . . . and this is the perfection of pyschological art.

There are two distinct kinds of fiction, or narrative literature, which for want of more apt terms, we may call the melodramatic and the

meditative; the former is in a great degree mechanical, and deals chiefly
with incidents and adventure; a few types of character, an approved
scenic material and what are called effective situations, make up the
story; the other species, on the contrary, is modelled upon no external
pattern, but seems evolved from the author's mind and tinged with his
idiosyncrasy; the circumstances related are often of secondary interest
—while the sentiment they unfold, the picturesque or poetic light in
which they are placed, throw an enchantment over them. We feel the
glow of individual consciousness even in the most technical description;
we recognize a significance beyond the apparent, in each character;
and the effect of the whole is that of life rather than history: we inhale
an atmosphere as well as gaze upon a landscape; the picture offered to
the mental vision has not outline and grouping, but color and expression, evincing an intimate and sympathetic relation between the moral
experience of the author and his work, so that, as we read, not only
scenes but sensations, not only fancies but experience seem borne in
from the entrancing page.

There is a charm also essential to all works of genius which for want
of a more definite term we are content to call the ineffable. It is a quality
that seems to be infused through the design of the artist after its mechanical finish—as life entered the statue at the prayer of the Grecian sculptor.
It is a secret, indescribable grace, a vital principle, a superhuman element imparting the distinctive and magnetic character to literature, art
and society, which gives them individual life; it is what the soul is to
the body, luminous vapour to the landscape, wind to sound, and light
to color. No analysis explains the phenomenon; it is recognized by
consciousness rather than through direct intellectual perception; and
seems to appeal to a union of sensibility and insight which belongs, in
the highest degree, only to appreciative minds. . . . There is a peculiar
zest about them which proves a vital origin; and this is the distinction
of Hawthorne's tales. They almost invariably possess the reality of tone
which perpetuates imaginative literature;—the same that endears to
all time De Foe, Bunyan, Goldsmith, and the old dramatists. . . .
Robinson Crusoe is objectively, and Pilgrim's Progress spiritually, true
to nature; the Vicar of Wakefield emanated from a mind overflowing
with humanity; and it is the genuine reproduction of passion in the old
English plays that makes them still awaken echoes in the soul.

It may be regarded as a proof of absolute genius to create a mood; to
inform, amuse, or even interest is only the test of superficial powers
sagaciously directed; but to infuse a new state of feeling, to change the

frame of mind and, as it were, alter the consciousness—this is the triumph of all art. It is that mysterious influence which beauty, wit, character, nature and peculiar scenes and objects exert, which we call fascination, a charm, an inspiration or a glamour, according as it is good or evil. It may safely be asserted that by virtue of his individuality every author and artist of genius creates a peculiar mood, differing somewhat according to the character of the recipient, yet essentially the same. If we were obliged to designate that of Hawthorne in a single word, we should call it metaphysical, or perhaps soulful. He always takes us below the surface and beyond the material; his most inartificial stories are eminently suggestive; he makes us breathe the air of contemplation, and turns our eyes inward. It is as if we went forth, in a dream, into the stillness of an autumnal wood, or stood alone in a vast gallery of old pictures, or moved slowly, with muffled tread, over a wide plain, amid a gentle fall of snow, or mused on a ship's deck, at sea, by moonlight; the appeal is to the retrospective, the introspective, to what is thoughtful and profoundly conscious in our nature and whereby it communes with the mysteries of life and the occult intimations of nature. And yet there is no painful extravagance, no transcendental vagaries in Hawthorne; his imagination is as human as his heart; if he touches the horizon of the infinite, it is with reverence; if he deals with the anomalies of sentiment, it is with intelligence and tenderness. His utterance too is singularly clear and simple; his style only rises above the colloquial in the sustained order of its flow; the terms are apt, natural and fitly chosen. Indeed, a careless reader is liable continually to lose sight of his meaning and beauty, from the entire absence of pretension in his style. It is requisite to bear in mind the universal truth, that all great and true things are remarkable for simplicity; the direct method is the pledge of sincerity, avoidance of the conventional, an instinct of richly-endowed minds; and the perfection of art never dazzles or overpowers, but gradually wins and warms us to an enduring and noble love. The style of Hawthorne is wholly inevasive; he resorts to no tricks of rhetoric or verbal ingeniuty; language is to him a crystal medium through which to let us see the play of his humor, the glow of his sympathy, and the truth of his observation.

Although he seldom transcends the limited sphere in which he so efficiently concentrates his genius, the variety of tone, like different airs on the same instrument, gives him an imaginative scope rarely obtained in elaborate narrative. Thus he deals with the tragic element, wisely and with vivid originality, in such pieces as 'Roger Malvin's Burial' and 'Young Goodman Brown;' with the comic in 'Mr. Higginbotham's Catastrophe,' 'A Select Party,' and 'Dr. Heidegger's Experiment,' and with the purely fanciful in 'David Swan,' 'The Vision of the Fountain,' and 'Fancy's Show Box.' Nor is he less remarkable for sympathetic observation of nature than for profound interest in humanity; witness such limning as the sketches entitled 'Buds and Bird Voices,' and 'Snow-Flakes'—genuine descriptive poems, though not cast in the mould of verse, as graphic, true and feeling as the happiest scenes of Bryant or Crabbe. With equal tact and tenderness he approaches the dry record of the past, imparting life to its cold details, and reality to its abstract forms. The early history of New England has found no such genial and vivid illustration as his pages afford. Thus, at all points, his genius touches the interests of human life, now overflowing with a love of external nature, as gentle as that of Thomson, now intent upon the quaint or characteristic in life with a humor as zestful as that of Lamb, now developing the horrible or pathetic with something of Webster's dramatic terror, and again buoyant with a fantasy as aerial as Shelley's conceptions. And, in each instance, the staple of charming invention is adorned with the purest graces of style. This is Hawthorne's distinction. We have writers who possess in an eminent degree, each of these two great requisites of literary success, but no one who more impressively unites them; cheerfulness as if caught from the sea-breeze or the green-fields, solemnity as if imbibed from the twilight, like colors on a palette, seem transferable at his will, to any legend or locality he chooses for a frame-work whereon to rear his artistic creation. . . . He has performed for New England life and manners the same high and sweet service which Wilson has for Scotland —caught and permanently embodied their 'lights and shadows.'

Brevity is as truly the soul of romance as of wit; the light that warms is always concentrated, and expression and finish, in literature as in painting, are not dependent upon space. Accordingly the choicest gems of writing are often the most terse; and as a perfect lyric or sonnet outweighs in value a mediocre epic or tragedy, so a carefully worked and richly conceived sketch, tale or essay is worth scores of diffuse novels and ponderous treatises. It is a characteristic of standard literature, both ancient and modern, thus to condense the elements of thought and style. Like the compact and well-knit frame, vivacity, efficiency and grace result from this bringing the rays of fancy and reflection to a focus. It gives us the essence, the flower, the vital spirit of mental enterprise; it is a wise economy of resources and often secures permanent renown by distinctness of impression unattained in efforts of great range. We, therefore, deem one of Hawthorne's great merits a sententious habit, a concentrated style. He makes each picture complete and does not waste an inch of canvass. Indeed the unambitious length of his tales is apt to blind careless readers to their artistic unity and suggestiveness; he abjures quantity, while he refines upon quality.

A rare and most attractive quality of Hawthorne, as we have already suggested, is the artistic use of familiar materials. The imagination is a wayward faculty, and writers largely endowed with it, have acknowledged that they could expatiate with confidence only upon themes hallowed by distance. It seems to us less marvellous that Shakespeare peopled a newly discovered and half-traditional island with such new types of character as Ariel and Caliban; we can easily reconcile ourselves to the enchanting impossibilities of Arabian fiction; and the superstitious fantasies of northern romance have a dream-like reality to the natives of the temperate zone. To clothe a familiar scene with ideal interest, and exalt things to which our senses are daily accustomed, into the region of imaginative beauty and genuine sentiment, requires an extraordinary power of abstraction and concentrative thought. Authors in the old world have the benefit of antiquated memorials which give to the modern cities a mysterious though often disregarded charm; and the very names of Notre Dame, the Rialto, London Bridge, and other time-hallowed localities, take the reader's fancy captive and prepare him to accede to any grotesque or thrilling narrative that may be associated with them. It is otherwise in a new and entirely practical country; the immediate encroaches too steadily on our attention; we can scarcely obtain a perspective. . . .

Yet with a calm gaze, a serenity and fixedness of musing that no outward bustle can disturb and no power of custom render hackneyed, Hawthorne takes his stand, like a foreign artist in one of the old Italian cities,—before a relic of the past or a picturesque glimpse of nature, and loses all consciousness of himself and the present, in transferring its features and atmosphere to canvass. In our view the most remarkable trait in his writings is this harmonious blending of the common and familiar in the outward world, with the mellow and vivid tints of his own imagination. It is with difficulty that his maturity of conception and his finish and geniality of style links itself, in our minds, with the streets of Boston and Salem, the Province House and even the White Mountains; and we congratulate every New Englander with a particle of romance, that in his native literature, 'a local habitation and a name,' has thus been given to historical incidents and localities;—that art has enshrined what of tradition hangs over her brief career—as characteristic and as desirable thus to consecrate, as any legend or spot, German or Scottish genius has redeemed from oblivion. The 'Wedding Knell,' the 'Gentle Boy,' the 'White Old Maid,' the 'Ambitious Guest,' the 'Shaker Bridal,' and other New England subjects, as embodied and glorified by the truthful, yet imaginative and graceful art of Hawthorne, adequately represent in literature, native traits, and this will ensure their ultimate appreciation. But the most elaborate effort of this kind, and the only one, in fact, which seems to have introduced Hawthorne to the whole range of American readers, is 'The Scarlet Letter.' With all the care in point of style and authenticity which mark his lighter sketches, this genuine and unique romance, may be considered as an artistic exposition of Puritanism as modified by New England colonial life. In truth to costume, local manners and scenic features, the Scarlet Letter is as reliable as the best of Scott's novels; in the anatomy of human passion and consciousness it resembles the most effective of Balzac's illustrations of Parisian or provincial life, while in developing bravely and justly the sentiment of the life it depicts, it is as true to humanity as Dickens. Beneath its picturesque details and intense characterization, there lurks a profound satire. The want of soul, the absence of sweet humanity, the predominance of judgment over mercy, the tyranny of public opinion, the look of genuine charity, the asceticism of the Puritan theology,—the absence of all recognition of natural laws, and the fanatic substitution of the letter for the spirit—which darken and harden the spirit of the pilgrims to the soul of a poet—are shadowed forth with a keen, stern and eloquent, yet indirect emphasis, that haunts us like 'the cry of the human.' Herein is evident and palpable the latent power which we have described as the most remarkable trait of Hawthorne's genius;—the impression grows more significant as we dwell upon the story; the states of mind of the poor clergyman, Hester, Chillingworth and Pearl, being as it were transferred to our bosoms through the intense sympathy their vivid delineation excites;—they seem to conflict, and glow and deepen and blend in our hearts, and finally work out a great moral problem. It is as if we were baptized into the consciousness of Puritan life, of New England character in its elemental state; and knew, by experience, all its frigidity, its gloom, its intellectual enthusiasm and its religious aspiration. 'The House of the Seven Gables' is a more elaborate and harmonious realization of these characteristics.

The scenery, tone and personages of the story are imbued with a local authenticity which is not, for an instant, impaired by the imaginative charm of romance. . . . So life-like in the minutiae and so picturesque in general effect are these sketches of still-life, that they are daguerreotyped in the reader's mind, and form a distinct and changeless background, the light and shade of which give admirable effect to the action of the story: occasional touches of humor, introduced with exquisite tact, relieve the grave undertone of the narrative and form vivacious and quaint images which might readily be transferred to canvass—so effectively are they drawn in words; take, for instance, the street-musician and the Pyncheon fowls, the judge balked of his kiss over the counter, Phoebe reading to Clifford in the garden, or the old maid, in her lonely chamber, gazing on the sweet lineaments of her unfortunate brother. Nor is Hawthorne less successful in those pictures that are drawn exclusively for the mind's eye and are obvious to sensation rather than the actual vision. Were a New England Sunday, breakfast, old mansion, easterly storm, or the morning after it clears, ever so well described? The skill in atmosphere we have noted in his lighter sketches, is also as apparent: around and within the principal scene of this romance, there hovers an alternating melancholy and brightness which is born of genuine moral life; no contrasts can be imagined of this kind, more eloquent to a sympathetic mind, than that between the inward consciousness and external appearance of Hepzibah or Phoebe and Clifford, or the Judge. They respectively symbolize the poles of human existence; and are fine studies for the psychologist. Yet this attraction is subservient to fidelity to local characteristics. Clifford represents, though in its most tragic imaginable phase, the man of fine organization and true sentiments environed by the material realities of New England life; his plausible uncle is the type of New England selfishness, glorified by respectable conformity and wealth; Phoebe is the ideal of genuine, efficient, yet loving female character in the same latitude; Uncle Venner, we regard as one of the most fresh, yet familiar portraits in the book; all denizens of our eastern provincial towns must have known such a philosopher; and Holgrave embodies Yankee acuteness and hardihood redeemed by integrity and enthusiasm. The contact of these most judiciously selected and highly characteristic elements, brings out not only many beautiful revelations of nature, but elucidates interesting truth; magnetism and socialism are admirably introduced; family tyranny in its most revolting form, is powerfully exemplified; the distinction between a mental and a heartfelt interest in another, clearly unfolded; and the tenacious and hereditary nature of moral evil impressively shadowed forth. The natural refinements of the human heart, the holiness of a ministry of disinterested affection, the gracefulness of the homeliest services when irradiated by cheerfulness and benevolence, are illustrated with singular beauty. . . .

Perhaps the union of the philosophic tendency with the poetic instinct is the great charm of his genius. It is common for American critics to estimate the interest of all writings by their comparative glow, vivacity and rapidity of action: somewhat of the restless temperament and enterprising life of the nation infects its taste: such terms as 'quiet,' 'gentle' and 'tasteful,' are equivocal when applied in this country, to a book; and yet they may envelope the rarest energy of thought and depth of insight as well as earnestness of feeling; these qualities, in reflective minds, are too real to find melo-dramatic development; they move as calmly as summer waves, or glow as noiselessly as the firmament; but not the less grand and mighty is their essence; to realize it, the spirit of contemplation, and the recipient mood of sympathy, must be evoked, for it is not external but moral excitement that is proposed; and we deem one of Hawthorne's most felicitous merits—that of so patiently educing artistic beauty and moral interest from life and nature, without the least sacrifice of intellectual dignity.

66. A[mory] D[wight] M[ayo]:
Hawthorne as a religious novelist, from
'The Works of Nathaniel Hawthorne', in
the *Universalist Quarterly*

July 1851, viii, 272–93

Mayo (1823–1907) was a Unitarian clergyman and educator.

Among the few American writers who have the peculiarity of genius which consists of insight into this fact of the soul, Mr. Hawthorne occupies a prominent position. We are convinced that the rarest quality of his mind is the power of tracing the relations of spiritual laws to character. He looks at the soul, life, and nature, from the stand-point of Providence. He follows the track of one of God's mental or moral laws. Every thing which appears along its borders is minutely investigated, though sometimes appreciated rather for its nearness to his path than its own value. If we mistake not, this is the clue to all his works. Even his lightest tale gains a peculiarity of treatment and depth of tone from it, though the tendency of his mind is better perceived in his more elaborate works. Wherever he goes, whoever he meets, or whatever may be the scenes amid which he mingles, this thought is uppermost:— How are these things related to each other, and to those great spiritual agencies which underlie and encompass them? Whatever else Mr. Hawthorne may be, and we do not deny to him great versatility of powers, he is, more than any thing else, a seer.

His view of human nature determines his treatment of individuals. He can hardly be called a truthful delineator of character. His men and women have the elements of life, though not arranged in harmonious proportions. Our interest is concentrated upon the point, in the nature of each, where the battle is raging between human will and spiritual laws. . . .

And his pictures of life are generally from the same point of view. He shows us a street, a domestic circle, a public assembly, or a whole village, describes them with wonderful fidelity, yet just as we think we have them securely located upon solid ground, by one magic sentence the whole is transmuted to a symbolic picture, and a witch element in the atmosphere makes us doubt whether we are not in dream-land. Even the beautiful introductions to the 'Mosses from an old Manse,' and the 'Scarlet Letter,' are tinged with this peculiarity. . . . An observing reader will be struck by this tendency to symbolism on every page of these books.

So nature is regarded oftener by him in its relations to the human mind, and mental and moral laws, than as existing for any independent purpose. His exquisite pencilling of her beautiful scenes is generally illustrative of the person who is the central figure of the landscape. His winds howl a warning through open doors on the advent of some critical moment. 'Alice's Posies,' and 'The Pyncheon Elm,' the garden of 'The House of the Seven Gables,' the wood where Hester and Dimmesdale talked, and the midnight sky, seen by the minister from the pillory, all prefigure in outline and detail the spiritual states of those who lived among them. . . .

This prominent tendency in Mr. Hawthorne's mind, at times assumes the form of disease. Doubtless the most profound, and from an angel's point of view, the truest estimate of man, life and nature, is that in which they are woven into a spectacle illustrative of spiritual laws. . . . A tendency to disease in his nature, appears in the fearful intensity of his narratives. There is also a sort of unnaturalness in his world. It is seen not in the noon-day sun, so often as by moon-beams, and by auroral or volcanic lights. All that he describes may and does actually happen, but something else happens, by the omission of which we fail sometimes to acknowledge the reality of his delineation. This tendency appears in many of the tales in the 'Mosses from an Old Manse,' and reached its climax in the 'Scarlet Letter'. In 'The House of the Seven Gables,' we see the author struggling out of its grasp, with a vigor which we believe ensures a final recovery.

The constitution of Mr. Hawthorne's mind, in other respects, is admirably calculated to fit him for his primary office of seer. For all danger of that godless or misanthropic spirit, which so often destroys men who know much of human nature, is averted by his great affections. He follows the track of a spiritual law into the darkest or wildest scene, without losing his faith in God, or his love for humanity. . . .

In addition to these qualities, Mr. Hawthorne is largely gifted with the higher forms of imagination. Were we a metaphysician, we might guess at its quality, and perhaps discover that the very spiritual insight of which we have been talking, is essentially imaginative. Be this as it may, he also possesses that form of the divine faculty which makes him alive in every corner of his soul, and that which gives him the power of vivid portraiture, also, to a considerable degree, the higher gift by which the poet weaves the deepest realities of life into an airy picture for artistic contemplation. A true poet is not ensnared in his own work, but has it at arm's length, and finally places it out of immediate contact with our sympathies, into the region of art. It is this which distinguishes the artist from the philanthropist. The latter gives us a picture of human happiness and wretchedness, which appeals only to our conscience and disturbs us sleeping and waking; the former uses the same materials, and creates the same groups, yet by a power of his own, forces it to appeal to our sense of beauty, and become a perpetual source of delight. There is no untruth in this. We do not ignore the moral relations of the work by thus acknowledging that God is both the all-good and the all-beautiful. We do not ascribe this power to Mr. Hawthorne in the highest degree. Portions of his work are faultless, yet we have not in any case the sense, either of that completeness or entire beauty which declares a man a poet. Even in creative imagination, Mr. Hawthorne is not deficient. Amid the throng of half human generalizations, we catch a glimpse occasionally of a true poetic creation. Phœbe is the only New England girl we ever met in a book, and Pearl is a newcomer into the world of poetry. We yet hope to witness greater evidences of our author's power in this direction. We must also speak of his style, as a development of his imaginative life. It is truly original and admirable. We read page after page, till, satiated with its harmony and beauty, we lose all hold upon the narrative, and make it a substitute for a diorama or a concert.

Yet, though we hazard a little in saying it, it does seem to us that the final impression of these books is not poetical so decidedly as religious. The author sings, but sings oratorios and hymns. He paints, yet paints the 'spiritual body' and the world of souls. We regard him as a religious novelist, in a high and peculiar sense. He does not, like the tribe of disguised parsons who have broken into the realm of letters, write books and sew together men and women of paste-board, to illustrate artificial and arbitrary creeds, or rules of conduct. Neither like the able class which swears by Goethe, does he give a picture of actual life faithful in every particular, leaving the reader to find its law and morality; but he lays bare those spiritual laws of God to which we must conform, and with wonderful distinctness describes the soul's relations to them. . . .

There are few books in English literature more valuable as a pledge of eminence than the 'Twice told Tales.' The sketches are short, and often carelessly executed, yet display remarkable felicity of handling, delicacy of outlining, purity and flexibility of style, and insight into the working of spiritual laws and the dark corners of life and character. The ruling propensity of the writer here assumes the form of a love for the mysterious, and becomes almost an element of fatalism in his philosophy. Each of his shadowy personages is the slave of a destiny, and we see him only an instant at the point of its culmination. The whole book is written in that uncertain region between the most profound religion and a poetic superstition; too true to be put off among volumes of ghost stories, too highly colored to be valuable as an accurate description of life. Other qualities of mind, to which we have already referred, are here manifested or foreshadowed. Of the forty articles in these volumes, we have been most strongly impressed by the 'Minister's Black Veil,' 'The Gentle Boy,' 'The Prophetic Pictures,' the entire series of 'Legends of the Province House,' 'The Village Uncle,' 'The Seven Vagabonds,' and 'Peter Goldthwaite's Treasure.'

In the 'Mosses from an old Manse,' the same mental characteristics appear in greater maturity of development. The tales of this series show a more decided treatment, more vivid and definite portrayal of character, and a deeper coloring than the writer's previous works. They are to the 'Twice Told Tales,' what paintings in oils are to sketches in water colors. The introductory description of the 'Old Manse' is not surpassed by any thing of its kind in English literature, and is the best part of the book. Perhaps the unhealthiness of the writer's mind is more prominently exhibited in a few of these stories, than elsewhere. 'The Birth-mark,' 'Rappaccini's Daughter,' and 'Roger Malvin's Burial,' are the nettles and mushrooms of Mr. Hawthorne's mind, and certainly should not be tied up with a bouquet of flowers for the public. Perhaps we hate these tales the more, that they are bound in the same covers with 'The Celestial Railroad,' and 'Drowne's wooden Image,' the happiest efforts of the author in sketch writing.

We should be ungrateful for a day of the purest pleasure, did we overlook the next work in this series. Though written for children, the little volume bearing the title of 'True Stories' is a book to be read by everybody. Here the author has given a striking and connected view of the early history of New England, in a few simple tales related by a grandfather to a group of children. We admire, particularly, the manner in which the salient points of the historical period are seized, the skill of the grouping, the suggestive style of the narrative, the shy, sharp hits at popular vices and follies, and the profound, yet genial morality of the book.

Standing as 'The Scarlet Letter' does, at the junction of several moral highways, it is not easy to grasp the central idea around which it instinctively arranged itself in the author's mind. The most obvious fact upon its pages is, that the only safety for a human soul consists in appearing to be exactly what it is. If holy, it must not wrench itself out of its sphere to become a part in any satanic spectacle; if corrupt, it must heroically stand upon the low ground of its own sinfulness, and rise through penitence and righteousness.

This law of life is exhibited in the contrasted characters of Dimmesdale and Hester. Whatever errors of head or heart, or infelicity of circumstances, prevent Hester from fully realizing the Christian ideal of repentance, she sternly respects her moral relations to society. . . .

Another fact which appears in this book, is the downward tendency of sin; once let a soul be untrue, even though half in ignorance of its duty, and its world is disorganized, so that every step in its new path involves it in greater difficulties. The cardinal error, in this maze of guilt and wretchedness, is Hester's marriage with Chillingworth. . . .

Another fact more perplexing to a Christian moralist is here illustrated,—that a certain experience in sin enlarges the spiritual energies and the power to move the souls of men to noble results. The effects of Dimmesdale's preaching are perfectly credible, and moral, although he stood in false relations to those he addressed. True, the limitation at last came in his public exposure, yet we had almost said he could not have left his mark so deep upon the conscience of that community, had he lived and died otherwise. And Hester's error was the downward step in the winding stair leading to a higher elevation. This feature of the work, so far from being a blemish, is only a proof of the writer's insight, and healthy moral philosophy. He has portrayed sin with all its terrible consequences, yet given the other side of a problem which must excite our wonder, rebuke our shallow theories, and direct us to an all-embracing, infinite love for its solution.

In the character of Chillingworth appears another law,—the danger of cherishing a merely intellectual interest in the human soul. . . .

Passing from these points of the book to its general moral tone, we find the author's delineation of spiritual laws equalled by his healthy and profound religious sentiment. In justice to human nature, he shows all the palliative circumstances to guilt, while he is sternly true to eternal facts of morality. . . .

As a work of art, this book has great merits, shaded by a few conspicuous faults. We cannot too much admire the skill with which the tangled skein of counteracting law and character is unravelled, the compact arrangement and suggestive disposition of the parts. The analysis of character is also inimitable, and the style is a fit dress for the strange and terrible history it rehearses. Yet we shall be disappointed if we look for any remarkable delineation of character, or portraiture of historical manners. There is a certain ghastliness about the people and life of the book, which comes from its exclusively subjective character and absence of humor. The world it describes is untrue to actual existence; for, although such a tragedy may be acting itself in many a spot upon earth, yet it is hidden more deeply beneath the surface of existence than this, modified by a thousand trivialities, and joys, and humorous interludes of humanity. No puritan city ever held such a throng as stalks through the 'Scarlet Letter;' even in a well conducted mad-house, life is not so lurid and intense. The author's love for symbolism occasionally amounts to a ridiculous melo-dramatic perversity, as when it fathers such things as the minister's hand over his heart, and the hideous disfigurement of his bosom, Dame Hibbins from Gov. Bellingham's window screeching after Hester to go into the forest and sign the black man's book, and the meteoric 'A' seen upon the sky during the midnight vigil. . . .

The 'House of the Seven Gables,' is inferior to the 'Scarlet Letter' in artistic proportion, compactness and sustained power. It is not a jet of molten ore from a glowing furnace, but a work elaborated in thoughtful leisure, characterized by a more sober coloring, and less intensity of life than its predecessor. Yet whatever value the book may have lost by the absence of one class of peculiarities, is almost restored by the presence of another; for it cannot be denied, that as a whole, it is nearer actual life, and more comprehensively true to human nature, than any former work of its author.

Mr. Hawthorne has here attempted to describe the operation of spiritual laws in the midst of the modern life in New England. The tale is the development of the providential retribution for gain unrighteously acquired, while the social problem of aristocracy and democracy naturally branches out from the main idea. . . .

In passages, this work is not inferior to any of the author's books. The picture of Maule's execution; the description of the house and garden; Hepzibah opening the shop; the crowd seen from the arched window; the analysis of Clifford; Phœbe waking, walking to church, and becoming conscious of her love in the moonlight arbor, and the death of Judge Pyncheon, present an everfresh claim upon our admiration. The style is every way worthy of the theme; and although in some respects inferior to the 'Scarlet Letter,' the book has peculiar merits of its own, and is by far the most pleasing of its author's productions.

67. Hawthorne, Preface to the 1851 Edition

11 January 1851

The Author of 'Twice-Told Tales' has a claim to one distinction, which, as none of his literary brethren will care about disputing it with him, he need not be afraid to mention. He was, for a good many years, the obscurest man of letters in America.

These stories were published in magazines and annuals, extending over a period of ten or twelve years, and comprising the whole of the writer's young manhood, without making (so far as he has ever been aware) the slightest impression on the public. One or two among them, the 'Rill from the Town Pump,' in perhaps a greater degree than any other, had a pretty wide newspaper circulation; as for the rest, he had no grounds for supposing that, on their first appearance, they met with the good or evil fortune to be read by anybody. Throughout the time above specified, he had no incitement to literary effort in a reasonable prospect of reputation or profit, nothing but the pleasure itself of composition—an enjoyment not at all amiss in its way, and perhaps essential to the merit of the work in hand, but which, in the long run, will hardly keep the chill out of a writer's heart, or the numbness out of his fingers. To this total lack of sympathy, at the age when his mind would naturally have been most effervescent, the public owe it (and it is certainly an effect not to be regretted on either part) that the Author can show nothing for the thought and industry of that portion of his life, save the forty sketches, or thereabouts, included in these volumes.

Much more, indeed, he wrote; and some very small part of it might yet be rummaged out (but it would not be worth the trouble) among the dingy pages of fifteen- or twenty-year-old periodicals, or within the shabby morocco covers of faded souvenirs. The remainder of the

works alluded to had a very brief existence, but, on the score of brilliancy, enjoyed a fate vastly superior to that of their brotherhood, which
succeeded in getting through the press. In a word, the author burned
them without mercy or remorse, and, moreover, without any subsequent regret, and had more than one occasion to marvel that such very
dull stuff, as he knew his condemned manuscripts to be, should yet have
possessed inflammability enough to set the chimney on fire!

After a long while the first collected volume of the 'Tales' was
published. By this time, if the Author had ever been greatly tormented
by literary ambition (which he does not remember or believe to have
been the case), it must have perished, beyond resuscitation, in the dearth
of nutriment. This was fortunate; for the success of the volume was not
such as would have gratified a craving desire for notoriety. A moderate
edition was 'got rid of' (to use the publisher's very significant phrase)
within a reasonable time, but apparently without rendering the writer
or his productions much more generally known than before. The
great bulk of the reading public probably ignored the book altogether.
A few persons read it, and liked it better than it deserved. At an interval of three or four years, the second volume was published, and encountered much the same sort of kindly, but calm, and very limited
reception. The circulation of the two volumes was chiefly confined to
New England; nor was it until long after this period, if it even yet be the
case, that the Author could regard himself as addressing the American
public, or, indeed, any public at all. He was merely writing to his
known or unknown friends.

As he glances over these long-forgotten pages, and considers his way
of life while composing them, the Author can very clearly discern why
all this was so. After so many sober years, he would have reason to be
ashamed if he could not criticise his own work as fairly as another man's;
and, though it is little his business, and perhaps still less his interest, he
can hardly resist a temptation to achieve something of the sort. If
writers were allowed to do so, and would perform the task with perfect
sincerity and unreserve, their opinions of their own productions would
often be more valuable and instructive than the works themselves.

At all events, there can be no harm in the Author's remarking that
he rather wonders how the 'Twice-Told Tales' should have gained what
vogue they did than that it was so little and so gradual. They have the
pale tint of flowers that blossomed in too retired a shade,—the coolness
of a meditative habit, which diffuses itself through the feeling and observation of every sketch. Instead of passion there is sentiment; and, even

in what purport to be pictures of actual life, we have allegory, not always so warmly dressed in its habiliments of flesh and blood as to be taken into the reader's mind without a shiver. Whether from lack of power, or an unconquerable reserve, the Author's touches have often an effect of tameness; the merriest man can hardly contrive to laugh at his broadest humor; the tenderest woman, one would suppose, will hardly shed warm tears at his deepest pathos. The book, if you would see anything in it, requires to be read in the clear, brown, twilight atmosphere in which it was written; if opened in the sunshine, it is apt to look exceedingly like a volume of blank pages.

With the foregoing characteristics, proper to the production of a person in retirement (which happened to be the Author's category at the time), the book is devoid of others that we should quite as naturally look for. The sketches are not, it is hardly necessary to say, profound; but it is rather more remarkable that they so seldom, if ever, show any design on the writer's part to make them so. They have none of the abstruseness of idea, or obscurity of expression, which mark the written communications of a solitary mind with itself. They never need translation. It is, in fact, the style of a man of society. Every sentence, so far as it embodies thought or sensibility, may be understood and felt by anybody who will give himself the trouble to read it, and will take up the book in a proper mood.

This statement of apparently opposite peculiarities leads us to a perception of what the sketches truly are. They are not the talk of a secluded man with his own mind and heart (had it been so, they could hardly have failed to be more deeply and permanently valuable), but his attempts, and very imperfectly successful ones, to open an intercourse with the world.

The Author would regret to be understood as speaking sourly or querulously of the slight mark made by his earlier literary efforts on the Public at large. It is so far the contrary, that he has been moved to write this Preface chiefly as affording him an opportunity to express how much enjoyment he has owed to these volumes, both before and since their publication. They are the memorials of very tranquil and not unhappy years. They failed, it is true,—nor could it have been otherwise,—in winning an extensive popularity. Occasionally, however, when he deemed them entirely forgotten, a paragraph or an article, from a native or foreign critic, would gratify his instincts of authorship with unexpected praise,—too generous praise, indeed, and too little alloyed with censure, which, therefore, he learned the better to inflict upon himself. And, by the by, it is a very suspicious symptom of a deficiency of the popular element in a book when it calls forth no harsh criticism. This has been particularly the fortune of the 'TWICE-TOLD TALES.' They made no enemies, and were so little known and talked about that those who read, and chanced to like them, were apt to conceive the sort of kindness for the book which a person naturally feels for a discovery of his own.

This kindly feeling (in some cases, at least) extended to the Author, who, on the internal evidence of his sketches, came to be regarded as a mild, shy, gentle, melancholic, exceedingly sensitive, and not very forcible man, hiding his blushes under an assumed name, the quaintness of which was supposed, somehow or other, to symbolize his personal and literary traits. He is by no means certain that some of his subsequent productions have not been influenced and modified by a natural desire to fill up so amiable an outline, and to act in consonance with the character assigned to him; nor, even now, could he forfeit it without a few tears of tender sensibility. To conclude, however: these volumes have opened the way to most agreeable associations, and to the formation of imperishable friendships; and there are many golden threads interwoven with his present happiness, which he can follow up more or less directly, until he finds their commencement here; so that his pleasant pathway among realities seems to proceed out of the Dreamland of his youth, and to be bordered with just enough of its shadowy foliage to shelter him from the heat of the day. He is therefore satisfied with what the 'TWICE-TOLD TALES' have done for him, and feels it to be far better than fame.

68. From a notice in *Harper's New Monthly Magazine*

April 1851, ii, 712

Ticknor, Reed, and Fields have issued a new edition of *Twice Told Tales*, by NATHANIEL HAWTHORNE, with an original preface, and a portrait of the author. The preface is highly characteristic, and will be read with as much interest as any of the stories. Mr. Hawthorne presents some details of his literary autobiography, in which he relates the ill success of his first adventures as an author, with irresistible unction and naïveté. He claims to have been for a good many years the obscurest literary man in America. His stories were published in magazines and annuals, for a period comprising the whole of the writer's young manhood, without making the slightest impression on the public, or, with the exception of 'The Rill from the Town-Pump,' as far as he is aware, having met with the good or evil fortune to be read by any body. When collected into a volume, at a subsequent period, their success was not such as would have gratified a craving desire for notoriety, nor did they render the writer or his productions much more generally known than before. The philosophy of this experience is unfolded by the author without the slightest affectation of concealment, or any show of querulousness on account of its existence. On the contrary, he views the whole affair with perfect good humor, and consoles himself in the failure of large popularity, with the sincere appreciation which his productions received in certain gratifying quarters. They were so little talked about that those who chanced to like them felt as if they had made a new discovery, and thus conceived a kindly feeling not only for the book but for the author. The influence of this on his future literary labors is set forth with his usual half-comic seriousness. . . .

69. [E. P. Whipple], a review in *Graham's Magazine*

May 1851, xxxviii, 469

The success of 'The Scarlet Letter' has created an increased demand for the author's other writings, and we accordingly have here to notice a new and elegant edition of his short romances and tales, every page teeming with thought and brightened by genius. The volumes are prefaced by a genial introduction, and adorned by a likeness of Hawthorne from an exquisite portrait by G. Thomson, in which the artist has embodied the mind as well as delineated the features of the man. No person can judge of the scope and character of Hawthorne's peculiar powers, without first giving the present work an attentive and, we need not add, a delighted perusal. We envy the man who reads it for the first time. The volumes are composed of forty tales, embodying the mental experience of an extraordinary mind, during some dozen years of its sequestered activity, and bear the decisive signs of original and originating genius. There is nothing in English letters which they resemble, and they are accordingly to be considered a new contribution to imaginative literature. The individuality of Hawthorne presents a novel combination of mental and moral traits, a combination sufficiently forcible to be creative; and if the reader will scrutinize his consciousness after these stories have left their mark upon it, he will find that the impression left on his mind is absolutely new. In addition to his originality and novelty, Hawthorne has the further merit of being pleasing, and no cultivated mind can resist the subtle fascination of his mind. His style is the fluent and varying medium of his sentiment, thought, humor, pathos, and imagination—of all those qualities, indeed, which look out upon the reader from the grand face and head which adorns the present edition.

A WONDER-BOOK FOR GIRLS AND BOYS

1851

70. Hawthorne, Preface

15 July 1851

The author has long been of opinion that many of the classical myths were capable of being rendered into very capital reading for children. In the little volume here offered to the public, he has worked up half a dozen of them, with this end in view. A great freedom of treatment was necessary to his plan; but it will be observed by every one who attempts to render these legends malleable in his intellectual furnace, that they are marvellously independent of all temporary modes and circumstances. They remain essentially the same, after changes that would affect the identity of almost anything else.

He does not, therefore, plead guilty to a sacrilege, in having sometimes shaped anew, as his fancy dictated, the forms that have been hallowed by an antiquity of two or three thousand years. No epoch of time can claim a copyright in these immortal fables. They seem never to have been made; and certainly, so long as man exists, they can never perish; but, by their indestructibility itself, they are legitimate subjects for every age to clothe with its own garniture of manners and sentiment, and to imbue with its own morality. In the present version they may have lost much of their classical aspect (or, at all events, the author has not been careful to preserve it), and have, perhaps, assumed a Gothic or romantic guise.

In performing this pleasant task,—for it has been really a task fit for hot weather, and one of the most agreeable, of a literary kind, which he ever undertook,—the author has not always thought it necessary to write downward, in order to meet the comprehension of children. He has generally suffered the theme to soar, whenever such was its tendency, and when he himself was buoyant enough to follow without an effort.

Children possess an unestimated sensibility to whatever is deep or high, in imagination or feeling, so long as it is simple, likewise. It is only the artificial and the complex that bewilder them.

71. Unsigned review in
Graham's Magazine

January 1852, xl, 111

Hawthorne may have written more powerful stories than those contained in this volume, but none so truly delightful. The spirit of the book is so essentially sunny and happy, that it creates a jubilee in the brain as we read. It is intended for children, but let not the intention cheat men and women out of the pleasure they will find in its sparkling and genial pages. The stories are told by a certain Eustice Bright to a mob of children, whose real names the author suppresses, but whom he re-baptizes with the fairy appellation of Primrose, Periwinkle, Sweet Fern, Dandelion, Blue-Eye, Clover, Huckleberry, Cowslip, Squash-blossom, Milk-weed, Plantain and Butter-cup. The individuality of these little creatures is happily preserved, especially in the criticisms and applications they make after each story is told; and the reader parts with them unwillingly, and with the hope (which the author should not disappoint) of resuming their acquaintance in another volume. The stories, six in number, are classical myths, re-cast to suit the author's purpose, and told with exquisite grace, simplicity and playfulness. The book will become the children's classic, and, to our taste, is fairly the best of its kind in English literature. It is a child's story-book informed with the finest genius.

72. [Henry F. Chorley], from a review in the *Athenaeum*

17 January 1852, pp. 81–2

. . . Among the sterling pleasures which, though few, make rich amends for the many grievances and misconstructions that await honest critics, there is none so great as the discovery and support of distant and unknown genius. Such pleasure the *Athenæum* may fairly claim in the case of Mr. Hawthorne. Like all men so richly and specially gifted, he has at last found his public,—he is at last looked to, and listened for:—but it is fifteen years since we began to follow him in the American periodicals, and to give him credit for the power and the originality which have since borne such ripe fruit in 'The Scarlet Letter' and 'The House of the Seven Gables.' Little less agreeable is it to see that acceptance after long years of waiting seems not to have soured the temper of the writer,—not to have encouraged him into conceit,—not to have discouraged him into slovenliness. Like a real artist, Mr. Hawthorne gives out no slightly planned nor carelessly finished literary handiwork. His '*Wonder Book*' is meant for children,—yet like the faëry tales of Hans Christian Andersen, grown people will be glad to devour its wonders themselves. Six of the old classical legends of Mythology,—those of Medusa, Midas, Pandora, the Golden Apples, Philœmon and Baucis, and Pegasus—are told by him in an entirely new fashion, and with such grace, humour and poetry, as few command. Mr. Hawthorne is sure that 'these old immemorial fables' are neither Greek nor Chaldæan, nor exclusively belonging to any country whatsoever,—and has accordingly claimed and substantiated his right to handle them in his own fashion. More delicious stories for children we have rarely seen. The framework, too, is at once pleasantly American and gracefully fantastic.

THE SNOW-IMAGE, AND OTHER TWICE-TOLD TALES

1851

73. Hawthorne, Preface

1 November 1851

TO HORATIO BRIDGE, ESQ., U.S.N.

My dear Bridge,—Some of the more crabbed of my critics, I understand, have pronounced your friend egotistical, indiscreet, and even impertinent, on account of the Prefaces and Introductions with which, on several occasions, he has seen fit to pave the reader's way into the interior edifice of a book. In the justice of this censure I do not exactly concur, for the reasons, on the one hand, that the public generally has negatived the idea of undue freedom on the author's part by evincing, it seems to me, rather more interest in those aforesaid Introductions than in the stories which followed; and that, on the other hand, with whatever appearance of confidential intimacy, I have been especially careful to make no disclosures respecting myself which the most indifferent observer might not have been acquainted with, and which I was not perfectly willing my worst enemy should know. I might further justify myself, on the plea that ever since my youth, I have been addressing a very limited circle of friendly readers, without much danger of being overheard by the public at large; and that the habits thus acquired might pardonably continue, although strangers may have begun to mingle with my audience.

But the charge, I am bold to say, is not a reasonable one, in any view which we can fairly take of it. There is no harm, but, on the contrary, good, in arraying some of the ordinary facts of life in a slightly idealized and artistic guise. I have taken facts which relate to myself, because they chance to be nearest at hand, and likewise are my own property. And, as for egotism, a person, who has been burrowing, to his utmost ability, into the depths of our common nature, for the purposes of psychological romance,—and who pursues his researches in that dusky region, as he

235

needs must, as well by the tact of sympathy as by the light of observation,—will smile at incurring such an imputation in virtue of a little preliminary talk about his external habits, his abode, his casual associates, and other matters entirely upon the surface. These things hide the man, instead of displaying him. You must make quite another kind of inquest, and look through the whole range of his fictitious characters, good and evil, in order to detect any of his essential traits.

Be all this as it may, there can be no question as to the propriety of my inscribing this volume of earlier and later sketches to you, and pausing here, a few moments, to speak of them, as friend speaks to friend; still being cautious, however, that the public and the critics shall overhear nothing which we care about concealing. On you, if on no other person, I am entitled to rely, to sustain the position of my Dedicatee. If anybody is responsible for my being at this day an author, it is yourself. I know not whence your faith came; but, while we were lads together at a country college,—gathering blueberries, in study-hours, under those tall academic pines; or watching the great logs, as they tumbled along the current of the Androscoggin; or shooting pigeons and gray squirrels in the woods; or bat-fowling in the summer twilight; or catching trouts in that shadowy little stream which, I suppose, is still wandering river-ward through the forest,—though you and I will never cast a line in it again,—two idle lads, in short (as we need not fear to acknowledge now), doing a hundred things that the Faculty never heard of, or else it had been the worse for us,—still it was your prognostic of your friend's destiny, that he was to be a writer of fiction.

And a fiction-monger, in due season, he became. But was there ever such a weary delay in obtaining the slightest recognition from the public, as in my case? I sat down by the wayside of life, like a man under enchantment, and a shrubbery sprung up around me, and the bushes grew to be saplings, and the saplings became trees, until no exit appeared possible, through the entangling depths of my obscurity. And there, perhaps, I should be sitting at this moment, with the moss on the imprisoning tree-trunks, and the yellow leaves of more than a score of autumns piled above me, if it had not been for you. For it was through your interposition—and that, moreover, unknown to himself—that your early friend was brought before the public, somewhat more prominently than theretofore, in the first volume of 'Twice-told Tales.' Not a publisher in America, I presume, would have thought well enough of my forgotten or never-noticed stories to risk the expense of print and paper; nor do I say this with any purpose of casting odium on the respectable fraternity of booksellers, for their blindness to my wonderful merit. To confess the truth, I doubted of the public recognition quite as much as they could do. So much the more generous was your confidence; and knowing, as I do, that it was founded on old friendship rather than cold criticism, I value it only the more for that.

So, now, when I turn back upon my path, lighted by a transitory gleam of public favor, to pick up a few articles which were left out of my former collections, I take pleasure in making them the memorial of our very long and unbroken connection. Some of these sketches were among the earliest that I wrote, and, after lying for years in manuscript, they at last skulked into the Annuals or Magazines, and have hidden themselves there ever since. Others were the productions of a later period; others, again, were written recently. The comparison of these various trifles—the indices of intellectual conditions at far separate epochs—affects me with a singular complexity of regrets. I am disposed to quarrel with the earlier sketches, both because a mature judgment discerns so many faults, and still more because they come so nearly up to the standard of the best that I can achieve now. The ripened autumnal fruit tastes but little better than the early windfalls. It would, indeed, be mortifying to believe that the summer-time of life has passed away, without any greater progress and improvement than is indicated here. But—at least so I would fain hope—these things are scarcely to be depended upon, as measures of the intellectual and moral man. In youth, men are apt to write more wisely than they really know or feel; and the remainder of life may be not idly spent in realizing and convincing themselves of the wisdom which they uttered long ago. The truth that was only in the fancy then may have since become a substance in the mind and heart.

I have nothing further, I think, to say; unless it be that the public need not dread my again trespassing on its kindness, with any more of these musty and mouse-nibbled leaves of old periodicals, transformed, by the magic arts of my friendly publishers, into a new book. These are the last. Or, if a few still remain, they are either such as no paternal partiality could induce the author to think worth preserving, or else they have got into some very dark and dusty hiding-place, quite out of my own remembrance, and whence no researches can avail to unearth them. So there let them rest.

Very sincerely yours,

N. H.

74. [E. A. Duyckinck], from a review in the *Literary World*

10 January 1852, x, 22–4

. . . how long this delicate genius of our countryman lay hidden from the world! Ten years ago—twenty years ago he was quite the man he is now, one in whom is now acknowledged one of the finest poetical products of America; and America, too, had then abundant need of such an exhibition in the meagre list of her stinted authorship—yet he remained unknown. . . .

[Quotes Preface 'On you, if' to 'mind and heart'.]

Kindly and feeling companions on our pilgrimage have been these tales of Nathaniel Hawthorne, touching this rough, noisy, every-day life with a gentle wand when the clash, and turmoil, and commonness disappear, and a fine spiritual structure arises, with all its accessories calm and purified from earth. The vulgarity of life is gone, but its truth and earnestness remain. It is no Chesterfieldian vacuum of politeness, but a world of realities, a camera obscura of the outer world delicately and accurately painted on the heart. Yes, it is the great honor of Nathaniel Hawthorne to be as far removed as the poles from vulgarity.

Every one knows the skill with which he links the spiritual to the material world. There is one story in this book which should have had a supernatural conclusion. It is 'My Kinsman Major Molineaux.' A youth comes down from the country, in old provincial times, to seek his relative, a man of consequence in Boston. His inquiries for him through the city are picturesquely and statuesquely rendered. Everybody bilks him. The joke winding up this series of beautifully drawn pictures is, that the traveller's distinguished kinsman is that night to be tarred and feathered. Most lame and impotent conclusion! Humor is not Hawthorne's forte, at least humor of the broad comic stamp; but for a bit of sentimental refinement, or life irradiated by the imagination, he is the man.

An apologue, The Man of Adamant, is artistically told—the feeling for proportion being strong through all Hawthorne's writings. It is an illustration of the misery and moral death of isolation; how a man's heart turns to stone when he is separated from his kind by spiritual pride. Richard Digby, the hero of this little story, takes refuge in a cave, where the process of petrifaction finally encrusts his body in its stony mantle:

[Quotes 'In this manner he' to 'symptom of the disease'.]

Ethan Brand, or, the Unpardonable Sin, is a story of similar moral—of the penalty of cultivating the intellect to the exclusion of the heart.

The Great Stone Face, like the Great Carbuncle, is an anecdote of the White Mountains, transmuted into a fine legend.

In Hawthorne's descriptive vein there are some admirable sketches in this book, as Main Street, Salem, Old News, and the Bell's Biography. We take the opening passage of the last:

[Quotes 'Harken to our' to 'an Indian chief'.]

For the sequel to this and a hundred other improvements of our common life, by the light of poetry, we must commend the reader to this attractive volume of the genius of Nathaniel Hawthorne.

75. [E. P. Whipple], a review in *Graham's Magazine*

April 1852, xl, 443

This is a collection of Mr. Hawthorne's Sketches and Stories which have not been included in any previous collection, and comprise his earliest and latest contributions to periodical literature. It can hardly add to his great reputation, though it fully sustains it. 'The Snow-Image,' with which the volume commences, is one of those delicate creations which no imagination less etherial and less shaping than Hawthorne's could body forth. 'Main Street,' a sketch but little known, is an exquisite series of historical pictures, which bring the persons and events in the history of Salem, vividly home to the eye and the fancy. 'Ethan Brand,' one of the most powerful of Hawthorne's works, is a representation of a man, tormented with a desire to discover the unpardonable sin, and ending with finding it in his own breast. 'The Great Stone Face,' a system of philosophy given in a series of characterizations, contains, among other forcible delineations, a full length of Daniel Webster. The volume contains a dozen other tales, some of them sunny in sentiment and subtile in humor, with touches as fine and keen as Addison's or Steele's: and others dark and fearful, as though the shadow of a thunder-cloud fell on the author's page as he wrote. All are enveloped in the atmosphere, cheerful or sombre, of the mood of mind whence they proceeded, and all convey that unity of impression which indicates a firm hold on one strong conception. As stories, they arrest, fasten, fascinate attention; but, to the thoughtful reader they are not merely tales, but contributions to the philosophy of the human mind.

THE BLITHEDALE ROMANCE

1852

76. Hawthorne, Preface

May 1852

In the 'BLITHEDALE' of this volume, many readers will probably suspect a faint and not very faithful shadowing of BROOK FARM, in Roxbury, which (now a little more than ten years ago) was occupied and cultivated by a company of socialists. The Author does not wish to deny, that he had this Community in his mind, and that (having had the good fortune, for a time, to be personally connected with it) he has occasionally availed himself of his actual reminiscences, in the hope of giving a more lifelike tint to the fancy-sketch in the following pages. He begs it to be understood, however, that he has considered the Institution itself as not less fairly the subject of fictitious handling, than the imaginary personages whom he has introduced there. His whole treatment of the affair is altogether incidental to the main purpose of the Romance; nor does he put forward the slightest pretensions to illustrate a theory, or elicit a conclusion, favorable or otherwise, in respect to Socialism.

In short, his present concern with the Socialist Community is merely to establish a theatre, a little removed from the highway of ordinary travel, where the creatures of his brain may play their phantasmagorical antics, without exposing them to too close a comparison with the actual events of real lives. In the old countries, with which Fiction has long been conversant, a certain conventional privilege seems to be awarded to the romancer; his work is not put exactly side by side with nature; and he is allowed a license with regard to every-day Probability, in view of the improved effects which he is bound to produce thereby. Among ourselves, on the contrary, there is as yet no such Faery Land, so like the real world, that, in a suitable remoteness, one cannot well tell the difference, but with an atmosphere of strange enchantment, beheld through which the inhabitants have a propriety of their own. This atmosphere is what the American romancer needs. In its absence, the beings of imagination are compelled to show themselves in the same category as actually living mortals; a necessity that generally renders the paint and pasteboard of their composition but too painfully discernible. With the idea of partially obviating this difficulty, (the sense of which has always pressed very heavily upon him,) the Author has ventured to make free with his old, and affectionately remembered home, at BROOK FARM, as being, certainly, the most romantic episode of his own life—essentially a day-dream, and yet a fact—and thus offering an available foothold between fiction and reality. Furthermore, the scene was in good keeping with the personages whom he desired to introduce.

These characters, he feels it right to say, are entirely fictitious. It would, indeed, (considering how few amiable qualities he distributes among his imaginary progeny,) be a most grievous wrong to his former excellent associates, were the Author to allow it to be supposed that he has been sketching any of their likenesses. Had he attempted it, they would at least have recognized the touches of a friendly pencil. But he has done nothing of the kind. The self-concentrated Philanthropist; the high-spirited Woman, bruising herself against the narrow limitations of her sex; the weakly Maiden, whose tremulous nerves endow her with Sibylline attributes; the Minor Poet, beginning life with strenuous aspirations, which die out with his youthful fervor—all these might have been looked for, at BROOK FARM, but, by some accident, never made their appearance there.

The Author cannot close his reference to this subject, without expressing a most earnest wish that some one of the many cultivated and philosophic minds, which took an interest in that enterprise, might now give the world its history. Ripley, with whom rests the honorable paternity of the Institution, Dana, Dwight, Channing, Burton, Parker, for instance—with others, whom he dares not name, because they veil themselves from the public eye—among these is the ability to convey both the outward narrative and the inner truth and spirit of the whole affair, together with the lessons which those years of thought and toil must have elaborated, for the behoof of future experimentalists. Even the brilliant Howadji might find as rich a theme in his youthful reminiscenses of BROOK FARM, and a more novel one—close at hand as it lies —than those which he has since made so distant a pilgrimage to seek, in Syria, and along the current of the Nile.

77. From an unsigned review in the *Spectator*

3 July 1852, xxv, 637–8

Nathaniel Hawthorne is an American writer of considerable repute in his own country, and of high though limited estimation here. Extensive *popularity* he is not perhaps likely to achieve, because his great merit lies rather in execution than in structure—in finish than in breadth. 'Materiem superabat opus'[1]: but the matter in a large sense is what strikes the generality, who have not taste, skill, or patience to relish minutiæ of execution, even if those minutiæ are combined into a complete whole, as is the case with Nathaniel Hawthorne.

Although Hawthorne undoubtedly belongs to the class of novelists, his novels are of a peculiar kind. A story there is, and in its principal characters and catastrophe generally a striking though singular one; but its conduct partakes more of the simplicity of the so-called classical drama than of the rapid narrative, the various incidents, and the mutations of fortune which distinguish the romantic school. So far as *story* is concerned, the effect is probably as good in an abridgment as in the work itself; the great merit of the writer arising from the manner in which the details are worked up, as with some of Washington Irving's sketches. This manner might probably run into tediousness, and the singularity verge upon plagiarism, were the themes European and hackneied. But Mr. Hawthorne, by taking his subjects from the actual life or traditions of America, gives to his detailed pictures an attraction of novelty to English readers, while the just delineation and easy elegance of his pen impart an air of vivid truthfulness to his reflections and elaborate descriptions.

The framework of *The Blithedale Romance* is founded on a Communist attempt of some enthusiasts at Blithedale farm, rather after the fashion of Godwin and other admirers of the principles of the first French Revolution than after modern Socialist schemes. At the head of this party, though hardly belonging to it, is Hollingsworth, a quondam

---

[1] *Materiem superabat opus*: The manner conquered the matter (Ovid, *Metamorphosis.* II.5).

blacksmith, of great heart and natural powers, whose whole soul is embarked in a project for reforming criminals. A woman called Zenobia, of full rich beauty, independent spirit, and high intellectual power, is also a principal; and represents the advocate of the 'rights of women,' chafing at the control which convention and the real or assumed superiority of man enforce upon the sex. There is also another conspicuous female, Priscilla, who exhibits the clinging, devoted, feminine character, seeing nothing but the person she loves. The real story turns upon the passion of Zenobia for Hollingsworth, his preference for Priscilla, and the suicide of the proud, passionate, ill-regulated, queenly Zenobia. The story, however, is expanded by many matters, and some mysteries not thoroughly cleared up; including a mesmerist adventurer, Westervelt, a veiled lady, a connexion between Westervelt and Zenobia, and some use of magnetism. The preface distinctly repudiates all idea of sketching the actors in a real project of philanthropy, which Blithedale was: but Margaret Fuller seems to have suggested the idea of Zenobia, as Hollingsworth may be a fancy sketch of Elihu Burritt.

One lesson impressed by the book is the danger of a woman, no matter what her gifts, deviating ever so little from the received usages of society; though this lesson is by no means new, and it had been done as conclusively already. Another, a newer and a more important moral, is the danger of earnest philanthropy swallowing up every other feeling, till your genuine philanthropist becomes as hard, as selfish, and as indifferent to the individual results of his conduct, if it forward his end, as the most adamantine conqueror or statesman. This feeling, the more extreme and engrossing in proportion to the comprehension of the philanthropist's nature and consciousness, without any sort of regard to the feasibility or importance of its project, is not perhaps so much illustrated by the catastrophe as noted by passing occurrences. It is a moral, however, that cannot be too strongly impressed; for it actuates classes as well as individuals, and with a less sense of responsibility. . . .

Mr. Hawthorne is not a disciple of that school of human perfectibility which has given rise to plans of pantisocracy and similar Arcadias.

78. [Henry F. Chorley], from a review in the *Athenaeum*

10 July 1852, pp. 741–3

When 'The Antiquary' was published, the large world of readers, disappointed on finding in the new novel no hero or heroine of the same quality as *Fergus* and *Flora M'Ivor*—and no scene of breathless interest to correspond with those in the *Kaim of Derncleugh*—were for a moment cold to the racy humour of *Monkbarns*, the spectral remorse of *Elspeth*, and the independant vagabondism of *Edie Ochiltree*. The criticism was, that the third Waverley Novel was inferior to its predecessors, because it was unlike them—and that the 'Great Unknown' had 'written himself out,' because he had produced a story in a new manner worked out by new creations.—Some temporary judgment of the kind, for similar reasons, may possibly be passed upon 'The Blithedale Romance.' Nevertheless, Mr. Hawthorne's third tale, in our judgment, puts the seal on the reputation of its author as the highest, deepest, and finest imaginative writer whom America has yet produced. Long years ago, ere the 'Twice-told tales' were collected, when we were tracing the anonymous author of 'David Swan' through the periodicals of the New Country, we were convinced that Mr. Hawthorne might become such a man.—It is with more than ordinary satisfaction, then, that we record his having justified that belief. He does not appear to be either spoiled or rendered inert by his success, so hardly won and so patiently waited for. He is courageous, versatile, solicitous to attain the highest artistic finish while he preserves his individuality—and, what is as much to the purpose, his nationality.

This 'Blithedale Romance' is eminently an American book;—not, however, a book showing the America of *Sam Slick* and *Leather-Stocking*,—the home of the money-making droll rich in mother-wit, or of the dweller in the wilderness rich in mother-poetry.—Mr. Hawthorne's America is a vast new country, the inhabitants of which have neither materially nor intellectually as yet found their boundaries,—a land heaving with restless impatience, on the part of some among its best spirits, to exemplify new ideas in new forms of civilized life. But

Mr. Hawthorne knows that in America, as well as in worlds worn more threadbare, poets, philosophers and philanthropists however vehemently seized on by such fever of vain-longing, are forced to break themselves against the barriers of Mortality and Time—to allow for inevitable exceptions—to abide unforeseen checks,—in short, to re-commence their dream and their work with each fresh generation, in a manner tantalizing to enthusiasts who would grasp perfection for themselves and mankind, and that instantaneously.—The author's sermon is none the less a sermon because he did not mean it as such. He must be fully believed when he tells us that, while placing the scene of his third tale in a Socialist community he had no intention of pronouncing upon Socialism, either in principle or in practice. Mr. Hawthorne's preface assures us that he conjured up his version of Brook Farm, Roxbury, merely as a befitting scene for the action of certain beings of his mind, without thought of lesson or decision on a question so grave and complex. This, however, makes him all the more valuable as a witness. The thoughtful reader will hardly fail to draw some morals for himself from a tale which, though made up of exceptional personages, is yet true to human characteristics and human feelings, and pregnant with universal emotion as well as with deep special meaning.

The imaginary narrator, a 'minor poet,' is the least earnest of the four persons who complicate and divide the interest of this romance. Though his heart is, like theirs, staked in the game, gain or loss is of less mortal moment to him than to his companions. He can observe the strife of passions, and write a ballad over the killed and the wounded. We note this peculiarity in Miles Coverdale, as illustrating Mr. Hawthorne's fine dramatic sense of what is fit and probable. 'The Blithedale Romance' could not have been told either by Hollingsworth the rugged, self-engrossed philanthropist, or by Zenobia the gorgeous theatrical beauty who aspired after female emancipation, or by Priscilla the pale, nervous *somnambule.*—The last paragraph has but incompletely sketched the *dramatis personæ:*—but let it pass. Three of these, the Poet, the wealthy and sumptuous Zenobia (who was, to boot, a woman of genius), and the one-idead Philanthropist, joined the experimental community at Blithedale, in weariness at the plight of old society, and in hope of being able to originate some state more Paradisaic and productive of good to all and to each. We must, by extracting a passage or two, show in how shrewd yet how loving a spirit Mr. Hawthorne deals with the fulfilment of such a project. Here is the first Socialist supper party.—

[Quotes ch. 4, 'We all sat' to 'sympathy like this'; ch. 8, 'On the whole' to 'into a faggot' and 'The peril of' to 'one substance'.]

The reader is not, however, to imagine that 'The Blithedale Romance' is a cold or prosy essay, done up after the fashion of a gilt pill, with a few incidents enabling the reader to swallow its wisdom. Though rich in thought and suggestion, the tale is full of mystery, suspense, and passion, exciting the strongest interest. Besides Zenobia, Hollingsworth, and the Poet-narrator, the Blithedale Community included, as we have said, the timid, pale girl Priscilla,—who appeared to have dropped into the midst of it from the clouds, and who joined the company with no idea higher or more general than that of satisfying her own heart's yearning for shelter and escape. Stern and self-engrossed as was Hollingsworth—nay, because of his stern earnestness,—he contrived to fascinate both Zenobia and Priscilla: the former resolving to place her wealth at his disposal,—the latter submitting her heart to him long ere she guessed that it was gone from her. The two women were thus brought into unconscious rivalry: and excellently true to nature is the manner—as tender as it is real—in which Mr. Hawthorne manages to maintain the individuality of each. We do not remember any study of the passionate woman of genius, in which her whole heart-struggle is so distinctly portrayed, without the impression of what is unfeminine and repulsive being produced as this of Zenobia. . . .

[Quotes three long passages illustrating Hawthorne's descriptive style.]

Long as are the above remarks and selections, they are far from illustrating all the phases of appeal to admiration and sympathy exhibited in this remarkable book of a remarkable writer. We have no fear as regards its ultimate fate in this country,—and much hope that its writer will make many more additions to the treasury of Fiction.—His tales, as we have already said, are national while they are universal,—his sentences are pregnant with meaning,—and his style is rich and original.

79. [Charles Hale], a review in *To-Day*

17 July 1852, ii, 42

Hale (1831-82), a politician and journalist, was the son of the editor of the *Boston Daily Advertiser* and founded *To-Day: A Boston Literary Journal* in 1852.

This book is marked with all the beauties and all the faults which Mr. Hawthorne's genius strews over his works. It is full of graceful description, dancing humor, delicate appreciation of character, and contemplative views of the relations of individuals to each other in confined societies. It has also the mysticism which adds a charm, and that which carries a gloom, to many of his writings. The story upon which the series of pictures and conversations is centred is shrouded with doubt, by being told by one who is a spectator, and not an actor; and a sort of supernatural glow is given to its results, by the ignorance in which the reader has been kept by the supposed ignorance of the narrator. Hawthorne does not give us his pictures or his battles covered by a fog; but there is an unnatural light, now so lurid that we cannot see distinctly by it, and now so glaring that we can scarcely see at all, except to recognize dark shadows, which makes even his smiles ghastly, and his mildest incidents catastrophes.

The scene is laid at 'Brook Farm,' the locality in this neighborhood of a 'community' now separated; but the author disavows having taken either character or incident from the parties who were actually there assembled. It is a romance supposed to be founded upon the life of persons gathered together with the purpose of first avoiding, but eventually improving, the world. In fact, however, the whole incident and action of the story is based upon the conventionalities of life, and the passions recognized as those most fostered by society as it is. We can hardly avoid the feeling that a covert sneer at that which is considered good by those who live 'in the world,' and also at those who would try to live above the things of the world, imbues every chapter.

Some parts of the book suggest unconscious imitations of 'Wilhelm Meister;' but its close, and perhaps its tenor, belong more to the Hoffman school. It cannot be read without pleasure, although the pleasure is constantly subdued by the presence of a constructed fatalism, which, though not incorrect perhaps in any instance, shadows and gives a sombre tone to the picture. If it were to rest pleasantly, as a whole, in the memory, the last sixty or seventy pages, with all their melodrama,— deeply studied and highly wrought, but melodrama still,—should be torn off.

With all this, we feel that Mr. Hawthorne has added a new laurel to his crown by this book. We have dwelt more upon what strikes us as its faults, than we should, did we not know that its beauties and its power would be recognized by every intelligent reader, and that no word of ours will dim the justly earned reputation of the author.

80. From an unsigned review in the *Literary World*

24 July 1852, xi, 52–4

Any one who expects to see Ripley of the Tribune, his companions Dana and Curtis, the Howadji, 'shown up' in this volume, had better reserve his coin in his breeches-pocket, and leave this book unpurchased. A Romance by Nathaniel Hawthorne means no such literal or decipher-able interpretation of the real world. It is a step into quite another existence, ghostly, ideal, unsubstantial, where thinly-draped spiritualities float hither and thither in their limbo of vanities.

For ourselves we should like to have seen this experiment at social life treated in a more matter-of-fact way—as an objective thing—a subject, after all the heroics were disposed of, for humor, good nature, and laughter. If Charles Dickens, for instance, with his large, healthy, observing eye, had been among the members for a fortnight, or that choice spirit, the author of 'Paul Pry,' had, in the best-natured way in the world, turned his steps to Roxbury after his celebrated visit to Little Pedlington! But this, as we have said, is a treatment which Hawthorne never could have contemplated. Still we cannot but think, for this world, the preservation of the flesh and blood texture about our ghostliness something very desirable. It may be a searching, conscientious operation on rare occasions to take our spirits out of their bodily cases and look at them nakedly, even in the thin, dry atmosphere of New England speculation; but we are convinced that, for the ordinary entertainment of life, such spectacles are, to say the least, unprofitable. Bodies are given to us for protection of the soul.

Hawthorne is a delicate spiritual anatomist, with scalpel and probe in hand, demonstrating to the minutest fibre the constitution of the human heart, and like every-day surgeons oftener and more curiously exhibiting disease than health.

The spiritualities and more powerful scenes of this book are not to be brought into the glare of a weekly newspaper. The reader will find them in the volume, of a strength and nicety of grasp not inferior to the writing of the Scarlet Letter, or the tragedy of the Seven Gables.

81. Unsigned review in the *Christian Examiner*

September 1852, lv, 292–4

The preface to this captivating volume is by no means the least important part of it. And yet we would advise all readers who wish to peruse the work under an illusion which will add an intense interest to its pages, to postpone the preface till they have gone through the book. Certainly one has reason to believe that Mr. Hawthorne is presenting in these pages a story, which, however it may depend for its decorative and fanciful details upon his rich imagination, is essentially a delineation of life and character as presented at 'Brook Farm.' It is well known that he was a member of that community of amiable men and women, who undertook there to realize their ideas of a better system of social relations. He fixes there the scene of his story, with frequent reference to the localities around, keeping up a close connection with the neighboring city of Boston; and the volume owes very much of its lifelike fidelity of representation to the reader's supposition that the characters are as real as the theory and the institution in which they have their parts. Yet in the preface Mr. Hawthorne, with a charming frankness which neutralizes much of the charm of his story, repudiates altogether the matter-of-fact view so far as regards his associates at 'Brook Farm,' and pleads necessity as his reason for confounding fact and fiction.

We cannot but regard the license which Mr. Hawthorne allows himself in this respect as open to grave objection. Seeing that many readers obtain all their knowledge of historical facts from the incidental implications of history which are involved in a well-drawn romance, we maintain that a novelist has no right to tamper with actual verities. His obligation to adhere strictly to historic truth is all the more to be exacted whenever the character and good repute of any real person are involved. Now Mr. Hawthorne is a daring offender in this respect. It is the only drawback upon our high admiration of him. We trust he will take no offence at this our free expression of opinion, when, while offering to him a respectful and grateful homage for all the spiritual glow and all the human wisdom which we find on his pages, we venture to question his right to misrepresent the facts and characters of assured history. If he shaded and clouded his incidents somewhat more obscurely, if he removed them farther back or farther off from the region of our actual sight and knowledge, he would be safer in using the privileges of the romancer. But he gives us such distinct and sharp boundary lines, and deals so boldly with matters and persons, the truth of whose prose life repels the poetry of his fiction, that we are induced to confide in him as a chronicler, rather than to indulge him as a romancer. Thus in his 'Scarlet Letter' he assures us in his preface that he has historical papers which authenticate the story that follows. That story involves the gross and slanderous imputation that the colleague pastor of the First Church in Boston, who preached the Election Sermon the year after the death of Governor Winthrop, was a mean and hypocritical adulterer, and went from the pulpit to the pillory to confess to that character in presence of those who had just been hanging reverently upon his lips. How would this outrageous fiction, which is utterly without foundation, deceive a reader who had no exact knowledge of our history! We can pardon the anachronism, in the same work, by which the little children in Boston are represented as practising for the game of annoying Quakers half a score of years before such a thing as a Quaker had been heard of even in Old England. But we cannot admit the license of a novelist to go the length of a vile and infamous imputation upon a Boston minister of a spotless character. In his 'Blithedale Romance,' Mr. Hawthorne ventures upon a similar freedom, though by no means so gross a one, in confounding fact and fiction. So vividly does he present to us the scheme at Brook Farm, to which some of our acquaintance were parties, so sharply and accurately does he portray some of the incidents of life there, that we are irresistibly impelled to fix the real names of men and women to the characters of his book. We cannot help doing this. We pay a tribute to Mr. Hawthorne's power when we confess that we cannot believe that he is drawing upon his imagination. We ask, Whom does he mean to describe as Zenobia? Is it Mrs. ——, or Miss ——? Then, as we know that no one of the excellent women who formed the community at 'Brook Farm' was driven to suicide by disappointed love, we find ourselves constructing the whole character from a combination of some half a dozen of the women whose talents or peculiarities have made them prominent in this neighborhood. We can gather up in this way all the elements of his Zenobia, except the comparatively unimportant one of queenly beauty which he ascribes to her. We leave to the help-meet of the author to settle with him the issue that may arise from his description of himself as a bachelor.

Having thus relieved our minds of the disagreeable part of a critic's duty, we are the more free to express our delight and gratitude, after the perusal of the book before us. Mr. Hawthorne is a writer of marvellous power, a most wise and genial philosopher, a true poet, and a skilful painter. We have gained instruction from his pages, of the most difficult kind to obtain, of the most valuable sort for use. The quiet humor, the good-tempered satire, which has no element of cynicism, the analysis of character, with the tracing of the deeper motives which fashion its outer workings and its inner growth, the clear vision for truth, and, above all, the sagacity which distinguishes between the really spiritual in thought and life and the morbid phenomena which so often propose themselves as spiritualities,—these are the tokens of a master-mind in our author. We thank him most heartily for this book, and gratefully acknowledge that it has offered to us wise and good lessons which ought to make us strong for faith and duty.

82. [E. P. Whipple], a review in *Graham's Magazine*

September 1852, xli, 333–4

Hawthorne wrote to Fields on 3 May 1852 to say that he had just handed over to Whipple the manuscript of *The Blithedale Romance* 'and stand ready to burn it or print it, just as he may decide' [MS., Berg Collection, New York Public Library].

In the first flush of a romancer's fame, there is rarely any distinct recognition of the peculiar originality of his powers as distinguished from other great novelists, who equally fasten the interest and thrill the hearts of their readers. The still, small voice of analysis is lost amid thunders of applause. In the case of Hawthorne this mode of reception does but little justice either to the force or refinement of his powers. It is only when we explore the sources of his fascination, when we go over the processes of his mind in creation, that we can realize the character and scope of his genius, and estimate, on true principles, the merit of each succeeding product of his pen. It is obvious to every reader that his mind is at once rich in various faculties, and powerful in its general action; that he possesses observation, fancy, imagination, passion, wit, humor; but a great writer can never be accurately described in those abstract terms which apply equally to all great writers, for such terms give us only the truth as it is *about* the author, not the truth as it is *in* him. The real question relates to the modification of his powers by his character; the tendency, the direction, the coloring, which his faculties receive in obeying the primary impulses of his individuality. This brings us at once to the sharpest test to which an author can be subjected, for it puts to him that searching query which instantly dissolves the most plausible bubbles—has he novelty of nature? Is he an absolutely new power in literature? It is Hawthorne's great felicity that he can stand the remorseless rigor of this test. He is not made up by culture, imitation, appropriation, sympathy, but has grown up in obedience to vigorous innate principles and instincts seated in his own nature; his power and peculiarity can be analyzed into no inspirations caught from other minds, but conduct us back to their roots in his original constitution. Thus he has imagination, and he has humor; but his imagination is not the imagination of Shelley or the imagination of Richter; neither is his humor the humor of Addison or the humor of Dickens; they are both essentially *Hawthorneish,* and resent all attempts to identify them with faculties in other minds. His style, again, in its clearness, pliability, and melodious ease of movement, reminds us of the style of Addison, of Scott, and of Irving, in making us forget itself in attending to what it conveys; but for that very reason every vital peculiarity of it is original, for what it conveys is the individuality of Hawthorne, and there is not a page which suggests, except to the word-mongers and period-balancers of mechanical criticism, even an unconscious imitation of any acknowledged master of diction. This contented movement within the limitations of his own genius, this austere confinement of his mind to that 'magic circle' where none can walk but he, this scorn of pretending to be a creator in regions of mental effort with which he can simply sympathize—all declare the sagacious honesty, the instinctive intellectual conscientiousness of original genius. Hunt him when and where you will—lay traps for him—watch the most secret haunts and cosiest corners of his meditative retirement—and you never catch him strutting about in borrowed robes, gorgeous with purple patches cut from transatlantic garments, or adroitly filching felicities from transcendental pockets. Inimitable in his own sphere, he has little temptation to be a poacher in the domains of other minds.

It is evident, if what we have said be true, that the criticism to be applied to Hawthorne's works must take its rules of judgment from the laws to which his own genius yields obedience; for if he differs from other writers, not in degree but in kind, if the process and purpose of his creations be peculiar to himself, and especially if he draws from an experience of life from which others have been shut out, and has penetrated into mysterious regions of consciousness, a pioneer in the unexplored wildernesses of thought—it is worse than ridiculous to prattle the old phrases, and apply the accredited rules of criticism to an entirely new product of the human mind. The objections of Hawthorne, if objections there be, do not relate to the exercise of his powers but to his nature itself. His works are the offspring of that; proceed as certainly from it as a deduction from a premise; and criticism can do little in detecting any break in the links of that logic of passion and imagination, any discordance in that unity of law, which presides over the organization of each product of his mind. But we are willing to admit, that criticism may advance a step beyond this, and after conceding the power and genuineness of a work of art, can still question the excellence of the spirit by which it is animated; can, in short, doubt the validity, denounce the character, and attempt to weaken the influence, of the *kind* of genius its analysis lays open.

The justice of such a criticism applied to Hawthorne would depend on the notion which the critic has of what constitutes excellence in kind. The ordinary demand of the mind in a work of art, serious as well as humorous, is for geniality—a demand which admits of the widest variety of kinds which can be included within a healthy and pleasurable directing sentiment. Now Hawthorne is undoubtedly exquisitely genial, at times, but in him geniality cannot be said to predominate. Geniality of general effect comes, in a great degree, from tenderness to persons; it implies a conception of individual character so intense and vivid, that the beings of the author's brain become the objects of his love; and this love somewhat blinds him to the action of those spiritual laws which really control the conduct and avenge the crimes of individuals.

In Hawthorne, on the contrary, persons are commonly conceived in their relations to laws, and hold a second place in his mind. In 'The Scarlet Letter,' which made a deeper impression on the public than any romance ever published in the United States, there is little true characterization, in the ordinary meaning of the term. The characters are not really valuable for what they are, but for what they illustrate. Imagination is predominant throughout the work, but it is imagination in its highest analytic rather than dramatic action. And this is the secret of the strange fascination which fastens attention to its horrors. It is not Hester or Dimmesdale that really interest us, but the spectacle of the human mind open to the retribution of violated law, and quivering in the agonies of shame and remorse. It is the law and not the person that is vitally conceived, and accordingly the author traces its sure operation with an unshrinking intellect that, for the time, is remorseless to persons. As an illustration of the Divine order on which our conventional order rests, it is the most moral book of the age; and is especially valuable as demonstrating the superficiality of that code of ethics, predominant in the French school of romance, which teaches obedience to individual instinct and impulse, regardless of all moral truths which contain the generalized experience of the race. The purpose of the book did not admit of geniality. Adultery has been made genial by many many poets and novelists, but only by considering it under a totally different aspect from that in which Hawthorne viewed it. Geniality in 'The Scarlet Letter' would be like an ice-cream shop in Dante's Inferno.

In 'The House of Seven Gables,' we perceive the same far-reaching and deep-seeing vision into the duskiest corners of the human mind, and the same grasp of objective laws, but the interest is less intense, and the subject admits of more relief. There is more of character in it, delineated however on some neutral ground between the grotesque and the picturesque, and with flashes of supernatural light darting occasionally into the picture, revealing, by glimpses, the dread foundations on which the whole rests. It contains more variety of power than 'The Scarlet Letter,' and in the characters of Clifford and Phebe exhibits the extreme points of Hawthorne's genius. The delineation of Clifford evinces a metaphysical power, a capacity of watching the most remote movements of thought, and of resolving into form the mere film of consciousness—of exhibiting the mysteries of the mind in as clear a light as ordinary novelists exhibit its common manifestations—which might excite the wonder of Kant or Hegel. Phebe, on the contrary, though shaped from the finest materials, and implying a profound insight into the subtilest sources of genial feeling, is represented dramatically, is a pure embodiment, and may be deemed Hawthorne's most perfect character. The sunshine of the book all radiates from her; and there is hardly a 'shady place' in that weird 'House,' into which it does not penetrate.

'The Blithedale Romance,' just published, seems to us the most perfect in execution of any of Hawthorne's works, and as a work of art, hardly equalled by anything else which the country has produced. It is a real organism of the mind, with the strict unity of one of Nature's own creations. It seems to have grown up in the author's nature, as a tree or plant grows from the earth, in obedience to the law of its germ. This unity cannot be made clear by analysis; it is felt in the oneness of impression it makes on the reader's imagination. The author's hold on the central principle is never relaxed; it never slips from his grasp; and yet every thing is developed with a victorious ease which adds a new charm to the interest of the materials. The romance, also, has more thought in it than either of its predecessors; it is literally crammed with the results of most delicate and searching observation of life, manners and character, and of the most piercing imaginative analysis of motives and tendencies; yet nothing seems labored, but the profoundest reflections glide unobtrusively into the free flow of the narration and description, equally valuable from their felicitous relation to the events and persons of the story, and for their detached depth and power. The work is not without a certain morbid tint in the general coloring of the mood whence it proceeds; but this peculiarity is fainter than is usual with Hawthorne.

The scene of the story is laid in Blithedale, an imaginary community on the model of the celebrated Brook Farm, of Roxbury, of which Hawthorne himself was a member. The practical difficulties in the way of combining intellectual and manual labor on socialist principles constitute the humor of the book; but the interest centres in three characters, Hollingsworth, Zenobia, and Priscilla. These are represented as they appear through the medium of an imagined mind, that of Miles Coverdale, the narrator of the story, a person indolent of will, but of an apprehensive, penetrating, and inquisitive intellect. This discerner of spirits only tells us his own discoveries; and there is a wonderful originality and power displayed in thus representing the characters. What is lost by this mode, on definite views, is more than made up in the stimulus given both to our acuteness and curiosity, and its manifold suggestiveness. We are joint watchers with Miles himself, and sometimes find ourselves disagreeing with him in his interpretation of an act or expression of the persons he is observing. The events are purely mental, the changes and crises of moods of mind. Three persons of essentially different characters and purposes, are placed together; the law of spiritual influence, the magnetism of soul on soul begins to operate; and the processes of thought and emotion are then presented in perfect logical order to their inevitable catastrophe. These characters are Hollingsworth, a reformer, whose whole nature becomes ruthless under the dominion of one absorbing idea—Zenobia, a beautiful, imperious, impassioned, self-willed woman, superbly endowed in person and intellect, but with something provokingly equivocal in her character—and Priscilla, an embodiment of feminine affection in its simplest type. Westervelt, an elegant piece of earthliness, 'not so much born as damned into the world,' plays a Mephistophelian part in this mental drama; and is so skilfully represented that the reader joins at the end, with the author, in praying that Heaven may annihilate him. 'May his pernicious soul rot half a grain a day.'

With all the delicate sharpness of insight into the most elusive move-ments of Consciousness, by which the romance is characterized, the drapery cast over the whole representation, is rich and flowing, and there is no parade of metaphysical acuteness. All the profound and penetrating observation seems the result of a certain careless felicity of aim, which hits the mark in the white without any preliminary posturing or elaborate preparation. The stronger, and harsher passions are represented with the same ease as the evanescent shades of thought and emotion. The humorous and descriptive scenes are in Hawthorne's best style. The peculiarities of New England life at the present day are admirably caught and permanently embodied; Silas Foster and Hollings-worth being both genuine Yankees and representative men. The great passage of the volume is Zenobia's death, which is not so much tragic as tragedy itself. In short, whether we consider 'The Blithedale Romance' as a study in that philosophy of the human mind which peers into the inmost recesses and first principles of mind and character, or a highly colored and fascinating story, it does not yield in interest or value to any of Hawthorne's preceding works, while it is removed from a comparison with them by essential differences in its purpose and mode of treatment, and is perhaps their superior in affluence and fineness of thought, and masterly perception of the first remote workings of great and absorbing passions.

83. Notice in the *Southern Quarterly Review*

October 1852, n.s., vi, 543

We are inclined to think this very pretty story quite as successful, as a work of art, as any of the preceding volumes of our author. It has all their defects, and these defects are such as seem inseparable from the writer's mind. These lie chiefly in the shaping and conception of the work, and in the inadequate employment of his characters. Their results do not co-operate with their natures; and the events are not always accommodated to the moral of the personage. The catastrophe rarely satisfies the reader, and seldom accords with poetical propriety. Instead of Zenobia committing suicide, an action equally shocking and unnecessary, he should have converted her, by marriage—the best remedy for such a case—from the error of her ways, and left her, a mother, with good prospects of a numerous progeny. Apart from faults such as this, the book is full of beauties. The character of Hollingsworth is admirably drawn in most respects.

84. From an unsigned essay, 'Contemporary Literature of America', in the *Westminster Review*

October 1852, lviii, 592–8

. . . From fact we pass to fiction, and to the examination of Hawthorne's last production, in order to which we must brush aside the whole brood of negro tales now swarming amongst us. 'Uncle Tom' has become a notoriety; and the success of the book is the great literary fact of the day. Sir Walter Scott and Charles Dickens never addressed as many readers, in the same space of time, as Harriet Beecher Stowe. The extraordinary sale in England, however, is due, first of all, to the *price*, secondly to the *subject*, and finally to the *novelty* of the thing. Meanwhile it is a hopeful omen for the slave, that a universal sympathy has been excited in his behalf. 'The Blithedale Romance' will never attain the popularity which is vouchsafed (to borrow a pulpit vocable) to some of its contemporaries, but it is unmistakably the finest production of genius in either hemisphere, for this quarter at least—to keep our enthusiasm within limits so far. Of its literary merits we wish to speak, at the outset, in the highest terms, inasmuch as we intend to take objection to it in other respects. . . .

With our limited space, we cannot pretend to give even a faint outline of a tale which depends for its interest altogether upon the way of telling it. Hawthorne's *forte* is the analysis of character, and not the dramatic arrangement of events. 'To live in other lives, and to endeavour—by generous sympathies, by delicate intuitions, by taking note of things too slight for record, and by bringing his spirit into manifold acquaintance with the companions whom God assigned him—to learn the secret which was hidden even from themselves,'—this, which is the estimate formed of Miles Coverdale, has its original in the author himself. The adoption of the autobiographical form (now so common in fictions) is, perhaps, the most suitable for the exercise of such peculiar powers. Not more than six or seven characters are introduced, and only four of them are prominent figures. They have, therefore, ample room for displaying their individuality, and establishing each an independent interest in the reader's regards. But this is not without disadvantages, which become more apparent towards the close. The analysis of the characters is so minute, that they are too thoroughly individualized for dramatic co-operation, or for that graduated subordination to each other which tends to give a harmonious swell to the narrative, unity to the plot, and concentrated force to the issue. They are simply contemporaries, obliged, somehow, to be on familiar terms with each other, and, even when coming into the closest relationship, seeming rather driven thereto by destiny, than drawn by sympathy. It is well that the *dramatis personæ* are so few. They are a manageable number, and are always upon the stage; but had there been more of them, they would only have presented themselves there in turns, which, with Hawthorne's slow movement, would have been fatal to their united action and combined effect. Even with a consecutive narrative, and a concentration of interest, the current flows with an eddying motion, which tends to keep them apart, unless, as happens once or twice, it dash over a precipice, and then it both makes up for lost time, and brings matters to a point rather abruptly. But the main tendency is toward isolation—for the ruling faculty is analytic. It is ever hunting out the anomalous; it discovers more points of repulsion than of attraction; and the creatures of its fancy are all morbid beings— all 'wandering stars,' plunging, orbitless, into the abyss of despair— confluent but not commingling streams, winding along to the ocean of disaster and death; for all have a wretched end—Zenobia and Priscilla, Hollingsworth and Coverdale—the whole go to wreck. The queenly Zenobia drowns herself in a pool; her ghost haunts Hollingsworth through life; and, as for Coverdale, he falls into a moral scepticism more desolating than death. Hear him at middle age: 'As regards human progress, let them believe in it who can, and aid in it who choose. If I could earnestly do either, it would be all the better for my comfort.'

Is this the moral of the tale? It is but too appropriate. Poor Miles Coverdale! so genial, so penetrative, so candid—he begins by mocking others, and he ends with mocking himself! Hollingsworth's life teaches a solemn lesson to traffickers in humanity, and with due solemnity is it enforced. Priscilla's life is too shadowy and colourless to convey any lesson. She is a mere straw upon the current. And what of Zenobia? It is difficult to say what we may gather from her life—so many lives were in her! She discusses it herself with Coverdale (quite characteristic) on the eve of her fall. It is a wise point to settle, but she makes it out thus:

'A moral? Why this: that in the battle-fields of life, the downright stroke that would fall only on a man's steel head-piece, is sure to light upon a woman's heart, over which she wears no breastplate, and whose wisdom it is, therefore, to keep out of the conflict. Or thus: that the whole universe, her own sex and yours, and Providence or destiny to boot, make common cause against the woman who swerves one hair's breadth out of the beaten track. Yes; and add (for I may as well own it now) that, with that one hair's breadth, she goes all astray, and never sees the world in its true aspect afterwards.'

There is something very unartistic in such formal applications of moral or social truths, reminding us of the old homiletic fashion of making a 'practical improvement' of a discourse to saints, sinners, and all sorts of folk. It indicates imperfection in the construction and colouring of the picture. So many morals—one a-piece for Coverdale and Hollingsworth, and two and a-half for Zenobia—are symptomatic of weak moral power, arising from feebleness of moral purpose. Hawthorne has a rich perception of the beautiful, but he is sadly deficient in moral depth and earnestness. His moral faculty is morbid as well as weak; all his characters partake of the same infirmity. Hollingsworth's project of a penitentiary at Blithedale is here carried out in imagination. Hawthorne walks abroad always at night, and at best it is a moonlight glimmering which you catch of reality. He lives in the region and shadow of death, and never sees the deep glow of moral health anywhere. He looks mechanically (it is a habit) at Nature and at man through a coloured glass, which imparts to the whole view a pallid, monotonous aspect, painful to behold. And it is only because Hawthorne can see beauty in everything, and will look at nothing but beauty in anything, that he can either endure the picture himself, or win for it the admiration of others. The object of art is the development of beauty—not merely sensuous beauty, but moral and spiritual beauty. Its ministry should be one of pleasure, not of pain; but our anatomist, who removes his subjects to Blithedale, that he may cut and hack at them without interference, clears out for himself a new path in art, by developing the beauty of deformity! He would give you the poetry of the hospital, or the poetry of the dissecting-room; but we would rather not have it. Art has a moral purpose to fulfil; its mission is one of mercy, not of misery. Reality should only be so far introduced as to give effect to the bright ideal which Hope pictures in the future. In fact, a poet is nothing unless also a prophet. Hawthorne is the former; but few poets could be less of the latter. He draws his inspiration from Fate, not from Faith. He is not even a Jeremiah, weeping amid the ruins of a fallen temple, and mourning over the miseries of a captive people. He is a Mephisto-philes, doubtful whether to weep or laugh; but either way it would be in mockery. 'It is genuine tragedy, is it not?' said Zenobia (referring to the fatal blow which laid her hopes prostrate), at the same time coming out 'with *a sharp, light laugh.*' Verily, a tragedy!—burlesqued by much of the same maniac levity. That 'Blithedale' itself should end in smoke, was, perhaps, fit matter for mirth; that Hollingsworth's huge tower of selfishness should be shattered to pieces was poetically just; but that the imperial Zenobia should be vanquished, was to give the victory to Despair. Zenobia is the only one in the group worthy to be the Trustee of Human Right, and the Representative of Human Destiny; and she, at least, should have come out of all her struggles in regal triumph. But, after the first real trial of her strength with adversity, and when there was resolution yet left for a thousand conflicts, to throw her into that dirty pool, and not even to leave her there, but to send her base-hearted deceiver, and that lout of a fellow, Silas Foster, to haul her out, and to let the one poke up the corpse with a boat-hook, and the other tumble it about in the simplicity of his desire to make it look more decent—these, and many other things in the closing scene, are an outrage upon the decorum of art, as well as a violation of its purpose. That such things do happen, is no reason why they should be idealized; for the Ideal seeks not to imitate Reality, but to perfect it. The use it makes of that which *is* true, is to develope that which *ought* to be true.

We are cautioned, in the preface, against the notion (otherwise very liable to be entertained) that this is a history of Brook Farm under a fictitious disguise. . . . Imaginary as the characters are, however, the supposition that Zenobia is an apograph of Margaret Fuller, may not be so far wrong. That extraordinary woman could not have been absent from the mind of the novelist—nay, must have inspired his pencil, whilst sketching 'the high-spirited woman bruising herself against the narrow limitations of her sex.' And, in so far as it is the embodiment of this sentiment or relation, we may have in the career of Zenobia (not in its details, but in its essential features), a missing chapter in Margaret

Fuller's life—unwritten hitherto, because never sufficiently palpable to come under the cognizance of the biographer, and only capable of being unveiled by the novelist, whose function it is to discern the intents of the heart, and to describe things that are not as though they were. We may, at least, venture to say that the study of Zenobia will form an excellent introduction to the study of her supposed prototype. There are problems both in biography and in history which imagination only can solve; and in this respect, 'Blithedale,' as a whole, may tell a truer tale with its fictions than Brook Farm with its facts. Hence it is that our author, while expressing an earnest wish that the world may have the benefit of the latter, felt that it belonged to him to furnish it with the former. . . .

But here, again, Hawthorne disappoints us, and again through his lack of moral earnestness. Everybody will naturally regard this story, whether fact or fiction, as a socialistic drama, and will expect its chief interest as such to be of a moral kind. 'Blithedale,' whatever may be its relation to Brook Farm, is itself a socialistic settlement, with its corresponding phases of life, and therefore involves points both of moral and material interest, the practical operation of which should have been exhibited so as to bring out the good and evil of the system. But this task Hawthorne declines, and does not 'put forward the slightest pretensions to illustrate a theory, or elicit a conclusion favourable or otherwise to Socialism.' He confines himself to the delineation of its picturesque phases, as a 'thing of beauty,' and either has no particular convictions respecting its deeper relations, or hesitates to express them. It was not necessary for him to pass judgment upon the theories of Fourier or Robert Owen. He had nothing to do with it as a theory; but as a phase of life it demanded appropriate colouring. Would he paint an ideal slave-plantation merely for the beauty of the thing, without pretending to 'elicit a conclusion favourable or otherwise' to slavery? Could he forget the moral relations of this system, or drop them out of his picture, 'merely to establish a theatre a little removed from the highway of ordinary travel, where the creatures of his brain may play their phantasmagorical antics without exposing them to too close a comparison with the actual events of real life?' In respect of involving moral relations, the two cases are analogous, and the one may be rendered morally colourless with no more propriety than the other. 'Blithedale,' then, as a socialistic community, is merely used here as a scaffolding—a very huge one—in the construction of an edifice considerably smaller than itself! And then, the artist leaves the scaffolding standing!

Socialism, in this romance, is prominent enough to fill the book, but it has so little business in it, that it does not even grow into an organic part of the story, and contributes nothing whatever toward the final catastrophe. It is a theatre—and, as such, it should have a neutral tint; but it should also be made of neutral stuff; and its erection, moreover, should not be contemporaneous with the performance of the play. But the incongruity becomes more apparent when we consider the kind of play acted in it. Take the moral of Zenobia's history, and you will find that Socialism is apparently made responsible for consequences which it utterly condemned, and tried, at least, to remedy. We say, apparently, for it is really not made responsible for anything, good, bad, or indifferent. It forms a circumference of circumstances, which neither mould the characters, nor influence the destinies, of the individuals so equivocally situated,—forms, in short, not an essential part of the picture, but an enormous fancy border, not very suitable for the purpose for which it was designed. Zenobia's life would have been exhibited with more propriety, and its moral brought home with more effect, in the 'theatre' of the world, out of which it really grew, and of which it would have formed a vital and harmonious part. Zenobia and Socialism should have been acted in the ready-made theatre of ordinary humanity, to see how it would fare with them there. Having occupied the ground, Hawthorne owed it to truth, and to a fit opportunity, so to dramatize his experience and observation of Communistic life, as to make them of practical value for the world at large.

85. [Orestes Brownson], from a review in *Brownson's Quarterly Review*

October 1852, n.s., vi, 561–4

Mr. Hawthorne has fully established his reputation as the first writer, in his favorite line, our American literature can boast, and we have nothing to do, when he publishes a new work, but to judge it without judging the general character, merits, or demerits of the author. . . . In the class of literature he has selected he has no superior amongst us, probably no equal, but we owe it to ourselves to say that the class is not the highest.

The Blithedale Romance we have read with a good deal of interest, for much in it is connected with some of our personal friends. . . . Mr. Hawthorne was for a brief period one of the communitarians, attracted more, we apprehend, by the romance of the thing, than by any real belief in the principles of the establishment, or deep sympathy with its objects. Under the name of Miles Coverdale he sketches in this little volume his experiences during his brief residence at Brook Farm as one of the regenerators of society, mingled with various romantic instances which did, and many more which did not happen, but which might have happened. He has treated the institution and the characters of his associates with great delicacy and tenderness. He enjoys a quiet laugh and indulges in a little gentle satire, now and then, and upon the whole makes the experiment appear, as it in reality was, a folly born of honest intentions and fervent zeal in behalf of society. But he brings none of the real actors in the comedy, or farce, or tragedy, whichever it may have been, upon the stage. We can recognize in the personages of his Romance individual traits of several real characters who were there, but no one has his or her whole counterpart in one who was actually a member of the community. There was no actual Zenobia, Hollingsworth, or Priscilla there, and no such catastrophe as described ever occurred there; yet none of these characters are purely imaginary. Hollingsworth, in relation to his one fixed purpose, had his counterpart there, and the author has given us in Miles Coverdale much that we dare affirm to have been true of himself. Still, there has been no encroachment on the sanctity of private character, and pain has been given, we presume, to no private feeling. The reader may collect from the Romance the general tone, sentiment, hopes, fears, and character of the establishment, but very little of the actual persons engaged in it, or of the actual goings-on at Brook Farm.

In the character of Hollingsworth the author has been exceedingly successful, as also in the sketch of Old Moody. They both stand out from his canvas lifelike, and impress us as real living and breathing men. Priscilla is too shadowy, and suffers by a comparison with the Alice and Fanny of Sir Edward Bulwer Lytton. It is a character which Hawthorne is too much of a man to delineate; he takes to it not naturally, and his likeness degenerates into a caricature. Zenobia stands in exact contrast to Priscilla, and is neither more complete nor truthful. Mr. Hawthorne succeeds better with men and boys than with women and girls. He knows that vanity is a characteristic of women, and that every woman must have something to love, and that she will love the strong-minded and strong-willed man who speaks to her as a master, if also a man of deep feeling and strong passions, in preference to the man remarkable chiefly for personal beauty, gentle manners, kind feelings, and the readiness with which he devotes himself to her will and makes her pleasure his own. But this denotes no great insight into the female character. Love in its proper sense is no more a want of woman's heart than of man's, and she is in general less capable of love, and less steady in it, than man. All the pretty things said of woman's love in novels and romances are mere moonshine. Woman has a more impulsive and passionate nature than man, and love with her is an emotion. She craves not so much love as a strong emotion of some sort, it matters little to her of what sort, and hence she is always captivated by the man who gives her the most excitement, produces in her the strongest emotions, though nine tenths of the time they are emotions of anger or grief. Any woman would die for a Hollingsworth sooner than bestow a single smile on a Miles Coverdale. But Zenobia was not the woman to commit suicide because disappointed,—she who had been, as novelists say, 'in love' no one knows how many times, and whose heart had become as tough as sole-leather. No, if that had been all, she would have taken a cathartic, and found herself as well as ever. Women of her large experience and free principles never kill themselves for disappointed affection. Hollingsworth did not cause her to commit so rash an act by rejecting her for Priscilla. It was not the loss of her lover, but the loss of her estate, and with it the means of indulging her tastes or gratifying her vanity, though even that is to suppose her exceedingly unwomanly, as in fact she was. Indeed, her suicide was a blunder, and had, according to all that we have been able to observe of woman's nature, no *ratio sufficiens*. There was nothing in what we are told that would cause her to commit it, and we think bluff old Silas Foster was quite right when he refused to believe it, and declared it impossible. It is always an æsthetic no less than a moral defect for an author to make his heroes or heroines commit suicide. It is an exceeding bungling way of disposing of a character you do not know what to do with, and shows poverty of invention as much as the common practice of novelists of making their lovers first-cousins. If the individual must die, why, give him a fever, the consumption, the plague, the cholera, the cholic; or if you can find no disease to carry him off, sure you can find a villain, a bravo, or an assassin kind enough to relieve you of your embarrassment. One of the best things Hawthorne says is, that, if Zenobia could have fore-seen what a fright she would appear after having drowned herself, she would never have done so foolish a thing. Then, again, self-murder is too great a sin, and leaves too little possibility of contrition before the soul leaves the body, to be decked out with all the charms of romance and the choicest flowers of poetry. To introduce it in popular literature thus decked out is to conceal its horror, and to render the young, the passionate, the giddy, and the vain familiar with the thought of seek-ing repose by plunging themselves into hell, where there is no rest for ever. We do not charge Mr. Hawthorne with approving suicide,—by no means; but he so manages the suicide of Zenobia that the shock we feel is not that of horror for her sin, but of indignation at the man who is assumed to have wronged her, and regret at the loss of so beauti-ful a woman.

Aside from the terrible catastrophe and a little too much tenderness for experiments like that of Brook Farm, *The Blithedale Romance* may be read by our Protestant community with great advantage, and per-haps nothing has been written among us better calculated to bring modern philanthropists into deserved disrepute, and to cure the young and enthusiastic of their socialistic tendencies and dreams of world reform. There is a quiet satire throughout the whole on all philanthropic and communitarian enterprises that will not fail to have a good effect on our community. In this point of view, we can commend *The Blithe-dale Romance*, not as unobjectionable, indeed, but as little so as we can expect any popular work to be that emanates from an uncatholic source.

86. From an unsigned review in the *American Whig Review*

November 1852, xvi, 417–24

We believe that if Mr. Hawthorne had intended to give a faithful por-trait of Brook Farm and its inmates, he would have signally failed. He has no genius for realities, save in inanimate nature. Between his characters and the reader falls a gauze-like veil of imagination, on which their shadows flit and move, and play strange dramas replete with second-hand life. An air of unreality enshrouds all his creations. They are either dead, or have never lived, and when they pass away they leave behind them an oppressive and unwholesome chill.

This sluggish antiquity of style may suit some subjects admirably. When, as in the Scarlet Letter, the epoch of the story is so far removed from the present day as to invest all the events with little more than a reminiscent interest; when characters and customs were so different to to all circumstance that jostles us in the rude, quick life of today, and when we do not expect to meet, in the long corridors of Time down which the author leads us, any company beyond the pale shadowy ancestry with whose names we are faintly familiar, but with whom we have no common sympathies. . . . Mr. Hawthorne deals artistically with shadows. There is a strange, unearthly fascination about the fair spectres that throng his works, and we know no man who can distort nature, or idealize abortions more cleverly than the author of the Scarlet Letter. But we question much, if we strip Mr. Hawthorne's works of a certain beauty and originality of style which they are always sure to possess, whether the path which he has chosen is a healthy one. . . . When an author sits down to make a book, he should not alone consult the inclinations of his own genius regarding its purpose or its construction. If he should happen to be imbued with strange, saturnine doctrines, or be haunted by a morbid suspicion of human nature, in God's name let him not write one word. Better that all the beautiful, wild thoughts with which his brain is teeming should moulder for ever in neglect and darkness, than that one soul was overshadowed by stern, uncongenial dogmas, which should have died with their Puritan fathers. It is not alone necessary to produce a work of art. The soul of beauty is Truth, and Truth is ever progressive. The true artist therefore endeavors to make the world better. He does not look behind him, and dig out of the graves of past centuries skeletons to serve as models for his pictures; but looks onward for more perfect shapes, and though sometimes obliged to design from the defective forms around him, he infuses, as it were, some of the divine spirit of the future into them, and lo! we love them with all their faults. But Mr. Hawthorne discards all idea of successful human progress. All his characters seem so weighed down with their own evilness of nature, that they can scarcely keep their balance, much less take their places in the universal march. . . . It is a pity that Mr. Hawthorne should not have been originally imbued with more universal tenderness. It is a pity that he displays nature to us so shrouded and secluded, and that he should be afflicted with such a melancholy craving for human curiosities. His men are either vicious, crazed, or misanthropical, and his women are either unwomanly, unearthly, or unhappy. His books have no sunny side to them. They are unripe to the very core.

We are more struck with the want of this living tenderness in the Blithedale Romance than in any of Mr. Hawthorne's previous novels. In the Scarlet Letter and the House of the Seven Gables, a certain gloominess of thought suited the antiquity of the subjects; but in his last performance, the date of the events, and the nature of the story, entitle us to expect something brighter and less unhealthy. The efforts of any set of hopeful, well-meaning people to shame society into better ways, are deserving of respect, as long as they do not attempt to interfere with those sacred foundation-stones of morality on which all society rests. . . . It is sad mistake to suppose them stern exponents of the gross and absurd system laid down by Fourier. They are not, at least as far as our knowledge goes, either dishonest or sensual. They do not mock at rational rights, or try to overturn the constitution of society. We believe their ruling idea to be that of isolating themselves from all that is corrupt in the congregations of mankind called cities, and seek in open country and healthy toil the sweets and triumphs of a purer life. One would imagine that dealing with a subject like this would in some degree counteract Mr. Hawthorne's ascetic humor. . . . From the beginning to the end, the Blithedale Romance is a melancholy chronicle, less repulsive, it is true, than its predecessors, but still sad and inexpressibly mournful. Not that the author has intended it to be uniformly pathetic. It is very evident that he sat down with the intention of writing a strong, vigorous book, upon a strong, vigorous subject; but his own baneful spirit hovered over the pages, and turned the ink into bitterness and tears.

Let us review his characters, and see if we can find anything genial among them. Hollingsworth in importance comes first. A rude fragment of a great man. Unyielding as granite in any matters on which he has decided, yet possessing a latent tenderness of nature that, if he had been the creature of other hands than Mr. Hawthorne's, would have been his redemption. But our author is deeply read in human imperfection, and lets no opportunity slip of thrusting it before his readers. . . .

Readers will perchance say that Mr. Hawthorne has a right to deal with his characters according to his pleasure, and that we are not authorized to quarrel with the length of their noses, or the angularities of their natures. No doubt. But, on the other hand, Mr. Hawthorne has no right to blacken and defame humanity, by animating his shadowy people with worse passions and more imperfect souls than we meet with in the world.

Miles Coverdale, the narrator of the tale, is to us a most repulsive being. A poet, but yet no poetry in his deeds. A sneering, suspicious, inquisitive, and disappointed man, who rejects Hollingsworth's advances because he fears that a connection between them may lead to some ulterior peril; who allows Zenobia to dominate over his nature, because she launches at him a few wild words, and who forsakes the rough, healthy life of Blithedale, because he pines for Turkey carpets and a sea-coal fire. Such is the man upon whose dictum Mr. Hawthorne would endeavor covertly to show the futility of the enterprise in whose favor he was once enlisted. . . .

The Zenobia of our author does not command our interest. Her character, though poetically colored, is not sufficiently powerful for a woman that has so far outstridden the even pace of society. She has a certain amount of courage and passion, but no philosophy. Her impulses start off in the wrong direction, nor does she seem to possess the earnestness necessary to induce a woman to defy public opinion. She is a mere fierce, wild wind, blowing hither and thither, with no fixity of purpose, and making us shrink closer every moment from the contact.

In truth, with the exception of Priscilla, who is faint and shadowy, the dramatis personæ at Blithedale are not to our taste. There is a bad purpose in every one of them—a purpose, too, which is neither finally redeemed nor condemned.

Notwithstanding the faults which we have alluded to, and which cling to Mr. Hawthorne tenaciously in all his works, there is much to be admired in the Blithedale Romance. If our author takes a dark view of society, he takes a bright one of nature. He paints truthfully and poetically, and possesses a Herrick-like fashion of deducing morals from flowers, rocks, and herbage, or any other little feature in his visionary landscape. . . .

On the socialist theory Mr. Hawthorne says little in the Blithedale Romance. . . . One of the most curious characteristics of the book is, that not one of the persons assembled at Blithedale treat the institution as if they were in earnest. Zenobia sneers at it—Coverdale grumbles at it—Hollingsworth condemns—Priscilla alone endures it. . . .

In Priscilla, Mr. Hawthorne has essayed a delicate character, but in his portraiture he has availed himself of an ingenious expedient, which we know not whether to rank as intentional or accidental. In drawing a portrait, there are two ways of attaining delicacy of outline. One is by making the outline itself so faint and indistinct that it appears as it were to mingle with the surrounding shadow; the other and more difficult one is, to paint, and paint detail after detail, until the whole becomes so finished a work of art, so harmoniously colored, that one feature does not strike us more forcibly than another; so homogeneous in its aspect that outline, background and detail are all painted perfectly on our perceptions in a manner that defies analysis. Now, there is no question that the man who employs the first means has infinitely easier work than the last. He has nothing to do but conjure you up a pretty-looking ghost, and lo! the work is done. Mr. Hawthorne is fond of these ghosts. Priscilla is a ghost; we do not realize her, even to the end. Her connection with Westervelt is shadowy and ill-defined. Zenobia's influence over her nature is only indistinctly intimated. Her own mental construction is left almost an open question; and even when, in the crowning of the drama, we find her the support, the crutch of the rugged Hollingsworth, there is no satisfactory happiness wreathed about her destiny. . . .

That Mr. Hawthorne can paint vividly when he likes it, few who have read his novels can doubt. He possesses all the requisites for the task—power of language, felicity of collateral incident, and a certain subdued richness of style which is one of his greatest charms. The . . . description of the death of Zenobia is exquisitely managed. . . .

A thought crosses us, whether Mr. Hawthorne would paint a wedding as well as a death; whether he could conjure as distinctly before our vision the bridal flowers, as he has done the black, damp weeds that waved around the grave of Zenobia. We fear not. His genius has a church-yard beauty about it, and revels amid graves, and executions, and all the sad leavings of mortality.

LIFE OF FRANKLIN PIERCE

1852–53

87. From an unsigned essay, 'Hawthorne's Life of Pierce—Perspective', in the *Democratic Review*

September 1852, xxxi, 276–88

Nathaniel Hawthorne, has kindly compelled us to return to the subject of the ensuing Presidency. He has appeared in the hurly-burly world of politics, and that with a great man's life upon his hands. We must honor him and ourselves with a notice—N. Hawthorne, politician, is welcome.

It falls not often to the lot of the literary character to be the biographer of a President; neither does it fall to the lot of most Presidents to have a literary character for a biographer. . . . In fact, and truth, the biographies of our great men have all been thrown into the hands of lawyers, disposed of as goods and chattels to an executor and legatee in a will, and then badly disposed. . . . The real business of a biographer, the question what is biography, never enters their ridiculously special-pleading heads. They never imagine that to be a true biographer, one must be the man—must make himself the man, and that what one looks for in biography is not the mere writer, but the actual worker. . . . It is only by the clearest perception, and the most assiduous study, that even a 'literary man,' that is one who can write, can approximate to the idea of history. Few have ever done so. . . .

In such dearth of genius, we welcome most heartily to the field of political biography the elegant novelist of the Blythedale Romance and the Scarlet Letter.

It omens well for Frank Pierce's administration, that his biography, modest, unassuming as it is, deficient as it is in everything which could attract the lucubrations of the high-falutin order of literary genii, is the first which has attracted the attention of a proved and elegant writer, and of one who, from his literary triumphs and his warm, genial nature, is respected abroad and beloved at home. Hawthorne's work has not a tittle of rhodomontade. There is not in it, from cover to cover, a single sentence perversive of fact, apologetic of fact, or written only for effect. It is bald in parts, yet always *simplex munditiis*. It is not 'adorned with cuts,' nor has it any feature or attribute which could warrant the severest or most envious Whig critic in classing it among the 'campaign lives,' and other ephemeral publications which a presidential election usually hurries into existence. It is rather a memoir, or what the French style a *brochure*, than a biography. Yet it possesses one attribute in which most of our writers are deficient—proportion. Neither the early youth, nor the manhood, nor the military services, nor the forensic triumphs of its subject, are drawn out to an extent tedious to the reader or injurious to the remaining portions of the volume. It is what it assumes to be, the simple statement of a man's life, by a schoolfellow and friend, who is anxious that the world should duly estimate the most marked characteristics of a retiring yet great career. We have all met men, nay, known men of whom each of us could say and may have said —'He would be great, were he known—he would show himself noble had he a chance.' We have all said so much of some one dear friend. It is Hawthorne's happiness to have seen the prophecy and the Democratic leader—it is Frank Pierce's happiness to have such a biographer. . . .

The small volume before us is not indeed as full as the admirer, either of the author or his subject might legitimately desire. It possesses order, and proportion, even in its minuteness; but the narrative portion may be considered to end with the capture of the Mexican capital. The succeeding and concluding chapters are rather of the character of essay, than biographical, and denote rather a well intentioned Democratic desire in the writer, than great political aptitude.

88. [E. A. Duyckinck], from a review in the *Literary World*

25 September 1852, xi, 195–6

Mr. Hawthorne introduces his *Life of Franklin Pierce* with a kind of deprecatory apology, stating that the work would not have been 'voluntarily' undertaken by him, that 'this species of writing is remote from his tastes,' and that it has cost a sacrifice of some 'foolish delicacy' to enter upon the undertaking. We confess that the squeamishness appears to us altogether superfluous, not at all overcoming our settled repugnance to prefatory apologies—the very worst introduction an orator or author can make of himself. We hold it to be quite within the range of the ordinary duties of a man of letters to write such a life; nor can we share in the regrets expressed by many, that Nathaniel Hawthorne has stooped from 'the high region of his fancies' to perform the work.

Persons who object to the author of the Scarlet Letter engaging in this enterprise, must think the work itself either vicious or unnecessary, the manner of its execution bad, or some obvious motive of entering upon it corrupt. For the first of these cases, we hold more nobly of the state, as Malvolio says of the soul, than to be of that opinion. We are willing to think that any man who has undergone the scrutiny of a nominating Congress of either of the two great party divisions of the country, and been appointed one of the two candidates for the Presidency, between whom the choice for that high office is likely to be made —we are confident in maintaining, is a proper and honorable subject for biography. The interests of the country demand an account of him, and the best talent may be worthily employed in writing it. There are two points here worth noticing. An idea prevails among certain persons, that the business of politics is so essentially corrupt that its touch is defilement; and, as if to justify this view, a great deal of the political writing falls into inferior hands. . . . The work requires ability of a high rank: it should be carefully sought out, well paid accordingly, and the best writers should frankly and faithfully serve the public in this way. It is a species of work for the people, in which the author who leaves for it his more inviting individual occupations, should receive a cordial support. We thank Mr. Hawthorne for the good precedent of his life of Pierce.

The work itself being honorable and desirable, has Mr. Hawthorne brought any discredit upon himself by his manner of performing it? Is he an exaggerated, violent, untrue partisan, or does he serve the great universal aims of biography, by presenting a true and interesting picture of human life? No one who knows Mr. Hawthorne would attribute to him any conscious departure from the right. The biography of a living man, under these party circumstances, is necessarily a matter of eulogy, but what Mr. Pierce gains from this work will be from no false rhetoric or false positions. He is seen in his own natural height. There is no effort to prove him a 'great' man, or make him out a first rate subject for biography—there is no character drawing, or comparative analysis after the manner of Clarendon and Plutarch, but the man such as he is, in the relations which he has borne to the American people, in his associations of birth, his education, his development, public and military life—is simply and clearly presented. As a composition, Hawthorne's life bears with it an air of modesty, reality, and truthfulness. We question whether any other American writer could have overcome the inevitable difficulties of a piece of biography of a living character, or met more reasonably and fairly to everybody the voracious claims of partisan eulogy. It would not have been possible for him to make an ordinary hack job of it, nor has he attempted it.

Allowing the work in itself to be good and to be well performed, the cavil is then made, 'It may be all very well, but the work is evidently written for an office. A pretty spectacle, a retired, self-denying poet bidding high for a share of the spoils of office.' So pretty, that we should like to see it happen oftener, and public life the gainer by the successful result. If the ends are good to mankind in general, and the means taken are good, it is all nonsense to exclude the poet from the work. A poet cannot write poetry for ever, nor would he be able to live upon the proceeds should he do so. Literary men may and ought to take an active part in the affairs of the world, and there is no province where they are more wanted than the political.

So much for the fallacy implied in the censure we have heard from many lips—'We are sorry Hawthorne has done it.' Moreover, there being no good reasons why he should not do it, there appears one very good reason why he should. 'Nor can,' says he, 'it be considered improper (at least the author will never feel it so, although some foolish delicacy be sacrificed in the undertaking), that when a friend, dear to him almost from boyish days, stands up before his country, misrepresented by indiscriminate abuse on the one hand, and by aimless praise on the other, he should be sketched by one who has had opportunities of knowing him well, and who is certainly inclined to tell the truth.'

On strictly personal grounds we think this work a desirable one from Hawthorne. It has brought him down from the subtle metaphysical analysis of morbid temperaments, in which his pen has had somewhat too limited and painful a range, to a healthy encounter with living interests. There is no obscure subtlety or attenuated moonshine to be endured in the life of a democratic candidate for the Presidency. The masses want facts and deeds, clear narration, and everyday probability of motive. We appeal to Mr. Hawthorne, whether the attainment of these things in living biography costs him less intellectual effort than the description of his imaginary Pyncheons and Dimmesdales.

Having said thus much of this Life of Pierce, there is little need for us to enter into a detailed analysis of the book—the more particularly, as its general interest had already made it a familiar volume throughout the country. . . .

[Quotes three long passages illustrating Hawthorne's style.]

. . . For a peculiarly neat piece of Hawthorne's characterization, which shows of what he is capable were he further to enter upon a field to which his genius certainly invites him—that of American History, we may refer the reader to the story of the vacillating New Hampshire canvas for Governor, of the Reverend John Atwood. It is as choice a bit as the sketches of the politicians prefixed to the Scarlet Letter, and which have excited the admiration and the hostility of many of Mr. Hawthorne's commentators.

89. From an unsigned essay, 'Contemporary Literature of America', in the *Westminster Review*

1 January 1853, n.s., iii, 295

. . . Hawthorne's 'Life of General Pierce,' belongs to that mongrel species of literature called 'political biography.' It does its author no credit. We should not deem it worthy of notice did we not wish to give emphatic expression to our regret that Hawthorne should have written it. Not that we object to him using his pen in political discussion, for he is an American citizen as well as an author. He is, moreover, one of the General's former fellow-students at college, and might have been prompted by a noble and magnanimous desire to do justice to an old friend, whose sudden celebrity exposed him to the risk of crucifixion between hostile abuse and partisan praise. But we discover nothing noble in the work itself—nothing to indicate that it is not the production of a partisan who has been paid for the job. The writer is clearly out of his element; his genius forsakes him; and his usual thoughtfulness is replaced by declamatory panegyric. Franklin Pierce may deserve all the compliments here paid to him; but what excites our surprise is, that a writer so discriminating as Hawthorne usually is, should deal in compliments at all.

90. Charles Hale: An attack on Hawthorne's politics and philosophy, from an unsigned essay, 'Nathaniel Hawthorne', in *To-Day*

18 September 1852, ii, 177–83

Mr. Hawthorne presents himself before us in the triple aspect of the novelist, biographer, and politician. It is not to be expected, even of a man of so much versatility, that he should appear quite so well in each character; and we cannot but think that it is as a novelist that he is destined to win immortality. However that may be, a man who professes to combine such varied, not to say conflicting, gifts, and who is so prominently before the public in each of these departments, is not to be despatched with a flourish of the pen. . . .

We know Mr. Hawthorne's popularity, and we fully believe that he deserves it. He stands at the head of all the living writers of fiction in this country; and, in his peculiar vein, probably he has no equal any where. He does not, it is true, like other great novelists,—Fielding and Thackeray, for example,—present that large view of society as it is, which we find in 'Tom Jones' and 'Pendennis.' He prefers to take a profound but narrow view of some unusual phase of men and things; but, once in it, he shows himself a master. . . . There is a something unearthly about all his characters, as if he had been groping for them in the land of dreams, and conceived of them while laboring under an incubus. . . . Mr. Hawthorne must be a German. No Yankee or Englishman could ever invest with so complete a fog of mystery the commonest objects of our daily experience. . . .

Thus, in the 'House with the Seven Gables,' who but Hawthorne would conceive, and who but he would be able to invest with such a mysterious interest, the miserable fowls that lived in the garden? A cock, two hens, and a chicken,—to another man they would have been just what they were,—peculiarly uninteresting, being lean, useless, and seldom laying an egg,—offering no food either to one's stomach or his imagination. Any other fowls, who have come down in history, have been famous either for laying golden eggs or for saving Rome, or at least been noticeable for some imaginary virtue in the breed, like those scraggy and tail-less monsters, rejoicing in the name of Shanghai, who, in these latter days, deform the picturesque appearance of the New England barn-yard. But in Hawthorne's hands, these old Pyncheon fowls become mysteriously connected with the fate of the Pyncheon family, and mixed up with its destiny,—symbols of the life of the old house, and having all the personal traits of its old inhabitant. They are tutelary sprites or Banshees, wizened and crack-brained humorists on account of their solitary way of life, and from sympathy for Hepzibah, their lady-patroness. And think of an itinerant daguerreotypist for a hero. . . .

Mr. Hawthorne wants dramatic power, or that mimic faculty, whatever it may be called, which enables an author to represent successfully the colloquial peculiarities of different classes of persons. All his characters—men and women, gentle and vulgar—talk in the same strain of measured elegance. Look through any of his dialogues, and it will appear that his most ambitious attempts in this way have been failures. We never could say of remarks in any of his books, that they were the peculiar property of any of his characters; but they might apply nearly as well perhaps to all. . . . He does not drag down the lofty ones by putting vulgar sentiments into their mouths, but he drags up the common herd to a high table-land of conversation, where all meet on an equality.

It has been made a common objection to Mr. Hawthorne, that he has no great purpose in his novels, no virtue to inculcate, or no vice to expose. We are not among the number of those who believe it necessary in every fiction-writer to magnify himself into a public censor, and never stoop to feed the public with entertainment without thrusting some wholesome pill down their throats at the same time. Little good is effected in that way; and, when the moral is by itself, we confess that we usually skip it. At the same time, the novelist should never forget that, in proportion to his popularity, he possesses more or less power to elevate or degrade the standard of the community; and that, for the proper exercise of that power, he is accountable. We do think that Mr. Hawthorne's stories fail to teach any good lesson. We have seen a well-written criticism of 'Blithedale' which styles it 'the most brilliant gem in the Satanic school of American literature;' and, though we consider that an overstatement, we must agree that there is nothing sincere and satisfactory about its tone, or that of the other novels which have preceded it. That is something defective in Hawthorne's philosophy. . . .

Hawthorne has no real sympathy with men. He doubtless strives to mingle with them, and he observes them narrowly; but it is not as one of them. 'Vanity and vexation of spirit' is the result of his reflections and the sum of his teachings.

There is one other characteristic of Mr. Hawthorne's which we desire to approach with great delicacy. We do not recollect to have seen it noticed by anyone else; and we should prefer on the whole to believe that we are mistaken, and that it does not exist. It is, in brief, a tendency towards voluptuousness, possibly coarseness, indicated by an over-coloring of his pictures of physical beauty, and in other ways which we need not particularize. We do not altogether object to a slight infusion of this into our literature, that it may the more conform to nature: at all events, it ought to be expected as a necessary re-action from the excessive prudishness which has characterized us of late. We are as far on one side of the true line as the old novelists were on the other. But any steps in this direction must be guided by a scrupulous refinement and a true delicacy. It would have been in better taste for Hawthorne to omit the feverish speculations of Coverdale the invalid upon the beauty of Zenobia. In view of the connection between Hollingsworth and Zenobia, it was artistic but repulsive to make him wound her dead body in the heart when raising her from the water. But, on this subject, a mere hint is sufficient.

Mr. Hawthorne's women are peculiar, and another illustration of our position that he cannot take a broad and entire view of human nature. They are all weird, and as much a peculiar creation of his fancy as the three sisters in Macbeth are of Shakespeare's. They are not such women as we see and know. They are not our relations and friends, and we never fell in love with such. In truth, they are not loveable; they are incomprehensible, and full of mystery. They are neither one thing nor another. . . . His old people are worse than his women. He seems to have a sort of venomous spite against them, and to dwell with a cruel delight on every unfortunate concomitant of age. . . . How he loves to linger over every item that can alienate poor Miss Hepzibah Pyncheon from our sympathies,—'the creaking joints of her stiffened knees,' her 'shrunken waist,' 'her rigid and rusty frame,' her 'long lank arm,' and her scowl. It may be that he means to excite our sympathy for her, notwithstanding the repulsive description with which he introduces her. But we doubt if that be really his intention. . . .

It would be quite useless in us to waste the reader's time and our own in attempting to criticize 'Twice-told Tales,' 'Mosses from an Old

Manse,' and the 'Wonder Book for Children.' They are universal favorites, and deservedly so. We, moreover, intend to notice but briefly his more elaborate productions.

. . . it is in his last work that Mr. Hawthorne appears as the biographer and politician. The good democrat may now purchase for thirty-seven and a half cents the life of Gen. Frank. Pierce, contained in a well-written and well-printed volume, and embellished with a portrait. This little book has been subject to a great deal of unjust criticism already. No man can give a good reason why Mr. Hawthorne, being a Democrat, should not write a life of the Democratic nominee for the Presidency if he sees fit so to do, and knows anything upon the subject. We have seen a leading Whig paper predicting that it will be the death of his literary fame, and that it is a miserable affair in itself considered; and a leading Democratic paper asserting that it possesses every literary excellence, and is calculated to add new laurels to the crown of the illustrious author. The indifferent reader knows how much to allow for any such criticisms. We cannot agree with the Democrat that it is Mr. Hawthorne's best work, nor with the Whig that it will incapacitate him from ever writing another good work, which is what must be meant by saying that it will be the death of his literary fame; for, of course, if he continues to write Scarlet Letters and Blithedale Romances, the public will continue to read them eagerly to the end of time. . . .

Considered as a piece of biography, this book has, of course, scarcely any value. When time enough has passed to allow the affairs of to-day to be seen in their true light, and the political questions which now agitate the country having yielded their place to others, cease to engross the attention of the people, some impartial pen may be called upon to write the biography of such of the men of the time as have left names behind them. But, since we must have contemporary biographies for the campaign, we are glad that General Pierce has fallen into the hands of so accomplished a writer as Mr. Hawthorne. . . .

Notwithstanding the pleasure we derived from the 'Life of General Pierce,' we have one request to make of its author; that when he comes to be an old man, and employs his leisure in editing a complete edition of his works with notes, he will omit the 'Life of General Pierce' (for that will do all its work this year), but insert everything else that he has written.

91. Hawthorne, from 'The Wayside'

13 March 1853

. . . Merely from the titles of the stories, I saw at once that the subjects were not less rich than those of the former volume; nor did I at all doubt that Mr. Bright's audacity (so far as that endowment might avail) had enabled him to take full advantage of whatever capabilities they offered. Yet, in spite of my experience of his free way of handling them, I did not quite see, I confess, how he could have obviated all the difficulties in the way of rendering them presentable to children. These old legends, so brimming over with everything that is most abhorrent to our Christianized moral sense,—some of them so hideous, others so melancholy and miserable, amid which the Greek tragedians sought their themes, and moulded them into the sternest forms of grief that ever the world saw; was such material the stuff that children's playthings should be made of! How were they to be purified? How was the blessed sunshine to be thrown into them?

But Eustace told me that these myths were the most singular things in the world, and that he was invariably astonished, whenever he began to relate one, by the readiness with which it adapted itself to the childish purity of his auditors. The objectionable characteristics seem to be a parasitical growth, having no essential connection with the original fable. They fall away, and are thought of no more, the instant he puts his imagination in sympathy with the innocent little circle, whose wide-open eyes are fixed so eagerly upon him. Thus the stories (not by any strained effort of the narrator's, but in harmony with their inherent germ) transform themselves, and reassume the shapes which they might be supposed to possess in the pure childhood of the world. When the first poet or romancer told these marvellous legends (such is Eustace Bright's opinion), it was still the Golden Age. Evil had never yet existed; and sorrow, misfortune, crime, were mere shadows which the mind fancifully created for itself, as a shelter against too sunny realities; or, at most, but prophetic dreams, to which the dreamer himself did not yield a waking credence. Children are now the only representatives of the men and women of that happy era; and therefore it is that we must raise the intellect and fancy to the level of childhood, in order to re-create the original myths.

92. From an unsigned review in *Graham's Magazine*

September 1853, xliii, 333–5

This little volume, in some respects the sequel, and in many respects the superior of the charming 'Wonder-Book,' presents Hawthorne's genius in its most attractive form. The subjects of the tales are taken from the ancient myths; and legends which furnished Homer, Hesiod, Æschylus and Sophocles with the materials of epic and dramatic poetry, Hawthorne has transformed into stories for children. In this he has exhibited consummate art. . . . The stories come from his imagination pure, delicate, consistent, full of moral beauty, and exceeding all fairy tales we can remember in interest and attractiveness. The style of narration is almost faultless. The obedient words seem to melt softly into the mould of the author's fine conceptions, and the attention is never dazzled away from the pictures and incidents which the style conveys, to be fixed on mere felicities of diction. The spirit of the narratives is always child-like, and never childish, and the most charming simplicity is attained without ever lapsing into puerility. Moral truths are insinuated into the texture of the stories with the most delightful innocence of moral parade, and without any intrusion of those 'do-me-good' truisms, which children see through with such instinctive tact, and sicken at with such instinctive taste. The book is, indeed, a work of art for children.

One peculiarity of the volume will surprise all who have not read its delightful predecessor, 'The Wonder Book,' namely, its sustained geniality of tone. It is absolutely without any signs of that inquisitive and piercing analysis and vivid representation of morbid mental phenomena, which lends a fascination, sometimes serpent-like, to Hawthorne's novels. He seems here to take all the virtues on trust, and has a child's faith in goodness and innocence, as well as in marvels and enchantments. This emancipation of his imagination from its introspective tendencies, gives free play to his humor, which peeps and smiles continually out in the sweetest and sunniest way, just satisfying the sense of merriment without allowing it to shock and surprise the reader out of his faith in the wonders of the narrative, or twist the ideal and picturesque grace of the story into a grotesque form. . . .

It is almost needless to say that all these stories evince the felicity and transforming power of genius, and are to be rigidly distinguished from ordinary books for children. They have nothing of the book-making, hack-writing, soul-lacking character of job work, but are true products of imagination—of the literary artist as discriminated from the literary artisan. It seems to us that if widely read they would exercise an admirable influence, not only on the forming morals but the forming taste of children, refining character as well as conveying lessons. They have evidently been tried on the fit audience, though few, of the author's own children, before being presented to the child-public. Though some of the words may occasionally puzzle very young boys and girls, we think that all who have learned to read can master the spirit and substance of the book. If not, their parents will find the work of translation a most pleasant occupation. Like all true children's books, it affords delightful reading to the old.

93. From an unsigned review in the *Knickerbocker Magazine*

October 1853, xlviii, 407–9

We quite agree with Mr. Eustace Bright, the imaginary author of the mythological stories contained in this beautiful volume, that they are 'better chosen and better handled' than those which proved so popular in the 'Wonder-Book,' by the same writer. We have not been accustomed, even when we were younger than at present, to regard mythological tales with much favor; nor, so far as our observation goes, do children generally esteem them to possess much attraction. But not so with the new, simple, and picturesque 'renderings' of them by Mr. Hawthorne. He has breathed anew into them the breath of life, and brought them freshly before the little people of 'this dim and ignorant present.' . . .

We quite agree with Mr. Bright's editor, that 'he really appears to have overcome the usual objections against these fables;' and the 'liberties with the original structure,' of which the editor speaks, are, as we have already intimated, the very charm of the volume.

94. Richard Henry Stoddard: The biographical interest, from an unsigned essay, 'Nathaniel Hawthorne', in the *National Magazine*

January 1853, ii, 17–24

Stoddard (1825–1903), a critic and editor as well as a popular poet of the day, came to know Hawthorne well and through his intercession was given a political appointment. He contributed reviews to various periodicals, among them *Godey's Lady's Book* and the *Southern Literary Messenger*. This essay is especially noteworthy because it includes an autobiographical letter from Hawthorne (with the substitution of the third person for the first), a letter which must be viewed as one of the chief sources of the myth of the withdrawn and secluded Hawthorne. The second paragraph of the following excerpt is taken from that letter.

We know not how it may be with others, but for our single selves, we have great faith in our being able to discover authors in their books; to discover their peculiarities of mind and person, and oftentimes the circumstances of their lives; building, as it were, complete forms from their fragmentary members scattered in many places. It may not be always intentional—in most cases we fancy it is not—but there is always something of an author in his books, even when he is most false to himself, or disguises himself the most. Any perfect and impenetrable disguise is impossible. . . . Disguise himself as he may, the musician is still revealed by some chord or combination of sound; the painter by some bit of color, some gleam of light or shade; the sculptor by the turn of a limb, or the fold of a robe; and the poet, or prose-writer, by the cadence of his sentences, or even by some favorite word, which has become a part and parcel of his soul. A tone, an atmosphere, a certain *Je ne sais quoi* lies under, broods over, and is the informing soul of every work of art. We speak now of works of art—of all true works of true artists—be they books, statues, pictures, or linked sounds: with the patch-work imitations of the mere copyist, and the lifeless original of the still more lifeless original, we have nothing to do. There are certain qualities in a true work of art which it is impossible to mistake; certain more or less recondite qualities which relate to, and relate the thoughts and life of its author. . . . If what we have advanced be true, and it will be granted, we think, in most cases, it is especially and emphatically true in the case of Nathanial Hawthorne. If ever author was revealed in his books, Hawthorne is the man. . . .

It was the fortune or misfortune, just as the reader pleases, of Hawthorne to have some slender means of supporting himself; and so, on leaving college, in 1825, instead of immediately studying a profession, he sat himself down to consider what pursuit in life he was best fit for. His mother had now returned, and taken up her abode in her deceased father's house, a tall, ugly, old, grayish building, (it is now the residence of half a dozen Irish families,) in which Hawthorne had a room; and year after year he kept on considering what he was fit for, and time and his destiny decided that he was to be the writer that he is. He had always a natural tendency (it appears to have been on the paternal side) toward seclusion, and this he now indulged to the utmost; so that, for months together, he scarcely held human intercourse outside of his own family, seldom going out except at twilight, or only to take the nearest way to the most convenient solitude, which was oftenest the seashore, the rocks and beaches in that vicinity being as fine as any in New-England. Once a year, or thereabouts, he used to make an excursion of a few weeks, in which he enjoyed as much of life as other people do in the whole year's round. Having spent so much of his youth and boyhood away from his native place, he had very few acquaintances in Salem, and during the nine or ten years that he spent there, in this solitary way, we doubt whether so much as twenty people in the town were aware of his existence. . . .

Quiet, unobtrusive, and retired, has been the life of Hawthorne, and such are his books. Had his life been different, his books could not have well been what they are. They mirror the man, and could not have been written by any other man, nor by Hawthorne himself, had he been city born and bred, and had his life been passed in the dust and noise of cities, and in close contact with mankind, instead of communion with his own soul, and the manifold-influences of nature. The freshness and stillness of nature breathe through his pages, and mingle like an odor with his there-expressed thoughts and feelings. Those years of seclusion and dreaming are all reproduced in his books, and in their quintessence only; he gives us the quintessence of everything; others give us processes with their results, he the results alone; in this respect he is like Tennyson. And he has another of Tennyson's fine peculiarities—that of seeing nature with the eyes of his mind. If he, or any of his characters passes through a landscape, the landscape is always in keeping with his or her idiosyncrasies, and in keeping with the essay or sketch in which it is introduced. There is an air of reserve about Hawthorne, even when most frank; as if he distrusted the propriety of frankness, or had left, and was feeling, much which could not and should not be revealed. He reveals, we are apt to think, the characteristics of an ideal man, rather than his own; talks oftentimes of pleasant but irrelevant matters, to lead the mind from himself; shutting himself up the while in his own heart and soul, like a sensitive plant in the depths of a shady wood.

There is a sort of unreality about his delineations of man and the world; or a reality very different from that of everyday life and thought. It is as if he surveyed both from a distance, calmly and coldly; or if warmly, with only a scientific warmth, such as an enthusiastic anatomist might experience in a rare case of dissection. . . . Hawthorne is a close student of country lore, from the grand phenomena of the seasons and years, down to the veriest details of insignificant rural objects. Nothing escapes his shy, wandering glance. And he has the rare faculty of reproducing his own sensations in the minds of his readers; we feel in reading his books what he must have felt in writing them. The walk of his genius, or that in which it pleases him to make his genius walk, is somewhat narrow, but it is far-reaching, ascending into skyey regions, and descending into chasms of darkness. It is a line—but a line which touches the verge of things. The chief drawback of his genius is its exceeding delicacy. It is too delicate, too shadowy, too spiritual in many of its manifestations, to be at once, or ever very widely recognized. It needs the study of a kindred mind, which the mass of readers have not, and the moods of mind which feed it, which but few have ever felt, or feeling have known how to classify and analyze. Had Hawthorne written worse, he would have written—for the world of readers we mean—better. His excellences have been his worst enemies.

One of the first things that strike us in his writings, is the simplicity, purity, and beauty of his style. He is not only correct—many authors who are nothing else are that—but he makes his correctness charming. There is an indescribable grace about his sentences, and a peculiar rhythm in their construction, which falls upon the ear like the voice of some one who is dear to us. We never forget his prose, because we never find anything like it out of his books. It is better than that of Irving, admirable as that is, because it is more fresh and unstudied, while equally correct; and better than was Addison's, the heretofore model of fine English prose. It is difficult to describe it, save as style; other writers are mannerists—Hawthorne is a stylist. Does he attempt description, the object or objects described stand before us clearly or dimly, as circumstances require, and always in their most obvious relations, which strike us the more from the veil of beauty that half conceals them, and the dramatic grouping in which they are shown. Does he become reflective, his thoughts are new and striking, often universal in their bearings; never obscure, even while expressing obscurity, but crystal-like in their clearness, and often gorgeous with imagery, threading the intricate labyrinths of fancy and imagination with the certain clew of poetry. Does he analyze the passions of his characters, his analysis is always sure and profound, bringing many dark things to light, and laying bare the heart of many mysteries. In the region of mystery, the wildernesses and caverns of the mind, he is at home—more at home, it seems to us, than in the upper and outer world. His personages are not so much men and women, as passions, simple or complex in their forms; ideas made palpable and familiar, sentiments clothed in flesh. A single character sometimes embodies the result of many years' thought and observation. Nothing is wanting to make many of his characters perfect, save that spontaneity which is the crown of human nature. They are either too bad or too good

For human nature's daily food.

But we always see—not always, however, 'with eye serene'—

The very pulse of the machine.

He aims to impart form, symmetry, harmony and beauty to whatever he touches; unless he does this, he does nothing. He conceives an idea which he wishes to work out in an essay or tale; broods over it, it may be for years, until it takes form; broods over the form until it suits and satisfies his conscience of taste; and then broods over its various parts, carefully adapting each to each, and linking all together with the most subtile threads of fact and feeling. A sentence or a single word sometimes gives one the clew to whole pages. A seemingly random speech or action, admits a flood of light into the chambers of the heart. 'Not only' —says Poe, in a critique on Hawthorne—'not only is all done that should be, but (what perhaps is an end with more difficulty attained) there is nothing done which should not be. Every word *tells*, and there is no word which does *not* tell.'

The form of Hawthorne's works is generally perfect, and many times highly original. Saving certain shadowy resemblances to some of the Germans, his manner of working out a sketch is unlike that of any other author. Often he gives us the sensation—the atmosphere and tone —the dream of his subject, rather than the subject itself. There is something dim and indistinct about his conceptions which affects us powerfully. The scene seems to be laid out of the real world in a kind of fancy realm; or if not out of the real world, away on its dim outer borders, a Shade-land—

> The land which lies, as legend saith,
> Between the worlds of life and death—

where the living and dead meet familiarly and equally. The ancient witch element of his native town pervades all that he has written. He seems to have brooded over it, until it has become a portion of his being. Not that he deals in witches, ghosts, or any of the unearthly agencies of Mrs. Radcliffe, or Monk Lewis; he has too pure and natural a taste, too keen a sense of the ludicrous for that; but rather that he gives us glimpses of existences and worlds, other and darker than our own. The strange moods of mind, the many temptations to sin, the feeling of the Evil One at his elbow, and in his heart, which, in 'The Scarlet Letter,' comes over the minister, Arthur Dimmesdale, after parting from Hester Prynne in the forest, will perhaps explain what we mean. In analysis of soul-torture, the struggle between the good and evil principles in man's nature, Hawthorne is very profound and instructive. Bunyan himself is not more at home in the mystical world of spirit-life and allegory. And Hawthorne has written allegories not unworthy the inspired tinker— not, like many, to show his ingenuity in that difficult field of composition, but to insinuate beautiful morals, and to teach beautiful truth, clothing truth herself

> In the quaint garments of a parable.

Bunyan, the reader will remember, was one of Hawthorne's earliest favorites.

The traditions and legends of New-England find in Hawthorne a fitting historian. The spirit of the early settlers glares fiercely in his pages, or glimmers like dull red flame. There is something of the old

Puritan about all that he writes; something stern, uncompromising, toned down and softened by touches of inherent melancholy. Melancholy—a quiet pensiveness, like the faint light of an autumn afternoon—is the atmosphere of Hawthorne's writings. Without palpably aiming at morality, and lugging it in by the ear, he is a severe moralist, and the tendency of all his books is to make men wiser and better. And herein lies his chiefest merit, without which his many beautiful intellectual qualities were as sounding brass and tinkling cymbals. For intellect is often depraved, while extremely beautiful. The beauty of an author's books does not always suffer from the depravity of his mind; sometimes it seems to increase as he becomes depraved.

Hence the danger to which its worshipers are exposed. 'It cannot mislead us,' say they, 'because it is beautiful.' It cannot be far wrong,—if we grant it wrong at all,—

> For even the light that leads astray,
> Is light from heaven.

A pernicious doctrine, and one that is utterly false. For no light from heaven ever did, or ever can lead astray; though many lights that may seem akin to it,—wandering Will-o'-the-Wisps, and beacon fires on lofty peaks of mind,—may entice thousands into the broad but downward paths of darkness, over which they shed a flickering, mocking brilliancy. For this reason many beautiful books—many philosophies, poems, and romances—are pernicious. None who have read can deny the brilliancy and beauty of most of the modern French and English novels, though but few are hardly enough to deny their unhealthy and evil tendency.

Of Hawthorne's works separately we have not left ourselves room to speak. We have confined ourselves to general, rather than to particular criticism, much to our regret and the reader's loss. Could we have selected some of our favorite extracts, and have allowed Hawthorne to speak for himself, it would have been better perhaps for both of us. But after all, specimen-bricks, the best that can be selected—even the block of granite, the corner-stone of a mansion, is a poor apology for the mansion itself; above all, for the mind-mansion of a man of genius—

> Who ransacks mines and ledges,
> And quarries every rock,
> And hews the famous adamant
> For each eternal block.

95. 'Sir Nathaniel': Hawthorne and the delineation of the abnormal, from 'American Authorship', in the *New Monthly Magazine*

June 1853, xcviii, 202–12

Already have we devoted a few pages of this Magazine to a general notice* of the writings of Mr. Hawthorne. The present series, however, affords an opportunity for resuming the subject—with a particular reference to one of his publications ('Twice-told Tales') which was then hardly mentioned, and to another ('The Blithedale Romance') which has been subsequently produced.

His reputation has advanced, is increasing, and ought still to be progressive. He is now read, in their own consonant-crazy tongue, by borderers on the Black Sea, and exiles of Siberia. There is an individual charm about his writings, not perhaps, to the minds most influenced by it, of a wholly unexceptionable kind; for it may be true that 'il fait que chacun, après l'avoir lu, est plus mécontent de son être.'[1] Indeed, it is impossible, we should think, to read him without becoming sadder if not wiser—in spite of an assumed air of *gaillardise*,[2] and a cheery moral tacked now and then to a sorrowful parable, he is essentially sad-hearted and confirms any similar tendency in his readers. We expect a hue-and-cry to be raised against him in this matter by the sanatory commissioners of criticism and guardians of the literary board of health. In his choice of subjects, he had already been indicted by them as himself a *mauvais sujet*.[3] He is charged with a fondness for the delineation of abnormal character; and it is a true bill. If guilt be involved in the indictment, guilty he will plead. Individuality, idiosyncrasy, *propria persona*-lity,[4] he must have at any price. Into the recesses and darker sub-surface nooks of human character he will penetrate at all hazards. 'This long while past,' says Zenobia to the Blithedale romancer, 'you have been follow-

---

* *New Monthly*, February 1852.

[1] *il faut que chacun, après l'avoir lu, est plus mécontent de son être*: he makes everyone, after having read him, more discontent with his own being.

[2] *gaillardise:* forced gaiety.

[3] *mauvais sujet:* hard case.

[4] *propria persona:* his own person.

ing up your game, groping for human emotions in the dark corners of the heart.' The romancer himself records his fear, that a certain cold tendency, between instinct and intellect, which made him 'pry with a speculative interest into people's passions and impulses,' had gone far towards unhumanising his heart. . . .

In harmony with this tendency—this 'making my prey of people's individualities, as my custom was'—is a fondness for merging ME (as the Germans have it) in NOT ME: as where one of Mr. Hawthorne's characters, in the wantonness of youth, strength, and comfortable condition, meeting with a forlorn, dejected, used-up old man, tries to identify his own mind with the old fellow's, and take his view of the world, as if looking through a smoke-blackened glass at the sun. In a curious disposition of mind, of which these habits are exponents, lies much of the author's power and weakness both. With special ability to depict exceptional modes of human nature, is conjoined special temptation to linger amid what is morbid, and to court intimacy with whatever deviates from the dull standard of conventionalism, and give to distortion and oddity the preference over 'harmonic union.' He has been described as walking abroad always at night, so that it is but a moonlight glimmering which you catch of reality. Applying to him what has been said of a countryman of his, we may pronounce his delight to lie in treading the border-land between the material and spiritual worlds— the debateable country of dreams, sleep-walking, and clairvoyance. . . . No wonder that Mr. Hawthorne should be so richly endowed, as some of his observers assure us he is,* with the divine faculty of silence, when mixing in social life. Small-talk, tea-table prattle, tripping gossip, versatile chit-chat—these are not for one whose cherished habit is to chew the cud of sweet and bitter fancies, and to sit in the shade to ruminate, while others traverse the gay meadow to graze. Nor is he to be appreciated but by those who, whatever their loquacity, are, *au fond*,[1] pensive and given to speculative broodings. The art with which

* When occupying the Old Manse, Mr. Hawthorne is said to have been, to his neighbours, as much a phantom and a fable as the old parson of the parish, dead half a century before, whose faded portrait in the attic was gradually rejoining its original in native dust. . . . Emerson, with the 'slow, wise smile' that breaks over his face, like day over the sky, said: 'Hawthorne rides well his horse of the night.' The same authority informs us, that during his three years' occupancy of the Old Manse, Mr. Hawthorne was not seen, probably, by more than a dozen villagers—choosing the river-side, where he was sure of solitude, for his walks—and loving to bathe every evening in the river after nightfall;—and other illustrations are added, in a 'very American' tone, of the romancer's manner of manhood. See that gaily-equipped gift-book, 'Homes of American Authors', published last year by Messrs. Putnam.

[1] *au fond:* at bottom.

he can lend a superstitious awe to his stories, and subtilise their grosser common-places into ghostly significance, will indeed always secure him a good company of readers. But to enter into his mood as well as meaning, and to gather from his sentences and suggestions all that was fermenting in his soul when he wrote them, is for an inner circle of disciples. Not that we arrogate a place there; but at least we can recognise this esoteric initiation.

The 'Twice-told Tales' have been criticised by the author himself. . . . And he asks us, if we would see anything in the book, to read it in the clear, brown, twilight atmosphere in which it was written; confessing that if opened in the sunshine it is apt to look exceedingly like a volume of blank pages. . . . But whenever read, at vespers or matins, on grass or in garret, by youth or by age, the pages are studded, *haud longis intervallis*,[1] with passages that pay their way. Amid so miscellaneous a 'store,' we can select for passing mention one or two only, which appear most characteristic of the narrator's manner of spirit. Such is 'The Minister's Black Veil,' which *could* have been written by none other than the hand that traced in burning furrows the 'Scarlet Letter:' there is truly, as Parson Hooper feels, a preternatural horror interwoven with the threads of the black crape covering his face—an ambiguity of sin or sorrow so enveloping the poor minister, that love or sympathy can no longer reach him—so that, with self-shudderings and outward terrors, his earthly fate is to be ever groping darkly within his own soul, or gazing through a medium that saddens the whole world. Such is also 'The Wedding Knell'—with that grotesquely repulsive rendezvous at the church-altar; the aged bride, an insatiate woman of the world, clad in brightest splendour of youthful attire, and suddenly startled, as she awaits the bridegroom, by the dreadful anachronism of a tolling bell, the only flourish to announce her affianced one, who arrives in the midst of a slow funeral procession, his vestment a shroud! Such, again, is 'Wakefield'—with its warning monition, that amid the seeming confusion of our mysterious world individuals are so nicely adjudged to a system, and systems to one another, and to a whole, that, by stepping aside for a moment, a man exposes himself to a fearful risk of losing his place for ever, and becoming the Outcast of the Universe. It is a capital touch in this story of an eccentric man's twenty years' desertion of his wife and home, without assignable cause, even to himself, while dwelling all the while in the next street,—that of his venturing out for the first time from his secret lodging, partly resolving to cross the head of

1 *haud longis intervallis:* not at all at long intervals.

the street, and send one hasty glance towards his forsaken domicile, when 'habit—for he is a man of habits—takes him by the hand, and guides him, wholly unaware, to his own door, where, just at the critical moment, he is aroused by the scraping of his foot upon the step'—and, in affright, little dreaming of the doom to which his first backward step devotes him, he hurries away, breathless with agitation, and afraid to look back. Not always, as in this case, is Mr. Hawthorne careful to furnish his tales or vagaries with a 'pervading spirit or moral,' either implicit and implied, or 'done up neatly, and condensed into the final sentence.' What, for instance, is the moral, what the spirit, what the meaning of 'The Great Carbuncle?' Thought may, as he alleges, always have its efficacy, and every striking incident its moral: but interpreted as some, and they not purblind, critics apprehend, that allegory of the crystal mountains is efficacious only as a premium to scepticism, and a *damper* to all imagination that would with the lofty sanctify the low, and sublimate the human with the divine. No such intention may the allegorist have had; but at least he might have guarded against so justifiable a gloss by using a more intelligible cypher.

In his best style is that brief fantasy of the mid-day slumberer beside the tuft of maples, 'David Swan'—during whose hour's sleep there successively visit him, as stray passengers on the highway, a pair of opulent elders, who half resolve to adopt him; and a heart-free maiden, who becomes a half lover at first sight; and a couple of scampish repro-bates, who more than half determine to rob and, if need be, dirk the dreaming lad. When the coach-wheels awaken him, and he mounts and rides away, David casts not one parting glance at the place of his hour's repose beside the maple-shaded fountain—unconscious of the three un-realised Acts of that hour's unacted Drama—ignorant that a phantom of Wealth had thrown a golden hue upon that fountain's waters, and that one of Love had sighed softly to their murmur, and that one of Death had threatened to crimson them with his blood: so true is it that, sleep-ing or waking, we hear not the airy footsteps of the strange things that almost happen. Very significant of the author's meditative habit is his description of the interruption of the two rascals' felonious design: 'They left the spot with so many jests and such laughter at their unac-complished wickedness, that they might be said to have gone on their way rejoicing. In a few hours they had forgotten the whole affair, nor once imagined that the recording angel had written down the crime of murder against their souls, in letters as durable as eternity.' This thought is illustrated more at length in the 'morality' called 'Fancy's Show-Box'

—which discusses, as a point of vast interest, the question whether the soul may contract stains of guilt, in all their depth and flagrancy, from deeds which may have been plotted and resolved upon, but which, physically, have never had existence—whether the fleshy hand, and visible frame of man, must set its seal to the evil designs of the soul, in order to give them their entire validity against the sinner. Casuistry of this sort is 'nuts' to Mr. Hawthorne.

'Dr. Heidegger's Experiment,' too, has the real Hawthorne odour. The quartette of withered worldlings who, by the doctor's magic art, enjoy a temporary rejuvenescence—with what cruel truth their weak points are exposed! First laughing tremulously at the ridiculous idea that, were youth restored them, they, with their experience of life, would or should or could ever go astray again—grey, decrepit, sapless, miserable creatures, without warmth enough in their souls or bodies to be animated even by the prospect of recovering their spring days. And then, when the spell began to work, lost in a delirium of levity, mad-dened with exuberant frolic, and disporting themselves in follies to be equalled only by their own absurdities half a century before. An apolo-gue, styled 'The Lily's Quest,' relates the rambles of two lovers in search of a site for their Temple of Happiness—they, the representatives of Hope and Joy, while there dogs them a darksome figure, type of all the woful influences which life can conjure up, and interposing a gloomy forbiddal whenever they think the site is found:—a site is at last found, which he forbids not; but it is—a grave. Touchingly beautiful, however, is the inference drawn by the bridegroom, despite the taunting words of the Dark Shadow over his bride's grave; for then he knew, we are told, what was betokened by the parable in which the Lily and himself had acted; and the mystery of Life and Death was opened to him; and he could throw his arms towards heaven and cry, 'Joy, joy! on a grave be the site of our temple; and now our happiness is for eternity!' Nor must we omit allusion to 'Edward Fane's Rosebud,' that retrospect of a mumbling crone's girlhood, when wrinkled Nurse Toothaker (now cowering in rheumatic crabbedness over her fire, and warming her old bones too by an infusion of Geneva) was a fresh and fair young maiden —so fresh and fair, that, instead of Rose, which seemed too mature a name for her half-opened beauty, her lover called her Rosebud;—nor again, and lastly, to the legend of the mantle of Lady Eleanore—fatal handiwork of a dying woman, which, perchance, owed the fantastic grace of its design to the delirium of approaching death, and with whose golden threads the last toil of stiffening fingers had interwoven plague and anguish, a spell of dreadful potency; itself a symbol of Eleanore's withdrawal from the sympathies of our common nature, and the instrument of her signal and utter humiliation. The subtlety and power of this legend are of the rarest.

'The Blithedale Romance' we esteem, in *spite* of its coming last, the highest and best of Mr. Hawthorne's works. The tale is narrated with more ingenuity and ease; the characters are at least equal to their predecessors, and the style is at once richer and more robust—more mellowed, and yet more pointed and distinct. A true artist has planned and has filled up the plot, ordering each conjunction of incidents, and interweaving the cross threads of design and destiny with masterly tact; skilled in the by-play of suggestion, hint, and pregnant passing intimation—in the provocative spell of suspense—in the harmonious development of once scattered and seemingly unrelated forces. His humour is fresher in quality, and his tragic power is exercised with almost oppressive effect—at times making the boldest, oldest romance-reader

> Hold his breath
> For a while;

at others, making all *but* him lose the dimmed line in blinding tears. There are scenes that rivet themselves on the memory—such as Coverdale's interview with Westervelt in the woodland solitude, followed by his observation of another rencontre from his leafy hermitage in the vine-entangled pine-tree; and the dramatic recital of Zenobia's Legend; and the rendezvous at Eliot's Pulpit; and above all, the dreadful errand by midnight in quest of the Dead—intensified in its grim horror by the contrasted temperaments of the three searchers, especially Silas Foster's rude matter-of-fact hardness, probing with coarse unconscious finger the wounds of a proud and sensitive soul. There are touches of exquisite pathos in the evolution of the tale of sorrow, mingled with shrewd 'interludes' of irony and humour which only deepen the distress. Antiperistasis, Sir Thomas Browne would call it.

Upon the bearing of the romance on Socialism we need not descant, the author explicitly disclaiming all intent of pronouncing *pro* or *con.* on the theories in question. As to the characters, too, he as explicitly repudiates the idea, which in the teeth of such disclaimer, and of internal evidence also, has been attributed to him, of portraying in the Blithedale actors the actual companions of his Brook Farm career—or other American celebrities (as though Margaret Fuller were Zenobia, because both living on 'Rights of Woman' excitement, and both dying by drowning!). The characters are few; but each forms a study. . . . Miles Coverdale himself is no lay figure in the group of actors. His character is replete with interest, whether as a partial presentment of the author's own person, or as a type of no uncommon individuality in this age of 'yeast.' We have in him a strange but most true 'coincidence' of warm feeling and freezing reflection, of the kind deep heart and the vexed and vacillating brain, of a natural tendency to faith and a constitutional taint of scepticism, of the sensuous, indolent epicurean and the habitual cynic, of the idealist—all hope, and the realist—all disappointment. It is this fusion of opposite, not contradictory qualities, which gives so much piquancy and flavour to Coverdale's character, and his author's writings in general. . . .

Of 'The Scarlet Letter,' 'The House of the Seven Gables,' the 'Mosses from an Old Manse,' &c., we have entered our verdict, such as it is, in a previous 'fly-leaf.' The 'Life of Franklin Pierce,' a confessedly time-serving palaver, is in no way worthy of that 'statute of night and silence' which Mr. Hawthorne has been called. It is meagre, hasty, and without distinctive merit of any kind. Prejudiced in his favour, we read it with full purpose of heart to like it exceedingly, and to find an immense deal in it; but it baffled us outright. . . .

A word or two, however, ere we leave him, upon his more genial and satisfactory contributions to the Literature of Childhood. The 'Wonder-Book,' like most true books for children, has a charm for their grave and reverend seniors. . . . Do you remember 'Little Annie's Ramble' in 'Twice-told Tales?'—where he tells us that if he prides himself on anything, it is because he has a smile that children love—and that few are the grown ladies that could entice him from the side of such as little Annie, so deep is his delight in letting his mind go hand in hand with the mind of a sinless child. For he wisely holds and sweetly teaches that, as the pure breath of children revives the life of aged men, so is our moral nature revived by their free and simple thoughts, their native feeling, their airy mirth, for little cause or none, their grief, soon roused and soon allayed.

96. Hawthorne as the favourite of the British, from an unsigned essay, 'American Novels', in the *North British Review*

November 1853, xx, 81–99

. . . America is a new thing upon the face of the earth. Great nations, in their youth, have commonly produced great poets; but America has had no youth. The youth of America was that of Britain; and the great poets who lived before, and even after, the national schism, belong as much to her literature as they do to ours. In fact, the very notion of two literatures in one language is an absurdity. If English literature, since the political independence of America, has flourished best at headquarters it is no more to be wondered at than that the press of London should have been more prolific of good books than that of Liverpool.

The spirit of romance, however, has not been so strictly metropolitan in its choice of an abiding place as that of poetry. If Coleridge, Words-worth, Burns, and Tennyson, have had no rivals in America, it is not so with Dickens, Marryat, Bulwer, and Currer Bell. Against these names America may boldly set her Stowes, Coopers, Longfellows, and Haw-thornes, in whom there is no mistaking an independence and originality which hold out high hopes of the share which the writers of America are destined to take in the English literature of the future. . . .

Nathaniel Hawthorne, a name that must be familiar to most of our readers, has distinguished himself in England chiefly by three very re-markable tales,—'The House with the Seven Gables,' 'The Scarlet Letter,' and 'The Blithedale Romance.' These works are the most forcible in the imaginative line that America has yet produced. Nothing in her poetry is half so poetical, and yet they are not more so than imaginative prose has a right to be. The most striking features in these tales are the extraordinary skill and masterly care which are displayed in their composition. 'The House with the Seven Gables' may be charged with a little redundance of description; but in the other stories named it would be difficult to pick out a page that could be omitted without loss to the development of the narrative and the idea, which are always mutually illustrative to a degree not often attained in any species of modern art. When Mr. Hawthorne begins one of his stories he seems to become so perfectly absorbed with his leading moral—which, by the way, is not always unexceptionable—that he no longer has eyes or memory for anything in the universe but for exactly those things which will serve him best for illustrations and arguments and steps in his poetical proof of the moral proposition he sets out with. With all this rigid adherence to his point, there is, however, no sense of hardness, difficulty, and confinement in his style. His language, though for an American extraordinarily accurate, is always light and free; his illustrations and incidents, though often startlingly odd, and, for the moment, apparently unrelated, have never the air of being far-fetched, but seem rather to be the best possible for the occasion; and the narrative, though curiously elaborated, is so well *contrasted* and *proportioned* in its several parts, that it makes, when we have finished, an impression full of simplicity and totality. His tales always deserve a double reading, one for the story and one for the art, which is so complete that it is scarcely possible to comprehend all its bearings on the first perusal, though that which we do comprehend on the first perusal is of itself entirely satisfactory and sufficient. This is a great test of the genuineness of an imaginative work. . . .

Notwithstanding all this artistic excellence there are certain very serious defects in Mr. Hawthorne's tales. We will notice the two faults which chiefly strike us. One is mainly artistic, the other mainly moral. The artistic fault is the continual, and certainly the very effective, though faulty, use of the *supernatural*. Now, the supernatural, as Mr. Hawthorne uses it, is perhaps an allowable means of effect in a work which is only meant to endure for the day and hour in which such work is written and read; but Mr. Hawthorne's tales are too permanently valuable to admit, legitimately, of so large an admixture of an element of effect which fails upon the second reading. Mr. Hawthorne manages the supernatural so well, he makes it so credible by refining away the line of demarcation between the natural and supernatural, he derives profit, so ingeniously from the existing tremor of the public mind, arising from what is seen and said of mesmerism, electro-biology, spirit-rappings, and Swedenborgian psychology, that we could have made no objection to one trial of his faculties for rendering nightmares compatible with daylight and open eyes; but when the thing is done over and over again, and the sober and admirable nature of his stories continually overwhelmed with this insane supernature, it loses its value. Nature being a

thing of beauty, is a joy for ever; but a trick, however skilful and astonishing, is not worth seeing more than once. Mr. Hawthorne should,
moreover, recollect that, in the course of a few years at most, the class
of phenomena upon which he relies for his most vivid colouring will
certainly either sink to the sober level of natural facts, or will be exploded as impostures and vapours of enfeebled brains. The 'supernatural'
is only interesting beyond other things so long as it continues to vibrate
between the credible and the incredible. The credible, however exalted,
is nature,—the absolutely incredible is a lie, and neither nature nor
supernature. If ever clairvoyance and spirit-rappings become established *facts*, they will immediately fall into the domains of nature;
spiritual nature, indeed, but still nature; and they will be no more
'extraordinary' or 'supernatural' than any of those moral phenomena
whose realities daily plague or pacify the conscience, although they fail
to present any very distinct and tangible substance to the eye of the
mere understanding. When this comes to pass all the 'supernatural'
colouring of Mr. Hawthorne's tales will resemble the prominent
'lights' of Sir Joshua Reynolds' pictures, which, through some fault of
the artist, have all changed to blackness and vacancy. It must be further
remarked, that Mr. Hawthorne's error in this matter is not wholly
artistical; he is damaging the cause of truth in endowing with such a
wonderful semblance of reality things in which he himself has no
settled faith. . . .

The other charge we have to make against Mr. Hawthorne is a far
graver one, and not unallied with that with which we have now been
engaged. The fault in question is that of making the moral subserve the
art, instead of the art the moral; and furthermore, of even distorting
moral truth, in order to obtain artistic effect. Mr. Hawthorne's mind is
much too discerning to allow of a verdict of 'not guilty,' or of 'quite
unintentional error.' In Mr. Hawthorne's hands, the Christian faith is
strangely mixed up with a nightmare feeling of fatality, a combination
which certainly produces a very strong artistic effect, but which, as it is
formed at the expense of Christian reality, we do not hesitate to condemn. Again, the great fundamental truth of all morality, that God's
violated laws vindicate themselves, is obscured by the frequent employment of supernatural means of restoring the equilibrium destroyed
by sin. Mesmerism, magic signs in heaven and earth, witches, and evil
persons endowed with a fiendish ubiquity and omniscience, are not
needed, or employed, to work out the moral harmony of the world;
and to use them as Mr. Hawthorne does, is to do as much as lies in his

power, to weaken his reader's apprehension of the most solid and self-sufficient of all realities. Those who have not perused any of Mr. Hawthorne's works, will scarcely understand or credit the statement of the very extraordinary impression which those works are calculated to leave upon the mind. Upon laying down one of these books, we seem to have been living in a world of bad dreams, and horribly consistent insanities; the author's wonderful power of describing, and of *harmonizing*, the strangest characters and incidents, gives, for the time, a strong impression of the possibility and reality of such events and persons; and so long as this impression remains, vibrating in the heart and mind, the ordinary realities of life seem to totter, and to become insubstantial. This impression is always of a strongly moral kind; but the morality is often partial and perverted, and sometimes unchristian, if not anti-christian. . . .

Mr. Hawthorne's *chef-d'œuvre* is . . . his last work 'The Blithedale Romance.' In this tale, the writer, with an irony of withering calmness, exposes the vanity and selfishness which underlies the seemingly worthy and benevolent purposes of the various *dramatis personæ*, who engage themselves in one of the many schemes of politico-moral reformation which moderns have invented as substitutes for the reformation of themselves. . . . A defect of this very remarkable book, is the absence of any sufficient glimpse of the realities whose opposites it is, we suppose, Mr. Hawthorne's desire to teach us to shun. Silas Foster, as we have said, is the only real person in the drama. Zenobia and Priscilla, in their several extremes, are alike destitute of true womanhood—Hollingsworth and Coverdale, in their opposite ways, equally unmanly. As is always the case with clever and selfish persons, Zenobia, Coverdale, Hollingsworth, and others in this tale, have a singular acuteness to one another's defects, and an obtuseness no less extraordinary to their own.

We have devoted the larger portion of our space to the writings of Mr. Hawthorne, because we believe that he is altogether the most remarkable prose writer yet produced by America. His writings are highly condensed, which is more than can be said of nine-tenths of the American novelists, essayists, historians, or theologians; and they are admirably consecutive and well brought out, which is more than we can say of any but one or two individuals of the remaining tenth, who, like Ralph Waldo Emerson and Longfellow, are condensed, but ejaculatory and incapable of pursuing a thought or a story with logic and determination. He also writes pure English, which is what the Americans ought, just now, chiefly to look to, for, as we shall shew, they are in danger of abusing their noble inheritance of a pure, sweet, and powerful language, by an admixture of slang, flippancies, and false grammar, which will become a chronic and even an incurable disease, unless it is seasonably withstood and checked by writers like Mr. Hawthorne.

MOSSES FROM AN OLD MANSE
1854

97. Hawthorne, from a letter to James T. Fields, in James T. Fields' *Yesterdays with Authors*
13 April 1854 [1871] pp. 75-6

I am very glad that the 'Mosses' have come into the hands of our firm; and I return the copy sent me after a careful revision. When I wrote those dreamy sketches, I little thought that I should ever preface an edition for the press amidst the bustling life of a Liverpool consul. Upon my honor, I am not quite sure that I entirely comprehend my own meaning in some of these blasted allegories; but I remember that I always had a meaning—or, at least, thought I had. I am a good deal changed since those times; and to tell you the truth, my past self is not very much to my taste, as I see myself in this book. Yet certainly there is more in it than the public generally gave me credit for, at the time it was written.

But I don't think myself worthy of very much more credit than I got. It has been a very disagreeable task to read this book. The story of 'Rappaccini's Daughter' was published in the Democratic Review, about the year 1844; and it was prefaced by some remarks on the celebrated French author (a certain M. de l'Aubepine) from whose works it was translated. I left out this preface, when the story was republished; but I wish you would turn to it in the Democratic; and see whether it is worth while to insert it in the new edition. . . .

98. Unsigned review in *Graham's Magazine*

November 1854, xlv, 492

This is a new edition, carefully revised by the author, of a work published in New York several years ago, and containing some of the ripest products of Hawthorne's mind. The account of the 'Old Manse,' the stories of the 'Birthmark,' 'Young Goodman Brown,' 'Rappaccini's Daughter,' 'Egotism,' 'The Artist of the Beautiful,' 'The Christmas Banquet,' 'Drowne's Wooden Image,' 'Roger Malvin's Burial,' will not soon be forgotten by any readers who have previously made their acquaintance. 'P.'s Correspondence,' is one of the most ingenious and striking of all Hawthorne's works. 'Earth's Holocaust,' (which we take pride in saying was originally published in this magazine,) 'The Celestial Railroad,' and 'The Procession of Life,' are profoundly philosophical in their meaning and purpose, while the ideas they expound are clothed in forms of equal vividness and simplicity. 'Feathertop,' and 'Passages from an Unpublished Work,' are new. The latter is Hawthorne all over—thoroughly steeped in his peculiar sentiment and humor. The publishers have issued the volumes in a shape which makes them agree with their uniform edition of Hawthorne's other works—'The Twice Told Tales,' 'The Snow Image,' 'The Scarlet Letter,' 'The House of Seven Gables,' and 'The Blithedale Romance,' eight volumes in all. We need not say that every American who has the least appreciation of literary art, and who desires to own all the great and original efforts of the American mind in the sphere of romance, should possess a complete edition of Hawthorne. Popular as this great writer is, and large as has been the circulation of his writings, we still think that if his merits were as widely known as they deserve, he would have ten readers where he now has one. In England his genius seems to be more deeply appreciated than in his own land. There he is considered the foremost man in our literature.

99. A British comparison of Poe and Hawthorne, from an unsigned essay, 'American Literature: Poe; Hawthorne', in *Tait's Edinburgh Magazine*

January 1855, xxii, 33–41

When we ask for the *most* original writer yet produced by America, we are at once directed to Edgar Allan Poe and reminded of 'The Raven: a Poem.' We, personally, have nothing to object against the statement that Poe is the most original of American authors, so long as in admitting the 'originality' we are not supposed to yield him the *very highest rank* in the literature of the New World. This is quite another thing, though, we fear, not generally understood to be so. We give Poe the foremost place in his class, but that class is not the highest. . . . A work of genius is the result of the spontaneous and harmonious exercise (or outflow) of any number of faculties, excited to such a degree of activity that the product shall be homogeneous (we mean no pun), and exclude the idea of *process*. With all that Poe has written (as far as we know) *fully* present to our minds, we are prepared to deny that he has left behind him any such work. We concede to him—

1. Extraordinary, perhaps unparalleled, powers of analysis, and of retention;

2. Great command of language;

3. Very great imitative and constructive tact;

4. An ideality sufficiently intense to tinge, (but not to saturate and deeply colour), all his conceptions;

5. All these receiving a special direction from a love of the wonderful and mysterious, and a gloomy *morale,* in which a sense of the terrible was an everpresent influence.

This combination of powerful elements does not, however, make the thing called *genius*. . . .

Our estimate of Poe would not be complete, if we omitted to specify what we deny, as well as what we concede to him. We cannot allow Poe to have possessed more than an infinitesmal endowment of either

306

Conscience or Affection. About the first of these items, there will perhaps be little dispute: it has, indeed, been pretty generally recognised
that the man was a creature of wonderful powers in whose composition
'conscience had been left out.' But we do not know that it has ever
been noticed that in all his writings there is no development of any
sentiment or idea that is strictly moral. . . .

Let us refresh ourselves by turning to Nathaniel Hawthorne, who is,
or was recently, the American Consul at Liverpool, and who has a
warm corner in English hearts wherever he is or may be. Many happy
new years to Nathaniel Hawthorne! Immeasurably Poe's inferior in
analytical talent, but as much his superior in insight; with less constructive tact and command of words, but with an intenser ideality; no
delver into day-dreading horrors, but a lover and reproducer of sunshine and all genial things; sweetly human in his sympathies, reverenc-
ing women and children, full of highest aspiration,—Hawthorne does
not rank so high among men of genius, as Poe among men of talent,—
but a man of *genius* he is, if words mean anything. He is a prose-poet, a
little too prone to 'metaphysical conceits.' A phrenologist would say,
he is Emerson over again, with a keener eye for (not simple existences,
but) incident; to speak 'by the card' . . . with a larger bump of
Eventuality. There are passages in Emerson—*e.g.* in the surpassing
Essays on Love and on Friendship—which might very well have been
written by Hawthorne; and if the sage of Concord had sat down to
write a short story, he would surely have produced Hawthorne's
'Artist of the Beautiful.' Mr. Hawthorne's writings belong, most
distinctly, to the nineteenth century; no other age than our own could
have produced them, and in some of them the vague suggestions arising
from topics of the day are too firmly woven into the texture of the
story for the author's acceptance with the majority of readers. . . .

The year 3000 may find the 'Blithedale Romance' an instructive as
well as interesting record of humanity in its go-cart, feeling its little way;
but the number is very small of the readers of to-day, who care for the
memorial of a social experiment woven into a romance. We doubt
whether the book is to be found at one in fifty of our circulating libra-
ries,—which is, of course, no reproach to a writer who does not wield
the pen for circulating library readers, or care for making his volume the
book of a season. Mr. Hawthorne 'fishes with a heavy sinker.'

The two stories by which Mr. Hawthorne is best known are, 'The
House of Seven Gables' and the 'Scarlet Letter'—the second being the
greater favourite with general readers, partly because there is more unity,

with less remoteness of design, in the story; and partly because it contains more pathos, while what some one has called 'metaphysical conceits' are fewer; but it cannot be doubted that the mysteriously-sounding title has led thousands to open the book, saying, 'What *can* the *Scarlet Letter* be?' . . .

To ourselves, the 'Scarlet Letter' has always been rather a painful book. Nothing is more unsatisfactory than to be taken by your author into a labyrinth of moral horrors, and left there when he leaves the narrative. . . . Did Mr. Hawthorne *mean* the 'Flood of Sunshine' to be the oftenest-read, and best-remembered chapter in the book? . . .

We are tempted to write that Mr. Hawthorne is the most pure-minded of story-tellers, absolutely *the* most free from all taint of grossness. Let him tell you about Phoebe, of Clifford noting 'the ripeness of her lips, and virginal development of her bosom,—all her little womanly ways budding out of her like blossoms on a young fruit-tree,' and you are only imparadised. But Eugéne Sue could not have written so minutely about a sweet girl, without making you feel the difference between a prose-poet and a prosing sensualist.

No attentive reader of Nathaniel Hawthorne, especially no reader of the 'Mosses from an Old Manse,' can fail to discern that there is always, or nearly always, a typical meaning running through Mr. Hawthorne's stories. Notable instances are to be found in the 'Birth-Mark,' and the 'Artist of the Beautiful.' In the former, there are features which point to the 'Scarlet Letter;' in the latter, to the 'House of Seven Gables.' . . .

Of various typical meanings capable of being given to the 'House of Seven Gables,' we give that which occurred to us first, and which seems best supported by a reference to the 'Mosses.' It is eminently a nineteenth-century story. All the way through, Law and Convention are presented as blind, stupid powers, siding with the strong, when strength *is* most unjust. The Pyncheon of olden times is surely the type of Might, wicked Might, grasping the heritage of Industry in the name of Religion, while the law hallows the wrong, and creates a nominally 'just' right for the 'owner' of things originally acquired by rapine and murder. The Maule family stands for Labour and Invention robbed of their birthright, and biding their time. Hepzibah for Aristocracy, become, as now, old-womanish, and driven, in days of 'unrestricted competition,' when the cotton-lord may buy up the land-lord, to ally itself with the very Industry which, in olden days, it contemned. Alice, with her posies and her harpsichord, represents the shadowy grace and beauty which haunt things that have 'hoar antiquity' and prescription in their favour. Clifford is the analogue of the Gentle and Beautiful, pushed aside or trodden upon by rampant Material Success, whose type is the 'Pyncheon of to-day.' Young Holgrave is the old, wronged Industry, backed by science and stirred by daring speculation, now coming forward, in fresh guise and fashion, to claim its own. Uncle Venner is extremest Poverty, pauperism, dignified in our eyes by contributing its own peculiar lessons of wisdom: 'You are welcome, friends, to my mess of dandelions!' Phoebe is—Phoebe, and has such a corner in our hearts that we do not like to make anything else of her, least of all an abstraction. But surely this pretty creation of Mr. Hawthorne's must stand for the Middle Classes of Society, to whom has been committed by Providence the mission of social reconciliation; which, once completed, the disunited are joined, the unblest, blest, and the 'wild reformer' becomes a Conservative after Heaven's own fashion. Moan no longer, old harpsichord! Home to thy rest, grieved Shade! Cease they prophecies, O whispering elm, and break into murmurous thanksgivings!

Turning a farewell thought to the humanity, purpose, and purity of Nathaniel Hawthorne's writings, our minds revert insensibly to poor, unhappy Edgar Allan Poe. Ah! we cry, what a burden of grief and shame lies in

L'immenza impieta, la vita indegna![1]

Far from all remembrance of Mr. Hawthorne be any thought of such a sacrilege.

[1] *L'immenza impieta, la vita indegna!*: The immense impiety, the unworthy life!

100. A British objection to Hawthorne and his audience, from an unsigned essay, 'Modern Novelists—Great and Small', in *Blackwood's Magazine*

May 1855, lxxvii, 562–6

The books of Mr Hawthorne are singular books: they introduce to us not only an individual mind, but a peculiar audience; they are not stories into which you enter and sympathise, but dramas of extraordinary dumb show, before which, in darkness and breathless silence, you sit and look on, never sure for a moment that the dimly-lighted stage before you is not to be visited by the dioramic thunders of an earthquake, falling houses, moaning victims, dismay and horror and gloom. Had the reputation of this gentleman been confined to his own country, it would have been out of our sphere of comment; but he has had great popularity on this side of the Atlantic, where we understand he is now resident, and his books have perhaps excited the public curiosity almost as much as the books of Miss Bronte. *The Scarlet Letter* glows with the fire of a suppressed, secret, feverish excitement; it is not the glow of natural life, but the hectic of disease which burns upon the cheeks of its actors. The proud woman, the fantastic and elfish child, the weak and criminal genius, and the injured friend, the husband of Hester, are exhibited to us rather as a surgeon might exhibit his pet 'cases,' than as a poet shows his men and women, brothers and sisters to the universal heart. In this book the imagination of the writer has been taxed to supply a world and a society in accordance with the principal actors in his feverish drama. . . .

The House of Seven Gables is not less remarkable nor less unwholesome than its predecessor. The affectation of extreme homeliness and commonplace in the external circumstances, and the mystery and secret of the family with which these circumstances are interwoven, is very effective in its way; and if it were not that its horrors and its wonders are protracted into tedious long-windedness, we would be disposed to admire the power with which these figures were posed and these situations made. But we are never contented with manufactured stories. If they do not grow with a sweet progression of nature, they may please our eye, or flatter, with a sense of superiority to the multitude, our critical faculties; but we cannot take such productions into our heart.

In the death-scene of Judge Pyncheon, we are wearied and worried out of all the horror and impressiveness which might have been in it, had its author only known when to stop. Perhaps there is scarcely such another piece of over-description in the language. The situation is fairly worn to pieces. Throughout the book this is the leading error. Everything is dwelt upon with a tedious minuteness. The motion is slow and heavy. The story-teller holds our buttons and pours out his sentences all in the same cadence. We feel ourselves compelled to submit and listen to the long story. But even the power and fascination it undoubtedly possesses, does not impel us to forgive the author for this interminable strain upon our patience. Like the wedding guest in the *Ancient Mariner*, we sit reluctantly to hear it out; and when it is done, and no adequate reward is forthcoming of either wisdom or pleasure, we are injured and indignant, and do not understand why we have been detained so long to so little purpose. For it is no particular gratification to us to know how Mr Hawthorne studies his subjects—how he sets them in different lights, like a child with a new toy, and gets new glimpses of their character and capabilities—we want the result, and not the process—the story completed, but not the photographs from which it is to be made.

In the *Blythedale Romance* we have still less of natural character, and more of a diseased and morbid conventional life. American patriots ought to have no quarrel with our saucy tourists and wandering notabilities, in comparison with the due and just quarrel they have with writers of their own. What extraordinary specimens of womankind are Zenobia and Priscilla, the heroines of this tale! What a meddling, curious, impertinent rogue, a psychological Paul Pry, is Miles Coverdale, the teller of the story! How thoroughly worn out and *blasé* must that young world be, which gets up excitements in its languid life, only by means of veiled ladies, mysterious clairvoyants, rapping spirits, or, in a milder fashion, by sherry-cobler and something cocktails for the men, and lectures on the rights of women for the ladies. We enter this strange existence with a sort of wondering inquiry whether any *events* ever take place there, or if, instead, there is nothing to be done but for everybody to observe everybody else, and for all society to act on the universal impulse of getting up a tragedy somewhere, for the pleasure of looking at it; or if that may not be, of setting up supernatural intercourse one way or another, and warming up with occult and forbidden influences the cold and waveless tide of life. We do not believe in Zenobia drowning herself. It is a piece of sham entirely, and never impresses us with the slightest idea of reality. Nor are we moved with any single emotion throughout the entire course of the tale. There is nothing touching in the mystery of old Moodie; nothing attractive in the pale clairvoyant Priscilla—the victim, as we are led to suppose, of Mesmerism and its handsome diabolical professor. We are equally indifferent to the imperious and splendid Zenobia, and to the weak sketchy outline of Hollingsworth, whose 'stern' features are washed in with the faintest water-colours, and who does not seem capable of anything but of making these two women fall in love with him. The sole thing that looks true, and seems to have blood in its veins, is Silas Foster, the farmer and manager of practical matters for the Utopian community, which proposes to reform the world by making ploughmen of themselves. Could they have done it honestly, we cannot fancy any better plan for the visionary inhabitants of the farm and the romance of Blythedale. Honest work might do a great deal for these languid philosophers; and Mr. Hawthorne himself, we should suppose, could scarcely be in great condition for dissecting his neighbours and their 'inner nature' after a day's ploughing or reaping; but mystery, Mesmerism, love, and jealousy, are too many for the placid angel of agriculture, and young America by no means makes a success in its experiment, either by reforming others or itself.

After all, we are not ethereal people. We are neither fairies nor angels. Even to make our conversation—and, still more, to make our life—we want more than thoughts and fancies—we want *things*. You may sneer at the commonplace necessity, yet it *is* one; and it is precisely your Zenobias and Hollingsworths, your middle-aged people, who have broken loose from family and kindred, and have no *events* in their life, who do all the mischief, and make all the sentimentalisms and false philosophies in the world. When we come to have no duties, except those we 'owe to ourselves' or 'to society,' woe to us! Wise were the novelists of old, who ended their story with the youthful marriage, which left the hero and the heroine on the threshold of the maturer dangers of life, when fiction would not greatly aid them, but when the battle-ground, the real conflict, enemies not to be chased away, and sorrows unforgetable, remained. The trials of youth are safe ground;

and so, to a considerable extent, are the trials of husbands and wives, when they struggle with the world, and not with each other; but the solitary maturer men and women, who have nothing happening to them, who are limited by no particular duties, and have not even the blessed necessity of working for their daily bread—these are the problem of the world; and the novelist had need to be wary who tries to deal with it.

We believe no one will deny great talent to Mr Hawthorne; and if he would but be brief, we would admit, with greater satisfaction, the power of his situations, and the effectiveness of his scenery. . . .

Mr Hawthorne, we are afraid, is one of those writers who aim at an intellectual audience, and address themselves mainly to such. We are greatly of opinion that this is a mistake and a delusion, and that nothing good comes of it. The novelist's true audience is the common people—the people of ordinary comprehension and everyday sympathies, whatever their rank may be.

THE MARBLE FAUN
[TRANSFORMATION]
1859–61

---

101. Hawthorne, Preface

15 October 1859

It is now seven or eight years (so many, at all events, that I cannot precisely remember the epoch) since the Author of this Romance last
appeared before the Public. It had grown to be a custom with him, to
introduce each of his humble publications with a familiar kind of Preface, addressed nominally to the Public at large, but really to a character
with whom he felt entitled to use far greater freedom. He meant it for
that one congenial friend—more comprehensive of his purposes, more
appreciative of his success, more indulgent of his short-comings, and, in
all respects, closer and kinder than a brother—that all-sympathizing
critic, in short, whom an author never actually meets, but to whom he
implicitly makes his appeal, whenever he is conscious of having done his
best.

The antique fashion of Prefaces recognized this genial personage as
the 'Kind Reader,' the 'Gentle Reader,' the 'Beloved,' the 'Indulgent,' or,
at coldest, the 'Honoured Reader,' to whom the prim old author was
wont to make his preliminary explanations and apologies, with the
certainty that they would be favourably received. I never personally
encountered, nor corresponded through the Post, with this Representative Essence of all delightful and desirable qualities which a Reader can
possess. But, fortunately for myself, I never therefore concluded him to
be merely a mythic character. I had always a sturdy faith in his actual
existence, and wrote for him, year after year, during which the great
Eye of the Public (as well it might) almost utterly overlooked my small
productions.

Unquestionably, this Gentle, Kind, Benevolent, Indulgent, and most
Beloved and Honoured Reader, did once exist for me, and (in spite of
the infinite chances against a letter's reaching its destination, without a

314

definite address) duly received the scrolls which I flung upon whatever wind was blowing, in the faith that they would find him out. But, is he extant now? In these many years, since he last heard from me, may he not have deemed his earthly task accomplished, and have withdrawn to the Paradise of Gentle Readers, wherever it may be, to the enjoyments of which his kindly charity, on my behalf, must surely have entitled him? I have a sad foreboding that this may be the truth. The Gentle Reader, in the case of any individual author, is apt to be extremely short-lived; he seldom outlasts a literary fashion, and, except in very rare instances, closes his weary eyes before the writer has half done with him. If I find him at all, it will probably be under some mossy gravestone, inscribed with a half-obliterated name, which I shall never recognize.

Therefore, I have little heart or confidence (especially, writing, as I do, in a foreign land, and after a long, long absence from my own) to presume upon the existence of that friend of friends, that unseen brother of the soul, whose apprehensive sympathy has so often encouraged me to be egotistical in my Prefaces, careless though unkindly eyes should skim over what was never meant for them. I stand upon ceremony, now, and, after stating a few particulars about the work which is here offered to the Public, must make my most reverential bow, and retire behind the curtain.

This Romance was sketched out during a residence of considerable length in Italy, and has been re-written and prepared for the press, in England. The author proposed to himself merely to write a fanciful story, evolving a thoughtful moral, and did not purpose attempting a portraiture of Italian manners and character. He has lived too long abroad, not to be aware that a foreigner seldom acquires that knowledge of a country, at once flexible and profound, which may justify him in endeavouring to idealize its traits.

Italy, as the site of his Romance, was chiefly valuable to him as affording a sort of poetic or fairy precinct, where actualities would not be so terribly insisted upon, as they are, and must needs be, in America. No author, without a trial, can conceive of the difficulty of writing a Romance about a country where there is no shadow, no antiquity, no mystery, no picturesque and gloomy wrong, nor anything but a common-place prosperity, in broad and simple daylight, as is happily the case with my dear native land. It will be very long, I trust, before romance-writers may find congenial and easily handled themes either in the annals of our stalwart Republic, or in any characteristic and probable events of our individual lives. Romance and poetry, like ivy, lichens, and wall-flowers, need Ruin to make them grow.

In re-writing these volumes, the Author was somewhat surprised to see the extent to which he had introduced descriptions of various Italian objects, antique, pictorial, and statuesque. Yet these things fill the mind, everywhere in Italy, and especially in Rome, and cannot easily be kept from flowing out upon the page, when one writes freely, and with self-enjoyment. And, again, while reproducing the book, on the broad and dreary sands of Redcar, with the gray German Ocean tumbling in upon me, and the northern blast always howling in my ears, the complete change of scene made these Italian reminiscences shine out so vividly, that I could not find in my heart to cancel them.

An act of justice remains to be performed towards two men of genius, with whose productions the Author has allowed himself to use a quite unwarrantable freedom. Having imagined a sculptor, in this Romance, it was necessary to provide him with such works in marble as should be in keeping with the artistic ability which he was supposed to possess. With this view, the Author laid felonious hands upon a certain bust of Milton and a statue of a Pearl-Diver, which he found in the studio of Mr. PAUL AKERS, and secretly conveyed them to the premises of his imaginary friend, in the Via Frezza. Not content even with these spoils, he committed a further robbery upon a magnificent statue of Cleopatra, the production of Mr. WILLIAM W. STORY, an artist whom his country and the world will not long fail to appreciate. He had thoughts of appropriating, likewise, a certain door of bronze, by Mr. RANDOLPH ROGERS, representing the history of Columbus in a series of admirable bas-reliefs, but was deterred by an unwillingness to meddle with public property. Were he capable of stealing from a lady, he would certainly have made free with Miss HOSMER's noble statue of Zenobia.

He now wishes to restore the above-mentioned beautiful pieces of sculpture to their proper owners, with many thanks, and the avowal of his sincere admiration. What he has said of them, in the Romance, does not partake of the fiction in which they are imbedded, but expresses his genuine opinion, which, he has little doubt, will be found in accordance with that of the Public. It is perhaps unnecessary to say, that, while stealing their designs, the Author has not taken a similar liberty with the personal characters of either of these gifted Sculptors; his own Man of Marble being entirely imaginary.

102. [Henry F. Chorley], from a review in the *Athenaeum*

3 March 1860, pp. 296–7

Both Hawthorne and Mrs. Hawthorne wrote to Chorley about this review, Hawthorne adding these remarks to his wife's:

You see how fortunate I am in having a critic close at hand, whose favorable verdict consoles me for any lack of appreciation in other quarters. Really, I think you were wrong in assaulting the individuality of my poor Hilda. If her portrait bears any resemblance to that of Phoebe, it must be the fault of my mannerism as a painter. But I thank you for the kind spirit of your notice; and if you had found ten times as much fault, you are amply entitled to do so by the quantity of praise heretofore bestowed. (Julian Hawthorne, *Nathaniel Hawthorne and His Wife* [1884], ii, 247–8).

Not with impunity can a novelist produce two such books—each, of its class, perfect—as 'The Scarlet Letter' and 'The House of the Seven Gables.' He is expected to go on; and his third and fourth romances will be measured by their two predecessors, without reference to the fact that there may be slow growth and solitary perfection in works of genius. The yew and the locust-tree have different natural habits. Then, for one to whom all Europe is looking for a part of its pleasure, to stop the course of his labours is a piece of independence hard to forgive. Thirdly, there is hazard in an attempt to change the scale of creative exercise when an artist has shown himself perfect in the one originally adopted. . . .

It is only fit, fair, and friendly that the above three considerations should be allowed their full weight in adjudging the merit of Mr. Hawthorne's fourth and longest work of fiction, produced after the pause of many years. It would be idle to appeal to them were the production which calls them forth not a remarkable one—one of the most remarkable novels that 1860 is likely to give us, whether from English, French, or American sources.

Mr. Hawthorne has drunk in the spirit of Italian beauty at every pore. The scene of this romance is principally at Rome, and the writer's intense yearning to reproduce and accumulate his recollections of that wonderful city appears to have again and again possessed itself of heart and pen, to the suspense, not damage, of his story. Who would object to wait for the progress of passion and the development of mystery on being beckoned aside into such a land of rich and melancholy enchantment as is disclosed in the following exquisite picture of the Borghese Gardens?—

[Quotes ch. 8, 'The entrance to' to 'they call life' and 'The scenery amid' to 'actual possessions'.]

. . . We have inadvertently touched on the great scenic power and beauty of this Italian Romance ere offering a word on its matter and argument. Whether the elevating influences of remorse on certain natures have ever been taken as the theme of a story so fearlessly as here, may be questioned. Casuists and moralists must discuss the truth of the data. To Mr. Hawthorne truth always seems to arrive through the medium of his imagination;—some far-off phantasy to suggest a train of thought and circumstance out of which philosophies are evolved and characters grow. His hero, the Count of Monte Beni, would never have lived had not the Faun of Praxiteles stirred the authors' admiration; and this mythical creature so engaged the dreamer's mind, that he draws out of the past the fancy of an old family endowed with certain constant attributes of Sylvan gaiety and careless, semi-animal enjoyments such as belonged to the dances and sunshine of Arcady. Such is Donatello at the beginning of the tale; and with these qualities are mixed up unquestioning, simple love and fidelity, which can take a form of unreasoning animal fury in a moment of emergency. He is hurried into sudden murder for the sake of the woman he loves; and with that the Faun nature dies out, and the sad, conscience-stricken human being begins, in the writhings of pain, to think, to feel,—lastly, to aspire. This, in a few words, is the meaning of 'Transformation'; and for the first moiety of the romance the story turns slowly, with windings clearly to be traced, yet powerfully, round its principal figure. The other characters Mr. Hawthorne must bear to be told are not new to a tale of his. Miriam, the mysterious, with her hideous tormentor, was indicated in the *Zenobia* of 'The Blithedale Romance,' —Hilda, the pure and innocent, is own cousin to *Phoebe* in 'The House of the Seven Gables,'—Kenyon, the sculptor, though carefully wrought out, is a stone image, with little that appeals to our experience of men. These are all the characters; and when it is added that Miriam is a magnificent paintress with a mystery, that Hilda is a copyist of pictures from New England, and that Kenyon is her countryman, enough has been told to define the brain creatures who figure in the wild 'Romance of Monte Beni'.

Mr. Hawthorne must be reckoned with for the second moiety of his book. In spite of the delicious Italian pictures, noble speculations, and snatches of arresting incident, which it contains, we know of little in Romance more inconclusive and hazy than the manner in which the tale is brought to its close. Hints will not suffice to satisfy interest which has been excited to voracity. Every incident need not lead to a mathematical conclusion nor *coup de theatre* (as in the comedies of M. Scribe), but the utter uncertainty which hangs about every one and every thing concerned in the strong emotions and combinations of half of this romance, makes us part company with them, as though we were awaking from a dream,—not bidding tearful farewell at the scaffold's foot to the convict,—not saying 'Go in peace' to the penitent who enters a religious house for the purposes of superstitious expiation,— not acquiring such late knowledge of the past as makes us lenient to crime, wrought by feeble human nature under the goad of long-drawn torture; and thus willing to forgive and accept the solution here proposed in so shadowy a fashion. Hilda and Kenyon marry, as it was to be seen they would do in the first page; but the secret of Miriam's agony and unrest, the manner of final extrication from it, for herself, and the gay Faun, who shed blood to defend her, then grew sad and human under the consciousness of the stain, are all left too vaporously involved in suggestion to satisfy any one whose blood has turned back at the admirable, clear and forcible last scenes of 'The Scarlet Letter.'

103. Hawthorne, from the Postscript

March 1860

On 9 March 1860 Hawthorne wrote to W. D. Ticknor: 'I intend to add a few pages to the concluding chapter, in order to make things a little clearer' (*Letters of Hawthorne to W. D. Ticknor, 1851–64* [1910], ii, 97).

There comes to the Author, from many readers of the foregoing pages, a demand for further elucidations respecting the mysteries of the story.

He reluctantly avails himself of the opportunity afforded by a new edition, to explain such incidents and passages as may have been left too much in the dark; reluctantly, he repeats, because the necessity makes him sensible that he can have succeeded but imperfectly, at best, in throwing about this Romance the kind of atmosphere essential to the effect at which he aimed. He designed the story and the characters to bear, of course, a certain relation to human nature and human life, but still to be so artfully and airily removed from our mundane sphere, that some laws and proprieties of their own should be implicitly and insensibly acknowledged.

The idea of the modern Faun, for example, loses all the poetry and beauty which the Author fancied in it, and becomes nothing better than a grotesque absurdity, if we bring it into the actual light of day. He had hoped to mystify this anomalous creature between the Real and the Fantastic, in such a manner that the reader's sympathies might be excited to a certain pleasurable degree, without impelling him to ask how Cuvier would have classified poor Donatello, or to insist upon being told, in so many words, whether he had furry ears or no. As respects all who ask such questions, the book is, to that extent, a failure.

Nevertheless, the Author fortunately has it in his power to throw light upon several matters in which some of his readers appear to feel an interest. To confess the truth, he was himself troubled with a curiosity similar to that which he has just deprecated on the part of his readers, and once took occasion to cross-examine his friends, Hilda and the sculptor, and to pry into several dark recesses of the story, with which they had heretofore imperfectly acquainted him. . . .

104. [James Russell Lowell], from a review in the *Atlantic Monthly*

April 1860, v, 509–10

The nineteenth century has produced no more purely original writer than Mr. Hawthorne. A shallow criticism has sometimes fancied a resemblance between him and Poe. But it seems to us that the difference between them is the immeasurable one between talent carried to its ultimate, and genius,—between a masterly adaptation of the world of sense and appearance to the purposes of Art, and a so thorough conception of the world of moral realities that Art becomes the interpreter of something profounder than herself. In this respect it is not extravagant to say that Hawthorne has something of kindred with Shakspeare. But that breadth of nature which made Shakspeare incapable of alienation from common human nature and actual life is wanting to Hawthorne. He is rather a denizen than a citizen of what men call the world. We are conscious of a certain remoteness in his writings, as in those of Donne, but with such a difference that we should call the one super- and the other subter-sensual. Hawthorne is psychological and metaphysical. Had he been born without the poetic imagination, he would have written treatises on the Origin of Evil. He does not draw characters, but rather conceives them and then shows them acted upon by crime, passion, or circumstance, as if the element of Fate were as present to his imagination as to that of a Greek dramatist. Helen we know, Antigone, and Benedick, and Falstaff, and Miranda, and Parson Adams, and Major Pendennis,—these people have walked on pavements or looked out of club-room windows; but what are these idiosyncrasies into which Mr. Hawthorne has breathed a necromantic life, and which he has endowed with the forms and attributes of men? And yet, grant him his premises, that is, let him once get his morbid tendency, whether inherited or the result of special experience, either incarnated as a new man or usurping all the faculties of one already in the flesh, and it is marvellous how subtilely and with what truth to as much of human nature as is included in a diseased consciousness he traces all the finest nerves of impulse and motive, how he compels every trivial circumstance into an accomplice of his art, and makes the sky flame with foreboding or the landscape chill and darken with remorse. It is impossible to think of Hawthorne without at the same time thinking of the few great masters of imaginative composition; his works, only not abstract because he has the genius to make them ideal, belong not specially to our clime or generation; it is their moral purpose alone, and perhaps their sadness, that mark him as the son of New England and the Puritans.

It is commonly true of Hawthorne's romances that the interest centres in one strongly defined protagonist, to whom the other characters are accessory and subordinate,—perhaps we should rather say a ruling Idea, of which all the characters are fragmentary embodiments. They remind us of a symphony of Beethoven's, in which, though there be variety of parts, yet all are infused with the dominant motive, and heighten its impression by hints and far-away suggestions at the most unexpected moment. As in Rome the obelisks are placed at points toward which several streets converge, so in Mr. Hawthorne's stories the actors and incidents seem but vistas through which we see the moral from different points of view,—a moral pointing skyward always, but inscribed with hieroglyphs mysteriously suggestive, whose incitement to conjecture, while they baffle it, we prefer to any prosaic solution.

Nothing could be more original or imaginative than the conception of the character of Donatello in Mr. Hawthorne's new romance. His likeness to the lovely statue of Praxiteles, his happy animal temperament, and the dim legend of his pedigree are combined with wonderful art to reconcile us to the notion of a Greek myth embodied in an Italian of the nineteenth century; and when at length a soul is created in this primeval pagan, this child of earth, this creature of mere instinct, awakened through sin to a conception of the necessity of atonement, we feel, that, while we looked to be entertained with the airiest of fictions, we were dealing with the most august truths of psychology, with the most pregnant facts of modern history, and studying a profound parable of the development of the Christian Idea.

Everything suffers a sea-change in the depths of Mr. Hawthorne's mind, gets rimmed with an impalpable fringe of melancholy moss, and there is a tone of sadness in this book as in the rest, but it does not leave us sad. In a series of remarkable and characteristic works, it is perhaps the most remarkable and characteristic. If you had picked up and read a stray leaf of it anywhere, you would have exclaimed, 'Hawthorne!'

The book is steeped in Italian atmosphere. There are many land-scapes in it full of breadth and power, and criticisms of pictures and statues always delicate, often profound. . . .

105. Unsigned review in the *Westminster Review*

April 1860, lxxiii, 624–7

The two most original novelists of America are unquestionably E. A. Poe and N. Hawthorne, and however great their difference in other points, and most of all in the moral impression of their works, they agree in one remarkable peculiarity; they both, as Hawthorne says of his last heroine, delight to brood on the verge of some great mystery, but their mode of treating the mysteries they delight in is of the most opposite character.

Poe loves to commence with some startling circumstance that has to be explained, and exhibits a most wonderful analysis of the attendant facts that are to elucidate, and to throw light upon it. Hawthorne, on the other hand, delights to start from the common and quiet events of life, and gradually to build up, with a skill that no one has approached, a structure of fear and wonder that partakes of the supernatural, and finds its root in the passions of his characters. The sharp and acute criticism which resolves the most perplexing problems into the commonplaces of life which distinguishes Poe's most remarkable productions, is the very opposite of that brooding over the mysteries of individual will which lend their chief charm to the works of Hawthorne.

In his last novel he has endeavoured to give a symbolic picture of the nature of Sin, to offer, though with diffidence, and as a mere suggestion, an opinion which evidently has greater weight to his imagination than he is openly willing to allow. He makes his most balanced character, the person who represents the cool and intellectual type of mankind, inquire,

'Is sin then—which we deem such a dreadful blackness in the universe—is it, like sorrow, merely an element of human education, through which we struggle to a higher and purer state than we could otherwise have attained? Did Adam fall that we might ultimately rise to a far loftier Paradise than his?'

This question wounds his pure heroine as it will wound many of his readers, but it is the ground idea of the Book.

Struck by the wide divergence between the moral conceptions of antiquity and those of the present time, he works out the thesis, which he only indicates as if he felt the ground was too awful to be trodden by the firm and assured step of free inquiry. The *personel* of his story is extremely simple, two women and two men. His women and one of the men we have met before in the Blythedale Romance.

He says of one of his heroines, 'It is very singular how her imagination seemed to run on stories of bloodshed in which a woman's hand was crimsoned by the stain;' the singularity is one with which Hawthorne fully sympathises, and causes Miriam to be too much a repetition of Zenobia in his last romance. This passionate and at last criminal woman, stands side by side with a pure and holy Hilda, 'a daughter of the Puritans.' Both artists at Rome, their only fellowship is with Kenyon, an American sculptor alluded to above, and Donatello the hero of the tale, and the supporter of the questionable moral problem which underlies it. Donatello, the Count of Monte Beni, has during a passing visit to Rome, fallen into this circle of artists; a simple uneducated nature, he resigns himself to an absolute and unresisting devotion to Miriam, whose past history is a mystery to all, but whose generosity and noble nature make her beloved by all the little circle.

The mystery which attends her takes gradual and oppressive shape, and at last culminates in a strange and unaccountable follower, who serves her as a model, but exercises over her a power which none can understand; he naturally becomes the object of Donatello's hate, a hate as unreasoning as the antipathies of animals, and at last when witnessing the tyrannous exercise of the model's power over his beloved, he in answer to her despairing and appealing glances, throws him from the summit of the Tarpeian Rock on which they stood. The murder once committed, the moral action of the fable opens upon the reader. This Donatello, the child of nature, the gay companion of every animated thing in field or wood, the fabled descendant of an ancient Faun, who, it was said in the legends of his own country, had seduced an ancestress in the old times of the Etruscan Kings; this man without a thought beyond the loveliness of the present, this type of the old world before conscience prostrated that it might elevate mankind, this relic of the golden age, this Donatello, now awakes to the 'before and after,' and the painful throes of a questioning reason open to him through the valley of the shadow of death, a path to a new and more exalted life. The first effect of his crime is absolute horror of the mistress he had so loved, and whose appealing look had prompted him to the deed. His horror, though it benumbs, does not destroy his love, he flies to his Tuscan castle on the slopes of the Appenines and leads a solitary and despairing life.

Hither, after a time, Miriam follows him, awaiting in concealment that softening of the first poignancy of his remorse, which will allow of her offering such comfort and consolation as a devoted can offer to a bruised heart. This time at last arrives, but we must confess that the problem is stated at the outset of the story with far greater clearness than its solution is ultimately worked out; mysterious hints of atonement, of lives devoted to universal benevolence, of duty to each other, of mutual support, of relinquishment of love and of ultimate internal peace, afford but suggestive hints of a solution that should at least be as detailed as the difficulties to be solved. Kenyon and Hilda are artificial opposites of the real hero and heroine; they have but little flesh and blood; Hilda is a pure and beautiful dream—fit companion of the white doves among whom she lives in the upper floor of an old tower in Rome, and Kenyon a mere antithesis to Donatello. To praise the romance for a remarkable power of psychological analysis, to say that it abounds in piquant remarks and striking views, is only to say that it is a book of Hawthorne's. There is, however, one particular in which it is widely different from its predecessors, and the difference is to its disadvantage. The scene is laid in Italy, and not in the New World. It is impossible to deny the beauty of the descriptions of Italian scenes and objects, with which the romance abounds; but, at the same time, it is equally impossible to resist a certain disagreeable impression they produce. These laboured pictures of Italian skies, of well-known spots, of world-renowned statues, and of some in American studios not yet so famous, have a strange flavour of the news letter; and not only so, but of news addressed to an American public.

Such passages as the following are by no means rare:—

'Not a nude figure, I hope. Every young sculptor seems to think he must give the world some specimen of indecorous womanhood, and call it Eve, Venus, a Nymph, or any name that may apologise for a lack of decent clothing. I am weary, even more than I am ashamed, of seeing such things. Now-a-days people are as good as born in their clothes, and there is practically not a nude human being in existence.

'An artist, therefore, as you must candidly confess, cannot sculpture nudity with a pure heart, if only because he is compelled to steal guilty glimpses at hired models. The marble inevitably loses its chastity under such circumstances. An old Greek sculptor, no doubt, found his models in the open sunshine, and among pure and princely maidens, and thus the nude statues of antiquity are as modest as violets, and sufficiently draped in their own beauty. But as for Mr. Gibson's coloured Venuses (stained, I believe, with tobacco-juice), and all other nudities of to-day, I really do not understand what they have to say to this generation, and would be glad to see as many heaps of quicklime in their stead.'

This is provincial narrowness which partakes neither of the purity of nature nor of reason, but belongs only to that intermediate purgatorial position through which Mr. Hawthorne endeavours to lead his hero, Donatello. There are also one or two peculiarities of expression which fall gratingly on an English ear. Hawthorne sometimes makes use of American words that positively require a dictionary on this side the Atlantic; few of our readers will, we dare say, understand what is meant by the Archangel's feeling the old Serpent *squirm* mightily under his armed heel; and unless to a native of our eastern counties, where many Anglo-Saxon words still survive, the term, a *wilted* heart, will convey but an indefinite idea. It is very true that these words may be found in Webster, that to *squirm* is to swarm or wreath, and the *wilted* hay is still used in Norfolk to denote the first fading of the crop, and is the past participle of *welcken*, but when such words as these occur in the midst of a poetical description or passionate outpouring, they produce a strange and almost ludicrous effect.

But setting these peculiarities aside, it must be confessed that there is an irresistible attraction about the romance of 'Monte Beni;' it is in our opinion by no means equal to either of the author's three previous works; there are, however, few books of the present season which will occupy, and deservedly, so large a portion of public attention.

106. Hawthorne, from a letter to John Lothrop Motley

1 April 1860

Motley (1814–77), an historian and diplomat, had written to Hawthorne (29 March 1860), praising several of the author's works, especially *The Marble Faun*. His remarks about the conclusion of the romance undoubtedly impressed Hawthorne:

With regard to the story, which has been somewhat criticised, I can only say that to me it is quite satisfactory. I like those shadowy, weird, fantastic, Hawthornesque shapes flitting through the book. I like the misty way in which the story is indicated rather than revealed; the outlines are quite definite enough from the beginning to the end to those who have imagination enough to follow you in your airy flights . . . it really moves my spleen that people should wish to bring down the volatile figures of your romance to the level of an every-day romance. (George Parsons Lathrop, *A Study of Hawthorne*, pp. 261–2.)

You are certainly that Gentle Reader for whom all my books were exclusively written. Nobody else (my wife excepted, who speaks so near me that I cannot tell her voice from my own) has ever said exactly what I loved to hear. It is most satisfactory to be hit upon the raw, to be shot straight through the heart. It is not the quantity of your praise that I care so much about (though I gather it all up most carefully, lavish as you are of it), but the kind, for you take the book precisely as I meant it; and if your note had come a few days sooner, I believe I would have printed it in a postscript which I have added to the second edition. . . . You work out my imperfect efforts, and half make the book with your warm imagination; and see what I myself saw, but could only hint at. Well, the romance is a success, even if it never finds another reader. . . .

107. From an unsigned review in *The Times*

7 April 1860, p. 5

It may be tempting to make sport of a poet's dream, and the occasion is here ready to our inclinations. Mr. Hawthorne is a poet, and his *Transformation* is a dream, airy and illusory, enticing us to hot pursuit or leaving us to a sense of emptiness and ridicule. What is our proper province in a case like this? What have *we* to do with shadows or ethereal semblances? Even art has more solid materials for our investigation and opinion. We have, at all events, a shadow or rarefaction here, evoked by a poetical imagination from its contact with known facts. It may be tempting, as we have said, to keep within the domain of these facts, and to pour a contemptuous commentary on the fancies which have sprung out of them. But it is a temptation which we shall wisely resist in the interests of a higher art than comes ordinarily to the reader's closet or the critic's tribunal. We will only state as a preliminary that this is an ideal romance, of which the dust of modern Rome is something more than the background, and in which its hoary monuments each play their part. The expectants of satire will understand our abstinence when we tell them that, among other transcendental processes, the Faun of Praxiteles walks down from its pedestal and becomes the most prominent of the *dramatis personæ*. On the other hand, those who welcome a work of pure phantasy will appreciate the ideal with reference to which it was moulded. A familiar marble statue is endued with a soul, and this soul is rigorously burdened with moral responsibilities beneath which it tends steadily to grow and develope itself. Strange as it may sound, this conception is not altogether new. The principle of this Roman dream is an echo of other dreams, and the *Transformation* of Mr. Hawthorne, thus freely effected, combines the feat of Pygmalion with the life ordeal of Undine.

We may wish to pass a balanced judgment on the artistic result, or at least to give the true *rationale* of the process. But when a work of imagination differs from the ordinary standard the task of the critic may be easy or it may be exceedingly difficult. It is easy to note and condemn certain deviations, which are unequivocal lapses, and the eccentricity, which is both an aberration and a weakness. The singularities of infirmity are the easiest blots to hit, for, like other blotches and distortions, they simply disfigure a type, and have nothing to commend their harsh departures from nature. But there are cases in which natural types have been and may be set aside for airy conceptions to which the world rightfully renders homage. Such conceptions belong to a truly ideal sphere, and their congruities of grace and proportion sufficiently vindicate their author's audacity. Criticism abdicates part of its functions, and accepts such conceptions as types, models—existences independent and absolute. It allows a true creative capacity to be a law to itself, nor does it dream of insisting on the anomalies of tricksy Ariels or Pucks or the impossible combination of qualities in an Apollo Belvedere.

The art which attains this high impunity is so subtle that it defies analysis, and yet so definite in its manifestation that it admits of no dispute. In a book like this before us we at once admit its presence, perplexing and yet pleasing us, startling and leading us captive. As far as our knowledge of the world's present literature extends Mr. Hawthorne possesses more of this rare capacity than any living writer. His art of expression is equal to the idealism of his conceptions, and his pure flexible English beguiles his readers into accepting them as among the sum of probable and natural things. But, none the less, they are pure transcendentalisms, impalpable to common sense and unamenable to law. Or rather, as we said, they are a law to themselves, beyond the convenanted rules and formulas of art, and externally independent of the critical scheme and dispensation.

If we conceive we are not entitled to assert our jurisdiction at their expense, we may nevertheless consider the *rationale* of their origin. There is a peculiar type of the American mind which is strongly in revolt against American utilities, and which is predisposed by the very monotony of its surroundings to hues of contrast and attitudes of antagonism. We have seen the manifestation of this revolt in American literature in Edgar Poe and even in Longfellow and Washington Irving. It is emphatically the desire of idealists like these and of Mr. Hawthorne to escape from the 'iron rule' of their country and the 'social despotism' of their generation. They disdain to be parts of a complicated scheme of progress, which can only result in their arrival at a colder and drearier region than that they were born in, and they refuse to add to 'an accumulated pile of usefulness, of which the only use will be, to burden their posterity with even heavier thoughts and more inordinate labour than their own.' This impulse induces them to become vagrants in imagination and reality, tourists in the old world of

Europe, dreamers and artificers in the older world of poetry and romance; and the contrast of that to which they attach themselves, as compared with that which they fly from, is more stimulating than early association with such influences is to us. We have, in truth, no parallel among ourselves to the freshness of their enthusiasm and no equivalent to its literary restlessness or *élan*. Send Mr. Thackeray to Rome, and he goes and comes with the average impressions of a man of the world, to whom art, history, and poetry are very passable *entrées*, in addition to, the ordinary pabulum of a 'fogey' or 'fat contributor.' But the American artist finds himself in Rome with eyes full of innocent wonder, and a heart thumping against his breast like that of Aladdin in the cave. He comes, as he observes, from a country where 'there is no shadow, no antiquity, no mystery, no picturesque and gloomy wrong nor, anything but a commonplace prosperity, in broad and simple daylight;' and he stands in the centre of the ruins of the historic world till their very dust, as it floats in the air, intoxicates him like wine—till the ghosts of the Capitol dance before him in infinite confusion, like the night concourse of spectres which the magician of the Coliseum displayed to the excited gaze of Benvenuto Cellini. The statues and pictures take form and walk, as their subjects quicken; or at least they seem to the poet's eye to be struggling out of the tombs into which they are crushed by a vast heap of vague and ponderous remembrances.

We can easily conceive that Mr. Hawthorne had no intention at the outset of working such impressions into a story or picture of his own constructing. In fact, from the extent to which he has introduced descriptions of various Italian objects, antique, pictorial, and statuesque, and, from the very miscellaneous nature of these items, we should rather infer that, in the first instance, he contemplated a work of descriptive criticism. Be this as it may, there is no work, even of this class, on Rome and its treasures which brings their details so closely and vividly before us. It is worth all the guide-books we ever met with, as regards the gems of Italian art, the characteristic features of Roman edifices, and the atmosphere of Roman life. In fact, we conceive it calculated, in many instances, to impart new views of objects with which travellers may have imagined themselves already too familiar. . . .

But, as we said, all these artistic and panoramic performances might have been easily turned to other account, and were probably sketched with another object, until Mr. Hawthorne, standing within the gallery of the Capitol, conceived this pregnant theory of the Faun of Praxiteles:

[Quotes ch. 1, 'The Faun is' to 'intimate and dear'.]

We conceive Mr. Hawthorne's purpose as shaping itself out of this impression, and as exacting aid from his creative ingenuity in this wise. To embody the Faun for an experiment of the influences of mortal sin and sorrow on its Pagan nature, he transports us to the recesses of the Tuscan hills, where he supposes the existence of a noble race of immemorial antiquity and of hereditary peculiarities. . . .

Around this *pedestal,* as it were, of his conception, Mr. Hawthorne weaves a variety of suggestive legends and Arcadian fillets appropriate to the main figure; and his dream of a modern Faun in the person of Donatello, the last Count of Monte Beni, actually grows into a portrait by the marvellous skill and consistency with which it is elaborated. At a later period we have a picture of Donatello in his Tuscan home, with accessories such as Horace may have cherished at his Sabine farm, and with the same internal light of a calm rustic felicity. But the description of Donatello in the gardens of the Villa Borghese is a more quotable specimen of the ingenious art which sustains Mr. Hawthorne in his extravagant audacity. The Faun has found his way to Rome, and has attached himself to a young female artist, about whose antecedents and position there is a mystery of criminality. . . .

[Summarizes story and quotes several long passages.]

The association of these two personages is the scaffolding by which Mr. Hawthorne proceeds to the 'Transformation' of the Faun's nature on a theory which seems to pervade his works, that you may so change any nature by burdening it with heavy responsibilities. It is represented of Miriam that she has been equivocally involved in some awful catastrophe, on account of which she is living in retirement and isolation. A sort of half-mad priest is the depositary of her secret, and persecutes her incessantly in spite of warnings and prayers. Donatello is a witness to one of these interviews on the brink of the Tarpeian Rock, and at a signal of half assent from Miriam he murders the priest by throwing him headlong. Thenceforth he and Miriam are bound together by the consciousness of their common crime, while this consciousness subdues and shatters the nature of Donatello and leads up by degrees to his so-called 'Transformation.' The last steps of this process are not very happy, nor is their result clear, but the harmony of the conception is sustained even when its outlines are blurred and Donatello is losing his affinity to the wild creatures of the woods. . . .

[Quotes ch. 27, ' "I doubt" ' to ' "come near me".']

From this point, which is midway in the second volume, Mr. Haw-thorne's purpose evidently falters, and there is comparatively a falling short of the intended result. The attentive reader cannot fail to perceive this miscarriage, and we suspect that Mr. Hawthorne is not only con-scious of it himself, but makes Kenyon, the artist, his spokesman in the difficulty:—

[Quotes ch. 41, 'He pointed to a ' to 'friend's adventures'.]

Thus, as we infer, Mr. Hawthorne has avowedly left us a vigorous sketch, instead of a finished work of art. His Transformation was too subtle a process for his skill to perfect in the range of pure mythological existences; or, possibly, he was conscious of a strain in contrasting such supernatural being with the common every-day life of the Rome around him. At all events, it is a startling effect to be got out of galleries and museums, from the hints and suggestions of classified, catalogued art. Our astonishment is moved by the near approach to a great compo-sition under such conditions, and out of such rigid materials. We are more impressed by Mr. Hawthorne's success up to a certain point than by the shortcomings which render this success imperfect; and, like the gazers on the sky in mythologic times, we are surprised that the wings of Icarus should bear him so far, instead of being amazed that they should dissolve so soon.

There is another female character, introduced as a foil to Miriam, and the happy issue of her intercourse with Kenyon is obviously designed as a contrast to the misery of the union which commences in crime. Otherwise Hilda is not worth much in our eyes, nor, we suspect, in Mr. Hawthorne's. Nor is there any explanation of the mystery which surrounds Miriam herself, which may or may not be considered a fault, at the option of the reader. Minor intricacies we do not remark, and minor blemishes we are indifferent to. Our desire has been to arrive at the central principle of a work of exceptional aim and singular beauty, and to convey this idea definitely to our readers. We find here the nu-cleus of a clear conception, which is for the most part luminous, though in its outer diffusion it lapses into vapour. So we recognize the power of an artistic Prospero over the cloudy forms and hues of dreamland; while there is so much originality in the shapes into which he attempts to mould them that, though the effect is incomplete, the effort is a work of genius.

108. From an unsigned essay, 'The Marble Faun: Completed', in the *Knickerbocker Magazine*

July 1860, lvi, 65–73

Hawthorne's addition of the Postscript did not satisfy all of the romance's critics and provoked this parody, the only such piece to be published in Hawthorne's lifetime.

There are, we doubt not, thousands of our readers who have perused with pleasure the fascinating romance of the 'Marble Faun,' lately given to the world by the accomplished HAWTHORNE. But though the novel is claimed to possess a remarkable amount of 'artistic finish,' it cannot be denied that a vast number of obtuse individuals declare themselves utterly unable to see where the finish comes in. Among these heathen who know nothing of Suggestive Art, one has gone so far as to say that the information that HILDA had a hopeful soul, and saw sun-light on the mountain-tops, is by no means a satisfactory clearing up of the darkness in which most of the *dramatis personæ* are left. Others have wished to have the obscure points of DONATELLO's ears cleared up, and the majority in fact appear to have been a little puzzled with this or that bit of chiaroscuro.

Great minds, however, never condescend to explain, but leave all that sort of thing to commentators. Therefore, I for one have ventured on a guess, leaving to others full liberty to write different conclusions if they choose. Should the conclusion here attempted be *really* different in any particular from what the author intended, the public will of course soon be informed of the deviation.

To the few who have not read 'the best guide-book for Italy,' it should be mentioned that as regards plot, Monte Beni is not, as has been popularly supposed, a variety of three-card monte, or of any other game, but is the name of a place in Italy, the birth-place of a family descended, according to legend, from a sylvan god. The members of this family show their origin by retaining the pointed ears of the

333

dii sylvestres. The last of the name, DONATELLO, goes to Rome, where he falls in love with a 'mysterious' beauty, named MIRIAM, and very properly throws over the Tarpeian rock a half-demoniac wretch, who has made her life miserable. Owing to this deed, which under the circumstances would in most parts of America be regarded as an act of common politeness, DONATELLO takes to being miserable and remorseful, 'agonizing' with all his might, and progressing generally toward the average standard of idiocy and popular vulgar melancholy. Mingled with their destinies are a 'pure soul', HILDA, who copies pictures and has art-religious, pre-Raphaelite tendencies, and KENYON, a sculptor. The arrest of MIRIAM and DONATELLO as principals in a murder, and of HILDA as witness, with the discharge of the latter, complete the romance. What became of them all, has been so far unanswered.

★

The gorgeous visions which seem to hang immutably reposeful over the heaven of the artist's soul, are never surely impelled on a preordained and unswerving track. The blind old man of Scio's rocky isle could indeed toil at the mid-night lamp, that he might give to posterity a chart and compass to aid it in unrolling the trackless waste of history, for the scholar is constant, but the artist never. So it came to pass that Kenyon changed his mind and resolved with heartful hopefulness not to pack his trunks and take the next steamer from Civita Vecchia, but to await his destiny in Rome. Could he have taken the white wings of Hilda's snowy doves, he would undoubtedly have gone back to New-York, though methinks that like aspirations, if closely scanned, would well deserve to be bridled, since they are evidently such horses as a grand old proverb defines beggars' wishes to be.

Hilda's soul was a medium of that penitential pathos through which hope gleams like a spoon through thin blue-milk. Her large orbs vibrated tenderly at the suggestion, for she looked upon life not as a stereoscope, but as a radiating mirror. The same old priest who had heard her first confession had left Rome on police business, to which he was ardently devoted, being enabled by his skill as a detective to eke out the slender pittance with which his extraordinary piety and singular austerity were so inadequately rewarded. . . . But before his departure, he had transferred the tender duty of arguing with Hilda to Father O'Whack, an Irish priest of the Propaganda. In the peculiar state of tearfulness in which Hilda's soul had adjusted itself to repose, this change was eminently beneficial. . . .

CHAPTER SECOND

Rome is a stupendous mass of over-clouded misery, where the stumbling foot-step of the sorrowful traveller flies from the cess-pool to take refuge in the tomb. To those gifted with finer feelings, its innumerable works of art, its sky, its violets, its palaces, its cultivated social circles, its grassy arches, and its trailing vines, are a wreck of desolation which crush the ruined heart with ponderous gloom. Man of marble though he was, Kenyon at times blenched before the irrevocable, and went a little way out of town to the gardens of the Villa Borghese. Here, though crime quivered in every leaf and eternal misery grated in the gravel-walks, he was, not happier; for there is no happiness on earth, especially for the good; but a little easier. Here, too, there were unquestionably, miles below his feet, rows under rows of unsuspected dungeons, where innocence shrieked in torture, and modern science raked amid the crumble of old crimes to devise nameless agonies. But this at least was out of sight, though Kenyon could never forget that the violets were rooted in decay, and that the ilexes sent their fibres down into blood. . . .

CHAPTER THIRD

. . . And Miriam condescendingly pressed her card into Hilda's hand and vanished amid the shimmering sunset light and the dancing leaves. After her went the faun made human; after the faun, the big bull-dog; after the big bull-dog, the glances of the impassioned Hilda and the philosophic Kenyon.

'Beloved! how beautiful they are!' sighed Hilda. 'There *was* a time,' she continued, 'when I dreamed that I was better than fashionable people such as they; better than worldlings; better, in fact, than any thing or any body who did not talk fine and think fine in the latest dilletanti style. But I now feel that while the teachers and preachers on art are such as *we*, the expression of culture and refinement in society must ever be such as *they* set forth. 'Tis part of a great social system, my beloved. Let us sentimentalize!'

And they arose and went home to tea.

109. From an unsigned essay, 'The Author of Adam Bede and Nathaniel Hawthorne', in the *North British Review*

August 1860, xxxii, 87–98

It is expedient to examine occasionally the more striking products of our romance literature. Many of our ablest writers seem to find the dramatic form most congenial to their own tastes, and best adapted to convey their convictions on morals, politics, and theology—on arts, science, and letters, to the public. The novel is unquestionably a marked and characteristic form of the literary activity of this century. For this, if for no other reason, the critic is bound not to neglect it. But we confess that other motives induce us at intervals to undertake such a review. There are many questions of social concernment which lie apart from politics, philosophy, theology, and the larger questions of national life. These cannot be more conveniently discussed than in connection with the literature which undertakes to represent them as they work themselves out among us. To attempt to solve, or at least to adjust, some of the more subtle and knotty problems in practical ethics, which meet us at every step we take, is a task that ought not to prove unprofitable. We can all repeat the ten commandments. Few of us are sinners on a large scale; thieves and murderers will not return a parliamentary representative until 'minorities' are enfranchised; but the minor moralities—the charities, and graces, and courtesies which sweeten life—are little understood, and habitually neglected.

Many people appear to suppose that the imagination is a faculty which necessarily manifests in its operations a certain falseness. One man has common sense,—another has imagination. The one sees things as they are,—the other sees things as they are not. Such is the current phraseology;—the fact being, that the man whose imagination is most intense and exalted, is the man whose impressions of things are, in general, the most truthful and exact. Doubtless, there is a grain of truth in the popular view. The imagination in different men works under different laws. The more powerful intellects keep it in subjection, but it takes the feebler captive. In the one case, it vitalizes and exalts; in the other, it discolours and exaggerates. The author of *Adam Bede* represents the first class; Nathaniel Hawthorne, the second.

The second class is, undoubtedly, the more numerous. . . . Many readers, we know, will resent the award. The grave sympathy, the homely insight, the classic Puritanism, the rich and meditative intellect, have commended their owner to a multitude of admirers, and kept a place of kindly greeting for him in many hearts and by many firesides. Nor can it be denied that his imagination is vivid and affluent, and capable of sustaining an impassioned and lofty flight. It is perhaps hardly fair, moreover, to assert without qualification, that the imagination, which takes the colour of what it feeds on, is necessarily inferior. The question is still an 'open' one—one on which the Cabinet is divided; and though, for our own part, we have never doubted that the tranquil supremacy of the 'Shakespearean' mind represents the very highest type, yet we all know that treatises have been written to prove the reverse. But to the class we have described—whether first-class or second-class—Mr. Hawthorne belongs. At present Rome masters him: he has been subdued by the vanquished Queen of Christendom. Nor need we wonder at this. Stronger men have yielded to the fascination. Uncrowned, dishevelled, and forlorn, she yet remembers a spell taught her in the old pagan ages, which takes us captive, and binds our hearts to her forever.

Mr. Hawthorne is an admirable writer; but his style (where both are so pre-eminently good) is curiously unlike that of the lady of whose works we have spoken. *Hers* has a crystal-like purity; his is dyed with rich and vivid colours. The rhetoric of *Adam Bede*, untouched by the heart or the imagination, might become bald; with these,—exactly as we have it, in short,—it is the perfection of natural eloquence. But even without original thought or deep feeling, Mr. Hawthorne's style—rich, fragrant, and mixed with flowers of many hues, like Attic honey— would be always delightful. Even in this matter of language the contrast we have insisted upon asserts itself; while, as respects the relative power of these writers to delineate *character*, the evidence is still more decisive. In the one book it grows like a flower; in the other, it is constructed like a machine. Mr. Hawthorne, starting with some moral or intellectual conception, adapts his characters to it, fits them into the framework he has prepared, and expands or compresses them until they fill the mould. Thus there is in his representations a want of the ease, *abandon,* and lawlessness of life,—they are too symmetrical to be natural, too exact to be true. A character may accidentally or incidentally illus-

337

trate a law; but the writer who models the character upon the law, produces a moral or intellectual monster. If there are no actual 'monsters' in *Transformation,* there is at least very little flesh and blood in it,—very little except the affluent fancy, the fine analysis, and the perfect taste, of an admirable *critic;* no life, but only a great deal of very delightful talk about life. . . .

As a guide to Rome, no pleasanter than Mr. Hawthorne could be wished. To pilgrims, like ourselves, who have trod the dust of the Holy City, and on whom the spell of her widowed beauty rests, his romance recalls vividly the associations and incidents of that delightful life.

[Quotes five long, descriptive passages.]

Of the strange story which binds these charming criticisms together, we have not time to speak at length. Only let it be noted that one trait very characteristic of Mr. Hawthorne's habit of thought reappears. Those who have read *The House with the Seven Gables,* and *The Scarlet Letter,* (the latter by far the most powerful and sustained imaginative effort that Mr. Hawthorne has yet made), will understand to what we allude. His fictions have, almost without exception, a peculiar *background.* The commonplace events of the present are shrouded in the ghost-like shadows of the past. The influences of the dead haunt and afflict the footsteps of living men. This new English earth has seen the Indian and the Puritan, and Monarchy and Revolution; and two centuries of English civilization and English crime cannot be lightly lost. It is the moral feeling, however, that he communicates to this association which is most peculiar to himself. The crime of yesterday is curiously interwrought with the retribution of today. It follows the present with menacing tenacity, and clings to it with an immitigable grasp. It is continually rising up in judgment against us. Why do the bright eyes lose their lustre, and why are the rosy lips paled, and how has a dark shadow fallen upon the fair brow of the young girl—darker than is meet for the blooming youth of an English maiden? We are told that her health is delicate and uncertain; and we know that her mother died of the same mysterious blight. Mr. Hawthorne finds another explanation,—an explanation not endorsed by the Faculty. It is *the family curse,*—the cruel sin of the grim Puritan grandfather,—that falls upon the maiden's head, and spoils her innocent youth. And so in *Transformation,* the Count of Monte Bene represents the pleasant rural life of old Etruria, and inherits the playful unreflective virtues of the ancestor who had piped to the Nymphs and caroused with Pan, 'while Italy was yet guiltless of Rome.' The marble of Praxiteles preserves to us in unfaded youth the form of this sylvan Sire; and with Mr. Hawthorne's picture of the famous statue,—striking, as it does, the key-note to his story,—we take our leave of a capricious and fantastic, but captivating romance:—

[Quotes ch. 1, 'The Faun is' to 'Faun of Praxiteles'.]

110. E. P. Whipple: His final assessment of Hawthorne, from an unsigned essay, 'Nathaniel Hawthorne', in the *Atlantic Monthly*

May 1860, v, 614–22

Hawthorne wrote to Fields that he had seen in the *Atlantic*
a really keen and profound article by Whipple, in which he goes
over all my works, and recognizes that element of unpopularity
which (as nobody knows better than myself) pervades them all.
I agree with almost all he says, except that I am conscious of not
deserving nearly so much praise. (Letter, 1 April 1860, James T.
Fields, *Yesterdays with Authors* [1871], p. 89.)

The romance of 'The Marble Faun' will be widely welcomed, not only
for its intrinsic merits, but because it is a sign that its writer, after a
silence of seven or eight years, has determined to resume his place in
the ranks of authorship. . . .

The publication of this new romance seems to offer us a fitting
occasion to attempt some description of the peculiarities of the genius
of which it is the latest offspring, and to hazard some judgments on its
predecessors. It is more than twenty-five years since Hawthorne began
that remarkable series of stories and essays which are now collected in
the volumes of 'Twice-Told Tales,' 'The Snow Image and other Tales,'
and 'Mosses from an Old Manse.' . . .

There would appear, on a slight view of the matter, no reason for the
little notice which Hawthorne's early productions received. The subjects were mostly drawn from the traditions and written records of
New England, and gave the 'beautiful strangeness' of imagination to
objects, incidents, and characters which were familiar facts in the popular mind. The style, while it had a purity, sweetness, and grace which
satisfied the most fastidious and exacting taste, had, at the same time,
more than the simplicity and clearness of an ordinary school-book.

But though the subjects and the style were thus popular, there was something in the shaping and informing spirit which failed to awaken interest, or awakened interest without exciting delight. Misanthropy, when it has its source in passion,—when it is fierce, bitter, fiery, and scornful,—when it vigorously echoes the aggressive discontent of the world, and furiously tramples on the institutions and the men luckily rather than rightfully in the ascendant,—this is always popular; but a misanthropy which springs from insight,—a misanthropy which is lounging, languid, sad, and depressing,—a misanthropy which remorselessly looks through cursing misanthropes and chirping men of the world with the same sure, detecting glance of reason,—a misanthropy which has no fanaticism, and which casts the same ominous doubt on subjectively morbid as on subjectively moral action,—a misanthropy which has no respect for impulses, but has a terrible perception of spiritual laws,—this is a misanthropy which can expect no wide recognition; and it would be vain to deny that traces of this kind of misanthropy are to be found in Hawthorne's earlier, and are not altogether absent from his later works. He had spiritual insight, but it did not penetrate to the sources of spiritual joy; and his deepest glimpses of truth were calculated rather to sadden than to inspire. A blandly cynical distrust of human nature was the result of his most piercing glances into the human soul. He had humor, and sometimes humor of a delicious kind; but this sunshine of the soul was but sunshine breaking through or lighting up a sombre and ominous cloud. There was also observable in his earlier stories a lack of vigor, as if the power of his nature had been impaired by the very process which gave depth and excursiveness to his mental vision. Throughout, the impression is conveyed of a shy recluse, alternately bashful in disposition and bold in thought, gifted with original and various capacities, but capacities which seemed to have developed themselves in the shade, without sufficient energy of will or desire to force them, except fitfully, into the sunlight. Shakspeare calls moonlight the sunlight *sick*; and it is in some such moonlight of the mind that the genius of Hawthorne found its first expression. A mild melancholy, sometimes deepening into gloom, sometimes brightened into a 'humorous sadness,' characterized his early creations. Like his own Hepzibah Pyncheon, he appeared 'to be walking in a dream'; or rather, the life and reality assumed by his emotions 'made all outward occurrences unsubstantial, like the teasing phantasms of an unconscious slumber.' Though dealing largely in description, and with the most accurate perceptions of outward objects, he still, to use again his own

341

words, gives the impression of a man 'chiefly accustomed to look inward, and to whom external matters are of little value or import, unless they bear relation to something within his own mind.' But that 'something within his own mind' was often an unpleasant something, perhaps a ghastly occult perception of deformity and sin in what appeared outwardly fair and good; so that the reader felt a secret dissatisfaction with the disposition which directed the genius, even in the homage he awarded to the genius itself. As psychological portraits of morbid natures, his delineations of character might have given a purely intellectual satisfaction; but there was audible, to the delicate ear, a faint and muffled growl of personal discontent, which showed they were not mere exercises of penetrating imaginative analysis, but had in them the morbid vitality of a despondent mood.

Yet, after admitting these peculiarities, nobody who is now drawn to the 'Twice-Told Tales,' from his interest in the later romances of Hawthorne, can fail to wonder a little at the limited number of readers they attracted on their original publication. For many of these stories are at once a representation of early New England life and a criticism on it. They have much of the deepest truth of history in them. 'The Legends of the Province House,' 'The Gray Champion,' 'The Gentle Boy,' 'The Minister's Black Veil,' 'Endicott and the Red Cross,' not to mention others, contain important matter which cannot be found in Bancroft or Grahame. They exhibit the inward struggles of New-England men and women with some of the darkest problems of existence, and have more vital import to thoughtful minds than the records of Indian or Revolutionary warfare. In the 'Prophetic Pictures,' 'Fancy's Show-Box,' 'The Great Carbuncle,' 'The Haunted Mind,' and 'Edward Fane's Rose-Bud,' there are flashes of moral insight, which light up, for the moment, the darkest recesses of the individual mind; and few sermons reach to the depth of thought and sentiment from which these seemingly airy sketches draw their sombre life. It is common, for instance, for religious moralists to insist on the great spiritual truth, that wicked thoughts and impulses, which circumstances prevent from passing into wicked acts, are still deeds in the sight of God; but the living truth subsides into a dead truism, as enforced by commonplace preachers. In 'Fancy's Show-Box,' Hawthorne seizes the prolific idea; and the respectable merchant and respected church-member, in the still hour of his own meditation, convicts himself of being a liar, cheat, thief, seducer, and murderer, as he casts his glance over the mental events which form his spiritual biography. Interspersed with serious histories

and moralities like these, are others which embody the sweet and playful, though still thoughtful and slightly saturnine action of Hawthorne's
mind,—like 'The Seven Vagabonds,' 'Snow-Flakes,' 'The Lily's Quest,'
'Mr. Higenbotham's Catastrophe,' 'Little Annie's Ramble,' 'Sights from
a Steeple,' 'Sunday at Home,' and 'A Rill from the Town-Pump.'

The 'Mosses from an Old Manse,' are intellectually and artistically
an advance from the 'Twice-Told Tales,' The twenty-three stories
and essays which make up the volume are almost perfect of their kind.
Each is complete in itself, and many might be expanded into long romances by the simple method of developing the possibilities of their
shadowy types of character into appropriate incidents. In description,
narration, allegory, humor, reason, fancy, subtilty, inventiveness, they
exceed the best productions of Addison; but they want Addison's
sensuous contentment and sweet and kindly spirit. Though the author
denies that he has exhibited his own individual attributes in these
'Mosses,' though he professes not to be 'one of those supremely hospitable people who serve up their own hearts delicately fried, with brain-
sauce, as a titbit for their beloved public,'—yet it is none the less apparent that he has diffused through each tale and sketch the life of the mental
mood to which it owed its existence, and that one individuality pervades and colors the whole collection. The defect of the serious stories
is, that character is introduced, not as thinking, but as the illustration of
thought. The persons are ghostly, with a sad lack of flesh and blood.
They are phantasmal symbols of a reflective and imaginative analysis
of human passions and aspirations. The dialogue, especially, is bookish,
as though the personages knew their speech was to be printed, and
were careful of the collocation and rhythm of their words. The author
throughout is evidently more interested in his large, wide, deep, indo-
lently serene, and lazily sure and critical view of the conflict of ideas
and passions, than he is with the individuals who embody them. He
shows moral insight without moral earnestness. He cannot contract his
mind to the patient delineation of a moral individual, but attempts to
use individuals in order to express the last results of patient moral
perception. Young Goodman Brown and Roger Malvin are not persons; they are the mere, loose, personal expression of subtile thinking.
'The Celestial Railroad,' 'The Procession of Life,' 'Earth's Holocaust,'
'The Bosom Serpent,' indicate thought of a character equally deep,
delicate, and comprehensive, but the characters are ghosts of men rather
than substantial individualities. In the 'Mosses from an Old Manse,' we
are really studying the phenomena of human nature, while, for the

time, we beguile ourselves into the belief that we are following the
fortunes of individual natures.

Up to this time the writings of Hawthorne conveyed the impression
of a genius in which insight so dominated over impulse, that it was
rather mentally and morally curious than mentally and morally impassioned. The quality evidently wanting to its full expression was
intensity. In the romance of 'The Scarlet Letter' he first made his
genius efficient by penetrating it with passion. This book forced itself
into attention by its inherent power; and the author's name, previously
known only to a limited circle of readers, suddenly became a familiar
word in the mouths of the great reading public of America and England.
It may be said, that it 'captivated' nobody, but took everybody captive.
Its power could neither be denied nor resisted. There were growls of
disapprobation from novel-readers, that Hester Prynne and the Rev.
Mr. Dimmesdale were subjected to cruel punishments unknown to the
jurisprudence of fiction,—that the author was an inquisitor who put his
victims on the rack,—and that neither amusement nor delight resulted
from seeing the contortions and hearing the groans of these martyrs of
sin; but the fact was no less plain that Hawthorne had for once compelled the most superficial lovers of romance to submit themselves to
the magic of his genius. The readers of Dickens voted him, with three
times three, to the presidency of their republic of letters; the readers of
Hawthorne were caught by a *coup d'etat*, and fretfully submitted to a
despot whom they could not depose.

The success of 'The Scarlet Letter' is an example of the advantage
which an author gains by the simple concentration of his powers on one
absorbing subject. In the 'Twice-Told Tales,' and the 'Mosses from an
Old Manse,' Hawthorne had exhibited a wider range of sight and insight than in 'The Scarlet Letter.' Indeed, in the little sketch of 'Endicott
and the Red Cross,' written twenty years before, he had included in a
few sentences the whole matter which he afterwards treated in his famous
story. In describing the various inhabitants of an early New-England
town, as far as they were representative, he touches incidentally on a

young woman, with no mean share of beauty, whose doom it was to wear the
letter A on the breast of her gown, in the eyes of all the world and her own
children. And even her own children knew what that initial signified. Sporting
with her infamy, the lost and desperate creature had embroidered the fatal
token in scarlet cloth, with golden thread and the nicest art of needle-work; so
that the capital A might have been thought to mean Admirable, or anything,
rather than Adulteress.

Here is the germ of the whole pathos and terror of 'The Scarlet Letter';
but it is hardly noted in the throng of symbols, equally pertinent, in
the few pages of the little sketch from which we have quoted.

Two characteristics of Hawthorne's genius stand plainly out, in the
conduct and characterization of the romance of 'The Scarlet Letter,'
which were less obviously prominent in his previous works. The first
relates to his subordination of external incidents to inward events. Mr.
James's 'solitary horseman' does more in one chapter than Hawthorne's
hero in twenty chapters; but then James deals with the arms of men,
while Hawthorne deals with their souls. Hawthorne relies almost entirely for the interest of his story on what is felt and done within the
minds of his characters. Even his most picturesque descriptions and
narratives are only one-tenth matter to nine-tenths spirit. The results
that follow from one external act of folly or crime are to him enough
for an Iliad of woes. It might be supposed that his whole theory of
Romantic Art was based on these tremendous lines of Wordsworth:—

> Action is momentary,—
> The motion of a muscle, this way or that:
> Suffering is long, obscure, and infinite.

The second characteristic of his genius is connected with the first.
With his insight of individual souls he combines a far deeper insight of
the spiritual laws which govern the strangest aberrations of individual
souls. But it seems to us that his mental eye, keen-sighted and far-
sighted as it is, overlooks the merciful modifications of the austere
code whose pitiless action it so clearly discerns. In his long and patient
brooding over the spiritual phenomena of Puritan life, it is apparent, to
the least critical observer, that he has imbibed a deep personal antipathy
to the Puritanic ideal of character; but it is no less apparent that his
intellect and imagination have been strangely fascinated by the Puritanic idea of justice. His brain has been subtly infected by the Puritanic
perception of Law, without being warmed by the Puritanic faith in
Grace. Individually, he would much prefer to have been one of his
own 'Seven Vagabonds' rather than one of the austerest preachers of
the primitive church of New England; but the austerest preacher of the
primitive church of New England would have been more tender and
considerate to a real Mr. Dimmesdale and a real Hester Prynne than this
modern romancer has been to their typical representatives in the world
of imagination. Throughout 'The Scarlet Letter' we seem to be follow-

ıidance of an author who is personally good-natured, but
ılly and morally relentless.

Iouse of the Seven Gables,' Hawthorne's next work, while it
ɔncentration of passion and tension of mind than 'The Scarlet
ncludes a wider range of observation, reflection, and character;
ᴀɴᴜ ... morality, dreadful as fate, which hung like a black cloud over
the personages of the previous story, is exhibited in more relief. Although the book has no imaginative creation equal to little Pearl, it still
contains numerous examples of characterization at once delicate and
deep. Clifford, especially, is a study in psychology, as well as a marvellously subtle delineation of enfeebled manhood. The general idea of the
story is this,—'that the wrong-doing of one generation lives into the
successive ones, and, divesting itself of every temporary advantage,
becomes a pure and uncontrollable mischief'; and the mode in which
this idea is carried out shows great force, fertility, and refinement of
mind. A weird fancy, sporting with the facts detected by a keen observation, gives to every gable of the Seven Gables, every room in the House,
every burdock growing rankly before the door, a symbolic significance.
. . . The whole representation, masterly as it is, considered as an effort
of intellectual and imaginative power, would still be morally bleak,
were it not for the sunshine and warmth radiated from the character
of Phœbe. In this delightful creation Hawthorne for once gives himself
up to homely human nature, and has succeeded in delineating a New-
England girl, cheerful, blooming, practical, affectionate, efficient, full
of innocence and happiness, with all the 'handiness' and native sagacity
of her class, and so true and close to Nature that the process by which
she is slightly idealized is completely hidden.

In his romance there is also more humor than in any of his other
works. It peeps out, even in the most serious passages, in a kind of
demure rebellion against the fanaticism of his remorseless intelligence.
In the description of the Pyncheon poultry, which we think unexcelled
by anything in Dickens for quaintly fanciful humor, the author seems
to indulge in a sort of parody on his own doctrine of the hereditary
transmission of family qualities. At any rate, that strutting chanticleer,
with his two meagre wives and one wizened chicken, is a sly side fleer
at the tragic aspect of the law of descent. Miss Hepzibah Pyncheon,
her shop, and her customers, are so delightful, that the reader would
willingly spare a good deal of Clifford and Judge Pyncheon and Holgrave, for more details of them and Phœbe. Uncle Venner, also, the old
wood-sawyer, who boasts 'that he has seen a good deal of the world,

not only in people's kitchens and back-yards, but at the street-corners, and on the wharves, and in other places where his business' called him, and who, on the strength of this comprehensive experience, feels qualified to give the final decision in every case which tasks the resources of human wisdom, is a very much more humane and interesting gentleman than the Judge. Indeed, one cannot but regret that Hawthorne should be so economical of his undoubted stores of humor,—and that, in the two romances he has since written, humor, in the form of character, does not appear at all.

Before proceeding to the consideration of 'The Blithedale Romance,' it is necessary to say a few words on the seeming separation of Hawthorne's genius from his will. He has none of that ability which enabled Scott and enables Dickens to force their powers into action, and to make what was begun in drudgery soon assume the character of inspiration. Hawthorne cannot thus use his genius; his genius always uses him. This is so true, that he often succeeds better in what calls forth his personal antipathies than in what calls forth his personal sympathies. His life of General Pierce, for instance, is altogether destitute of life; yet in writing it he must have exerted himself to the utmost, as his object was to urge the claims of an old and dear friend to the Presidency of the Republic. The style, of course, is excellent, as it is impossible for Hawthorne to write bad English, but the genius of the man has deserted him. General Pierce, whom he loves, he draws so feebly, that one doubts, while reading the biography, if such a man exists; Hollingsworth, whom he hates, is so vividly characterized, that the doubt is, while we read the romance, whether such a man can possibly be fictitious.

Midway between such a work as the 'Life of General Pierce', and 'The Scarlet Letter', may be placed 'The Wonder-Book' and 'Tanglewood Tales.' In these Hawthorne's genius distinctly appears, and appears in its most lovable, though not in its deepest form. These delicious stories, founded on the mythology of Greece, were written for children, but they delight men and women as well. Hawthorne never pleases grown people so much as when he writes with an eye to the enjoyment of little people.

Now 'The Blithedale Romance' is far from being so pleasing a performance as 'Tanglewood Tales,' yet it very much better illustrates the operation, indicates the quality, and expresses the power, of the author's genius. His great books appear not so much created by him as through him. They have the character of revelations,—he, the instrument, being often troubled with the burden they impose on his mind. His profoundest glances into individual souls are like the marvels of clair-voyance. It would seem, that, in the production of such a work as 'The Blithedale Romance,' his mind had hit accidentally, as it were, on an idea or fact mysteriously related to some morbid sentiment in the inmost core of his nature, and connecting itself with numerous scattered observations of human life, lying unrelated in his imagination. In a sort of meditative dream, his intellect drifts in the direction to which the subject points, broods patiently over it, looks at it, looks into it, and at last looks through it to the law by which it is governed. Gradually individual beings, definite in spiritual quality, but shadowy in substantial form, group themselves around this central conception, and by degrees assume an outward body and expression corresponding to their internal nature. On the depth and intensity of the mental mood, the force of the fascination it exerts over him, and the length of time it holds him captive, depend the solidity and substance of the individual characterizations. In this way Miles Coverdale, Hollingsworth, Westervelt, Zenobia, and Priscilla become real persons to the mind which has called them into being. He knows every secret and watches every motion of their souls, yet is, in a measure, independent of them, and pretends to no authority by which he can alter the destiny which consigns them to misery or happiness. They drift to their doom by the same law by which they drifted across the path of his vision. Individually, he abhors Hollingsworth, and would like to annihilate Westervelt, yet he allows the superb Zenobia to be their victim; and if his readers object that the effect of the whole representation is painful, he would doubtless agree with them, but profess his incapacity honestly to alter a sentence. He professes to tell the story as it was revealed to him; and the license in which a romancer might indulge is denied to a biographer of spirits. Show him a fallacy in his logic of passion and character, point out a false or defective step in his analysis, and he will gladly alter the whole to your satisfaction; but four human souls, such as he has described, being given, their mutual attractions and repulsions will end, he feels assured, in just such a catastrophe as he has stated.

Eight years have passed since 'The Blithedale Romance' was written, and during nearly the whole of this period Hawthorne has resided abroad. 'The Marble Faun,' which must, on the whole, be considered the greatest of his works, proves that his genius has widened and deepened in this interval, without any alteration or modification of its characteristic merits and characteristic defects. The most obvious excellence of the work is the vivid truthfulness of its descriptions of Italian life, manners, and scenery; and, considered merely as a record of a tour in Italy, it is of great interest and attractiveness. The opinions on Art, and the special criticisms on the masterpieces of architecture, sculpture, and painting, also possess a value of their own. The story might have been told, and the characters fully represented, in one-third of the space devoted to them, yet description and narration are so artfully combined that each assists to give interest to the other. Hawthorne is one of those true observers who concentrate in observation every power of their minds. He has accurate sight and piercing insight. When he modifies either the form or the spirit of the objects he describes, he does it either by viewing them through the medium of an imagined mind or by obeying associations which they themselves suggest. We might quote from the descriptive portions of the work a hundred pages, at least, which would demonstrate how closely accurate observation is connected with the highest powers of the intellect and imagination.

The style of the book is perfect of its kind, and, if Hawthorne had written nothing else, would entitle him to rank among the great masters of English composition. Walter Savage Landor is reported to have said of an author whom he knew in his youth, 'My friend wrote excellent English, a language now obsolete.' Had 'The Marble Faun' appeared before he uttered this sarcasm, the wit of the remark would have been pointless. Hawthorne not only writes English, but the sweetest, simplest, and clearest English that ever has been made the vehicle of equal depth, variety, and subtility of thought and emotion. His mind is reflected in his style as a face is reflected in a mirror; and the latter does not give back its image with less appearance of effort than the former. His excellence consists not so much in using common words as in making common words express uncommon things. Swift, Addison, Goldsmith, not to mention others, wrote with as much simplicity; but the style of neither embodies an individuality so complex, passions so strange and intense, sentiments so fantastic and preternatural, thoughts so profound and delicate, and imaginations so remote from the recognized limits of the ideal, as find an orderly outlet in the pure English of Hawthorne. He has hardly a word to which Mrs. Trimmer would primly object, hardly a sentence which would call forth the frosty anathema of Blair, Hurd, Kames, or Whately, and yet he contrives to embody in his simple style qualities which would almost excuse the verbal extravagances of Carlyle.

In regard to the characterization and plot of 'The Marble Faun,' there is room for widely varying opinions. Hilda, Miriam, and Donatello will be generally received as superior in power and depth to any of Hawthorne's previous creations of character; Donatello, especially, must be considered one of the most original and exquisite conceptions in the whole range of romance; but the story in which they appear will seem to many an unsolved puzzle, and even the tolerant and interpretative 'gentle reader' will be troubled with the unsatisfactory conclusion. It is justifiable for a romancer to sting the curiosity of his readers with a mystery, only on the implied obligation to explain it at last; but this story begins in mystery only to end in mist. The suggestive faculty is tormented rather than genially excited, and in the end is left a prey to doubts. The central idea of the story, the necessity of sin to convert such a creature as Donatello into a moral being, is also not happily illustrated in the leading event. When Donatello kills the wretch who malignantly dogs the steps of Miriam, all readers think that Donatello committed no sin at all; and the reason is, that Hawthorne has deprived the persecutor of Miriam of all human attributes, made him an allegorical representation of one of the most fiendish forms of unmixed evil, so that we welcome his destruction with something of the same feeling with which, in following the allegory of Spenser or Bunyan, we rejoice in the hero's victory over the Blatant Beast or Giant Despair. Conceding, however, that Donatellos' act was murder, and not 'justifiable homicide,' we are still not sure that the author's conception of his nature and of the change caused in his nature by that act, are carried out with a felicity corresponding to the original conception.

In the first volume, and in the early part of the second, the author's hold on his design is comparatively firm, but it somewhat relaxes as he proceeds, and in the end it seems almost to escape from his grasp. Few can be satisfied with the concluding chapters, for the reason that nothing is really concluded. We are willing to follow the ingenious processes of Calhoun's deductive logic, because we are sure, that, however severely they task the faculty of attention, they will lead to some positive result; but Hawthorne's logic of events leaves us in the end bewildered in a labyrinth of guesses. The book is, on the whole, such a great book, that its defects are felt with all the more force.

In this rapid glance at some of the peculiarities of Hawthorne's genius, we have not, of course, been able to do full justice to the special merits of the works we have passed in review; but we trust that we have said nothing which would convey the impression that we do not place them among the most remarkable romances produced in an age in which romance-writing has called forth some of the highest powers of the human mind. In intellect and imagination, in the faculty of discerning spirits and detecting laws, we doubt if any living novelist is his equal; but his genius, in its creative action, has been heretofore attracted to the dark rather than the bright side of the interior life of humanity, and the geniality which evidently is in him has rarely found adequate expression. In the many works which he may still be expected to write, it is to be hoped that his mind will lose some of its sadness of tone without losing any of its subtilty and depth; but, in any event, it would be unjust to deny that he has already done enough to insure him a commanding position in American literature as long as American literature has an existence.

III. A British view of Hawthorne and an authentic American literature, from an unsigned essay, 'Nathaniel Hawthorne', in the *Universal Review*

June 1860, iii, 742–71

American literature is always an interesting subject, not only because it is literature, but because it is one of the elements in the solution of a problem which is important in a greater or less degree to the whole world—the moral and intellectual influence of democratic government. . . . We see a nation, one of the mightiest on the earth, in the yet early years of its existence, and undergoing the process of formation and self-development under influences scarcely less various than those which could have been invented for it by the most imaginative speculator. If we look at one aspect of the United States, we may see many things which constitute an admirable success, and which may make us emulous, if not envious, of the means by which results are achieved which, with us, seem as distant as they are confessedly desirable. If we look on another, we are reminded of a child who has possessed himself of a handful of powerful drugs, and perched himself out of reach of any one who can control him. We know that he will make experiments for himself much more extraordinary than any we should have courage to make on his constitution, and we await the issue with feelings in which sympathy and compassion are not without their alloy of scientific curiosity. Thus we are not forced, as in most instances of historic speculation, to search out, by more or less imperfect means, the obscure and latent causes which have originated what we see before us. In almost all other cases we have to draw our conclusion from the results—to argue from effects to causes. . . . But in America the traces of all that has contributed to form her state and shape her destiny, are patent to the view. . . .

An imaginative mind—such as that of Mr. Hawthorne himself, for instance—might discern in both the illustrations we have used, some analogy to the elements of national life. . . . Whether, however, we look at the matter, in this fanciful light or from a purely rational point of view, all would agree in thinking that that efflorescence of a nation's being which finds its expression in its literature is as well worthy of attention for what it points to, even if not for its own positive merit, as any other product of its institutions.

In the case of America, the light which art and literature throw on the character of a nation has been to a great extent denied, because the country can hardly be said to possess in this respect any thing peculiarly and distinctively its own. . . . What the Greeks were to the Romans in a literary point of view, that the English are to the Americans. We have long supplied them with the greater part of what they require in this respect. Not that there is any deficiency of printed books in the United States, but the part which is not a reflection of something in the old country appears to be very small indeed. For almost every work of note which has been produced there, the mother nation can show a better counterpart. How can a national literature flourish when this is the case? It can scarcely do so, until the nation undergoes so great a change that the literature it imports no longer finds any thing responsive to it in the national mind. By the time that such a result is accomplished, something also will have arisen which will find its appropriate literary vent. Till then, probably, the most distinctive feature of American literature will be that which has often been pointed out as its most remarkable feature now—the element of humor. Humor is universal enough in itself; but the manner of its expression is so dependent upon local peculiarities that it will hardly bear to travel. . . . If we wished to preserve for posterity some idea of what the Americans are, and how they differ from us, we should choose not Irving or Longfellow, but Lowell and Sam Slick.

Are there, then, no signs of a national American literature in any department except that of humor? It must be confessed there are but few. If we exclude from consideration all who have not gained sufficient fame to be read beyond their own limits, the number of American writers who are any thing more than Englishmen in America does not amount to much. Irving dealt with national traditions, and devoted himself to national subjects. But his whole cast of thought, and of the dress of his thought, was formed upon English models. Longfellow is equally indebted to Germany; and the poem in which he is sometimes said to be most original is a homage to the traditions of the red man rather than of his own white brethren. About Emerson, indeed, there is something which one does not think would have been written in Europe, but it is not his strongest part. Poe seems altogether incapable of being classified; and if his works (omitting the American phrases and positive local allusions) had been published as translations from the French, German, or Danish, we do not think any one would have disbelieved in their assumed origin. This is not quite the case with the writer before us. Mr. Hawthorne is, we are inclined to think, the most national writer, of a serious kind, whom the country has yet produced in the department of fiction. He seems to us to reflect many of the characteristics of the American mind more exactly than any of his predecessors. He has evidently a warm as well as an enlightened love for his country. He likes to dwell on the picturesque part of its early struggles, just as we like to hover about the region of the civil war. The primitive habits of the first settlers—the stern Puritanic training of the infant states—the conflict of asceticism with the old jovial English spirit—the legends which cluster, like bats around a ruined tower, about the decaying period of the English rule—are all familiar denizens of his mind, and the channels through which many of his ideas spontaneously flow. He reflects more unconsciously, perhaps, some of the, perhaps transitional, characteristics of the America that is; the contrasts which are always presenting themselves between the material and the moral side of civilization, and the singular combination of knowingness and superstition, which some at least of the present phases of American life offer to our notice.

Mr. Hawthorne has written upwards of sixty stories and sketches, and four novels, all of various kinds and degrees of merit. There is no necessity for regarding the classification under which these appeared, which seems accidental, and dependent on the fact that he found he had, at certain times, written enough to compose a volume. We may also disregard the fact of their being longer or shorter—of their being mere stories, or three-volume novels. It will for our present purpose, be most convenient to divide them into three classes:—I. Studies of Historic Events, or of Every-day Characters. II. Scenes and Stories purely imaginative and fantastic. III. Allegories and Moral Sketches or Narratives. The first of these classes, as far as the shorter pieces are concerned, is not that in which Mr. Hawthorne's originality is most apparent. Except for the delicacy of observation which distinguishes all he writes, there is little about them to separate them from such sketches as those of Washington Irving. One kind are pictures of events in American annals, which he has striven to reproduce with a certain imaginative coloring, rather than as transcripts of what might actually have happened. There is no study of costume as costume; it is introduced for the purpose of heightening the impression rather than of completing the portrait. Indeed, we may say generally, though there is much about Mr. Hawthorne's writings of what would be called 'the picturesque,' and though he has a strong feeling for the thing itself, he has not the gift —perhaps has not the desire—of setting a landscape or a scene before our eyes in its unity as well as its variety. He has a certain power of selection, but he uses it to deepen the feeling that he wishes to inspire, not to dash down those few strong touches which form a living whole. His effect is produced by an accumulation of details, all of which converge to a certain impression, but we do not carry away from them a mental photograph. The effect rather resembles the result of what addresses itself to the ear than the feelings which are left by exercising the sense of sight. After reading a story of this kind we feel more as if we had been at a concert than at a play. There is the same sense of vague harmony, touching chords of feeling which it requires some subtle hand to reach; the same sense of occasional incompleteness in an intellectual point of view, and the same sort of semi-physical gratification which is produced by listening to music, or inhaling perfume. In other respects these sketches have but slight value, and we shall offer no excuse for passing on to the more important ones.

Under the head of 'Imaginative and Fantastic' sketches we should include all he has written which does not, on the one hand, represent any actual fact, external circumstance, or character, and, on the other, involves no distinct moral lesson. In stories of this kind we are as far as possible from any thing realistic. There is nothing about them which bears any relation to life as we habitually know it. The people have no more substantiality than the personages of a fairy tale; and though the recital of their fate may thrill us with a transient horror, or their characters excite a tepid fondness, they seldom rouse any deeper sentiment than that of wonder. It is in these stories that Mr. Hawthorne bears the greatest resemblance to Poe, because it is in these that he is least moral, though always far more so than that singular writer. In the 'New Adam and Eve,' for instance, we observe a similar power of taking some odd idea and working out the suggested hypothesis into all possible consequences. The author, in that sketch, imagines the whole human race to be destroyed—obliterated from the face of the earth, leaving no actual form of man, woman, or child, even dead, behind it; but leaving all the traces of its existence—its public and private buildings, its furniture and utensils, its untasted food, its ornaments and clothes, its books and pictures—as if the whole world were turned into one vast Pompeii. Into this strange solitude are introduced the two new beings who are to repeople it, and who survey, with perplexity, the vestiges of their predecessors. The point of the sketch consists in the contrast between primeval simplicity and the multifarious appliances with which civilization surrounds us—not without a sigh of regret at the kind of heavy weight which the rolling ages of this hoary old world have left upon its brows. No other moral than this is perceptible, but one may fancy a sort of appropriateness in the picture to an inhabitant of a land which embraces all degrees of the world's progress within the circuit of its territories, and which can show us, as it were, fainter and fainter zones of civilization melting away by imperceptible degrees into the primitive wildness of nature. Such a fancy would hardly have occurred to a dweller in one of the old continents. In 'David Swan' we find an apologue such as Parnell might have versified, though without the ethical force which would have recommended it to him. A youth falls asleep at a fountain, and, during his slumber, various persons approach him who each intend, for a brief moment, to do something which, were it done, would entirely change the course of his destiny. . . . This story is only so far moral that it suggests on what trifles the course of our life may depend; but though the thought is a solemn one, and forcibly put, it gives us nothing more than this to carry away. No moralist can teach us to control fate. In 'The Prophetic Pictures'—is illustrated the idea—which is a favorite one with our author—that an artist has the power of calling on to the canvas the latent capacities, for good or evil, of his

355

sitter, and fixing him with the expression which he will wear when those capacities have developed themselves into habits. . . . The effect of the tale is wild and ghastly in the author's way of telling it, and reminds us of some parts of the writings both of Poe and Wilkie Collins, though it does not aim at the matter-of-fact air which stands for so much in the power of the two latter writers. 'The Ambitious Guest'—which describes the violent death of a whole family, together with a stranger, all of whom have been making plans for the future to the moment of their fate—by the sudden fall of part of a mountain—owes its telling character to a similar feeling—that of the irresistibleness of our destiny. The most ghastly of all the stories in this class, however, is 'The Hollow of the Three Hills.' An old witch descends at sunset into one of those weird and lonely spots which have always been the scene of unholy operations. She is joined by a beautiful, but faded lady, who kneels down and places her head in her lap. The hag summons up three pictures relating to the guilty woman's life; her forsaken parents, in their solitary grief; her betrayed husband, telling the story of his dishonor to the associates of his mad-house; and, lastly, the burial which is awaiting herself amid the curses and revilings of her former friends. The story concludes; 'But when the old woman stirred the kneeling lady, she lifted not her head. "Here has been a sweet hour's sport!" said the withered crone, chuckling to herself.' 'The Hall of Fantasy,' and 'P.'s Correspondence,' are sketches of a lighter character. The former describes a sort of limbo, peopled with the shapes of inventors, theorists, and reformers—the representatives of all the wasted intellect and ingenuity that has ever existed. The latter purports to be the description, by a half madman, of all manner of celebrated people—a strange jumble of the dead and the living—Byron and Shelley grown old, fat, and converted to respectability; Napoleon I a denizen of Pall Mall; Canning, a peer, and Keats in middle age, with a completed epic. The wit of this latter fantasy is merely that of cross-readings ingeniously enough worked out. 'The Select Party,' which is much of the same kind, introduces us to such entities as the Oldest Inhabitant, the Clerk of the Weather, Old Harry, Davy Jones, and Posterity. In this section we may also, perhaps, include 'The Celestial Railroad,' which is a kind of travestie of the *Pilgrim's Progress*. There, however, the moral element is more distinctively brought out. . . . Over the remaining pieces of this kind there is no need to linger. They are all marked by ingenuity, cleverness, and Mr. Hawthorne's grace of style and sentiment, but many of them are air-drawn shapes, which leave but little impression when we have closed the book. We pass on to the third class, which comprehends the author's most impressive and important productions.

Upon looking over them, in connexion, we have been struck with the fact that they almost all represent one or other of two ideas, which appear to have a remarkable prominence in the author's mind.

One of these ideas is the notion expressed to a certain extent by Persius in a line, which Kant took as a kind of motto to his great metaphysical work,—*Tecum habita, et nôris quam sit tibi curta supellex*[1]— the warning (in a larger sense) against attempting to transcend in any way the conditions of our being. Hartley Coleridge has attempted to show that a phase of this idea is the basis of *Hamlet*. The Prince of Denmark, he tells us, stepped out of the limits of our proper nature by placing himself in connexion with the unseen world, and thereby immediately assumed a false relation towards actual life, and ultimately found his mind unable to support the weight of the new experience laid upon him in a region for which our faculties are too weak. Mr. Hawthorne, in about half of the tales we should include under our third section, teaches either a similar lesson, or its corollary, viz., that, seeing we cannot pass the bounds which encircle this human system, we should make the best of it as it is. Thus in 'The Birthmark,' he describes a man of science whose wife is all perfection, except that her cheek is marked with the figure of a tiny hand. He is annoyed by this defect, and persuades the lady to allow him to eradicate it by resorting to subtle devices of chemistry. He succeeds; but the same potent elixir which destroys the eyesore destroys life also, and the woman fades out of the existence which had just received what the presumptuous experimentalist thought its finishing touch. In 'Rappaccini's Daughter' is described a beautiful girl, whose father puts her out of the pale of humanity by nourishing her on poisons till her whole nature is saturated with them, so that she inhales with pleasure the noxious odors, which kill animals that breathe them, and causes flowers to wither by holding them in her hand. The youth who wins her heart is in process of being endowed, by sympathy and contact, with the same mysterious power, but is persuaded by a physician, the rival of her father, to give her a potion to neutralize the effect of all the poison she has imbibed. It is, in fact, an efficacious antidote; but her physiological nature is so completely reversed that what would be a remedy to any one else, acts as a poison on her; she takes the draught, and falls dead in her lover's arms. 'Earth's

---

[1] *Tecum habita, et nôris quam sit tibi curta supellex:* Live in your own house, and recognize how poorly it is furnished (Persius, *Satires,* IV, 52).

Holocaust' describes—somewhat after the manner of the Vision of Mirza—a bonfire in which mankind had determined to get rid of all the rubbish and worn-out 'properties' that had accumulated in the history of the world, so as to begin entirely afresh and 'turn over a new leaf.' But, we are told, in spite of every thing having been burnt, all that is valuable will reappear in the ashes the succeeding day, while, unless the human heart itself is thrown on to the pile, every thing for the sake of which the fire was kindled will spring up again as luxuriantly as ever. In 'Dr. Heidegger's Experiment' (which we fancy may have been suggested by a scene in Dumas' *Memoires d'un Medecin*), we are taught that, if we could renew our youth by some Medean draught, we should, unless altered in other respects, commit the same follies as we have now to look back to. 'Peter Goldthwaite's Treasure'—where a man pulls down his whole house, to find a concealed hoard which turns out worthless on discovery,—and 'The Threefold Destiny,' where the hero, after roaming over the world to meet with a lot such as he conceives suitable for him, after returning unsuccessful, finds it on the spot whence he set out,—both convey the same moral as the old fable of the sons who dug over their land to find the money which its improved fertility was really to give them. Nearly a similar lesson is enforced in 'The Great Carbuncle,' which like the 'Jewel of Giamschid,' eludes all those who set out to search for it, except one who dies at the instant of discovery, and two, who become aware that they can do much better without it. 'The Celestial Railroad,' which we have already looked at as a mere work of fancy, may probably also be meant to imply that there are no short cuts in spiritual matters. 'Mrs. Bullfrog' is a comic sketch (not our author's happiest vein), symbolizing the philosophy which teaches us to 'make the best of it,' in the case of matrimonial as well as other disappointments. 'Egotism, or the Bosom Serpent,' needs no explanation. All these stories have great variety in treatment, and it is not until we look over them with a view to establishing some kind of classification, that we see how very many of them express different *facets*, so to speak, of the same idea. It is not, perhaps a novel one—no moral ideas are—but, it is sound as far as it goes, and if, to apply an oft-quoted sentence, its author has not 'solved the mystery of the universe,' he has, nevertheless, taught us 'to keep within the limits of the knowable.'

The other leading notion to which we referred as pervading a great number, and among them the most important, of Mr. Hawthorne's moral tales, is the idea of secret guilt. Though the former point in his philosophy might not, in its manifold diversities of presentation, at once strike a casual reader, we should imagine that every one at all acquainted with his writings must have recognized the predominance of the one of which we now speak. It re-appears so often as almost to make us fancy that he must have had at some time or other the office of a confessor, or have enjoyed some peculiar opportunity for studying this phase of morbid moral anatomy. We will mention some of the phases under which the idea is presented—the garments in which it is clothed in the various sketches, quoting at the same time some of the passages in which we may trace its development through the author's mind in its progress towards the proportions it has assumed in some of his later works. 'The Haunted Mind' is a study of the miscellaneous fancies which occur to us on waking in the middle of the night. Among these the following passage is remarkable, not only as being a good speciment of Mr. Hawthorne's style, but as containing the germ of much which we find elsewhere hinted at or expressed in a concrete form. After experiencing and revelling in the sensation of warmth in bed— 'that idea,' he continues, 'has brought a hideous one in its train:'—

[Quotes 'You think how' to 'darkness of the chamber'.]

'Young Goodman Brown' describes a man setting out to attend a witches' sabbath, leaving his young wife (Faith) behind. On his way he becomes conscious that the most respectable persons of his acquaintance are bound in the same direction. At his initiation into the unhallowed mysteries, he is confronted by his fair young spouse, who has come there on a similar errand; but before he is able to learn whether she has the stain of guilt which would entitle her to admission, the scene dissolves, and he is at home again—to become a cynic and a disbeliever in human virtue for the rest of his life. The following is from the speech of the archfiend to the intending proselytes:—

[Quotes ' "There," resumed' to ' "look upon each other" '.]

In 'The Procession of Life,' which is a sort of classification of mankind according to their real not their conventional value, by their intellectual gifts, their virtue, or their vice, the same idea is pursued:—

[Quotes 'Come, all ye' to 'brotherhood of crime' and 'Here comes a murderer' to 'meant for them'.]

In 'Egotism,' which describes an unfortunate person who has swallowed a snake, which is constantly preying on his vitals, we are reminded, in a slightly different form, of the freemasonry which exists between one guilty being and another. The victim wanders about the streets as if to establish a species of brotherhood between himself and the world. . . . In 'The Christmas Banquet,' supposed to be a convivial gathering of the ten most miserable persons that could be found in the world at one time, is introduced a misanthrope who had been soured by the failure of his trust in mankind. . . . In 'Fancy's Show-Box' the idea is carried still further, and Fancy, Memory, and Conscience are represented as bringing before the mental vision of a man who has committed none but the most venial faults, throughout his life, a variety of sins which at one time or other he had a passing wish to perpetrate. . . . 'The Minister's Black Veil' conveys a very similiar idea, and is a sort of foreshadowing of the 'Scarlet Letter' . . . 'The Intelligence Office,' which is one of those fantastic sketches in which the allegory is made more quaint by being conveyed through a common and familiar channel, embodies much the same notion as that of 'Fancy's Show-Box.' . . .

By far the most powerful of Mr. Hawthorne's shorter works in this class, however, is the one entitled 'Roger Malvin's Burial'—both for the picturesque power of the colouring and the ghastly vividness with which the central idea is presented. . . .

The Scarlet Letter, is, probably, the best known of Mr. Hawthorne's works, and it is unnecessary to recount the plot. . . . But it may be interesting to trace, in various passages, the developments of the same ideas which have been associated by the author in former works with this favorite phase of moral experience, for which they seem in such points to have been studies. In the following passage we recognize the moral enforced in 'Young Goodman Brown:'

[Quotes ch. 1, 'Hester felt or' to 'guilty like herself'.]

. . . The *House of the Seven Gables* is a little less impressive than the earlier work, but it makes up for this in its greater variety and more life-like and real character. In the *Scarlet Letter* the chief personages seem to be almost as far removed from us as the characters in some old Greek tragedy; there is a halo of romance thrown round them which, to a degree, isolates them from our entire sympathies, however forcibly the record of their doom may come home to our hearts.

The *House of the Seven Gables* is a story of contemporary life, and though we scarcely feel that we are in the every-day world, the people are such as might be met with there. While preserving the romantic cast of the narrative in all that pertains to its essentials, nothing can surpass the art with which the familiar figures of the street and the shop are embroidered, as it were, on this dusky background, which seems to throw them into more prominent relief. The character of Hepzibah, with her faded gentility, her warmth of affection, and her struggles in assuming her new life, are painted with extraordinary skill. Judge Pyncheon is not described at so much length as most of Mr. Hawthorne's characters, but the touches which picture him to us, though few, are strong, and seem to give the man's inner nature. Were we on the look-out for merely descriptive passages, we should probably choose this novel as the best specimen of its author's power. Nowhere has he written with so much force and with so little apparent effort. The eighteenth chapter of this novel, in which the author describes all the schemes of an ambitious man cut short by his sudden death, is full of a grim irony such as we find nowhere so well sustained except in some of the best passages of Dickens. Mr. Hawthorne falls far short of the rich variety and comic power of the latter writer, but he may occasionally compete with him in the intensity wherewith certain strong emotions or situations are kneaded into the reader's mind, so as to leave an indelible impression.

The basis of this story, too, is the idea of secret guilt—and working on a broader scale than elsewhere in the author's creations. . . .

[Quotes ch. 15, 'The judge, beyond' to 'the death-hour', but with several deletions.]

In reading the story from which these extracts are taken, we are apt to be so fascinated by the narrative, as to be unconscious of a certain disproportionateness in its construction which forces itself on us after we lay it down. The *dénouement* seems to be over-balanced by the characters and descriptions, and to be a little hurried over. Not that it is otherwise than a perfectly allowable one in a romance of the kind. The descendant of the man who was burnt through Pyncheon's agency having been in the secret of the house all through the story, comes forward at last to marry the heiress and remove the spell. His part, however, is rather too much that of a spectator all through, and we have a sort of feeling that his agency ought to have been of a more active character as regards the Judge; though how this could have been effected we do not presume to suggest. . . .

Before we pass on to Mr. Hawthorne's most recent work, a few words must be said about *The Blithedale Romance*—though we are inclined to think, that this is the book which, of all he has written, is least likely to contribute to his fame. It was the result, we believe, of its author's experience at Brook Farm, a kind of Utopian or Fourierist agricultural community, which came to grief after a short trial. It was natural enough that the characters, who had self-reliance and singularity enough to quit the world for such experiment, should have had many traits which an observer of human nature would be glad to study, and which a writer like Mr. Hawthorne would feel almost irresistibly compelled to draw out in some consistent framework. If, however, as we suspect, it was the characters which suggested the story, this would be enough to account for its inferior success to that of the author's former novels. A work of fiction may start from the central idea, and work outwards by means of characters which the author looks for to embody it in; or it may work towards some idea from the outside, because a number of characters have presented themselves which look as if they ought to do something if brought together. The best novels are those in which idea, plot, and character, all spring up together in the mind, one knows not how, but mutually dependent, and incapable of expressing a being expressed in any other form. To this degree of excellence, however, few attain. Mr. Hawthorne's successes, we think, have arisen from the fact that his genius is of the former class. An idea has possessed him, and he has striven to bring it out in the most appropriate and forcible way he could devise; if aerial and exceptional, by fantastic and merely imaginative machinery; if more substantial and more based on the facts of life, then by a more realistic and living narrative. To have elaborated the notion of the freemasonry of guilt, which is conveyed in 'Young Goodman Brown,' by a series of mundane characters would have resulted in a monstrous and impossible work. . . . In *The Blithedale Romance* he appears, as we have said, to have pursued a different plan. The result is, that there is a want of point and unity in the story. We are sensible of the power of particular scenes, such as the night-search by the river for the missing heroine, and the force and delicacy with which her character, and that of her stern and rugged friend, are drawn. But we close the book with a certain feeling of dissatisfaction, only mitigated by that halo which a man of genius contrives to throw round any creation of his pen, and transfer us by means of it into the enchanted region of which he keeps the key.

Of the latest work for which we are indebted to Mr. Hawthorne, we scarcely know whether we can give a more favorable account. It is full of graceful and beautiful thoughts, and its finish and ease of style are greater than any former writing of the author. But it is largely deficient in the vigor which has held us spell-bound over many of his other pages. We question whether many persons have finished *Transformation* at a sitting, unless they really had nothing else to do. One might fancy that the Italian atmosphere which has lent color and brilliancy to the book, had also imparted something of the enervating softness, with which it often affects those who breathe it not as their native air. The nervous American fibre with its remote under-strength of stalwart British organization, seems to have been relaxed, or led away from its former strivings after positive results. The effect appears in a sort of feebleness of purpose, which makes the book a compromise between an art novel and a psychological study, without a thoroughly complete working out of either, and without the attractiveness of narrative, structure, and pointed interest, which have distinguished the two best of the novels above described. . . .

[Summarizes the story and quotes six long passages.]

As a novel in the ordinary sense of the term it is undoubtedly defective. To those who read 'for the story' it will be found tedious, for there is but little action, and the mystery relating to the influence exercised by Miriam's victim over her career, is left unsolved, except by vague hints which we are at liberty to fill up in any way we like. We think this a fault in art; for, the greatest writers, whatever might be the weight of the moral they meant to inculcate, or the significance of the problem they wished to discuss, have always seen the necessity of also condescending to a lower order of appreciation, and of making the vesture and outward presentation of the truth attractive in itself, and competent to satisfy, as a narrative of incident, the minds of those who would not be at first, or perhaps even at all, awake to its inner meanings. . . . Of this dramatic vigor Mr. Hawthorne has in his former works shown himself so capable a master, that we must conclude that it is of set purpose and design that he has now constructed his story so loosely, and encumbered it with matter not directly germane to its primary conception. He seems to have been possessed with the idea, on the one hand, of embodying his Italian impressions in something like an 'art-novel'—a form of literature which has yet to become naturalized among us—a amphibious creation, to which nothing but some example of transcendent excellence will persuade us to be reconciled; and, on the other, to bring before us the suggestive idea, the theory of which is most fully presented in our last extract. With the fullest admiration for Mr. Hawthorne's genius, and the entire recognition of the power with which this notion, in its concrete shape, is exhibited in the shifting aspects of the romance, we question after all, the propriety of the form under which it has come to light. It seems more properly belonging to the class of ideas with which the author has dealt in his imaginative and fantastic tales. We seem to see the same incongruity in its present extensive and elaborate attire that there would have been in drawing out, for instance, the theme of *Rappacini's Daughter* to a similar length. The conception, indeed, is one more fit for verse than prose. To tie it down to the limits and conditions of a three-volume novel is like imprisoning Ariel in the oak-tree. The matter-of-fact solidity which we require in a prose story might be dispensed with in a poem, and the vagueness to which we have objected, though it would not be a merit, would be far less of a defect than it is in the actual case; while the philosophic or ethical aspect of the question, which is now unavoidably postponed to the incidents, might have been developed in a manner more calculated to do it justice. We may say, in conclusion, that those who read *Transformation* for its interest as a romance, in the usual sense of the expression, will be disappointed. But, having got through it, those readers whose intelligent appreciation an author chiefly values, will return again and again to its pages for correct and striking thoughts on art expressed in the happiest languages—for scenes of Arcadian beauty—and for glimpses into the moral *arcana* of our nature such as few novelists afford. . . .

We have said, at the outset of this article, that we think Mr. Hawthorne one of the most national writers that the United States have produced; and the tone and temper of mind which seem to us to have given birth to his latest work, if we are correct in our estimate of them, bear out a part of this opinion. Mr. Hawthorne belongs to the historic side of American life by his patriotic feeling, by his vivid local coloring, by his choice of subjects, such as (except in the last instance) no English writer would be competent to deal with, and by his freedom, so far as is possible consistently with his writing in the English language at all, from any restrictions through deference to European models. He has taken what material he could find in his own country, and, to a great extent, peculiar to it, has looked at it with an artist's imaginative eye, and made as much of it probably as any one could do. That there are not the materials in American history for grand mediæval romances is not his fault. To breathe life into the dry bones of dusty chroniclers, to flash the ray of genius on historic problems, as Scott did in *Ivanhoe*, to summon into visible mixture of earth's mould the mythic phantoms which flit round a nation's cradle, is not given to the citizen of the land the pedigree of whose liberties is far younger than the time of legal memory, and whose annals are written, not in grass-grown entrenchments, mouldering castles, and half-effaced monuments, but in treaties and declarations and newspapers. To have produced so much from such materials is a triumph of which a much greater writer might well be proud.

If, as we have tried to show, Mr. Hawthorne may be held to represent, with some faithfulness, the historic and picturesque side of the life of America, no less we think, does he embody, much more unconsciously, perhaps, some of the peculiar characteristics of her mental condition. His writings in the first place, are those of a recluse, and bring before us the cultivated tone of thought of the class which, in the United States has usually kept aloof from politics. Acquainted with practical life, so far as it can be learnt in an official situation, he shows but little sympathy with anything but its artistic side. He seems essentially a man of letters; his humor is that of a spectator *ab extra*, and is of the school of Addison and Charles Lamb rather than of Sam Slick. Endowed with a genial sympathy, and the power as well as the disposition to penetrate into the feelings, and ideally assume the position of people quite different from himself, he has shown no tendency to make use of this faculty for any thing like class representation of contemporary life in the way, for instance, which Mr. Disraeli has done in *Sybil*. The spirit of his time comes out through him in quite a different manner. He represents the *youthfulness* of America—not in respect of its physical vigor and energy, but of its vague aspirations, its eager curiosity, its syncretism, its strainings after the perception of psychologic mysteries, its transitory phases of exhausted cynicism, its tendency to the grotesque in taste and character, and its unscrupulous handling of some of the deepest secrets of our nature. His philosophy, on its practical side, seems to combine a resignation to the pressure of the inevitable (when it is *really* destiny which causes our failure), with a moral elasticity which teaches us to 'make the best of it' when a way of escape can be found, and which latter feeling connects him with that large class of his countrymen whom he has represented in his portrait of Holgrave, who have a sort of Protean faculty of turning their powers to account under all varieties of circumstances, and a prehensile instinct which breaks their fall and furnishes a fresh starting-point for more hopeful enterprises. On its religious side it seems to be deeply tinged with that Puritan and Calvinistic element which has left such deep traces wherever it has had any root. The idea of remorse—of the hell which the soul may bear within itself, transfiguring all outward things with the deep shadows and lurid lights cast by its own internal flames, is the one which seems to have obtained the firmest hold on his mind, and to have inspired his strongest and best writing. No feeling, perhaps, in the range of those with which a writer of fiction may deal, is more available for powerful effects, and for that accumulation of external detail mingled with deep psychological insight which has constituted the basis of Mr. Hawthorne's fame. We would only take leave to warn him that such a theme holds out temptations to morbid treatment more than almost any other, and that a writer of his great acuteness and wide observation, ought not to be at a loss for future subjects, not necessarily of a more shallow, but, we may hope, of a cheerful and varied tendency. And, as regards more particularly the novel which has suggested our survey of him, we suspect—even with a 'third edition' before us—that another, on such a plan, would be an experiment which it would not be safe for his popularity to repeat.

112. Richard Holt Hutton: Hawthorne and the Calvinist imagination, from an unsigned essay, 'Nathaniel Hawthorne', in the *National Review*

October 1860, xi, 453–81

Hutton (1826–97) was, with Walter Bagehot, co-editor of the *National Review* from 1861 to 1897. His collected works include four volumes of theological and literary criticism.

Mr. Hawthorne speaks more than once in his various thoughtful and artistic tales of the 'moonlight of romance,' and the phrase has a special applicability to the fictions which it is his delight to weave. It is one of his favorite theories that there must be a vague, remote, and shadowy element in the subject-matter of any narrative with which his own imagination can successfully deal. Sometimes he apologizes for this idealistic limitation to his artistic aims. 'It was a folly,' he says in his preface to the *Scarlet Letter*, 'with the materiality of this daily life pressing so intrusively upon me, to attempt to fling myself back into another age, or to insist on creating the semblance of a world out of airy matter, when, at every moment, the impalpable beauty of my soap-bubble was broken by the rude contact of some actual circumstance.' . . . But the dissatisfaction with his own idealism which he here expresses has at least not sufficed to divert his efforts into the channel indicated. In the *Blithedale Romance* he tells us that he chose the external scenery of the socialist community at Brook Farm

merely to establish a theatre, a little removed from the highway of ordinary travel, where the creatures of his brain may play their phantasmagorical antics without exposing them to too close a comparison with the actual events of real lives. In the old countries with which fiction has long been conversant, a certain conventional privilege seems to be awarded to the romancer; his work is not put exactly side by side with nature; and he is allowed a license with regard to every-day probability, in view of the improved effects which he is bound to produce thereby. Among ourselves, on the contrary, there is as yet no Faëry-land so like the real world that, in a suitable remoteness, one cannot well tell the difference, but with an atmosphere of strange enchantment, beheld through which, the inhabitants have a propriety of their own. This atmosphere is what the American romancer wants. In its absence, the beings of imagination are compelled to show themselves in the same category as actually living mortals,—a necessity that generally renders the paint and pasteboard of their composition but too painfully discernible.

And once more, in the preface to his latest work, *Transformation*, he reiterates as his excuse for laying the scene in Italy, that

no author without a trial can conceive of the difficulty of writing a romance about a country where there is no shadow, no antiquity, no mystery, no picturesque and gloomy wrong, nor any thing but a commonplace prosperity in broad and simple daylight, as is happily the case with my dear native land. It will be very long, I trust, before romance writers may find congenial and easily handled themes either in the annals of our stalwart republic, or in any characteristic and probable event of our individual lives. Romance and poetry, ivy, lichens, and wall-flowers, need ruin to make them grow.

These passages throw much light on the secret affinities of Mr. Hawthorne's genius. But it would be a mistake to conclude from them, as he himself would apparently have us, that he is a mere romantic idealist, in the sense in which these words are commonly used,—that he is one all whose dramatic conceptions are but the unreal kaleidoscopic combinations of fancies in his own brain.

We may perhaps accept Mr. Hawthorne's own phrase,—'the moonlight of romance,'—and compel it to help us to a distinction which will explain something of the secret of his characteristic genius. There are writers—chiefly poets, but also occasionally writers of fanciful romances like Mr. Longfellow's *Hyperion*—whose productions are purely ideal, not only seen by the light of their own imagination but constituted out of it,—made of moonshine,—and rendered vivid and beautiful, if they are vivid and beautiful, merely with the vividness and beauty of the poet's own mind. In these cases there is no distinction at all between the delineating power and the delineated object; the dream is indistinguishable from the mind of the dreamer, and varies wholly with its laws. Again, at the opposite extreme there is a kind of creative imagination which has its origin in a deep sympathy with, and knowledge of, the real world. That which it deals with is actual life as it has existed, or still exists, in forms so innumerable that it is scarcely possible to assert that its range is more limited than life itself. Of course the only adequate example of such an imagination is Shakspeare's; and this kind of imaginative power resembles sunlight, not only in its brilliancy, but especially in this, that it casts a light so full and equable over the universe it reveals, that we never think of its source at all. . . . Between these two kinds of creative imagination there is another, which also shows a real world, but shows it so dimly in comparison with the last as to keep constantly before our minds the unique character of the light by which we see. The ideal light itself becomes a more prominent element in the picture than even the objects on which it shines; and yet is made so, chiefly by the very fact of shining on those objects which we are accustomed to think of as they are seen in their own familiar details in full daylight. If the objects illuminated were not real and familiar, the light would not seem so mysterious; it is the pale uniform tint, the loss of color and detail, and yet the vivid familiar outline and the strong shadow, which produces what Mr. Hawthorne calls the 'moonlight of romance.'

[Quotes 'The Custom-House': 'Moonlight in a' to 'nature of the other',]

Sir Walter Scott's delineative power partakes of both this moonlight imagination and the other more powerful and brilliant and realistic kind. Often it is a wide, genial sunshine, of which we quite forget the source in the vividness of the common life which it irradiates. At other times, again, when he is in his Black Douglas mood, as we may call it, it has all the uniformity of tint and the exciting pallor, of what Mr. Hawthorne terms the moonlight of romance.

At all events, there is no writer to whose creations the phrase applies more closely than to Mr. Hawthorne's own. His characters are by no means such unreal webs of moonshine as the idealists proper constitute into the figures of their romance. They are real and powerfully conceived, but they are all seen in a single light,—the contemplative light of the particular idea which has floated before him in each of his stories, —and they are seen, not fully and in their integrity, as things are seen by daylight, but like things touched by moonlight, *only so far* as they are lighted up by the idea of the story. The thread of unity which connects his tales is always some pervading thought of his own; they are not written mainly to display character, still less for the mere narrative interest, but for the illustration they cast on some idea or conviction of their author. Amongst English writers of fiction, we have many besides Shakspeare whose stories are merely appropriate instruments for the portraiture of character, and who therefore never conceive themselves bound to confine themselves scrupulously to the one aspect most naturally developed by the tale. Once introduced, their characters are given in full,—both that side of them which is, so to say, turned *towards* the story, and others which are not. Other writers, again, make the characters quite subsidiary to the epical interest of the plot, using them only to heighten the coloring of the action it describes. Mr. Hawthorne's tales belong to neither of these classes. Their unity is ideal. His characters are often real and vivid, but they are illuminated only from one centre of thought. So strictly is this true of them, that he has barely *room* for a novel in the ordinary sense of the word. If he were to take his characters through as many phases of life as are ordinarily comprised in a novel, he could not keep the ideal unity of his tales unbroken; he would be obliged to delineate them from many different points of view. Accordingly, his novels are not novels in the ordinary sense; they are ideal situations expanded by minute study and trains of closely related thought into the dimensions of novels. A very small group of figures is presented to the reader in some marked ideal relation; or if it be in consequence of some critical event, then it must be some event which has struck the author as rich in ideal or moral suggestion. But it is not usually in his way—though his latest novel gives us one remarkable exception to this observation—to seize any glowing crisis of action when the passion is lit or the blow is struck that gives a new mould to life, for his delineation; he prefers to assume the crisis past, and to delineate as fully as he can the ideal situation to which it has given rise, when it is beginning to assume more of a chronic character.

But, however this may be, almost all his tales embody single ideal situations, scarcely ever for a moment varied in their course in any essential respect. For instance, to take his shorter tales, the mockery of the attempt to renew in wasted age the blasted hopes of youth is crystallized into a *tableau vivant* in the *Wedding-Knell*. The absolute spiritual isolation of every man's deepest life, and the awe which any visible assertion of that isolation inspires, even when made by the mildest of our guilty race, is translated into an ideal picture in the *Minister's Black Veil*. So in the *Great Stone Face* we have an embodiment of the conviction that *he* is best fitted to fulfil any great human hope or trust whose heart is constantly fed upon the yearning to find the perfect fulfilment of it in another. So in *Roger Malvin's Burial* we are shown how an innocent man, who is too cowardly to face the mere appearance of guilt, may thereby incur a remorse and guilt as deep as that from the faintest suspicion of which he shrank. And so we may run through almost all the *tales* properly so called. We do not mean that in any of them the author thinks the thought first in its abstract form, and then condenses it into a story. We should suppose, on the contrary, that the artistic form is the one in which the idea of the tale first flashes on him, and that the work of elaboration only gives more substance and greater variety of color to the parts. But not the less is the essence originally ideal, since every touch and line in his imagined picture is calculated to impress some leading thought on the reader.

But it is only when we look at his longer tales, whose dimensions would lead us to expect more variety of aspect in the characters, more circumstance, and less sameness of leading *thought*, that this characteristic of Mr. Hawthorne's tales becomes striking. The stories of the *Scarlet Letter*, of the *House of the Seven Gables*, and of *Transformation*, might all have been included, in their full ideal integrity, and with all the *incident* they contain, in the *Twice-told Tales* without adding more than a few pages to the book. We do not mean that thus compressed they would produce the same, or any thing like the same, imaginative impression, but only that, as far as either the *aspect* of his characters or the circumstantial interest of the stories is concerned, there need be no compression in thus shortening them. The omissions would be most important, indeed, to the effect, but they would be the omission of minute contemplative touches, imaginative self-repetitions, and so forth, which seldom indeed give us a single glimpse of any other than the one side of his characters, or add a second thread to the one interest of the tale.

In the *Scarlet Letter*, for instance, there is but one conception, which is developed in three—perhaps we should say four—scenes of great power, and that is the analysis of the deranging effect of the sin of adultery on the intrinsically fine characters of those principally affected by it, with a special view to its different influence on the woman, who is openly branded with the shame, and on the man, whose guilt is not published and who has a double remorse to suffer, for the sin, and for the growing burden of insincerity. The effect of the sin on the child who is the offspring of it is made a special study, as are the false relations it introduces between the mother and child. Throughout the tale every one of the group of characters studied is seen in the lurid light of this sin and in no other. The only failure is in the case of the injured and vindictive husband, whose character is subordinated entirely to the artistic development of the other three.

In the same way the predominant idea of the *Blithedale Romance* is to delineate the deranging effect of an absorbing philanthropic idea on a powerful mind,—the unscrupulous sacrifices of personal claims which it induces, and the misery in which it ends. There is scarcely one *incident* in the tale properly so called except the catastrophe, and what there is, is so anxiously shrouded in mystery as to have really all the enigmatic character of a *tableau vivant* of clear general meaning but doubtful interpretation as to details. The author seems to say to the reader, 'Here is a group of characters in relations tending to illustrate how much more sacred are personal affections than any abstract *cause* however noble; what these relations exactly are, except as they illustrate my idea, I will not say, as that is quite non-essential; you may imagine them what you please,—I tell you only enough to impress you with my predominant conviction.'

Again, in the *House of the Seven Gables* we have a picture studied to impress on us that both personal character, and the malign influences of evil action, are transmitted, sometimes with accumulating force, even through centuries, blighting every generation through which they pass. This subject would apparently involve a series of sketches; but only two are introduced from the past, and the family characteristics are so anxiously preserved as to make even these seem like slight modifications of some of the living group. But Mr. Hawthorne with rare art, pictures the shadow of the past as constantly hanging, like a baneful cloud, over the heads of his figures; and every detail, even the minutest, is made to point backwards to the weary past from which it has derived its constitutional peculiarities. Even the little shop which 'old maid Pyncheon' re-opens in the dark old house is not new. A miserly ancestor of the family had opened it a century before, who is supposed to haunt it, and the scales are rusty with the rust of generations. The half-effaced picture of the ancestral Pyncheon which hangs on the walls, the garden-mould, black with the vegetable decay of centuries, the exhausted breed of aristocratic fowls which inhabit the garden,—every touch is studied to condense the dark past into a cloud hanging over the living present, and make the reader feel its malign influence. The only incident in the tale is the light thrown upon a crime,—which had been committed thirty years before the story opens,—by the sudden death of the principal representative of the family, from the same specific disease, in the same chair, and under the same circumstances, as that of the old ancestor and founder of the family whose picture hangs above the chair.

The same criticism may be made on Mr. Hawthorne's latest work. The sole idea of *Transformation* is to illustrate the intellectually and morally awakening power of a sudden impulsive sin, committed by a simple, joyous, instinctive, 'natural' man. The whole group of characters is imagined solely with a view to the development of this idea. Mr. Hawthorne even hints, though rather hesitatingly, that without sin the higher humanity of man could not be taken up at all; that sin may be essential to the first conscious awakening of moral freedom and the possibility of progress. The act of sin itself is the only distinct incident of the tale; all the rest is either extraneous dissertation on Art, or the elaboration and study of the group of characters requisite to embody this leading idea. A tale containing the whole ideal essence of the book, and in this instance, though only in this instance, almost equally power-ful, might have been told in a few pages.

And yet we are very far indeed from meaning to say that the microscopic diffuseness with which Mr. Hawthorne enlarges these ideal studies into the length of an ordinary novel is wasted. For the secret of his power lies in the great art with which he reduplicates and reflects and re-reflects the main idea of the tale from the countless faces of his imagination, until the reader's mind is absolutely saturated and haunted by it. There are many among his shorter tales, which now occupy per-haps only five or ten pages, which would have gained infinitely in power by similar treatment, without the addition of a single fresh incident or scene. As they read now they have almost a feeble effect; they give the writer's idea and no more; they do not fill the reader with it; and Mr. Hawthorne's peculiar genius lies in the power he possesses to be haunted, and in his turn to haunt the reader, with his conceptions, far more than in their intrinsic force. Look at the central notion of his various minor tales, and you will be perhaps struck with a certain ideal simplicity, and a strange dash of lurid color in them that will impress you as promising, but no more. But let him summon this idea before you in the innumerable Protean shapes of his own imagination, with alterations of form just striking enough to make it seem at once the same and something fresh; and before he has done with you you are pursued, you are possessed, you are beset with his notion: it is in your very blood; it stares at you with ghastly force from every word of his narrative; it is in the earth and in the air; and every mouth that opens among his characters, however little they may be involved in the mystery of the tale, only sends it thrilling with greater force through your heart. What a story, for instance, might he not have made out of the very eerie tales called *Roger Malvin's Burial*, or *Rappacini's Daughter*, if he had elaborated them with any thing like the art shown in the *House of the Seven Gables*!

Mr. Hawthorne was quite aware of the slight ideal structure of his earlier and shorter tales. He has himself criticised them with rare candor and subtlety, though not with a fair appreciation of the promise of deeper power which they contained, in his preface to one of the editions of the *Twice-Told Tales*.

[Quotes 'At all events' to 'intercourse with the world'.]

This passage contains some of the truest and finest touches in the way of literary self-criticism with which we are acquainted; but it does not, as we said, do justice to the undeveloped germs of power in many of the pieces comprised in this and Mr. Hawthorne's other collections of shorter tales. It is true, indeed, that, throughout almost all he has yet written, sentiment takes the place of passion, and it is not seldom true, though it by no means holds of the majority of his finished studies of character, that, in the place of 'pictures of actual life, we have allegory not always so warmly dressed in its habiliments of flesh and blood as to be taken into the reader's mind without a shiver.' But there is enough even in the early tales of which Mr. Hawthorne here speaks to prove that the allegorical turn which his tales are apt to take was not with him, as it often is, a sign of meagre or shallow imaginative endowments,—a proof that fancy predominates in him rather than genuine imagination. When a man sits down professing to paint human life and character, and in place thereof succeeds only in representing abstract virtues, vices, passions, and the like, under human names, we may fairly say that with him the allegorical vein proves the general poverty of his spiritual blood. He has peeled off the outer surface where he professed to model the substance. But when, on the other hand, the same truth, which by an ordinary intellect would be expressed in a purely abstract form, naturally takes shape in a man's mind under an imaginative clothing which savors of allegory, no inference of the kind is legitimate. In the one case the allegory is the degenerate romance, in the other it is a thought expressing itself in the language of the imagination. The weakness in the former case is measured by the inability of the imagination to see the broad chasm between the reality and the allegorical shadow. In the latter case there is no such inability, but the thought which would have entered an ordinary mind in a purely abstract form presents itself to this in the form of a vivid shadow-picture.

And it is a sign that Mr. Hawthorne's genius has not the weakness usually belonging to allegorists, that the longer a subject rests in his mind, the more certainly do the allegorical shadows of its first outline gather solidity of form and variety of color, and gradually substantiate themselves into real living men. In the ideal situation or conception, as it first presents itself to the author's mind, the places of the human actors are perhaps occupied by appropriate symbols of some predominant sentiment or characteristic which each of the group subsequently embodies. If written down in that faint early form, the tale seems allegorical. But if allowed to lie by in the imagination, it deepens into a real dramatic situation; a body of real human life and character gathers round, and clothes, each of the ideal skeletons in the original plan, turning the faint allegory into a chapter of vivid human experience. So clearly did Mr. Edgar Poe perceive this vein of genuine imaginative power in Mr. Hawthorne's writings, even at a time when he had published only his shorter tales, that he boldly asserted,—in this, as we think, overleaping the truth,—that the conspicuously ideal scaffoldings of Mr. Hawthorne's stories were but the monstrous fruits of the bad transcendental atmosphere which he had breathed so long,—the sign of the Emersonian school of thought in which he had studied:

He is infinitely too fond of allegory [said Edgar Poe], and can never hope for popularity so long as he persists in it. This he will *not* do, for allegory is at war with the whole tone of his nature, which disports itself never so well as when escaping from the mysticism of his Goodman Browns and White Old Maids into the hearty, genial, but still Indian summer sunshine of his Wakefields and Little Annie's Rambles. Indeed, *his* spirit of metaphor run mad is clearly imbibed from the phalanx and phalanstery atmosphere in which he has been so long struggling for truth. He has not half the material for the exclusiveness of authorship that he possesses for its universality. He has the purest style, the finest taste, the most available scholarship, the most delicate humor, the most touching pathos, the most radiant imagination, the most consummate ingenuity, and with these varied good qualities he has done *well* as a mystic. But is there any one of these qualities which should prevent his doing doubly well in a career of honest, upright, sensible, prehensible, and comprehensible things? Let him mend his pen, get a bottle of visible ink, come out from the Old Manse, cut Mr. Alcott, hang (if possible) the editor of the *Dial,* and throw out of the window to the pigs all his odd numbers of the *North-American Review.*

The caustic American critic was, we think, confusing two things in this brief summary of Mr. Hawthorne's qualifications and deficiencies. He saw that Mr. Hawthorne could produce the most skilful studies from real life, as, for instance—to take one amongst many—in his sketch of the old Apple Dealer; he saw also that almost all his tales proper embodied an idea or a truth, and he thought the former the natural bent of Mr. Hawthorne's mind, the latter the imported mannerism of a clique. But the truth is, that both are equally natural to him, the ideal framework being quite as essential to him in putting together a tale as an unlimited store of unforeseen coincidences and exciting emergencies is to Fennimore Cooper or G. P. R. James, or a picturesque episode in history to Sir Walter Scott. Mr. Hawthorne could never weave his studies of human nature into a continuous narrative, based on mere circumstantial incident and striking adventure. The constructive talent, probably the special tastes and interests, requisite for that kind of framework of a tale are not a part of his genius. He must have an ideal centre and an ideal bond for his characters, or they would fall asunder into loose unconnected atoms. He has either no power or else no desire to construct what is ordinarily meant by a plot; that is, a chain of circumstantial coincidences in which the interest depends on the unusual and unforeseen character of the contingent events. The purely ideal clue of his stories supersedes entirely the function of the ordinary circumstantial thread.

But notwithstanding the simplicity and ideality which invariably mark the outline of Mr. Hawthorne's stories, the most notable characteristic of his genius distinguishes him widely from the school of allegorists.

His imagination only departs from that basis of New England simplicity which is the foundation and staple of its creations, to represent in his figures and excite in the reader those fearfully blended and yet mutually repellent emotions which thrill us with a sense of something at once real and preternatural,—true to a life and a moral state which has in it a dash of sin and of ghastly contradictions, and yet exciting those fitful pulses, those flushings and shiverings of the spirit, which testify to an uncanny or unholy origin. If we want to find Mr. Hawthorne's power at the very highest, we must look to this instinctive knowledge of what we may call the laws, not exactly of *discordant* emotions, but of emotions which *ought* to be mutually exclusive, and which combine with the thrill and the shudder of disease. This is almost the antithesis of Allegory. And he makes his delineation of such 'unblest unions' the more striking, because it stands out from a background of healthy life, of genial scenes and simple beauties, which renders the contrast the more thrilling. We have often heard the term, 'cobweby' applied to his romances; and their most marking passages certainly give the same sense of unwelcome shrinking to the spirit which a line of unexpected cobweb suddenly drawn across the face causes physically when one enters a deserted but familiar room. Edgar Poe, indeed, is much fuller of uncanny terrors; but then there is nothing in his writings of the healthy, simple, and natural background which gives sin and disease all its horror. It is the pure and severe New England simplicity which Mr. Hawthorne paints so delicately that brings out in full relief the adulterous mixture of emotions on which he spends his main strength. We might almost say that he has carried into human affairs the old Calvinistic type of imagination. The same strange combination of clear simplicity, high faith, and reverential reality, with one reluctant, but for that very reason intense and devouring, conviction of the large comprehensiveness of the Divine Damnation which that grim creed taught its most honest believers to consider as the true trust in God's providence, Mr. Hawthorne copies into his pictures of human life. He presents us with a scene of clear severe beauty, full of truthful goodness, and then he uncovers in some one point of it a plague-spot that, half concealed as he keeps it, yet runs away with the imagination till one is scarcely conscious of any thing else. Just as Calvinism, with all its noble features, can never keep its eyes off that one fact, as it thinks it, of God's calm foreknowledge of a wide-spread damnation; and this gradually encroaches on the attention till the mind is utterly absorbed in the fascinating terror of the problem how to combine the clashing emotions of love and horror which its image of Him inspires;—so Mr. Hawthorne's finest tales, with all the fair simplicity of their general outline, never detain you long from some uneasy mixture of emotions which only deep disease can combine on one object, until at last you ask for nothing but the disentangling of the infected web.

There are many illustrations of this peculiarity of Mr. Hawthorne's genius in his earlier and shorter tales. In one of them he exclaims, and it is the key to his genius, 'Blessed are all simple emotions, be they dark or bright! It is the lurid intermixture of the two that produces the illuminating blazes of the infernal regions.' The tale in which Mr. Hawthorne makes this remark, *Rappacini's Daughter*, itself exemplifies in a somewhat fanciful but striking form this constant bent of his imagination. Dr. Rappacini is a professor of medical science in the university of Padua. He has devoted himself to the study of deadly poisons, and learnt how to infuse them so subtly into both animal and vegetable natures as to render that which would be fatal in the ordinary way, essential to life and health, and even productive of unusual lustre and bloom. Mr. Hawthorne has evidently based his tale on the physiological fact—which, at least in the case of arsenic, is well attested—that a malignant poison, if gradually administered, may at length become a condition of life and conducive to beauty. Dr. Rappacini has filled his garden with flowers so poisonous that he himself dare not touch them, and can scarcely venture to breathe the air around them. But the life of his daughter Beatrice has been imbued and fed with the same poisons which gave so rich a bloom and so sweet but deadly a perfume to these rare plants; and to her they are health and added loveliness. Her breath is instantly fatal to the insect or the butterfly that drinks it in, and even her touch is deadly. But her heart is stainless and noble, and she shudders herself at the malign influences which she involuntarily puts forth as insects fall dead around her. Her great beauty fascinates one of the students, whose lodging looks out above this strange garden; and by Rappacini's skill, exercised without the young man's knowledge, he is gradually imbued with the same poisons which enter so deeply into the life and constitution of Beatrice. The point and art of this eerie tale lie in the conflict of emotions which Beatrice's true spiritual beauty and malignant physical influences raise in the mind of her lover, filling him with a passion blended equally of love and horror; and in the description of the despair with which he discovers that the same malignant influences are already part of himself.

The same tendency of imagination, in perhaps quite as characteristic, but in a far more unpleasant form, is shown in the tale called the *Birth-Mark*, which turns on the morbid horror inspired by a slight birth-mark on the cheek of a beautiful woman in the mind of her husband, who is at the same time passionately attached to her and bent on eradicating it. This tale has no imaginative beauty, and is only remarkable for the diseased mixture of emotions which it depicts. Again, in the tale concerning 'The Man with the Snake in his Bosom' and 'Young Goodman Brown,' with all the most remarkable of Mr. Hawthorne's shorter tales, the same prominent feature, in some form or other, may be discerned.

But it is in the more elaborate tales that Mr. Hawthorne has most scope, at once for the relieving elements which these morbid interests, if they are to be artistically treated at all, especially require, and for the fuller development and *justification*, so to say, of emotions so subtle and unhealthy. In the *Scarlet Letter* he has a subject naturally so painful as exactly to suit his genius. He treats it with perfect delicacy, for his attention is turned to the morbid anatomy of the relations which have originated in the sin of adultery, rather than to the sin itself. There are two points on which Mr. Hawthorne concentrates his power in this remarkable book. The first is the false position of the minister, who gains fresh reverence and popularity as the very fruit of the passionate anguish with which his heart is consumed. Frantic with the stings of unacknowledged guilt, he is yet taught by those very stings to understand the hearts and stir the consciences of others. His character is a pre-Raphaelite picture of the tainted motives which fill a weak but fine and sensitive nature when placed in such a position; of self-hatred quite too passionate to conquer self-love; of a quailing conscience smothered into insane cravings for blasphemy; of the exquisite pain of gratified ambition conscious of its shameful falsehood. The second point on which Mr. Hawthorne concentrates his power is the delineation of anomalous characteristics in the child who is the offspring of this sinful passion. He gives her an inheritance of a lawless, mischievous, and elvish nature, not devoid of strong affections, but delighting to probe the very sorest points of her mother's heart, induced in part by some mysterious fascination to the subject, in part by wanton mischief. The scarlet A, which is the brand of her mother's shame, is the child's delight. She will not approach her mother unless it be on her bosom; and the unnatural complication of emotions thus excited in Hester Prynne's heart present one of the most characteristic features of the book, and are painfully engraved on the reader's mind. The scene of most marvellous power which the book contains contrives to draw to a focus all the many clashing affections portrayed. Mr. Dimmesdale, the unhappy minister, eager to invent vain penances in expiation of the guilt which he dares not avow, creeps out at midnight in his canonical robe to stand for an hour on the scaffold on which Hester and her child had been pilloried years before. It is the night when many are watching by the dying-bed of the governor of Massachusetts, and one of the minister's reverend colleagues, who has been praying with the governor, passes under the scaffold, lantern in hand. In his nervous and excited mood, Dimmesdale almost addresses him aloud, and then, paralyzed by dread and his limbs stiffened by cold, it occurs to him that he will never be able to descend the steps of the scaffold, and that morning will break to show him there to all his revering flock:—

[Quotes ch. 12, 'Morning would break' to ' "tomorrow noontide?" '.]

This strange vigil, the grim hysteric humor of the minister, the proud and silent fortitude of Hester, the mocking laughter of the child as she detects her unknown father's cowardice, together make as weird-like a tangle of human elements as ever bubbled together in a witches' caldron. Yet this scene, though probably the most powerful which Mr. Hawthorne has ever painted, scarcely exemplifies his uncanny fashion of awakening the most mutually repellent feelings at the same moment towards the same person so characteristically as many of his other tales.

In the most striking chapter in the *House of the Seven Gables*, he makes Judge Pyncheon, who has died in his chair from some sudden effusion of blood, holding his still ticking watch in his hand, a subject at once for awe and scorn. He recalls all the judge's engagements for the day,—the bank-meeting at which he was to take the chair,—the business appointment he was to keep,—the private purchases he was to make,—the little act of charity which he had thought of, time and purse permitting,—the half-formal call on his physician concerning some trifling symptoms of indisposition,—the political dinner to discuss the election of the next state governor; and then he taunts the judge with his forgetfulness. . . .

[Quotes ch. 18, 'Half an hour' to 'gubernatorial one?' but with several deletions.]

Thus Mr. Hawthorne goes on throughout the twenty-four hours during which the judge's body remains undiscovered,—mingling with the most powerful picture of the supernatural side of death, which he never ceases to keep vividly before us, the feelings that cluster round petty business, the sarcasms that might sting the sensitive, the urgency that might hasten the dilatory, the incentives that would spur the ambitious, flinging them all in cold irony at the corpse with an eerie effect that only Mr. Hawthorne could produce.

But the most characteristic instance of Mr. Hawthorne's power in studying combinations of emotions that are as it were at once abhorrent to nature and true to life, is in *Transformation*. The one powerful scene in that distended work is the scene of crime.

[Summarizes the scene and quotes ch. 19, ' "Did you not" ' to 'blood-stained city', but with several deletions.]

This is very finely conceived and yet revolting. Have we not reason for saying, that Mr. Hawthorne's chief power lies in the delineation of unnatural alliances of feeling, which are yet painfully real, of curling emotions that may mix for a moment, but shrink apart again quickly, as running water from clotted blood?

But it would be very unjust to Mr. Hawthorne to represent him as in any degree addicted, like Edgar Poe, to the invention of monstrosities and horrors. We only mean that his genius naturally leads him to the analysis and representation of certain outlying moral anomalies, which are not the anomalies of ordinary evil and sin, but have a certain chilling unnaturalness of their own. But under Mr. Hawthorne's treatment these anomalies are only the subtle flaws or passionate taints of natures full of fine elements; they are never superlatives of iniquity and abomination, like Edgar Poe's. They are the dark spots in a fine picture, never the very substance of the whole. There is, for instance, every palliation which a charitable imagination can invent for Hester's sin and Dimmesdale's cowardice in the *Scarlet Letter*; and even the child's elfish wantonness, though in some degree preternatural, is not demoniacal, but the mere lawless taint in an otherwise warm and open heart. So too in *Transformation* there is every excuse that circumstances can give to the crime which Donatello commits and Miriam sanctions;—after the first moment of mad excitement is over, it fills them with unspeakable anguish; it rouses all the tender devotion of the woman in Miriam for the man who had thus stained his conscience under the impulse of love to her; it awakens the sleeping soul of Donatello;—and the book is meant to record their uninterrupted upward progress from that moment. Moreover, in the two other characters we find a peaceful contrast to the turbid hearts of the sinful lovers. Neither in this nor in any other tale does Mr. Hawthorne cast any slur on human nature. He loves to picture it in its highest and tenderest aspects. And when he delineates what is revolting, one of the main elements that makes it so revolting is the Manichean incarceration of some noble and half-angelic affection in a malignant body of evil, from which it vainly seeks to be divorced.

This bent of Mr. Hawthorne's genius is no doubt in great degree determined by the speculative character of his mind. Even his *imagination* is inquisitive and—shall we call it what he calls it himself in the *Blithedale Romance?*—rather *prying* than ardent. It is fertile, but in a cold and restless way. It is used more to help him to explore mysteries than from the glowing creative impulse that cannot choose but paint. He states to himself a problem, and sets his imagination to work to solve it. How was it the woman felt who wore publicly the symbol of her own sin and shame fancifully embroidered on her bosom? What would be the state of mind of one who had unhappily killed another, and could never clearly determine in his own conscience whether his *will* had consented to the deed or not? What would be the result of a wrongful life-imprisonment on a soft æsthetic nature made for the enjoyment of the beautiful? How would a sin of passion work on a healthy, innocent, natural man of unawakened spirit? These are the kind of hypotheses on which Mr. Hawthorne's imagination works; and from the nature of the case, images summoned up in obedience to such questionings cannot always be of a very wholesome kind. The problems that Mr. Hawthorne starts are usually connected with the deepest mysteries of the human mind and conscience; and the imagination which attempts to keep pace with the inquisitive intellect cannot but paint strange and thrilling anomalies in reply to its queries. 'That cold tendency,' says Mr. Coverdale, the hero of the *Blithedale Romance*, who has many points of intellectual affinity with its author,—'that cold tendency between instinct and intellect, which made me pry with a speculative interest into people's passions and impulses, appeared to have gone far towards unhumanizing my heart.' We do not mean to say that it has gone far, or any way at all, towards unhumanizing Mr. Hawthorne's heart, which is evidently tender. But no doubt, he is led by the speculative bias of his mind to steep his imagination in *arcana* on which it is scarcely good to gaze at all.

It is remarkable, and perhaps a symptom of the same imaginative constitution, that while Mr. Hawthorne has the most eager desire to penetrate the secret attitudes of minds painfully or anomalously situated, he has little or no interest in picturing the exact combination of circumstances which brought them into these attitudes. His imagination is the very converse of De Foe's. De Foe seizes the outer fact with the most vivid force; indirectly only, by the very force and minuteness of his conception of the visible circumstances, actions, and gestures he narrates, do you get at the inward mind of his characters. Mr. Hawthorne, on the contrary, is often positively anxious to *suppress* all distinct account of the actual facts which have given rise to his ideal situations. He wishes to save the mental impression from being swallowed up, so to say, in the interest of the outward facts and events. He sees that people of a matter-of-fact turn of mind attach more value to knowing the exciting causes than to knowing the state of mind which results. If they hear what seems to them an insufficient cause for a heroine's misery, they set her down as feeble-minded, and give up their interest in her fate. If they hear a *too* sufficient cause, they say she deserved all she suffered, and for that reason discard her from their sympathies. Mr. Hawthorne sees the difficulty of inventing facts that will exactly hit the shade of feeling that he desires to excite in his readers' minds, and so he often refuses to detail the facts distinctly at all. He often gives us our choice of several sets of facts which might be adequate to the results, declines to say which he himself prefers, and insists only on the attitude of mind produced. Thus, in the *Blithedale Romance*, he precludes a far from explanatory or lucid conversation with this mystifying sentence, 'I hardly could make out an intelligible sentence on either side. What I seem to remember I yet suspect may have been patched together by my fancy in brooding over the matter afterwards.' Again, in another part of the same book, 'The details of the interview that followed being unknown to me, while notwithstanding it would be a pity quite to lose the picturesqueness of the situation, I shall attempt to sketch it mainly from fancy, although with some general grounds of surmise in regard to the old man's feelings.' But he has carried this preference for delineating states of mind, and obscurely suggesting the class of facts which may have given rise to them, to the furthest point in his new work, *Transformation*.

Owing, it may be [he tells us, in a chapter justly headed 'Fragmentary Sentances,' at a critical conjunction in the tale], to this moral estrangement,—this chill remoteness of their position,—there have come to us but a few vague whisperings of what passed in Miriam's interview that afternoon with the sinister personage who had dogged her footsteps ever since her visit to the catacomb. In weaving these mystic utterances into a continuous scene, we undertake a task resembling in its perplexity that of gathering up and piecing together the fragments of a letter which has been torn and scattered to the winds. Many words of deep significance,—many entire sentences, and these probably the most important ones,—have flown too far on the winged breeze to be recovered. If we insert our own conjectural amendments, we may perhaps give a purport utterly at variance with the true one.

And then Mr. Hawthorne continues,

Of so much we are sure, that there seemed to be a sadly mysterious fascination in the influence of this ill-omened person over Miriam; it was such as beasts and reptiles of subtle and evil natures sometimes exercise over their victims. . . . Yet let us trust there may have been no crime in Miriam, but only one of those fatalities which are among the insoluble riddles propounded to mortal comprehension—the fatal doom by which every crime is made to be the agony of many innocent persons, as well as of the single guilty one.

In other words, Mr. Hawthorne wishes us to picture a mind perturbed, flushed, on the verge of despair, but does not wish us to know how far the exciting causes had involved her in real guilt, or merely in misery. It is not essential, he thinks, to the purpose of the book, which is rather to trace the effects of the subsequent guilt on the relation between Miriam and Donatello than to develop fully the previous character of the woman who draws the poor young count into crime. As far as regards Miriam, the problem set himself by the author in this book is only to delineate the influence exerted over her heart by Donatello's plunge into guilt on her behalf. He thinks it enough to indicate that she who led Donatello into guilt was either herself guilty, or at least intimately imbued with all the infectious fever of a guilty atmosphere. More is not essential to the author's purpose, and more he will not tell us. He seems to hint, perhaps truly, that the chasm between guilt and wretchedness in a woman's mind is not always so clear as in a man's; and that, at all events, there is as much power in any deeply roused affection to extricate her from the one as from the other. For like reasons, we suppose, the end of the tale is as shadowy as the beginning. The *transformation* is accomplished; the Faun is no longer a Faun; and all the author contemplated is therefore attained. The wreath of mist which hangs over Miriam's past is allowed also to settle over her own and Donatello's future. The problem has been solved in the dissolving colors of two richly painted minds. And their earthly destiny is nothing to the reader; to know it might even divert his attention from the artist's true purpose, to concentrate it on the *dénouement* of a commonplace story.

This predominance of moral coloring over the definite forms of actual fact in Mr. Hawthorne's novels is to us, we confess, unsatisfactory. And the degree to which it is absent or prevails in his several works, seems to us a fair measure of their relative artistic worth. The *Scarlet Letter*, in which there is by far the most solid basis of fact, is, we think, also considerably the finest and most powerful of his efforts. The *House of the Seven Gables*, in itself nearly a perfect work of art, is yet composed of altogether thinner materials. Yet the details are worked up with so much care and finish,—the whole external scenery of this, as well as of the *Scarlet Letter*, is so sharply defined, so full of the clear air of New England life,—that we can bear better the subtle moral coloring and anatomy with which they both abound. In the *Blithedale Romance* we observe the first tendency to shroud certain portions of the narrative in an intentional veil, and to attempt to paint a distinct moral *expression* without giving a distinct outline of fact. The effect is powerful, but vague and not satisfying. The figures wander vagrant-like through the imagination of the reader. They seem to have no distinct place of their own assigned to them. You know what sort of characters you have beheld, but not when and under what circumstances you have beheld them. In *Transformation* these defects are at their maximum; and the evil is exaggerated by the mass of general padding—artistic criticisms, often powerful, and always subtle, upon Italian art:—puffs, not in very good taste, of the works of American sculptors;—silly attacks upon nude figures, and the like,—which distend, alloy, and ungracefully speckle the ideal tenor of the tale.

But we must draw to a conclusion. The most distinguishing deficiency in Mr. Hawthorne's mind, which is also in close connection with its highest power, is his complete want of sympathy not only with the world of voluntary action, but with the next thing to action, namely, the world of impulsive passion. With exceedingly rare exceptions,—the scene of crime and passion which we have quoted from *Transformation* is the only exception we can recall,—the highest power of Mr. Hawthorne is all spent on the delineation of *chronic* suffering or sentiment, in which all desire to act on others is in a measure paralyzed. He likes to get past the rapids any way he can;—as we have seen, he not seldom introduces you to his tale with only the distant rush of them still audible behind you, his delight being to trace the more lasting perturbations which they effect for winding miles below. But what he does paint for you, he likes to study thoroughly; he loves to get beneath the surface, to sound the deeper and mysterious pools, measure the power of the fretted waters, and map carefully out the sandy shallows. The result is necessarily a considerable limitation in the field of his genius. The excitement which other writers find in delineating the swaying fortunes of an active career, he is—we will not say *obliged* to find, for of course the positive capacity of his genius, not its incapacity for other fields, leads him in this direction—but he is obliged to find *only* in rare and often painful pictures of unhealthy sentiment. This is what circles so closely the range of his characters. They are necessarily very limited both in number and in moral attitude. We have but two studies, in his tales, of characters with any active bent—Hollingsworth in the *Blithedale Romance*, and Phœbe in the *House of the Seven Gables*. Both are carefully drawn, but both are far slighter sketches, and more evidently taken from observation only, than his other characters. His nearest approach to the delineation of impulsive passion is seen in the sketch of Zenobia in the *Blithedale Romance*, and of Miriam in *Transformation*. But in neither case is it real impulse to act on others which he draws well; it is rather the turbid tossing of a rich mind ill at ease with itself, and casting about for sympathy and help. The characters which he draws most completely,—though they are not always the pleasantest,—are those which, like Mr. Coverdale in the *Blithedale Romance*, and Holgrave in the *House of the Seven Gables*, have 'no impulse to help or to hinder,' caring only 'to look on, to analyze, to explain matters to themselves.' Clifford too, in the latter tale,—who evidently represents the sensitive and æsthetic side of the author's own mind, 'that squeamish love of the beautiful' (to use his own expressive phrase) which is in him, when stripped of that cold centre of contemplative individuality, which seems to us to be at the centre of Mr. Hawthorne's literary genius and personality,—is a fine study.

But one criticism more. The moral ideal which Mr. Hawthorne keeps before himself and his readers throughout his works is on the whole not only pure but noble. It is defective, however, as we might expect, on the same side on which his genius seems to fail. He is, in political and social conviction, a democratic quietist; one might almost say a fatalist. Is it not a part of this fatalistic disposition, we may ask in passing, to encourage the cultivated and thinking portion of society to resign to the masses the duty of forming the political judgment of his nation, and to permit himself to be quietly sucked in by that fatally fascinating and overmastering tide called the Will of the democracy? However this may be, in political and social life, he is one who deprecates all spasmodic reforms, and attaches little value to reformatory efforts at all, except as the indispensable conditions of generous hopes and youthful aspirations. Speaking of such an experiment of social reform, he says, 'After all, let us acknowledge it wise, if not more sagacious, to follow out one's day-dream to its natural consummation, although, if the vision have been worth the having, it is certain never to be consummated otherwise than by a failure.' Again he says, in another tale, and with much of true moral insight, though it be the one-sided moral insight of the quietist recluse, 'the haughty faith with which he [the enthusiastic practical reformer] began life would be well bartered for a far humbler one at its close, in discerning that man's best-directed effort accomplishes a kind of dream, while God is the sole worker of realities.' Nor should we find fault with him for his very deeply rooted conviction that, so far as any real and deep reform is accomplished, it may in a certain sense be said to *accomplish itself* instead of being forced on society by the enthusiastic patronage of crusading philanthropists, could he but confine this theory within modest limits,—did he not press it into the service of what seems to us the grossest political immorality. We can sympathize with him when he so finely moralizes at the end of the *Blithedale Romance* on the dangers of philanthropy:—

[Quotes ch. 28, 'Admitting what is' to 'blessed end'.]

Yet more; we can even go with him, quite as far as he wishes his readers to go, when he ironically prescribes a universal slumber as the only cure for the world's overstretched nerves:—

[Quotes 'The Old Manse': 'The world should' to 'afflict the universe'.]

For none of these thoughts and sayings, however depreciative of effort, or destructive of the sanguine hopes with which effort spurs itself on, do we reproach Mr. Hawthorne. It is fitting that, after the preacher of one-sided action and overstrained vigilance has spoken, this too restless age should also hear the invitation to distrust its own 'earnestness,' and renew its highly strung energies by rest. Nay we are quite willing to admit that the function of the contemplative man, who keeps clear of the many streams of human energy, and passes his solitary criticisms upon their tendency from some nook of seemingly selfish retirement, is justified in the scheme of Providence by the very existence of the philanthropic class of one-sided workers. But it is when Mr. Hawthorne comes to apply his quietistic creed to the actual political world in which he lives, that we find his moral shortcomings painfully evident, and see that he has permitted a mere theory to confuse 'that simple perception of what is right, and the single-hearted desire to achieve it,' of which he speaks so well, as grievously as ever did the one dominant idea of a professional philanthropist.

[Criticizes Hawthorne's *Life of Pierce*.]

113. Hawthorne, from 'To a Friend', introductory to *Our Old Home*

2 July 1863

Because of Franklin Pierce's unpopularity, Fields advised Hawthorne against dedicating the volume to his old friend. Hawthorne answered:

. . . if he is so exceedingly unpopular that his name is enough to sink the volume, there is so much the more need that an old friend should stand by him. I cannot, merely on account of pecuniary profit or literary reputation, go back from what I have deliberately felt and thought it right to do; and if I were to tear out the dedication, I should never look at the volume again without remorse and shame. As for the literary public, it must accept my book precisely as I think fit to give it, or let it alone. Nevertheless, I have no fancy for making myself a martyr when it is honorably and conscientiously possible to avoid it; and I always measure out my heroism very accurately according to the exigencies of the occasion, and should be the last man in the world to throw away a bit of it needlessly. So I have looked over the concluding paragraph and have amended it in such a way that, while doing what I know to be justice to my friend, it contains not a word that ought to be objectionable to any set of readers (Letter, 18 July 1863, James T. Fields, *Yesterdays with Authors* [1871], p. 108.

I have not asked your consent, my dear General, to the foregoing inscription, because it would have been no inconsiderable disappointment to me had you withheld it; for I have long desired to connect your name with some book of mine, in commemoration of an early friendship that has grown old between two individuals of widely dissimilar pursuits and fortunes. I only wish that the offering were a worthier one than this volume of sketches, which certainly are not of a kind likely to prove interesting to a statesman in retirement, inasmuch as they meddle with no matters of policy or government, and have very little to say about the deeper traits of national character. In their humble way, they belong entirely to æsthetic literature, and can achieve no higher success than to represent to the American reader a few of the external aspects of English scenery and life, especially those that are touched with the antique charm to which our countrymen are more susceptible than are the people among whom it is of native growth.

I once hoped, indeed, that so slight a volume would not be all that I might write. These and other sketches, with which in a somewhat rougher form than I have given them here, my journal was copiously filled, were intended for the side-scenes and back-grounds and exterior adornment of a work of fiction of which the plan had imperfectly developed itself in my mind, and into which I ambitiously proposed to convey more of various modes of truth than I could have grasped by a direct effort. Of course, I should not mention this abortive project, only that it has been utterly thrown aside and will never now be accomplished. The Present, the Immediate, the Actual, has proved too potent for me. It takes away not only my scanty faculty, but even my desire for imaginative composition, and leaves me sadly content to scatter a thousand peaceful fantasies upon the hurricane that is sweeping us all along with it, possibly, into a Limbo where our nation and its polity may be as literally the fragments of a shattered dream as my unwritten Romance. But I have far better hopes for our dear country; and for my individual share of the catastrophe, I afflict myself little, or not at all, and shall easily find room for the abortive work on a certain ideal shelf, where are reposited many other shadowy volumes of mine, more in number, and very much superior in quality, to those which I have succeeded in rendering actual.

To return to these poor Sketches: some of my friends have told me that they evince an asperity of sentiment towards the English people which I ought not to feel, and which it is highly inexpedient to express. The charge surprises me, because, if it be true, I have written from a shallower mood than I supposed. I seldom came into personal relations with an Englishman without beginning to like him, and feeling my favorable impression wax stronger with the progress of the acquaintance. I never stood in an English crowd without being conscious of hereditary sympathies. Nevertheless, it is undeniable that an American is continually thrown upon his national antagonism by some acrid quality in the moral atmosphere of England. These people think so loftily of themselves, and so contemptuously of everybody else, that it requires more generosity than I possess to keep always in perfectly good-humor with them. Jotting down the little acrimonies of the moment in my journal, and transferring them thence (when they happened to be tolerably well expressed) to these pages, it is very possible that I may have said things which a profound observer of national character would hesitate to sanction, though never any, I verily believe, that had not more or less of truth. If they be true, there is no reason in the world why they should not be said. Not an Englishman of them all ever spared America for courtesy's sake or kindness; nor, in my opinion, would it contribute in the least to our mutual advantage and comfort if we were to besmear one another all over with butter and honey. At any rate, we must not judge of an Englishman's susceptibilities by our own, which likewise, I trust, are of a far less sensitive texture than formerly. . . .

114. Unsigned review in the *North American Review*

October 1863, xcvii, 588–9

We have enough objective knowledge of the Old World, those of us who have not travelled in it, and the narrative of any new sight-seer who is nothing more is as vapid as the gossip of the street-corner. The interest which we now feel in a book about England, or France, or the Pyramids, is in precise proportion to the worth of the book as an autobiography, and to the worth of the life that it records. In this respect a narrative of experiences in a foreign land is more precious than it ever was before; for our enhanced familiarity with the background of the sketch enables us to enter with added zest into the self-consciousness of the writer.

By the standard of judgment which we have thus indicated Mr.

Hawthorne's 'English Sketches' are unsurpassed, if not unequalled, in merit. We can hardly conceive of a book of nearly four hundred pages containing so little and so much,—so little of any mark or interest about men and places and things in England, and so much about himself in those aspects in which the personality of a man of genius is always gladdening, instructive, and inspiring. We do not believe that with the outward eye he saw a great deal. There are two or three bits of exquisite sky and landscape painting; but the few attempts at elaborate architectural description are professedly unfinished, and might as well have been unbegun. But there are inimitably happy outlines of scenes and spots, odd buildings and strange nooks, which had some specific relation of harmony or incongruity with the author's mind,—outlines not drawn from notes or from reminiscences painfully recalled, but phototyped from the very retina of the inward eye, and filled in with the very hues and shadings supplied at the moment by the author's taste, wit, sympathy, or disgust. As to the characters brought upon the stage, we see them, too, not in their own persons, but in the images reflected from the mirror curved and mottled with the intense idiosyncrasies of the writer,—now convex, now concave,—here distorting, there beautifying,—on which each figure was caught, and thence thrown upon the printed sheet. The two properties of the work which seem to us the most striking are its humor and its kindliness. The humor is unforced, we think generally unconscious. Things present themselves grotesquely to Mr. Hawthorne. He takes hold of them by some other than the usual handle, and offers to our view just the parts and aspects of them which it is conventionally fit to keep out of sight. It is a humor always delicate, frequently even serious, and never more manifest than when the writer is most in earnest. His kindliness, too, if not unconscious, is expressed unintentionally. There is, indeed, no little pretence of an opposite sort, an affectation (shall we call it?) of roughness and unsociableness; but it is very feebly maintained,—the ill-fitted mask keeps dropping from the face, in which we see the tokens of a tenderness of human fellow-feeling, such as it is equally impossible to counterfeit and to disguise.

391

115. Unsigned essay, 'A Handful of Hawthorne', in *Punch*

17 October 1863, lxxix, 339–40

Nathaniel Hawthorne, author of the *Scarlet Letter* and the *House with the Seven Gables* (you see we at once endeavour to create a prejudice in your favour) you are a 'cute man of business besides being a pleasing writer. We have often credited you with literary merit, and your style, dear boy, puts to shame a good many of our own writers who ought to write better than they do. But now let us have the new pleasure of congratulating you on showing that you are as smart a man, as much up to snuff, if you will pardon the colloquialism, as any Yankee publisher who ever cheated a British author. You have written a book about England, and into this book you have put all the caricatures and libels upon English folk, which you collected while enjoying our hospitality. Your book is thoroughly saturated with what seems ill-nature and spite. You then wait until the relations between America and England are unpleasant, until the Yankee public desires nothing better than good abuse of the Britisher, and then like a wise man, you cast your disagreeable book into the market. Now we like adroitness, even when displayed at our own expense, and we hope that the book will sell largely in America, and put no end of dollars to your account. There was once a person of your Christian name, who was said to be without guile. Most American pedigrees are dubious, but we think you would have a little extra trouble to prove your descent from Nathaniel of Israel. In a word, you are a Smart Man, and we can hardly say anything more likely to raise you in the esteem of those for whom you have been composing. Come, there is none of the 'insular narrowness,' on which you compliment us all, in this liberal tribute to your deserts. You see that in spite of what you say, 'these people' (the English) do not all 'think so loftily of themselves and so contemptuously of everybody else that it requires more generosity than you possess to keep always in perfectly good humour with them.' You will have no difficulty in keeping in perfectly good humour with us.

We are pleased with you, too, on another point. You stick at nothing, and we like earnestness. Not content with smashing up our male population in the most everlasting manner, you make the most savage onslaught upon our women. This will be doubly pleasant to your delicate-minded and chivalrous countrymen. And we are the more inclined to give you credit here, because you do not write of ladies whom you have seen at a distance, or in their carriages, or from the point of view of a shy and awkward man who sculks away at the rustle of a crinoline, and hides himself among the ineligibles at the ball-room door. Everybody knows that you have had ample opportunity of cultivating ladies' society, and have availed yourself of that opportunity to the utmost. Everybody in the world knows that the gifted American Consul at Liverpool is an idoliser of the ladies, and is one of the most ready, fluent, accomplished talkers of lady-talk that ever fascinated a sofa-full of smiling beauties. His gay and airy entrance into a drawing-room, his pleasant assurance and graceful courtesy, his evident revel in the refined atmosphere of perfume and *persiflage,* are proverbial, and therefore he is thoroughly acquainted with the nature and habits of English women. Consequently his tribute has a value which would not appertain to the criticisms of a sheepish person, either so inspired with a sense of his own infinite superiority, or so operated on by plebeian *mauvaise honte,* that he edges away from a lady, flounders and talks nonsense when compelled to answer her, and escapes with a red face, like a clumsy hobbadehoy, the moment a pause allows him to do so. No, no, this is the testimony of the lady-killer, the sparkling yet tender Liverpool Lovelace, Nathaniel Hawthorne, to the merits of our English women.

English girls seemed to me all homely alike. They seemed to be country lasses, of sturdy and wholesome aspect, with coarse-grained, cabbage-rosy cheeks, and, I am willing to suppose, a stout texture of moral principle, such as would bear a good deal of rough usage without suffering much detriment. But how unlike the trim little damsels of my native land! I desire above all things to be courteous.

Courteous. Of course. How can the drawing-room idol be anything but courteous? He simply sketches our young ladies truthfully. Indeed he says so:

Since the plain truth must be told, the soil and climate of England produce feminine beauty as rarely as they do delicate fruit, and though admirable specimens of both are to be met with, they are the hot-house ameliorations of refined society, and apt, moreover, to relapse into the coarseness of the original stock. The men are man-like, but the women are not beautiful, though the female Bull be well enough adapted to the male.

'The female Bull.' Cow would have been neater, and more entertaining, perhaps, to Broadway; but one would not mend after a master.

But our matrons. We rather, in our weakness, piqued ourselves upon
our matrons, with what we've thought their handsome faces, ready
smiles, cheerful kindness, and tongues that talk freely because the hearts
are innocent. Thanks to our Lovelace-Adonis, we now know that we
must abandon this superstition. Here is his sketch of the English married
lady of middle age:

She has an awful ponderosity of frame, not pulpy, like the looser development
of our few fat women, but massive with solid beef and streaky tallow; so that
(though struggling manfully against the idea) you inevitably think of her as
made up of steaks and sirloins. When she walks, her advance is elephantine.
When she sits down, it is on a great round space of her Maker's footstool, where
she looks as if nothing could ever move her. She imposes awe and respect by the
muchness of her personality, to such a degree that you probably credit her with
far greater moral and intellectual force than she can fairly claim. Her visage is
usually grim and stern, seldom positively forbidding, yet calmly terrible.

Calmly terrible. Is not this a momentary weakness, Nathaniel? Can
any created woman be terrible to you? Away, eater of hearts. You don't
fear any matron. You show it in your next passage:

You may meet this figure in the street, and live, and even smile at the recollection. But conceive of her in a ball-room, with the bare brawny arms that she invariably displays there, and all the other corresponding development, such as is
beautiful in the maiden blossom, but a spectacle to howl at in such an overblown
cabbage-rose as this.

Well painted, Nathaniel, with a touch worthy of Rubens, who was
we think, your great uncle, or was it Milton, or Thersites, or somebody
else, who, in accordance with American habit, was claimed as your
ancestor. Never mind, you are strong enough in your own works to
bear being supposed a descendant from a gorilla, were heraldry unkind.
Mr. Punch makes you his best compliments on your smartness, and on
the gracious elegance of your descriptions of those with whom you are
known to have been so intimate, and he hopes that you will soon give
the world a sequel to *Transformation,* in the form of an autobiography.
For his is very partial to essays on the natural history of half-civilised
animals.

116. [Henry Bright], from a review in the *Examiner*

17 October 1863, pp. 662–3

Bright (1830–84), a critic who contributed regularly to the *Examiner* and the *Athenaeum,* was the centre of a large and enthusiastic literary circle in Liverpool and sustained an extensive correspondence with various literary figures. He and Hawthorne became close friends during the latter's consular days.

These sketches of English life and scenery are by a master's hand; they are somewhat fragmentary indeed, and there is something of caprice in the choice of subject and of treatment. But, with all their wilfulness, they are full of grace and beauty, of a tender pathos, and of subtle humour. They are no mere hard photographs of external nature— accurately cold and unimpassioned. If only some grass-grown grave or country market-place is being drawn, it is richly coloured by the peculiar tints which Mr. Hawthorne's imagination has cast over it. He does not describe things as they are, but rather as they appear to him; and he takes no pains to disguise the fact that he saw things as an American with strong prejudices, and as a retiring man with dreamy tendencies was sure to see them.

And then again, he does not always dwell most upon the more important or striking scenes. He tells us what affected him, and cares very little whether the outside world sympathizes with him or not. He passes silently over the docks of Liverpool to paint minutely his dreary little Consul's office. He declines to linger among the ruins of Kenilworth, while he spends a long morning with some old pensioners at Warwick. He has no word for Cambridge, which he visited, but he tells us of Uttoxeter and Lillington, and other places, which perhaps, no stranger ever troubled to see before. He has, he tells us, 'a sad and quaint kind of enjoyment in defeating the probabilities of oblivion,' so far as he can do it, for what would otherwise be forgotten; and this may partly have guided him to the choice of several among his subjects. In any case we see how much we have in England, little known or thought about by us, which strikes the imagination and warms the heart of so accomplished an American as Mr. Hawthorne.

But we will at once turn to the one part in this book (in other respects so charming) which somewhat surprises us in our English self-complacency. Whatever Mr. Hawthorne may like in England, he certainly does not like us Englishmen. With us he is neither struck nor pleased. Englishmen, and English women more especially, seem to be his positive aversion. Nothing, it is true, can be kinder or more generous than the words in which he distantly alludes to individuals; nothing can be more cynical and contemptuous than the expressions he uses of us as a race.

We do not profess to understand how and why this is so. Of course we have all our own theories of female beauty, and of course an American may prefer the New England type to that which prevails with us. Of course, too, an American may consider us 'stolid' and 'beefy,' and unworthy to be compared, for dash and energy, with a genuine Yankee. But we do not see why it was necessary to express these unpleasant opinions so unpleasantly,—and we see still less why we are to be cordially disliked because a Lancashire witch appears less graceful than a Yankee girl, and because we are inferior creatures to our trans-atlantic cousins. A man can like a dog. The only way we can find of explaining Mr. Hawthorne's temper towards England is to suppose that he is jealous of us. He loves England so much, that he cannot endure those who possess her as their country. He contrasts his own love for what is old and venerable with our apparent indifference. He envies us our grey cathedrals, our old monuments, our relics of the past. 'For my part,' he says, 'I used to wish we could annex their island, transferring their thirty millions of inhabitants to some convenient wilderness in the great West, and putting half or a quarter as many of ourselves into their places.' In another passage he passes, unconsciously it may be, from his love to England to his dislike for her proprietors:

I felt, indeed, like the stalwart progenitor in person, returning to the hereditary haunts after more than two hundred years, and finding the church, the hall, the farm-house, the cottage, hardly changed during his long absence,—the same shady by-paths and hedge-lanes, the same veiled sky, and green lustre of the lawns and fields,—while his own affinities for these things, a little obscured by disuse, were reviving at every step.

An American is not very apt to love the English people, as a whole, on whatever length of acquaintance.

We cannot but feel for the 'progenitor' when he finds himself treated like a stranger,—the 'Old Home' knowing him no more,—the new owners ready to show courtesy but not obedience,—not a soul recognizing in him any of the rights of a proprietor, and perhaps at times forgetting that any real relationship ever did exist.

Certainly under such treatment we should smart ourselves, and as we live in the sunshine of the substantial comforts and privileges we enjoy, we can readily pardon a sharp word or two from the stranger from across the seas. Nay, we carry our Christian forgiveness so far that nothing would please us better than to see Mr. Hawthorne permanently 'annexed' to us, and having to endure, as one of us, the sarcasms of some future American consul.

Meanwhile let Mr. Hawthorne retaliate as he will any harsh judgment that any English traveller may have, in his or her turn, passed upon America, we in England are too well content to be sensitive; and let us turn again to the many beauties that lie thickly scattered through his book.

Here are a few lines, full of eloquent fancy, about our English summer weather:

[Quotes 'A London Suburb': 'For each day' to 'another of prophesy'.]

The following criticism on Wilberforce's statue in Westminster Abbey is very humorous and very sound:

[Quotes 'Up the Thames': 'This excellent man' to 'illustrious the individual'.]

Mr. Hawthorne's descriptions of English country scenery are in their way perfect. They are less genial, so to speak, than those of Washington Irving; but his, after all, were chiefly the background to scenes of English life, and therefore appealed more directly to human sympathies. On the other hand Mr. Hawthorne's descriptions are wonderfully faithful, and never artificial, as Irving's often are. Through them all, too, there runs a vein of graceful thought, which sometimes turns to pathos, sometimes flashes out in quaint fancies, sometimes breaks into gentle irony.

See how, by the mere witchery of the writer, some commonplace public gardens at Leamington become full of interest and of beauty:

[Quotes 'Leamington Spa': 'The Jephson Garden' to 'no genuine progress'.]

There is a point still left on which we have a word to say before closing volumes, in which we have found so much to admire and to dwell upon. One great reproach to American writers on England has been the disgraceful way in which they have violated every rule of courteous reserve, and have repaid English hospitality by detailing the domestic details of private families. . . . In this respect Mr. Hawthorne has set an example to some among us. While he was in England he saw and knew many eminent men, but he has not thought that their position was any reason why he should amuse his readers with descriptions of their private life. He says, with a good taste now too rare, 'I assume no liberties with living men.' Once only does he directly mention any English friend by name,—and that once is in order to lay a wreath of tenderest regrets, of most endearing praise, upon Leigh Hunt's grave. . . .

117. From an unsigned essay, 'Hawthorne on England', in *Blackwood's Magazine*

November 1863, xciv, 610–23

. . . All of us form, almost unconsciously, an idea of the personal character of a writer with whose works we are familiar, when his walk in literature is, like Hawthorne's, such as to admit of the display of individuality; and few have impressed their audience with a more distinct stamp of their personality than this author. We think of him as a man unusually shy and reserved, both because he habitually prefers to draw on imagination and on a narrow circle of reality for his subjects, rather than to look abroad on the actual world; and because an acquaintance with that world could only be maintained at the expense of that delicate bloom and wild fragrance which are the chief among his charms. Dreamy he must be, listless of aim, as seeing little to allure him in the ordinary material objects of men, and given to look at common things in an uncommon light, which transfigures and even sometimes distorts them; yet capable of the shrewd glance that penetrates into surrounding realities, and saves him from being a visionary. But, above

all, whatever else he might turn out to be, we should have predicted
that he was eminently, with all his shyness and reserve, a gentle and a
genial man. For, while he is stern as a prophet in denouncing crime and
sin, he has the most tender indulgence for the criminal and sinner,
judging him extenuatingly, setting forth his temptations, and sorrow-
ing greatly as he abandons him to the inevitable law;—a kind of soft-
hearted Rhadamanthus, held by an unhappy fascination on the judicial
bench, and forced in conscience to punish the culprits whom he would
willingly set free; so that we know not what degree of iniquity a
character must attain to, absolutely to deprive it of his sympathy. Looking thus on the tragic parts of his subject, he prefers, in treating of
simple and common matters, to regard them in their graceful and
sunny aspect. His sharpest satire is kindlier than the geniality of a really
sarcastic man; and for mere weaknesses which do not amount to vice
—indolence, vagabondism, and suchlike—he does not conceal his
partiality. Kindly, clear, picturesque, graceful, quaint—such are the
epithets which define his path in literature.

When, therefore, a work from his pen was announced, giving
England the specially genial title of 'Our Old Home,' we might
well expect to see ourselves, if shrewdly, yet favourably and indul-
gently depicted. For was not he the man who, in his Romance of
'Monte Beni,' had painted the perishing splendours of Rome so truthfully and with such art, that those who have not beheld them may
almost fancy that they have, while those already familiar with them
feel their influence more keenly than before in reading his descriptions?
And would not he, so skilful to observe and depict the magnificent
ruins which were no more to him than to the rest of the world, be unfailing to perceive and to describe the grandeurs of the land which was
the old home of his countrymen? That imagination which evidently
delights to expatiate in the past, and which could scarce get elbow-room
in the narrow bounds of American History, would find here fresh fields
and pastures new. The expansive cordiality which could include the old
Puritans, the modern men of Massachusetts, and the cosmopolitan
population of Rome, might surely find in the varieties of English life
ample matter for its widest embrace. Here, we might have felt assured,
was no Yankee come among us laden with all the prejudices of his
nation, the exaggeration of which, by present circumstances, amounts
almost to insanity—no brazen shouter for subjugation, nor extermina-
tion, nor devastation—no rabid denouncer of English sympathies with
rebels, nor threatening claimant of English sympathies with Federals;

here was no Frenchman about to jabber, for the benefit of other French-
men, nonsense about the Lord Mayor and Sir Peel; but a kindly
philosopher who, setting aside, as foreign to his nature and his purpose,
those matters which make up the subject of our own local politics—
condition of the poor, parish unions, and so forth—would turn upon
us a shrewd mild eye, lit with the deep inward light of imagination,
sparkling with the play of pleasant fancy, and give us a representation
of ourselves which, if it should show us as less agreeable than we had
hoped, would leave us nothing to object to, and, if it should raise us in
our own estimation, would do so on some grounds better than conceit.

With such expectations then it was that we opened the book, and
found that, whatever its merits, we had to lament the loss of something
still better, as was apparent from the following extract:

[Quotes 'To a Friend': 'I once hoped' to 'rendering actual'.]

What pleasant possibilities were blighted when so pregnant a
thought miscarried! A romance of ancient English life by Hawthorne
—there would indeed be something which would insure the despatch
of millions of order to Mr Mudie and his congeners. Would he have
selected a period near our own into which to work the details he had
acquired among us? Probably his taste for the antique would draw him
farther back. The wigged and sworded gallants of the days of the
Georges—'the tea-cup times of hood and hoop, or while the patch was
worn'—days of Johnson and the, to him, more congenial Goldsmith—
how familiarly would he have entered on the scene, and paced it like
a man in his own domain! Or would he step back a century, and show
us the Roundhead fathers of his Boston Puritans in full conflict with
the Cavaliers? Or yet back again, over the boundary of an age, into the
times of Elizabeth and her splendid group of subject worthies? Having
no ground given to us on which to build a reply, we are compelled,
instead of lamenting one lost romance, to mourn for a whole series of
irrecoverable novels, ranging through our history from the Tudors
down to Victoria.

Closing our eyes after reading the foregoing passage of his book, we
tried to imagine what could be the unfortunate circumstances in the
American troubles which had so disconcerted him, and robbed both
America and England of what might have been a common possession. . . .

Resuming the book, we were somewhat startled at the next paragraph, which stands thus:

[Quotes 'To a Friend': 'To return to 'to 'humour with them'.]

At this last sentence we paused, and turned back, that we might be quite sure what country he was speaking of, and, finding it was our own, we went on:

[Quotes 'To a Friend': 'Jotting down' to 'texture than formerly'.]

Asperities and little acrimonies of Nathaniel Hawthorne! It seemed a contradiction in terms. It was like talking of the asperity of a July evening, the acrimony of a bubbling fountain. We thought it might be either an intentional jesting with his own mild nature, or a delusion such as an ultra good-natured man might chance to fall into. But presently we underwent a new shock at finding him talking politics something in the style of a New York paper. The friend he addresses in his preface is the ex-President, General Franklin Pierce; and he tells him that the presidential chair, when he filled it, was 'the most august position in the world.' This was not exactly what we looked for from Hawthorne in the preface to a book about England; but still, august positions are matters of fancy rather than of fact, and why should not a man of genius have his phantasy on the subject? . . . We should hesitate even now to call Nathaniel Hawthorne a sour-tempered or ill-natured man; but it is certain that, in the present case, his good-nature has taken the unfortunate form of perpetual carping and much virulence. The change in him, if change there be, must be owing probably to some sense of injury received at our hands, either personal or national. Now, as we have said, distinguished Americans have little reason to complain of their reception here, and we cannot suppose that so general a favourite as Mr Hawthorne has been treated less kindly than others. We rather believe that the sense of injury under which he seems to labour is national, because the feeling, as we very well know, is general among Americans, and because passages in his book seem to tell us so. . . . we infer that Mr Hawthorne shares, in far greater degree than we could possibly have anticipated in a man of his character, the prejudices and animosities which now make up the political creed of Federal Americans. He evidently thinks that the vitality of his country depends on the existence of the Union and the Federal system. . . .

However, having, as we think, pointed out the grounds of Mr Hawthorne's animus towards us, we need not dwell longer on the not agreeable subject. We must count it as another misfortune inflicted on us by the American war, that, besides depriving us of his romance, it has prejudiced him into such opinions as we have quoted. Still we may draw some comfort from the fact, that our optical powers will not be materially affected by his representation that we are blind on one eye and can't see with the other—that we shall not be more bulbous, longer-bodied, or shorter-legged, in consequence of the publication of his book —and that our women will still charm our purblind race though they have not the stamp of Mr Hawthorne's approbation. We wish we could quote some pleasanter passages respecting our people, but there are really none; those we have given, and others to the same purport, contain all he has to say in a general way about England and the English.

But there are chapters in his book as excellent as any of the excellent things that he has written. He occupied in this country the post of American consul at Liverpool, and one of his very best chapters describes the people with whom his official duties brought him into contact. . . . Mr Hawthorne's duties appear to have allowed him plenty of leisure for seeing places more pleasant than Liverpool: Leamington seems to have been for a time his headquarters, and from thence he made trips to Warwick and Stratford-on-Avon. These quiet places, filled with ancient memories, seem to suit his genius far better than scenes, the description of which demands more effort from a writer, forces him into a display of enthusiasm; such as Greenwich Hospital, rich with recollections of our naval triumphs, and Westminster Abbey, with its thronged assembly of illustrious dead. There is a remarkably pleasant account of the Leicester Hospital at Warwick. . . .

Again the remark occurs, in reading his chapter on Stratford, that Mr Hawthorne is better fitted to deal with an unpretending than with a lofty theme. His remarks on Shakespeare and on Burns, whose birth-place and other memorials he afterwards visited, are not beyond the reach of many writers of an intellectual stature much inferior to his own. But at Lichfield, amid the scenes associated with Johnson's early life, he is more at home, and is specially good on the subject of the Doctor's penance in the marketplace at Uttoxeter, when an elderly man, for disobedience in his youth to his father, Michael Johnson; while in the old town of Boston, parent of the New England city, his foot is on his native heath, and he discourses of the streets and church, once alive with the figures of the old Puritans who emigrated to Massachusetts, in a spirit worthy of the author of the 'Scarlet Letter.'

The admirers of a popular writer always take especial interest in noting the circumstances, when they peep into light, whereby may be traced the germs of those creations which specially bear the image and superscription of his genius. . . .

Through all these subjects, however well treated, there runs a carping depreciatory thread by no means improving the pattern. And there is one feature of English manners which seems to have cast a peculiarly gloomy and disastrous shadow on his mind: it is the practice of expecting a fee, indulged in by those domestics or other persons charged with the office of conducting strangers about the precincts of remarkable places. . . .

The most powerful, though not the most pleasant, of his chapters (for we doubt if he would have hit on the topic at all in his kindliest mood), is that called 'Outside Glimpses of English Poverty.'. . . The strain of implication which is heard in an undertone in this chapter, is intended to suggest the fact that America has no such scenes of poverty blotting *her* noon-day prosperity, because her institutions and her people are so superior to ours. There is a belief, prevalent even among intelligent Americans, men well acquainted with agricultural theories, with the blessings of draining, of guano, and of top-dressing, that the fertility of their native soil is owing to the Union and the Constitution, whose beneficent influences descended upon it like a rich dew. . . .

What a deal of delicate machinery has been put in requisition to produce this book! A man of fine scholarly mind has been trained by time and thought and practice into a good novelist and a most excellent writer, whose finer fancies are never marred in expression for want of fittest language. He then spends several leisurely years among us, with an infinity of opportunity for studying us, and of dreaming and poring over what he saw, till it should be sublimated in the subtle essences of the brain, and come to light idealised. Such are the elaborate means— and, so far as the picture produced of the 'Old Home' goes, with what result? All these complicated excellences have been put in motion to tell us that people who show public places in England expect money for their trouble, and that Englishmen cannot exist without that diet of beef and beer which renders them the earthiest of the earthy. Truly a remarkable sketch of a great people, and showing an insight into their characteristics worthy of a profound philosopher.

But still there is a great deal of allowance to be made for the fact, that the work he had in hand, and which may have been very dear to him, was marred by distracting influences, which he was wroth at, and resented, perhaps, without due discrimination. There are occupations in which no biped likes to be disturbed, and hatching is one of them. Tread with ever so innocent intention near the sacred precincts where the maternal fowl broods on the nest, and be she Dorking or Shanghae, bantam or gallina, she will, as she flaps and scrambles from the nursery behind the orchard fence, proclaim her injuries, and denounce you as a wrong-doer to the whole neighbourhood. Mr Hawthorne, who is, as we suppose, not rapid in elaborating his conceptions, had, after a few years' residence in England, germinated an egg which, could he have sat quietly upon it for a few years longer, would doubtless have produced a charming chick. But lo! long before it could see the light, a great turmoil arose in the West, and footsteps and voices were heard around, moving to investigate and discuss the matter, and growing loud and shrill, and even angry; till, scared by the increasing clamour, Nathaniel hurries from the nest, screaming to the heavens a protest against the vile disturbers of the incubation, and leaving them to comfort themselves as best they may with a view of the empty shell of his addled romance.

118. Edward Dicey: A British defence of Hawthorne's politics and philosophy, from 'Nathaniel Hawthorne', in *Macmillan's Magazine*

July 1864, x, 241–6

Dicey (1832–1911), a journalist and historian, met Hawthorne in 1861 and became interested in the problem of the writer's politics. One of his studies is *Six Months in the Federal States* (1863).

. . . As I write, I can see him now, with that grand, broad forehead, fringed scantily by the loose worn wavy hair, passing from black to grey, with the deep-sunk flashing eyes—sometimes bright, sometimes sad, and always 'distrait'-looking—as if they saw something beyond what common eyes could see, and with the soft feminine mouth,

which, at its master's bidding—or, rather, at the bidding of some
thought over which its master had no control—could smile so wondrous
pleasantly. It was not a weak face—far from it. A child, I think, might
have cheated Hawthorne; but there were few men who could have
cheated him without his knowing that he was being cheated. He was
not English-looking except in as far as he was not American. When
you had once gazed at his face or heard him speak, the very idea that he
ever could have gone a-head in any way, or ever talked bunkum of any
kind seemed an absurdity in itself. How he ever came to have been born
in that bustling New World became, from the first moment I knew
him, an increasing mystery to me. If ever a man was out of his right
element it was Hawthorne in America. He belonged, indeed, to that
scattered Shandean family, who never are in their right places wherever
they happen to be born—to that race of Hamlets, to whom the world is
always out of joint anywhere. His keen poetic instinct taught him to
appreciate the latent poetry lying hid dimly in the great present and the
greater future of the country in which his lot was thrown; and, though
keenly, almost morbidly, sensitive to the faults and absurdities of his
countrymen, he appreciated their high sterling merit with that instinctive justice which was the most remarkable attribute of his mind.
England itself suited him but little better than the States—more
especially that part of England with which his travels had made him
most familiar. To have been a happy man, he should, I think, have been
born in some southern land, where life goes onwards without changing,
where social problems are unknown, and what has been yesterday is
to-day, and which will be to-morrow. Never was a man less fitted to
buffet out the battle of life amidst our Anglo-Saxon race. He held his
own, indeed, manfully, and kept his head above those waters in which
so many men of genius have sunk. But the struggle was too much for
him, and left him worn-out and weary. Had, however, the conditions
of his life been more suited to his nature, he would, I suspect, have
dreamed the long years away—and what he gained the world would
have lost. . . .

Now, it was impossible for a man like Hawthorne to be an enthusiastic partisan. When Goethe was attacked, because he took no part in
the patriotic movement which led to the war of German independence,
he replied, "I love my country, but I cannot hate the French." So
Hawthorne, loving the North, but not hating the South, felt himself
altogether out of harmony with the passion of the hour. If he spoke his
own mind freely, he was thought by those around him to be wanting

in attachment to his country. . . . Of two lines of action, he was perpetually in doubt which was the best; and so, between the two, he always inclined to letting things remain as they are. Nobody disliked slavery more cordially than he did; and yet the difficulty of what was to be done with the slaves weighed constantly upon his mind. . . . Moreover, if I am to speak the truth, the whole nature of Hawthorne shrank from the rough wear and tear inseparable from great popular movements of any kind. His keen observant intellect served to show him the weaknesses and vanities and vulgarities of the whole class of reformers. He recognised that their work was good; he admired the thoroughness he could not imitate; but somehow the details of popular agitation were strangely offensive to him. . . . And so this fastidiousness often, I think, obscured the usual accuracy of his judgment. The impression, for instance, made upon him by the personal manner and behaviour of President Lincoln was so inconsistent with his own ideas of dignity, that he longed, as I know, to describe him as he really appeared and only failed to do so, in his 'Sketches of the War,' in consequence of the representations of his friends. Still, I can recall how, after he had been describing to me the impression left upon him by his visit to the White House, an eminently characteristic doubt crossed his mind as to whether he was not in the wrong. 'Somehow,' he said, 'though why I could never discern, I have always observed that the popular instinct chooses the right man at the right time. But then,' he added, 'as you have seen Lincoln, I wish you could have seen Pierce too; you would have seen a real gentleman.'. . .

Never was a man more strangely misplaced by fate than Hawthorne in that revolutionary war-time. His clear powerful intellect dragged him one way, and his delicate sensitive taste the other. That he was not in harmony with the tone of his countrymen was to him a real trouble, and he envied keenly the undoubting faith in the justice of their cause, which was possessed by the brother men-of-letters among whom he lived. To any one who knew the man, the mere fact that Hawthorne should have been able to make up his mind to the righteousness and expediency of the war at all, is evidence of the strength of that popular passion which has driven the North into conflict with the South. . . .

Here, in England, people accused Hawthorne, as I think, unfairly, for the criticisms contained in his last book upon our national habits and character. The abuse was exaggerated, after our wont; but I admit, freely, that there were things in the 'Old Home' which I think its author would not have written if his mind had not been embittered by the harsh and unsparing attacks that, ever since the outbreak of the war, have been poured upon everything and everybody in the North. With all his sensitiveness, and all his refinement, and all his world-culture, Hawthorne was still a Yankee in heart. He saw the defects of his own countrymen only too clearly; he was willing enough to speak to them unsparingly; but, when others abused his country, then the native New England blood was roused within that thoughtful nature.

119. Richard Holt Hutton: Hawthorne, the 'ghost of New England', from an unsigned essay, 'Nathaniel Hawthorne' in the *Spectator*

18 July, xxxvii, 705–6
37

The ghostly genius of Hawthorne is a great loss to the American people. He has been called a mystic, which he was not, and a psychological dreamer, which he was in very slight degree. He was really the ghost of New England,—we do not mean the 'spirit,' nor the 'phantom,' but the ghost in the older sense in which that term is used as the thin, rarefied essence which is to be found somewhere behind the physical organization,—embodied, indeed, and not by any means in a shadowy or diminutive earthly tabernacle, but yet only half embodied in it, endowed with a certain painful sense of the gulf between his nature and its organization, always recognizing the gulf, always trying to bridge it over, and always more or less unsuccessful in the attempt. His writings are not exactly spiritual writings; for there is no dominating spirit in them. They are ghostly writings. He was, to our minds, a sort of sign to New England of the divorce that has been going on there (and not less perhaps in old England) between its people's spiritual and earthly nature, and of the impotence which they will soon feel, if they are to be absorbed more and more in that shrewd, hard earthly sense which is one of their most striking characteristics, in *communicating* even with the

ghost of their former self. Hawthorne, with all his shyness and tenderness, and literary reticence, shows very distinct traces also of understanding well the cold, curious, and shrewd spirit which besets the
Yankees even more than other commercial peoples. His heroes have
usually not a little of this hardness in them. Coverdale, for instance, in
the 'Blithedale Romance,' confesses that 'that cold tendency between
instinct and intellect which made me pry with a speculative interest into
people's passions and impulses appeared to have gone far towards unhumanizing my heart.' Holgrave, in the 'House of the Seven Gables,'
is one of the same class of shrewd, cold, curious heroes. Indeed, there
are few of the tales without a character of this type. But though
Hawthorne had a deep sympathy with the practical as well as the
literary genius of New England, it is always in a far-removed and
ghostly kind of way, as though he were stricken by some spell which
half-paralyzed him from communicating with the life around him, as
though he saw it only by a reflected light. His spirit haunted rather than
ruled his body; his body hampered his spirit. Yet his external career was
not only not romantic, but identified with all the dullest routine of
commercial duties. That a man who consciously *telegraphed*, as it were,
with the world, transmitting meagre messages through his material
organization, should have been first a custom-house officer in Massachusetts, and then the consul in Liverpool, brings out into the strongest
possible relief the curiously representative character in which he stood
to New England as its literary or intellectual ghost. There is nothing
more ghostly in his writings than his account, in his recent book, of the
consulship in Liverpool,—how he began by trying to communicate
frankly with his fellow-countrymen, how he found the task more and
more difficult, and gradually drew back into the twilight of his reserve,
how he shrewdly and somewhat coldly watched 'the dim shadows as
they go and come,' speculated idly on their fate, and all the time
discharged the regular routine of consular business, witnessing the usual
depositions, giving captains to captainless crews, affording costive
advice or assistance to Yankees when in need of a friend, listening to
them when they were only anxious to offer, not ask, assistance, and
generally observing them from that distant and speculative outpost
whence all common things looked strange.

Hawthorne, who was a delicate critic of himself, was well aware of
the shadowy character of his own genius, though not aware that precisely here lay its curious and thrilling power. In the preface to 'Twice-
told Tales' he tells us frankly, 'The book, if you would see anything

in it, requires to be read in the clear brown twilight atmosphere in which it was written; if opened in the sunshine, it is apt to look exceedingly like a volume of blank pages.' And then he adds, coming still nearer to the mark, 'They are not the talk of a secluded man with his own mind and heart, *but his attempts, and very imperfectly successful ones, to open an intercourse with the world.*' That is, he thinks, the secret of his weakness; but it is also the secret of his power. He carries with him always the air of trying to manifest himself; and the words come faintly, not like whispers so much as like sounds lost in the distance they have traversed. A common reader of Mr. Hawthorne would say that he took a pleasure in mystifying his readers, or weaving cobweb threads, not to bind their curiosity, but to startle and chill them, so gravely does he tell you in many of his tales that he could not quite make out the details of a fictitious conversation, and that he can only at best hint its purport. For instance, in 'Transformation,' he says of his heroine and her temper,

Owing to this moral estrangement, this chill remoteness of their position, there have come to us but a few vague whisperings of what passed in Miriam's interview that afternoon with the sinister personage who had dogged her footsteps ever since her visit to the catacomb. In weaving these mystic utterances into a continuous scene, we undertake a task resembling in its perplexity that of gathering up and piecing together the fragments of a letter which has been torn and scattered to the winds. Many words of deep significance—many sentences, and these probably the most important ones—have flown too far on the winged breeze to be recovered.

This is a favorite device of Mr. Hawthorne's, and does not, we think, proceed from the wish to mystify, so much as from the refusal of his own imagination so to modify his own conception to make it clearly conceivable to the mind of his readers. He had a clear conception of his own design, and a conception, too, of the world for which he was writing, and was ever afraid of not conveying his own conception, but some other distinct from it and inconsistent with it, to the world, if he expressed it in his own way. He felt that he could not reproduce in others his own idea, but should only succeed in spoiling the effect he had already, by great labor, produced. He had manifested himself partially; but the next stroke, if he made it at all, would spoil everything, mistranslate him, and reverse the impression he hoped to produce. It was the timidity of an artist who felt that he had, as it were, to translate all his symbols from a language he knew thoroughly into one he knew less perfectly, but still so perfectly as to be nervously sensible to the slightest fault. . . . And sometimes, like a ghost that moves its lips but cannot be heard, he simply acquiesced in the incapacity, only using expressive gestures and vague beckonings to indicate generally a subject for awe or fear. From a similar cause Hawthorne was continually expressing his regret that his native country has as yet no Past, and he seems always to have been endeavoring to supply the want by peopling his pictures of life with shadowy presences, which give them some of the eerie effect of a haunted house or a mediaeval castle. We doubt much, however, whether it was really a Past after which he yearned. When he laid his scene in Italy, or wrote about England he certainly made little or no use of their Past in his art, and, we imagine, that all he really craved for was that interposing film of thought between himself and the scene or characters he was delineating, which spared his isolated imagination the necessity of trying to paint in the exact style of the people he was addressing. He wanted an apparent excuse for the far-off and distant tone of thought and feeling which was most natural to him.

And when we turn from the manner to the thoughts of this weird New England genius, we find the subjects on which Hawthorne tries to 'open intercourse' with the world are just the subjects on which the ghost of New England would like to converse with New England,—the workings of guilt, remorse, and shame in the old Puritan times, as in the 'Scarlet Letter;' the morbid thirst to discover and to sin the un-pardonable sin, as in the very striking little fragment called 'Ethan Brand,' which we have always regretted keenly that Hawthorne never completed; the eternal solitude of every individual spirit, and the terror with which people realize that solitude, if they ever do completely realize it, as in the extraordinary tale of the awe inspired by a mild and even tender-hearted man, who has made a vow which puts a black veil forever between his face and that of all other human beings, and called the 'Minister's Black Veil;'—the mode in which sin may develop the intellect treated imaginatively both in 'Ethan Brand,' and at greater length and with even more power in 'Transformation;'—the mysteri-ous links between the flesh and the spirit, the physical and the spiritual nature, a subject on which all original New England writers have displayed a singular and almost morbid interest, and which Haw-thorne has touched more or less in very many of his tales, especially in the strange and lurid fancy called 'Rappacini's Daughter,' where Hawthorne conceives a girl accustomed by her father's chemical skill to the use of the most deadly poisons, whose beauty of mind and body is equal and perfect, but who, like deadly nightshade or the beautiful purple flowers whose fragrance she inhales, breathes out a poison which destroys every insect that floats near her mouth, shudders at her own malign influence on everything she touches, and gives rise, of course, to the most deadly conflict of emotions in those who love her;—these and subjects like these, indigenous in a mind steeped in the metaphysical and moral lore of New England endowed with much of the cold simplicity of the Puritan nature, and yet insulated from the world for which he wished to write, and too shy to press into it, are the favorite themes of Hawthorne's brooding and shadowy moods.

His power over his readers arises from much the same cause as that of his own fanciful creation,—the minister who wore the black veil as a symbol of the veil which is on all hearts, and who startled men less because he was hidden from their view than because he made them aware of their own solitude. . . . Hawthorne, with the pale, melancholy smile that seems ever to be always on his lips, seems to speak from a somewhat similar solitude. Indeed, we suspect the story was a kind of parable of his own experience. Edgar Poe, though by no means a poor critic, made one great blunder, when he said of Hawthorne,

He has not half the material for the exclusiveness of authorship that he has for its universality. He has the purest style, the finest taste, the most available scholarship, the most delicate humor, the most touching pathos, the most radiant imagination, the most consummate ingenuity, and with these varied good qualities he has done *well* as a mystic. But is there any one of these qualities which should prevent his doing doubly well in a career of honest, upright, sensible, prehensible, and comprehensible literature? Let him mend his pen, get a bottle of visible ink, come out from the Old Manse, cut Mr. Alcott, hang (if possible) the editor of the *Dial*, and throw out of window to the pigs all his old numbers of the *North American Review*.

The difficulty did not lie in these sacrifices, but in the greater feat of escaping from himself; and could he have done so, of course he would as much have lost his imaginative spell as a ghost would do who really returned into the body. That pallid, tender, solitary, imaginative treatment of characteristics and problems which have lain, and still lie, very close to the heart of New England,—that power of exhibiting them lit up by the moonlight of a melancholy imagination,—that ghostly half appeal for sympathy, half offer of counsel on the diseases latent in the New England nature,—were no eccentricity, but of the essence of his literary power. What gave him that pure style, that fine taste, that delicate humor, that touching pathos, in a great degree even that

radiant imagination and that consummate ingenuity, was the consciously separate and aloof life which he lived. Without it he might
have been merely a shrewd, hard, sensible, conservative, success-
worshipping, business-loving Yankee democrat, like the intimate
college friend, Ex-President Pierce, whom he helped to raise to a somewhat ignominious term of power, and who was one of the mourners
beside his death-bed. Hawthorne had power to *haunt* such men as these
because he had nursed many of their qualities, thoughts, and difficulties,
in a ghostly solitude, and could so make them feel, as the poor folks said
figuratively of themselves after communing with the veiled minister,
that 'they had been with him behind the veil.'

120. George William Curtis: Hawthorne, the Salem recluse, from an unsigned review in the *North American Review*

October 1864, xcix, 539–57

Curtis (1824–92), a journalist and reformer, took part in the Brook
Farm experiment and was later a travel correspondent for the *New
York Tribune*. In 1856, with his oration on *The Duty of the American
Scholar to Politics and the Times,* he became one of the most influential voices against slavery. His essay represents his effort to
relate Hawthorne's art to what he felt were current political
necessities.

. . . The old witch-hanging city had no weirder product than this
dark-haired son. He has certainly given it an interest which it must
otherwise have lacked; but he speaks of it with small affection, considering that his family had lived there for two centuries. 'An unjoyous
attachment,' he calls it. And, to tell the truth, there was evidently little
love lost between the little city and its most famous citizen. Stories still

float in the social gossip of the town, which represent the shy author as inaccessible to all invitations to dinner and tea; and while the pleasant circle awaited his coming in the drawing-room, the impracticable man was—at least so runs the tale—quietly hobnobbing with companions to whom his fame was unknown. Those who coveted him as a phoenix could never get him, while he gave himself freely to those who saw in him only a placid barn-door fowl. The sensitive youth was a recluse, upon whose imagination had fallen the gloomy mystery of Puritan life and character. Salem was the inevitable centre of his universe more truly than he thought. The mind of Justice Hathorn's descendant was bewitched by the fascination of a certain devilish subtlety working under the comeliest aspects in human affairs. It overcame him with strange sympathy. It colored and controlled his intellectual life.

Devoted all day to lonely reverie and musing upon the obscurer spiritual passages of the life whose monuments he constantly encountered, that musing became inevitably morbid. With the creative instinct of the artist, he wrote the wild fancies into form as stories, many of which, when written, he threw into the fire. Then, after nightfall, stealing out from his room into the silent streets of Salem, and shadowy as the ghosts with which to his susceptible imagination the dusky town was thronged, he glided beneath the house in which the witch-trials were held, or across the moonlight hill upon which the witches were hung, until the spell was complete. Nor can we help fancying that, after the murder of old Mr. White in Salem, which happened within a few years after his return from college, which drew from Mr. Webster his most famous criminal plea, and filled a shadowy corner of every museum in New England, as every shivering little man of that time remembers, with an awful reproduction of the scene in wax-figures, with real sheets on the bed, and the murderer in a glazed cap stooping over to deal the fatal blow,—we cannot help fancying that the young recluse who walked by night, the wizard whom as yet none knew, hovered about the house, gazing at the windows of the fatal chamber, and listening in horror for the faint whistle of the confederate in another street.

Three years after he graduated, in 1828, he published anonymously a slight romance with the motto from Southey, 'Wilt thou go with me?' Hawthorne never acknowledged the book, and it is now seldom found; but it shows plainly the natural bent of his mind. It is a dim, dreamy tale, such as a Byron-struck youth of the time might have written, except for that startling self-possession of style and cold analysis of passion, rather than sympathy with it, which showed no imitation, but remarkable original power. The same lurid gloom over-hangs it that shadows all his works. It is uncanny; the figures of the romance are not persons, they are passions, emotions, spiritual specula-tions. So the 'Twice-told Tales,' that seem at first but the pleasant fancies of a mild recluse, gradually hold the mind with a Lamia-like fascination; and the author says truly of them, in the Preface of 1851, 'Even in what purport to be pictures of actual life, we have allegory not always so warmly dressed in its habiliments of flesh and blood as to be taken into the reader's mind without a shiver.' There are sunny gleams upon the pages, but a strange, melancholy chill pervades the book. In 'The Wedding Knell,' 'The Minister's Black Veil,' 'The Gentle Boy,' 'Wakefield,' 'The Prophetic Pictures,' 'The Hollow of the Three Hills,' 'Dr. Heidegger's Experiment,' 'The Ambitious Guest,' 'The White Old Maid,' 'Edward Fane's Rose-bud,' 'The Lily's Quest,'—or in the 'Legends of the Province House,' where the courtly provincial state of governors and ladies glitters across the small, sad New England world, whose very baldness jeers it to scorn,—there is the same fateful atmos-phere in which Goody Cloyse might at any moment whisk by upon her broomstick, and in which the startled heart stands still with un-speakable terror.

The spell of mysterious horror which kindled Hawthorne's imagina-tion was a test of the character of his genius. The mind of this child of witch-haunted Salem loved to hover between the natural and the super-natural, and sought to tread the almost imperceptible and doubtful line of contact. He instinctively sketched the phantoms that have the figures of men, but are not human; the elusive, shadowy scenery which, like that of Gustave Doré's pictures, is Nature sympathizing in her forms and aspects with the emotions of terror or awe which the tale excites. His genius broods entranced over the evanescent phantasmagoria of the vague debatable land in which the realities of experience blend with ghostly doubts and wonders.

But from its poisonous flowers what a wondrous perfume he distilled! Through his magic reed, into what penetrating melody he blew that deathly air! His relentless fancy seemed to seek a sin that was hopeless, a cruel despair that no faith could throw off. Yet his naive and well-poised genius hung over the gulf of blackness, and peered into the pit with the steady nerve and simple face of a boy. The mind of the reader follows him with an aching wonder and admiration, as the bewildered old mother forester watched Undine's gambols. As

Hawthorne describes Miriam in 'The Marble Faun,' so may the character of his genius be most truly indicated. Miriam, the reader will remember, turns to Hilda and Kenyon for sympathy.

Yet it was to little purpose that she approached the edge of the voiceless gulf between herself and them. Standing on the utmost verge of that dark chasm, she might stretch out her hand and never clasp a hand of theirs; she might strive to call out, 'Help, friends! help!' but, as with dreamers when they shout, her voice would perish inaudibly in the remoteness that seemed such a little way. This perception of an infinite, shivering solitude, amid which we cannot come close enough to human beings to be warmed by them, and where they turn to cold, chilly shapes of mist, is one of the most forlorn results of any accident, misfortune, crime, or peculiarity of character, that puts an individual ajar with the world.

Thus it was because the early New England life made so much larger account of the supernatural element than any other modern civilized society, that the man whose blood had run in its veins instinctively turned to it. But beyond this alluring spell of its darker and obscurer individual experience, it seems neither to have touched his imagination nor even to have aroused his interest. To Walter Scott the romance of feudalism was precious, for the sake of feudalism itself, in which he believed with all his soul, and for that of the heroic old feudal figures which he honored. He was a Tory in every particle of his frame, and his genius made him the poet of Toryism. But Hawthorne had apparently no especial political, religious, or patriotic affinity with the spirit which inspired him. It was solely a fascination of the intellect. And although he is distinctively the poet of the Puritans, although it is to his genius that we shall always owe that image of them which the power of 'The Scarlet Letter' has imprinted upon literature, and doubtless henceforth upon historical interpretation, yet what an imperfect picture of that life it is! All its stern and melancholy romance is there,— its picturesque gloom and intense passion; but upon those quivering pages, as in every passage of his stories drawn from that spirit, there seems to be wanting a deep, complete, sympathetic appreciation of the fine moral heroism, the spiritual grandeur, which overhung that gloomy life, as a delicate purple mist suffuses in summer twilights the bald crags of the crystal hills. It is the glare of the Scarlet Letter itself, and all that it luridly reveals and weirdly implies, which produced the tale. It was not beauty in itself, nor deformity, not virtue nor vice, which engaged the author's deepest sympathy. It was the occult relation between the two. Thus while the Puritans were of all men pious, it was the instinct of

Hawthorne's genius to search out and trace with terrible tenacity the dark and devious thread of sin in their lives.

Human life and character, whether in New England two hundred years ago or in Italy to-day, interested him only as they were touched by this glamour of sombre spiritual mystery; and the attraction pursued him in every form in which it appeared. It is as apparent in the most perfect of his smaller tales, 'Rappaccini's Daughter,' as in 'The Scarlet Letter,' 'The Blithedale Romance,' 'The House of the Seven Gables,' and 'The Marble Faun.' You may open almost at random, and you are as sure to find it, as to hear the ripple in Mozart's music, or the pathetic minor in a Neapolitan melody. Take, for instance, 'The Birth-Mark,' which we might call the best of the smaller stories, if we had not just said the same thing of 'Rappaccini's Daughter,'—for so even and complete is Hawthorne's power, that, with few exceptions, each work of his, like Benvenuto's, seems the most characteristic and felicitous. . . . The point of interest in both stories is the subtile connection, in the first, between the beauty of Georgiana and the taint of the birth-mark; and, in the second, the loveliness of Beatrice and the poison of the blossom.

This, also, is the key of his last romance, 'The Marble Faun,' one of the most perfect works of art in literature. . . . Donatello, indeed, is the true centre of interest, as he is one of the most striking creations of genius. But the perplexing charm of Donatello, what is it but the doubt that does not dare to breathe itself, the appalled wonder whether, if the breeze should lift those clustering locks a little higher, he would prove to be faun or man? It never does lift them; the doubt is never solved, but it is always suggested. The mystery of a partial humanity, morally irresponsible but humanly conscious, haunts the entrancing page. It draws us irresistibly on. But as the cloud closes around the lithe figure of Donatello, we hear again from its hidden folds the words of 'The Birth-Mark': 'Thus ever does the gross fatality of earth exult in its invariable triumph over the immortal essence, which, in this dim sphere of half-development, demands the completeness of a higher state.' Or still more sadly, the mysterious youth, half vanishing from our sympathy, seems to murmur, with Beatrice Rappaccini, 'And still as she spoke, she kept her hand upon her heart,—"Wherefore didst thou inflict this miserable doom upon thy child?" '. . .

It is not strange, certainly, that a man such as has been described, of a morbid shyness, the path of whose genius diverged always out of the sun into the darkest shade, and to whom human beings were merely psychological phenomena, should have been accounted ungenial, and sometimes even hard, cold, and perverse. From the bent of his intellectual temperament it happens that in his simplest and sweetest passages he still seems to be studying and curiously observing, rather than sympathizing. You cannot help feeling constantly that the author is looking askance both at his characters and you, the reader; and many a young and fresh mind is troubled strangely by his books, as if it were aware of a half-Mephistophelean smile upon the page. Nor is this impression altogether removed by the remarkable familiarity of his personal disclosures. There was never a man more shrinkingly retiring, yet surely never was an author more naively frank. He is willing that you should know all that a man may fairly reveal of himself. The great interior story he does not tell, of course, but the introduction to 'The Mosses from an Old Manse,' the opening chapter of 'The Scarlet Letter,' and the 'Consular Experiences,' with much of the rest of 'Our Old Home,' are as intimate and explicit chapters of autobiography as can be found. Nor would it be easy to find anywhere a more perfect idyl than that introductory chapter of the Mosses. Its charm is perennial and indescribable; and why should it not be, since it was written at a time in which, as he says, 'I was happy'? It is, perhaps, the most softly-hued and exquisite work of his pen. So the sketch of 'The Custom-House,' although prefatory to that most tragically powerful of romances, 'The Scarlet Letter,' is an incessant play of the shyest and most airy humor. It is like the warbling of bobolinks before a thunder-burst. How many other men, however unreserved with the pen, would be likely to dare to paint, with the fidelity of Teniers and the simplicity of Fra Angelico, a picture of the office and the companions in which and with whom they did their daily work? The Surveyor of Customs in the port of Salem treated the town of Salem, in which he lived and discharged his daily task, as if it had been, with all its people, as vague and remote a spot as the town of which he was about to treat in the story. He commented upon the place and the people as modern travellers in Pompeii discuss the ancient town. It made a great scandal. He was accused of depicting with unpardonable severity worthy folks, whose friends were sorely pained and indignant. But he wrote such sketches as he wrote his stories. He treated his companions as he treated himself and all the personages in history or experience with which he dealt, merely as phenomena to be analyzed and described, with no more private malice or personal emotion than the sun, which would have photographed them, warts and all.

Thus it was that the great currents of human sympathy never swept him away. The character of his genius isolated him, and he stood aloof from the common interests. Intent upon studying men in certain aspects, he cared little for man; and the high tides of collective emotion among his fellows left him dry and untouched. So he beholds and describes the generous impulse of humanity with sceptical courtesy rather than with hopeful cordiality.

He does not chide you if you spend effort and life intself in the ardent van of progress, but he asks simply, 'Is six so much better than half a dozen?' He will not quarrel with you if you expect the millennium to-morrow. He only says, with that glimmering smile, 'So soon?' Yet in all this there was no shadow of spiritual pride. Nay, so far from this, that the tranquil and pervasive sadness of all Hawthorne's writings, the kind of heart-ache that they leave behind, seem to spring from the fact that his nature was related to the moral world, as his own Donatello was to the human. 'So alert, so alluring, so noble,' muses the heart as we climb the Apennines toward the tower of Monte Beni;—'alas! is he human?' it whispers, with a pang of doubt.

How this directed his choice of subjects, and affected his treatment of them, when drawn from early history, we have already seen. It is not, therefore, surprising, that the history into which he was born interested him only in the same way.

When he went to Europe as Consul, 'Uncle Tom's Cabin' was already published, and the country shook with the fierce debate which involved its life. Yet eight years later Hawthorne wrote with calm ennui, 'No author, without a trial, can conceive of the difficulty of writing a romance about a country where there is no shadow, no antiquity, no mystery, no picturesque and gloomy wrong, nor anything but a commonplace prosperity, in broad and simple daylight, as is happily the case with my dear native land.' Is crime never romantic, then, until distance ennobles it? Or were the tragedies of Puritan life so terrible that the imagination could not help kindling, while the pangs of the plantation are superficial and commonplace? Charlotte Brontë, Dickens, and Thackeray were able to find a shadow even in 'merrie England.' But our great romancer looked at the American life of his time with these marvellous eyes, and could see only monotonous sunshine. That the Devil, in the form of an elderly man clad in grave and decent attire, should lead astray the saints of Salem village, two centuries ago, and confuse right and wrong in the mind of Goodman Brown, was something that excited his imagination, and produced one of his weirdest stories. But that the same Devil, clad in a sombre sophism, was confusing the sentiment of right and wrong in the mind of his own countrymen he did not even guess. The monotonous sunshine disappeared in tremendous war. What other man of equal power, who was not intellectually constituted precisely as Hawthorne was, could have stood merely perplexed and bewildered, harassed by the inability of positive sympathy, in the vast conflict which tosses us all in its terrible vortex?

In political theories and in an abstract view of war men may differ. But this war is not to be dismissed as a political difference. Here is an attempt to destroy the government of a country, not because it oppressed any man, but because its evident tendency was to secure universal justice under law. It is therefore a conspiracy against human nature. Civilization itself is at stake; and the warm blood of the noblest youth is everywhere flowing in as sacred a cause as history records,—flowing not merely to maintain a certain form of government, but to vindicate the rights of human nature. Shall there not be sorrow and pain, if a friend is merely impatient or confounded by it,—if he sees in it only danger or doubt, and not hope for the right,—or if he seem to insinuate that it would have been better if the war had been avoided, even at that countless cost to human welfare by which alone the avoidance was possible?

Yet, if the view of Hawthorne's mental constitution which has been suggested be correct, this attitude of his, however deeply it may be regretted, can hardly deserve moral condemnation. He knew perfectly well that, if a man has no ear for music, he had better not try to sing. But the danger with such men is, that they are apt to doubt if music itself be not a vain delusion. This danger Hawthorne escaped. There is none of the shallow persiflage of the sceptic in his tone, nor any affectation of cosmopolitan superiority. . . .

The truth is, that his own times and their people and their affairs were just as shadowy to him as those of any of his stories, and his mind held the same curious, half-wistful poise among all the conflicts of principle and passion around him, as among those of which he read and mused. If you ask why this was so,—how it was that the tragedy of an old Italian garden, or the sin of a lonely Puritan parish, or the crime of a provincial judge, should so stimulate his imagination with romantic appeals and harrowing allegories, while either it did not see a Carolina slave-pen, or found in it only a tame prosperity,—you must take your answer in the other question, why he did not weave into any of his stories the black and bloody thread of the Inquisition. His genius obeyed its law. When he wrote like a disembodied intelligence of events with which his neighbors' hearts were quivering,—when the same half-smile flutters upon his lips in the essay 'About War Matters,' sketched as it were upon the battle-field, as in that upon 'Fire Worship,' written in the rural seclusion of the mossy Manse,—ah me! it is Donatello, in his tower of Monte Beni, contemplating with doubtful interest the field upon which the flower of men are dying for an idea. Do you wonder, as you see him and hear him, that your heart, bewildered, asks and asks again, 'Is he human? Is he a man?'

Now that Hawthorne sleeps by the tranquil Concord, upon whose shores the old Manse was his bridal bower, those who knew him chiefly there revert beyond the angry hour to those peaceful days. How dear the old Manse was to him, he has himself recorded; and in the opening of the 'Tanglewood Tales' he pays his tribute to that placid landscape, which will always be recalled with pensive tenderness by those who, like him, became familiar with it in happy hours.

To me [he writes], there is a peculiar, quiet charm in these broad meadows and gentle eminences. They are better than mountains, because they do not stamp and stereotype themselves into the brain, and thus grow wearisome with the same strong impression, repeated day after day. A few summer weeks among mountains, a lifetime among green meadows and placid slopes, with outlines forever new, because continually fading out of the memory,—such would be my sober choice.

He used to say, in those days,—when, as he was fond of insisting, he was the obscurest author in the world, because, although he had told his tales twice, nobody cared to listen,—that he never knew exactly how he contrived to live. But he was then married, and the dullest eye could not fail to detect the feminine grace and taste that ordered the dwelling, and perceive the tender sagacity that made all things possible.

Such was his simplicity and frugality, that, when he was left alone for a little time in his Arcadia, he would dismiss 'the help,' and, with some friend of other days who came to share his loneliness, he cooked the easy meal, and washed up the dishes. No picture is clearer in the memory of a certain writer than that of the magician, in whose presence he almost lost his breath, looking at him over a dinner-plate which he was gravely wiping in the kitchen, while the handy friend, who had been a Western settler, scoured the kettle at the door. Blithe-dale, where their acquaintance had begun, had not allowed either of them to forget how to help himself. It was amusing to one who knew this native independence of Hawthorne, to hear, some years afterward, that he wrote the 'campaign' Life of Franklin Pierce for the sake of getting an office. That such a man should do such a work was possibly incomprehensible, to those who did not know him, upon any other supposition, until the fact was known that Mr. Pierce was an old and constant friend. Then it was explained. Hawthorne asked simply how he could help his friend; and he did the only thing he could do for that purpose. But although he passed some years in public office, he had neither taste nor talent for political life. He owed his offices to works quite other than political. His first and second appointments were virtually made by his friend Mr. Bancroft, and the third by his friend Mr. Pierce. His claims were perceptible enough to friendship, but would hardly have been so to a caucus.

In this brief essay we have aimed only to indicate the general character of the genius of Hawthorne, and to suggest a key to his peculiar relation to his time. The reader will at once see that it is rather the man than the author who has been described; but this has been designedly done, for we confess a personal solicitude, shared, we are very sure, by many friends of Nathaniel Hawthorne, that there shall not be wanting to the future student of his works such light as acquaintance with the man may throw upon them, as well as some picture of the impression his personality made upon his contemporaries.

Strongly formed, of dark, poetic gravity of aspect, lighted by the deep, gleaming eye that recoiled with girlish coyness from contact with your gaze; of rare courtesy and kindliness in personal intercourse, yet so sensitive that his look and manner can be suggested by the word glimmering; giving you a sense of restrained impatience to be away; mostly silent in society, and speaking always with an appearance of effort, but with a lambent light of delicate humor playing over all he said in the confidence of familiarity, and firm self-possession under all, as if the glimmering manner were only the tremulous surface of the sea,—Hawthorne was personally known to few, and intimately to very few. But no one knew him without loving him, or saw him without remembering him; and the name Nathaniel Hawthorne, which, when it was first written, was supposed to be fictitious, is now one of the most enduring facts of English literature.

POSTHUMOUS PUBLICATIONS:
THE FRAGMENTS
(A) PANSIE
1864

121. Unsigned review in the *Athenaeum*
10 September 1864, p. 338

In this little book are the last lines penned by the late American writer, Mr. Hawthorne. They form the first and only chapter of an unfinished novel, and are as minute, touching, delicate and perfect as anything the author ever wrote. The chapter will have wide acceptance. In its way, it is as valuable as the first sketch which an inspired artist might draw,—the noble instalment towards a grand and mysterious picture. All the signs, and therewith the warrant, of a great master may be found in this sketch; if we may so name a portrait that seems to want no touch to render it more finished, or to win with it sympathy and admiration. But the sketch to which we now allude is not that of 'Pansie,' of whom we get but a charming glance, full of promise of the enjoyment that is never to come. We speak of the one other personage who figures in this exquisite picture, Pansie's great-grandfather, Dr. Dollover, who stands in this composition like a rich, dark, mellow, mystic, and yet real, figure before a grand but gloomy background of a picture by Rembrandt. We cannot give this sketch higher praise. It does not merit less.

(B) SEPTIMIUS; A ROMANCE

1872

122. Unsigned review in the British Quarterly Review

October 1872, lvi, 540

This romance was found among the unpublished manuscripts of Nathaniel Hawthorne, and never underwent his final revision. This is obvious, in the circumstance that the hero of the story is represented as making love to a girl whose simple, guileless affection he is utterly incompetent to reciprocate. Further consideration transposed this betrothed bride into a sister, whom he contentedly resigns to a rival. This romance of an earthly immortality is grotesque and weird in its details. The passionate desire to discover and obtain the elixir of life is stirred in the breast of one Septimius Felton, an aimless student, who is brought into violent contrast with a young patriot, who fights bravely in the first struggle for American independence. Felton is forced into a duel with a young English officer; he kills his man, but receives from his dying hand various bequests, some curious secrets, and the key of an old casket, which by a strange coincidence has previously come into his own possession, and which furnishes the proof of his being the heir to the English estates, and the name of his victim. The dying officer leaves a miniature of his betrothed in the hands of his slayer; a circumstance which leads her to discover his grave. She fans the wild conceit in the mind of the man who has killed her lover, that some precious flower, blooming out of a bloody grave, was the one ingredient needed to complete the elixir of which he was in quest. To this end, with the aid of a crimson flower, that she had herself planted on her lover's grave, she tempts him to concoct a deadly poison, and when—as Septimius supposes—the moment has arrived for them both to quaff the nectar, and secure the gift of immortality, she drinks the poison, and dies before his eyes. The speculations concerning the possibilities of an endless life on earth are curious, but neither original nor impressive; and the wild, improbable story in which the blood of Septimius Felton is mingled with that of an Indian sachem, who has been hung for witchcraft, and that of an English baronet, is only partially worked out. Throughout the romance we feel there is lacking 'the touch of a vanished hand.' The eerie supernatural machinery that Mr. Hawthorne laid under contribution in his 'Scarlet Letter' and his 'Transformations' is again employed here; but we think, without any great effect or conspicuous purpose. Septimius is a *'study'* for brother artists, but hardly more.

123. From an unsigned review in the *New Englander*

October 1872, xxxi, 785–6

. . . The proposal, made soon after Mr. Hawthorne's death, to print his note-books, though coming from his own family, met with wide disapprobation and in some quarters severe remonstrance as making merchandise of his private papers and endangering his literary fame. There was some reason for such misgivings in this case, as in that of any admired author. In the absence of his own directions, his desk might claim to be sacredly guarded, if only through jealousy for his name. But his family were safe custodians. And, as it turned out, no harm was done, but on the contrary, while the private informal character of the papers, as materials for the writer's workmanship rather than his finished works, gave them peculiar interest, they were found to be in themselves readable and characteristic of his mind. . . .

Of course had he lived he would have chosen to revise and finish it if it was to be published, but no injustice is done to him, since it is manifestly incomplete and printed in view of that fact, and can be judged by no higher standard than it will bear. . . . In the phraseology of artists, the work is 'a study,' only carried further than the note-books, which were materials for building secured in case they should be needed, while this is already a house only here and there incomplete, and still enabling us to understand what the architect's last touches would have made it. As a story, its machinery, stages, and catastrophe are fairly brought before us. For the most part it needs no revision, and the main effect could hardly be enhanced by completing some of the details. As the title indicates, it is the story of a gifted young man seeking an earthly immortality and disenchanted when his dream seems about to be fulfilled. It is Hawthorne's workmanship throughout, with his clear-cut transparent style, weird suggestions, and picturesque and sometimes grotesque descriptions. And not the least interesting, though subordinate, aspect of the story is in the hero's outside relation to the war of our Revolution. Could the author have intended here a hint of his own life-work in cloudland or dreamland going on aloof from his country's later strife?

124. From an unsigned review in *Harper's New Monthly Magazine*

November 1872, xlv, 784

The marks of Hawthorne's inimitable genius are on *Septimius Felton*. . . . It is a story of the search for the elixir of life—a story of a wild, weird imagination, diseased yet pure, chaste, morally free from every thing that can contaminate. Certainly neither life nor literature affords any such characters as walk in shadowy forms upon this stage— Septimius Felton, Dr. Portsoaken, Aunt Keziah, and Sybil Dacy; certainly, outside of the lunatic asylum, no such imaginings were ever indulged in as those in which Septimius Felton indulges just as he is about to drink what he imagines to be the elixir of life; and certainly the consummation of the plot in the death of Sybil and the flight of Septimius is as unexpected as its course is unparalleled in fiction. Yet with all the genius which characterizes the book, it can hardly be popular; not even the pen of Hawthorne can give a semblance of reality to so weird and ghostly a story; every thing is, as it were, a shadow; the very characters are impalpable spectres; their aims and thoughts and purposes are those of dream-land, not of actual life; and we judge the book will achieve its reputation rather as a literary curiosity than as a popular romance.

(C) *FANSHAWE* AND *THE DOLLIVER ROMANCE*

1876

---

125. From an unsigned review in *Appletons' Journal*

August 1876, n.s., i, 190

The fatality of fame has fallen heavily upon Hawthorne during the past month. Nothing was more repugnant to him during his life than the idea that some one would write a biography of him after his death, and he did all in his power to prevent it; but a biographer has now appeared who was not content to relate the short and simple story of Hawthorne's life, but endeavors by the most minute scrutiny and comparison of what he did, and wrote, and recorded of himself, to penetrate the inmost sanctuary of his genius, and lay bare the very pulse of the machine. Doubtless, too, Hawthorne thought he had secured for 'Fanshawe' the oblivion to which he consigned all his immature productions, but the tireless industry of his admirers has not only secured for it a posthumous lease of life, but has disinterred from the pages of sundry old magazines and newspapers enough of the random and miscellaneous 'pot-boilers' of his younger days to fill two volumes. . . .

Perhaps not the least enjoyable and instructive of these works of Hawthorne's will be found in the two volumes of miscellaneous pieces which the fastidious author had suppressed and forgotten, and for the resurrection of which we are indebted, it is said, to the indefatigable researches of the late Mr. J. E. Babson. 'Fanshawe,' Hawthorne's earliest attempt at novel-writing, fills the greater portion of one of the volumes, and the fragments of 'The Dolliver Romance' occupy a considerable part of the other. Of neither of these is it necessary to say much here, though we may remark, in passing, that Mr. Lathrop's abstract and analysis of 'Fanshawe' is almost the best part of a book in which the purely interpretive criticism is nearly always strikingly good. The remaining contents of the volumes consist of shorter pieces, mostly essays and biographical sketches, contributed by Hawthorne to the *Salem Gazette*, the *New England Magazine*, and the *American Magazine of Useful and Entertaining Knowledge*, during the ten years of seclusion which followed upon his leaving college. Some of these are almost as perfect as anything of the kind he ever wrote, but others are peculiarly interesting as exhibiting Hawthorne's method and style in their formative stage. Crude Hawthorne never was, even his boyish compositions showing something of the precision and grace of his maturer works; but somehow it is encouraging to find that such consummate and exquisite literary art was not wholly an endowment of Nature. As an acquirement it does not seem so far removed and unattainable as when it had the exclusive semblance of a 'gift.'

126. From an unsigned review in the *British Quarterly Review*

October 1876, lxiv, 540–5

Anything that may throw light on so strange and elusive a personality as that of Hawthorne must be welcome to not a few readers. To get to enjoy him is like the acquiring of a new taste. He is far from exciting us by means of incident or anything of that kind, but he fascinates us by his unique way of unveiling what is mysterious and yet common,— what all have felt as terrible *possibilities* in humanity and in themselves, —and he surrounds these with a weirdness, a glamour, that at once intensifies and magnifies them. But we are not sure that these recent additions to the Hawthorne library are calculated to have altogether the effect that his friends and representatives should be most concerned to produce. 'Fanshawe' is one of his very early efforts. He himself deliberately withdrew it, as Mr. J. T. Fields tells us rather regretfully, and would never hear of its being again put before the public. Indeed he was impatient of its being even named in his presence. And one does not need to read far to find the reason. It has little that is marked by Hawthorne's later characteristics. It abounds in incident distinctively after the style of Scott; it is so loosely written that it may be referred to as an encouragement to the young who are willing to labour to attain a finished style, and thus may have a high use; it is weak in climax and without any skill in character-drawing. . . . There are instances of clumsiness and even of positive error in the writing, which, for Hawthorne's sake, should surely have been corrected. . . .

How very different is this from the sweet musical delicacy of the additional but *unrevised* sections of 'The Dolliver Romance,' which are presented to us in the second of these volumes! True, they do not conduct us to any definite point in the story, but the glimpse of Pansie's father is interesting, and we have some further instances of the efficacy of that wondrous cordial. It is strange to observe how here, too, an undecipherable, half-mystical document, like that in 'Septimius,' was meant to play its part. But the charm of many of the sentences remains in the ear like the echoes of sweet music. . . .

The 'Tales and Sketches,' and the short biographies with which the two volumes are eked out, are very unequal, the most characteristic sketch being that of 'Graves and Goblins,' which is full of a quaint and dusky suggestiveness that would have fully justified its place among the 'Twice-told Tales.'

. . . Hawthorne was singularly deficient in what we may call dramatic identifying power. By this we mean that his characters are discriminated more by what they say than by their manner of saying it. Dr. Johnson would have made his little fishes all talk like whales; Hawthorne makes all his people talk like—*Hawthorne*. And this, taken strictly by itself, is a matter in which it is clear he showed no growth. . . . However much they talk, they talk *through* him; it is still Hawthorne who comes before us. In truth, his characters are masks for his own moods. Through them all he is wistfully contemplating his own personality in its varied possibility. . . . The interest directly connects itself with the writer, who thus makes himself fascinating, if not awful, by hiding his face behind a shadowy projection of his own phantasy. He is an egotist, though of a supremely attractive order. The true point of interest in any one of his characters is not found till its relation to his own mood is clearly established in the reader's mind. The thin intangibility of his characters for the most part, the lack of flesh and blood and genuine personal traits in them, is thus to be accounted for. More reality in them would have conflicted with his self-revelation and spoiled the tone and pitch of his story. . . .

Now, when we have said this much, it is clear that we are very near to the source at once of Hawthorne's strength and of his peculiar limitations. He has no dramatic grasp, he cannot discriminate character by passing faithfully from its essential mode to its outward characteristics, and again from outward manifestation to essential mode, concerned only to make it dramatically self-consistent and real. His conceptions were alien to this, as we have seen; his language, clear and beautiful as it is, was, so far as we can judge, inadequate for this purpose. . . .

(D) DR. GRIMSHAWE'S SECRET

1883

127. From an unsigned review in the *Athenaeum*

6 January 1883, pp. 9–11

The discovery of an unpublished story by Nathaniel Hawthorne would indeed be matter for congratulation. His writings are too few, not for his own fame, but for our delight. Perfect as are the pictures on the tapestry of 'scarlet web our wild Romancer weaves,' there was room for more, and had he lived to finish 'The Dolliver Romance' it would—so Mr. Fields, who had been told the plot, believed—have been the greatest of all his works. But, as everybody knows, the first chapter of 'The Dolliver Romance' alone was published, and then the pen fell for ever from the wearied hand. Naturally enough, after his death Mrs. Hawthorne and his daughters looked over his MSS. to see if there was anything more that could be published. They found three rough sketches, of which the most nearly complete, though that was incomplete enough, was 'Septimius,' which appeared in 1872, as edited by Miss Hawthorne. . . .

The last of the sketches is 'Dr. Grimshawe's Secret,' and it is impossible to ignore the fact that it has come into the world in a somewhat questionable shape. That such a sketch exists nobody denies, but it is strongly denied by Mrs. Lathrop that it can be 'truthfully published as anything more than an experimental fragment.' Now the announcement in the *Boston Daily Advertiser* of August 12th last distinctly states that 'the plot is carried out, and the work is practically finished.' This announcement must evidently have been sanctioned by Mr. Julian Hawthorne, for it goes into details of the history of the manuscript. . . . [He] tells us in the preface that he considers it 'practically complete': 'The story as a story is complete as it stands; it has a beginning, a middle, and an end. There is no break in the narrative and the legitimate

430

conclusion is reached.' He owns it is not complete 'as a work of art,' but this he evidently thinks of but slight importance. He believes the second or English part was first written, and that the first or American part was 'a rewriting of an original first part'; and he thinks that though the parts 'overlap' there is a real unity in the whole. This judgment, or want of judgment, is simply wonderful. There is no cohesion whatever between the parts, and the second part sometimes becomes absolutely unmeaning. The first part is written in Hawthorne's most careful style, though even there we find much that needs correction and revision. The second part is full of inconsistencies and extravagances. We fail to see the middle of the story, and there is no end at all.

It is, of course, difficult for a critic to be absolutely certain in matters of internal evidence of genuineness. . . . It would, then, no doubt be possible to imitate Hawthorne's style so that detection would be some-what difficult. At the same time, in spite of the great unevenness in quality which this book shows, and partly on account of that uneven-ness, we have very little doubt that (with possibly some exceptions of no great importance) Nathaniel Hawthorne was the author of 'Dr. Grimshawe's Secret.' Whether it was a right thing to publish so in-complete a work we will not inquire. . . .

Certainly Hawthorne has been the worst used of men. He particularly desired that no biography of himself should appear, and four have already been written, all curiously inadequate, and two more have been announced. He was most fastidious and painstaking in his work, and had a horror of imperfection, and now every scrap and fragment he ever wrote is collected and published, to the detriment (were it possible) rather than to the increase of his reputation. . . .

The first half of 'Dr. Grimshawe's Secret', is excellent, but much of it has already appeared in a slightly different form in 'Septimius.' Dr. Grimshawe himself is Dr. Fortsoaken again, and 'crusty Hannah' is first cousin to Aunt Keziah. The same strange room, hung round with cobwebs, is common to both, and the great spider 'Orontes' reappears in a still more terrific form. . . .

The smaller inconsistencies—the whole book is full of them—are hardly worth noticing after the inconsistency of the plot itself. What is the meaning of the picture of the man with a noose round his neck? Why did Colcord tell the doctor that he had some papers 'still recover-able by search,' and a few hours afterwards say, 'I have them about my person'? What was the gold ornament that resembled the article held in the hand of the statue of the founder of the almshouses? Why did not

Redclyffe claim acquaintance with the warden? But we might fill a column with such questions.

However, this incoherency is in one aspect satisfactory, as it seems another warrant for the genuineness of this fragment, or rather these fragments. Hawthorne might hereafter have worked up these rough notes for an English story. Surely no one could deliberately set himself to write for publication such crude nonsense as some of it undoubtedly is. Besides in nearly all we can recognize Hawthorne's touch, and even where that seems occasionally to fail, as in the dull political conversation with the warden, we can still see traces of Hawthorne's thought. Delightful descriptions of scenery, quaint pathetic suggestions, wild imaginings of every kind, lie strewn about; but, without form and void as it now is, no one who respected Hawthorne's memory should have permitted the publication of this book.

128. Eugene Benson: Hawthorne and Poe, From 'Poe and Hawthorne', in the *Galaxy*

December 1868, vi, 742–8

Benson (1837–1908), an American painter, spent most of his life on the Continent, and established his studio first in Florence and later in Rome. He frequently contributed to periodicals, and he published a book-length study about art in Italy.

Poe and Hawthorne are two brilliant exceptions in American literature. Among Americans, they are the only two literary men who have had the sense of beauty and the artist's conscience in a supreme degree. They belonged to the haughty and reserved aristocracy of letters. Hawthorne was like a magician, hidden from the world, creating his beautiful phantasms; Poe was like a banished spirit, abased among men, exercising an intellect, and drawing upon a memory that implied a clearer and higher state of being than that of material and common life. His mental perspicacity and unerringness suggest a super-mortal quality, and make the simple narrative of 'The Gold Bug' appalling; for you will remark that the sentiment of strangeness and terror which it begets is excited without any of Poe's usual resources—that is, of death or murder in any form. One is appalled by the *precision* of the intellect revealed, which is unmatched by any English story-writer.

But it is because of the beauty that Poe created, because of his knowledge of its harmonious conditions, because of his admirable style, the pure and strange elements of his nature, his general and minute method, rather than because of his puzzles, or curious intellectual *inventions* that he is a type of exquisite and brilliant genius. The interest of his inventions would be exhausted at the first reading, if they were not contained in a beautiful literary form—if they were not set before us with a fine literary art, that charms even while it is the medium of the exceptional, and often of the repugnant!

Poe was dominated by intellectual conscience; Hawthorne was dominated by moral conscience. For the proper objects of intellect, Poe had an intellectual *passion*. Hawthorne's passion, on the contrary, spent itself upon moral subjects; you will notice that the texture of his stories is woven about a question of moral responsibility and the transmission of traits. The problem of sin engaged Hawthorne; the processes of crime—that is, pure intellect in action—engaged Poe.

Very few persons have a definite idea of the difference between the unique and unrivalled genius of these two men, who still had positive, if hidden, bonds of sympathy with each other. They were radically, though not obviously different in their work and in the spring of their being. Both had an exquisite sense of the music of thought; both loved the mysterious and *bizarre*; both labored to paint the exceptional and dominate our intellects with an intimate sense of the spiritual and unseen.

Poe began his work in a natural but emphatic tone. He was direct. He took his reader from particular to particular, exercising a power like that of the Ancient Mariner upon the wedding guest. He arrested his reader upon a particular *word*. The emphasis with which he pronounces it, gives a foretaste of the lurking *dénouement*. With particular words he struck the key-tone of his tale; with particular words he rapidly and ominously indicated the unaccustomed road upon which he urged your mind.

Hawthorne works in a different fashion. He deepens the tone of *his* stories by flowing and unnoticeable phrases. He avoids emphasis; by gentle speech he lures you on and on into the depressing labyrinth of human motives and human character, touching with exquisite grace, elaborating a trait, at all times letting you but faintly see the connection of events, but always establishing the fact of the subtle relationships of his characters, and making you feel that his subject has its roots deep in the fluid depths of the ancient, unseen, and baffling world of the past, which the intellect cannot sound, but only dive into, and come forth to tell strange tales of its shadowy experience. To Poe, nothing was shadowy. On the contrary, everything was fearfully distinct and real and positive to his tenacious and penetrating intellect. In Hawthorne, moral conscience was abnormal in its development. In Poe, it did not even exist. Hawthorne, in his method, was an idealist; Poe, in his method, was a realist. But Poe realized the unreal, and Hawthorne idealized the real. But for Poe's poetic sense, he would have been as prosaic and literal, *at all times*, as De Foe. But for Hawthorne's poetic sense, he would have been a droning moralist. Poe confronted the mind with the appalling; Hawthorne begot in it a sense of the unstableness and ungraspableness of human experience. He aimed to give us glimpses of the moral ramifications and far-reaching influence of human actions.

Both Poe and Hawthorne were alike and splendidly endowed with imagination; but Poe had more *invention*—in fact, a most marvellous faculty of invention—and he was the more purely intellectual of the two. Hawthorne was a man of delicate sentiment, of mystical imagination; Poe was a man of little sentiment, but great delicacy of intellectual perception, and had a realistic imagination. Hawthorne incessantly lures the mind from the visible and concrete to the invisible and spiritual. To him, matter was transparent; in his stories he paints material bodies, and gradually resolves them into abstractions; they become allegorical, typical—uncertain incarnations of certain affinities, traits, qualities. Poe never is vague, never indefinite. His most weird and arbitrary imagination is made palpable and positive to the reader. The predominating sentiment of Hawthorne is sad and depressing; that of Poe is melancholy and ominous.

Poe's intellect was direct, inevitable, and unerring; Hawthorne's was indirect, easily turned from its object, and *seemed* purposeless; Poe's always seemed instinct with intense purpose. Hawthorne would have preferred to *hide* all his processes of creation; he shunned observation; he was isolated; happy in evoking beautiful figures, but having no desire to let you see *how* he did it. But Poe, like all *inventors*, took pains to let you see the whole process of his mind; he laid bare his mechanism; he took his listener step by step with him, well aware that he *must* admire a skill and ingenuity so superior to all he had known.

The action of Hawthorne's mind was like a limpid stream that, fed from hidden springs, glints and glides through sunshine, darkens in shadow, loses itself only to surprise you again with the same placid and dark-flowing waters. In point of style Hawthorne is serene and elusive. Poe is nervous, and terse, and positive. Hawthorne's style is characterized by exquisite sequence of thought and imperceptible gradations of tone and sentiment. Poe's is more salient, has a more rapid and impassioned, and always tense expression.

We are to understand Poe by his stories of 'The Gold Bug,' 'Légeia,' 'Eleanora,' 'The Oblong Box,' 'The Murders of the Rue Morgue,' 'The Fall of the House of Usher,' and 'The Black Cat;' we are to understand Hawthorne by 'The House of the Seven Gables,' 'The Scarlet Letter' 'The Minister's Black Veil,' and 'Mosses from an Old Manse.'

Poe's 'House of Usher,' 'Légeia' and 'Eleanora' are the most beautiful examples of his prose, and show the positive influence of De Quincey's 'Opium Eater'. They have great beauty of diction, as well as great *precision* of expression, which is the chief characteristic of the style of 'The Gold Bug.' His word-palette seems to be full and rich, and he uses it to produce sombre and beautiful pictures. He produces all the effects of poetry, save that of flowing and musical sounds.

Poe was unquestionably under the first impression of De Quincey's magazine writings when he wrote his most imaginative stories. They have the same full and impressive diction—long and mournful breathings of an over-burdened *memory*, associated with a wish to define, to explain, to analyze. In 'The Gold Bug,' in 'The Murders of the Rue Morgue,' and in 'The Black Cat,' Poe attained an original expression, and his own mind, pure from all foreign influence, seems to be in full action. It is them that he narrates and analyzes, but gives no room for the reverie and the dream which add so much to the haunting beauty of his 'House of Usher' and 'Légeia.'

De Quincey and Poe had a remarkable tendency to reverie, which was, in both cases, always checked by a passion for analysis. De Quincey, who is the subtlest of all English critics, often broke out of his finest dreams, and interrupted his most perfect analyses, to indulge a trivial and colloquial habit of his mind. Poe never made the same mistake. He never was trivial or garrulous in a story designed to produce a particular impression. . . .

Hawthorne's earlier style shows no positive foreign influence. He was always subdued and restrained; he was pervaded by a fine thoughtfulness. The action of his thought was not intense and incessant, like Poe's, but gentle and diffused. Hawthorne indicated himself at the beginning as a man of intellectual *sentiment*; Poe as a man of intellectual *passion*. The distinction to be made between the *effect* of the literary expression of the two minds is, that Hawthorne charms, and Poe enchains the reader. That Hawthorne has left us a larger quantity of perfect artistic work than Poe, we must attribute to the happier conditions of his life. Hawthorne may have been a little chilled by the want of the pleasant sun of popularity; but Poe was embittered by the success of others, and preminently unfortunate in his destiny. Nothing that he ever wrote begot a sentiment of love; but the gentle and friendly genius of Hawthorne awakens a responsive spirit in the reader.

Hawthorne never seems to feel or think very deeply; he thought comprehensively. Compared with hearty writers like Dickens or Irving, or with impassioned writers like De Quincey or George Sand, he is the chilliest, the most elusive of spirits, and his only merit seems to be that of a graceful habit of thinking, and of a temperate illustration and expression of his subject. His delicate humor oftenest is like the fantasy of an invalid; the merriment is pathetically contrasted with a sad and time-stricken face.

Hawthorne was not closely related to his contemporaries. The vivid and near, and all that characterizes the social life of New England today, seem as remote from him as the ghost of a memory. He is our American type of the 'Dreamer'—a being who could have no place in our thoughts of American life but for Hawthorne.

While Theodore Parker was accumulating facts, and fulminating against a people swayed hither and thither by conscience and selfishness; while Emerson was affronting the formalists and the literalists, Hawthorne was dreaming. He *brooded over* his thoughts; he spent season after season in *reverie*—reverie which is foreign to our idea of the American man. Out of his loneliness, out of his reveries, out of his dreams, he wove the matchless web of a style which shows what Lowell calls the rarest creative intellect, in some respects, since Shakespeare.

The 'Passages from Hawthorne's Note Books' let us see how he perfected his art, and taught himself to use, with such inimitable clearness and delicacy, his means of expression. They are the answer to the question why we never discover shallow or dry or meagre places in his perfectly sustained, evenly flowing, harmoniously and exquisitely *toned* style. Hawthorne seems to have had but one activity, and that activity was the activity of the artist. He used his mind to mirror nature. To see, to feel, to reflect, was his whole life—all of which is contained in the single word *reverie*. The observations of nature which enrich his literary work are not the observations of an active, restless, or acquisitive mind; in his work they seem accidental; they lend themselves, without any effort on his part, to accent his work, to break the monotony of his mood. Many of his pages show great sweetness of temper, an almost feminine feeling toward nature and life.

The alembic of his genius gave forth the material consigned to it colored and mellowed, and oftened saddened in hue, by his unique and pervading personality.

Hawthorne, a descendant of the Puritans, living in a Puritan state, in a Puritan town, without making himself the historian of Puritanism, rendered it with force, gave the spirit and sentiment of its life, in an intense and powerful story which contains the very soul of its faith. Hawthorne, in 'The Scarlet Letter,' has made the work of the historian and judge superfluous as an examination and decision upon Puritanism as a *social fact*. The most intense work of our greatest romancer, without a word of indignation, without an aggressive phrase, embodies Puritanism in a story, and leaves it with a stigma more terrible than the scarlet letter it seared upon the heart of the wretched Dimmesdale, and fixed upon the black robe of the heroic martyr, Hester Prynne. With what fine and beautiful art he lets you *see* the monstrous pretensions of the legal spirit, which was the soul of Puritanism, and its brutal blunder in intruding itself between a woman's heart and its most sacred need— 'sacred even in its pollution.' In the treatment of his theme, how fine, how elevated, how comprehensive is Hawthorne! With what indulgence and sympathy, with what reverence does he consider the mournful and mute woman, blank-eyed and helpless before her judges, who seek to unmask the secret of her heart. Poor Hester Prynne! how different her treatment from the treatment of the Syrian Magdalen! Noble and outraged, much suffering, silent woman! victim of legal, obtuse, and mechanical minds, she shall forever exist as the type of her sex wronged by bigotry, victim of a harsh, unelastic social faith!

Among Hawthorne's *creations*, it seems to me that Clifford in 'The House of Seven Gables,' and Donatello in 'The Marble Faun,' are the most remarkable. Clifford is an example of portrait art; Donatello is a beautiful and palpable creation. They illustrate the two phases of his genius. The portrait of Clifford in the chapter entitled 'The Guest,' is in every particular an uncommon and impressive piece of work. Poe never did anything so subtle, so floating and vague, and at the same time vivid and sure, as the description and analysis of Clifford. . . .

[Quotes ch. 7, 'The expression of' to 'to destroy it', with several deletions.]

After this matchless rendering of traits, Hawthorne gives a matchless analysis of Clifford's nature—than which I know of nothing more finely distilled in expression, more discriminating in thought. It is Hawthorne's masterpiece, with which his Faun only is comparable.

You will observe that in all of Hawthorne's works the remarkable and characteristic thing is the incessant action of the moral faculty, exquisitely toned by the artistic sentiment! The moral sense and the artistic sense make of him a channel of issue, and it is their incessant play of expression which begets the distrust and doubt of the reader upon all the old, creed-closed questions of life. He is the finest distillation of the New England mind, and he has idealized all that is local in New England life. No marble can be too white or too exquisitely sculptured to symbolize his pure and beautiful genius, and suggest the gratitude which his countrymen owe to him.

Edgar A. Poe, the gift of the South to American liteature, was more selfish, and more unfortunate in his life than Hawthorne. In him the moral faculty had no play—everything was concentrated to feed his sense of beauty and strangeness. He was no shifting questioner and elusive thinker, but ardent, intense; and his mind was the intellectual centre of the anomalous! But what an imperial imagination, and how august and music-voiced was his memory! 'The Raven' and the prose poem, 'Légeia,' are magical in their influence. All that there is of beauty and regret and strangeness to be employed by the literary artist was employed by Poe in 'Légeia.' He awakens the imagination, touches the profoundest emotions of an impassioned lover, and by associating his creation with the idea of death, produces that wild melancholy, that rebellious and protesting sentiment of regret, which possesses us at the memory of a beautiful, beloved, but vanished object! . . . Poe had what I may call, preëminently, a *beautiful* mind—all its highest and characteristic manifestations were harmonious and enchaining. His combination of the strange or the unusual with the lovely or symmetrical, is his claim to be considered original. No writer ever reached a more personal expression of the beautiful than Poe. He was modern in all his traits, romantic as no other American writer, delighting in the horrible as the natural antithesis of his radiant and mournful ideal beauty. The women that live in his stories, the ideal women of a modern epoch, pale, sick, luminous, wide-eyed, preyed upon by 'incurable melancholy,' versed in the most recondite knowledge, vibrative, and 'speaking with a voice that resembles music,' and as from profound depths, have no existence outside of Poe's beautiful and strange imagination. He created them as Eugene Delacroix created his women, who are remarkable, impassioned, profound, and make you think. Poe's 'Lenore,' 'Légeia,' and 'Morella,' are the creations of a poet—ideal and natural as the Venus of Milo is ideal and natural, but in no sense *realistic*, and having no relation to the photographic and literal portraits of women such as we find in modern novels. It is for them that Poe has drawn upon his poetical nature; they are the issue of his sense of beauty, which in him was more imperative in its needs, and more creative in its energy than the same sense in Hawthorne. Among Americans, I repeat, Poe and Hawthorne are the only two literary men who have had the sense of beauty and the artist's conscience in a supreme degree; and in Poe it was more isolated, or unalloyed, than in Hawthorne.

POSTHUMOUS PUBLICATIONS:
THE NOTE-BOOKS
(A) PASSAGES FROM THE AMERICAN NOTE-BOOKS

1868–9

129. Unsigned review in the *Westminster Review*

1869, xci, 135

The biographical element in the passages from the American Note-books of Nathaniel Hawthorne is but slender. There is a meagre un-satisfactory notice of his sojourn at Brook Farm, touched throughout with a spirit of irony and quizzical humour; there are also some pleasing half poetical accounts of his children's life, doings and sayings, and numerous sketchings of the men and women that crossed his path on the journey of life, Emerson, Thoreau, Ticknor, Margaret Fuller and others. There is, moreover, in these 'Note-books,' evidence of much minute laborious observation and vigilant inspection of natural and social phenomena, but mainly of the superficial character. There is picturesque gossip too about woods, waters, and skies, whimsical comment and grotesque and ghastly fancy. 'What is the price of a day's labour in Lapland (he asks), where the sun never sets for six months.' Solomon dies, (he assumes) during the building of the temple, but his body remains leaning on a staff, and overlooking the workmen as if it were alive. The 'Note-books' on the whole make a curious study for admirers of the author, but they will add nothing to his reputation, and are suited rather to kill time than to inform or invigorate the understanding.

130. From an unsigned review in the *British Quarterly Review*

April 1869, xlix, 574–5

We are inclined to think that injustice is done to an author by the publication of a book like this. The memoranda of a literary man are fragments corresponding to the rough 'studies' of an artist, which may or may not be worked up into pictures yet to be. The author of 'Our Old Home,' in the preparation of which many rough sketches hastily dashed off were afterwards polished and edited, would never have sanctioned the issue of a selection so crude and miscellaneous as that now offered to his admirers.

There is, however, in these copious extracts much that is interesting to an English reader. They are of two kinds: some are portions of a diary relating the events of the writer's life, others are entries in an intellectual day-book; jottings of thoughts which passed through the mind, and of facts met with in reading or conversation. For the reader's relief these are alternated—a few pages of very miscellaneous paragraphs coming in here and there as a variation from the journal. We do not hesitate to give the preference to the *narrative* portions of the volumes. Many of the fancies put on record are curious and grotesque; some of them are ingeniously and painfully unnatural. But Mr. Hawthorne's observant faculty was vigilant and acute, and his command of words ready and felicitous. He took a great pleasure in inferring, from the dress, language, and demeanour of persons whom he casually met, their occupation, culture, and character; and his remarks were often discriminating. His descriptions of New England scenery under the changing seasons of the year are graphic, and sometimes as elaborate and minute as a water-colour study of William Hunt. Hence as they stand by themselves they are occasionally tedious; though, if worked up by the literary artist, they would doubtless have added interest and meaning to his tales.

The second of these volumes is decidedly the more entertaining, embracing, as it does, the period of Mr. Hawthorne's literary activity, but terminating before his removal to England. Not that there are many allusions to his works or to his habits of composition; but he was, at this period of his life, brought into association with several distinguished men. . . .

One of the most interesting portions of these 'Notes' is that which relates to the writer's share in the experiment of the community at Brook Farm—the basis, in fact, of the 'Blithedale Romance'. . . . The sunniest portion of the Diary is that which concerns Mr. Hawthorne's early married life near Concord. There is also a pleasing account of a summer holiday spent in the pretty islands off the New Hampshire coast.

(B) PASSAGES FROM THE ENGLISH NOTE-BOOKS

1870

---

131. G[eorge] S. Hillard, from a review in the *Atlantic Monthly*

September 1870, xxvi, 257–72

Hillard (1808–79), a lawyer and man of letters, was one of Hawthorne's closest friends, contributing to his support during the difficult years of the 1840s. His essays frequently appeared in the *North American Review*.

. . . The English and the American Note-Books have alike a peculiar value as illustrating the mind and character of the author. They form, indeed, a sort of autobiography. The question has been sometimes asked, Why have we no memoir of a man of such eminent rank in literature as Hawthorne? and the answer is, first, that it was his own emphatic and frequently expressed desire that nothing of the kind should be done; and, second, that in his case there are few materials for biography. The facts of his life could be put into two such pages as the reader now has before him. It was a very uneventful life, marked by long intervals of silence, wherein, however, the fruits of observation and reflection were slowly ripening on the bough. His birth, his college life, his service in the Custom-House at Boston, his brief experience at Brook Farm, his marriage, his official life in Salem, his consulship in Liverpool, his residence in Italy, his return home, his death,—these are really all the events in his life. For long years, while his classmates were busy in their several professions, making money, earning distinction, he was content to be a dreamer and seem to be an idler in the land. But idler he was not, and hardly a dreamer: he was an observer and a thinker. He was always a diligent worker, and at no easy calling. His

443

work was with the pen,—careful, conscientious, painstaking work, of all forms of intellectual labor that which is attended with the greatest waste of nervous energy. His matchless style was the product of long and laborious training. Much of what he wrote was never published, and much does not now exist in manuscript. He had no weak fondness for his own intellectual offspring, and never were his productions submitted to so merciless a criticism as his own. Hawthorne's life is to be read in his works, and especially in his Note-Books. His biography is simply a record of the growth of his mind. His Note-Books paint him as he was, his reserve included. He does not bare himself to the public gaze like Montaigne and Rousseau; but the essays of Montaigne and the confessions of Rousseau do not present a mind and character of more marked individuality than do the journals of Hawthorne. More of his life and conversation than these give the public is never likely to know, but he who reads them carefully can form a correct estimate of what manner of man he was. . . .

132. Unsigned review, in the *North British Review*

October 1870, liii, 149–50

The publication of *Passages from the English Note Books of Nathaniel Hawthorne* is described by the editor as the best answer that can be made to the demand for a life of that author. With the omission of the passages afterwards worked up into *Our Old Home*, the journals are published as they were written; and, though they throw less light on the literary method of the writer than the American notes belonging to the time of his greatest fertility in composition, they perhaps do more to illustrate his personal character. But their chief merit is that of reflecting without disguise the prepossessions of an average American travelling in Europe. In his own country, Hawthorne's appetite for strange emotions led him to treasure up notes of the external oddities of the persons he met with, such oddities being, on the whole, more numerous in America than in England, and also to record the slightest fancy, suggested by external objects, which gave promise of producing, when sufficiently laboured, the quaint weird effect in which he excelled. What he seems to have sought in England is sensations, or, as he phrased it, 'impressions' of a general character, which he looked forward to converting subsequently into so much eloquent or picturesque writing for his countrymen. Like most ordinary travellers, he was not in search of any particular pleasure or advantage; one piece of knowledge is much the same to him as another. But he had a true traveller's sense of duty. Without caring for architecture, he gazed at cathedrals till he thought he admired York Minster; without any taste for art, he haunted the National Gallery and the British Museum till he had persuaded himself that there might be beauty in Italian painting and the Elgin Marbles; though sincerely convinced that the present fashion for the picturesque in scenery is an ephemeral one, he rambled about the English and Scottish lakes till he was fairly tired of admiring. And as he recorded with impartial candour both disappointment and delight, and was seized by both alternately on nearly every occasion, it is not easy to say what conclusions he had arrived at by the end of his stay.

In some respects there is not much difference between these notes and the ordinary books which half-educated travellers often publish on their return from a short visit to some foreign land. Hawthorne makes the mistake common to tourists, of looking upon the country he was visiting as one large show-room. He suspects every public character who is pointed out to him of being conscious of his observation; and he has a comical sense of injury when any famous sight falls short, as he thinks, of what the new world has a right to expect from the old. He had formed beforehand a general notion of what the ideal English village or town or country-house ought to be like, and also of the emotions which the sight of them ought to call up in the breast of an imaginative author; if the result answers to his expectations, he extols the spectacle in terms which no mere spectacle can exactly deserve, whilst in the more common case of disenchantment he thinks it necessary to find a reason deep in the nature of things. The Zoological Gardens in London he condemns as not coming up to the utopian idea of 'a garden of Eden, where all the animal kingdom had regained a happy home.' The Crystal Palace fares still worse, as 'uncongenial with the English character, without privacy, destitute of mass, weight, and shadow, unsusceptible of ivy, lichens, or any mellowness from age.' The notion that a nation shows its historical antiquity by some visible equivalent for wrinkles and grey hair is prominent throughout; and the author avows that Conway Castle and the other Welsh ruins 'quite fill up one's idea.' He does not seem to suspect that the 'idea' in question is not only purely subjective but also a little mechanical; and when he goes the length of complaining that the Douglas whose body was thrown out of the window at Stirling Castle only fell fifteen or twenty feet, instead of 'tumbling headlong from a great height,' he recalls Goethe's sentimental prince, who wanted rocks, ruins, moonlight, and history, all made to order. But ancient castles and abbeys are on the whole fair game for the imagination: he attempts a more arduous task when he endeavours to seize the 'general effect' of the Exhibition of Pictures at Manchester or the Natural History Collections at the British Museum. From the streets of London to the first barefooted beggar he saw in Liverpool, he was bent upon studying everything, entering into the spirit of everything, and lastly, and principally, describing everything in terms worthy of his literary reputation. He would have thought it treason to his imaginative faculties to suspect that miles of glass-cases or painted canvas really have no dominant idea, and that they were simply put together for the convenience of classes to which he did not belong—the students, that is, of science and art.

The social impressions of a tolerably candid stranger are always instructive; and Hawthorne, who never forgets that he *is* a stranger, may probably be trusted when, in spite of his prepossessions, the only national characteristics that strike him as strange are such trifles as the arrangement of butchers' shops, the dress of women of the working classes, easier intercourse between rich and poor, and such traveller's wonders as a labouring man eating oysters in a ferry-boat. He regards England as constantly posing to herself and her colonies as a model of dignified and venerable old age; and, in the main, he misrepresents her as little as is compatible with this idea. The notes are the work of a good-tempered, impressionable man, who succeeded in one narrow field of literature; but they show little real ability, and none of that artificial mastery of men and things which a liberal education seldom fails to give, at least in appearance.

133. [Henry James], from a review in *The Nation*

14 March 1872, xiv, 172–3

This review, the first of several lengthy comments James was to make on Hawthorne, appeared when James was living in America and yearning to return to Europe. It reflects, among other things, his dissatisfaction with the materials America offered for fiction.

Mr. Hawthorne is having a posthumous productivity almost as active as that of his lifetime. Six volumes have been compounded from his private journals, an unfinished romance is doing duty as a 'serial,' and a number of his letters, with other personal memorials, have been given to the world. These liberal excisions from the privacy of so reserved and shade-seeking a genius suggest forcibly the general question of the proper limits of curiosity as to that passive personality of an artist of which the elements are scattered in portfolios and table-drawers. It is becoming very plain, however, that whatever the proper limits may be, the actual limits will be fixed only by a total exhaustion of matter. There is much that is very worthy and signally serviceable to art itself in this curiosity, as well as much that is idle and grossly defiant of the artist's presumptive desire to limit and define the ground of his appeal to fame. The question is really brought to an open dispute between this instinct of self-conservatism and the general fondness for squeezing an orange dry. Artists, of course, as time goes on, will be likely to take the alarm, empty their table-drawers, and level the approachers to their privacy. The critics, psychologists, and gossip-mongers may then glean amid the stubble.

447

Our remarks are not provoked by any visible detriment conferred on Mr. Hawthorne's fame by these recent publications. He has very fairly withstood the ordeal; which, indeed, is as little as possible an ordeal in his case, owing to the superficial character of the documents. His journals throw but little light on his personal feelings, and even less on his genius *per se*. Their general effect is difficult to express. They deepen our sense of that genius, while they singularly diminish our impression of his general intellectual power. There can be no better proof of his genius than that these common daily scribblings should unite so irresistible a charm with so little distinctive force. They represent him, judged with any real critical rigor, as superficial, un-informed, incurious, inappreciative; but from beginning to end they cast no faintest shadow upon the purity of his peculiar gift. Our own sole complaint has been not that they should have been published, but that there are not a dozen volumes more. The truth is that Mr. Haw-thorne belonged to the race of magicians, and that his genius took its nutriment as insensibly—to our vision—as the flowers take the dew. He was the last man to have attempted to explain himself, and these pages offer no adequate explanation of him. They show us one of the gentlest, lightest, and most leisurely of observers, strolling at his ease among foreign sights in blessed intellectual irresponsibility, and weav-ing his chance impressions into a tissue as smooth as fireside gossip. Mr. Hawthorne had what belongs to genius—a style individual and delight-ful; he seems to have written as well for himself as he did for others— to have written from the impulse to keep up a sort of literary tradition in a career singularly devoid of the air of professional authorship; but, as regards substance, his narrative flows along in a current as fitfully diffuse and shallow as a regular correspondence with a distant friend— a friend familiar but not intimate—sensitive but not exacting. With all allowance for suppressions, his entries are never confidential; the author seems to have been reserved even with himself. They are a record of things slight and usual. Some of the facts noted are incredibly minute; they imply a peculiar *leisure* of attention. How little his journal was the receptacle of Mr. Hawthorne's deeper feelings is indicated by the fact that during a long and dangerous illness of his daughter in Rome, which he speaks of later as 'a trouble that pierced into his very vitals,' he never touched his pen.

These volumes of Italian notes, charming as they are, are on the whole less rich and substantial than those on England. The theme, in this case, is evidently less congenial. 'As I walked by the hedges yesterday,' he writes at Siena, 'I could have fancied that the olive trunks were those of apple-trees, and that I were in one or other of the two lands that I love better than Italy.' There are in these volumes few sentences so deeply sympathetic as that in which he declares that 'of all the lovely closes that I ever beheld, that of Peterborough Cathedral is to me the most delightful; so quiet is it, so solemnly and nobly cheerful, so verdant, so sweetly shadowed, and so presided over by the stately minster and surrounded by the ancient and comely habitations of Christian men.' The book is full, nevertheless, of the same spirit of serene, detached contemplation; equally full of refined and gently suggestive description. Excessively detached Mr. Hawthorne remains, from the first, from Continental life, touching it throughout mistrust-fully, shrinkingly, and at the rare points at which he had, for the time, unlearnt his nationality. The few pages describing his arrival in France betray the irreconcilable foreignness of his instincts with a frank simplicity which provokes a smile. 'Nothing really thrives here,' he says of Paris; 'man and vegetables have but an artificial life, like flowers stuck in a little mould, but never taking root.' The great city had said but little to him; he was deaf to the Parisian harmonies. Just so it is under protest, as it were, that he looks at things in Italy. The strange-ness, the remoteness, the Italianism of manners and objects, seem to oppress and confound him. He walks about bending a puzzled, in-effective gaze at things, full of a mild, genial desire to apprehend and penetrate, but with the light wings of his fancy just touching the surface of the massive consistency of fact about him, and with an air of good-humored confession that he is too simply an idle Yankee *flâneur* to conclude on such matters. The main impression produced by his observations is that of his simplicity. They spring not only from an unsophisticated, but from an excessively natural mind. Never, surely, was a man of literary genius less a man of letters. He looks at things as little as possible in that composite historic light which forms the atmosphere of many imaginations. There is something extremely pleasing in this simplicity, within which the character of the man rounds itself so completely and so firmly. His judgments abound in common sense; touched as they often are by fancy, they are never distorted by it. His errors and illusions never impugn his fundamental wisdom; even when (as is almost the case in his appreciation of works of art) they provoke a respectful smile, they contain some saving particle of sagacity. Fantastic romancer as he was, he here refutes conclusively the common charge that he was either a melancholy or a morbid genius.

449

He had a native relish for the picturesque greys and browns of life; but these pages betray a childlike evenness and clearness of intellectual temper. Melancholy lies deeper than the line on which his fancy moved. Toward the end of his life, we believe, his cheerfulness gave way; but was not this in some degree owing to a final sense of the inability of his fancy to grope with fact?—fact having then grown rather portentous and overshadowing. . . . There seems from the first to have been nothing inflammable in his perception of things; there was a comfortable want of *eagerness* in his mind. Little by little, however, we see him thaw and relent, and in his desultory strolls project a ray of his gentle fancy, like a gleam of autumnal American sunshine, over the churches, statues, and ruins. From the first he is admirably honest. He never pretends to be interested unless he has been really touched; and he never attempts to work himself into a worshipful glow because it is expected of a man of fancy. He has the tone of expecting very little of himself in this line, and when by chance he is pleased and excited, he records it with modest surprise. He confesses to indifference, to ignorance and weariness, with a sturdy candor which has far more dignity, to our sense, than the merely mechanical heat of less sincere spirits. Mr. Hawthorne would assent to nothing that he could not understand; his understanding on the general æsthetic line was not comprehensive; and the attitude in which he figures to the mind's eye throughout the book is that of turning away from some dusky altar-piece with a good-humored shrug, which is not in the least a condemnation of the work, but simply an admission of personal incompetency. The pictures and statues of Italy were a heavy burden upon his conscience; though indeed, in a manner, his conscience bore them lightly—it being only at the end of three months of his Roman residence that he paid his respects to the 'Transfiguration,' and a month later that he repaired to the Sistine Chapel. He was not, we take it, without taste; but his taste was not robust. He is 'willing to accept Raphael's violin-player as a good picture'; but he prefers 'Mr. Brown,' the American landscapist, to Claude. He comes to the singular conclusion that 'the most delicate, if not the highest, charm of a picture is evanescent, and that we continue to admire pictures prescriptively and by tradition, after the qualities that first won them their fame have vanished.' The 'most delicate charm' to Mr. Hawthorne was apparently simply the primal freshness and brightness of paint and varnish, and—not to put too fine a point upon it—the new gilding of the frame. 'Mr. Thompson,' too, shares his admiration with Mr. Brown: 'I do not think there is a better painter

... living—among Americans at least; not one so earnest, faithful, and religious in his worship of art. I had rather look at his pictures than at any, except the very old masters; and taking into consideration only the comparative pleasure to be derived, I would not except more than one or two of those.' From the statues, as a general thing, he derives little profit. Every now and then he utters a word which seems to explain his indifference by the Cis-Atlantic remoteness of his point of view. He remains unreconciled to the nudity of the marbles. 'I do not altogether see the necessity of our sculpturing another nakedness. Man is no longer a naked animal; his clothes are as natural to him as his skin, and we have no more right to undress him than to flay him.' This is the sentiment of a man to whom sculpture was a sealed book; though, indeed, in a momentary 'burst of confidence,' as Mr. Dickens says, he pronounces the Pompey of the Spada Palace 'worth the whole sculpture gallery of the Vatican'; and when he gets to Florence, gallantly loses his heart to the Venus de' Medici and pays generous tribute to Michael Angelo's Medicean sepulchres. He has indeed, throughout, that mark of the man of genius that he may at any moment surprise you by some extremely happy 'hit,' as when he detects at a glance, apparently, the want of force in Andrea del Sarto, or declares in the Florentine cathedral that 'any little Norman church in England would impress me as much and more. There is something, I do not know what, but it is in the region of the heart, rather than in the intellect, that Italian architecture, of whatever age or style, never seems to reach.' It is in his occasional sketches of the persons—often notabilities—whom he meets that his perception seems finest and firmest. We lack space to quote, in especial, a notice of Miss Bremer and of a little tea-party of her giving, in a modest Roman chamber overhanging the Tarpeian Rock, in which in a few kindly touches the Swedish romancer is herself suffused with the atmosphere of romance, and relegated to quaint and shadowy sisterhood with the inmates of the 'House of the Seven Gables.'

Mr. Hawthorne left Rome late in the spring, and travelled slowly up to Florence in the blessed fashion of the days when, seen through the open front of a crawling *vettura*, with her clamorous beggars, her black-walled mountain-towns, the unfolding romance of her landscape, Italy was seen as she really needs and deserves to be seen. Mr. Hawthorne's minute and vivid record of this journey is the most delightful portion of these volumes, and, indeed, makes well-nigh as charming a story as that of the enchanted progress of the two friends in the Marble Faun from Monte Beni to Perugia. He spent the summer in Florence—first

451

in town, where he records many talks with Mr. Powers, the sculptor, whom he invests, as he is apt to do the persons who impress him, with a sort of mellow vividness of portraiture which deepens what is gracious in his observations, and gains absolution for what is shrewd; and afterwards at a castellated suburban villa—the original of the dwelling of his Donatello. This last fact, by the way, is a little of a disenchantment, as we had fancied that gentle hero living signorial-wise in some deeper Tuscan rurality. Mr. Hawthorne took Florence quietly and soberly—as became the summer weather; and bids it farewell in the gravity of this sweet-sounding passage, which we quote as one of many:

[Quotes entry of 29 September 1858: 'This evening I' to 'evening as this'.]

Mr. Hawthorne returned to Rome in the autumn, spending some time in Siena on his way. His pictures of the strange, dark little mountain-cities of Radicofani and Bolsena, on his downward journey, are masterpieces of literary etching. It is impossible to render better that impression as of a mild nightmare which such places make upon the American traveller. 'Rome certainly draws itself into my heart,' he writes on his return, 'as I think even London, or even Concord itself, or even old sleepy Salem never did and never will.' The result of this increased familiarity was the mature conception of the romance of his 'Marble Faun.' He journalizes again, but at rarer intervals, though his entries retain to the last a certain appealing charm which we find it hard to define. It lies partly perhaps in what we hinted at above—in the fascination of seeing so potent a sovereign in his own fair kingdom of fantasy so busily writing himself simple, during such a succession of months, as to the dense realities of the world. Mr. Hawthorne's, however, was a rich simplicity. These pages give a strong impression of moral integrity and elevation. And, more than in other ways, they are interesting from their strong national flavor. Exposed late in life to European influences, Mr. Hawthorne was but superficially affected by them—far less so than would be the case with a mind of the same temper growing up among us to-day. We seem to see him strolling through churches and galleries as the last pure American—attesting by his shy responses to dark canvas and cold marble his loyalty to a simpler and less encumbered civilization. This image deepens that tender personal regard which it is the constant effect of these volumes to produce.

134. Dorville Libby: Hawthorne and the supernatural, from 'The Supernatural in Hawthorne', in the *Overland Monthly*

February, 1869, ii, 138–43

Although Libby is a totally unknown writer, his essay is included here because it expresses a widespread attitude toward an aspect of Hawthorne's work that was much discussed. Bret Harte was the editor of the *Overland Monthly*, a San Francisco journal, at this time.

It would be hard to find a man or woman who does not cherish some superstition. Every day of the year, every event of life, however fortuitous and insignificant, by the busy imagination of somebody is sacredly held as a sign of something else, with which it has no possible connection by any known laws. Moreover, whether we attribute it to childish credulity or an instinctive recognition of other spheres of life, there is a deep-seated and wide-spread belief in what is spoken of in general as the Supernatural. Most of us have had our own experiences; little skirmishes on the boundaries of what we know as the real with the dwellers in the vague realm beyond. The man must be strangely unimaginative who can pass a country graveyard alone, at midnight, with no more dread than a village market, at mid-day; and surely the hush and awe with which even the rude and thoughtless approach the body of the dead, cannot be born entirely of religion.

The ghost-story, with its superabundance of marvels and horrors, is told with zest, and heard with eagerness in town and country. Nearly every neighborhood has its own. Old sailors gather in some loft on shore when the storm is raging, and spin their yarns with many a mingled thread of signs and wonders and wild adventures with the spirits that roam about the mysterious sea. Farmers' sons gather closely about the hearth-fire, when the solemn stillness of the night arouses anew their desire to have their wits scared out of them by some ghostly tale, and their sleep invaded by spectre-troubled dreams. Haunted

453

houses abound; and neighbors' voices take a solemn tone as they tell of doors opening without human hands, and sepulchral groans, and cold, white feet that steal across the floors with a sound like rigid marble.

From the Witch of Endor, with her 'familiar spirit,' to the clairvoyant of to-day, the race of fortune-tellers has never died out. The faith of the King of Israel still fills the heart of the trembling visitor, in the presence of one who claims to read the future, and hold communion with the dead.

It must be remembered that the supernatural, from its very nature, admits no proof, and hence challenges doubt. When, in addition to this, credulity on the one side coöperates with design and interest on the other, this faith easily runs into the most utter absurdities. Spiritualists have seized upon this ready-made faith, swept together a multitude of occult and out-of-the-way phenomena, roughly classified the crude material, with a little addition of theory, and assumed for their so-called system the holy name of a religion. And this, too, has its devoted adherents and unquestioning believers.

Indeed, the supernatural is an inseparable element in all religions, true as well as false. As for Heathenism, superstitition is but another name for it in all its thousand forms. The higher culture of the Greeks and Romans embodied it in a more engaging way in their beautiful mythology. The boundaries between the worlds of life and of spirit were but ill defined. The mountain-tops were common to men and gods; caves opened into the realm of shades; fountains were peopled with beings, part human, part divine, cheering them with smiles or darkening them with tears. And in our own Christianity, where both science and revelation have come to our aid, the same element is involved, and to an equal degree, giving us only the advantage of knowing better where Nature stops and miracles begin.

Such an element could not fail to be abundantly presented in literature. This is especially true in the writings of Nathaniel Hawthorne. We do not mean to say, that in this he has pandered to the popular taste—for popular, in the common acceptation of the term, his books have never been, and probably never will be. Had he introduced a genuine ghost or two into each of his stories, with the conventional peculiarities of step and attire, it would have been much to the advantage of his publishers. His ghosts (if such we may call them), and all his ghostly paraphernalia, have too little of the startling to meet the general taste. In these stirring days the people demand something active and fast about their ghosts, as well as everything else—ranting, roaring ghosts, that can perform feats of rapping and table-tipping, and make themselves practical. His characters resemble men and women acting like sensible ghosts, rather than ghosts acting like crazy men and women.

Hawthorne never introduces the supernatural awkwardly—never *lugs* it in. There is none of the cheap machinery of the sensation story-writer about it, nor the trickery and smoke and concave mirror of stage tragedy. He never even brings it in directly. He rather makes it felt as a spirit than seen as a real presence. There is not in all his works a veritable ghost, presented as such, appearing at opportune moments, and giving indispensable warnings. He never even does violence to the probable. Forests, rivers, clouds, shadows, are never other than their true and natural selves under his pen; but all their varying expressions, their sub-tile suggestions, and reciprocal relations to the mood of the beholder, are portrayed with such consummate art, that the reader feels that they are as well entitled to be called characters as the strange men and women who move among them.

There are other relations which we sustain to the world around us than those coming through the medium of the senses. Nor are these relations of external nature to whatever is spiritual within us incompat-ible with its strictly material relations. What are commonly known as 'fairy tales' assume this incompatibility, and portray the spiritual rela-tions—often fantastically overwrought—to the utter subversion of all natural laws. Hawthorne's are not fairy stories. In dealing with either nature or art he never violates physical laws. He would never have had Hamlet's dead father walk; and yet the strong influences of the night would have aroused an equal spirit of revenge. He would never have told the weird story of the Ancient Mariner—and yet from earth, air, sea, he would have drawn the kindly lesson. He would never have made Poe's Raven speak a word—and yet a bowing of the head and a droop-ing of the wings would have told all that is said in 'nevermore.'

A superficial reader would be likely to urge, as an objection to our author, the unquestionable fact that he never presents what we com-monly call a natural character. The characters of Dickens, with all their grotesque exaggeration, never fail to suggest to us individuals whom they resemble, or classes which they typify. This can by no means be said of Hawthorne's. Some of them have scarcely any trait of humanity but the outward form, and 'even that not always so warmly clad in its habiliments of flesh and blood as to be taken into the reader's mind without a shiver.'

The criticism arises from a misapprehension of the design of the author. His characters are not to be considered men and women so much as motives and passions personified, with just enough human nature to fulfil the demands of plot, and take them through to the ultimate establishment of the principle at which he aims. His books are not written merely to sell; to catch the popular favor by sounding words, showy imagery and clap-trap incident; to unfold an intricate plot which has no valuable relation to any of the real concerns of life; to flatter national pride, or promote a moral reform. Their province is more exalted. They treat of the most intricate problems of human nature in all its higher relations. They are not so much novels as allegories, not allegories so much as ethical treatises, and perhaps rather religious than ethical. The Scarlet Letter is not a mere story of Hester Prynne, Rev. Arthur Dimmesdale, little Pearl, and old Roger Chillingworth. It is rather a masterly exposition of the normal relations of sin, hate, human justice, and Divine retribution. Here is to be found the great reason why he is not more generally read. His books mean too much. Many are interested in stories with natural characters and thrilling incidents, but few can appreciate a serious, and perhaps disagreeable, lesson, cunningly conveyed through characters, each one essential to its deduction.

We have said that religion and the supernatural are intimately connected, or rather, that the supernatural is involved in religion, and its existence presupposed by it. As might be expected, nearly all of Hawthorne's works deals with themes essentially religious, as involving our relations and responsibilities to a higher power. A few of them are cheerful in tone. Of his more important works, the Marble Faun is the best illustration of this class. The aim seems to be to show how sin and penitence therefor can develop a soul. Evil passions, through much sorrow, work their own cure. The shriek that came quivering up from the Model as he was hurled over the Tarpeian Rock by murderous hands, awoke the sleeping soul of Donatello. The sight of the dead Capuchin, the sad parting from Miriam, the sorrowful days at Monte Beni, all were stern teachers. His soul grew to a strength and beauty it had never known or conceived before. And when at length the Bronze Pontiff has bestowed his benediction, and they, the guilty and penitent, once more brought together, are parting from their friends forever, with Hilda we have 'hopeful hearts and see sunlight on the mountain-tops.'

Most of his stories, however, are sombre in style and gloomy in moral. Worthy descendant of the Pilgrims, he portrays a Divine government of the world by penalties alone, as man governs a rebellious province. Of the garden of Eden, he thinks only of the curse; of Calvary, he dwells only on the wickedness that called for and consummated the inconceivable sacrifice; of all God's attributes he has an oppressive sense of his terrible power and uncompromising justice. He has a love that appears almost morbid for the darker mysteries of our spiritual relations. He especially dwells upon the mission of sin in its manifold relations to us, both temporal and eternal; hunts the question through the past; grapples with it in the present, and peers eagerly after it into the dim future—'that immenser mystery which encircles our little life, and into which our friends vanish from us one by one.'

In the preface to The House of the Seven Gables he sets forth its moral in the following words: 'The truth that the wrong-doing of one generation lives into the successive ones, and, divesting itself of every temporary advantage, becomes a pure and uncontrollable mischief.' The ill-gotten gains fall upon the holders. Decay settles resistlessly upon both house and family, bringing to the one all its spectral attributes, and all its petty miseries to the other. A favorite topic is the evil resultant from one idea in life, as science in 'Rapaccini's Daughter,' and the 'Birth-Mark'; selfishness in the 'Bosom Serpent,' the unpardonable sin in 'Ethan Brand,' and a particular moral reform in Blithedale Romance. Indeed, he seems to have very little love for the whole genus of reformers, for, in the last-named book, he speaks of 'that steam-engine of the devil's own contrivance—a philanthropist.'

But he often gives us still gloomier lessons. No dark-browed divine ever set forth more uncompromising doctrine than this modern storyteller. He represents conscience not as a kind and genial guide, but an avenger, keen and swift. Roger Malvin's Burial portrays life-long misery for neglect of what might seem a very questionable duty. For having even dreamed of witchcraft and scandalous wickedness, all gladness faded utterly from the life of young Goodman Brown and 'his dying hour was gloom.' Nothing could be more painful than the vivid portrayal of the relentlessness of sin in the story of the Scarlet Letter. The flaming emblem of her crime burnt into the very heart of Hester Prynne, and the old physician was the very incarnation of merciless and systematic retribution. The pervading gloom of the picture is even deepened by the gleam of delusive hope that momentarily cheered the two sufferers at their meeting in the forest, and the whims, now child-like, now elfish, of little Pearl.

There is always a kind of dreaminess about his characters which reminds one of the wonderful descriptions in Undine. The characters in the Marble Faun well illustrate this trait. Kenyon, perhaps, is quite human, but ugly phantoms sometimes steal out of his brain, and crouch in marble in his studio. Hilda is a pure, conscientious girl, but spirits attended her in the shape of beautiful doves—spirits ready at her will to flutter from her trembling finger and touch the throbbing cheek of Kenyon, and return with both thrills in their snowy wings. Miriam is not a ghost herself, but sadly haunted by one. Donatello is the true Faun of the ancients, but humanized and spiritualized with all Hawthorne's inimitable art. But the Model—how ghostly was his unwelcome guidance of the lost Miriam from the recesses of the tombs! How fiendishly did he shriek as he was hurled over the Tarpeian Rock! How did his wicked presence fill the church as the guilty pair looked upon him, and saw the little rill of blood trickle from his mouth and hide in his dusky beard!

Here it may be well to answer the objection often urged, that Hawthorne does not clear up his mysteries. The truly supernatural admits no clearing up. It is the especial privilege of the romancer to make this departure from the strictly probable, and thus avail himself of the charm of mystery. If you take this away, the romance degenerates into a novel, and probably a very tame one at that.

This peculiarity is perceptible not in his characters alone, but in all their surroundings. His landscapes, true to life as they may be in a certain sense, have yet a vagueness that well befits the dreamy people who flit about them. Everything has meaning. The woods, the brook, the quaint old streets of the city, seem almost of themselves to tell the story of Hester and her paramour, while the scarlet badge figures as one of the chief actors, so many attributes has it of conscious, thinking life. The House of the Seven Gables is a dismal old thing, haunted by a dead man's curse. Old Hepzibah, who moves so dolefully about it in its latter days with her forbidding frown, is a fitting emblem of its faded gentility and wretched hospitality. The old house could not have smiled into semblance of a home had a hundred light-hearted Phœbes flitted about it. One even wonders how the artist found sunlight enough among its mists of a century to ply his cheerful trade, or how Alice's posies drew beauty and fragrance from its unsightly and unwholesome decay.

> O'er all there hung a shadow and a fear;
> A sense of mystery the spirit daunted,

And said, as plain as whisper in the ear,
The place is haunted.

These characteristics have given rise to the common criticism of
misanthropy. There are many people in the world who construe all
plain truth-telling as ill-natured fault-finding. It is true that he has left
the cheerful lessons to other pens, but a man may even put a low
estimate on all the powers, aspirations and deserts of humanity, and yet
be a cordial lover of the race.

The scene of all his earlier romances is laid in New England. However far the life of New England is removed at the present day from the
ideal and romantic, there was much of those elements in the days of the
Puritans. The stern devotion of the Fathers, the lofty faith which
referred every question directly to the all-wise Lawgiver, the whole
system of signs and warnings, the belief in the personal, actual presence
of the Devil in their midst tempting and destroying, all these traits of
their religion invest their life and homes with a weirdness which
comports well with the tone of the stories he has to tell. Besides, there is
something essentially romantic in the mere idea of ancient times. A
civilization two hundred years old can scarcely be said to have an
antiquity, and yet to the New Englander of to-day the war-whoop of
the Indians on the spot where his cities now stand resounds as indistinctly as the war-cry of the Crusaders in the Holy Land. Those days
appear but wan and spectral as we look back to them from the broad
blaze of our present prosperity. The shrewd and worldly Yankee of
to-day adds, by contrast, a new ghostliness to his fanatical ancestor, who
cut out Quakers' tongues, hung witches, and then blessed God with a
self-complacent devoutness. All this element suits Hawthorne's mental
constitution and his purpose well, and he has availed himself of it with
peculiar skill. Indeed, he has so intensified it that we may well doubt
whether life was ever to the Puritans themselves so serious and sombre
as the conception we get of it from his pages.

Referring to the scene of the Marble Faun, he says in his preface:
'Romance and poetry, ivy, lichens and wallflowers need ruin to make
them grow.' Italy, with its wild traditions, its poetical superstitions,
and its authentic history sounding like a romance, all mellowed by the
dimness and mists of many centuries, furnished every facility for the
exercise of his art. It is true that romancers, like poets, are licensed to
create as well as describe; but in choosing a background on which to
project one's creations, it surely is well to select one with which they will
harmonize. Even the genius of Hawthorne could not have managed a

Model in New York, or a Donatello in San Francisco. All the main accessories of the story are either peculiar to the old civilization of the country, or artistically wrought to harmonize so perfectly with it as to render it impossible to distinguish how much he owes to history, and how much to imagination. So we find in the book those peculiarly Italian scenes which can envelop it with the true atmosphere of romance: the catacombs, from which the Model, more malicious than other ghosts, could haunt his victim both night and day; Rome, with all its sad magnificence of ruin; the picture galleries, still visited by the spirits of the mighty masters; St. Peter's, where all that is solemn in religion is deepened by all that is imposing in art; the tower of Monte Beni, still wreathed with somewhat of the glory of the days when gods and men dwelt there together, with the sunshine still shut up within its sparkling wine.

Hawthorne had neither predecessor nor rival, and he has left no successor. Original in conception, aim, and diction, his writings constitute a class of themselves. So unique were his powers that in all the range of our American literature there is no author whose characteristics approach his near enough to justify a comparison. Who could develop the hints for stories so lavishly given in his note-book? Or who could complete the Dolliver Romance? The queer old shop, with its odor of medicinal herbs; the old Doctor, in his sprightly dotage; the fitful child, with all her elfish ways; who now can weave them into the deep, significant romance fit to bear the name of Hawthorne?

135. Hawthorne, the New England artist, from an unsigned review in the *Southern Review*

April 1870, vii, 328-54

New England has produced one satirist, in the person of James Russell Lowell. . . . She has produced one genuine poet, John Greenleaf Whittier. . . . She has produced a comfortable number of second-rate singers, parodists in rhythm, dainty echoes, who warble, not without melody, albeit at second hand, and in the buckram fashion that proceeds out of a plethora of self-consciousness. But she has produced only one artist to her manner born and indigenous to her soil—we mean, of course, Nathaniel Hawthorne.

Hawthorne is in many respects the legitimate successor of Washington Irving. He has not Irving's sunny enjoyment of life, nor his cheery, buoyant humor, but he has all his grace, and much more than all his power. Irving represents a generation that is past and gone, and a tone of thought now quite archaic. Hawthorne belongs to a generation that is living and present, and antiquity is to him but a medium through which he catches the multiform lights and shadows of modern life. His hectic morbidness, his subtle allegory, his weird fancy, and the plaintive minor tones that play fitfully among the exquisitely modulated cadences of his incomparable style, are proof enough that his paper bark, which he would fain launch upon the broad ocean of the absolute and infinite, to wander whither it lists, is ever grating harshly upon the narrow and inadequate shores of the present, anchored, but not at rest. As in some degree a typical writer of these times, as a novelist of unusual powers, as one of the few American authors who have cultivated art for art's sake, and have studied to express themselves worthily rather than ostentatiously, it has seemed eminently proper to us that his merits should be canvassed in the pages of the SOUTHERN REVIEW.

No estimate of Hawthorne's genius can go for much unless it takes into the account the fact that he was born and nurtured in New England. . . . The soil, the climate, the religion, if not the genius, of the people, are peculiarly hostile to artistic impulses. . . .

461

But Hawthorne felt this influence of New England upon the development of his genius much more poignantly than most of his contemporaries did, and much more keenly than the above paragraph would seem to indicate. His works abound in internal evidence to this fact, and, in regard to these works, we must remember that, while positively disclaiming the imputation that he had infused too much of his personality into his prefaces and introductions, he admits that the 'essential traits' of his character are to be discerned nevertheless, in his main writings, the *ensemble* of which, at any rate, indirectly reflects the color of his actual thought. Now the especial personality which is revealed to us in Hawthorne's works, is that of a genius subdued into a melancholy that is only too nigh akin to morbidness; and so subdued by the chilling, the bewildering, the prostrating consciousness of having to live a life necessarily 'at variance with his country and his time.' 'To persons whose pursuits are insulated from the common business of life,' says our author in one of his most elaborate tales, 'who are either in advance of mankind, or apart from it,—there often comes a sensation of moral cold, that makes the spirit shiver, as if it had reached the frozen latitude around the pole.' In this story, indeed, under the characters of Robert Danforth and Peter Hovenden, he has portrayed the opposite poles of the New England nature; hard, uncouth materialism, and a narrow, grovelling, sneering selfishness, showing the crushing influence of such a contact to the lover of beauty. . . . So, likewise, in that profound and saddest of allegories, *Young Goodman Brown*, our author bodies forth his writhing and impotent consciousness of the secret hollowness and Pharisaic iniquity of New England life. . . . In the same way he gives the key-note to the melancholy that predominates over the tone of his sketches. . . .

But this is still not all. We must contemplate this gentle spirit, cast adrift in this uncongenial atmosphere as it is, and feebly struggling against the hard and sour austerities of the surrounding life that clash so rudely with its artistic aspirations, and weigh so gloomily upon its brooding melancholy—we must contemplate this timid and shrinking spirit brought face to face with the consciousness of a retribution which it must *personally* pay, and from the penalties of which it can in no wise escape. There is no article of faith in all his creed that Hawthorne has dwelt upon so often, so earnestly, so painfully, as that which he styles emphatically 'the truth, that the wrong-doing of one generation lives into the successive ones, and divesting itself of every temporary advantage, becomes a pure and uncontrollable mischief.' He repeats this idea more often than any other in his tales; he allegorizes it elaborately and under a hundred protean shapes, and he has made it the key-note to his two most extensive books, the *House of the Seven Gables*, and the *Romance of Monte Beni*. Not only this; he seems to brood over the notion with a subtle dread, and a sense of doom. . . . Again, observe how, in the Old Manse, he speaks of the boy who killed the wounded soldier upon the battle-field of Concord. . . . Compare, likewise, the intense morbidness of *Roger Malvin's Burial*. . . .

Such, then, is Hawthorne's relation to New England.

It is as an artist that Hawthorne must be studied most. Whatever the limitations of his genius—and these limitations are many—he was emphatically an artist, whose materials are always subdued to, and plastic in, his hand. His sphere is a narrow one, and remote, but within it he is completely sovereign. His material is achromatic, and somewhat thin, but he assimilates it thoroughly, and weaves it smoothly and easily into the texture of his thought. He is exigent with himself, also; his standard is very high: he waits for the moment of invention, and, like Leonardo da Vinci, cannot be driven to work until the happy inspiration is upon him. Thus, his idea is always completely wrought, as far as it goes, and we find in him nothing fragmentary, nothing of guess-work, nothing tentative and premonitory of things to come. The peculiarly artistic impression that his works create, is furthered by his instinctive ideality, his constructive skill, and the careful finish he gives to everything he touches. He has the most poignantly acute susceptibility to every form of mystic sentiment and weird consciousness—a susceptibility that enables him to fling his peculiar glamour of ethereal but pensive fancy about the most trivial circumstances and pettiest incidents of life. He conjoins to this delicate receptivity the power of transmuting his most aerial thought into an image of speech that preserves all its fragile tenderness, and all its minute perfection of contour and of tone. . . . His Note-Book reveals to us what the quality of his performance would have constrained us to infer: his deep, thorough, patient study, his zealous and elaborate preparation, and the fidelity with which he worked out each hint, each detail, until, touch by touch, he wrought each little tale and sketch into a cabinet piece of exquisite finish. . . .

It is in this susceptible conscientiousness, this wearisome desire to overlay each thought with perfection, this utter impatience of all half-way processes, that we must seek for the cause of the limitation of Hawthorne's powers; for limited they are, and upon many sides. His invention is sobered continually, and his quickening fancy held in reins, by the fastidiousness of his conception, and by the ingrained reserve and timidity of his disposition. His observation is minute, but his judgment is indeterminate. He never quite makes up his mind upon which side of an idea to place himself, and often fails in his picture through his reluctance to present its central thought in a decisive light. You cannot make yourself sure in regard to any of his atmospheres, he has such a propensity to neutralize every effect with the contrary one, to temper lurid glare with pallid moonlight, and make it uncertain whether they be veritable witches that chase Tam o' Shanter and Kirk Alloway Brig, or only shadows of the night manipulated by an apprehensive fancy. He has none of Tieck's robustness of faith in the supernatural, nor any of Fouqué's simple and implicit spirituality, nor of Hoffmann's shuddering horror lest the figments of his too active brain should really be standing there behind him, looking over his shoulder. So, these writers are able always to excel him in breadth of effect. His self-consciousness likewise costs him much, for it leads constantly in his case to the query so fatal to the orator, 'Pleads he in earnest?' In the same way, as was early re-marked by Edgar Poe, he overwhelms the most of his subjects in a strain of allegory which destroys everything like dramatic effect. But, indeed, there is nothing dramatic in Hawthorne. In the *Snow Image*, which is imitated from Goethe's *Erl-King*, and is the most dramatic of his pieces, one cannot help being irritated the whole time he is reading it, to see so many opportunities for forcible effect let slip, as if his grasp had no nervousness whatsoever in it. He approaches most of his subjects by intimation and suggestion, not directly; he is never dogmatic, but constantly informs you he has no decided convictions in the premises, and is prepared to abandon those he has—glimmering speculations as they are—if you make strenuous demand upon him. . . . You are drawn to him, however, irresistibly; and you seek from him something that will suffice to soften 'the iron facts of life;' in lieu thereof, with a faint, half pensive, half ironic smile, he flings over you a tissue of shadows and a veil of unrealities, hiding himself the while. You are uncertain whether to weep or not; you are very certain not to laugh. There is nothing so genuine as a hearty laugh in all his writings. Withal, he impresses you irresistibly with the consciousness of immense forces held in reserve—forces never brought up, never shown, never heard from, yet whose existence you predicate with mathematical certainty. . . .

The *Note-Book* more than bears out the impression of exuberant fertility of thought and imagination which lies perdu in the authorized works, behind the veil of his subdued, reticent, and timid manner; but at the same time, it confirms the final estimate to which every student of Hawthorne's art must come: That he did not depict, nor attempt to depict, nor even conceive of, men and women as such, but only certain attributes, which he clad in the garb of shadowy but fascinating form. His characters are essentially phantasmagoria, and he looks upon them as such, and develops them as such; nay, more, he transforms to suit his mood even the real people whom he puts into his magic lantern, so that the instrument shows you only their shadows, definitely outlined, it is true, but thin and unsubstantial. . . .

Part of this shadowy, unreal, and dejected texture of all that he writes is due to the causes of which we have already spoken; part is due to that 'unconquerable reserve' to which he himself pleads guilty; part must be explained by the chilling influences of the neglect with which his earlier writings were received by an unappreciative public. It is quite apparent that much of Hawthorne's shyness and timidity of statement is constitutional. Curtis, in the *Homes of American Authors*, has told us that during his three years' residence at the 'Old Manse' in Concord, Hawthorne was not seen by a dozen people of the place altogether. . . . Hawthorne seems to work freest behind a veil. But he purchases this freedom too dear, when he shadows himself thus completely.

That something of life and fire was pressed out of Hawthorne by the dead weight of a blind and unapprehensive public, is very certain. No spirit as sensitive as his could preserve its perfect health under such a burthen of obscurity as he had to endure.

The philosophy of popularity has yet to be written, but it is not difficult to see why Hawthorne was so slow in being recognized. . . . Hawthorne, while principally an artist, was still a good deal of a moralist, and something of a philosopher. Much of his best art is 'caviare to the general.' It is a harmonious and beautiful art, to be sure; but it is not spontaneous, and so misses something of the impulsive charm of naturalness and directness. No premeditated art, no matter how cunning, can simulate that which gushes by the first intention, warm and fluid, from the heart. Neither taste nor culture can supply the place of that glowing power of nature, which seizes upon the soul by the mere force of sympathy. Taste and culture, in fact, the outgrowths of educated thought, are drawbacks to popularity, so far forth at least as they tend to add angles reflective and refractive to the media through which people see works of art. The law is, the more transparent the medium, the more instinctive the recognition. . . .

A shallower spirit than Hawthorne would have changed his style, gone into more sensational walks, or sought eclat in some shape or other of simulated *hysterica passio*. A more dishonest spirit might have stooped still lower, even to the mud and mire, as we have seen a contemporary do, who, to revive a notoriety waning for lack of sustenance, violated the sanctity of the grave, and battened her prurient fancy in nauseous libels of the helpless dead. But Hawthorne upheld his art with unblenching fidelity, patiently waiting for the only kind of popularity that is worth having. . . . What he writes must be his own, not the populace's; if it do not suit them, he cannot help it, but will go on, trusting to create an audience on whom his appeal will finally have its effect; if it bring name, fame, fortune, so much the better for him. . . .

Hawthorne did not even modify his vehicle of expression, deeming that he had no business to swerve from what he regarded the most appropriate form for his art, which was at once a worthy art in itself, and the best he could do in the premises. . . . So that we may say, without paradox, that, if Hawthorne's obscurity injured the tone of his genius, by quenching in some degree the fire of his temper, it at the same time enabled him to approve the strength of his fidelity to art, and contributed, besides, sensibly to *purify* it. If he is fastidious to an extreme, he is yet perfect in his class; if he confines himself within too restrictive limits, within those limits each performance of his is a gem almost flawless. . . .

136. Henry T. Tuckerman: The years of seclusion established, from 'Nathaniel Hawthorne', in *Lippincott's Magazine*

May 1870, v, 498–507

This essay is typical of the large number of statements in private memoirs in the decades after Hawthorne's death.

Half a decade has elapsed since Hawthorne died, and in the retrospect we find his literary example emphasized by a survey of our limited native field of artistic development in letters; for he eminently possessed the patience of the true artist; he obeyed the laws of intellectual achievement; he subdued that vivacity of temperament which is only content with immediate and obvious results; he turned resolutely aside from the thoroughfare and the arena, and in solitude wrought out his conceptions with conscientious skill and calm reflection; and therefore it is they still appeal to us, still conserve for us not only his name, but his nature—not his fancies merely, but his life; therefore it is they are a permanent trophy, and not a casual memorial, and, amid so much that is incomplete and ephemeral, retain intact their graceful individuality and normal interest. Nor is this an accidental result. It was assured by the earliest as it was confirmed by the latest of his productions; for both are alike distinguished by pure taste in expression, high finish, distinct aim and artistic fidelity—the conservative elements of literature. Years ago, when Hawthorne's name was scarcely known beyond his native region, we wrote of him in an old diary thus:

'I have passed this long, balmy forenoon delightfully—reading Hawthorne. How considerate in B—— to send these winsome volumes to refresh my exile! I remember, when I first encountered one of his sketches in a Boston annual, I thought Hawthorne was an assumed name quaintly devised for an Elia-ish incognito; and it struck me as quite appropriate, for is not hawthorn the favorite hedge, and is not its very mention suggestive of verdure, home and a cheering wayside? I know not how long I remained under this delusion, but being accustomed to haunt the Athenæum, I would sometimes look up from my book and speculate upon the silent figures around me in the reading-room. I cannot affirm that there was often anything in them upon which imagination might complacently repose; neither did their habitual attitudes emulate the graces of Praxiteles. They were chiefly retired merchants who dozed or mumbled over the newspapers, and whose physiognomies betokened Mammon's votaries:

> Across whose brain scarce dares to creep
> Aught but Thrift's parent pair—to get, to keep.

'There was occasionally, indeed, a sprinkling of professional youths whose fees were inadequate to their office rents, and whose leisurely movements betokened a hopeless ignorance of patients or clients. Sometimes, too, a well-to-do physician, with that air of self-esteem consequent upon being a domestic necessity to sundry prosperous families, would step rapidly in, whip in hand, and stand a few moments at the table carelessly glancing at an English Review; or a popular divine would ensconce himself in an arm-chair and very snugly gloat over Hook's jokes or *Blackwood's* sneers, peering ever and anon about, to assure himself he was unobserved by any prying member of "our parish." Into this heterogeneous assembly I more than once observed a personage glide with a very unobtrusive step, and a certain gentle self-withdrawal of bearing that awakened in my breast a vague sympathy. His figure was completely enveloped in a cloak—the high cape almost concealing his features. He walked, as I have said, very modestly in, seated himself noiselessly by the table, drew a magazine toward him, and, leaning his head with a kind of subdued content above it, seemed to read like a man who could fold an author's thoughts up in his own with an affectionate patience. He never looked around. There was a harmonized quietude in his position. In fact he wore that aspect which makes one of lively sympathies instinctively say, "A penny for your thoughts"—only there was that about him which repelled all idle curiosity. You felt there was a rich human sweetness in the silent oracle that forbade untimely interrogation, but if it were to breathe spontaneously, could not but "discourse most excellent music." Repose of manner is not common among us, and to an observant mind its rarity makes it very welcome. It betokens inward resources. Perhaps this is why it is deemed characteristic of a gentleman—as one whose position secures him from that eagerness of outward aim that marks the demeanor of the vulgar. There is something that whispers of faith, too, in repose. We are apt, and with justice, to imagine that a quiet conscience, a satisfied affection or a serene trust thus diffuses calmness over the pilgrim of life. I saw a dark and lustrous eye gleam from under my quiet neighbor's brow, and knew thereby that his was not the tranquillity of a stagnant or indifferent spirit. One day, for the first time, I saw him acknowledge, by a slight inclination, the greeting of a friend of mine as he left the reading-room. I hastily followed and inquired the name of the unknown. It was Hawthorne, and thus those dreamy sketches that had charmed me in the annuals as they gracefully reposed, like Goldsmith's memory, under the hawthorn "for whispering lovers made," became associated with my gentle mystery of the Athenæum.

'What charms me in this writer's genius is his felicity in the use of common materials. It is very difficult to give an imaginative scope to a scene or a topic which familiarity has robbed of illusion. It is by the association of ideas, by the halo of remembrance and the magic of love, that an object usually presents itself to the mind under fanciful relations. From a foreign country our native spot becomes picturesque, and from the hill of manhood the valley of youth appears romantic; but that is a peculiar and rare mental alchemy which can transmute the dross of the common and the immediate into gold. Yet so doth Hawthorne. His "Old Apple-dealer" yet sits by the old South Church, and "The Willey House" is inscribed every summer-day by the penknives of ambitious cits. He is able to illustrate by his rich invention, places and themes that are before our very eyes and in our daily speech. His fancy is as free of wing at the North-end or on Salem turnpike as that of other poets in the Vale of Cashmere or amid the Isles of Greece. He does not seem to feel the necessity of distance either of time or space or realize his enchantments. He has succeeded in attracting an etheral interest to home subjects, which is no small triumph. Somewhat of that poetic charm which Wilson has thrown over Scottish life in his *Lights and Shadows*, and Irving over English in his *Sketch Book,* and Lamb over metropolitan in his *Elia*, has Hawthorne cast around New England, and his tales here and there blend, as it were, the traits which endear these authors. His best efforts, I think, are those in which the human predominates. Ingenuity and moral significancy are finely displayed, it is true, in his allegories; but sometimes they are coldly fanciful, and do not win the sympathies as in those instances where the play of the heart relieves the dim workings of the abstract and the supernatural. Hawthorne, like all individualities, must be read in the appropriate mood. This secret of appreciation is now understood as regards Wordsworth. It is due to all genuine authors. To many whose mental ailment has been exciting and coarse, the delicacy, meek beauties and calm spirit of these writings will but gradually unfold themselves; but those capable of placing themselves in relation with Hawthorne will discover a native genius for which to be grateful and proud, and a brother whom to know is to love. He certainly has done much to obviate the reproach which a philosophical writer, not without reason, has cast upon our authors, when he asserts their object to be to astonish rather than please.'

Although Hawthorne, the man, was comparatively so little known in his lifetime in that social way that affords such available material for gossip and criticism in the case of so many contemporary authors, yet in another sense few writers of the time are more thoroughly revealed in their inmost personality to such as meditate his record; for this is essentially the history of his mind—the revelation of his consciousness; and as if to complete and confirm it, copious extracts from his notebooks and letters have been published since his decease. A leading English critical journal sneered at these data of observation and experience as too unimportant to be interesting; but to the student of literature and the analyst of character they are eminently so, for thereby we learn the process of his authorship, the fidelity of his observation, and his manner of regarding the most familiar elements of life. Taken in connection with his finished works, in these notes we trace his development and his career step by step: we see the details of his daily experience, and realize how he garnered and arranged them for purposes of art. That these are often the reverse of extraordinary, that they are such as thousands are familiar with, and to an unreflecting and unobservant mind they convey no romantic hints, ethical truths or infinite possibilities, only render their statement more suggestive of the latent significance of the most common lot and surroundings when noted by patient intelligence or meditated by an earnest soul. To such, Nature is an ever-new and inspiring picture, sentiment and sensation a conscious relation to the universe and to destiny, and life itself a wonderful drama. From old Salem to Brook Farm, thence to Berkshire valleys and a Massachusetts village, or across the ocean; at an English seaport and in the heart of Italy; as an officer of the customs, a Socialistic novice, a consul, farmer, author; in an old manse of New England or lone villa in Tuscany; wandering in his native fields, along the green lanes of old England or beside moonlit Roman fountains,—we follow his thoughtful step and his dreamy eye, and feel anew the mysterious process through which life is interpreted, Nature described and Art illustrated by Experience. What strikes us in these desultory notes is the variety of his observation, the facility of his psychological sympathies. Not only secluded dell and radiant sunset, historic scenes and the trophies of genius, but the homeliest details and least inspiring facts of daily life find mention—a wharf and a bar-room not less than a wood or a lake; the weather, a garden, an orchard, a roadside encounter with vagrants, the talk of the gifted, a solitary ramble, the advent of apple blossoms or the ripening of a gourd—whatever the eye beholds or the heart responds to yields food for speculation or a glimpse into the philosophy of life. Open the casual record at hazard and you light on a glimpse that hints a picture, a humorous sketch or idea, an anecdote that may be expanded into a tale, a fantasy which is the germ of an allegory, a trait of human character to be wrought into dramatic interest. Slight as are the incidents, familiar as are the scenes, we can imagine that to such a mind they have a meaning and a use, and learn to appreciate the great truth that 'a man's best things are nearest him—lie close about his feet.' Hawthorne noted moods of mind as well as external facts: he elicited with zest the ideas of diverse human beings, to compare and contrast them; and found suggestive alike the talk of critic and vagabond, sailor and farmer, politician and bigot. The Notch in the White Hills, the limited view from a city window, and the sights and sounds of a lunatic asylum, were each and all to him sources of curious knowledge and avenues of truth. How simple the habits, intent the observation and patient the record of the reticent man thus humbly yet profoundly occupied in the study of life; which, to most of his fellows, was and is a whirlpool absorbing consciousness and whelming individuality! 'I bathed in the cave o'erhung with maples and walnuts—the water cool and thrilling;' 'what a beautiful afternoon this has been!' 'men of cold passions have quick eyes;' 'the natural tastes of man for the original Adam's occupation is fast developing in me: I find I am a good deal interested in our garden;' 'O perfect day! It opens the gates of heaven, and gives us glimpses far inward;' 'I found one cracker in the tureen, and exulted over it as if it had been gold;' 'I take an interest in all the nooks and crannies and every development of cities;' 'a morning mist fills up the whole length and breadth of the valley between my house and Monument Mountain;' 'the wind-turn—the lightning-catch—a child's phrases for weathercock and lightning-rod;' 'a walk with the children: we went through the wood: they found Houstonias there more than a week ago;' 'one thing, if no more, I have gained by my custom-house experience—to know a politician. It is a knowledge which no previous thought or power of sympathy could have taught me, because the animal, or the machine rather, is not in Nature.'

There is one remarkable passage in these note-books which tells the whole story of Hawthorne's authorship, and tells it from his inmost heart: there is a great lesson to be thence learned, and a singular pathos and power involved therein. On one of his visits to the home of his childhood, just as prosperity began faintly to dawn upon his long and sequestered life-work, local associations, always strong in their appeal to his nature, seem to have inspired him to unwonted self-revelation; and he thus recorded his baffled zeal and self-reliant loyalty, so unconsciously indicative of rare natural gifts and an intensely reflective character:

Salem, Oct. 4, 1840—*Union St. Family Mansion.* If ever I should have a biographer, he ought to mention this chamber in my memoirs. Here I sit in my old accustomed chair, where I used to sit in days gone by. Here I have written many tales—many that have been burned to ashes, many that doubtless deserved the same fate. This claims to be a haunted chamber, for thousands upon thousands of visions have appeared to me in it; and some few of them have become visible to the world, because so much of my lonely youth was wasted here, and here my mind and character were formed; and here I have been glad and hopeful, and here I have been despondent; and here I sat a long, long time waiting for the world to know me, and sometimes wondering why it did not know me sooner, or whether it would ever know me at all—at least till I was in my grave. And sometimes it seemed as if I were already in the grave, with only life enough to be chilled and be numbed. But often I was happy—at least as happy as I then knew how to be or was aware of the possibility of being. By and by the world found me out in my lonely chamber, and called me forth—not, indeed, with a roar of acclamation, but rather with a still, small voice—and forth I went, and found nothing in the world I thought preferable to my old solitude till now. And now I begin to understand why I was imprisoned so many years in this lonely chamber, and why I could never break through the viewless bolts and bars; for if I had sooner made my escape into the world, I should have grown hard and rough, and been covered with earthly dust, and my heart might have become callous by rude encounters with the multitude. But living in solitude till the fullness of time was come, I still kept the dew of my youth and the freshness of my heart. I used to think I could imagine all passion, all feeling, all states of the heart and mind; but how little did I know! We are not endowed with real life, and all that seems real about us is but the thinnest substance of a dream till the heart be troubled: that touch creates us; then we begin to be; thenceforth we are beings of reality and inheritors of eternity.

This last conviction lies at the basis of all genuine productiveness in

Art—verbal, plastic and pictorial—and fidelity thereto is a test of the integrity of genius. De Quincey has well defined the two great divisions of literature—that of power and that of knowledge; the former, being in its essence creative, implies an absolute inward experience as the condition and inspiration of original and geniune work: all earnest natures recognize the law, and are not to be lured into factitious labour or ingenious imitation as a substitute for what must be born of personal emotion and imperative consciousness. These were the traits which made Charlotte Brontë's few novels memorable; and her biographer tells us that 'she thought every serious delineation of life ought to be the product of personal experience and observation—experience naturally occurring, and observation of a normal kind.' 'I have not accumulated since I published *Shirley*,' she said. 'What makes it needful for me to speak again? and till I do so, may God give me grace to be dumb.' There are special temptations for an American author to evade this ethical condition—the demands of the immedaite are so pertinacious, while vanity and gain conspire to compromise both fame and faculty. It is a rare distinction of Hawthorne that he was so true to himself in this regard. . . .

Thoroughly American, and of the geniune Eastern type, were the antecedents of Hawthorne: his nature and surroundings were fitted to deepen the traditional idiosyncrasies of his birthplace, and endow him to become their most characteristic interpreter. Born in the old New England town whose colonial history is so tragically memorable, on the fourth of July, 1804, his progenitors had emigrated from England and participated in the persecution of the Quakers so pathetically illustrated by their descendant in his first successful sketch as a verbal artist—'The Gentle Boy.' On the father's side his ancestors were seafaring men—'a gray-haired shipmaster, in each generation, returning from the quarter-deck to the homestead, while a boy of fourteen took the hereditary place before the mast.' Here we have the origin of the adventurous and observant vein in the future author, over whose young soul a domestic bereavement cast no transitory shadow, when, in 1810, his father died of yellow fever at Havana, and made his mother a sorrowful recluse for life. She is described as beautiful, and this widowed loyalty proves her rare sensibility, which her son inherited. She sent him, when ten years old, to a farm belonging to the family on Sebago Lake, in Maine, to regain his health: he returned invigorated, and completed his studies in a year, so as to enter Bowdoin College in that State in 1825, with Longfellow, Cheever and Franklin Pierce. After graduating, Hawthorne

lived retired in his native town—a hermit, a dreamer and a thinker—
'passing the day alone in his room, writing wild tales, most of which he
destroyed; and walking out at night.' In 1832 he published an anonymous romance, which he never claimed, and the public could not
identify. Such a youth is exceptional in America, where the struggle for
life's prizes begins at its threshold, and the exigencies of the hour
usually launch the collegian into the world prematurely to work for
bread and fame. The inestimable benefit of an interval of rest—for the
mind to lie fallow and the faculties to strengthen—in our busy land,
between academic education and the career of manhood, is obvious,
especially in the instance of such refined aspirations as those of Hawthorne. This episode, so unusual then and there, has been described as a
'wandering uncertain and mostly unnoticed life;' but that it was
auspicious to the author's development and conservative of the man's
best nature, he, as we have seen, long after recorded as his grateful conviction. After his contributions to the *Token* and the *Democratic Review*
had made manifest his rare gifts, he received an appointment from the
Boston collector, but lost it on Harrison's inauguration in 1841: then
passed a few months in a co-operative community in West Roxbury,
Massachusetts, which furnished him with several types of character—
'the self-conceited philanthropist; the high-spirited woman bruising
herself against the narrow limitations of her sex; the weakly maiden
whose trembling nerves endowed her with Sibylline attributes; the
minor poet beginning life with strenuous aspirations which die out
with his youthful fervor.' In 1843 he married and settled at Concord,
where he lived for three years, when a change in the political world
made him surveyor of the port of Salem, where, for another three years,
he was the chief executive officer of 'the decayed old custom-house.'
When, in 1850, the Whigs were once more in the ascendant, Hawthorne
lost his office and retired to Lenox, Massachusetts, to dwell on the
borders of the lake called the Stockbridge Bowl, and resume, with new
zest and success, his literary pursuits. In 1852 he returned to Concord,
and on the election of Franklin Pierce as President of the United States
was appointed United States consul at Liverpool, where he remained
eight years; and after visiting the Continent and passing a winter in
Rome and a summer in Tuscany, returned to his native land, crowned
with fame in literature, and so far prosperous in circumstances as, for
the first time, to feel himself independent. A long and happy evening
to his days was anticipated by all who knew and honored him; but his
pleasure in being once more at home was embittered by the sanguinary,

and, as he long thought, hopeless, struggle that convulsed the nation. Still, in the serene exercise of his rare powers, in the congenial retrospect of his foreign experience, and the comfort and cheer of assured success as the reward of past waiting and vicissitude—in domestic happiness and social recognition and genial activity—benign were the closing years of Hawthorne; but their close none the less seemed sadly premature. A future for him and for us had shaped itself nobly from the firm and faithful basis of past achievement, and to the natural grief for the departure of a gifted spirit and an illustrious countryman, was added the pang which attends the abrupt ending of a happy dream.

Introspective authors, known intimately as such, excite singular personal interest, and we eagerly desire to be admitted to their consciousness when the crises of life occur or the shadow of death is upon them. All who followed Hawthorne with sympathetic insight as a man through the discipline and self-distrust of hope deferred, and as an author in his psychological and picturesque delineations of life, character and their environments, felt a tender and reverent curiosity, when his own existence on earth closed, to realize his feelings and faith in those waning hours which had become too sacred for the familiar record he used to keep in more vital and observant days. Such knowledge is only obtainable through the confidence of intimate friends. Reticent as Hawthorne was by nature and habit, and few as were his associates, we have sought not in vain to follow his patient and faltering steps as he descended into the dark valley. The friend of his youth was alone the witness of his departure. It has been thought and said that Hawthorne's friendships were unaccountable: it had created surprise that he found apparent congeniality in men of totally diverse tastes and temperaments from his own. This, however, is explicable if we consider that men of genius, especially of the kind which distinguished him, are feminine in this—that they find solace and satisfaction in 'variety of the accustomed.' Constitutional shyness makes the process of intimacy and confidence long and often irksome with them. They may enjoy, to the full, intercourse with kindred minds, and appreciate the regard and fellowship of those devoted to the same pursuits, but they shrink from self-revelation to such; they reserve their 'abandon' for those with whom old and early habit has made them perfectly at home. In college, as we know, Hawthorne and Franklin Pierce grew into the most intimate relations—first, through constant association, and then by virtue of the very diversity of their natures. This kind of fellowship, if it survives youth, is rarely superseded by later ties; and it is therefore quite natural that the friend

Hawthorne chose to be near him in the days of his decline, and who felt himself drawn specially to that sad ministry, should be he who learned to love the reserved student, and, when politically successful, sought and secured prosperity for the gifted author. . . .

137. William Brighty Rands: The problem of Hawthorne's ambivalence, from 'Nathaniel Hawthorne', in *St. Paul's Magazine*

May 1871, viii, 150–61

Rands (1823–82), who wrote this essay under the pseudonym 'Matthew Browne', was best known for his poems and fairy tales for children.

. . . There was a time when 'The Scarlet Letter' had some claim to be considered a popular book; but it owed a large part of its general diffusion to the fact that it could be and was sold in this country for a shilling. And it is undoubtedly true that Hawthorne is essentially a writer for select readers. Beyond the inner circle there is a pretty considerable public who turn over his books, or, at least, 'The Scarlet Letter;' but to the majority of these good people he is of necessity a man so much misknown that he might himself have preferred not being read at all by them. At least one would say so, if it were not for the strong proofs afforded by his memoranda posthumously published of the pleasure he took in being widely, if remotely, known. He could not have missed seeing the frequent declarations of English critics, that he was, on the whole, the most original man of genius America had produced. When we bear in mind the names which this verdict placed second to him—Bryant, Lowell, Longfellow, Emerson, and Poe—we cannot wonder that he took pleasure in the verdict; though he undoubtedly did so in a shy way that had a smack of humor in it. It was a verdict that might be a little disputed in favor of Emerson; some people would say, in favor of Poe; but, after all, there was something mechanical about the movement of the fine faculties of the latter, and, as Lowell says of him, in his writings 'the heart is all squeezed out by the mind.' There are, no doubt, critics at present who would affirm that the advent of Walt Whitman has changed the conditions, and that *he* is now the most original man of genius that America has produced. There is something to be said for this last claim; for whether we decide that Whitman is a great poet who will live, or only the splendid Apollo of rowdies, he is the most truly American of the writers of merit that America has produced. Emerson, indeed, is American; so, in a way, is Lowell, under the *persona* of Hosea Biglow; so, in a way, is Longfellow, in the 'Song of Hiawatha;' so, again, is Cooper in his novels. But, indeed, the whole question of 'Americanism' involves some curious matters that are well worth looking at.

To begin with, it is exceedingly difficult for us English to catch in a new literature the distinct impress of another nationality when the language employed by the writers is our own, written idiomatically and with perfect purity; as, for example, Poe, Hawthorne, Prescott, Longfellow, and Bryant wrote. The first accents of nationality that strike our ears are usually such as relate to scenery and minor circumstances. We perceive that a writer is an American (the title is not exhaustively accurate as a definition) if he writes squash instead of pumpkin, and talks familiarly of the blue-bird and the hickory-pole, or of caucuses and mass-meeting, dollars and dimes, and so on. These are accidents of a kind which may turn up in literature of any quality, in America or elsewhere. But when a writer like Lowell seizes a peculiar type of character which we at once recognize as national, or when Hawthorne describes the scenery of the Assabeth (in the introduction to the 'Mosses from an Old Manse'), or Emerson paints a landscape such as we can nowhere see on this side of the Atlantic, we find him American in another and a higher sense. He is American just as a man who is always letting out about the Rhine (and, perhaps, his grandmother) is German. But there are other ways yet of being American.

Hawthorne painted American scenery beautifully, but he painted that of Italy with equal beauty, and sometimes that of England. Only he seems to have been the first of his countrymen whose literary self-consciousness, so to speak, was American. It was almost irritably so. His mind stands back, and looks around, and realizes its traditions, and the relation of his people to the parent people, and deliberately formulates itself as American. He always shows himself distinctly wide-awake to the particulars in which America has broken with the old traditions; and yet he hardly appears resigned to her privations—to the absence of the wall-flower, the ivy, and the lichen on the walls of her civilization, for example; or, again, to the absence of a supremely cultured and 'leisured' class in America; or to that of 'the untouched and ornamental' in general in her social fabric. In 'The House of the Seven Gables' he has very vividly, and evidently with only partial consciousness of what he was about, shown us the way in which his mind had been at work upon the old problems in the new forms in which they appear to him in the growth of his country under the shadow of English tradition. He writes as if he resented the fact that he could not be an American and an Englishman all at once. People may deny this as long as they please, and maintain that it is our national conceit which makes us think these things; but Hawthorne would not have denied it if it had been pressed home to him in a quiet hour by an Englishman of genial humor and true love of American freedom. There are perpetually recurring traces in his writings of a sense that the 'go-ahead' spirit seemed, for the present at least, to involve a kind and degree of impermanence which was painful. In 'The House of the Seven Gables,' which we now know he preferred to 'The Scarlet Letter'—a very significant fact—we have a striking embodiment of all this. The young 'Red Republican' daguerreotypist, descendant of Maule, who baffled and mesmerized the ancient Pyncheon, is the representation of Labor and Progress, and he marries Phœbe Pyncheon. Here is the reconciliation of the aristocratic spirit with the spirit of modern equality. But though the young man has been not long previously quarrelling with the kind of permanence which is symbolized by antiquated houses like that of the Seven Gables, he is no sooner betrothed than he, too, contemplates the permanent, and proposes a new wing to the Pyncheon hose.

This is one instance, too, out of a hundred that could be cited to illustrate the way and the degree in which Hawthorne, without becoming cynical, so often *seems* to approach the confines of cynicism,— the hazy border-land in which we so often find him stealing along, softly, with his face towards the light, but with a slant look at the gloom beyond. Another instance occurs at the opening of 'The Scarlet Letter', where the author notices, quite unnecessarily as it appears, the fact that wherever men go and sit down in large numbers, there are two things which they are compelled to set up—namely, a prison and a graveyard.

Take, again, the remark of the sexton when he hands to Arthur Dimmesdale, on the pulpit-stairs, the minister's glove which he had picked
up on the pillory. Again, the various readings which different people
give to the letter A said to be seen in the sky in the night upon which
Arthur mounts that place of shame in the dark by himself. Again, the
different versions which tradition gave of the wonderful closing scene
of the story, and of the minister's dying speech to the people. Again, the
sudden confession at the end of 'The Blithedale Romance,' that the
narrator of the story was himself in love with Priscilla—an announcement which throws backward upon the narrative a most peculiar
coloring. Again, the story of Goodman Brown. In all these and in many
other instances, we feel the presence of a fine genius which flies, and
mounts heavenwards, but which yet looks as if it *might* have singed its
wing at some time. There are two ways, and only two, in which such
awkward corners as his mind is always running against can be, in
military phrase, 'turned;' by a very *dogmatic* moral faculty, or by a much
stronger sense of humor than Hawthorne possessed. Richter, Sterne, or
Molière would have wrapped up that touch about the prison and the
graveyard in such a nice, warm laugh that we should not have been
stung by it. When some Yankee 'jokist' the other day told us that a
certain district was so healthy, that when they 'inaugurated' the cemetery they had to shoot a man on purpose, we were reminded of the
inevitableness of that institution; but the humor took away all possibility
of pain. It is not Hawthorne's fault that he had not humor adapted to
the effort in question, though he had a fine, quiet humor of his own.
Nor is it his fault that he has not dogmatic or intellectual force enough,
or even sufficient depth of passion, to enable him to 'turn' the corners
which yet he appears unable to avoid. 'The Scarlet Letter' is the most
intense of his writings, or, at least, it can only be rivalled in that particular by 'Transformation;' but in neither is the passion quite strong
enough to communicate to the reader that sense of absolute and final
moral victory which, after so much pain, the heart craves. It by no
means follows that a picture of the very last despairs of the human soul,
with only just light enough to exhibit them, should depress. If the
picture be only strong enough, it may ensure a reaction of triumph in
the soul of the spectator. But the strength is essential; and of that has
Hawthorne quite enough, even for purposes of passion? . . .

The defect is no doubt partly of the intellect. His writings, with
small exceptions, start the deepest difficulties, and then rather worry
them than shake the life out of them. Nowhere is the *statement* of a

problem complete, or even as complete as it might be. In 'The House of the Seven Gables,' if Holgrave, the daguerreotypist, must needs start that question between the old and the new, he should have more to say about it than what he delivers with a sad smile. In 'The Blithedale Romance,' the question of the relation of what may be called vocational philanthropy to the exercise of the private affections is left in a highly unsatisfactory condition, and the book closes with the most dismal picture of a man of noble aspirations utterly broken down by remorse—morally crushed because he could not at any time rally his conscience into action after having caused the suicide of the beautiful Zenobia. Generally speaking, indeed, remorse and failure play too prominent a part in these writings. It is not well to exhibit remorse as having power to kill, or almost to kill, the soul of a man, and there to leave the matter. Nor, as we shall see in a moment, can we wholly admit the plea that Hawthorne was primarily an artist, not a moralist. In 'The Scarlet Letter,' the climax of the story is grand indeed, and the general result more wholesome. But even here we occasionally feel stifled. Remorse is not allowed to kill the soul of Arthur Dimmesdale; but, again, we have an immense problem started, and a most lurid exhibition of its difficulties, and then we are put off at the end with a hint that some day 'a new truth' will be disclosed which will put the whole relation of man and woman on a better footing. . . . Still less hopeful is the state of the case at the close of 'Transformation.' In that story, Donatello, the Faun, is supposed to have risen to a higher moral life in consequence of a crime, and Kenyon, the painter, puts the question whether sin may not be a necessary condition of moral and spiritual growth. Hilda flinches with horror from the notion, Kenyon utterly disavows it, and there the matter ends. But we all perceive that 'Transformation' was written for the very purpose of putting *some such* question, and we naturally ask that if such problems are to be dealt with at all they should at least be stripped bare and boldly grasped. As it is, we are not even left with a problem—we get a mere perplexity.* A little resolute reflection would have brought a mind of a certain degree (not necessarily the highest) of speculative force face to face with the ultimate question in terms which would not have shocked even Hilda. And then, though we should not have got a solution (for the problem is insoluble), we should have got a

---

* The same difficulty is started in the beautifully finished story of 'The Birth-Mark.' It is characteristic of Hawthorne and illustrative of what we are now saying, that he admitted, or rather smilingly avowed, having forgotten what some of these short stories meant!

problem instead of a perplexity, and that would have, so to speak, wrung out the defiance of the conscience, in company with the last word of the intellect, upon the subject.

Had Hawthorne that certain degree of speculative force? We think not. His imagination, along with much speculative apprehensiveness, is always bringing up questions which he never seizes by the throat. . . . We should say that this was a necessary result of one essential quality of Hawthorne's genius—namely, inconclusiveness, if it were not really apparent in many places that there is something more in it. For example, Arthur Dimmesdale, a Puritan divine in the days of Governor Winthrop, talks to Hester Prynne of adultery as a crime in which they had violated their reverence for each other's soul; and says, in another place, that what they did had a consecration of its own which made it less a crime than that of the physician, persistently torturing two hearts and trying to bring one of them to perdition. Now, all this is quite true. But what can we make of a Puritan divine in the seventeenth century speaking of reverence for the soul, and the 'consecration' that may lie even in a love which the conscience condemns? The first of these two ideas is natural enough in a Channing, and the second in a Robert Browning; but in Arthur Dimmesdale! Take, again, that very powerful but incongruous and impossible scene in which Arthur Dimmesdale pleads with the stern conscript fathers of New England for Hester, gives reasons for leaving the custody of the child Pearl with its mother, and actually tells these Puritan magistrates to their face that there was a peculiar sacredness in the relation of Pearl to Hester. If it were at all conceivable—it is not—that under the conditions of the theological and moral culture of those days a man like Arthur Dimmesdale, and suffering as he was, should have succeeded in wringing out of his soul some of the truth which he spoke to the grim old fellows, it is simply incredible that they should ask him to 'make that plain,' and placidly profess themselves convinced by his pleading. They would not have understood a word he said, and if they had understood they would assuredly have answered him—'Much learning, Master Dimmesdale, hath made thee mad.' These are instances, which could be paralleled by the score, of Hawthorne's imperfect grasp of speculative conditions, even in matters which he might have been supposed thoroughly to understand. . . .

It may, indeed, be called the brand of the Hawthorne genius. The way in which it most powerfully works is this. He never allows you to make up your mind, and seems never to have made up his own, whether there is a preternatural element at work in the narrative or not. The manner in which he takes up a wild tradition or an awful superstition (*e.g.*, that the body of the wounded will bleed at the approach of the murderer), or some startling unexplained phenomena (*e.g.*, those of mesmerism), and impacts, so to speak, ordinary events and persons into such things, is familiar to all his readers. His scenery and his persons are wrought out with the utmost distinctness, but every now and then he lets down a curtain of lurid haze all round, or sends a shudder over the page, before you well know where you are. This is the characteristic way in which the indeterminateness of his mind works for us. To the last we are not quite sure that we have got to 'the rights' of the connection or identity of Priscilla and the Veiled Lady, or the connection between Zenobia and the tropical flower she wore, or the 'Maule's blood' of the Pyncheon tradition, or the harpsichord music in the old Pyncheon house, or Donatello's faun-like ears, or the 'red letter A' as the Oxford gentleman called it. Again, this indeterminateness will be found to be of the essence of the Hawthorne humor. The best example of that is the exquisite account of the Salem custom-house, or, rather, of its people. In Hawthorne's mind, everything seemed capable of meaning something else, and the endless filaments of suggestion sent out in search of symbolic meanings,—you can see them trembling all round at every capture like a spider's web. There is one other source of the extreme fascination of this man's writings. A plain word for it would be concentration, or pertinacity; but in the lurid haze under which his genius so often works it becomes something for which we really want a name. Perhaps we might call it a fatality of method which carries an almost awfully impersonal look with it. When Judge Pyncheon sits dead in his chair in the dark room all night, and the genius of the author, through all that most terrible time, walks round and round him in the gloom, gradually closing in on the solemn fact that you well know all the while, you feel with a shudder, that this bad man is not only dead, he is dead-dead—fatally dead, so to speak. Now, the movement of Hawthorne as a narrator is always of this kind. He gradually *closes in* upon his idea; but as you feel that his imagination is doing this spontaneously, the effect is like that of some preternatural fatality.*

* Contrast Hawthorne's manner with that of Fielding. Here and there a sensitive woman, or a sharp critic, guesses at the outset who is the mother of 'Tom Jones:' but to the majority of readers the discovery comes suddenly at last, like a clap of thunder. In 'The Scarlet Letter', the dullest reader knows, from the very first scene, who is Pearl's father; but in spite of this, we follow with breathless interest (not suspense or curiosity) the author's gradual beleaguering of the dreadful truth.

Of the fine artistic finish of Hawthorne's work, of his beautifully
transparent style, of his exquisite descriptions of natural scenery and
works of art, much has already been written. They are beyond praise,
and they are known to all the world. Upon minor peculiarities of his
style something might be said, if there were space. But I may repeat, in
passing, a question I have put before—Why is it that painters have
seldom, if ever, taken subjects from his novels? The only reason that
occurs to me is that Hawthorne so entirely seizes the scene, when he
wishes to do it, and so finely and exhaustively paints it, that a painter
would be under too much restraint in working at the canvas. I have in
my mind the two opening chapters of 'The Scarlet Letter.' What could
any pencil do with them but just copy?

Of the personal qualities that are exhibited in the writings of Hawthorne, something might in any case be said, and the last notes from his
diaries have gone far to make his character public property. His fine
feelings towards women and children, his compassion for suffering, his
utter harmlessness, his radical patience of nature (though he *must* have
been irritable in the scientific sense of the word), his love of his native
country and his friends—all these lie upon the surface of his books, and
they receive abundant illustration in the diaries. Upon the surface, also,
lies what, if this genius and character had not made good their high
privileges of exemption, we might call some want of 'grit.' We discern
this in his flinching from the solid cabbage-rose beauty of a full-grown
Englishwoman, and we fancy that he was never, from his birth to his
death, quite at home with ordinary human nature. Most kind and
affectionate he evidently was, and made, above all things, for home; but
he never quite realized the solidity of human life and human beings, and
was not capable of social abandonment. For this he was not to blame,
but it must be borne in mind in giving due value to his estimates of men
and things.

When deductions have been made, we find the Note-Book most
delightful reading. It is very soothing to follow this fine novelist in his
quiet rambles about England, and particularly about London, usually
with his wife and children, but almost always happy, and quite always
minutely observant. It is pleasant to find that the more he sees of us
English the better he likes us. He begins by finding our weather cold
and bad, and ends by finding it sunny and exquisite—too hot, in fact.
He always tells us what he had to eat, and, when out and about, appears
to have drunk a pint of ale at every lunch or dinner. A great part of the
volumes consist of memoranda of his own acts of kindness to the poor

and suffering. There are charming descriptions and anecdotes, told in his best manner, and he is always delightful in speaking of children: which would make us wonder why his 'Tanglewood Tales' were not better, if it were not plain, in spite of 'Transformation,' that Hawthorne's mind was not particularly well fitted to manipulate Greek legend.

There is a passage in Mrs. Hawthorne's preface which ought not to be suppressed here:—

It is very earnestly hoped that these volumes of Notes—American, English, and by-and-by Italian—will dispel an often expressed opinion that Mr. Hawthorne was gloomy and morbid. He had the inevitable pensiveness and gravity of a person who possessed what a friend of his called 'the awful power of insight;' but his mood was always cheerful and equal, and his mind peculiarly healthful, and the airy splendor of his wit and humor was the light of his home. He saw too far to be despondent, though his vivid sympathies and shaping imagination often made him sad in behalf of others. He also perceived morbidness, wherever it existed, instantly, as if by the illumination of his own steady cheer; and he had the plastic power of putting himself into each person's situation, and of looking from every point of view, which made his charity most comprehensive. From this cause he necessarily attracted confidences, and became confessor to very many sinning and suffering souls, to whom he gave tender sympathy and help, while resigning judgment to the Omniscient and All-wise.

This is highly significant in its bearing upon the burrowing, or almost inquisitorial character of Hawthorne's studies of humanity; and a word or two more in the way of following up points already raised may not be undesirable. That peculiar shyness which a coarse person might have called want of grit, running as it did into incapacity for even *imaginative* social abandonment, had much to do with both the burrowing and the—what shall we call it?—the encircling, or beleaguering, movement of Hawthorne's mind. The truth is, that if he had had a more easy, natural flesh-and-blood grasp, both of living and of imaginary persons, he would have created much stronger and simpler figures. As it is, we can see that at first there is a sort of flinching, or falling-back movement of the whole of his nature, and then, after a time, he begins a kind of *teredo* action upon the character or the subject. Mr. Browning's manner may be called inquisitorial too, but how different in its boldness and flesh-and-blood grasp. You almost touch the hands and rub the shoulders of his people! On the other hand, we should have lost that weird indecision of the imagination which yet persists, returning to its point again and again, yet delaying to strike the final blow, in a way which to a victim threatened by him would be torture. We should also have lost that portion—the largest and most valuable—of Hawthorne's humor, which consists in what I might call the zest of shyness. Destiny herself could not drag him out to dinner, he himself tells us, and to such a man there must have been a keen delight in the involuntary exercise of his faculty of minute observation of others; himself unseen as a ghost. The subtle aroma of this felt delight is great part of Hawthorne's humor. Another element—diffused, like the first—is in his amused and amusing sense of the contrast there was between his own homely tastes and the awful lights with which his imagination so often painted. He could wash up plates and dishes with the best of us, and has recorded certain domestic triumphs in that kind; yet, at the bottom of his most lurid writing there is a sort of subtle plates-and-dishes consciousness. In other words, he felt that there was a certain humor in his writing romances, and the feeling is disclosed in his manner.

One of the things, by-the-by, which Mr. Hawthorne, in these 'Notes,' professed himself puzzled about is Mr. Browning's preference of 'The Blithedale Romance' to the other tales. The reason is not far to seek, however. The lesson of that powerful romance is, mainly, that the natural affections will not submit to be trampled on by systematized benevolence, but will turn and rend the trampler. This is a lesson after Mr. Browning's own heart, and no wonder that the author of 'The Flight of the Duchess,' and 'A Soul's Tragedy,' took kindly to the romance which embodied it. Considered, however, as a critical dictum upon the comparative merit of that work in the Hawthorne library, Mr. Browning's opinion is not worth a moment's thought. . . .

We hope, too, now that the accomplished lady who shared his life has followed him to the silent land, there is no indecorum in saying what a pleasure it is to be furnished by actual memoranda of his own with proofs, as strong as unobtrusive, that in one more distinguished example the common talk that men of genius are not fitted for a happy home-life was utterly inapplicable. We believe the accepted notion to be quite untrue; that whatever scintilla of excuse it may have is founded on facts which are favorable to men of letters; and that there are just as many unhappy married cheesemongers as poets, only we do not hear so much of the cheesemongers, nor do they possess the same trick and necessity of expression. One thing, meanwhile, is abundantly clear—namely, that the lady whose remains were recently laid in Kensal Green Cemetery did truly *share* the life of her husband.

Turning, out of mere respect, from her grave, before we make the remark, we may just ask those who repeat by rote the usual merciless criticisms of the married life of persons of exceptional faculty, to consider for a moment what would have been the consequence if Hawthorne had been unhappily married? No human being can possibly tell, but probably it would have been the destruction of his delicate genius, and the entire perversion of his career.

138. Leslie Stephen: Hawthorne and the lessons of romance, from an unsigned essay, 'Nathaniel Hawthorne', in the *Cornhill Magazine*

December 1872, xxvi, 717–34

Stephen (1832–1904), critic and historian, after contributing to many leading journals, became editor of *Cornhill Magazine* in 1871 and later undertook the editorship of the *Dictionary of National Biography*. His most important criticism includes several biographies and the *History of Thought in the Eighteenth Century* (1876).

. . . Some central truth should be embodied in every work of fiction, which cannot indeed be compressed into a definite formula, but which acts as the animating and informing principle, determining the main lines of the structure and affecting even its most trivial details. Critics who try to extract it as a formal moral, present us with nothing but an outside husk of dogma. The lesson itself is the living seed which, cast into a thousand minds, will bear fruit in a thousand different forms. These remarks, certainly obvious enough, are but a clumsy comment on part of Hawthorne's preface to the *House of the Seven Gables*; they roughly express, therefore, Hawthorne's theory of his own art; and they are preparatory to the question, so far as it is a rational question, what do his romances prove? . . . one may . . . attempt to indicate what is for some persons the most conspicuous tendency of writings in which the finest, if not the most powerful genius of America has embodied itself. Compressing the answer to its narrowest limits, one may say that Hawthorne has shown what elements of romance are discoverable amongst the harsh prose of this prosaic age. And his teaching is of importance, because it is just what is most needed at the present day. How is the novelist who, by the inevitable conditions of his style, is bound to come into the closest possible contact with facts, who has to give us the details of his hero's clothes, to tell us what he had for breakfast, and what is the state of the balance at his banker's—how is he to introduce the ideal element which must, in some degree, be present in all genuine art? A mere photographic reproduction of this muddy, money-making, bread-and-butter-eating world would be intolerable. At the very lowest, some effort must be made at least to select the most promising materials, and to strain out the coarse or the simple prosaic ingredients. Various attempts have been made to solve the problem since Defoe founded the modern school of English novelists by giving us what is in one sense a servile imitation of genuine narrative, but which is redeemed from prose by the unique force of the situation. Defoe painting mere every-day pots and pans is as dull as a modern blue-book; but when his pots and pans are the resource by which a human being struggles out of the most appalling conceivable 'slough of despond,' they become more poetical than the vessels from which the gods drink nectar in epic poems. Since he wrote novelists have made many voyages of discovery, with varying success, though they have seldom had the fortune to touch upon so marvellous an island as that still sacred to the immortal Crusoe. They have ventured far into cloud-land, and returning to *terra firma*, they have plunged into the trackless and savage-haunted regions which are girdled by the Metropolitan Railway. They have watched the magic coruscations of some strange *Aurora Borealis* of dim romance, or been content with the domestic gas-light of London streets. Amongst the most celebrated of all such adventures were the band which obeyed the impulse of Sir Walter Scott. For a time it seemed that we had reached a genuine Eldorado of novelists, where solid gold was to be had for the asking, and visions of more than earthly beauty rewarded the labours of the explorer. Now, alas! our opinion is a good deal changed; the fairy treasures which Scott brought back from his voyages have turned into dead leaves according to custom; and the curiosities, upon which he set so extravagant a price, savour more of Wardour Street than of the genuine mediæval artists. Nay, there are scoffers, though I am not of them, who think that the tittle-tattle which Miss Austen gathered at the country-houses of our grandfathers is worth more than the showy but rather flimsy eloquence of the 'Ariosto of the North.' Scott endeavoured at least, if with in-different success, to invest his scenes with something of—

> The light that never was on sea or land,
> The consecration and the poet's dream.

If he too often indulged in mere theatrical devices and mistook the glare of the footlights for the sacred glow of the imagination, he professed, at least, to introduce us to an ideal world. Later novelists have generally abandoned the attempt, and are content to reflect our work-a-day life with almost servile fidelity. They are not to be blamed; and doubtless the very greatest writers are those who can bring their ideal world into the closest possible contact with our sympathies, and show us heroic figures in modern frock-coats and Parisian fashions. The art of story-telling is manifold, and its charm depends greatly upon the infinite variety of its applications. And yet, for that very reason, there are moods in which one wishes that the modern story-teller would more frequently lead us away from the commonplace region of newspapers and railways to regions where the imagination can have fair play. Haw-thorne is one of the few eminent writers to whose guidance we may in such moods most safely entrust ourselves; and it is tempting to ask what was the secret of his success. The effort, indeed, to investigate the materials from which some rare literary flavour is extracted is seldom satisfactory. . . . And yet, with this warning as to the probable success of our examination, let us try to determine some of the peculiarities to which Hawthorne owes this strange power of bringing poetry out of the most unpromising materials.

In the first place, then, he had the good fortune to be born in the most prosaic of all countries—the most prosaic, that is, in external ap-pearance, and even in the superficial character of its inhabitants. Haw-thorne himself reckoned this as an advantage, though in a very different sense from that in which we are speaking. It was as a patriot, and not as an artist, that he congratulated himself on his American origin. There is a humorous struggle between his sense of the rawness and ugliness of his native land and the dogged patriotism befitting a descendant of the genuine New England Puritans. Hawthorne the novelist writhes at the discords which torture his delicate sensibilities at every step; but in-

stantly Hawthorne the Yankee protests that the very faults are symptomatic of excellence. He is like a sensitive mother, unable to deny that
her awkward hobbledehoy of a son offends against the proprieties, but
tacitly resolved to see proofs of virtues present or to come even in his
clumsiest tricks. He forces his apologies to sound like boasting. 'No
author' he says ,'can conceive of the difficulty of writing a romance
about a country where there is no shadow, no antiquity, no mystery, no
picturesque and gloomy wrong, nor anything but a commonplace prosperity, as is happily' (it must and shall be happily) 'the case with my dear
native land. It will be very long, I trust, before romance-writers may
find congenial and easily-handled themes either in the annals of our
stalwart republic, or in any characteristic and probable events of our
individual lives. Romance and poetry, ivy, lichens and wallflowers need
ruins to make then grow.' If, that is, I am forced to confess that poetry
and romance are absent, I will resolutely stick to it that poetry and
romance are bad things, even though the love of them is the strongest
propensity of my nature. To my thinking, there is something almost
pathetic in this loyal self-deception; and therefore I have never been
offended by certain passages in *Our Old Home* which appear to have
caused some irritation in touchy Englishmen. There is something, he
says by way of apology, which causes an American in England to take
up an attitude of antagonism. 'These people think so loftily of themselves, and so contemptuously of everybody else, that it requires more
generosity than I possess to keep always in perfect good-humour with
them.' That may be true; for, indeed, I believe that deep down in the
bosom of every Briton, beneath all superficial roots of cosmopolitan
philanthropy, there lies an ineradicable conviction that no foreigner is
his equal; and to a man of Hawthorne's delicate perceptions, the presence of that sentiment would reveal itself through the most careful
disguises. But that which really caused him to cherish his antagonism
was, I suspect, something else: he was afraid of loving us too well; he
feared to be tempted into a denial of some point of his patriotic creed;
he is always clasping it, as it were, to his bosom, and vowing and protesting that he does not surrender a single jot or tittle of it. Hawthorne
in England was like a plant suddenly removed to a rich soil from a dry
and thirsty land. He drinks in at every pore the delightful influences of
which he has had so scanty a supply. An old cottage, an ivy-grown wall,
a country churchyard with its quaint epitaphs, things that are commonplace to most Englishmen and which are hateful to the sanitary inspector, are refreshing to every fibre of his soul. He tries in vain to take

489

the sanitary inspector's view. In spite of himself he is always falling into the romantic tone, though a sense that he ought to be sternly philosophical just gives a humorous tinge to his enthusiasm. . . . He feels the charm of our historical continuity, where the immemorial past blends indistinguishably with the present, to the remotest recesses of his imagination. But then the Yankee nature within him must put in a sharp word or two; he has to jerk the bridle for fear that his enthusiasm should fairly run away with him. . . .

The true theory, it appears, is that which Holgrave expresses for him in the *Seven Gables*, namely, that we should free ourselves of the material slavery imposed upon us by the brick-and-mortar of past generations, and learn to change our houses as early as our coats. We ought to feel—only we unfortunately can't feel—that a tent or a wigwam is as good as a house. The mode in which Hawthorne regards the Englishman himself is a quaint illustration of the same theory. An Englishwoman, he admits reluctantly and after many protestations, has some few beauties not possessed by her American sisters. A maiden in her teens has 'a certain charm of half blossom and delicately-folded leaves, and tender womanhood shielded by maidenly reserves, with which, somehow or other, our American girls often fail to adorn themselves during an appreciable moment.' But he revenges himself for this concession by an almost savage onslaught upon the full-blown British matron with her 'awful ponderosity of frame. . . massive with solid beef and streaky tallow,' and apparently composed 'of steaks and sirloins.' He laments that the English violet should develop into such an overblown peony, and speculates upon the whimsical problem, whether a middle-aged husband should be considered as legally married to all the accretions which have overgrown the slenderness of his bride. Should not the matrimonial bond be held to exclude the three-fourths of the wife that had no existence when the ceremony was performed? A question not to be put without a shudder. The fact is, that Hawthorne had succeeded only too well in misleading himself by a common fallacy. That pestilent personage, John Bull, has assumed so concrete a form in our imaginations, with his top-boots and his broad shoulders and vast circumference, and the emblematic bull-dog at his heels, that for most observers he completely hides the Englishman of real life. Hawthorne had decided that an Englishman must and should be a mere mass of transformed beef and beer. No observation could shake his preconceived impression. . . . But the problem recurs—for everybody likes to ask utterly unanswerable questions—whether Hawthorne would not have developed into a still greater artist if he had been more richly supplied with the diet so dear to his inmost soul? Was it not a thing to weep over, that a man so keenly alive to every picturesque influence, so anxious to invest his work with the enchanted haze of romantic association, should be confined till middle age amongst the bleak granite rocks and the half-baked civilization of New England? 'Among ourselves,' he laments, 'there is no fairy land for the romancer.' What if he had been brought up in the native home of the fairies—if there had been thrown open to him the gates through which Shakspeare and Spencer caught their visions of ideal beauty? Might we not have had an appendix to the *Midsummer Night's Dream*, and might not a modern *Faerie Queen* have brightened the prosaic wilderness of this nineteenth century? The question, as I have said, is rigidly unanswerable. We have not yet learnt how to breed poets, though we have made some progress in regard to pigs. Nobody can tell, and perhaps, therefore, it is as well that nobody should guess, what would have been the effect of transplanting Shakspeare to modern Stratford, or of exiling him to the United States. And yet—for it is impossible to resist entirely the pleasure of fruitless speculation— we may guess that there are some reasons why there should be a risk in transplanting so delicate a growth as the genius of Hawthorne. . . .

Hawthorne, if his life had passed where the plough may turn up an antiquity in every furrow, and the whole face of the country is enamelled with ancient culture, might have wrought more gorgeous hues into his tissues, but he might have succumbed to the temptation of producing mere upholstery. The fairy land for which he longed is full of dangerous enchantments, and there are many who have lost in it the vigour which comes from breathing the keen air of every-day life. From that risk Hawthorne was effectually preserved in his New England home. Having to abandon the poetry which is manufactured out of mere external circumstances, he was forced to draw it from deeper sources. With easier means at hand of enriching his pages, he might have left the mine unworked. It is often good for us to have to make bricks without straw. Hawthorne, who was conscious of the extreme difficulty of the problem, and but partially conscious of the success of his solution of it, naturally complained of the severe discipline to which he owed his strength. We who enjoy the results may feel how much he owed to the very sternness of his education and the niggard hand with which his imaginative sustenance was dealt out to him. . . .

The story which perhaps generally passes for his masterpiece is *Transformation*, for most readers assume that a writer's longest book must necessarily be his best. In the present case, I think that this method, which has its conveniences, has not led to a perfectly just conclusion. In *Transformation*, Hawthorne has for once the advantage of placing his characters in a land where 'a sort of poetic or fairy precinct,' as he calls it, is naturally provided for them. The very stones of the streets are full of romance, and he cannot mention a name that has not a musical ring. Hawthorne, moreover, shows his usual tact in confining his aims to the possible. He does not attempt to paint Italian life and manners; his actors belong by birth, or by a kind of naturalization, to the colony of the American artists in Rome; and he therefore does not labour under the difficulty of being in imperfect sympathy with his creatures. Rome is a mere background, and surely a most felicitous background, to the little group of persons who are effectually detached from all such vulgarizing associations with the mechanism of daily life in less poetical countries. The centre of the group, too, who embodies one of Hawthorne's most delicate fancies, could have breathed no atmosphere less richly perfumed with old romance. . . . Perhaps it may be thought by some severe critics that, with all his merits, Donatello stands on the very outside verge of the province permitted to the romancer. But without cavilling at what is indisputably charming, and without dwelling upon certain defects of construction which slightly mar the general beauty of the story, it has another weakness which it is impossible quite to overlook. Hawthorne himself remarks that he was surprised, in rewriting his story, to see the extent to which he had introduced descriptions of various Italian objects. 'Yet these things,' he adds, 'fill the mind everywhere in Italy, and especially in Rome, and cannot be kept from flowing out upon the page when one writes freely and with self-enjoyment.' The associations which they called up in England were so pleasant, that he could not find it in his heart to cancel. Doubtless that is the precise truth, and yet it is equally true that they are artistically out of place. There are, to put it bluntly, passages which strike us like masses of undigested guide-book. To take one instance—and, certainly, it is about the worst—the whole party is going to the Coliseum, where a very striking scene takes place. On the way, they pass a baker's shop.

'"The baker is drawing his loaves out of the oven,' remarked Kenyon. "Do you smell how sour they are? I should fancy that Minerva (in revenge for the desecration of her temple) had slyly poured vinegar into the batch, if I did not know that the modern Romans prefer their bread in the acetous fermentation."'

The instance is trivial, but it is characteristic. Hawthorne had doubtless remarked the smell of the sour bread, and to him it called up a vivid recollection of some stroll in Rome; for, of all our senses, the smell is the most powerful in awakening associations. But then what do we who read him care about the Roman taste for bread 'in acetous fermentation?' When the high-spirited girl is on the way to meet her tormentor, and to receive the provocation which leads to his murder, why should we be worried by a gratuitous remark about Roman baking? It somehow jars upon our taste, and we are certain that, in describing a New England village, Hawthorne would never have admitted a touch which has no conceivable bearing upon the situation. There is almost a super-abundance of minute local colour in his American romances, as, for example, in the *House of the Seven Gables*; but still, every touch, however minute, is steeped in the sentiment and contributes to the general effect. In Rome the smell of a loaf is sacred to his imagination, and intrudes itself upon its own merits, and, so far as we can discover, without reference to the central purpose. If a baker's shop impresses him unduly because it is Roman, the influence of ancient ruins and glorious works of art is of course still more distracting. The mysterious Donatello, and the strange psychological problem which he is destined to illustrate, are put aside for an interval, whilst we are called upon to listen to descriptions and meditations, always graceful, and often of great beauty in themselves, but yet, in a strict sense, irrelevant. Hawthorne's want of familiarity with the scenery is of course responsible for part of this failing. Had he been a native Roman, he would not have been so pre-occupied with the wonders of Rome. But it seems that for a romance bearing upon a spiritual problem, the scenery, however tempting, is not really so serviceable as the less prepossessing surroundings of America. The objects have too great an intrinsic interest. A counter-attraction distorts the symmetry of the system. In the shadow of the Coliseum and St. Peter's you cannot pay much attention to the troubles of a young lady whose existence is painfully ephemeral. Those mighty objects will not be relegated to the background, and condescend to act as mere scenery. They are, in fact, too romantic for a romance. . . . A human soul, even in America, is more interesting to us than all the churches and picture-galleries in the world; and, therefore, it is as well that Hawthorne should not be tempted to the too easy method of putting fine description in place of sentiment.

But how was the task to be performed? How was the imaginative glow to be shed over the American scenery, so provokingly raw and deficient in harmony? A similar problem was successfully solved by a writer whose development, in proportion to her means of cultivation, is about the most remarkable of recent literary phenomena. Miss Brontë's bleak Yorkshire moors, with their uncompromising stone walls, and the valleys invaded by factories, are at first sight as little suited to romance as New England itself, to which, indeed, both the inhabitants and the country have a decided family resemblance. Now that she has discovered for us the fountains of poetic interest, we can all see that the region is not a mere stony wilderness; but it is well worth while to make a pilgrimage to Haworth, if only to discover how little the country corresponds to our preconceived impressions, or, in other words, how much depends upon the eye which sees it, and how little upon its intrinsic merits. Miss Brontë's marvellous effects are obtained by the process which enables an 'intense and glowing mind' to see everything through its own atmosphere. The ugliest and most trivial objects seem, like objects heated by the sun, to radiate back the glow of passion with which she has regarded them. Perhaps, this singular power is still more conspicuous in *Villette*, where she had even less of the raw material of poetry. An odd parallel may be found between one of the most striking passages in *Villette* and one in *Transformation*. Lucy Snowe in one novel, and Hilda in the other, are left to pass a summer vacation, the one in Brussels and the other in pestiferous Rome. Miss Snowe has no external cause of suffering but the natural effect of solitude upon a homeless and helpless governess. Hilda has to bear about with her the weight of a terrible secret, affecting, it may be, even the life of her dearest friend. Each of them wanders into a Roman Catholic church, and each, though they have both been brought up in a Protestant home, seeks relief at the confessional. So far the cases are alike, though Hilda, one might have fancied, has by far the strongest cause for emotion. And yet, after reading the two descriptions—both excellent in their way—one might fancy that the two young ladies had exchanged burdens. Lucy Snowe is as tragic as the innocent confidante of a murderess; Hilda's feelings never seem to rise above that weary sense of melancholy isolation which besieges us in a deserted city. It is needless to ask which is the best bit of work artistically considered. Hawthorne's style is more graceful and flexible; his descriptions of the Roman Catholic ceremonial and its influence upon an imaginative mind in distress are far more sympathetic, and imply a wider range of intellect. But Hilda does not touch and almost overawe us like Lucy. There is too much delicate artistic description of picture-galleries and of the glories

of St. Peter's to allow the poor little American girl to come prominently
to the surface. We have been indulging with her in some sad but charming speculations, and not witnessing the tragedy of a deserted soul. Lucy
Snowe has very inferior materials at her command; but somehow we
are moved by a sympathetic thrill: we taste the bitterness of the awful
cup of despair which, as she tells us, is forced to her lips in the night-
watches; and are not startled when so prosaic an object as the row of
beds in the dormitory of a French school suggest to her images worthy
rather of stately tombs in the aisles of a vast cathedral, and recall dead
dreams of an elder world and mightier race long frozen in death.
Comparisons of this kind are almost inevitably unfair; but the difference between the two illustrates one characteristic—we need not regard
it as a defect—of Hawthorne. His idealism does not consist in conferring
grandeur upon vulgar objects by tinging them with the reflection of
deep emotion. He rather shrinks than otherwise from describing the
strongest passions, or shows their working by indirect touches and
under a side-light. An excellent example of his peculiar method occurs
in what is in some respects the most perfect of his works, the *Scarlet
Letter*. There, again, we have the spectacle of a man tortured by a life-
long repentance. The Puritan clergyman, reverenced as a saint by all
his flock, conscious of a sin which, once revealed, will crush him to the
earth, watched with a malignant purpose by the husband whom he has
injured, unable to summon up the moral courage to tear off the veil,
and make the only atonement in his power, is undoubtedly a striking
figure, powerfully conceived and most delicately described. He yields
under terrible pressure to the temptation of escaping from the scene of
his prolonged torture with the partner of his guilt. And then, as he is
returning homewards after yielding a reluctant consent to the flight, we
are invited to contemplate the agony of his soul. The form which it
takes is curiously characteristic. No vehement pangs of remorse, or
desperate hopes of escape, overpower his faculties in any simple and
straightforward fashion. The poor minister is seized with a strange
hallucination. He meets a venerable deacon, and can scarcely restrain
himself from uttering blasphemies about the communion-supper. Next
appears an aged widow, and he longs to assail her with what appears
to him to be an unanswerable argument against the immortality of the
soul. Then follows an impulse to whisper impure suggestions to a fair
young maiden, whom he has recently converted. And, finally, he longs
to greet a rough sailor with a 'volley of good round, solid, satisfactory,
and heaven-defying oaths.' The minister, in short, is in that state of

mind which gives birth in its victim to a belief in diabolical possession; and the meaning is pointed by an encounter with an old lady, who, in the popular belief, was one of Satan's miserable slaves and dupes, the witches, and is said—for Hawthorne never introduces the supernatural without toning it down by a supposed legendary transmission—to have invited him to meet her at the blasphemous sabbath in the forest. The sin of endeavouring to escape from the punishment of his sins had brought him into sympathy with wicked mortals and perverted spirits.

This mode of setting forth the agony of a pure mind, tainted by one irremovable blot, is undoubtedly impressive to the imagination in a high degree; far more impressive, we may safely say, than any quantity of such rant as very inferior writers could have poured out with the utmost facility on such an occasion. Yet I am inclined to think that a poet of the highest order would have produced the effect by more direct means. Remorse overpowering and absorbing does not embody itself in these recondite and, one may almost say, over-ingenious fancies. Hawthorne does not give us so much the pure passion as some of its collateral effects. He is still more interested in the curious psychological problem than moved by sympathy with the torture of the soul. We pity poor Mr. Dimmesdale profoundly, but we are also interested in him as the subject of an experiment in analytical psychology. We do not care so much for his emotions as for the strange phantoms which are raised in his intellect by the disturbance of his natural functions. The man is placed upon the rack, but our compassion is aroused, not by feeling our own nerves and sinews twitching in sympathy, but by remarking the strange confusion of ideas produced in his mind, the singularly distorted aspect of things in general introduced by such an experience, and hence, if we please, inferring the keenness of the pangs which have produced them. This turn of thought explains the real meaning of Hawthorne's antipathy to poor John Bull. That worthy gentleman, we will admit, is in a sense more gross and beefy than his American cousin. His nerves are stronger, for we need not decide whether they should be called coarser or less morbid. He is not, in any proper sense of the word, less imaginative, for a vigorous grasp of realities is rather a proof of a powerful than a defective imagination. But he is less accessible to those delicate impulses which are to the ordinary passions as electricity to heat. His imagination is more intense and less mobile. The devils which haunt the two races partake of the national characteristics. John Bunyan, Dimmesdale's contemporary, suffered under the pangs of a remorse equally acute, though with apparently far less cause. The devils who tormented him whispered blasphemies in his ears; they pulled at his clothes; they persuaded him that he had committed the unpardonable sin. They caused the very stones in the streets and tiles on the houses, as he says, to band themselves together against him. But they had not the refined and humorous ingenuity of the American fiends. They tempted him, as their fellows tempted Dimmesdale, to sell his soul; but they were too much in earnest to insist upon queer breaches of decorum. They did not indulge in their quaint play of fancy which tempts us to believe that the devils in New England had seduced the 'tricksy spirit,' Ariel, to indulge in practical jokes at the expense of a nobler victim than Stephano or Caliban. They were too terribly diabolical to care whether Bunyan blasphemed in solitude or in the presence of human respectabilities. Bunyan's sufferings were as poetical, but less conducive to refined speculation. His were the fiends that haunt the valley of the shadow of death; whereas Hawthorne's are to be encountered in the dim regions of twilight, where realities blend inextricably with mere phantoms, and the mind confers only a kind of provisional existence upon the 'airy nothings' of its creation. Apollyon does not appear armed to the teeth and throwing fiery darts, but comes as an unsubstantial shadow threatening vague and undefined dangers, and only half detaching himself from the background of darkness. He is as intangible as Milton's Death, not the vivid reality which presented itself to mediæval imaginations.

This special aptitude of mind is probably easier to the American than to the English imagination. The craving for something substantial, whether in cookery or in poetry, was that which induced Hawthorne to keep John Bull rather at arm's length. We may trace the working of similar tendencies in other American peculiarities. Spiritualism and its attendant supersitions are the gross and vulgar form of the same phase of thought as it occurs in men of highly-strung nerves but defective cultivation. Hawthorne always speaks of these modern goblins with the contempt they deserve, for they shocked his imagination as much as his reason; but he likes to play with fancies which are not altogether dissimilar, though his refined taste warns him that they become disgusting when grossly translated into tangible symbols. Mesmerism, for example, plays an important part in the *Blithedale Romance* and the *House of the Seven Gables*, though judiciously softened and kept in the background. An example of the danger of such tendencies may be found in his countryman, Edgar Poe, who, with all his eccentricities, had a most unmistakable vein of genius. Poe is a kind of Hawthorne and *delirium tremens.* What is exquisitely fanciful and airy in the genuine artist is replaced in his rival by an attempt to overpower us by dabblings in the charnel-house and prurient appeals to our fears of the horribly revolting. After reading some of Poe's stories one feels a kind of shock to one's modesty. We require some kind of spiritual ablution to cleanse our minds of his disgusting images; whereas Hawthorne's pure and delightful fancies, though at times they may have led us too far from the healthy contact of every-day interests, never leave a stain upon the imagination, and generally succeed in throwing a harmonious colouring upon some objects in which we had previously failed to recognize the beautiful. To perform that duty effectually is perhaps the highest of artistic merits; and though we may complain of Hawthorne's colouring as too evanescent, its charm grows upon us the more we study it.

Hawthorne seems to have been slow in discovering the secret of his own power. The *Twice-Told Tales*, he tells us, are only a fragmentary selection from a great number which had an ephemeral existence in long-forgotten magazines, and were sentenced to extinction by their author. Though many of the survivors are very striking, no wise reader will regret that sentence. It could be wished that other authors were as ready to bury their innocents, and that injudicious admirers might always abstain from acting as resurrection-men. The fragments which remain, with all their merits, are chiefly interesting as illustrating the intellectual developments of their author. Hawthorne, in his preface to the collected edition (all Hawthorne's prefaces are remarkably instructive) tells us what to think of them. . . . We see him trying various experiments to hit off that delicate mean between the fanciful and the prosaic which shall satisfy his taste and be intelligible to the outside world. Sometimes he gives us a fragment of historical romance, as in the story of the stern old regicide who suddenly appears from the woods to head the colonists of Massachusetts in a critical emergency; then he tries his hand at a bit of allegory, and describes the search for the mythical carbuncle which blazes by its inherent splendour on the face of a mysterious cliff in the depths of the untrodden wilderness, and lures old and young, the worldly and the romantic, to waste their lives in the vain effort to discover it—for the carbuncle is the ideal which mocks our pursuit, and may be our curse or our blessing. Then perhaps we have a domestic piece,—a quiet description of a New England country scene—touched with a grace which reminds us of the creators of Sir Roger de Coverley or the Vicar of Wakefield. Occasionally there is a fragment of pure *diablerie*, as in the story of the lady who consults the witch in the hollow of the three hills; and more frequently he tries to work out one of those strange psychological problems which he afterwards treated with more fulness of power. The minister, who for an unexplained reason, puts on a black veil one morning in his youth and wears it until he is laid with it in his grave—a kind of symbolical prophecy of Dimmesdale; the eccentric Wakefield (whose original, if I remember rightly, is to be found in *King's Anecdotes*), who leaves his house one morning for no particular reason, and though living in the next street, does not reveal his existence to his wife for twenty years; and the hero of the *Wedding Knell*, the elderly bridegroom whose early love has jilted him, but agrees to marry him when she is an elderly widow and he an old bachelor, and who appals the marriage-party by coming to the church in his shroud, with the bell tolling as for a funeral, —all these bear the unmistakable stamp of Hawthorne's mint, and each is a study of his favourite subject, the borderland between reason and insanity. In many of these stories appears the element of interest, to which Hawthorne clung the more closely both from early associations and because it is the one undeniably poetical element in the American character. Shallow-minded people fancy Puritanism to be prosaic, because the laces and ruffles of the Cavaliers are a more picturesque costume at a masked ball than the dress of the Roundheads. The Puritan has become a grim and ugly scarecrow, on whom every buffoon may break his jest. But the genuine old Puritan spirit ceases to be picturesque only because of its sublimity: its poetry is sublimed into religion. The great poet of the Puritans fails, so far as he fails, when he tries to transcend the limits of mortal imagination. . . .

To represent the Puritan from within was not, indeed, a task suitable to Hawthorne's powers. Mr. Carlyle has done that for us with more congenial sentiment than could have been well felt by the gentle romancer. Hawthorne fancies the grey shadow of a stern old forefather wondering at his degenerate son. 'A writer of story-books! What kind of business in life, what mode of glorifying God, or being serviceable to mankind in his day and generation may that be? Why, the degenerate fellow might as well have been a fiddler!' And yet the old strain remains, though strangely modified by time and circumstance. Every pure Yankee represents one or both of two types—the descendant of the Puritans and the shrewd peddler; one was embodied in the last century in Jonathan Edwards, and the other in Benjamin Franklin; and we may still trace both in literature and politics the blended currents of feeling. It is an equal mistake—as various people have had to discover before now—to neglect the existence of the old fanaticism or enthusiasm—whichever you please to call it—in the modern Yankee, or to fancy that a fanatic is a bad hand at a bargain. In Hawthorne it would seem that the peddling element had been reduced to its lowest point; the more spiritual element had been refined till it is probable enough that the ancestral shadow would have refused to recognize the connection. The old dogmatical framework to which he attached such vast importance had dropped out of his descendant's mind, and had been replaced by dreamy speculation, obeying no laws save those imposed by its own sense of artistic propriety. But we may often recognize, even where we cannot express in words, the strange family likeness which exists in characteristics which are superficially antagonistic. The man of action may be bound by subtle ties to the speculative metaphysician; and Hawthorne's mind, amidst the most obvious differences, had still an affinity to his remote forefathers. Their bugbears had become his play-things; but the witches, though they have no reality, have still a fascination for him. The interest which he feels in them, even in their now shadowy state, is a proof that he would have believed in them in good earnest a century and a half earlier. The imagination, working in a different intellectual atmosphere, is unable to project its images upon the external world; but it still forms them in the old shape. His solitary musings necessarily employ a modern dialect, but they often turn on the same topics which occurred to Jonathan Edwards in the woods of Connecticut. Instead of the old Puritan speculations about predestination and freewill, he dwells upon the transmission by natural laws of an hereditary curse, and upon the strange blending of good and evil, which may cause sin to be an awakening impulse in a human soul. The change which takes place in Donatello in consequence of his crime is a modern symbol of the fall of man and the eating the fruit of the knowledge of good and evil. As an artist he gives concrete images instead of abstract theories; but his thoughts evidently delight to dwell in the same regions where the daring speculations of his theological ancestors took their origin. Septimius, the rather disagreeable hero of his last romance, is a peculiar example of a similar change. Brought up under the strict discipline of New England, he has retained the love of musing upon insoluble mysteries, though he has abandoned the old dogmatic guide-posts. When such a man finds that the orthodox scheme of the universe provided by his official pastors has somehow broken down with him, he forms some audacious theory of his own, and is perhaps plunged into an unhallowed revolt against the Divine order. Septimius, under

such circumstances, develops into a kind of morbid and sullen Hawthorne. He considers—as other people have done—that death is a disagreeable fact, but refuses to admit that it is inevitable. The romance
tends to show that such a state of mind is unhealthy and dangerous, and
Septimius is contrasted unfavourably with the vigorous natures who
preserve their moral balance by plunging into the stream of practical
life. Yet Hawthorne necessarily sympathizes with the abnormal being
whom he creates. Septimius illustrates the dangers of the musing
temperament, but the dangers are produced by a combination of an
essentially selfish nature with the meditative tendency. Hawthorne,
like his hero, sought refuge from the hard facts of commonplace life by
retiring into a visionary world. He delights in propounding much the
same questions as those which tormented poor Septimius, though, for
obvious reasons, he did not try to compound an elixir of life by means
of a recipe handed down from Indian ancestors. The strange mysteries
in which the world and our nature are shrouded are always present to
his imagination; he catches dim glimpses of the laws which bring out
strange harmonies, but, on the whole, tend rather to deepen than to
clear the mysteries. He loves the marvellous, not in the vulgar sense of
the word, but as a symbol of the perplexity which encounters every
thoughtful man in his journey through life. Similar tenets at an earlier
period might, with almost equal probability, have led him to the stake
as a dabbler in forbidden sciences, or have caused him to be revered as
one to whom a deep spiritual instinct had been granted.

Meanwhile, as it was his calling to tell stories to readers of the English
language in the nineteenth century, his power is exercised in a different
sphere. No modern writer has the same skill in so using the marvellous
as to interest without unduly exciting our incredulity. He makes, indeed,
no positive demands on our credulity. The strange influences which are
suggested rather than obtruded upon us, are kept in the background so
as not to invite, nor, indeed, to render possible the application of
scientific tests. We may compare him once more to Miss Brontë, who
shows us, in *Villette*, a haunted garden. She shows us a ghost who is for
a moment a very terrible spectre indeed, and then, rather to our annoyance, rationalizes him into a flesh and blood lover. Hawthorne would
neither have allowed the ghost to intrude so forcibly, nor have expelled
him so decisively. The garden in his hands would have been haunted
by a shadowy terror of which we could render no precise account to
ourselves. It would have refrained from actual contact with professors
and governesses; and as it would never have taken bodily form, it would

never have been quite dispelled. His ghosts are confined to their proper sphere, the twilight of the mind, and never venture into the broad glare of daylight. We can see them so long as we do not gaze directly at them; when we turn to examine them they are gone, and we are left in doubt whether they were realities or an ocular delusion generated in our fancy by some accidental collocation of half-seen objects. So in the *House of the Seven Gables* we may hold what opinion we please as to the reality of the curse which hangs over the family of the Pyncheons and the strange connection between them and their hereditary antagonists; in the *Scarlet Letter* we may, if we like, hold that there was really more truth in the witch legends which colour the imaginations of the actors than we are apt to dream of in our philosophy; and in *Transformation* we are left finally in doubt as to the great question of Donatello's ears, and the mysterious influence which he retains over the animal world so long as he is unstained by bloodshed. In *Septimius* alone, it seems to me that the supernatural is left in rather too obtrusive a shape in spite of the final explanations; though it might possibly have been toned down had the story received the last touches of the author. The artifice, if so it may be called, by which this is effected, and the romance is just sufficiently dipped in the shadow of the marvellous to be heightened without becoming offensive, sounds, like other things, tolerably easy when it is explained: and yet the difficulty is enormous, as may appear on reflection as well as from the extreme rarity of any satisfactory work in the same style by other artists. With the exception of a touch or two in Scott's stories, such as the impressive Bodach Glas in *Waverley* and the apparition in the exquisite *Bride of Lammermoor*, it would be difficult to discover any parallel.

In fact Hawthorne was able to tread in that magic circle only by an exquisite refinement of taste, and by a delicate sense of humour, which is the best preservative against all extravagance. Both qualities combine in that tender delineation of character which is, after all, one of his greatest charms. His Puritan blood shows itself in sympathy, not with the stern side of the ancestral creed, but with the feebler characters upon whom it weighed as an oppressive terror. He resembles, in some degree, poor Clifford Pyncheon, whose love of the beautiful makes him suffer under the stronger will of his relatives and the prim stiffness of their home. He exhibits the suffering of such a character all the more effectively because, with his kindly compassion, there is mixed a delicate flavour of irony. The more tragic scenes affect us, perhaps, with less sense of power; the playful, though melancholy, fancy seems to be less at home when the more powerful emotions are to be excited; and yet once, at least, he draws one of those pictures which engrave themselves instantaneously on the memory. The grimmest or most passionate of writers could hardly have improved the scene where the body of the magnificent Zenobia is discovered in the river. Every touch goes straight to the mark. The narrator of the story, accompanied by the man whose coolness has caused the suicide, and the shrewd, unimaginative Yankee farmer, who interprets with coarse, downright language the suspicions which they fear to confess to themselves, are sounding the depths of the river by night in a leaky punt with a long pole. Silas Foster interprets the brutal commonplace comments of the outside world, which jar so terribly on the more sensitive and closely interested actors in the tragedy. . . .

. . . Hawthorne is specially interesting because one fancies that, in spite of the marked idiosyncracies which forbid one to see in him the founder of a school—as, indeed, any rivalry would be dangerous—he is, in some sense, a characteristic embodiment of true national tendencies. If so, we may hope that, though America may never produce another Hawthorne, yet other American writers may arise who will apply some of his principles of art, and develop the fineness of observation and delicate sense of artistic propriety for which he was so conspicuous. On that matter, at least, we can have no jealousies; and if our cousins raise more Hawthornes, we may possibly feel more grateful than for some of their other productions. . . .

139. George Parsons Lathrop, The family version of Hawthorne, from *A Study of Hawthorne*

1876, pp. 284–99

Lathrop (1851–98), Hawthorne's son-in-law, was a writer of popular novels and travel books. Associate editor of the *Atlantic Monthly* from 1875 to 1877, he edited the 1883 Riverside Edition of Hawthorne's works, until recently the standard scholarly text.

What has thus far been developed in this essay, concerning Hawthorne's personality, though incidental, has, I hope, served the end in view,—that of suggesting a large, healthy nature, capable of the most profound thought and the most graceful and humorous mental play. The details of his early life already given show how soon the inborn honor of his nature began to shine. The small irregularities in his college course have seemed to me to bring him nearer and to endear him, without in any way impairing the dignity and beauty of character which prevailed in him from the beginning. It is good to know that he shared the average human history in these harmless peccadilloes; for they never hurt his integrity, and they are reminders of that old but welcome truth, that the greatest men do not need a constant diet of great circumstances. He had many difficulties to deal with, as unpicturesque and harassing as any we have to encounter in our daily courses,—a thing which people are curiously prone to forget in the case of eminent authors. The way in which he dealt with these throws back light on himself. We discover how well the high qualities of genius were matched by those of character.

Fragmentary anecdotes have a value, but so relative that to attempt to construct the subject's character out of them is hazardous. Conceptions of a man derived only from such matter remind one of Charles Lamb's ghosts, formed of the particles which, every seven years, are replaced throughout the body by new ones. Likewise, the grossest errors have been committed through the assumption that particular passages in Hawthorne's writings apply directly and unqualifiedly to himself. There is so much imagination interfused with them, that only a reverent and careful imagination can apply them aright. Nor are private letters to be interpreted in any other way than as the talk of the hour, very inadequately representative, and often—unless read in many lights —positively untrue, to the writer. It gives an entirely false notion, for example, to accept as a trait of character this modest covering up of a noble sentiment, which occurs in a letter refusing to withdraw the dedication of 'Our Old Home' to Pierce, in the time of the latter's unpopularity:—

Nevertheless, I have no fancy for making myself a martyr when it is honorably and conscientiously possible to avoid it; and I always measure out my heroism very accurately according to the exigencies of the occasion, and should be the last man in the world to throw away a bit of it needlessly.

Such a passage ought never to have been printed without some modifying word; for it has been execrably misused. 'I have often felt,' Hawthorne says, 'that words may be a thick and darksome veil of mystery between the soul and the truth which it seeks.' What injustice, then, that he should be judged by a literal construction of words quickly chosen for the transient embodiment of a mood!

The first and most common opinion about the man Hawthorne is, that he must have been extremely gloomy, because his mind nourished so many grave thoughts and solemn fancies. But this merely proves that, as he himself says, when people think he is pouring himself out in a tale or an essay, he is merely telling what is common to human nature, not what is peculiar to himself. 'I sympathize with them, not they with me.' He sympathizes in the special direction of our darker side. A creative mind of the higher order holds the thread which guides it surely through life's labyrinths; but all the more on this account its attention is called to the erratic movement of other travellers around it. The genius who has the clew begins, therefore, to study these errors and to describe them for our behoof. It is a great mistake to suppose that the abnormal or preposterous phases which he describes are the fruit of *self*-study,— personal traits disguised in fiction; yet this is what has often been affirmed of Hawthorne. We don't think of attributing to Dickens the multiform oddities which he pictures with such power, it being manifestly absurd to do so. As Dickens raises the laugh against them, we at once perceive that they are outside of himself. Hawthorne is so serious, that we are absorbed in the sober earnest of the thing, and forget to apply the rule in his case. Dickens's distinct aim is to excite us with something uncommon; Hawthorne's, to show us that the elements of all tragedies lie within our individual natures; therefore we begin to attribute in undue measure to *his* individual nature all the abnormal conditions that he has shown to be potential in any of us. But in truth he was a perfectly healthy person.

You are, intellectually speaking, quite a puzzle to me, his friend George Hillard wrote to him, once. How comes it you have such a taste for the morbid anatomy of the human heart, and such a knowledge of it, too? I should fancy, from your books, that you were burdened with some secret sorrow, that you had some blue chamber in your soul, into which you hardly dared to enter yourself; but when I see you, you give me the impression of a man as healthy as Adam in Paradise.

This very healthiness was his qualification for his office. By virtue of his mental integrity and absolute moral purity, he was able to handle unhurt all disintegrated and sinful forms of character; and when souls in trouble, persons with moral doubts to solve and criminals wrote to him for counsel, they recognized the healing touch of one whose pitying immaculateness could make them well.

She who knew best his habitual tone through a sympathy such as has rarely been given to any man, who lived with him a life so exquisitely fair and high, that to speak of it publicly is almost irreverent, has written:—

He had the inevitable pensiveness and gravity of a person who possessed what a friend has called his 'awful power of insight'; but his mood was always cheerful and equal, and his mind peculiarly healthful, and the airy splendor of his wit and humor was the light of his home. He saw too far to be despondent, though his vivid sympathies and shaping imagination often made him sad in behalf of others. He also perceived morbidness wherever it existed instantly, as if by the illumination of his own steady cheer.

His closest friends, too, speak with delight of his genial warmth and ease in converse with them. He could seldom talk freely with more than two or three, however, on account of his constitutional shyness, and perhaps of a peculiarly concentrative cast of mind; though he possessed a ready adaptability. 'I talk with everybody: to Mrs. T—— good sense; to Mary, good sense, with a mixture of fun; to Mrs. G——, sentiment, romance, and nonsense.'* A gentleman who was with him at Brook Farm, and knew him well, tells me that his presence was very attractive,

*American Note-Books, 1837.

and that he inspired great esteem among all at the farm by his personal qualities. On a walking trip to Wachusett, which they once made together, Hawthorne showed a great interest in sitting in the barrooms of country taverns, to listen to the talk of the attendant farmers and villagers. The manner in which he was approached had a great deal to do with his response. If treated simply and wisely, he would answer cordially; but he was entirely dismayed, as a rule, by those who made demonstrations of admiration or awe. 'Why do they treat me so?' he asked a friend, in one case of this sort. 'Why, they're afraid of you.' 'But I tremble at *them*,' he said. 'They think,' she explained, 'that you're imagining all sorts of terrible things.' 'Heavens!' he answered; 'if they only knew what I *do* think about.' . . .

He was simple in his habits, and fond of being out of doors, but not —after his college days—as a sportsman. While living beside the Concord, he rowed frequently, with a dreamy devotion to the pastime, and was fond of fishing; swimming, too, he enjoyed. But his chief exercise was walking; he had a vast capacity for it, and was, I think, never even seen upon horseback. At Brook Farm he 'belabored the rugged furrows' with a will; and at the Old Manse he presided over his garden in a paradisiacal sort of way. Books in every form he was always eager for, sometimes, as has been reported, satisfying himself with an old almanac or newspaper, over which he would brood as deeply as over richly stored volumes of classic literature. At other times he was fastidious in his choice, and threw aside many books before he found the right one for the hour. An impression has been set afloat that he cared nothing for books in themselves, but this is incorrect. . . . He was, as we have seen, a cordial admirer of other writers, seldom vexing himself with a critical review of their merits and defects, but applying to them instead the test of his own catholic capacity for enjoyment. The deliberate tone in which he judges his own works, in his letters, shows how little his mind was impressed by the greatness of their fame and of the genius found in them. There could not have been a more modest author, though he did not weakly underrate his work. 'Recognition,' he once said to Mr. Howells, 'makes a man very modest.'

An attempt has also been made to show that he had little interest in animals, partly based, ludicrous as it may seem, on his bringing them into only one of his books. In his American journals, however, there is abundant evidence of his acute sympathy in this direction; at the Old Manse he fried fish for his dog Leo, when he says he should not have done it for himself; and in the Trosachs he finds a moment for pitying some little lambs startled by the approach of his party.* I have already mentioned his fondness for cats. It has further been said that he did not enjoy wild nature, because in the 'English Note-Books' there is no out-gushing of ecstatic description. But in fact he had the keenest enjoy-ment of it. He could not enter into the spectacle when hurrying through strange regions. Among the English lakes he writes:—

To say the truth, I was weary of fine scenery, and it seemed to me that I had eaten a score of mountains and quaffed as many lakes, all in the space of two or three days, and the natural consequence was a surfeit.

I doubt if anybody ever does really see a mountain, who goes for the set and sole purpose of seeing it. Nature will not let herself be seen in such cases. You must patiently bide her time; and by and by, at some unforeseen moment, she will quietly and suddenly unveil herself and for a brief space allow you to look right into the heart of her mystery. But if you call out to her peremptorily, 'Nature! unveil yourself this very moment!' she only draws her veil the closer; and you may look with all your eyes, and imagine that you see all that she can show, and yet see nothing.

But this was because his sensibility was so great that he drew from little things a larger pleasure than many feel when excited by grand ones; and knowing this deeper phase, he could not be content with the hasty admiration on which tourists flatter themselves. The beauty of a scene which he could absorb in peace was never lost upon him. Every year the recurrent changes of season filled him with untold pleasure; and in the spring, Mrs. Hawthorne has been heard to say, he would walk with her in continuous silence, his heart full of the awe and delight with which the miracle of buds and new verdure inspired him. Nothing could be more accurate or sensitive than the brief descriptions of nature in his works. But there is nothing sentimental about them; partly owing to the Anglo-Saxon instinct which caused him to seek precise and detailed statement first of all, and partly because of a certain classic, awe-inspired reserve, like that of Horace and Virgil.

There was a commendable indolence in his character. It was not a constitutional weakness, overcoming will, but the instinctive precaution of a man whose errand it was to rise to great emergencies of exertion. He always waited for an adequate mood, before writing. But these intervals, of course, were richly productive of revery which afterward entered into the creative moments. He would sometimes become deeply abstracted in imagination; and while he was writing 'The Scarlet Letter' it is related by a trustworthy person that, sitting in the

*English Note-Books (May, 1856).

room where his wife was doing some sewing, he unconsciously took up a part of the work and cut it into minute fragments with the scissors, without being aware that he had done so. At some previous time, he had in the same way gradually chipped off with a knife portions of a table, until the entire folding-leaf was worn away by the process. The opinion was sometimes advanced by him that without a certain mixture of uncongenial labor he might not have done so much with the pen; but in this he perhaps underestimated the leisure in his blood, which was one of the elements of his power. Men of smaller calibre are hollowed out by the fire of ideas, and decay too quickly; but this trait preserved him from such a fate. Combined with his far-reaching foresight, it may have had something to do with his comparative withdrawal from practical affairs other than those which necessity connected him with. Of Holgrave he writes:—

His error lay in supposing that this age more than any past or future one is destined to see the garments of antiquity exchanged for a new suit, instead of gradually renewing themselves by patchwork; . . . and more than all, in fancying that it mattered anything to the great end in view whether he himself should contend for it or against it.

The implied opinion of the author, here, is not that of a fatalist, but of an optimist (if we must connect him with any 'ism') who has a very profound faith in Providence; not in any 'special providence,' but in that operation of divine laws through unexpected agencies and conflicting events, which is very gradually approximating human affairs to a state of truthfulness. Hawthorne was one of the great believers of his generation; but his faith expressed itself in the negative way of showing how fragile are the ordinary objects of reverence in the world, how subject the best of us are to the undermining influence of very great sin; and on the other hand, how many traits of good there are, by consequence, even in the worst of us. This, however, is a mere skeleton statement: the noblest element in his mood is that he believes with his heart. A good interpreter has said that he *feels* with his *brain*, and *thinks* with his *heart*, to show the completeness with which he mingled the two elements in his meditations on existence. A warm, pure, living sympathy pervaded all his analysis of mankind, without which that analysis would have taken no hold upon us. It is a crude view which reckons him to have been wanting in moral enthusiasm: he had not that kind which can crush out sympathy with suffering, for the sake of carrying out an idea. Perhaps in some cases this was a fault; but one cannot dwell on the mistaken side of such a phase, when it possesses another side so full of beneficent aid to humanity. And it must be remembered that with all this susceptibility, he was not a suffering poet, like Shelley, but distinctly an endurer. His moral enthusiasm was deeper that that of any scheme or system.

His distaste for society has been declared to proceed from the fact that, when he once became interested in people, he could no longer chemically resolve them into material for romance. But this assumption is also erroneous; for Hawthorne, if he felt it needful, could bring to bear upon his best friends the same qualitative measuring skill that he exercised on any one. I do not doubt that he knew where to place his friends and acquaintance in the scale of relative excellence. All of us who have not an equal analytic power with his own can at least reverence his discretion so far as to believe that he had stand-points not open to every one, from which he took views often more essentially just than if he had assumed a more sweeping estimate. In other cases, where he bestowed more friendship and confidence than the object of them especially deserved, he no doubt sought the simple pleasure of accepting what circumstances offered him. He was not a suspicious person; although, in fear of being fooled by his fancy, he cultivated what he often spoke of to a friend as 'morose common-sense,' deeming it a desirable alloy. There was even, in many relations, an unquestioning trust on his part; for he might well be called

> As the greatest only are,
> In his simplicity sublime

The connection between Pierce and himself involved too many considerations to make it possible to pass them with indifference; and he perhaps condemned certain public acts of the President, while feeling it to be utter disloyalty to an old friend to discuss these mistakes with any one. As to other slighter connections, it is very likely he did not take the trouble that might have saved him from being imposed upon.

But it is impossible to define Hawthorne's personality precisely. A poet's whole effort is to indirectly express this, by expressing the effect of things upon him; and we may read much of Hawthorne in his books, if we have the skill. But it is very clear that he put only a part of himself into them; that part which best served the inexorable law of his genius for treating life in a given light. For the rest, his two chapters on 'The Custom-House' and 'The Old Manse' show us something of his mode of taking daily affairs. But his real and inmost character was a mystery even to himself, and this, because he felt so profoundly the impossibility of sounding to the bottom any human heart. 'A cloudy veil stretches over the abyss of my nature,' he writes, at one time. 'I have, however, no love of secrecy or darkness.' At another time: 'Lights and shadows are continually flitting across my inward sky, and I know neither whence they come nor whither they go; nor do I look too closely into them.' A mind so conscious as his of the slight reality of appearances would be dissatisfied with the few tangible qualities which are all of himself that a man can discern: at the same time he would hesitate to probe the deeper self assiduously, for fear of turning his searching gaze too intently within, and thus becoming morbid. In other persons, however, he could perceive a contour, and pursue his study of investigation from without inward,—a more healthy method. His *instinctive* knowledge of himself, being brought into play, would of course aid him. Incidentally, then, something of himself comes to light in his investigation of others. And it is perhaps this inability to define their own natures, except by a roundabout method, which is the creative impulse of all great novelists and dramatists. I doubt whether many of the famous delineators of character could give us a very distinct account of their own individualities; and if they did, it would probably make them out the most uninteresting of beings. It would certainly be divested of the special charm of their other writing. Imagine Dickens clearly accounting for himself and his peculiar traits: would he be able to excite even a smile? How much of his own delicious personality could Thackeray have described without losing the zest of his other portraitures? Hawthorne has given a kind of picture of himself in Coverdale, and was sometimes called after that character by his friends; but I suspect he has adroitly constructed Coverdale out of the *appearance* which he knew himself to make in the eyes of associates. I do not mean that Hawthorne had not a very decisive personality; for indeed he had. But the essence of the person cannot be compressed into a few brief paragraphs, and must be slowly drawn in as a pervasive elixir from his works, his letters, his note-books. In the latter he has given as much definition of his interior self as we are likely to get, for no one else can continue the broken jottings that he has left, and extend them into outlines. We shall not greatly err if we treat the hidden depths of his spirit with as much reverence as he himself used in scrutinizing them. Curiously enough, many of those who have studied this most careful and delicate of definers have embraced the madness of attempting to bind him down in unhesitating, absolute statements. He who mastered words so completely that he learned to despise their obscurity, has been made the victim of easy epithets and a few conventional phrases. But none can ever be said to know Hawthorne who do not leave large allowances for the unknowable.

140. Anthony Trollope: The novelist's view of the romancer, from 'The Genius of Nathaniel Hawthorne', in the *North American Review*

September 1879, cclxxiv, 203–22

Hawthorne's well-known comments on Trollope's novels (see p. 514)—that they are precisely to his taste—have been taken to be a testament of his unqualified admiration. The context of those remarks, however, which Trollope himself was apparently unaware of, suggests a somewhat different meaning. Hawthorne was telling his publisher of his own lack of popularity and his lack of confidence in *The Marble Faun*:

> My own opinion is, that I am not really a popular writer, and that what popularity I have gained is chiefly accidental, and owing to other causes than my own kind or degree of merit. Possibly I may (or may not) deserve something better than popularity; but looking at all my productions, and especially this latter one, with a cold and critical eye, I can see that they do not make their appeal to the popular mind. (Letter, 11 February 1860, to James T. Fields, *Yesterdays with Authors* [1871], p. 87.)

Fields, ever sensitive about public relations, may have sensed an ironic undertow in the remarks on Trollope that followed. At any rate, he deleted all the references to Trollope. Only three weeks later, in a letter to John Lothrop Motley, Hawthorne used the same language to complain that 'These beer-sodden English beef-eaters do not know how to read a Romance; neither can they praise it rightly, if ever so well disposed' (1 April 1860, MS., Berg Collection, New York Public Library). Critics have always supposed that Hawthorne had been contrasting his own romances with Trollope's realism. It seems more likely that he was, with some bitterness, contrasting the romance with popular fiction which he could enjoy but could not altogether respect as serious literature.

There never surely was a powerful, active, continually effective mind less round, more lop-sided, than that of Nathaniel Hawthorne. If there were aught of dispraise in this, it would not be said by me,—by an Englishman of an American whom I knew, by an Englishman of letters of a brother on the other side of the water, much less by me, an English novelist, of an American novelist. . . . from Hawthorne we could not have obtained that weird, mysterious, thrilling charm with which he has awed and delighted us had he not allowed his mind to revel in one direction, so as to lose its fair proportions.

I have been specially driven to think of this by the strong divergence between Hawthorne and myself. It has always been my object to draw my little pictures as like to life as possible, so that my readers should feel that they were dealing with people whom they might probably have known, but so to do it that the every-day good to be found among them should allure, and the every-day evil repel; and this I have attempted, believing that such ordinary good and ordinary evil would be more powerful in repelling or alluring than great and glowing incidents which, though they might interest, would not come home to the minds of readers. Hawthorne, on the other hand, has dealt with persons and incidents which were often but barely within the bounds of possibility, —which were sometimes altogether without those bounds,—and has determined that his readers should be carried out of their own little mundane ways, and brought into a world of imagination in which their intelligence might be raised, if only for a time, to something higher than the common needs of common life.

I will venture here to quote an extract from a letter written by Hawthorne to an American gentleman, a friend of his,—and of mine, though, if I remember rightly, I did not get it from him,—which he will recognize should he see this paper. As it is altogether about myself, perhaps I should do better to keep it to myself, but I will give it because it explains so accurately his own condition of mind in regard to novels:

It is odd enough that my own individual taste is for quite another class of novels than those which I myself am able to write. If I were to meet with such books as mine by another writer, I don't believe I should be able to get through them. Have you ever read the novels of Anthony Trollope? They precisely suit my taste; solid and substantial, written on strength of beef and through the inspiration of ale, and just as real as if some giant had hewn a great lump out of the earth, and put it under a glass case, with all its inhabitants going about their daily business, and not suspecting that they were made a show of.

This is what he could read himself, but could not possibly have produced,—any more than I could have produced that 'Marble Faun' which has been quite as much to my taste as was to his the fragment of common life which he has supposed me to put under a glass case in order that the frequenters at my little show might inspect at their ease all that was being done on that morsel of the earth's surface. . . .

Hawthorne is severe, but his severity is never of a nature to form laws for life. His is a mixture of romance and austerity, quite as far removed from the realities of Puritanism as it is from the sentimentalism of poetry. He creates a melancholy which amounts almost to remorse in the minds of his readers. . . . When he has operated upon you, you would not for worlds have foregone it. You have been ennobled by that familiarity with sorrow. You have been, as it were, sent through the fire and purged of so much of your dross. For a time, at least, you have been free from the mundane touch of that beef and ale with which novelists of a meaner school will certainly bring you in contact. No one will feel himself ennobled at once by having read one of my novels. But Hawthorne, when you have studied him, will be very precious to you. He will have plunged you into melancholy, he will have overshadowed you with black forebodings, he will almost have crushed you with imaginary sorrows; but he will have enabled you to feel yourself an inch taller during the process. Something of the sublimity of the transcendent, something of the mystery of the unfathomable, something of the brightness of the celestial, will have attached itself to you, and you will all but think that you too might live to be sublime, and revel in mingled light and mystery.

The creations of American literature generally are no doubt more given to the speculative,—less given to the realistic,—than are those of English literature. On our side of the water we deal more with beef and ale, and less with dreams. Even with the broad humor of Bret Harte, even with the broader humor of Artemus Ward and Mark Twain, there is generally present an undercurrent of melancholy, in which pathos and satire are intermingled. There was a touch of it even with the simple-going Cooper and the kindly Washington Irving. Melancholy and pathos, without the humor, are the springs on which all Longfellow's lines are set moving. But in no American writer is to be found the same predominance of weird imagination as in Hawthorne. There was something of it in M. G. Lewis—our Monk Lewis as he came to be called, from the name of a tale which he wrote; but with him, as with many others, we feel that they have been weird because they have desired to be so. They have struggled to achieve the tone with which their works are pervaded. With Hawthorne we are made to think that he could not have been anything else if he would. It is as though he could certainly have been nothing else in his own inner life. We know that such was not actually the case. Though a man singularly reticent,—what we generally call shy,—he could, when things went well with him, be argumentative, social, and cheery. I have seen him very happy, over canvas-back ducks, and have heard him discuss, almost with violence, the superiority of American vegetables. Indeed, he once withered me with a scorn which was anything but mystic or melancholy because I expressed a patriotic preference for English peas. And yet his imagination was such that the creations of his brain could not have been other than such as I have described. . . .

I will take a few of his novels,—those which I believe to be the best known,—and will endeavor to illustrate my idea of his genius by describing the manner in which his stories have been told.

'The Scarlet Letter' is, on the English side of the water, perhaps the best known. It is so terrible in its pictures of diseased human nature as to produce most questionable delight. The reader's interest never flags for a moment. There is nothing of episode or digression. The author is always telling his one story with a concentration of energy which, as we can understand, must have made it impossible for him to deviate. The reader will certainly go on with it to the end very quickly, entranced, excited, shuddering, and at times almost wretched. His consolation will be that he too has been able to see into these black deeps of the human heart. The story is one of jealousy,—of love and jealousy,—in which love is allowed but little scope, but full play is given to the hatred which can spring from injured love. . . .

The personages in it with whom the reader will interest himself are four,—the husband, the minister who has been the sinful lover, the woman, and the child. The reader is expected to sympathize only with the woman,—and will sympathize only with her. . . . I can fancy a reader so loving the image of Hester Prynne as to find himself on the verge of treachery to the real Hester of flesh and blood who may have a claim upon him. Sympathy can not go beyond that; and yet the author deals with her in a spirit of assumed hardness, almost as though he assented to the judgment and the manner in which it was carried out. In this, however, there is a streak of that satire with which Hawthorne always speaks of the peculiar institutions of his own country. The worthy magistrates of Massachusetts are under his lash throughout the story, and so is the virtue of her citizens and the chastity of her matrons, which can take delight in the open shame of a woman whose sin has been discovered. Indeed, there is never a page written by Hawthorne not tinged by satire.

The fourth character is that of the child, Pearl. Here the author has, I think, given way to a temptation, and in doing so has not increased the power of his story. The temptation was, that Pearl should add a picturesque element by being an elf and also a charming child. Elf she is, but, being so, is incongruous with all else in the story, in which, unhuman as it is, there is nothing of the ghost-like, nothing of the unnatural. The old man becomes a fiend, so to say, during the process of the tale; but he is a man-fiend. And Hester becomes sublimated almost to divine purity; but she is still simply a woman. The minister is tortured beyond the power of human endurance; but neither do his sufferings nor his failure of strength adequate to support them come to him from any miraculous agency. But Pearl is miraculous,—speaking, acting, and thinking like an elf,—and is therefore, I think, a drawback rather than an aid. The desolation of the woman, too, would have been more perfect without the child. It seems as though the author's heart had not been hard enough to make her live alone;—as sometimes when you punish a child you can not drive from your face that gleam of love which shoots across your frown and mars its salutary effect.

But through all this intensity of suffering, through this blackness of narrative, there is ever running a vein of drollery. As Hawthorne himself says, 'a lively sense of the humorous again stole in among the solemn phantoms of her thought.' He is always laughing at something with his weird, mocking spirit. The very children when they see Hester in the streets are supposed to speak of her in this wise: 'Behold, verily, there is the woman of the scarlet letter. Come, therefore, and let us fling mud at her.' Of some religious book he says, 'It must have been a work of vast ability in the somniferous school of literature.' 'We must not always talk in the market-place of what happens to us in the forest,' says even the sad mother to her child. Through it all there is a touch of burlesque,—not as to the suffering of the sufferers, but as to the great question whether it signifies much in what way we suffer, whether by crushing sorrows or little stings. Who would not sooner be Prometheus than a yesterday's tipsy man with this morning's sick-headache? In this way Hawthorne seems to ridicule the very woes which he expends himself in depicting.

As a novel 'The House of the Seven Gables' is very inferior to 'The

Scarlet Letter.' The cause of this inferiority would, I think, be plain to any one who had himself been concerned in the writing of novels. When Hawthorne proposed to himself to write 'The Scarlet Letter,' the plot of his story was clear to his mind. He wrote the book because he had the story strongly, lucidly manifest to his own imagination. In composing the other he was driven to search for a plot, and to make a story. 'The Scarlet Letter' was written because he had it to write, and the other because he had to write it. The novelist will often find himself in the latter position. He has characters to draw, lessons to teach, philosophy perhaps which he wishes to expose, satire to express, humor to scatter abroad. These he can employ gracefully and easily if he have a story to tell. If he have none, he must concoct something of a story laboriously, when his lesson, his characters, his philosophy, his satire, and his humor will be less graceful and less easy. All the good things I have named are there in 'The House of the Seven Gables'; but they are brought in with less artistic skill, because the author has labored over his plot, and never had it clear to his own mind. . . .

Two or three of the characters here drawn are very good. The wicked and respectable gentleman who *drees* the doom of his family, and dies in his chair all covered with blood, is one Judge Pyncheon. The persistent, unbending, cruel villainy of this man,—whose heart is as hard as a millstone, who knows not the meaning of conscience, to whom money and respectability are everything,—was dear to Hawthorne's heart. He likes to revel in an excess of impossible wickedness, and has done so with the Judge. . . .

But the personage we like best in the book is certainly Miss Hepzibah Pyncheon. . . . Her timidity, her affection, her true appreciation of herself, her ugliness, her hopelessness, and general incapacity for everything,—cent-shop-keeping included,—are wonderfully drawn. There are characters in novels who walk about on their feet, who stand upright and move, so that readers can look behind them, as one seems to be able to do in looking at a well-painted figure on the canvas. There are others, again, so wooden that no reader expects to find in them any appearance of movement. They are blocks roughly hewed into some more or less imperfect forms of humanity, which are put into their places and which there lie. Miss Hepzibah is one of the former. The reader sees all round her, and is sure that she is alive,—though she is so incapable.

Then there is her brother Clifford, who was supposed to have committed the murder, and who, in the course of the chronicle, comes home to live with his sister. There are morsels in his story, bits of telling in the description of him, which are charming, but he is not so good as his sister, being less intelligible. Hawthorne himself had not realized the half-fatuous, dreamy, ill-used brother, as he had the sister. In painting a figure it is essential that the artist should himself know the figure he means to paint.

There is yet another Pyncheon,—Phœbe Pyncheon, who comes from a distance, Heaven knows why, to live with her far-away cousin. She is intended as a ray of sunlight,—as was Pearl in 'The Scarlet Letter,' —and is more successful. As the old maid Pyncheon is capable of nothing, so is the young man Pyncheon capable of everything. She is, however, hardly wanted in the story, unless it be that the ray of sunlight was necessary. And there is a young 'daguerreotypist,'—as the photographer of the day used to be called,—who falls in love with the ray of sunlight, and marries her at the end; and who is indeed the lineal descendant of the original ill-used poor man who was hung as a witch. There is just one love-scene in the novel, most ghastly in its details; for the young man offers his love, and the girl accepts it, while they are aware that the wicked, respectable old Judge is sitting, all smeared with blood, and dead, in the next room to them. The love-scene, and the hurrying up of the marriage, and all the dollars which they inherit from the wicked Judge, and the 'handsome dark-green barouche' prepared for their departure, which is altogether unfitted to the ideas which the reader has formed respecting them, are quite unlike Hawthorne, and would seem almost to have been added by some every-day, beef-and-ale, realistic novelist, into whose hands the unfinished story had unfortunately fallen.

But no one should read 'The House of the Seven Gables' for the sake of the story, or neglect to read it because of such faults as I have described. It is for the humor, the satire, and what I may perhaps call the philosophy which permeates it, that its pages should be turned. Its pages may be turned on any day, and under any circumstances. To 'The Scarlet Letter' you have got to adhere till you have done with it; but you may take this volume by bits, here and there, now and again, just as you like it. . . .

'Mosses fron an Old Manse' will be caviare to many. By this I intend no slight to the intelligence of the many readers who may not find themselves charmed by such narratives. In the true enjoyment of Hawthorne's work there is required a peculiar mood of mind. The reader should take a delight in looking round corners, and in seeing how places and things may be approached by other than the direct and obvious route. No writer impresses himself more strongly on the reader who will submit to him; but the reader must consent to put himself altogether under his author's guidance, and to travel by queer passages, the direction of which he will not perceive till, perhaps, he has got quite to the end of them. . . . This, as the name implies, is a collection of short stories,—and of course no thread or general plot is expected in such a compilation. But here the short narratives are altogether various in their style, no one of them giving any clew as to what may be expected to follow. They are, rather than tales, the jottings down of the author's own fancies, on matters which have subjected themselves to his brain, one after the other, in that promiscuous disorder in which his manner of thinking permitted him to indulge. He conceives a lovely woman, who has on her cheek a 'birth-mark,' so trifling as to be no flaw to her beauty. But her husband sees it, and, seeing it, can not rid himself of the remembrance of it. . . . This is transcendental enough; but it is followed, a few pages on, by the record of Mrs. Bullfrog, who had got herself married to Mr. Bullfrog, as the natural possessor of all feminine loveliness, and then turns out to be a hideous virago, with false hair and false teeth, but who is at last accepted graciously by Bullfrog, because her money is real. The satire is intelligible, and is Hawthornean, but why Hawthorne should have brought himself to surround himself with objects so disagreeable the reader does not understand.

'The Select Party' is pleasant enough. . . . The student of Hawthorne will understand what quips and quirks will come from this mottled company.

Then there is an Italian, one Rappacini, and his daughter, weird, ghostlike, and I must own very unintelligible. The young lady, however, has learned under the teaching of her father, who is part doctor, part gardener, and part conjurer, to exist on the essence of a flower which is fatal to everybody else. She becomes very detrimental to her lover, who has no such gifts, and the story ends as a tragedy. There is a very pretty prose pastoral called 'Buds and Bird-Voices,' which is simply the indulgence of a poetic voice in the expression of its love of nature. 'The Hall of Fantasy' is a mansion in which some unfortunates make their whole abode and business, and 'contract habits which unfit them for all the real employments of life. Others,—but these are few,— possess the faculty, in their occasional visits, of discovering a purer truth than the world can impart.' The reader can imagine to himself those who, under Hawthorne's guidance, would succeed and those who would fail by wandering into this hall. 'The Procession of Life' is perhaps the strongest piece in the book,—the one most suggestive and most satisfactory.

There is a droll story, with a half-hidden meaning, called 'Drowne's Wooden Image,' in which Copley the painter is brought upon the scene, so that I am led to suppose that there was a Drowne who carved head-pieces for ships in Boston, and who, by some masterpiece in his trade and by the help of Hawthorne, has achieved a sort of immortality. . . . 'P.'s Correspondence' is the last I will mention.

Such is the nature of the Mosses from the old Manse each morsel of moss damp, tawny, and soft, as it ought to be, but each with enough of virus to give a sting to the tender hand that touches it.

In speaking of 'The Marble Faun,' as I will call the story, I hardly know whether, as a just critic, to speak first of its faults or of its virtues. As one always likes to keep the sweetest bits for the end of the banquet, I will give priority of place to my caviling. The great fault of the book lies in the absence of arranged plot. The author, in giving the form of a novel to the beautiful pictures and images which his fancy has enabled him to draw, and in describing Rome and Italian scenes as few others have described them, has in fact been too idle to carry out his own purpose of constructing a tale. We will grant that a novelist may be natural or supernatural. Let us grant, for the occasion, that the latter manner, if well handled, is the better and the more efficacious. And we must grant also that he who soars into the supernatural need not bind himself by any of the ordinary trammels of life. His men may fly, his birds may speak. His women may make angelic music without instruments. His cherubs may sit at the piano. This wide latitude, while its adequate management is much too difficult for ordinary hands, gives facility for the working of a plot. But there must be some plot, some arrangement of circumstances, with an intelligible conclusion, or the reader will not be satisfied. . . . 'The gentle reader,' says our author as he ends his narrative, 'would not thank us for one of those minute elucidations which are so tedious and after all so unsatisfactory in clearing up the romantic mysteries of a story.' There our author is, I think, in error. His readers will hardly be so gentle as not to require from him some explanation of the causes which have produced the romantic details to which they have given their attention, and will be inclined to say that it should have been the author's business to give an explanation neither tedious nor unsatisfactory. The critic is disposed to think that

Hawthorne, as he continued his narrative, postponed his plot till it was too late, and then escaped from his difficulty by the ingenious excuse above given. As a writer of novels, I am bound to say that the excuse can not be altogether accepted. But the fault, when once admitted, may be well pardoned on account of the beauty of the narrative.

In 'The Marble Faun,' as in all Hawthorne's tales written after 'The Scarlet Letter,' the reader must look rather for a series of pictures than for a novel. It would, perhaps, almost be well that a fastidious reader should cease to read when he comes within that border, toward the end, in which it might be natural to expect that the strings of a story should be gathered together and tied into an intelligible knot. This would be peculiarly desirable in regard to 'The Marble Faun,' in which the delight of that fastidious reader, as derived from pictures of character and scenery, will be so extreme that it should not be marred by a sense of failure in other respects.

In speaking of this work in conjunction with Hawthorne's former tales, I should be wrong not to mention the wonderful change which he effected in his own manner of writing when he had traveled out from Massachusetts into Italy. As every word in his earlier volumes savors of New England, so in 'The Marble Faun' is the flavor entirely that of Rome and of Italian scenery. His receptive imagination took an impress from what was around him, and then gave it forth again with that wonderful power of expression which belonged to him. Many modern writers have sought to give an interest to their writings by what is called local coloring; but it will too often happen that the reader is made to see the laying on of the colors. In Hawthorne's Roman chronicle the tone of the telling is just as natural,—seems to belong as peculiarly to the author,—as it does with 'The Scarlet Letter' or 'The House of the Seven Gables.'

141. A reply to Trollope, from an unsigned essay, 'Polar Opposites in Fiction', in the *Dublin University Magazine*

October 1879, xciv, 437–42

In the September number of the *North American Review* is an article entitled 'The Genius of Nathaniel Hawthorne,' which possesses a peculiar interest for all admirers of that genius, being written by one who dwells content in the opposite pole of mind. It requires some effort, at first, to convince oneself that there is before one an elaborate critique upon Hawthorne written by so unlikely a person as Anthony Trollope. But the result of this strange combination is particularly instructive. Trollope has made a noteworthy attempt to understand and admire Hawthorne, and in so doing has afforded a charming illustration of the fact that between the realist and the idealist there is a great gulf fixed, which the former can no wise cross unless he learn to fly.

Mr. Trollope is very anxious to make us clearly understand, at starting, that he and Hawthorne were great admirers each of the other. Mr. Trollope appreciates the 'Marble Faun' because, or in spite of, its being so unlike anything which he could himself have produced; while he acquaints us also with Hawthorne's feelings towards himself. . . . Mr. Trollope seems inclined to accept this as a kind of praise given by one artist to another of a different order. Truth to tell, we see little but the amused interest and humorous regard of an ideal artist for a worker in earthen pots. Mr. Trollope does not seem to suspect that his work may stand in the same relation to the intense imagination of Hawthorne, as the veriest trash to the tired thinker, to whom it sometimes affords the relief of cessation of thought. What is a work of art? Is it solid and substantial, as if some giant had hewn a great lump out of the earth?

The actual marble of the statue, the touchable canvas and paint of the picture, the piece of reality which is used as scaffolding for the artist's work, this Mr. Trollope can appreciate, and does appreciate heartily: the Turneresque atmosphere which Hawthorne could fling about his characters, is to him but a 'preserved extract of moonshine and mist.'

523

Just that part which, instead of being built out of beef and ale, is produced from strength of spirit and inspiration of soul, misses his apprehension. In speaking of the 'House of the Seven Gables,' Mr. Trollope says, 'The personage we like best in the book is certainly Miss Hephzibah Pyncheon.' . . . Mr. Trollope says Clifford 'is not so good as his sister, being less intelligible.' Does Mr. Trollope really never meet with people who are not intelligible, and if he attempted to reproduce them, who must needs be described as unintelligible, or not at all? It is just in the fact that Hawthorne has not attempted to make Clifford intelligible that he has shown himself a true artist.

Mr. Trollope has one great advantage over many of his brother authors; he deals in the respectabilities of life. Church dignitaries and commonplace housewives adorn his pages. These people are as intelligible as poor Hephzibah. But a crazed soul like Clifford Pyncheon, who, though a grown man, can find strange childlike joy in a gleam of sunshine, and cowers in childish fear before the superior cunning of his stern kinsman—such a soul he wots not of. Yet even his favourite, poor rusty Hephzibah, though she had to guard her brother like a baby, recognised dimly that his mind reached into regions to which she could not raise her own.

'The Scarlet Letter' meets much more fully with our critic's admiration. He appreciates with keenness the vivid pictures of 'diseased human nature.' The phrase seems rather a severe one to apply to some of the characters in the book.

Mr. Trollope finds fault with the fourth character—that of Pearl, the child of the minister and Hester Prynne—the living symbol of the Scarlet Letter. Mr. Trollope says she is an elf, unnatural, and therefore a drawback to the reality of the book. She certainly is unnatural, and it difficult to believe that Hawthorne ever intended her as a real child. . . .

From these two novels Mr. Trollope goes on to dissect some of the stories which, as he says, though he intends 'no slight to the intelligence of the many,' will be, to them, caviare. In this Mr. Trollope is very right: and in the criticisms which follow he reveals, innocently enough, that some of these stories are decidedly caviare to himself. To a true Hawthorne-lover, the curious, straightforward dissections to which Mr. Trollope treats us are like the analysis of a new novel by a 'prentice hand put on to review for a country paper.

Mr. Trollope, as a critic, seems to have a pet word. It is 'unintelligible.' Of course he swears by Shakespeare—who, by the way, he considers to have had an 'equal' mind, while Nathaniel Hawthorne's he describes, with considerable impoliteness, as lop-sided:—does he find Hamlet a perfectly intelligible character?

'Rappaccini's Daughter' is set down by this word unintelligible by our critic, and obtains no further attention from him. . . . Mr. Trollope chooses some others of Hawthorne's most trivial stories to dissect, such as 'Mrs. Bullfrog' and 'P.'s Correspondence,' the mere quips and quirks of a productive pen. But he says nothing of that marvellous story, 'The Artist of the Beautiful,' in which Hawthorne's peculiar powers are so markedly visible. Is it too much to expect a writer who avowedly reproduces the commonplace characters in life with the fidelity of the photographer, and who is so devoid of all sense, both of the absurd as well as of the artistic, as to entitle a book, 'Is he Popenjoy?' to study a story which is full of the purest artistic feeling? What cares he for the useless butterfly wings? he loves what Hawthorne somewhere calls the solid unrealities of life. Art is outside of these; she is not solid, she is often unintelligible, but she is real. 'If there were nothing mystical in human destiny, if mere instincts and the impulses of sheer emotion never struck truer than cool common sense,' then perhaps we might accept Mr. Trollope as our prophet, and put aside the inner longing for something less intelligible than Archdeacon Grantly or Mrs. Proudie. But we cannot; man does not live by beef and ale alone. . . .

142. Henry James: The young writer's view, from *Hawthorne*

1879, pp. 144–5

James had already published *The American*, *The Europeans*, and *Daisy Miller* and was deeply involved in the discoveries of his 'international theme' when he completed this study for the 'English Men of Letters Series'. Intended as an introduction for the English reader into the American literary scene, it has been looked upon as a classic in American criticism. It represents not an original statement about Hawthorne's art, but instead a summary and a synthesis of attitudes that had been only gradually revealed in several decades of criticism. The final paragraph is printed here.

. . . He was a beautiful, natural, original genius, and his life had been singularly exempt from worldly preoccupations and vulgar efforts. It had been as pure, as simple, as unsophisticated, as his work. He had lived primarily in his domestic affections which were of the tenderest kind; and then—without eagerness without pretension but with a great deal of quiet devotion—in his charming art. His work will remain; it is too original and exquisite to pass away; among the men of imagination he will always have his niche. No one has had just that vision of life and no one has had a literary form that more successfully expressed his vision. He was not a moralist, and he was not simply a poet. The moralists are weightier, denser, richer, in a sense; the poets are more purely inconclusive and irresponsible. He combined in a singular degree the spontaneity of the imagination with a haunting care for moral problems. Man's conscience was his theme, but he saw it in the light of a creative fancy which added, out of its own substance, an interest, and, I may almost say, an importance.

Select Index

Figures in bold type indicate quotations
Topics are listed under Hawthorne, Nathaniel

INDEX